MATTHEW HENRY'S COMMENTARY

ACTS TO REVELATION

D0333043

A companion volume

Matthew Henry's Commentary: The Four Gospels

MATTHEW HENRY'S COMMENTARY

ACTS TO REVELATION

Edited by David Winter

HODDER AND STOUGHTON

LONDON SYDNEY AUCKLAND TORONTO

CONTENTS

INTRODUCTION

Why another edition of Matthew Henry's Commentary on the New Testament—and why an abridged one, at that? They are perfectly reasonable questions. It is hard to think of another area of knowledge where a "text book" nearly two hundred years old would be considered worth re-issuing for general use. Yet the undeniable fact is that this monumental work from another age—and another world, almost—has maintained its appeal for the modern reader. In terms of sales, and in terms of genuine affection and spiritual impact, there is probably no Bible commentary to equal it . . . for all that it represents a voice from the distant past.

It is worth asking why this should be so. After all, there are plenty of better commentaries, as commentaries. Since Henry's day much has come to light about biblical manuscripts, about exegesis, and about New Testament Greek. In some of these areas, Matthew Henry is, frankly, an unreliable guide. His style—repetitive and at times irritatingly over-elaborate—is hardly calculated to endear him to the modern reader. And at times he is quite inexcusably prejudiced, not to say bigoted—Baptists and "Papists" get very short shrift, for example.

.Yet, having lived with this Commentary for the best part of two years, I have to record that Matthew Henry has done more for my "soul" than any modern Commentary. However intrusive the voice of Henry, the voice of God comes through: and comes through with a force and clarity unequalled in the most minutely researched, meticulously scholarly modern equivalent. The only commentary of modern times which is in any way comparable is William Temple's magnificent devotional commentary on St. John's Gospel. There, too, God speaks, the heart is warmed, the spirit rises.

Matthew Henry's idea of a commentary is rather different from that of most modern theologians. Questions of authorship, textual criticism, historical background, dating and literary sources do not concern him very much. Unlike his successors, he is less concerned with why, when and how. His overriding concern is *what*—what has God said? What does it mean (in general), and what does it mean *to me*? His aim is to help the reader hear the voice of God through the Scriptures, and authorship, text, history and background are only important as they serve that end.

So the effect of reading Matthew Henry is to be directed to the Scriptures themselves, and especially the Scriptures applied to the human condition. Nobody has worked out how many embryonic sermons there are to a page of this Commentary, but no preacher ever came up dry from Henry's well. That alone would be reason enough for keeping it in print.

But why in an abridged version? What is gained by cutting out great swathes of a book that has been such a help to so many? The answer, I think, lies in the different uses to which this work can be put. There are undoubtedly readers who will find the entire work—all the millions of words of it—immensely fascinating and helpful. But for most readers today, the need is for something more precise and streamlined. They want the devotional insights, the flashes of illumination that make a familiar parable, or an obscure verse in Romans, come across with totally new force. They want help in preparing talks and sermons, and help in applying the message of the New Testament to their lives as individuals, and as men and women in society. But they do not want to have to plough through pages of polemic, or illustration piled upon illustration, or lengthy examples drawn from the master-servant relationship in the time of Queen Anne. Much can go with no loss at all to the general reader of today.

So in this edited version the reader will find the essential Matthew Henry, but not all the trimmings. Passages of purely antiquarian interest have gone. So have passages where he argues through problems which are largely irrelevant today—slavery, or the courtesies due to the gentry.

The polemical passages caused some heart-searching, because clearly Matthew Henry felt strongly about some issues which divide Christians, and it is misleading, in a way, to excise his harsh words and sometimes sweeping judgments. On the other hand, religious controversy was conducted in his day with a degree of vituperation and even venom which most of us would regard as sub-Christian today. We are used to a more muted, apologetic style of dissent, and have, perhaps, learnt that some things which once seemed of the essence of the Gospel are not in fact so.

In the event, the polemic has, for the most part, been omitted from this edition. With it, necessarily, has gone some valuable material relating to controversies about baptism, the Christian ministry, confirmation, ordination and the papacy. On the other hand, Matthew Henry's positive views on these subjects will be crystal clear to the discerning reader.

What we are left with, in the end, is a work of rare spiritual quality, one of the few books on the Bible which drives the reader all the time back to the scriptural text, and magnifies its message without distorting it. Time and again, and sometimes in the unlikeliest places, Matthew Henry strikes true mystical gold. As often, he puts an uncannily perceptive finger on human frailty and inconsistency. But always the Scripture itself is the source and inspiration. He is a servant of the Word.

THE ACTS OF THE APOSTLES

CHAPTER ONE

PROLOGUE (*vv.* 1–5)

In these verses, I. Theophilus is put in mind, and we in him, of St. Luke's gospel.

His gospel is here called *the former treatise which he had made,* which he had an eye to in writing this, intending this for a continuation and confirmation of that.

The contents of his gospel were *that, all that, which Jesus began both to do and teach*; and the same is the subject of the writings of the other three evangelists.

A general hint is given of the instructions he furnished his disciples with, now that he was about to leave them, and they, since *he breathed on them* and *opened their understandings*, were better able to receive them. 1. He instructed them concerning the work they were to do: *He gave commandments to the apostles whom he had chosen.* 2. He instructed them concerning the doctrine they were to preach: *He spoke to them of the things pertaining to the kingdom of God.* He had given them a general idea of that kingdom, and the certain time it should be set up in the world (in his parable, Mark xiii.), but here he instructed them more in the nature of it, as a kingdom of grace in this world and of glory in the other, and opened to them that covenant which is the great charter by which it is incorporated.

A particular assurance is given them that they should now shortly receive the Holy Ghost, with orders given them to expect it (*vv.* 4, 5), he *being assembled together with them,* probably in the interview at the mountain in Galilee which he had appointed before his death; for there is mention of their *coming together again* (*v.* 6), to attend his ascension. Though he had now ordered them to Galilee, yet they must not think to continue there; no, they must return to Jerusalem, and not depart thence.

Now this gift of the Holy Ghost he speaks of,

[1] As *the promise of the Father, which they had heard of him,* and might therefore depend upon. *First,* The Spirit was given by promise, and it was at this time the great promise, as that of the Messiah was before (Luke i. 72), and that of eternal life is now, 1 John ii. 25. *Secondly,* It was *the promise of the Father,* 1. Of Christ's Father. Christ, as Mediator, had an eye to God as his Father, fathering his design, and owning it all along. 2. Of our Father, who, if he give us *the adoption of sons,* will certainly give us *the Spirit of adoption,* Gal. iv. 5, 6.

[2] As the prediction of John Baptist; for so far back Christ here directs them to look (*v.* 5): "You have not only heard it from me, but you had it from John; when he turned you over to me, he said

1

(Matt. iii. 11), *I indeed baptize you with water, but he that comes after me shall baptize you with the Holy Ghost.*" It is a great honour that Christ now does to John, not only to quote his words, but to make this great gift of the Spirit, now at hand, to be the accomplishment of them.

THE ASCENSION (*vv.* 6–11)

In Jerusalem Christ, by his angel, had appointed his disciples to meet him in Galilee; there he appointed them to meet him in Jerusalem again, such a day. Thus he would try their obedience, and it was found ready and cheerful; *they came together*, as he appointed them, to be *the witnesses* of his ascension, of which we have here an account. Observe,

I. The question they asked him at this interview. *Lord, wilt thou at this time restore again the kingdom to Israel?*

Now two things were amiss in this question:

1. Their expectation of the thing itself. They thought Christ would *restore the kingdom to Israel*, that is, that he would make the nation of the Jews as great and considerable among the nations as it was *in the days of Dàvid and Solomon*.

2. Their enquiry concerning the time of it: "*Lord, wilt thou* do it *at this time?*" Now herein they missed their mark, [1] That they were inquisitive into that which their Master had never directed nor encouraged them to enquire into. [2] That they were impatient for the setting up of that kingdom in which they promised themselves so great a share, and would anticipate the divine counsels.

II. The check which Christ gave to this question, like that which he had a little before given to Peter's enquiry concerning John, *What is that to thee? v.* 7, *It is not for you to know the times and seasons.* He does not contradict their expectation that the kingdom would be restored to Israel, because that mistake would soon be rectified by the pouring out of the Spirit, after which they never had any more thoughts of the temporal kingdom; and also because there is a sense of the expectation which is true, the setting up of the gospel kingdom in the world; and their mistake of the promise shall not make it of no effect; but he checks their enquiry after the time.

The knowledge of it is reserved to God as his prerogative; it is what *the Father hath put in his own power;* it is hid with him. None besides can reveal the times and seasons to come. *Known unto God are all his works,* but not to us, *ch.* xv. 18.

III. He appoints them their work, and with authority assures them of an ability to go on with it, and of success in it. "*It is not for you to know the times and the seasons* — this would do you no good; but know this (*v.* 8) that you shall receive a spiritual *power*, by the *descent of the Holy Ghost upon you* and shall not receive it in vain, for *you shall be witnesses unto me* and my glory; and your testimony shall not be in vain, for it shall be received here in Jerusalem, in the country about, and all the world over," *v.* 8. Christ here tells them,

1. That their work should be honourable and glorious: *You shall be witnesses unto me.*

2. That their power for this work

2

should be sufficient. *"But you shall receive the power of the Holy Ghost coming upon you"* (so it may be read), *"shall* be animated and actuated by a better spirit than your own; you shall have power to preach the gospel, and to prove it out of the scriptures of the Old Testament"* (which, when they were *filled with the Holy Ghost,* they did to admiration, *ch.* xviii. 28), *"and to confirm it both by miracles and by sufferings."*

3. That their influence should be great and very extensive: *" You shall be witnesses* for Christ, and shall carry his cause," (1) *"In Jerusalem*; there you must begin, and many there will receive your testimony; and those that do not will be left inexcusable." (2) "Your light shall thence shine throughout all Judea, where before you have laboured in vain." (3) "Thence you shall proceed *to Samaria,* though at your first mission you were forbidden to preach in *any of the cities of the Samaritans."* (4) "Your usefulness shall reach *to the uttermost part of the earth,* and you shall be blessings to the whole world."

IV. Having left these instructions with them, he leaves them (*v.* 9). We have here Christ's ascending on high; not fetched away, as Elijah was, with *a chariot of fire and horses of fire,* but rising to heaven, as he rose from the grave, purely by his own power, his body being now, as the bodies of the saints will be at the resurrection, a spiritual body, and raised in power and incorruption.

V. The disciples, when he had gone out of their sight, yet still continued *looking up stedfastly to*

heaven (*v.* 10), and this longer than it was fit they should; and why so? 1. Perhaps they hoped that Christ would presently come back to them again, to restore the kingdom to Israel, and were loth to believe they should now part with him for good and all. 2. Perhaps they expected to see some change in the visible heavens now upon Christ's ascension, that either *the sun should be ashamed or the moon confounded* (Isa. xxiv. 23), as being out-shone by his lustre; or, rather, that they should show some sign of joy and triumph; or perhaps they promised themselves a sight of the glory of the invisible heavens, upon their opening to receive him. Christ had told them that hereafter they should *see heaven opened* (John i. 51), and why should not they expect it now?

VI. Two angels appeared to them, and delivered them a seasonable message from God. Now we are told what the angels said to them, 1. To check their curiosity: *You men of Galilee, why stand you gazing up into heaven?* Christ's disciples should never stand and gaze, because they have a sure rule to go by, and a sure foundation to build upon. 2. To confirm their faith concerning Christ's second coming. (1) *"This same Jesus* shall come again in his own person, clothed with a glorious body. (2) *"He shall come in like manner.* He is gone away in a *cloud,* and *attended with angels*; and, *behold, he comes in the clouds, and with him an innumerable company of angels!"* When we stand gazing and trifling, the consideration of our Master's second coming should quicken and awaken us; and, when we stand gazing and trembling, the consideration of it should comfort and encourage us.

THE UPPER ROOM
(vv. 12–14)

We are here told, I. Whence Christ ascended—*from the mount of Olives* (v. 12), from that part of it where the town of Bethany stood, Luke xxiv. 50.

II. Whither the disciples returned: They came to Jerusalem, according to their Master's appointment, though there they were in the midst of enemies. At Jerusalem they *went up into an upper room, and there abode*; not that they all lodged and dieted together in one room, but there they assembled every day, and spent time together in religious exercises, in expectation of the descent of the Spirit.

III. Who the disciples were, that kept together. The eleven apostles are here named (v. 13), so is Mary the mother of our Lord (v. 14), and it is the last time that ever any mention is made of her in the scriptures. There were others that are here said to be the brethren of our Lord, *his kinsmen according to the flesh*; and, to make up *the hundred and twenty* spoken of (v. 15), we may suppose that all or most of *the seventy disciples* were with them, that were associates with the apostles, and were employed as evangelists.

IV. How they spent their time: *They all continued with one accord in prayer and supplication*. Those are in the best frame to receive spiritual blessings that are in a praying frame. Christ had promised now shortly to send the Holy Ghost; now this promise was not to supersede prayer, but to quicken and encourage it. God will be enquired of for promised mercies, and the nearer the performance seems to be the more earnest we should be in prayer for it.

DEATH OF JUDAS (vv. 15–26)

The sin of Judas was not only his shame and ruin, but it made a vacancy in the college of the apostles. Now being twelve when they were learners, if they were but eleven when they were to be teachers, it would occasion every one to enquire what had become of the twelfth, and so revive the remembrance of the scandal of their society; and therefore care was taken, before the descent of the Spirit, to fill up the vacancy, of the doing of which we now have an account, our Lord Jesus, probably, having given directions about it, among other things which he spoke *pertaining to the kingdom of God*. Observe,

I. The persons concerned in this affair. 1. The house consisted of *about a hundred and twenty*. The speaker was Peter, who had been, and still was, the most forward man; and therefore notice is taken of his forwardness and zeal, to show that he had perfectly recovered the ground he lost by his denying his Master.

II. The proposal which Peter made for the choice of another apostle. Now in his speech we may observe,

1. The account he gives of the vacancy made by the death of Judas, in which he is very particular, and, as became one that Christ had breathed upon, takes notice of the fulfilling of the scriptures in it.

2. The motion he makes for the choice of another apostle, *vv.* 21, 22. Here observe, (1) How the person must be qualified that must fill up the vacancy. None shall be an apostle but one that has companied with the apostles, and that continually; not that has visited them now and then, but been intimately conversant with them. (2) To what work he is called that must fill up the vacancy: He must be *a witness with us of his resurrection.* By this it appears that others of the disciples were with the eleven when Christ appeared to them, else they could not have been *witnesses with them,* as competent witnesses as they, of his resurrection. The great thing which the apostles were to attest to the world was Christ's resurrection, for this was the great proof of his being the Messiah, and the foundation of our hope in him. See what the apostles were ordained to, not to a secular dignity and dominion, but to preach Christ, and the power of his resurrection.

III. The nomination of the person that was to succeed Judas in his office as an apostle.

1. Two, who were known to have been Christ's constant attendants, and men of great integrity, were set up as candidates for the place (*v.* 23). The two they nominated were *Joseph* and *Matthias,* of neither of whom do we read elsewhere. These two were both of them such worthy men, and so well qualified for the office, that they could not tell which of them was the fitter, but all agreed it must be one of these two.

2. They applied to God by prayer for direction, not which of the seventy, for none of the rest could

stand in competition with these in the opinion of all present, but *which of these two? vv.* 24, 25. (1) They appeal to God as the searcher of hearts. (2) They desire to know which of these God had chosen: *Lord, show us this,* and we are satisfied. (3) They are ready to receive him as a brother whom God hath chosen. (4) The doubt was determined by lot (*v.* 26), which is an appeal to God, and lawful to be used for determining matters not otherwise determinable, provided it be done in a solemn religious manner, and with prayer, the prayer of faith. Matthias was not ordained by the imposition of hands, as presbyters were, for he was chosen by lot, which was the act of God; and therefore, as he must be baptized, so he must be ordained, by the Holy Ghost, as they all were not many days after. Thus the number of the apostles was made up, as afterwards, when James, another of the twelve, was martyred, Paul was made an apostle.

CHAPTER TWO

PENTECOST (*vv.* 1–4)

We have here an account of the descent of the Holy Spirit upon the disciples of Christ. Observe,

I. When, and where, this was done, which are particularly noted, for the greater certainty of the thing.

1. It was *when the day of pentecost was fully come,* in which there seems to be a reference to the manner of the expression in the institution of this feast, (Lev. xxiii. 15). This day was *fully come,* that is, the night preceding, with a part of the

day, was fully past. (1) The Holy Ghost came down at the time of a solemn feast, because there was then a great concourse of people to Jerusalem from all parts of the country, and the proselytes from other countries, which would make it the more public, and the fame of it to be spread the sooner and further, which would contribute much to the propagating of the gospel into all nations. (2) This feast of pentecost was kept in remembrance of the giving of the law upon mount Sinai, whence the incorporating of the Jewish church was to be dated, which Dr. Lightfoot reckons to be just one thousand four hundred and forty-seven years before this. Fitly, therefore, is the Holy Ghost given at that feast, in fire and in tongues, for the promulgation of the evangelical law, not as that to one nation, but to every creature. (3) This feast of pentecost happened on the *first day of the week*, which was an additional honour put on that day, and a confirmation of it to be the Christian sabbath.

2. It was when *they were all with one accord in one place*. The disciples were in one place, and they were not as yet so many but that one place, and no large one, would hold them all. And here they were *with one accord*. We cannot forget how often, while their Master was with them, there were *strifes among them, who should be the greatest*; but now all these strifes were at an end, we hear no more of them. Would we have the Spirit *poured out upon us from on high*? Let us be all of one accord, and, notwithstanding variety of sentiments and interests, as no doubt there was among those disciples, let us agree to love one another; for, where *brethren dwell together in unity*, there it is that *the Lord commands his blessing*.

II. How, and in what manner, the Holy Ghost came upon them.

1. Here is an audible summons given them to awaken their expectations of something great, *v.* 2. It is here said, (1) That it came *suddenly*, did not rise gradually, as common winds do, but was at the height immediately. (2) It was *a sound from heaven*, like a thunder-clap, Rev. vi. 1. (3) It was the sound of a wind, for the way of the Spirit is like that of the wind (John iii. 8), *thou hearest the sound thereof, but canst not tell whence it comes nor whither it goes*. (4) It was a *rushing mighty wind*; it was strong and violent, and came not only with a great noise, but with great force, as if it would bear down all before it. This was to signify the powerful influences and operations of the Spirit of God upon the minds of men, and thereby upon the world. (5) *It filled* not only the room, but *all the house where they were sitting*. This wind filling the house would strike an awe upon the disciples, and help to put them into a very serious, reverent, and composed frame, for the receiving of the Holy Ghost.

2. Here is a visible sign of the gift they were to receive. They saw *cloven tongues, like as of fire* (*v.* 3), and *it sat*—he, that is the Spirit (signified thereby), rested upon each of them, as he is said to rest upon the prophets of old. Observe, (1) There was an outward sen-

sible sign, for the confirming of the faith of the disciples themselves, and for the convincing of others. Thus the prophets of old had frequently their first mission confirmed by signs, that all Israel might know them to be established prophets.

(2) The sign given was fire, that John Baptist's saying concerning Christ might be fulfilled, *He shall baptize you with the Holy Ghost and with fire*; with the Holy Ghost as with fire.

(3) This fire appeared in cloven tongues. The operations of the Spirit were many; that of speaking with divers tongues was one, and was singled out to be the first indication of the gift of the Holy Ghost, and to that this sign had a reference. [1] They were tongues; for from the Spirit we have the word of God, and by him Christ would speak to the world, and he gave the Spirit to the disciples, not only to endue them with knowledge, but to endue them with a power to publish and proclaim to the world what they knew; for *the dispensation of the Spirit is given to every man to profit withal*. [2] These tongues were cloven, to signify that God would hereby divide unto all nations the knowledge of his grace, as he is said to have divided to them by his providence the light of the heavenly bodies, Deut. iv. 19. The tongues were divided, and yet they still continued all of one accord; for there may be a sincere unity of affections where yet there is a diversity of expression.

(4) This fire sat upon them for some time, to denote the constant residence of the Holy Ghost with them. The prophetic gifts of old were conferred sparingly and but at some times, but the disciples of Christ had the gifts of the Spirit always with them, though the sign, we may suppose, soon disappeared.

III. What was the immediate effect of this? 1. *They were all filled with the Holy Ghost*, more plentifully and powerfully than they were before. It seems evident to me that not only the twelve apostles, but all the hundred and twenty disciples were *filled with the Holy Ghost* alike at this time—all the seventy disciples, who were apostolic men, and employed in the same work, and all the rest too that were to preach the gospel; for it is said expressly (Eph. iv. 8, 11). *When Christ ascended on high* (which refers to this, *v.* 33), *he gave gifts unto men*, not only *some apostles* (such were the twelve), but *some prophets* and *some evangelists* (such were many of the seventy disciples, itinerant preachers), and *some pastors and teachers* settled in particular churches, as we may suppose some of these afterwards were. The *all* here must refer to the *all* that were together, *v.* 1; *ch.* i. 14, 15. 2. *They began to speak with other tongues*, besides their native language, though they had never learned any other. They spoke not matters of common conversation, but the word of God, and the praises of his name, *as the Spirit gave them utterance*, or gave them to speak *apophthegms*, substantial and weighty sayings, worthy to be had in remembrance. They spoke not from any previous thought or meditation, but *as the Spirit gave them utterance*; he furnished them with the matter as well as the language.

Now this was, (1) A very great
miracle; it was a miracle upon the
mind (and so had most of the nature
of a gospel miracle), for in the
mind words are framed. (2) A very
proper, needful, and serviceable
miracle. The language the disciples
spoke was Syriac, a dialect of the
Hebrew; so that it was necessary
that they should be endued with the
gift, for the understanding, both of
the original Hebrew of the Old
Testament, in which it was written,
and of the original Greek of the
New Testament, in which it was
to be written. But this was not all;
they were commissioned to *preach
the gospel to every creature, to disciple all nations.* But here is an
insuperable difficulty at the thres-
hold. How shall they master the
several languages so as to speak
intelligibly to all nations? It will be
the work of a man's life to learn
their languages. And therefore, to
prove that Christ could give
authority to preach to the nations,
he gives ability to preach to them in
their own language. And it should
seem that this was the accomplishment of that promise which Christ
made to his disciples (John xiv. 12),
*Greater works than these shall you
do.* For this may well be reckoned,
all things considered, a greater
work than the miraculous cures
Christ wrought. Christ himself did
not speak with other tongues, nor
did he enable his disciples to do so
while he was with them: but it was
the first effect of the *pouring out of
the Spirit* upon them. And archbishop Tillotson thinks it probable
that if the conversion of infidels to
Christianity were now sincerely and
vigorously attempted, by men of

honest minds, God would extraordinarily countenance such an
attempt with all fitting assistance,
as he did the first publication of the
gospel.

NEW WINE (*vv.* 5-13)

We have here an account of the
public notice that was taken of this
extraordinary gift with which the
disciples were all on a sudden
endued. Observe,

I. The great concourse of people
that there was now at Jerusalem, it
should seem more than was usual at
the feast of pentecost. *There were
dwelling* or abiding *at Jerusalem*
Jews that were *devout men, out of
every nation under heaven,* whither
the Jews were dispersed, or whence
proselytes were come. Now, 1. We
may here see what were some of
those countries whence those strangers came (*vv.* 9-11).

II. The amazement with which
these strangers were seized when
they heard the disciples speak in
their own tongues. It should seem,
the disciples spoke in various languages before the people of those
languages came to them; for it is
intimated (*v.* 6) that the spreading
of the report of this abroad was that
which *brought the multitude together,* especially those of different
countries, who seem to have been
more affected with this work of
wonder than the inhabitants of
Jerusalem themselves.

1. They observe that the speakers
are all Galileans, they know no
other than their mother tongue (*v.*
7); they are despicable men, from
whom nothing learned nor polite is
to be expected.

2. They acknowledge that they spoke intelligibly and readily their own language (which they were the most competent judges of), so correctly and fluently that none of their own countrymen could speak it better: *We hear every man in our own tongue wherein we were born* (*v.* 8), that is, we hear one or other of them speak our native language. (1) The things they heard the apostles discourse of were the *wonderful works of God*. It is probable that the apostles spoke of Christ, and redemption by him, and the grace of the gospel; and these are indeed the *great things of God*, which will be for ever *marvellous in our eyes*. (2) They heard them both praise God for these great things and instruct the people concerning these things, *in their own tongue*, according as they perceived the language of their hearers, or those that enquired of them to be.

3. They wonder at it, and look upon it as an astonishing thing (*v.* 12): *They were all amazed*, they were in an *ecstasy*, so the word is; and they were in doubt what the meaning of it was, and whether it was to introduce the kingdom of the Messiah, which they were big with the expectation of.

III. The scorn which some made of it who were natives of Judea and Jerusalem, probably the scribes and Pharisees, and chief priests, who always resisted the Holy Ghost; they said, *These men are full of new wine*, or *sweet wine*; they have drunk too much this festival-time, *v.* 13. And, if they called the Master of the house a wine-bibber, no marvel if they so call those of his household.

PETER'S SERMON
(*vv.* 14–36)

We have here the first-fruits of the Spirit in the sermon which Peter preached immediately, directed, not to those of other nations in a strange language (we are not told what answer he gave to those that were amazed, and said, *What meaneth this?*) but to the Jews in the vulgar language, even to those that mocked; for he begins with the notice of that (*v.* 15), and addresses his discourse (*v.* 14) *to the men of Judea and the inhabitants of Jerusalem*. Observe,

I. His introduction or preface, wherein he craves the attention of the auditory, or demands it rather. He applied himself to *the men of Judea—the men that were Jews*; so it should be read; "and you especially *that dwell at Jerusalem*, who were accessory to the death of Jesus, *be this known unto you*, which you did not know before, and which you are concerned to know now, *and hearken to my words.*"

II. His answer to their blasphemous calumny (*v.* 15): "*These men are not drunken, as you suppose.* You cannot think they are drunk, for *it is but the third hour of the day,*" nine of the clock in the morning; and before this time, on the sabbaths and solemn feasts, the Jews did not eat nor drink.

III. His account of the miraculous effusion of the Spirit, which is designed to awaken them all to embrace the faith of Christ, and to join themselves to his church. Two things he resolves it into:—that it was the fulfilling of the scripture, and the fruit of Christ's resurrection

9

and ascension, and consequently the proof of both.

1. That it was the accomplishment of the prophecies of the Old Testament which related to the kingdom of the Messiah, and therefore an evidence that this kingdom is come, and the other predictions of it are fulfilled. He specifies one, that of *the prophet Joel, ch.* ii. 28. Observe,

(1) The text itself that Peter quotes, *vv.* 17–21. It refers to *the last days*, the times of the gospel, which are called *the last days* because the dispensation of God's kingdom among men, which the gospel sets up, is the last dispensation of divine grace, and we are to look for no other than the continuation of this to the end of time.

(2) The application of this prophecy to the present event (*v.* 16): *This is that which was spoken by the prophet Joel*; it is the accomplishment of that, it is the full accomplishment of it.

2. That it was the gift of Christ, and the product and proof of his resurrection and ascension. From this *gift of the Holy Ghost*, he takes occasion to preach unto them Jesus. Here is,

(1) An abstract of the history of the life of Christ, *v.* 22. He calls him *Jesus of Nazareth*, because by that name he was generally known, but (which was sufficient to roll away that reproach) he was *a man approved of God among you*, censured and condemned by men, but approved of God: God testified his approbation of his doctrine by the power he gave him to work miracles. See what a stress Peter lays upon Christ's miracles. [1] The

matter of fact was not to be denied: "They were done *in the midst of you*, in the midst of your country, your city, your solemn assemblies, *as you yourselves also know*." [2] The inference from them cannot be disputed; the reasoning is as strong as the evidence; if he did those miracles, certainly God approved him, *declared him to be*, what he declared himself to be, *the Son of God* and *the Saviour of the world*; for the God of truth would never set his seal to a lie.

(2) An account of his death and sufferings which they were witness of also but a few weeks ago; and this was the greatest miracle of all, that a man approved of God should thus seem to be abandoned of him; and a man thus approved among the people, and in the midst of them, should be thus abandoned by them too. But both these mysteries are here explained (*v.* 23), and his death considered, [1] As God's act; and in him it was an act of wonderful grace and wisdom. For it was done by *the determinate counsel and foreknowledge of God*, in infinite wisdom, and for holy ends, which Christ himself concurred in, and in the means leading to them. [2] As the people's act; and in them it was an act of prodigious sin and folly; it was fighting against God to persecute one whom he approved as the darling of heaven; and fighting against their own mercies to persecute one that was the greatest blessing of this earth.

(3) An attestation of his resurrection, which effectually wiped away the reproach of his death (*v.* 24): *Whom God raised up*; the same that delivered him *to death*

delivers him *from death*, and thereby gave a higher approbation of him than he had done by any other of *the signs and wonders wrought by him*, or by all put together. This therefore he insists most largely upon.

[1] He describes his resurrection: God *loosed the pains of death, because it was impossible that he should be holden of it.* Christ was imprisoned for our debt, was thrown into the bands of death; but, divine justice being satisfied, it was not possible he should be detained there, either by right or by force; for he had life in himself, and in his own power, and had conquered the prince of death.

[2] He attests the truth of his resurrection (*v.* 32): *God hath raised him up, whereof we all are witnesses.*

[3] He showed it to be the fulfilling of the scripture, and, because the scripture had said that he must rise again before he saw corruption, therefore *it was impossible that he should be holden* by *death* and *the grave; for David speaks* of his being raised, so it comes in, *v.* 25. The scripture he refers to is that of David (Ps. xvi. 8–11), which, though in part applicable to David as a saint, yet refers chiefly to Jesus Christ, of whom David was a type.

To prove that when he spoke of the resurrection he meant it of Christ, he observes that when in another psalm he speaks of the next step of his exaltation he plainly shows that he spoke of another person, and such another as was his Lord (Ps. cx. 1): *"The Lord said unto my Lord,* when he had raised him from the dead, *Sit thou at my right hand,* in the highest dignity and dominion there; be thou entrusted with the administration of the kingdom both of providence and grace; *sit there* as king, *until I make thy foes* either thy friends or *thy footstool," v.* 35. Christ rose from the grave to rise higher, and therefore it must be of his resurrection that David spoke, and not his own, in the 16th Psalm; for there was no occasion for him to rise out of his grave who was not to ascend to heaven.

(4) The application of this discourse concerning the death, resurrection, and ascension of Christ.

[1] This explains the meaning of the present wonderful effusion of the Spirit in those extraordinary gifts. *The gift of the Holy Ghost* was, *First,* A performance of divine promises already made; here it is called *the promise of the Holy Ghost.* Christ received *the promise of the Holy Ghost,* that is, the promised gift of the Holy Ghost, and has given it to us; for all *the promises are yea and amen in him. Secondly,* It was a pledge of all divine favours further intended; what you now see and hear is but an earnest of greater things.

[2] This proves what you are all bound to believe, *that* Christ Jesus is the true Messiah and Saviour of the world. *Therefore let all the house of Israel know assuredly* that this truth has now received its full confirmation, and we our full commission to publish it, *That God has made that same Jesus whom you have crucified both Lord and Christ.* This is the great truth of the gospel which we are to believe, *that that same Jesus,* the very same *that was crucified at Jerusalem,* is he to

whom we owe allegiance, and from whom we are to expect protection, as *Lord and Christ*.

THREE THOUSAND CONVERTS
(*vv.* 37–41)

In these verses we find the word of God the means of beginning and carrying on a good work of grace in the hearts of many, *the Spirit of the Lord working by it*. Let us see the method of it.

I. They were startled, and convinced, and put upon a serious enquiry, *v.* 37. Peter had charged them with having a hand, a *wicked hand*, in his death, which was likely to have exasperated them against him; yet, when they heard this plain scriptural sermon, they were much affected with it.

1. It put them in pain: *They were pricked in their hearts*.

2. It put them upon enquiry. *Out of the abundance of the heart, the mouth spoke*. Observe,

(1) To whom they thus addressed themselves: *To Peter and to the rest of the apostles*.

(2) What the address is: *What shall we do?* [1] They speak as men at a stand, that did not know what to do; in a perfect surprise: "*Is that Jesus* whom we have crucified both *Lord and Christ?* Then what will become of us who crucified him? We are all undone!" [2] They speak as men at a point, that were resolved to do any thing they should be directed to immediately.

II. Peter and the other apostles direct them in short what they must do, and what in so doing they might expect, *vv.* 38, 39.

1. He here shows them the course they must take. (1) *Repent*; this is a plank after shipwreck. "*Repent, repent*; change your mind, change your way; admit an after-thought." (2) *Be baptized every one of you in the name of Jesus Christ*. They must be baptized *in the name of Jesus Christ*. They did believe in the Father and the Holy Ghost speaking by the prophets; but they must also believe in the name of Jesus, that he is the Christ, the Messiah promised to the fathers. (3) This is pressed upon each particular person: *Every one of you*.

2. He gives them encouragement to take this course:—(1) "It shall be for *the remission of sins*. Repent of your sin, and it shall not be your ruin; be baptized into the faith of Christ, and in truth you shall be justified, which you could never be by the law of Moses." (2) "You shall *receive the gift of the Holy Ghost* as well as we; for it is designed for a general blessing." Note, All that receive the remission of sins *receive the gift of the Holy Ghost*. All that are justified are sanctified. (3) "Your children shall still have, as they have had, an interest in the covenant, and a title to the external seal of it. Come over to Christ, to receive those inestimable benefits; for the promise of the remission of sins, and the gift of the Holy Ghost, is *to you and to your children*," *v.* 39. It was very express (Isa. xliv. 3): *I will pour my Spirit upon thy seed*. And (Isa. lix. 21), *My Spirit and my word shall not depart from thy seed, and thy seed's seed*. (4) "Though the promise is still extended to your children as it has been, yet it is not, as it has been,

confined to you and them, but the benefit of it is *designed* for *all that are afar off.*" To this general the following limitation must refer, *even as many of them,* as many particular persons in each nation, *as the Lord our God shall call* effectually into the fellowship of Jesus Christ.

III. These directions are followed with a needful caution (*v.* 40): *With many other words,* to the same purport, *did he testify* gospel truths, and exhort to gospel duties; now that the word began to work he followed it; he had said much in a little (*vv.* 38, 39), and that which, one would think, included all, and yet he had more to say.

IV. Here is the happy success and issue of this, *v.* 41. The Spirit wrought with the word, and wrought wonders by it. These same persons that had many of them been eye-witnesses of the death of Christ, and the prodigies that attended it, and were not wrought upon by them, were yet wrought upon by the preaching of the word, for it is this that is the *power of God unto salvation.* 1. They received the word; and *then* only the word does us good, when we do receive it, embrace it, and bid it welcome. 2. They gladly received it. Herod *heard* the word gladly, but these gladly *received* it. 3. They were baptized; believing with the heart, they made confession with the mouth, and enrolled themselves among the disciples of Christ by that sacred rite and ceremony which he had instituted. 4. Hereby there were added to the disciples to the number of about *three thousand souls that same day.*

THE INFANT CHURCH
(*vv.* 42–47)

We often speak of the primitive church, and appeal to it, and to the history of it; in these verses we have the history of the *truly primitive church,* of the *first days* of it, its state of infancy indeed, but, like that, the state of its greatest *innocence.*

I. They kept close to holy ordinances, and abounded in all instances of piety and devotion, for Christianity, admitted in the power of it, will dispose the soul to communion with God in all those ways wherein he has appointed us to meet him and promised to meet us.

1. They were diligent and constant in their attendance upon the *preaching of the word.* They *continued in the apostles' doctrine,* and never disowned nor deserted it.

2. They kept up the *communion of saints.* They continued *in fellowship* (*v.* 42), and *continued daily with one accord in the temple, v.* 46. They had fellowship with one another in religious worship. They met *in the temple*: there was their rendezvous; for joint-fellowship with God is the best fellowship we can have with one another, 1 John i. 3.

3. They frequently joined in the ordinance of the Lord's supper. They continued *in the breaking of bread,* in celebrating that memorial of their Master's death, as those that were not ashamed to own their relation to, and their dependence upon, Christ and him crucified. They did not think fit to celebrate the eucharist in the temple, for that was peculiar to the Christian institutes, and therefore they adminis-

tered that ordinance in private houses, choosing such houses of the converted Christians as were convenient, to which the neighbours resorted; and they went from one to another of these little synagogues or domestic chapels, houses that had churches in them, and there celebrated the eucharist with those that usually met there to worship God.

4. They continued *in prayers*. *After* the Spirit was poured out, as well as before, while they were waiting for him, they continued instant in prayer; for prayer will never be superseded till it comes to be swallowed up in everlasting praise.

5. They abounded in thanksgiving; were continually *praising God, v.* 47. This should have a part in every prayer, and not be crowded into a corner. Those that have received the gift of the Holy Ghost will be much in praise.

II. They were loving one to another, and very kind; their charity was as eminent as their piety, and their joining together in holy ordinances knit their hearts to each other, and very much endeared them to one another.

1. They had frequent meetings for Christian converse (*v.* 44). They associated together, and so both expressed and increased their mutual love.

2. They had *all things common*. There was such a concern for one another, and such a readiness to help one another as there was occasion, that it might be said, They had *all things common*, according to the law of friendship; one wanted not what another had; for he might have it for the asking.

3. They were very cheerful, and very generous in the use of what they had. Besides the religion that was in their sacred feasts, (their *breaking bread from house to house*) a great deal of it appeared in their common meals; they did *eat their meat with gladness and singleness of heart*.

4. They raised a fund for charity (*v.* 45): They *sold their possessions and goods*; some sold their lands and houses, others their stocks and the furniture of their houses, and *parted* the money to their brethren, *as every man had need*. This was to destroy, not property (as Mr. Baxter says), but selfishness. Herein, probably, they had an eye to the command which Christ gave to the rich man, as a test of his sincerity, *Sell that thou hast, and give to the poor*.

III. God owned them, and gave them signal tokens of his presence with them (*v.* 43): *Many wonders and signs were done by the apostles* of divers sorts, which confirmed their doctrine, and incontestably proved that it was from God.

But the Lord's giving them power to work miracles was not all he did for them; he *added to the church daily*. The word in their mouths *did wonders*, and God blessed their endeavours for the increase of the number of believers. Note, It is God's work to add souls to the church; and it is a great comfort both to ministers and Christians to see it.

IV. The people were influenced by it; those that were without, the standers by, that were spectators. 1. They *feared them*, and had a veneration for them (*v.* 43). 2. They

14

favoured them. Though we have reason to think there were those that despised them and hated them (we are sure the Pharisees and chief priests did), yet far the greater part of the common people had a kindness for them—they *had favour with all the people.* 3. They *fell over* to them. Some or other were daily coming in, though not so many as the first day; and they were such as *should be saved.* Note, Those that God has designed for eternal salvation shall one time or other be effectually brought to Christ: and those that are brought to Christ are *added to the church* in a holy covenant by baptism, and in holy communion by other ordinances.

CHAPTER THREE
LAME MAN HEALED
(*vv.* 1–11)

We were told in general (*ch.* ii. 43) that *many signs and wonders were done by the apostles,* which are not written in this book; but here we have one given us for an instance.

I. The persons by whose ministry this miracle was wrought were Peter and John, two principal men among the apostles.

II. The time and place are here set down. 1. It was in *the temple,* whither *Peter and John went up together,* because it was the place of concourse. 2. It was *at the hour of prayer,* one of the hours of public worship commonly appointed and observed among the Jews.

III. The patient on whom this miraculous cure was wrought is here described, *v.* 2. He was a poor lame beggar at the temple gate. 1. He was a cripple, not by accident, but born

so; he was *lame from his mother's womb,* as it should seem, by a paralytic distemper, which weakened his limbs; for it is said in the description of his cure (*v.* 7), *His feet and ankle bones received strength.* 2. He was a beggar. Being unable to work for his living, he must live upon alms; such are God's poor. He was *laid daily* by his friends at *one of the gates of the temple,* a miserable spectacle, unable to do any thing for himself but to *ask alms of those that entered into the temple* or came out. 3. He begged of Peter and John (*v.* 3), begged an alms; this was the utmost he expected from them, who had the reputation of being charitable men, and who, though they had not much, yet did good with what they had.

IV. We have here the method of the cure.

1. His expectations were raised. Peter, instead of turning his eyes from him, as many do from objects of charity, turned his eyes to him, nay, he *fastened his eyes upon him,* that his eye might affect his heart with compassion towards him, *v.* 4. John did so too, for they were both guided by one and the same Spirit, and concurred in this miracle; they said, *Look on us.*

2. His expectation of an alms was disappointed. Peter said, "*Silver and gold have I none,* and therefore none to give thee;" yet he intimated that if he had had any he would have given him an alms, not brass, but silver or gold.

3. His expectations, notwithstanding, were quite outdone. Peter had no money to give him; but, (1) He had that which was better, such an interest in heaven, such a power

from heaven, as to be able to cure his disease. (2) He gave him that which was better—the cure of his disease, which he would gladly have given a great deal of silver and gold for, if he had had it, and the cure could have been so obtained.

Let us now see how the cure was wrought. [1] Christ *sent his word and healed him* (Ps. cvii. 20); for healing grace is given by the word of Christ: this is the vehicle of the healing virtue derived from Christ. Christ spoke cures by himself; the apostles spoke them in his name. Peter bids a lame man *rise up and walk*, which would have been a banter upon him if he had not premised *in the name of Jesus Christ of Nazareth*. [2] Peter lent his hand, and helped him (*v.* 7). Not that this could contribute any thing to his cure; but it was a sign, plainly intimating the help he should receive from God, if he exerted himself as he was bidden. *His feet and ankle-bones received strength*, which they had not done if he had not attempted to rise, and been helped up; he does his part, and Peter does his, and yet it is Christ that does all: it is he that puts strength into him.

V. Here is the impression which this cure made upon the patient himself, which we may best conceive of it we put our soul into his soul's stead. 1. He leaped up, in obedience to the command, *Arise*. He leaped, as one glad to quit the bed or pad of straw on which he had lain so long lame. 2. He stood, and walked. He stood without either leaning or trembling, stood straight up, and walked without a staff. 3. He *held Peter and John*, *v.* 11. We need not ask why he held them. I

believe he scarcely knew himself: but it was in a transport of joy that he embraced them as the best benefactors he had ever met with. 4. He *entered with them into the temple*. His strong affection to them held them; but it could not hold them so fast as to keep them out of the temple, whither they were going to preach Christ. 5. He was there *walking*, *and leaping*, *and praising God*. All true converts walk and praise God; but perhaps young converts leap more in his praises.

VI. How the people that were eye-witnesses of this miracle were influenced by it we are next told. 1. They were entirely satisfied in the truth of the miracle, and had nothing to object against it. *They knew it was he that sat begging at the beautiful gate of the temple*, *v.* 10. 2. They were astonished at it: They were *filled with wonder and amazement* (*v.* 10); *greatly wondering*, *v.* 11. They were in an *ecstasy*. 3. They gathered about Peter and John: *All the people ran together unto them in Solomon's porch*.

PETER'S EXPLANATION
(*vv.* 12–26)

We have here the sermon which Peter preached after he had cured the lame man. In the sermon,

I. He humbly disclaims the honour of the miracle as not due to them, who were only the ministers of Christ, or instruments in his hand for the doing of it. Two things he asks them: 1. Why they were so surprised at the miracle itself. It was but a little before that Christ had *raised Lazarus from the dead*; and why should this then seem so strange? 2. Why they gave so much of the praise of it to them, who were only the instruments of it: *Why look you so earnestly on us?* They did not do it by any *power or holiness of their own*. It was not done by any might of their own, any skill they had in physic or surgery, nor any virtue in their word: the power they did it by was wholly derived from Christ.

II. He preaches Christ to them; this was his business, that he might lead them into obedience to Christ.

1. He preaches Christ, as the true Messiah promised to the fathers (*v.* 13).

2. He charges them flatly and plainly with the murder of this Jesus, as he had done before. *You killed the prince of life.* Observe the antithesis: "You preserved *a murderer*, a destroyer of life; and destroyed the Saviour, *the author of life*."

3. He attests his resurrection as before, *ch.* ii. 32.

4. He ascribes the cure of this impotent man to the power of Christ (*v.* 16). Here, (1) He appeals to themselves concerning the truth of the miracle; the man on whom it was wrought is one *whom you see, and know, and have known.* (2) He acquaints them with the power by which it was wrought. [1] It is done by the name of Christ, not merely by naming it as a spell or charm, but it is done by us as professors and teachers of his name, by virtue of a commission and instructions we have received from him and a power which he has invested us with. [2] The power of Christ is fetched in *through faith in his name*, a confidence in him, a dependence on him, a believing application to him.

III. He encourages them to hope that, though they had been guilty of putting Christ to death, yet they might find mercy; he does all he can to convince them, yet is careful not to drive them to despair. The guilt was very great, but, 1. He mollifies their crime by a candid imputation of it to their ignorance. 2. He mollifies the effects of their crime—the death of *the prince of life*; this sounds very dreadful, but it was *according to the scriptures* (*v.* 18), the predictions of which, though they did not necessitate their sin, yet did necessitate his sufferings. Now, though this is no extenuation at all of their sin in hating and persecuting Christ *to the death* (this still appears exceedingly sinful), yet it was an encouragement to them to repent, and hope for mercy upon their repentance; not only because in general God's gracious designs were carried on by it, but because in particular the death and sufferings of Christ were for *the remission of sins*, and the ground of that display of mercy for which he now encouraged them to hope.

IV. He exhorts them all to turn Christians, and assures them it would be unspeakably for their advantage to do so; it would be the making of them for ever. This is the application of his sermon.

1. He tells them what they must believe. (1) They must believe that Jesus Christ is the promised seed, that seed in which God had told Abraham *all the kindreds of the earth should be blessed, v.* 25. (2) They must believe that Jesus Christ is a prophet, *that prophet like unto Moses* whom God had promised to

raise up to them from among their brethren, v. 22. This refers to that promise, Deut. xviii. 18. (3) They must believe *that times of refreshing will come from the presence of the Lord* (v. 19), and that they will be *the times of the restitution of all things*, v. 21. There is a future state, another life after this; those times will come from the presence of the Lord, from his glorious appearance at that day, his coming at the end of time. The presence of the Lord will introduce, [1] *The restitution of all things* (v. 21); *the new heavens, and the new earth*, which will be the product of the dissolution of all things (Rev. xxi. 1), the renovation of the whole creation. [2] With this will come *the times of refreshing* (v. 19), of consolation to the Lord's people, like a cool shade to those *that have borne the burden and heat of the day*

2. He tells them what they must do. (1) They must *repent*, must bethink themselves of what they have done amiss, must return to their right mind, admit a second thought, and submit to the convictions of it; they must begin anew. (2) They must *be converted*, must face about, and direct both their faces and steps the contrary way to what they had been; they must *return to the Lord their God*, from whom they had revolted. (3) They must hear Christ, the great prophet. Attend his dictates, receive his doctrine, submit to his government.

3. He tells them what they might expect.

(1) That they should have the pardon of their sins; this is always spoken of as the great privilege of all those that embrace the gospel

(v. 19): *Repent, and be converted, that your sins may be blotted out.*

(2) That they should have the comfort of Christ's coming (vv, 20, 21). For, though *the heavens must receive him till the times of the restitution of all things*; yet, if you *repent and be converted*, you shall find no want of him; some way or other he shall be seen of you.

4. He tells them what ground they had to expect these things, if they were converted to Christ. Though they had denied him, and put him to death, yet they might hope to find favour through him, upon the account of their being Israelites. For,

(1) As Israelites, they had the monopoly of the grace of the Old Testament; they were, above any other, God's favourite nation, and the favours God bestowed upon them were such as had a reference to the Messiah, and his kingdom: *You are the children of the prophets, and of the covenant.*

(2) As Israelites, they had the first offer of the grace of the New Testament. Because *they were the children of the prophets and the covenant*, therefore to them the Redeemer was first sent, which was an encouragement to them to hope that if they did repent, and were converted, he should be yet further sent for their comfort (v. 20): *He shall send Jesus Christ*, for to you first he hath sent him, v. 26.

CHAPTER FOUR

PETER AND JOHN ARRESTED
(vv. 1–4)

I. The apostles, Peter and John, went on in their work, and did not labour in vain. The Spirit enabled the ministers to do their part, and the people theirs.

1. The preachers faithfully deliver the doctrine of Christ: *They spoke unto the people*, to all that were within hearing, *v.* 1.

The hearers cheerfully receive it (*v.* 4): *Many of those who heard the word believed*; not all—perhaps not the most, yet many, *to the number of about five thousand*, over and above the three thousand we read of before.

II. The chief priests and their party now made head against them, and did what they could to crush them; their hands were tied awhile, but their hearts were not in the least changed. It grieved them that the apostles *preached through Jesus the resurrection from the dead*. The Sadducees were grieved that the resurrection from the dead was preached; for they opposed that doctrine, and could not bear to hear of a future state, to hear it so well attested. The chief priests were grieved that they preached the resurrection of the dead through Jesus, that he should have the honour of it.

PETER AND JOHN EXAMINED (*vv.* 5–14)

We have here the trial of Peter and John before the judges of the ecclesiastical court.

I. Here is the court set. An extraordinary court, it should seem, was called on purpose upon this occasion. Here were Annas and Caiaphas, ringleaders in this persecution; Annas the president of the sanhedrim, and Caiaphas the high priest (though Annas is here called so) and *father of the house of judgment*. It should seem that Annas and Caiaphas executed the high priest's office alternately, year for year.

II. The prisoners are arraigned, *v.* 7. 1. They are brought to the bar; they *set them in the midst*, for the sanhedrim sat in a circle, and those who had any thing to do in the court stood or sat in the midst of them (Luke ii. 46), so Dr. Lightfoot. 2. The question they asked them was, "*By what power, or by what name, have you done this?* By what authority do you these things?" (the same question that they had asked their Master, Matt. xxi. 23.)

III. The plea they put in, the design of which was not so much to clear and secure themselves as to advance the name and honour of their Master. Observe,

1. By whom this plea was drawn up: it was dictated by the Holy Ghost, who fitted Peter more than before for this occasion. Mark xiii. 11.

2. To whom it was given in: Peter, who is still the chief speaker, addresses himself to the judges of the court, as the *rulers of the people, and elders of* Israel; for the wickedness of those in power does not divest them of their power.

3. What the plea is: it is a solemn declaration,

(1) That what they did was in the name of Jesus Christ, which was a direct answer to the question the court asked them (*vv.* 9, 10). Here [1] He justifies what he and his colleague had done in curing the lame man. It was a *good deed*; it was a kindness to the man that had begged, but could not work for his

living. [2] He transfers all the praise and glory of this good deed to Jesus Christ. "It is by him, and not by any power of ours, that this man is cured." [3] He charges it upon the judges themselves, that they had been the murderers of this Jesus. [4] He attests the resurrection of Christ as the strongest testimony for him, and against his persecutors. [5] He preaches this to all the bystanders, to be by them repeated to all their neighbours, and commands all manner of persons, from the highest to the lowest, to take notice of it at their peril.

(2) That the name of this Jesus, by the authority of which they acted, is that name alone by which we can be saved. It is not an indifferent thing, but of absolute necessity, that people believe in this name, and call upon it. We are lost if we do not take shelter in this name, and make it our refuge and strong tower; for we cannot be saved but by Jesus Christ, and, if we be not eternally saved, we are eternally lost (*v.* 12): *Neither is there salvation in any other.* As there is no other name by which diseased bodies can be cured, so there is no other by which sinful souls can be saved.

IV. The stand that the court was put to in the prosecution, by this plea, *vv.* 13, 14.

1. They could not deny the cure of the lame man to be both a good deed and a miracle.

2. They could not, with all their pomp and power, face down Peter and John. Probably there was something extraordinary and very surprising in their looks; they appeared not only undaunted by the rulers, but daring and daunting to them. Now, (1) We are here told what increased their wonder: They *perceived that they were unlearned and ignorant men.* Yet speak to them of the Messiah and his kingdom, and they speak with so much clearness, evidence, and assurance, so pertinently and so fluently, and are so ready in the scriptures of the Old Testament relating to it, that the most learned judge upon the bench is not able to answer them, nor to enter the lists with them. (2) We are told what made their wonder in a great measure to cease: they *took knowledge of them that they had been with Jesus.* When they understood that *they had been with Jesus,* had been conversant with him, attendant on him, and trained up under him, they knew what to impute their boldness to; nay, their boldness in divine things was enough to show with whom they had had their education.

RELEASE (*vv.* 15–22)

We have here the issue of the trial of Peter and John before the council.

I. Here is the consultation and resolution of the court about this matter, and their proceeding thereupon.

1. The prisoners were ordered to withdraw (*v.* 15).

2. A debate arose upon this matter: *They conferred among themselves*; every one is desired to speak his mind freely, and to give advice upon this important affair.

3. They came at last to a resolution, in two things:

(1) That it was not safe to punish the apostles for what they had done.

Very willingly would they have done it, but they had not courage to do it, because the people espoused their cause, and cried up the miracle; and they stood now in as much awe of them as they had done formerly, when they durst not lay hands on Christ *for fear of the people*.

(2) That it was nevertheless necessary to silence them for the future, *vv.* 17, 18. They could not prove that they had said or done any thing amiss, and yet they must no more say nor do what they have done. All their care is that the doctrine of Christ *spread no further among the people*; as if that healing institution were a plague begun, the contagion of which must be stopped. Now, to prevent the further spreading of this doctrine, [1] They charge the apostles never to preach it any more. [2] They threaten them if they do, strictly threaten them: it is at their peril. This court will reckon itself highly affronted if they do, and they shall fall under its displeasure.

II. Here is the courageous resolution of the prisoners to go on in their work, notwithstanding the resolutions of this court, and their declaration of this resolution, *vv.* 19, 20. They do, in effect, tell them that they are resolved to go on in preaching, and justify themselves in it with two things: 1. The command of God. If men's commands and God's interfere God's commands must take place.

III. Here is the discharge of the prisoners (*v.* 21): *They further threatened them*, and thought they frightened them, and then *let them go*.

THE CHURCH GIVES THANKS
(*vv.* 23–31)

We hear no more at present of the chief priests, what they did when they had dismissed Peter and John, but are to attend those *two witnesses*. And here we have,

I. Their return to their brethren, the apostles and ministers, and perhaps some private Christians (*v.* 23).

II. The account they gave them of what had passed. They related it to them, 1. That they might know what to expect both from men and from God in the progress of their work. 2. That they might have it recorded in the history of the church, for the benefit of posterity, particularly for the confirmation of our faith touching the resurrection of Christ. 3. That they might now join with them in prayers and praises; and by such a concert as this God would be the more glorified, and the church the more edified.

III. Their address to God upon this occasion. *They lifted up their voice to God with one accord*, *v.* 24. Now in this solemn address to God we have,

1. Their adoration of God as the Creator of the world (*v.* 24). Thus we Christians distinguish ourselves from the heathen, that, while they worship gods which they have made, we are worshipping the God that made us and all the world.

2. Their reconciling themselves to the present dispensations of Providence, by reflecting upon those scriptures in the Old Testament which foretold that the kingdom of the Messiah would meet with such opposition as this at the

first setting of it up in the world, *vv.* 25, 26.

3. Their representation of the present accomplishment of those predictions in the enmity and malice of the rulers against Christ. What was foretold we see fulfilled, *vv.* 27, 28. See here, (1) The wise and holy designs God had concerning Christ. He is here called the *child Jesus*, as he was called (Luke ii. 27, 43) in his infancy, to intimate that even in his exalted state he is not ashamed of his condescensions for us, and that he continues meek and lowly in heart. In the height of his glory he is the *Lamb of God*, and the *child Jesus*. But he is the *holy child Jesus* (so he was called, Luke i. 35, *that holy thing*), and *thy* holy child; the word signifies both a son and a servant. He was the Son of God; and yet in the work of redemption he acted as his Father's servant (Isa. xlii. 1), *My servant whom I uphold*. Now the God that anointed Christ determined what should be done to him, pursuant to that anointing. He was anointed to be a Saviour, and therefore it was determined he should be a sacrifice to make atonement for sin. God's *hand*, which properly denotes his executive power, is here put for his purpose and decree, because with him saying and doing are not two things, as they are with us. (2) The wicked and unholy instruments that were employed in the executing of this design, though they *meant not so, neither did their hearts think so*.

4. Their petition with reference to the case at this time. The enemies *were gathered together against Christ*, and then no wonder

that they were so against his ministers: *the disciple is not better than his Master*, nor must expect better treatment; but, being thus insulted, they pray,

(1) That God would take cognizance of the malice of their enemies.

(2) That God, by his grace, would keep up their spirits, and animate them to go on cheerfully with their work.

(3) That God would still give them power to work miracles for the confirmation of the doctrine they preached, which, by *the cure of the lame man*, they found to contribute very much to their success, and would contribute abundantly to their further progress: *Lord, grant us boldness, by stretching forth thy hand to heal*.

IV. The gracious answer God gave to this address, not in word, but in power. 1. God gave them a sign of the acceptance of their prayers (*v.* 31). The place was shaken, that their faith might be established and unshaken. 2. God gave them greater degrees of his Spirit, which was what they prayed for. Their prayer, without doubt, was accepted, for it was answered: *They were all filled with the Holy Ghost*, more than ever. When *they were filled with the Holy Ghost, they spoke the word with all boldness;* for *the ministration of the Spirit is given to every man, to profit withal*. Talents must be traded with, not buried.

ALL THINGS IN COMMON (*vv.* 32–37)

We have a general idea given us in these verses, and it is a very beautiful one, of the spirit and state of this truly primitive church.

I. The disciples loved one another dearly. Observe here, 1. There were multitudes that believed; even in Jerusalem, where the malignant influence of the chief priests was most strong, *there were three thousand* converted on one day, and *five thousand* on another, and, besides these, *there were added to the church daily.* 2. They *were all of one heart, and of one soul.* Though there were many, very many, of different ages, tempers, and conditions, in the world, who perhaps, before they believed, were perfect strangers to one another, yet, when they met in Christ, they were as intimately acquainted as if they had known one another many years.

II. The ministers went on in their work with great vigour and success (*v.* 33). The doctrine they preached was, the resurrection of Christ.

III. The beauty of the Lord our God shone upon them, and all their performances: *Great grace was upon them all,* not only all the apostles, but all the believers.

IV. They were very liberal to the poor, and dead to this world. This was as great an evidence of the grace of God in them as any other, and recommended them as much to the esteem of the people.

1. They insisted not upon property, which even children seem to have a sense of and a jealousy for, and which worldly people triumph in. These believers were so taken up with the hopes of an inheritance in the other world that this was as nothing to them. They did not take away property, but they were indifferent to it. What we have in the world is more God's than our own; we have it from him, must use it for him, and are accountable for it to him.

2. They abounded in charity, so that, in effect, *they had all things common*; for (*v.* 34) *there was not any among them that lacked,* but care was taken for their supply.

3. Many of them sold their estates, to raise a fund for charity. Now,

(1) We are here told what they did with the money that was so raised: They *laid it at the apostles' feet*—they left it to them to be disposed of as they thought fit. Being laid there, it was not hoarded up, but *distribution was made,* by proper persons, *unto every man according as he had need.*

(2) Here is one particular person mentioned that was remarkable for this generous charity: it was *Barnabas,* afterwards Paul's colleague. Observe, [1] The account here given concerning him, *v.* 36. It is probable that he was one of the seventy disciples, and, as he increased in gifts and graces, grew eminent, and was respected by the apostles, who, in token of their value for him, gave him a name, *Barnabas—the son of prophecy* (so it properly signifies), he being endued with extraordinary gifts of prophecy. *A son of exhortation* (so some), one that had an excellent faculty of healing and persuading; we have an instance of it, *ch.* xi. 22–24. *A son of consolation* (so we read it); one that did himself walk very much in *the comforts of the Holy Ghost*—a cheerful Christian, and this enlarged his heart in charity to the poor; or one that

was eminent for comforting the Lord's people, and speaking peace to wounded troubled consciences; he had an admirable facility that way. [2] Here is an account of his charity, and great generosity to the public fund.

CHAPTER FIVE

ANANIAS AND SAPPHIRA
(*vv*. 1–11)

The chapter begins with a melancholy *but*, which puts a stop to the pleasant and agreeable prospect of things which we had in the foregoing chapters; as every man, so every church, in its best state has its *but*. Observe here,

I. The sin of Ananias and Sapphira his wife. Now their sin was, 1. That they were ambitious of being thought eminent disciples, and of the first rank, when really they were not true disciples. 2. That they were covetous of the wealth of the world, and distrustful of God and his providence. Thus they thought to serve both God and mammon—God, by bringing part of the money to the apostles' feet, and mammon, by keeping the other part in their own pockets. 3. That they thought to deceive the apostles, and make them believe they brought the whole purchase-money, when really it was but a part. They dissembled with God and his Spirit, with Christ and his church and ministers; and this was their sin.

II. The indictment of Ananias, which proved both his condemnation and execution for this sin. When he brought the money, and expected to be commended and encouraged, as others were, Peter took him to task about it. Had it been a sin of infirmity, through the surprise of a temptation, Peter would have taken Ananias aside, and have bidden him go home, and fetch the rest of the money, and repent of his folly in attempting to put this cheat upon them; but he knew *that his heart was fully set in him to do this evil*, and therefore allowed him not space to repent. He here showed him,

1. The origin of his sin: *Satan filled his heart*.

2. The sin itself: *He lied to the Holy Ghost*; a sin of such a heinous nature that he could not have been guilty of it if Satan had not filled his heart.

3. The aggravations of the sin (*v*. 4). Which may be understood two ways: (1) "Thou wast under no temptation *to keep back part of the price*; before it was sold it was thy own, and when it was sold it was in thy own power to dispose of the money at thy pleasure." Or, (2) "Thou wast under no necessity of selling thy land at all, nor bringing any of the money to the apostles' feet. Thou mightest have kept the money, if thou hadst pleased, and the land too, and never have pretended to this piece of perfection."

4. All this guilt, thus aggravated, is charged upon him: *Why hast thou conceived this thing in thine heart?*

III. The death and burial of Ananias, *vv*. 5, 6.

1. He died upon the spot. It does not appear whether Peter designed and expected that this would follow upon what he said to him; it is probable that he did, for to Sapphira his wife Peter particularly spoke death, *v*. 9. This punishment

24

of Ananias may seem severe, but we are sure it was just. (1) It was designed to maintain the honour of the Holy Ghost, as now lately poured out upon the apostles, in order to the setting up of the gospel kingdom. (2) It was designed to deter others from the like presumptions, now at the beginning of this dispensation.

2. He was buried immediately, for this was the manner of the Jews (*v.* 6).

IV. The reckoning with Sapphira, the wife of Ananias, who perhaps was first in the transgression, and tempted her husband to eat this forbidden fruit. *She came in about three hours after*, expecting to share in the thanks of the house for her coming in, and consenting to the sale of the land, of which perhaps she was entitled to her dower or thirds; for *she knew not what had been done.*

1. She was found guilty of sharing with her husband in his sin, by a question that Peter asked her (*v.* 8). Ananias and his wife agreed to tell the same story, and the bargain being private, and by consent kept to themselves, nobody could disprove them, and therefore they thought they might safely stand in the lie, and should gain credit to it.

2. Sentence was passed upon her, that she should partake in her husband's doom, *v.* 9.

(1) Her sin is opened: *How is it that you have agreed together to tempt the Spirit of the Lord?* Before he passes sentence, he makes her to know her abominations, and shows her the evil of her sin.

(2) Her doom is read: *Behold, the feet of those who have buried*

thy husband are at the door (perhaps he heard them coming, or knew that they could not be long): *and* they *shall carry thee out.*

3. The sentence executed itself. There needed no executioner, a killing power went along with Peter's word, as sometimes a healing power did.

V. The impression that this made upon the people. Notice is taken of this in the midst of the story (*v.* 5): *Great fear came upon all that heard these things*, that heard what Peter said, and saw what followed; or upon all that heard the story of it; for, no doubt, it was all the talk of the city. And again (*v.* 11), *Great fear came upon all the church, and upon as many as heard these things.*

PROGRESS OF THE GOSPEL
(*vv.* 12–16)

We have here an account of the progress of the gospel, notwithstanding this terrible judgment inflicted upon two hypocrites.

I. Here is a general account of the miracles which the apostles wrought (*v.* 12). Now the gospel power returned to its proper channel, which is that of mercy and grace.

II. We are here told what were the effects of these miracles which the apostles wrought.

1. The church was hereby kept together, and confirmed in its adherence both to the apostles and to one another. *They* of the church *were all with one accord in Solomon's porch.* (1) They met in the temple, in the open place that was called Solomon's porch. They all met in public worship; so early was the institution of religious assemblies observed in the church, which must

by no means be forsaken or let fall, for in them a profession of religion is kept up. (2) They were there with one accord, unanimous in their doctrine, worship, and discipline; and there was no discontent nor murmuring about the death of Ananias and Sapphira.

2. It gained the apostles, who were the prime ministers in Christ's kingdom, very great respect. (1) The other ministers kept their distance: *Of the rest* of their company *durst no man join himself to them*, as their equal or an associate with them; though others of them were endued with the Holy Ghost, and spoke with tongues, yet none of them at this time did such signs and wonders as the apostles did: and therefore they acknowledged their superiority, and in every thing yielded to them. (2) All *the people magnified them*, and had them in great veneration, spoke of them with respect, and represented them as the favourites of Heaven, and unspeakable blessings to this earth.

3. The church increased in number (*v.* 14). Observe, (1) Believers are added to the Lord Jesus, joined to him, and so joined to his mystical body, from which nothing can separate us and cut us off, but that which separates us and cuts us off from Christ. (2) Notice is taken of the conversion of *women* as well as *men*; more notice than generally was in the Jewish church.

4. The apostles had abundance of patients, and gained abundance of reputation both to themselves and their doctrine by the cure of them all, *vv.* 15, 16. So many *signs and wonders were wrought by the apostles* that all manner of people

put in for the benefit of them, both in city and country, and had it. (1) In the city: They *brought forth their sick into the streets*. And they *laid them on beds and couches, that at the least the shadow of Peter, passing by, might overshadow some of them*, though it could not reach them all; and, it should seem, it had the desired effect, as the woman's touch of the hem of Christ's garment had; and in this among other things, that word of Christ was fulfilled, *Greater works than these shall you do.* (2) In the country towns: Multitudes came to Jerusalem from *the cities round about, bringing sick folks* that were afflicted in body, and *those that were vexed with unclean spirits*, that were troubled in mind, and they were *healed every one.*

PRISON DOORS OPENED
(*vv.* 17–25)

Never did any good work go on with any hope of success, but it met with opposition.

I. The priests were enraged at them, and shut them up in prison, *vv.* 17, 18. Observe, 1. Who their enemies and persecutors were. The high priest was the ringleader, Annas or Caiaphas, who saw their wealth and dignity, their power and tyranny, that is, their all, at stake, and inevitably lost, if the spiritual and heavenly doctrine of Christ should get ground and prevail among the people. Those that were most forward to join with the high priest herein were the *sect of the Sadducees*, who had a particular enmity to the gospel of Christ, because it confirmed and established the doctrine of the invisible world, the resurrection of the dead, and the future state, which they denied. 2. How they were affected towards them, ill affected, and exasperated to the last degree. 3. How they proceeded against them (*v.* 18). Hereby they designed, (1) To put a restraint upon them; though they could not lay any thing criminal to their charge worthy of death or of bonds, yet while they had them in prison they kept them from going on in their work, and this they reckoned a good point gained. Thus early were the ambassadors of Christ in bonds. (2) To put a terror upon them, and so to drive them off from their work. (3) To put a disgrace upon them, and therefore they chose to clap them up in the common prison, that, being thus vilified, the people might not, as they had done, magnify them.

II. God sent his angel to release them out of prison, and to renew their commission to preach the gospel.

1. The apostles are discharged, legally discharged, from their imprisonment (*v.* 19): *The angel of the Lord by night*, in spite of all the locks and bars that were upon them, *opened the prison doors*, and, in spite of all the vigilance and resolution of the keepers that *stood without before the doors*, *brought forth* the prisoners (see *v.* 23), gave them authority to go out without crime, and led them through all opposition. This deliverance is not so particularly related as that of Peter (*ch.* xii. 7, &c.); but the miracle here was the very same.

2. They are charged, and legally charged, to go on with their work,

so as thereby to be discharged from the prohibition which the high priest laid under them; the angel bade them, *Go, stand, and speak in the temple to the people all the words of this life, v.* 20.

III. They went on with their work (*v.* 21). 1. It was a great satisfaction to them to have these fresh orders. Perhaps they began to question whether, if they had their liberty, they should preach as publicly in the temple as they had done, because they had been told, when they were *persecuted in one city, to flee to another*. But, now that the angel ordered them to go preach in the temple, their way was plain, and they ventured without any difficulty, entered into the temple, and feared not the face of man. (2) They set themselves immediately to execute them, without dispute or delay.

IV. The high priest and his party went on with their prosecution, *v.* 21. See here,

1. How they were prepared, and how big with expectation, to crush the gospel of Christ and the preachers of it, for they raised the whole posse.

2. How they were disappointed, and had their faces filled with shame. See how they are baffled. (1) The officers come, and tell them that they are not to be found in the prison, *vv.* 22, 23. It occasioned various speculations, some suggesting that they were conjured out of the prison, and made their escape by magic arts; others that the keepers had played tricks with them, knowing how many friends these prisoners had, that were so much the darlings of the people. Some feared that, having made such a

27

wonderful escape, they would be the more followed. (2) Their doubt is, in part, determined; and yet their vexation is increased by another messenger, who brings them word that their prisoners are preaching in the temple (*v.* 25). Prisoners, that have broken prison, usually abscond, for fear of being retaken; but these prisoners, that here made their escape, dare to show their faces even where their persecutors have the greatest influence.

GAMALIEL'S ADVICE
(*vv.* 26–42)

Now here we have,

I. The seizing of the apostles a second time. We may think, if God designed this, "Why were they rescued from their first imprisonment?" But this was designed to humble the pride, and check the fury, of their persecutors; and now he would show that they were discharged, not because they feared a trial, for they were ready to surrender themselves and make their appearance before the greatest of their enemies.

II. Their examination. Being brought before this august assembly, the high priest, as the mouth of the court, told them what it was they had to lay to their charge, *v.* 28. 1. That they had disobeyed the commands of authority, and would not submit to the injunctions and prohibitions given them (*v.* 28). 2. That they had spread false doctrine among the people, or at least a singular doctrine, which was not allowed by the Jewish church, nor agreed with what was delivered from Moses's chair. 3. That they

had a malicious design against the government, and aimed to stir up the people against it, by representing it as wicked and tyrannical, and as having made itself justly odious both to God and man.

III. Their answer to the charge exhibited against them.

1. They justified themselves in their disobedience to the commands of the great sanhedrim, great as it was (*v.* 29): *We ought to obey God rather than men.* God had commanded them to teach in the name of Christ, and therefore they ought to do it, though the chief priests forbade them.

2. They justified themselves in doing what they could to fill Jerusalem with the doctrine of Christ.

(1) The chief priests are told to their faces the indignities they did to this Jesus: "*You slew him and hanged him on a tree,* you cannot deny it." The apostles, instead of making an excuse, or begging their pardon, for bringing the guilt of this man's blood upon them, repeat the charge, and stand to it.

(2) They are told also what honours God put upon this Jesus, and then let them judge who was in the right, the persecutors of his doctrine or the preachers of it. He calls God the *God of our fathers*, not only *ours*, but *yours*, to show that in preaching Christ they did not preach a new god, nor entice people to come and worship other gods; nor did they set up an institution contrary to that of Moses and the prophets, but they adhered to the God of the Jewish fathers; and that name of Christ which they preached answered the promises made to the fathers, and the

covenant God entered into with them, and the types and figures of the law he gave them. The God of *Abraham, Isaac,* and *Jacob,* is the *God and Father of our Lord Jesus Christ*; see what honour he did him. [1] He *raised him up*; he qualified him for, and called him to, his great undertaking, [2] He *exalted him with his right hand, hath lifted him up.* [3] "He has appointed him to be *a prince and a Saviour."* [4] He is appointed, as a prince and a Saviour, to *give repentance to Israel and remission of sins.* [5] All this is well attested, *First,* by the apostles themselves; they are ready to testify upon oath, if required, that they saw him alive after his resurrection, and saw him ascend into heaven. *Secondly,* By the Spirit of God. And, *Lastly,* The giving of the Holy Ghost to those that obey Christ, both for their assistance in their obedience and as a present recompence for their obedience, is a plain evidence that it is the will of God that Christ should be obeyed; "judge then whether we ought to obey you in opposition to him."

IV. The impression which the apostles' defence of themselves made upon the court. Instead of yielding to it, they raged against it, and were filled, 1. With indignation at what the apostles said. 2. With malice against the apostles themselves.

V. The grave advice which Gamaliel, a leading man in the council, gave upon this occasion, the scope of which was to moderate the fury of these bigots, and check the violence of the prosecution. Now observe here,

1. The necessary caution he gives to the council, with reference to the case before them. It is not a common case, and therefore should not be hastily determined.

2. The cases he cites, to pave the way to his opinion. Two instances he gives of factious seditious men (such as they would have the apostles thought to be), whose attempts came to nothing of themselves; whence he infers that if these men were indeed such as they represented them their cause would sink with its own weight, and Providence would infatuate and defeat them, and then they needed not persecute them.

3. His opinion upon the whole matter.

(1) That they should not persecute the apostles (*v.* 38).

(2) That they should refer this matter to Providence: "Wait the issue, and see what it will come to. *If it be of men, it will come to nought* of itself; *if of God, it will stand,* in spite of all your powers and policies." It may be the comfort of all who are sincerely on God's side, who have a single eye to his will as their rule and his glory as their end, that whatsoever is of God cannot be overthrown totally and finally, though it may be very vigorously opposed; it may be run upon, but cannot be run down.

VI. The determination of the council upon the whole matter, *v.* 40. 1. Thus far they agreed with Gamaliel that they let fall the design of putting the apostles to death. 2. Yet they could not forbear giving some vent to their rage (so outrageous was it) contrary to the convictions of their judgments and consciences; for, though they were advised to let them alone, yet, (1) *They beat them*, scourged them as malefactors, stripped them, and whipped them, as they used to do in the synagogues, and notice is taken (*v.* 41) of the ignominy of it. (2) *They commanded them that they should not speak* any more *in the name of Jesus*, that, if they could find no other fault with their preaching, they might have this ground to reproach it, that it was against law, and not only without the permission, but against the express order of their superiors.

VII. The wonderful courage and constancy of the apostles in the midst of all these injuries and indignities done them.

1. They bore their sufferings with an invincible cheerfulness. (*v.* 41).

2. They went on in their work with indefatigable diligence (*v.* 42): They were punished for preaching, and were commanded *not to preach*, and *yet they ceased not to teach and preach*; they omitted no opportunity, nor abated any thing of their zeal or forwardness.

CHAPTER SIX

DEACONS APPOINTED
(*vv.* 1–7)

Having seen the church's struggles with her enemies, and triumphed with her in her victories, we now come to take a view of the administration of her affairs at home; and here we have,

I. An unhappy disagreement among some of the church-members, which might have been of ill consequence, but was prudently accommodated and taken up in time (*v.* 1).

(1) The complainants were *the Grecians*, or Hellenists, *against the Hebrews*—the Jews that were scattered in Greece, and other parts, who ordinarily spoke the Greek tongue, and read the Old Testament in the Greek version, and not the original Hebrew, many of whom being at Jerusalem at the feast embraced the faith of Christ, and were added to the church, and so continued there. These complained against the Hebrews, the native Jews, that used the original Hebrew of the Old Testament.

(2) The complaint of these Grecians was *that their widows were neglected in the daily administration*, that is, in the distribution of the public charity, and the Hebrew widows had more care taken of them.

II. The happy accommodating of this matter, and the expedient pitched upon for the taking away of the cause of this murmuring. Now observe,

1. How the method was proposed by the apostles: They *called the multitude of the disciples unto them*, the heads of the congregations of Christians in Jerusalem, the principal leading men. The twelve themselves would not determine any thing without them, for *in multitude of counsellors there is safety*; and in an affair of this nature those might be best able to advise who were more conversant in the affairs of this life than the apostles were.

(1) The apostles urge that they could by no means admit so great a diversion, as this would be, from their great work (*v.* 2): *It is not reasonable that we should leave the word of God and serve tables.*

(2) They therefore desire *that seven men* might be chosen, well qualified for the purpose, whose business it should be *to serve tables, to be deacons to the tables, v.* 2. Now,

[1] The persons must be duly qualified. The people are to choose, and the apostles to ordain; but the people have no authority to choose, nor the apostles to ordain, men utterly unfit for the office: *Look out seven men;* so many they thought might suffice for the present, more might be added afterwards if there were occasion. These must be, *First, Of honest report,* men free from scandal, that were looked upon by their neighbours as men of integrity. *Secondly,* They must be *full of the Holy Ghost,* must be filled with those gifts and graces of the Holy Ghost which were necessary to the right management of this trust. *Thirdly,* They must be *full of wisdom.* It was not enough that they were honest, good men, but they must be discreet, judicious men, that could not be imposed upon, and would order things for the best, and with consideration.

[2] The people must nominate the persons. They might be presumed to know better, or at least were fitter to enquire, what character men had, than the apostles; and therefore they are entrusted with the choice.

[3] The apostles will ordain them to the service, will give them their charge, that they may know what they have to do and make conscience of doing it, and give them their authority, that the persons concerned may know whom they are to apply to, and submit to, in affairs of that nature.

(3) The apostles engage to addict themselves wholly to their work as ministers, and the more closely if they can but get fairly quit of this troublesome office (*v.* 4): *We will give ourselves continually to prayer, and to the ministry of the word.*

2. How this proposal was agreed to, and presently put in execution, by the disciples.

(1) They pitched upon the persons. An apostle, who was an extraordinary officer, was chosen by lot, which is more immediately the act of God; but the overseers of the poor were chosen by the suffrage of the people, in which yet a regard is to be had to the providence of God, who has all men's hearts and tongues in his hand. We have a list of the persons chosen. Some think they were such as were before of the seventy disciples; but this is not likely, for they were ordained by Christ himself, long since, *to preach the gospel;* and there was no more reason that they should leave the word of God to serve tables than that the apostles should. It is therefore more probable that they were of those that were converted since the pouring out of the Spirit; for it was promised to all that would be baptized that they should *receive the gift of the Holy Ghost;* and the gift, according to that promise, is that fulness of the Holy Ghost which was required in those that were to be chosen to this service. The first named is *Stephen, a man full of faith and of the Holy Ghost;* he had a strong faith in the doctrine of Christ, and was full of it above most; *full of fidelity, full of courage* (so some), for he was *full of the Holy Ghost,* of his gifts and

graces. He was an extraordinary man, and excelled in every thing that was good; his name signifies *a crown. Philip* is put next, because he, having *used this office of a deacon well, thereby obtained a good degree*, and was afterwards ordained to the office of an evangelist, a companion and assistant to the apostles, for so he is expressly called, *ch.* xxi. 8.

(2) The apostles appointed them to this work of serving tables for the present, *v.* 6. The people presented them to the apostles, who approved their choice, and ordained them. Having by prayer implored a blessing upon them, they did by the laying on of hands assure them that the blessing was conferred in answer to the prayer; and this was giving them authority to execute that office, and laying an obligation upon the people to be observant of them therein.

III. The advancement of the church hereupon. When things were thus put into good order in the church (grievances were redressed and discontents silenced) then religion got ground, *v.* 7. 1. *The word of God increased.* Now that the apostles resolved to stick more closely than ever to their preaching, it spread the gospel further, and brought it home with the more power. 2. Christians became numerous. 3. *A great company of the priests were obedient to the faith. Then* is the word and grace of God greatly magnified when those are wrought upon by it that were least likely, as the priests here, who either had opposed it, or at least were linked in with those that had.

STEPHEN ACCUSED (*vv.* 8–15)

Stephen, no doubt was diligent and faithful in the discharge of his office as distributor of the church's charity. And, being faithful in a little, he was entrusted with more.

I. He proved the truth of the gospel, by working miracles in Christ's name, *v.* 8. 1. He was *full of faith and power*, that is, of a strong faith, by which he was enabled to do great things. Those that are full of faith are full of power, because by faith the power of God is engaged for us.

II. He pleaded the cause of Christianity against those that opposed it, and argued against it (*vv.* 9, 10).

1. We are here told who were his opponents, *v.* 9. They were Jews, but Hellenist Jews, Jews of the dispersion, who seem to have been more zealous for their religion than the native Jews. They were *of the synagogue which is called the synagogue of the Libertines*; the Romans called those *Liberti*, or *Libertini*, who either, being foreigners, were naturalized, or, being slaves by birth, were made freemen. Some think that these Libertines were such of the Jews as had obtained the Roman freedom, as Paul had (*ch.* xxii. 27, 28); and it is probable that he was the most forward man of this synagogue of the Libertines in disputing with Stephen, and engaged others in the dispute, for we find him busy in the stoning of Stephen, and consenting to his death.

2. We are here told how he carried the point in this dispute (*v.* 10): *They were not able to resist the wis-*

dom and the Spirit by which he spoke. They could neither support their own arguments nor answer his. They were not able to resist the *wisdom and the Spirit by which he spoke*, that Spirit of wisdom which spoke by him. They thought they had only disputed with Stephen, and could make their part good with him; but they were disputing with the Spirit of God in him, for whom they were an unequal match.

III. At length, he sealed it with his blood; so we shall find he did in the next chapter; here we have some steps taken by his enemies towards it. When they could not answer his arguments as a disputant, they prosecuted him as a criminal, and suborned witnesses against him, to swear blasphemy upon him. By their rude and violent treatment of him, they would represent him, both to the people and to the government, as a dangerous man, that would either flee from justice if he were not watched, or fight with it if he were not put under a force. Having caught him, they brought him triumphantly into the council, and, as it should seem, so hastily that he had none of his friends with him.

3. How they were prepared with evidence ready to produce against him. They were resolved that they would not be run a-ground, as they were when they brought our Saviour upon his trial, and then had to seek for witnesses. These were got ready beforehand, and were instructed to make oath that they had *heard him speak blasphemous words against Moses and against God* (v. 11)—against this *holy place and the law* (v. 13); for

they heard him say what Jesus would do to their place and their customs, v. 14. It is probable that he had said something to that purport; and yet those who swore it against him are called *false witnesses*, because, though there was something of truth in their testimony, yet they put a wrong and malicious construction upon what he had said, and perverted it.

IV. We are here told how God owned him when he was brought before the council, and made it to appear that he stood by him (v. 15). Now Stephen appeared at the bar with the countenance *as of an angel*. 1. Perhaps it intimates no more than that he had an extraordinarily pleasant, cheerful countenance, and there was not in it the least sign either of fear for himself or anger at his persecutors. 2. It should rather seem that there was a miraculous splendour and brightness upon his countenance, like that of our Saviour when he was transfigured—or, at least, that of Moses when he came down from the mount—God designing thereby to put honour upon his faithful witness and confusion upon his persecutors and judges, whose sin would be highly aggravated, and would be indeed a rebellion against the light, if, notwithstanding this, they proceeded against him.

CHAPTER SEVEN

STEPHEN'S DEFENCE
(vv. 1–16)

Stephen is now at the bar before the great council of the nation, indicted for blasphemy. Now here,

I. The high priest calls upon him to answer for himself, *v.* 1.

II. He begins his defence, and it is long; but it should seem by his breaking off abruptly, just when he came to the main point (*v.* 50), that it would have been much longer if his enemies would have given him leave to say all he had to say. Observe,

(1) His preface: *Men, brethen, and fathers, hearken.* He gives them, though not flattering titles, yet civil and respectful ones, signifying his expectation of fair treatment with them; from men he hopes to be treated with humanity, and he hopes that brethren and fathers will use him in a fatherly brotherly way.

(2) His entrance upon the discourse.

[1] He begins with the call of Abraham out of Ur of the Chaldees, by which he was set apart for God to be the trustee of the promise, and the father of the Old-Testament church.

First, From this call of Abraham we may observe, 1. That in all our ways we must acknowledge God, and attend the directions of his providence, as of the pillar of cloud and fire. 2. Those whom God takes into covenant with himself he distinguishes from the children of this world.

Secondly, But let us see what this is to Stephen's case. 1. They had charged him as a blasphemer of God, and an apostate from the church; therefore he shows that he is a son of Abraham. 2. They were proud of their being circumcised; and therefore he shows that Abraham was taken under God's guidance, and into communion with him, before he was circumcised, for that was not till *v.* 8. 3. They had a mighty jealousy for this holy place. "Now," says Stephen, "you need not be so proud of it; for," (1) "You came originally out of *Ur of the Chaldees,* where *your fathers served other gods* (Josh. xxiv. 2), and you were not the first planters of this country." (2) "God appeared in his glory to Abraham a great way off in Mesopotamia, before he came near Canaan, nay, before he dwelt in Charran; so that you must not think God's visits are confined to *this land*.

[2] The unsettled state of Abraham and his seed for many ages after he was called out of Ur of the Chaldees.

[3] The building up of the family of Abraham, with the entail of divine grace upon it, and the disposals of divine Providence concerning it, which take up the rest of the book of Genesis.

Let us now see what this is to Stephen's purpose. 1. He still reminds them of the mean beginning of the Jewish nation, as a check to their priding themselves in the glories of that nation; and that it was by a miracle of mercy that they were raised up out of nothing to what they were, from so small a number to be so great a nation; but, if they answer not the intention of their being so raised, they can expect no other than to be destroyed. Their holy land, which they doted so much upon, their fathers were long kept out of the possession of, and met with dearth and great affliction in it; and therefore le them not think it strange if, after it has been so long polluted with sin, it be at length destroyed. The faith of the patriarchs in desiring to be buried in the land of Canaan plainly showed that they had an eye to the heavenly country, to which it was the design of this Jesus to lead them.

STEPHEN'S DEFENCE
Contd. (*vv.* 17–29)

Stephen here goes on to relate,

I. The wonderful increase of the people of Israel in Egypt; it was by a wonder of providence that in a little time they advanced from a family into a nation.

II. The extreme hardships which they underwent there, *vv.* 18, 19.

III. The raising up of *Moses to be their deliverer*. Stephen was charged with having spoken blasphemous words against Moses, in answer to which charge he here speaks very honourably of him.

IV. The attempts which Moses made to deliver Israel, which they spurned, and would not close in with. This Stephen insists much upon, and it serves for a key to this story (Exod. ii. 11–15), as does also that other construction which is put upon it by the apostle, Heb. xi. 24–26.

Now let us see how this serves Stephen's purpose. 1. They charged him with blaspheming Moses, in answer to which he retorts upon them the indignities which their fathers did to Moses, which they ought to be ashamed of, and humbled for, instead of picking quarrels thus, under pretence of zeal for the honour of Moses, with one that had as great a veneration for him as any

of them had. 2. They persecuted him for disputing in defence of Christ and his gospel, in opposition to which they set up Moses and his law: "But," saith he, "you had best take heed," (1) "Lest you hereby do as your fathers did, refuse and reject one *whom God has raised up to be to you a prince and a Saviour*; you may understand, if you will not wilfully shut your eyes against the light, that God will, by this Jesus, deliver you out of a worse slavery than that in Egypt; take heed then of thrusting him away, but receive him as a ruler and a judge over you." (2) "Lest you hereby fare as your fathers fared, who for this were very justly left to die in their slavery, for the deliverance came not till forty years after. This will be the issue of it, you put away the gospel from you, and it will be *sent to the Gentiles*; you will not have Christ, and you shall not have him, so shall your doom be." Matt. xxiii. 38, 39.

STEPHEN'S DEFENCE
Contd. (*vv.* 30–41)

Stephen here proceeds in his story of Moses; and let any one judge whether these are the words of one that was a blasphemer of Moses or no; nothing could be spoken more honourably of him. Here is,

I. The vision which he saw of the glory of God at the bush (*v.* 30).

II. The declaration which he heard of the covenant of God (*v.* 32). Now the preachers of the gospel preached up this covenant, *the promise made of God unto the fathers; unto which promise* those of *the twelve tribes* that did continue *serving God hoped to come, ch.*

xxvi. 6, 7. And shall they, under colour of supporting the holy place and the law, oppose the covenant which was made with Abraham and his seed, his spiritual seed, before the law was given, and long before the holy place was built?

III. The commission which God gave him to deliver Israel out of Egypt. The Jews set up Moses in competition with Christ, and accused Stephen as a blasphemer because he did not do so too. But Stephen here shows that Moses was an eminent type of Christ, as he was Israel's deliverer.

IV. His acting in pursuance of this commission, wherein he was a figure of the Messiah. And Stephen takes notice here again of the slights they had put upon him, the affronts they had given him, and their refusal to have him to reign over them, as tending very much to magnify his agency in their deliverance.

V. His prophecy of Christ and his grace, *v.* 37. He not only was a type of Christ (many were so that perhaps had not an actual foresight of his day), but Moses spoke of him (*v.* 37).

VI. The eminent services which Moses continued to do to the people of Israel, after he had been instrumental to bring them out of Egypt, *v.* 38. And herein also he was a type of Christ, who yet so far exceeds him that it is no blasphemy to say, "He has authority to change the customs that Moses delivered."

VII. The contempt that was, after this, and notwithstanding this, put upon him by the people. Those that charged Stephen with speaking against Moses would do well to answer what their own ancestors had done, and they tread in their ancestors' steps.

STEPHEN'S DEFENCE
Cont. (*vv.* 42–50)

Two things we have in these verses:

I. Stephen upbraids them with the idolatry of their fathers, which God gave them up to, as a punishment for their early forsaking him in worshipping the golden calf; and this was the saddest punishment of all for that sin, as it was of the idolatry of the Gentile world *that God gave them up to a reprobate mind.*

II. He gives an answer particularly to the charge exhibited against him relating to the temple, *that he spoke blasphemous words against that holy place, vv.* 44–50. He was accused for saying that Jesus would destroy this holy place: "And what if I did say so?" (saith Stephen) "the glory of the holy God is not bound up in the glory of this holy place, but that may be preserved untouched, though this be laid in the dust;" for, 1. It was not till our fathers came into the wilderness, in their way to Canaan that they had any fixed place of worship. 2. The holy place was at first but a tabernacle, mean and movable, showing itself to be short-lived, and not designed to continue always. 3. That tabernacle was *a tabernacle of witness*, or of testimony, *a figure for the time then present* (Heb. ix. 9), *a figure of good things to come, of the true tabernacle which the Lord pitched, and not men*, Heb. viii. 2. 4. That tabernacle was framed just as God appointed, and *according to the fashion which Moses saw in the mount*, which plainly intimates that it had reference to good things to come. 5. That tabernacle was pitched first in the wilderness; it was not a native of this land of yours (to which you think it must for ever be confined), but was brought in in the next age, by our fathers, who came after those who first erected it, into the possession of the Gentiles, into the land of Canaan, which had long been in the possession of the devoted nations *whom God drove out before the face of our fathers.* And why may not God set up his spiritual temple, as he had done the material tabernacle, in those countries that were now the possession of the Gentiles? That tabernacle was brought in by those who came *with Jesus*, that is, *Joshua.* And I think, for distinction sake, and to prevent mistakes, it ought to be so read, both here and Heb. iv. 8. Yet in naming *Joshua* here, which in Greek is *Jesus*, there may be a tacit intimation that as the Old-Testament Joshua brought in that typical tabernacle, so the New-Testament Joshua should bring in the true tabernacle into the possession of the Gentiles. 6. That tabernacle continued for many ages, *even to the days of David*, above four hundred years, before there was any thought of building a temple, *v.* 45. 7. God had his heart so little upon a temple, or such a holy place as they were so jealous for, that, when David desired to build one, he was forbidden to do it. 8. God often declared that temples made with hands were not his delight, nor could add any thing to the perfection of his rest and joy. Solomon,

when he dedicated the temple, acknowledged that God *dwelleth not in temples made with hands*; he has not need of them, is not benefited by them, cannot be confined to them.

STEPHEN'S DEFENCE
Contd. (*vv.* 51–53)

Stephen was going on in his discourse (as it should seem by the thread of it) to show that, as the temple-service must come to an end, and it would be the glory of both to give way to that worship of the Father in spirit and in truth which was to be established in the kingdom of the Messiah. It is probable that he perceived that they were going to silence him; and therefore he breaks off abruptly in the midst of his discourse, and by that spirit of wisdom, courage, and power, wherewith he was filled, he sharply rebuked his persecutors, and exposed their true character; for, if they will not admit the testimony of the gospel to them, it shall become a testimony against them.

I. They, like their fathers, were stubborn and wilful, and would not be wrought upon by the various methods God took to reclaim and reform them; they were like their fathers, inflexible both to the word of God and to his providences.

II. They, like their fathers, were not only not influenced by the methods God took to reform them, but they were enraged and incensed against them: *You do always resist the Holy Ghost.*

III. They, like their fathers, persecuted and slew those whom God sent unto them to call them to duty, and make them offers of mercy.

They had been the *betrayers and murderers of the just One* himself, as Peter had told them, *ch.* iii. 14, 15; v. 30. They had hired Judas to betray him, and had in a manner forced Pilate to condemn him; and therefore it is charged upon them that they were his betrayers and murderers. To which of the prophets would those have shown any respect who had no regard to the Son of God himself?

IV. They, like their fathers, put contempt upon divine revelation, and would not be guided and governed by it; and this was the aggravation of their sin, that God had given, as to their fathers his law, so to them his gospel, in vain. They would not yield to the plainest demonstrations, any more than their fathers before them did; for they were resolved not to comply with God either in his law or in his gospel.

We have reason to think Stephen had a great deal more to say, and would have said it if they would have suffered him; but they were wicked and unreasonable men with whom he had to do, that could no more hear reason than they could speak it.

STEPHEN MARTYRED
(*vv.* 54–60)

We have here the death of the first martyr of the Christian church.

Let us observe here the wonderful discomposure of the spirits of his enemies and persecutors, and the wonderful composure of his spirit.

I. See the strength of corruption in the persecutors of Stephen—malice in perfection, hell itself broken loose, men become incar-nate devils, and the serpent's seed spitting their venom.

1. *When they heard these things they were cut to the heart* (*v.* 54), the same word that is used Heb. xi. 37, and translated *they were sawn asunder*. They were put to as much torture in their minds as ever the martyrs were put to in their bodies.

2. They *gnashed upon him with their teeth.* This denotes, (1) Great malice and rage against him. (2) Great vexation within themselves; they fretted to see in him such manifest tokens of a divine power and presence, and it vexed them to the heart.

3. *They cried out with a loud voice* (*v.* 57), to irritate and excite one another, and to drown the noise of the clamours of their own and one another's consciences; when he said, *I see heaven opened*, they cried with a loud voice, that he might not be heard to speak.

4. They *stopped their ears*, that they might not hear their own noisiness; or perhaps under pretence that they could not bear to hear his blasphemies.

5. They *ran upon him with one accord*—the people and the elders of the people, judges, prosecutors, witnesses, and spectators, they all flew upon him, as beasts upon their prey.

6. They *cast him out of the city, and stoned him*, as if he were not worthy to live in Jerusalem; nay, not worthy to live in this world, pretending herein to execute the law of Moses (Lev. xxiv. 16). Now, the stoning of a man being a laborious piece of work, the witnesses took off their upper garments, that they might not hang in

38

their way, *and they laid them down at a young man's feet, whose name was Saul,* now a pleased spectator of this tragedy. It is the first time we find mention of his name; we shall know it and love it better when we find it changed to *Paul,* and him changed from a persecutor into a preacher. This little instance of his agency in Stephen's death he afterwards reflected upon with regret (*ch.* xxii. 20): *I kept the raiment of those that slew him.*

II. See the strength of grace in Stephen, and the wonderful instances of God's favour to him, and working in him. As his persecutors were full of Satan, so was he *full of the Holy Ghost.* Now here we have a remarkable communion between this blessed martyr and the blessed Jesus in this critical moment. We may observe,

1. Christ's gracious manifestation of himself to Stephen, both for his comfort and for his honour, in the midst of his sufferings.

(1) He, *being full of the Holy Ghost, looked up stedfastly into heaven, v.* 55.

(2) He saw the glory of God (*v.* 55); for *he saw the heavens opened, v.* 56. Some think his eyes were strengthened, and the sight of them so raised above its natural pitch, by a supernatural power, that he saw into the third heavens, though at so vast a distance, as Moses's sight was enlarged to see the whole land of Canaan. Others think it was a representation of the glory of God set before his eyes, as, before, Isaiah and Ezekiel; heaven did as it were come down to him, as Rev. xxi. 2.

(3) He *saw Jesus standing on the right hand of God* (*v.* 55), *the Son of man,* so it is *v.* 56. Now, [1] Here is a proof of the exaltation of Christ to the Father's right hand; the apostles saw him ascend, but they did not see him sit down. We are told that he sat down on the right hand of God; but was he ever seen there? Yes, Stephen saw him there, and was abundantly satisfied with the sight. [2] He is usually said to *sit* there; but Stephen sees him *standing* there, as one more than ordinarily concerned at present for his suffering servant; he stood up as a judge to plead his cause against his persecutors. He stands ready to receive him and crown him, and in the mean time to give him a prospect of the joy set before him. [3] This was intended for the encouragement of Stephen. He sees Christ is for him, and then no matter who is against him.

(4) He told those about him what he saw (*v.* 56): *Behold, I see the heavens opened.* If some were exasperated by it, others perhaps might be wrought upon to consider this Jesus whom they persecuted, and to believe in him.

2. Stephen's pious addresses to Jesus Christ. Two short prayers Stephen offered up to God in his dying moments, and in them as it were breathed out his soul:

(1) Here is a prayer for himself: *Lord Jesus, receive my spirit.* Thus Christ had himself resigned his spirit immediately into the hands of the Father. We are here taught to resign ours into the hands of Christ as Mediator, by him to be recommended to the Father. Stephen saw Jesus standing at the Father's right hand, and he thus

calls to him: "Blessed Jesus, do that for me now which thou standest there to do for all thine, receive my departing spirit into thy hand."

(2) Here is a prayer for his persecutors, *v.* 60.

[1] The circumstances of this prayer are observable; for it seems to have been offered up with something more of solemnity than the former. *First*, He *knelt down*, which was an expression of his humility in prayer. *Secondly*, He *cried with a loud voice*, which was an expression of his importunity.

[2] The prayer itself: *Lord, lay not this sin to their charge.* Herein he followed the example of his dying Master, who prayed thus for his persecutors, *Father, forgive them;* and set an example to all following sufferers in the cause of Christ thus to pray for those that persecute them.

3. His expiring with this: *When he had said this, he fell asleep;* or, as he was saying this, the blow came that was mortal. Note, Death is but a sleep to good people; not the sleep of the soul (Stephen had given that up into Christ's hand), but the sleep of the body; it is its rest from all its griefs and toils; it is perfect ease from toil and pain. Stephen died as much in a hurry as ever any man did, and yet, when he died, he fell asleep.

CHAPTER EIGHT

MORE PERSECUTION

(*vv.* 1–3)

In these verses we have,

I. Something more concerning

Stephen and his death. Accordingly here is, 1. Stephen's death rejoiced in by one—by many, no doubt, but by one in particular, and that was Saul, who was afterwards called Paul; he was *consenting to his death, he consented to it with delight* (so the word signifies); he was pleased with it. 2. Stephen's death bewailed by others (*v.* 2)—*devout men*, which some understand of those that were properly so called, *proselytes*, one of whom Stephen himself probably was. Or, it may be taken more largely; some of the church that were more devout and zealous than the rest went and gathered up the poor crushed and broken remains, to which they gave a decent interment, probably in the *field of blood*, which was bought some time ago to bury strangers in. They buried him solemnly, and made great lamentation over him.

II. An account of this persecution of the church, which begins upon the martyrdom of Stephen. Observe,

1. Against whom this persecution was raised: It was *against the church in Jerusalem*, which is no sooner planted than it is persecuted, as Christ often intimated that tribulation and persecution would arise *because of the word.*

2. Who was an active man in it; none so zealous, so busy, as Saul, a young Pharisee, *v.* 3. As for Saul (who had been twice mentioned before, and now again for a notorious persecutor) *he made havoc of the church*; he did all he could to lay it waste and ruin it; he cared not what mischief he did to the disciples of Christ, nor knew when to stop. He aimed at no less than the cutting off of the gospel Israel, that

the name of it should be no more in remembrance, Ps. lxxxiii. 4.

3. What was the effect of this persecution: *They were all scattered abroad* (v. 1), not all the believers, but all the preachers, who were principally struck at, and against whom warrants were issued out to take them up. The preachers were all scattered *except the apostles*, who, probably, were directed by the Spirit to continue at Jerusalem yet for some time, they being, by the special providence of God, screened from the storm, and by the special grace of God enabled to face the storm.

PHILIP'S MINISTRY
(vv. 4–13)

I. Here is a general account of what was done by them all (v. 4): *They went every where, preaching the word.* They did not go to hide themselves for fear of suffering, no, nor to show themselves as proud of their sufferings; but they went up and down to scatter the knowledge of Christ in every place where they were scattered. They went every where, into the way of the Gentiles, and the cities of the Samaritans, which before they were forbidden to go into, Matt. x. 5.

II. A particular account of what was done by Philip. Stephen was advanced to the degree of a martyr, Philip to the degree of an evangelist, which when he entered upon, being obliged by it to *give himself to the word and prayer*, he was, no doubt, discharged from the office of a deacon. Now observe,

1. What wonderful success Philip had in his preaching, and what reception he met with.

(1) The place he chose was the city of Samaria.

(2) The doctrine he preached was Christ; for he determined to know nothing else. The Samaritans had an expectation of the Messiah's coming, as appears by John iv. 25. Now Philip tells them that he is come, and that the Samaritans are welcome to him.

(3) The proofs he produced for the confirmation of his doctrine were miracles, v. 6. And the nature of the miracles was such as suited the intention of his commission, and gave light and lustre to it.

(4) The acceptance which Philip's doctrine, thus proved, met with in Samaria (v. 6): *The people with one accord gave heed to those things which Philip spoke.* The common people gave heed to Philip, — *a multitude of them*, not here and there one, but with one accord; they were all of a mind, that it was fit the doctrine of the gospel should be enquired into, and an impartial hearing given to it.

(5) The satisfaction they had in attending on, and attending to, Philip's preaching, and the success it had with many of them (v. 8).

2. What there was in particular at this city of Samaria that made the success of the gospel there more than ordinarily wonderful.

(1) That Simon Magus had been busy there, and had gained a great interest among the people, and *yet they believed the things that Philip spoke.* To unlearn that which is bad proves many times a harder task than to learn that which is good. These Samaritans, though they were not idolaters as the Gentiles, nor prejudiced against the

gospel by traditions received from their fathers, yet had of late been drawn to follow Simon, a conjurer (for so *Magus* signifies) who made a mighty noise among them, and had strangely *bewitched them*.

But Simon Magus himself became a convert to the faith of Christ, in show and profession, for a time. *Is Saul also among the prophets?* Yes (*v.* 13), *Simon himself believed also*. He was convinced that Philip preached a true doctrine, because he saw it confirmed by real miracles, of which he was the better able to judge because he was conscious to himself of the trick of his own pretended ones.

SIMON REBUKED
(*vv.* 14–25)

Two apostles were sent, the two most eminent, to Samaria, 1. To encourage Philip, to assist him, and strengthen his hands. 2. To carry on the good work that was begun among the people, and, with those heavenly graces that had enriched them, to confer upon them spiritual gifts. Now observe,

I. How they advanced and improved those of them that were sincere. It is said (*v.* 16), *The Holy Ghost was as yet fallen upon none of them*, in those extraordinary powers which were conveyed by the descent of the Spirit upon the day of pentecost. They were none of them endued with the gift of tongues, which seems then to have been the most usual immediate effect of the pouring out of the Spirit. See *ch.* x. 45, 46. This was both an eminent sign to those that believed not, and of excellent service to those that did. This, and

other such gifts, they had not, *only they were baptized in the name of the Lord Jesus*, and so engaged in him and interested in him, which was necessary to salvation, and in this they had joy and satisfaction (*v.* 8), though they could not speak with tongues. Those that are indeed given up to Christ, and have experienced the sanctifying influences and operation of the Spirit of grace, have great reason to be thankful, and no reason to complain, though they have not those gifts that are for ornament, and would make them bright. But it is intended that they should go on to the perfection of the present dispensation, for the greater honour of the gospel. We have reason to think that Philip had received these gifts of the Holy Ghost himself, but had not a power to confer them; the apostles must come to do this; and they did it not upon all that were baptized, but upon some of them, and, it should seem, such as were designed for some office in the church, or at least to be eminent active members of it; and upon some of them *one gift of the Holy Ghost*, and upon others *another*. See 1 Cor. xii. 4, 8; xiv. 26. Now in order to this, 1. *The apostles prayed for them, v.* 15. The Spirit is given, not to ourselves only (Luke xi. 13), but to others also, in answer to prayer: *I will put my Spirit within you* (Ezek. xxxvi. 27), *but I will for this be enquired of, v.* 37. We may take encouragement from this example in praying to God to give the renewing graces of the Holy Ghost to those whose spiritual welfare we are concerned for—for our children, for our friends, for our ministers. We should pray, and pray earnestly, *that they may receive the Holy Ghost*; for this includes all blessings. 2. They laid their hands on them, to signify that their prayers were answered, and *that the gift of the Holy Ghost was conferred upon them*; for, upon the use of this sign, *they received the Holy Ghost, and spoke with tongues*. The laying on of hands was anciently used in blessing, by those who blessed with authority. Thus the apostles blessed these new converts, ordained some to be ministers, and confirmed others in their Christianity. We cannot now, nor can any, thus give the Holy Ghost by the laying on of hands; but this may intimate to us that those whom we pray for we should use our endeavours with.

II. How they discovered and discarded him that was a hypocrite among them, and this was Simon Magus; for they knew how to *separate between the precious and the vile*.

(1) Peter shows him his crime (*v*. 20): *Thou hast thought that the gift of God may be purchased with money*; and thus, [1] He had overvalued the wealth of this world. [2] He had undervalued the gift of the Holy Ghost and put it upon a level with the common gifts of nature and providence.

(2) He shows him his character, which is inferred from his crime. And therefore Peter tells him plainly, [1] That his heart was *not right in the sight of God*, *v*. 21. "Though thou professest to believe, and art baptized, yet thou art not sincere." [2] That he is *in the gall of bitterness, and in the bond of iniquity: I perceive that thou art* so,

v. 23. Indwelling sin is *a root of bitterness*, that *bears gall and wormwood*, Deut. xxix. 18. The faculties are corrupted, and the mind embittered against all good, Heb. xii. 15. It intimates likewise the pernicious consequences of sin; the *end is bitter as wormwood*.

(3) He reads him his doom in two things:

[1] He shall sink with his worldly wealth, which he overvalued: *Thy money perish with thee*.

[2] He shall come short of the spiritual blessings which he undervalued (*v*. 21): "*Thou hast neither part nor lot in this matter*."

(4) He gives him good counsel, notwithstanding, *v*. 22. Observe,

[1] What it is that he advises him to: He must do his first works. *First*, He must *repent*,—must see his error and retract it,—must change his mind and way,—must be humbled and ashamed for what he has done. His repentance must be particular: "Repent of this, own thyself guilty in this, and be sorry for it." *Secondly*, He must *pray* to God, must pray that God would give him repentance, and pardon upon repentance.

[2] What encouragement he gives him to do this: *If perhaps the thought of thy heart*, this wicked thought of thine, *may be forgiven thee*. When Peter here puts a *perhaps* upon it, the doubt is of the sincerity of his repentance, not of his pardon if his repentance be sincere.

[3] Simon's request to them to pray for him, *v*. 24. He was startled and put into confusion by that which Peter said, finding that resented thus which he thought

would have been embraced with both arms; and he cries out, *Pray you to the Lord for me, that none of the things which you have spoken come upon me.*

Lastly, Here is the return of the apostles to Jerusalem, when they had finished the business they came about; for as yet they were not to disperse; but, though they came hither to do that work which was peculiar to them as apostles, yet, opportunity offering itself, they applied themselves to that which was common to all gospel ministers. 1. There, in the city of Samaria, they were preachers: *They testified the word of the Lord.* 2. In their road home they were itinerant preachers; as they passed through many villages of the Samaritans they preached the gospel.

THE ETHIOPIAN EUNUCH
(*vv.* 26–40)

We have here the story of the conversion of an Ethiopian eunuch to the faith of Christ, by whom, we have reason to think, the knowledge of Christ was sent into that country where he lived, and that scripture fulfilled, *Ethiopia shall soon stretch out her hands* (one of the first of the nations) *unto God,* Ps. lxviii. 31.

I. Philip the evangelist is directed into the road where he would meet with this Ethiopian, *v.* 26.

II. An account is given of this eunuch (*v.* 27), who and what he was, on whom this distinguishing favour was bestowed. 1. He was a foreigner, *a man of Ethiopia.* 2. He was a person of quality, a great man in his own country, *a eunuch,* not in body, but in office—lord

chamberlain or steward of the household. He *had the charge of all her treasure*; so great a trust did she repose in him. *Not many mighty, not many noble, are called*; but some are. 3. He was a proselyte to the Jewish religion, for *he came to Jerusalem to worship.*

III. Philip and the eunuch are brought together into a close conversation; and now Philip shall know the meaning of his being sent into a desert, for there he meets with a chariot, that shall serve for a synagogue, and one man, the conversion of whom shall be in effect, for aught he knows, the conversion of a whole nation.

1. Philip is ordered to fall into company with this traveller that is going home from Jerusalem towards Gaza, thinking he has done all the business of his journey, when the great business which the overruling providence of God designed in it was yet undone.

2. He finds him reading in his Bible, as he sat in his chariot (*v.* 28). Perhaps the eunuch was now reading over again those portions of scripture which he had heard read and expounded at Jerusalem, that he might recollect what he had heard.

3. He puts a fair question to him: *Understandest thou what thou readest?* Not by way of reproach, but with design to offer him his service.

4. The eunuch in a sense of his need of assistance, desires Philip's company (*v.* 31).

IV. The portion of scripture which the eunuch recited, with some hints of Philip's discourse upon it.

1. The chapter he was reading was the fifty-third of Isaiah, two verses of which are here quoted (*vv.* 32, 33), part of the seventh and eighth verses. These verses foretold concerning the Messiah, (1) That he should die, should be *led to the slaughter*, as sheep that were offered in sacrifice—that his life should be taken from among men, taken from the earth. (2) That he should die wrongfully, should die by violence, should be hurried out of his life, and *his judgment shall be taken away*—no justice done to him; for he must be *cut off, but not for himself.* (3) That he should die patiently. Like *a lamb dumb before the shearer*, nay, and before the butcher too, *so he opened not his mouth.* Never was there such an example of patience as our Lord Jesus was in his sufferings. (4) That yet he should live for ever, to ages which cannot be numbered; for so I understand those words, *Who shall declare his generation?* The Hebrew word properly signifies *the duration of one life*, Eccl. i. 4. Now who can conceive or express how long he shall continue, notwithstanding this; *for his life is taken* only *from the earth*; in heaven he shall live to endless and innumerable ages, as it follows in Isa. liii. 10, *He shall prolong his days*.

2. The eunuch's question upon this is, *Of whom speaketh the prophet this? v.* 34. It is a material question he asks, and a very sensible one.

3. Philip takes this fair occasion given him to open to him the great mystery of the gospel concerning Jesus Christ, *and him crucified.* He *began at this scripture*, took this for his text (as Christ did another passage of the same prophecy, Luke iv. 21), and *preached unto him Jesus, v.* 35. This is all the account given us of Philip's sermon, because it was the same in effect with Peter's sermons, which we have had before.

V. The eunuch is baptized in the name of Christ, *vv.* 36–38. Now here we have,

1. The modest proposal which the eunuch made of himself for baptism (*v.* 36). "*See, here is water*, which perhaps we may not meet with a great while again; *what doth hinder me to be baptized?* Canst thou show any cause why I should not be admitted a disciple and follower of Christ by baptism?" Those who have received the thing signified by baptism should not put off receiving the sign.

2. The fair declaration which Philip made him of the terms upon which he might have the privilege of baptism (*v.* 37): "*If thou believest with all thy heart, thou mayest.*"

3. The confession of faith which the eunuch made in order to his being baptized. It is very short, but it is comprehensive and much to the purpose, and what was sufficient: *I believe that Jesus Christ is the Son of God.* He was before a worshipper of the true God, so that all he had to do now was to *receive Christ Jesus the Lord.* (1) He believes that Jesus is *the Christ*, the true Messiah promised, the *anointed One*. (2) That Christ is *Jesus—a Saviour*, the only Saviour of his people from their sins. And, (3) That this Jesus Christ is the *Son of God*, that he has a divine nature, as the Son is of the same nature with

45

the Father; and that, being the Son of God, he is the *heir of all things*. This is the principal peculiar doctrine of Christianity, and whosoever believe this with all their hearts, and confess it, they and their seed are to be baptized.

4. The baptizing of him hereupon. If some hypocrites crowd into the church, who afterwards prove a grief and scandal to us, yet we must not therefore make the door of admission any straiter than Christ has made it; they shall answer for their apostasy, and not we.

VI. Philip and the eunuch are separated presently; and this is as surprising as the other parts of the story. One would have expected that the eunuch should either have staid with Philip, or have taken him along with him into his own country, and, there being so many ministers in those parts, he might be spared, and it would be worth while: but God ordered otherwise.

CHAPTER NINE

CONVERSION OF SAUL
(vv. 1–9)

We found mention made of Saul twice or thrice in the story of Stephen, for the sacred penman longed to come to his story; and now we are come to it, not quite taking leave of Peter, but from henceforward being mostly taken up with Paul the apostle of the Gentiles, as Peter was of the circumcision. We are here told,

I. How bad he was, how very bad, before his conversion; just before he was an inveterate enemy to Christianity, did his utmost to root it out, by persecuting all that

embraced it. In other respects he was well enough, as *touching the righteousness which is of the law, blameless*, a man of no ill morals, but a blasphemer of Christ, a persecutor of Christians, and injurious to both, 1 Tim. i. 13. And so ill informed was his conscience that he thought he ought to do what he did against the name of Christ (*ch.* xxvi. 9) and that he did God service in it, as was foretold, John xvi. 2. Saul cannot be easy if he knows a Christian is quiet; and therefore, hearing that the Christians in Damascus were so, he resolves to give them disturbance. In order to this, he applies to the high priest for a commission (*v.* 1) to go to Damascus, *v.* 2.

II. How suddenly and strangely a blessed change was wrought in him, not in the use of any ordinary means, but by miracles. The conversion of Paul is one of the wonders of the church. Here is,

1. The place and time of it: *As he journeyed, he came near to Damascus*; and there Christ met with him.

2. The appearance of Christ to him in his glory. Here it is only said that there *shone round about him a light from heaven*; but it appears from what follows (*v.* 17) that the Lord Jesus was in this light, and appeared to him by the way.

3. The arresting of Saul, and his detachment: *He fell to the earth, v.* 4. This may be considered, (1) As the effect of Christ's appearing to him, and of the light which shone round about him. (2) As a step towards this intended advancement. He is designed not only to be a Christian, but to be a minister, an apostle, a great apostle, and

therefore he must thus be cast down.

4. The arraigning of Saul. Being by the fall taken into custody, and as it were set to the bar, he heard a voice saying to him (and it was distinguishing, to him only, for though those that were with him heard a sound (v. 7) yet they knew not the words, *ch.* xxii. 9), *Saul, Saul, why persecutest thou me?* Observe here,

(1) Saul not only saw a light from heaven, but heard a voice from heaven; wherever the glory of God was seen, the word of God was heard (Exod. xx. 18); and to Moses (Num. vii. 89); and to the prophets.

(2) What he heard was very awakening.

[1] He was called by his name, and that doubled: *Saul, Saul.*

[2] The charge exhibited against him is, *Why persecutest thou me?* Observe, 1. The person sinning: "It is thou; thou, that art hast the knowledge of the scriptures, which, if duly considered, would show thee the folly of it: It is worse in thee than in another." 2. The person sinned against: "It is I, who never did thee any harm, who came from heaven to earth to do thee good, who was not long since crucified for thee; and was not that enough, but must I afresh be crucified by thee?" *Why persecutest thou me?* He thought he was persecuting only a company of, poor, weak, silly people, that were an offence and eye-sore to the Pharisees, little imagining that it was one in heaven that he was all this while insulting; for surely, if he had known, he would not have persecuted the Lord of glory.

5. Saul's question upon his indictment, and the reply to it, *v.* 5.

(1) He makes enquiry concerning Christ: *Who art thou, Lord?* He who had been a blasphemer of Christ's name now speaks to him as his Lord. The question is proper: *Who art thou?* This implies his present unacquaintedness with Christ. Note, There is some hope of people when they begin to enquire after Jesus Christ.

(2) He has an answer immediately, in which we have,

[1] Christ's gracious revelation of himself to him. He is always ready to answer the serious enquiries of those who covet an acquaintance with him: *I am Jesus whom thou persecutest.*

[2] His gentle reproof of him: *It is hard for thee to kick against the pricks,* or *goads*—to spurn at the spur. It is hard, it is in itself an absurd and evil thing, and will be of fatal consequence to him that does it. Those that revolt more and more when they are stricken by the word or rod of God, that are enraged at reproofs and fly in the face of their reprovers, kick against the pricks and will have a great deal to answer for.

6. His surrender of himself to the Lord Jesus at length, *v.* 6. See here,

(1) The frame and temper he was in, when Christ had been dealing with him. [1] He trembled, as one in a great fright. [2] He was astonished, was filled with amazement, as one brought into a new world, that knew not where he was.

(2) His address to Jesus Christ, when he was in this frame: *Lord, what wilt thou have me to do?* The great change in conversion is

wrought upon the will, and consists in the resignation of that to the will of Christ.

(3) The general direction Christ gave him, in answer to this: *Arise, go into the city of Damascus*, which thou art now near to, *and it shall be told thee what thou must do*. It is encouragement enough to have further instruction promised him. Christ manifests himself to his people by degrees; and both what he does and would he have them to do, though they know not now, they shall know hereafter.

7. How far his fellow travellers were affected with this, and what impression it made upon them. They fell to the earth, as he did, but rose without being bidden, which he did not, but lay still till it was said to him, *Arise*; for he lay under a heavier load than any of them did; but when they were up, (1) *They stood speechless*, as men in confusion, and that was all, *v.* 7. (2) *They heard a voice, but saw no man*; they heard Paul speak, but saw not him to whom he spoke, nor heard distinctly what was said to him: which reconciles it with what is said of this matter, *ch.* xxii. 9.

8. What condition Saul was in after this, *vv.* 8, 9. (1) *He arose from the earth*, when Christ commanded him, but probably not without help, the vision had made him so faint and weak. (2) *When his eyes were opened*, he found that his sight was gone. Thus a believing sight of the glory of God in the face of Christ dazzles the eyes to all things here below. Christ, in order to the further discovery of himself and his gospel to Paul, took him off from the sight of other things, which he must look off, that he may look unto Jesus, and to him only. (3) *They led him by the hand into Damascus*. He was thus taught what need he had of the grace of Christ to lead his soul (being naturally blind and apt to mistake) into all truth. (4) He lay *without sight*, and without food, *neither did eat nor drink for three days*, *v.* 9.

SAUL BAPTIZED (*vv.* 10–22)

I. Ananias is here ordered to go and look after him, to heal and help him; for he that causeth grief will have compassion.

1. The person employed is *Ananias, a certain disciple at Damascus*, not lately driven thither from Jerusalem, but a native of Damascus; for it is said (*ch.* xxii. 12) *that he had a good report of all the Jews who dwelt there, as a devout man according to the law*.

2. The direction given him is to go and enquire at such a house, probably an inn, for one *Saul of Tarsus*. Christ, in a vision, called to Ananias by name, *v.* 10. *Go then*, saith Christ, *into the street which is called Straight, and enquire in the house of Judas* (where strangers used to lodge) *for one called Saul of Tarsus*.

3. Two reasons are given him why he must go and enquire for this stranger, and offer him his service:

(1) Because he prays, and his coming to him must answer his prayer. Observe what condition Saul was now in. He was under conviction of sin, trembling and astonished; the setting of sin in order before us should drive us to prayer. He was under a bodily

affliction, blind and sick; and, *Is
any afflicted? Let him pray.* Christ
had promised him that it should be
further told him what he should do
(*v.* 6), and he prays that one may
be sent to him to instruct him.

(2) Because he hath seen in a
vision such a man coming to him,
to restore him to his sight; and
Ananias's coming to him must
answer his dream, for it was of
God (*v.* 12).

II. Ananias objects against going
to him, and the Lord answers the
objection.

1. Ananias pleads that this Saul
was a notorious persecutor of the
disciples of Christ, *vv.* 13, 14.

2. Christ overrules the objection
(*vv.* 15, 16). The vessel God uses
he himself chooses; and it is fit he
should himself have the choosing
of the instruments he employs
(John xv. 16). He is designed, (1)
For eminent services: *He is to bear
my name before the Gentiles,* is to
be the apostle of the Gentiles, and
to carry the gospel to heathen
nations. (2) For eminent sufferings
(*v.* 16). He that has been a persecutor shall be himself persecuted.

III. Ananias presently goes on
Christ's errand to Saul, and with
good effect.

1. Ananias delivered his message
to Saul, *v.* 17. Probably he found
him in bed, and applied to him as a
patient. (1) *He put his hands on him.*
It was promised, as one of the signs
that should follow those that
believe, that they should lay hands
on the sick, and they should recover (Mark xvi. 18), and it was for
that intent that he put his hands
on him. (2) He called him *brother,*
because he was made a partaker of

the grace of God, though not yet
baptized. (3) He produces his
commission from the same hand
that had laid hold on him by the
way, and now had him in custody.
The hand that wounded heals. (4)
He assures him that he shall not
only have his sight restored, but be
filled with the Holy Ghost: he must
himself be an apostle, and must in
nothing come behind the chief of
the apostles, and therefore must
receive the Holy Ghost immediately,
and not, as others did, by the inter-
position of the apostles; and Ananias's putting his hands upon him
before he was baptized was for the
conferring of the Holy Ghost.

2. Ananias saw the good issue of
his mission. (1) In Christ's favour
to Saul. Saul is delivered from the
spirit of bondage by his receiving
sight (*v.* 18), which was signified by
the falling of scales from his eyes;
and this immediately, and forth-
with: the cure was sudden, to show
that it was miraculous. (2) In
Saul's subjection to Christ: He was
baptized, and thereby submitted
to the government of Christ, and
cast himself upon the grace of
Christ.

IV. The good work that was
begun in Saul is carried on wonderfully; this new-born Christian,
though he seemed *as one born out of
due time,* yet presently comes to
maturity.

1. He received his bodily strength,
v. 19.

2. He associated with the disciples that were at Damascus, fell
in with them, conversed with them,
went to their meetings, and joined
in communion with them.

3. *He preached Christ in the*

synagogues, *v.* 20. To this he had an extraordinary call, and for it an extraordinary qualification, God having immediately revealed his Son to him and in him, that he might preach him, Gal. i. 15, 16. He preached concerning Christ, *that he is the Son of God*, his beloved Son, in whom he is well pleased, and with us in him, and not otherwise. *All that heard him were amazed, and said, "Is not this he that destroyed those who called on this name in Jerusalem*, and now does he call on his name himself, and persuade others to call upon it, and strengthen the hands of those that do?"

4. He confuted and confounded those that opposed the doctrine of Christ, *v.* 22. And we have reason to think he was instrumental in converting many to the faith of Christ, and building up the church at Damascus, which he went hither to make havoc of.

PAUL, THE CHRISTIAN
(*vv.* 23–31)

As soon as God *had revealed his Son in him, that he might preach him, he went not up to Jerusalem*, to receive instructions from the apostles (as any other convert would have done, that was designed for the ministry), but he went to Arabia (Gal. i. 16) where he would have opportunity of teaching, but not of learning; thence he returned to Damascus, and there, three years after his conversion, this happened, which is here recorded.

I. He met with difficulties at Damascus, and had a narrow escape of being killed there. Saul was no sooner a Christian than a preacher, no sooner a preacher than a sufferer; so quickly did he rise to the summit of his preferment.

II. He met with difficulties at Jerusalem the first time he went thither, *v.* 26. He came to Jerusalem. This is thought to be that journey to Jerusalem of which he himself speaks (Gal. i. 18). But I rather incline to think that this was a journey before that. Now observe,

1. How shy his friends were of him (*v.* 26). (1) See what was the cause of their jealousy of him: *They believed not that he was a disciple*, but that he only pretended to be so, and came among them as a spy or an informer. The disciples of Christ had need to be cautious whom they admit into communion with them. *Believe not every spirit.* (2) See how it was removed (*v.* 27): *Barnabas took him to the apostles* themselves, who were not so scrupulous as the inferior disciples, *to whom he first assayed to join himself, and he declared to them,* [1] What Christ had done for him. [2] What he had since done for Christ. So it was that, being satisfied himself, he gave satisfaction to the apostles concerning him, he having brought no testimonials from the disciples at Damascus, thinking *he needed not, as some others, epistles of commendation*, 2 Cor. iii. 1.

2. How sharp his enemies were upon him. (1) He was admitted into the communion of the disciples, which was no little provocation to his enemies. (2) He appeared vigorous in the cause of Christ, and this was yet more provoking to them (*v.* 29). (3) This brought him into peril of his life, with which he narrowly escaped: *The Grecians*,

when they found they could not deal with him in disputation, contrived to silence him another way; *they went about to slay him,* as they did Stephen when *they could not resist the Spirit by which he spoke, ch.* vi. 10. That is a bad cause that has recourse to persecution for its last argument. But notice was given of this conspiracy too, and effectual care taken to secure this young champion (*v.* 30): *When the brethren knew* what was designed against him *they brought him down to Cesarea.*

III. The churches had now a comfortable gleam of liberty and peace (*v.* 31): *Then had the churches rest.* Observe,

1. *The churches had rest.* After a storm comes a calm.

2. They made a good use of this lucid interval. (2) They *walked in the fear of the Lord*—were more exemplary themselves for a holy, heavenly way of life. (3) They *walked in the comfort of the Holy Ghost*—were not only faithful, but cheerful, in religion; they stuck to the ways of the Lord, and sang in those ways.

3. God blessed it to them for their increase in number: They *were multiplied.*

ENEAS HEALED (*vv.* 32–35)

Here we have, I. The visit Peter made to the churches that were newly planted by the dispersed preachers, *v.* 32.

II. The cure Peter wrought on *Eneas,* a man that had been bed-ridden eight years, *v.* 33. Peter does not pretend to do it himself by any power of his own, but declares it to be Christ's act and deed, directs

him to look up to Christ for help, and assures him of an *immediate* cure—not, "He *will* make thee," but, "He *does* make thee, whole;" and a *perfect* cure—not, "He makes thee *easy,*" but "He makes thee *whole.*" He does not express himself by way of prayer to Christ that he would make him whole, but as one having authority from Christ, and that knew his mind, he declares him made whole. (2) He ordered him to bestir himself, to exert himself: "*Arise and make thy bed,* that all may see thou art thoroughly cured.*" (3) Power went along with this word: he arose immediately, and no doubt very willingly made his own bed.

III. The good influence this had upon many (*v.* 35): *All that dwelt at Lydda and Saron saw him, and turned to the Lord.*

DORCAS RAISED (*vv.* 36–43)

Here we have another miracle wrought by Peter, for the confirming of the gospel, and which exceeded the former—the raising of Tabitha to life when she had been for some time dead. Here is,

I. The life, and death, and character of Tabitha, on whom this miracle was wrought, *vv.* 36, 37.

II. The request which her Christian friends sent to Peter to come to them with all speed, not to attend the funeral, but, if it might be, to prevent it, *v.* 38. Lydda, where Peter now was, was nigh to Joppa, and the disciples at Joppa had heard that Peter was there, and that he had raised Eneas from a bed of languishing; and therefore they *sent him two men,* to make the message the more solemn and respectful, *desiring him that he would not delay to come to them*; not telling him the occasion, lest he should modestly decline coming upon so great an errand as to raise the dead: if they can but get him to them, they will leave it to him.

III. The posture in which he found the survivors, when he came to them (*v.* 39). He found the corpse laid in the upper chamber, and attended by widows, probably such as were in the communion of the church, poor widows; there they were,

1. Commending the deceased—a good work, when there was that in them which was truly commendable, and worthy of imitation, and when it is done modestly and soberly, and without flattery of the survivors or any sinister intention, but purely for the glory of God and the exciting of others to that which is virtuous and praiseworthy.

2. They were here lamenting the loss of her: The widows stood by Peter, weeping. They need not weep for her; she is taken from the evil to come, *she rests from her labours and her works follow her*, besides those she leaves behind her: but they weep for themselves and for their children, who will soon find the want of such a good woman, that has not left her fellow.

IV. The manner in which she was raised to life. 1. Privately. Thus Peter declined everything that looked like vainglory and ostentation; they came to see, but he did not come to be seen. 2. By prayer. In his healing Eneas there was an implied prayer, but in this greater work he addressed himself to God by solemn prayer, as Christ when

he raised Lazarus; but Christ's prayer was with the authority of a Son, who *quickens whom he will*; Peter's with the submission of a servant, who is under direction, and therefore he *knelt down and prayed*. 3. By the word, a quickening word, a word which is spirit and life. When he had prayed, he *turned to the body*, and spoke in his Master's name, according to his example: "*Tabitha, arise*; return to life again." Power went along with his word, and she came to life, *opened her eyes* which death had closed.

V. The good effect of this miracle. 1. Many were by it convinced of the truth of the gospel, that it was from heaven, and not of men, and believed in the Lord, *v.* 42. 2. Peter was hereby induced to continue some time in this city, *v.* 43. Finding that a door of opportunity was opened for him there, he tarried there many days, till he was sent thence, and sent for thence upon business to another place.

CHAPTER TEN

CORNELIUS PRAYS (*vv.* 1–8)

It is not unlikely that some Gentiles might before now have stepped into a synagogue of the Jews, and heard the gospel preached; but the gospel was never yet designedly preached to the Gentiles, nor any of them baptized—Cornelius was the first; and here we have,

I. An account given us of this Cornelius, who and what he was, who was the first-born of the Gentiles to Christ. He was, according to the measure of the light he had, a religious man. It is a very good character that is given of him, *v.* 2. (1) He was possessed with a principle of regard to the true and living God. He was *a devout man and one that feared God*. He believed in one God, the Creator of heaven and earth, and had a reverence for his glory and authority, and a dread of offending him by sin. (2) He kept up religion in his family. He *feared God with all his house*. (3) He was a very charitable man: He *gave much alms to the people*, the people of the Jews, notwithstanding the singularities of their religion. (4) He was much in prayer: He *prayed to God always*. He kept up stated times for prayer, and was constant to them.

II. The orders given him from heaven, by the ministry of an angel, to send for Peter to come to him, which he would never have done if he had not been thus directed to do it. Observe,

1. How, and in what way, these orders were given him. He had a vision, in which an angel delivered them to him. It was about the *ninth hour of the day*, at three of the clock in the afternoon, which is with us an hour of business and conversation; but then, because it was in the temple the time of offering the evening sacrifice, it was made by devout people an *hour of prayer*, to intimate that all our prayers are to be offered up in the virtue of the great sacrifice.

2. What the message was that was delivered to him.

(1) He is assured that God accepts him in walking according to the light he had (*v.* 4). Observe, Prayers and alms must go together. The sacrifices under the law are said to be *for a memorial.* See Lev. ii. 9, 16; v. 12; vi. 15. And prayers and alms are our spiritual offerings, which God is pleased to take cognizance of, and have regard to.

(2) He is appointed to enquire after a further discovery of divine grace, now lately made to the world, *v.* 5, 6. Not, He may do it if he pleases; it will be an improvement and entertainment to him. But, He must do it; it is indispensably necessary to his acceptance with God for the future, though he has been accepted in his services hitherto. He that believed the promise of the Messiah must now believe the performance of that promise. Cornelius has now an angel from heaven talking to him, and yet he must not receive the gospel of Christ from this angel, nor be told by him what he ought to do, but all that the angel has to say is, "Send for Peter, and he shall tell thee."

III. His immediate obedience to these orders, *vv.* 7, 8. He sent with all speed to Joppa, to fetch Peter to him.

PETER'S VISION (*vv.* 9–18)

The scriptures of the Old Testament had spoken plainly of the bringing in of the Gentiles into the church. Christ had given plain intimations of it when he ordered them to *teach all nations*; and yet even Peter himself, who knew so much of his Master's mind, could not understand it, till it was here revealed by vision, *that the Gentiles should be fellow-heirs*, Eph. iii. 6. Now here observe,

I. The circumstances of this vision.

1. It was when the messengers sent from Cornelius were now *nigh the city*, v. 9. Peter knew nothing of their approach, and they knew nothing of his praying; but he that knew both him and them was preparing things for the interview, and facilitating the end of their negociation.

2. It was when *Peter went up upon the housetop to pray*, about noon.

3. It was when he became *very hungry*, and was waiting for his dinner (*v.* 10). Now this hunger was a proper inlet to the vision about meats, as Christ's hunger in the wilderness was to Satan's temptation to turn stones into bread.

II. The vision itself, which was not so plain as that to Cornelius, but more figurative and enigmatical, to make the deeper impression. 1. He *fell into a trance or ecstasy*, not of terror, but of contemplation, with which he was so entirely swallowed up as not only not to be regardful, but not to be sensible, of external things. He saw *a great sheet full of all manner of living creatures, which descended from heaven, and was let down to him to the earth*, that is, to the roof of the house where he now was. By this vision we are taught to see all the benefit and service we have from the inferior creatures coming down to us from heaven; it is the gift of God who made them. Peter was ordered by a voice from heaven to make use of this plenty and variety which God had sent him (*v.* 13): "*Rise, Peter, kill and eat*: without putting any difference between clean and unclean, take which thou

hast most mind to." The distinction of meats which the law made was intended to put a difference between Jew and Gentile, that it might be difficult to them to dine and sup with a Gentile, because they would have that set before them which they were not allowed to eat; and now the taking off of that prohibition was a plain allowance to converse with the Gentiles, and to be free and familiar with them. Now they might fare as they fared, and therefore might eat with them, and be fellow-commoners with them. He stuck to his principles, and would by no means hearken to the motion, though he was hungry (*v.* 14): *Not so, Lord.* God, by a second voice from heaven, proclaimed the repeal of the law in this case (*v.* 15): *What God hath cleansed, that call thou not common.* He that made the law might alter it when he pleased, and reduce the matter to its first state. *This was done thrice*, v. 16. The sheet was drawn up a little way, and let down again the second time, and so the third time, with the same call to him, to kill, and eat, and the same reason, that what God hath cleansed we must not call common; but whether Peter's refusal was repeated the second and third time is not certain; surely it was not, when his objection had the first time received such a satisfactory answer. But at last *the vessel was received up into heaven.*

III. The providence which very opportunely explained this vision, and gave Peter to understand the intention of it, *vv.* 17, 18. 1. What Christ did, Peter knew not just then

(John xiii. 7): *He doubted within himself what this vision which he had seen should mean.* 2. Yet he was made to know presently, for *the men who were sent from Cornelius* were just now come to *the house*, and were at *the gate enquiring whether Peter lodged there*; and by their errand it will appear what was the meaning of this vision.

PETER GOES TO CORNELIUS (*vv.* 19–33)

We have here the meeting between Peter the apostle, and Cornelius the centurion. Now here,

I. Peter is directed by the Spirit to go along with Cornelius's messengers (*vv.* 19, 20), and this is the exposition of the vision; now the riddle is unriddled: *While Peter thought on the vision*; he was musing upon it, and then it was opened to him.

II. He receives both them and their message: *He went down to them, v.* 21. Peter lodged them, though they were Gentiles, to show how readily he complied with the design of the vision in eating with Gentiles; for he immediately took them to eat with him. Though they were two of them servants, and the other a common soldier, yet Peter thought it not below him to take them into his house.

III. He *went with them* to Cornelius, whom he found ready to receive and entertain him. 1. Peter, when he went with them, was *accompanied by certain brethren from Joppa*, where he now was, *v.* 23. Six of them went along with him, as we find, *ch.* xi. 12. Either Peter desired their company, that

they might be witnesses of his proceeding cautiously with reference to the Gentiles, and of the good ground on which he went, and therefore he invited them (*ch.* xi. 12), or they offered their service to attend him, and desired they might have the honour and happiness of being his fellow-travellers. Now when they came into the house of Cornelius Peter found, (1) That he was expected, and this was an encouragement to him. (2) That he was expected by many, and this was a further encouragement to him. As Peter brought some with him to partake of the spiritual gift he had now to dispense, so *Cornelius had called together*, not only his own family, but *kinsmen and near friends*, to partake with him of the heavenly instructions he expected from Peter, which would give Peter a larger opportunity of doing good.

IV. Here is the first interview between Peter and Cornelius, in which we have, 1. The profound and indeed undue respect and honour which Cornelius paid to Peter (*v.* 25). His worshipping a man was indeed culpable; but, considering his present ignorance, it was excusable, nay, and it was an evidence of something in him that was very commendable—and that was a great veneration for divine and heavenly things. 2. Peter's modest and indeed just and pious refusal of this honour that was done him (*v.* 26). Peter did not entertain a surmise that his great respect for him, though excessive, might contribute to the success of his preaching, and therefore if he will be deceived let him be deceived;

no, let him know that Peter is a man, that *the treasure is in earthen vessels*, that he may value the treasure for its own sake.

V. The account which Peter and Cornelius give to each other, and to the company, of the hand of Heaven in bringing them together. Now,

1. Peter declares the direction God gave to him to come to those Gentiles, *vv.* 28, 29. "*God hath shown me*, by a vision, *that I should not call any man common or unclean*, nor refuse to converse with any man for the sake of his country."

2. Cornelius declares the directions God gave to him to send for Peter, and that it was purely in obedience to those directions that he had sent for him. Now,

(1) Cornelius gives an account of the angel's appearing to him, and ordering him to send for Peter; not as glorying in it, but as that which warranted his expectation of a message from heaven by Peter.

(2) He declares his own and his friends' readiness to receive the message Peter had to deliver (*v.* 33).

PETER'S SERMON (*vv.* 34–43)

We have here Peter's sermon preached to Cornelius and his friends. This excellent sermon of Peter's is admirably suited to the circumstances of those to whom he preached it; for it was a new sermon.

I. Because they were Gentiles to whom he preached. He shows that, notwithstanding this, they were interested in the gospel of Christ, which he had to preach, and entitled to the benefit of it, upon an equal footing with the Jews. He therefore lays down this as an undoubted principle, *that God is no respecter of persons; doth not know favour in judgment*, as the Hebrew phrase is; which magistrates are forbidden to do (Deut. i. 17; xvi. 19; Prov. xxiv. 23), and are blamed for doing, Ps. lxxxii. 2. God never perverts judgment upon personal regards and considerations, nor countenances a wicked man in a wicked thing for the sake of his beauty, or stature, his country, parentage, relations, wealth, or honour in the world. Now, (1) This was always a truth, before Peter perceived it. Yet now it was made more clear than it had been. Now *in Christ Jesus*, it is plain, *neither circumcision availeth any thing, nor uncircumcision*, Gal. v. 6; Col. iii. 11.

II. Because they were Gentiles inhabiting a place within the confines of the land of Israel, he refers them to what they themselves could not but know concerning the life and doctrine, the preaching and miracles, the death and sufferings of our Lord Jesus: for these were things the report of which spread into every corner of the nation, *vv.* 37, &c.

1. They knew in general, *the word*, that is, the gospel, *which God sent to the children of Israel: That word, I say, you know, v.* 37.

2. They knew the several matters of fact relating to this word of the gospel sent to Israel. (1) They knew the baptism of repentance which John preached by way of introduction to it, and in which the gospel first began, Mark i. 1. (2) They knew that immediately after

John's baptism the gospel of Christ, that word of *peace, was published throughout all Judea*, and that it took its rise from Galilee. (3) They knew that Jesus of Nazareth, when he was here upon earth, *went about doing good.* (4) They knew more particularly that he *healed all that were oppressed of the devil*, and helped them from under his oppressing power. (5) They knew that the Jews put him to death; they *slew* him by *hanging him on a tree.*

3. They did know, or might know, by all this, that he had a commission from heaven to preach and act as he did. This he still harps upon in his discourse, and takes all occasions to hint it to them. Let them know, (1) That this Jesus *is Lord of all*; it comes in in a parenthesis, but is the principal proposition intended to be proved, that Jesus Christ, by whom peace is made between God and man, *is Lord of all*; not only as *God over all blessed for evermore*, but as Mediator, *all power both in heaven and on earth* is put into his hand, and all judgment committed to him. (2) That *God anointed him with the Holy Ghost and with power*; he was both authorized and enabled to do what he did by a divine anointing, whence he was called *Christ—the Messiah, the anointed One.* (3) That *God was with him, v.* 38. His works were wrought in God.

III. Because they had had no more certain information concerning this Jesus, Peter declares to them his resurrection from the dead, and the proofs of it, that they might not think that when he was slain there was an end of him. 1.

The power by which he arose is incontestably divine (*v.* 40). 2. The proofs of his resurrection were incontestably clear; for God *showed him openly.*

IV. He concludes with an inference from all this, that therefore that which they all ought to do was to believe in this Jesus: he was sent to tell Cornelius what he must do, and it is this; his praying and his giving alms were very well, but one thing he lacked, he must believe in Christ. Observe,

1. Why he must believe in him. Faith has reference to a testimony, and the Christian faith is *built upon the foundation of the apostles and prophets*, it is built upon the testimony given by them.

2. What they must believe concerning him. (1) That we are all accountable to Christ as our Judge; this the apostles were commanded to testify to the world, that this Jesus is *ordained of God to be the Judge of the quick and dead, v.* 42. (2) That if we believe in him we shall all be justified by him as our righteousness, *v.* 43. The prophets, when they spoke of the death of Christ, did witness this, *that through his name,* for his sake, and upon the account of his merit, *whosoever believeth in him*, Jew or Gentile, *shall receive remission of sins.*

CORNELIUS BAPTIZED
(*vv.* 44–48)

Here we have,

I. God's owning Peter's word, by conferring the Holy Ghost upon the hearers of it, and immediately upon the hearing of it (*v.* 44). Observe, 1. When the Holy Ghost fell upon them—while Peter was preaching. 2. How it appeared that the Holy Ghost had fallen upon them (*v.* 46): *They spoke with tongues* which they never learned, perhaps the Hebrew, the holy tongue; as the preachers were enabled to speak the vulgar tongues, that they might communicate the doctrine of Christ to the hearers, so, probably, the hearers were immediately taught the sacred tongue, that they might examine the proofs which the preachers produced out of the Old Testament in the original. Or their being enabled to speak with tongues intimated that they were all designed for ministers, and by this first descent of the Spirit upon them were qualified to preach the gospel to others, which they did but now receive themselves. But, observe, when they spoke with tongues, they *magnified God*, they spoke of Christ and the benefits of redemption, which Peter had been preaching to the glory of God. Thus did they on whom the Holy Ghost first descended, *ch.* ii. 11. Note, Whatever gift we are endued with, we ought to honour God with it, and particularly the gift of speaking, and all the improvements of it. 3. What impression it made upon the believing Jews that were present (*v.* 45): *Those of the circumcision who believed were astonished*—those six that came along with Peter; it surprised them exceedingly, and perhaps gave them some uneasiness, because *upon the Gentiles also was poured out the gift of the Holy Ghost*, which they thought had been appropriated to their own nation. Had they understood the scriptures of the Old Testament, which

pointed at this, it would not have been such an astonishment to them; but by our mistaken notions of things we create difficulties to ourselves in the methods of divine providence and grace.

II. Peter's owning God's work in baptizing those on whom the Holy Ghost fell. Observe, 1. Though they had received the Holy Ghost, yet it was requisite they should be baptized; though God is not tied to instituted ordinances, we are; and no extraordinary gifts set us above them, but rather oblige us so much the more to conform to them. Some in our days would have argued. 2. Though they were Gentiles, yet, having received the Holy Ghost, they might be admitted to baptism (*v.* 47).

III. Their owning both Peter's word and God's work in their desire for further advantage by Peter's ministry: *They prayed him to tarry certain days.*

CHAPTER ELEVEN

PETER EXPLAINS (*vv.* 1–18)

Here we find,

I. Intelligence was presently brought of it to the church in Jerusalem, and thereabouts; for Cesarea was not so far from Jerusalem but that they might presently hear of it. Some for good-will, and some for ill-will, would spread the report of it; so that before he himself had returned to Jerusalem *the apostles and the brethren* there and *in Judea heard that the Gentiles also had received the word of God*, that is, the gospel of Christ.

II. That offence was taken at it by the believing Jews (*vv.* 2, 3).

58

III. Peter gave such a full and fair account of the matter of fact as was sufficient, without any further argument or apology, both to justify him, and to satisfy them (*v.* 4).

That which put the matter past all dispute was the descent of the Holy Ghost upon the Gentile hearers; this completed the evidence that it was the will of God that he should take the Gentiles into communion.

THE CHURCH AT ANTIOCH
(*vv.* 19–25)

We have here an account of the planting and watering of a church at Antioch, the chief city of Syria, reckoned afterwards the third most considerable city of the empire, only Rome and Alexandria being preferred before it, next to whose patriarch that of Antioch took place. Now concerning the church at Antioch observe,

I. The first preachers of the gospel there were such as were dispersed from Jerusalem by persecution, that persecution which arose five or six years ago (as some compute), at the time of Stephen's death (*v.* 19). Thus the wrath of man is made to praise God. Observe,

1. Those that *fled from persecution* did not flee from their work.

2. They pressed forward in their work, finding that the *good pleasure of the Lord prospered in their hands*.

3. They *preached the word to none but to the Jews only* who were dispersed in all those parts, and had synagogues of their own, in which they met with them by themselves, and preached to them. They did not yet understand that the Gentiles

were to be fellow-heirs, and of the same body; but left the Gentiles either to turn Jews, and so come into the church, or else remain as they were.

4. They particularly applied themselves to the Hellenist Jews, here called the Grecians, that were at Antioch. To them they preached the Lord Jesus. This was the constant subject of their preaching.

5. They had wonderful success in their preaching, *v.* 21. (1) Their preaching was accompanied with a divine power: *The hand of the Lord was with them.* (2) Abundance of good was done: *A great number believed, and turned unto the Lord*— many more than could have been expected, considering the outward disadvantages they laboured under: some of all sorts of people were wrought upon, and brought into obedience to Christ. Observe, What the change was. [1] They believed; they were convinced of the truth of the gospel, and subscribed to the record God had given in it concerning his Son. [2] The effect and evidence of this was that they *turned unto the Lord.* They turned to the Lord Jesus, and he became all in all with them. This was the work of conversion wrought upon them, and it must be wrought upon every one of us.

II. The good work thus begun at Antioch was carried on to great perfection; and the church, thus founded, grew to be a flourishing one, by the ministry of Barnabas and Saul, who built upon the foundation which the other preachers had laid, and *entered into their labours*, John iv. 37, 38.

1. The church at Jerusalem sent

Barnabas thither, to nurse this new-born church, and to strengthen the hands both of preachers and people, and put a reputation upon the cause of Christ there.

2. Barnabas went to fetch Saul, to join with him in the work of the gospel at Antioch. The last news we heard of him was that, when his life was sought at Jerusalem, he was sent away to Tarsus, the city where he was born, and, it should seem, he continued there ever since, doing good, no doubt. But now Barnabas takes a journey to Tarsus on purpose to see what had become of him, to tell him what a door of opportunity was opened at Antioch, and to desire him to come and spend some time with him there, *vv.* 25, 26. And here also it appears that Barnabas was a good sort of a man in two things: (1) That he would take so much pains to bring an active useful man out of obscurity. (2) That he would bring in Saul at Antioch, who, being a *chief speaker* (*ch.* xiv. 12), and probably a more popular preacher, would be likely to eclipse him there, by outshining him; but Barnabas is very willing to be eclipsed when it is for the public service.

3. We are here further told,

(1) What service was now done to the church at Antioch. Paul and Barnabas continued there a whole year, presiding in their religious assemblies, and preaching the gospel, *v.* 26.

(2) What honour was now put upon the church *at Antioch: There the disciples were first called Christians.* Hitherto those who gave up their names to Christ were called *disciples, learners, scholars,* trained up under him, in order to their being employed by him; but henceforward they were called *Christians.* They took their denomination not from the name of his person, *Jesus,* but of his office, *Christ—anointed,* so putting their creed into their names, *that Jesus is the Christ.*

FAMINE RELIEF (*vv.* 27–30)

Now here we have,

I. A visit which some prophets made to Antioch (*v.* 27): *In these days,* during that year that Barnabas and Saul lived at Antioch, there *came prophets from Jerusalem to Antioch.*

II. A particular prediction of a famine approaching, delivered by one of these prophets, his name *Agabus*; we read of him again prophesying Paul's imprisonment, *ch.* xxi. 10, 11. Here he stood up, probably in one of their public assemblies, and prophesied, *v.* 28. Observe, 1. Whence he had his prophecy. What he said was not of himself, but *he signified it by the Spirit, the Spirit of prophecy, that there should be* a famine. 2. What the prophecy was: *There should be great dearth throughout all the world,* by unseasonable weather, that corn should be scarce and dear, so that many of the poor should perish for want of bread. This should be not in one particular country, but *through all the world,* that is, all the Roman empire, which they in their pride, like Alexander before them, called *the world.* 3. The accomplishment of it: *It came to pass in the days of Claudius Cesar*; it began in the second year of his reign, and continued to the fourth, if not longer.

Several of the Roman historians make mention of it, as does also Josephus.

III. The good use they made of this prediction. When they were told of a famine at hand, they did not do as the Egyptians, hoard up corn for themselves; but, as became Christians, laid by for charity to relieve others, which is the best preparative for our own sufferings and want. Observe,

1. What they determined—that *every man, according to his ability*, should *send relief to the brethren that dwelt in Judea*, v. 29. (1) The persons that were recommended to them as objects of charity were *the brethen that dwelt in Judea*. Though we must, as we have opportunity, *do good to all men*, yet we must have a special regard *to the household of faith*, Gal. vi. 10. No poor must be neglected, but God's poor most particularly regarded. (2) The agreement there was among the disciples about it, that *every man* should contribute, *according to his ability*, to this good work.

2. What they did—they did as they determined (v. 30). *Which also they did*. They not only talked of it, but they did it.

CHAPTER TWELVE

JAMES MARTYRED (vv. 1–4)

Herod, though originally of an Edomite family, yet seems to have been a proselyte to the Jewish religion; for Josephus says he was zealous for the Mosaic rites, a bigot for the ceremonies. He was not only (as Herod Antipas was) tetrarch of Galilee, but had also the government of Judea committed to him by Claudius the emperor, and resided most at Jerusalem, where he was at this time. Three things we are here told he did:

I. He *stretched forth his hands to vex certain of the church*, v. 1. See how he advances gradually. 1. He began with some of the members of the church, certain of them that were of less note and figure; played first at small game, but afterwards flew at the apostles themselves. 2. He began with vexing them only, or afflicting them, imprisoning them, finding them, spoiling their houses and goods, and other ways molesting them; but afterwards he proceeded to greater instances of cruelty.

II. *He killed James the brother of John with the sword*, v. 2. We are here to consider, 1. Who the martyr was: it was *James the brother of John*; so called to distinguish him from the other James the brother of Joses. This who was here crowned with martyrdom was one of the first three of Christ's disciples, one of those that were *the witnesses of his transfiguration and agony*, whereby he was prepared for martyrdom. 2. What kind of death he suffered: he was slain *with the sword*, that is, his head was *cut off with a sword*, which was looked upon by the Romans to be a more disgraceful way of being beheaded than with an axe; so Lorinus. It is strange that we have not a more full and particular account of the martyrdom of this great apostle, as we had of Stephen. But even this short mention of the thing is sufficient to let us know that the first preachers of the gospel were so well assured of the truth of it that they sealed it with their blood, and thereby have encouraged us, if at any time we are called to it, *to resist unto blood too.*

III. He imprisoned Peter, of whom he had heard most, as making the greatest figure among the apostles and whom therefore he would be proud of the honour of taking off. Notice is taken of the time when Herod laid hold on Peter. It was at the feast of the passover, when their celebrating the memorial of their typical deliverance should have led them to the acceptance of their spiritual deliverance; instead of this, they, under pretence of zeal for the law, were most violently fighting against it.

Here is an account of Peter's imprisonment (*v.* 4). He was *delivered to four quaternions of soldiers,* that is, to sixteen, who were to be a guard upon him, four at a time, that he should not make his escape, nor be rescued by his friends. Thus they thought they had him fast. Herod's design was, *after Easter, to bring him forth unto the people.* He would do this *after Easter, after the passover,* certainly so it ought to be read, for it is the same word that is always so rendered; and to insinuate the introducing of a gospel-feast, instead of the passover, when we have nothing in the New Testament of such a thing, is to mingle Judaism with our Christianity.

PETER RELEASED (*vv.* 5–19)

We have here an account of Peter's deliverance out of prison, by which the design of Herod against him

was defeated, and his life preserved for further service, and a stop given to this bloody torrent. Now,

I. One thing that magnified his deliverance was that it was a signal answer to prayer (*v.* 5): *Peter was kept in prison* with a great deal of care, so that it was altogether impossible, either by force or by stealth, to get him out. *But prayer was made without ceasing of the church unto God for him,* for prayers and tears are the church's arms; therewith she fights, not only against her enemies, but for her friends: and to these means they have recourse. *Prayer was made without ceasing;* it was *fervent prayer.* It is the word that is used concerning Christ's praying in his agony *more earnestly;* it is *the fervent prayer of the righteous man, that* is effectual, and *availeth much.*

II. Let us observe when his deliverance came. 1. It was the very night before Herod designed to bring him forth, which made it to be so much the greater consolation to his friends and confusion to his enemies. 2. It was when he was *fast bound with two chains, between two soldiers;* so that if he offer to stir he wakes them; and, besides this, though the prison-doors, no doubt, were locked and bolted, yet, to make sure work, *the keepers before the door kept the prison,* that no one might so much as attempt to rescue him. Never could the art of man do more to secure a prisoner. 3. It was when he was *sleeping between the soldiers,* fast asleep.

III. It also magnified his deliverance very much that an *angel was*

62

sent from heaven on purpose to rescue him, which made his escape both practicable and warrantable.

1. *The angel of the Lord came upon him;—stood over him.* He seemed as one abandoned by men, yet not forgotten of his God; *the Lord thinketh upon him.*

2. *A light shone in the prison.* Though it is a dark place, and in the night, Peter shall see his way clear.

3. The angel awoke Peter, by giving him *a blow on his side*, a gentle touch. The language of this stroke was, *Arise up quickly*; not as if the angel feared coming short by his delay, but Peter must not be indulged in it.

4. *His chains fell off from his hands.* It seems they had hand-cuffed him, to make him sure, but *God loosed his bands.*

5. He was ordered to dress himself immediately, and follow the angel; and he did so, *vv.* 8, 9. Those who are delivered out of a spiritual imprisonment must follow their deliverer, as Israel when they went out of the house of bondage did; they *went out, not knowing whither they went*, but whom they followed.

6. He was led safely by the angel out of danger, *v.* 10. But still there is an iron gate, after all, that will stop them. However, up to that gate they march, and, like the Red Sea before Israel, it *opened to them*.

7. When this was done, *the angel departed from him*, and left him to himself.

IV. Having seen how his deliverance was magnified, we are next to see how it was manifested both to himself and others, and

how, being made great, it was made known. We are here told,

1. How Peter came to himself, and so came himself to the knowledge of it, *v.* 11. So many strange and surprising things coming together upon a man just awoke out of sleep put him for the present into some confusion; so that he knew not where he was, nor what he did, nor whether it was fancy or fact; but at length Peter *came to himself*, was thoroughly awake, and found that it was not a dream, but a real thing.

2. How Peter came to his friends, and brought the knowledge of it to them.

(1) He *considered the thing* (*v.* 12), considered how imminent his danger was, how great his deliverance; and now what has he to do?

(2) He went directly to a friend's house, which, it is likely, lay near to the place where he was; it was the house of Mary, a sister of Barnabas, and mother of John Mark, whose house, it should seem, was frequently made use of for the private meeting of the disciples.

(3) There he found *many* that were *gathered together praying*, at the dead time of the night, praying for Peter, who was the next day to come upon his trial, that God would find out some way or other for his deliverance.

(4) He knocked at the gate, and had much ado to get them to let him in (*vv.* 13–16). Now when he knocked there, [1] A *damsel came to hearken*; not to open the door till she knew who was there, a friend or a foe, and what their business was, fearing informers. [2] She knew Peter's voice, having

often heard him pray, and preach, and discourse, with a great deal of pleasure. But, instead of letting him in immediately out of the cold, *she opened not the gate for gladness.* [3] She ran in, and probably went up to an upper room where they were together, and told them that Peter was certainly at the gate, though she had not courage enough to open the gate, for fear she should be deceived, and it should be the enemy. But, when she spoke of Peter's being there, they said, *"Thou art mad*; it is impossible it should be he, for he is in prison." Sometimes that which we most earnestly wish for we are most backward to believe, because we are afraid of imposing upon ourselves, as the disciples, who, when Christ had risen, *believed not for joy*. However, she stood to it that it was he. Then said they, *It is his angel, v.* 15. *First,* "It is a *messenger* from him, that makes use of his name;" so some take it. *Secondly,* "It is his *guardian angel,* or some other angel that has assumed his shape and voice, and stands at the gate in his resemblance."

(5) At length they let him in (*v.* 16). The iron gate which opposed his enlargement opened of itself, without so much as once knocking at it; but the door of his friend's house that was to welcome him does not open of its own accord, but must be knocked at, long knocked at; lest Peter should be puffed up by the honours which the angel did him, he meets with this mortification, by a seeming slight which his friends put upon him. But, *when they saw him, they were astonished,* were filled with wonder

and joy in him, as much as they were but just now with sorrow and fear concerning him.

(6) Peter gave them an account of his deliverance. *He declared unto them how the Lord Jesus had* by an angel *brought him out of prison*; and it is very likely, having found them praying for his deliverance, he did not part with them till he and they had together solemnly given thanks to God for his enlargement.

(7) Peter sent the account to others of his friends. He would have James and his company to know of his deliverance, not only that they might be eased of their pain and delivered from their fears concerning Peter, but that they might return thanks to God with him and for him.

(8) Peter had nothing more to do for the present than to shift for his own safety, which he did accordingly: He *departed, and went into another place more obscure,* and therefore more safe.

V. Having seen the triumph of Peter's friends in his deliverance, let us next observe the confusion of his enemies thereupon, which was so much the greater because people's expectation was so much raised of the putting of him to death. Herod himself retired upon it: *He went down from Judea to Cesarea, and there abode.* He was vexed to the heart, as a lion disappointed of his prey; and the more because he had so much raised the *expectation of the people of the Jews* concerning Peter, had told them how he would very shortly gratify them with the sight of Peter's head in a charger, which would oblige them as much as John Baptist's did Herodias; it made him ashamed to be robbed of this boasting, and to see himself, notwithstanding his confidence, disabled to make his words good. This is such a mortification to his proud spirit that he cannot bear to stay in Judea, but away he goes to Cesarea.

DEATH OF HEROD
(*vv.* 20–25)

In these verses we have,

I. The death of Herod. God reckoned with him, not only for his putting James to death, but for his design and endeavour to put Peter to death; for sinners will be called to an account, not only for the wickedness of their deeds, but for the wickedness of their endeavours (Ps. xxviii. 4), for the mischief they have done and the mischief they would have done. It was but a little while that Herod lived after this. Some sinners God makes quick work with.

II. The progress of the gospel after this. 1. *The word of God grew and multiplied*, as seed sown, which comes up with a great increase, thirty, sixty, a hundred fold; wherever the gospel was preached, multitudes embraced it, and were added to the church by it, *v.* 24. After the death of James, the word of God grew; for the church, the more it was afflicted, the more it multiplied, like Israel in Egypt. 2. Barnabas and Saul returned to Antioch as soon as they had despatched the business they were sent upon: *When they had fulfilled their ministry*, had paid in their money to the proper persons, and taken care about the due distribution of

it to those for whom it was collected, they *returned from Jerusalem*. Barnabas and Saul, when they went to *Antioch*, *took with them John, whose surname was Mark*, at whose mother's house they had that meeting for prayer which we read of *v.* 12. She was sister to Barnabas. It is probable that Barnabas lodged there, and perhaps Paul with him, while they were at Jerusalem, and it was that that occasioned the meeting there at that time (for wherever Paul was he would have some good work doing), and their intimacy in that family while they were at Jerusalem occasioned their taking a son of that family with them when they returned, to be trained up under them, and employed by them, in the service of the gospel.

CHAPTER THIRTEEN
PAUL AND BARNABAS COMMISSIONED (*vv.* 1–3)

We have here a divine warrant and commission to Barnabas and Saul to go and preach the gospel among the Gentiles, and their ordination to that service by the imposition of hands, with fasting and prayer.

I. Here is an account of the present state of the church at Antioch, which was planted *ch.* xi. 20.

1. How well furnished it was with good ministers; there were there *certain prophets and teachers* (*v.* 1), men that were eminent for gifts, graces, and usefulness. Barnabas is first named, probably because he was the eldest, and Saul last, probably because he was the youngest; but afterwards the last became first,

and Saul more eminent in the church.

2. How well employed they were (*v.* 2): *They ministered to the Lord, and fasted.* Observe, (1) Diligent faithful teachers do truly minister unto the Lord. Those that instruct Christians serve Christ; they really do him honour, and carry on the interest of his kingdom. (2) Ministering to the Lord, in one way or other, ought to be the stated business of churches and their teachers. What have we to do as Christians and ministers but to *serve the Lord Christ*? Col. iii. 24; Rom. xiv. 18. (3) Religious *fasting* is of use in our ministering to the Lord, both as a sign of our humiliation and a means of our mortification. Though it was not so much practised by the disciples of Christ, *while the bridegroom was with them*, as it was by the disciples of John and of the Pharisees; yet, after the bridegroom was taken away, they abounded in it, as those that had well learned to deny themselves and to endure hardness.

II. The orders given by the Holy Ghost for the setting apart of Barnabas and Saul, while they were engaged in public exercises, the ministers of the several congregations in the city joining in one solemn fast or day of prayer: The *Holy Ghost said,* either by a voice from heaven, or by a strong impulse on the minds of those of them that were prophets, *Separate me Barnabas and Saul for the work whereunto I have called them.* He does not specify the work, but refers to a former call of which they themselves knew the meaning, whether others did or no: as for

Saul, he was particularly told that he must *bear Christ's name to the Gentiles* (*ch.* ix. 15), that *he must be sent to the Gentiles* (*ch.* xxii. 21); the matter was settled between them at Jerusalem before this, that as Peter, James, and John laid out themselves among those of the circumcision, so Paul and Barnabas should *go to the heathen,* Gal. ii. 7–9. Barnabas, it is likely, knew himself designed for this service as well as Paul. Yet they would not thrust themselves into this harvest, though it appeared plenteous, till they received their orders from the Lord of the harvest. The orders were, *Separate me Barnabas and Saul.* Observe here, 1. Christ by his Spirit has the nomination of his ministers; for it is by the Spirit of Christ that they are qualified in some measure for his services, inclined to it, and taken off from other cares inconsistent with it. 2. Christ's ministers are separated to him and to the Holy Ghost: *Separate them to me*; they are to be employed in Christ's work and under the Spirit's guidance, to the glory of God the Father. 3. All that are separated to Christ as his ministers are separated to work; Christ keeps no servants to be idle. 4. The work of Christ's ministers, to which they are to be separated, is work that is already settled, and that which all Christ's ministers hitherto have been called to.

III. Their ordination, pursuant to these orders: not to the ministry in general (Barnabas and Saul had both of them been ministers long before this), but to a particular service in the ministry, which had something peculiar in it, and which required a fresh commission, which commission God saw fit at this time to transmit by the hands of *these prophets and teachers*, for the giving of this direction to the church, that teachers should ordain teachers (for prophets we are not now any longer to expect), and that those who have the dispensing of the oracles of Christ committed to them should, for the benefit of posterity, *commit the same to faithful men, who shall be able also to teach others*, 2 Tim. ii. 2. They implored a blessing upon them in their present undertaking, begged that God would be with them, and give them success; and, in order to do this, that *they might be filled with the Holy Ghost* in their work.

ELYMAS THE SORCERER
(*vv*. 4–13)

In these verses we have,

I. A general account of the coming of Barnabas and Saul to the famous island of Cyprus. Observe, 1. Their being sent forth by the Holy Ghost was the great thing that encouraged them in this undertaking, *v.* 4. 2. They came to Seleucia, the sea-port town opposite to Cyprus, thence crossed the sea to Cyprus, and in that island the first city they came to was Salamis, a city on the east side of the island (*v.* 5); and, when they had sown good seed there, *thence they* went onward *through the isle* (*v.* 6) till they came to Paphos, which lay on the western coast. 3. *They preached the word of God* wherever they came, *in the synagogues of the Jews*; so far were they from excluding them that they gave them the preference, and so left those

among them who believed not inexcusable. 4. *They had John for their minister*; not their servant in common things, but their assistant in the things of God.

II. A particular account of their encounter with *Elymas the sorcerer*, whom they met with at Paphos, where the governor resided.

1. There the *deputy*, a Gentile, *Sergius Paulus* by name, encouraged the apostles, and was willing to hear their message.

2. There Elymas, a Jew, a *sorcerer*, opposed them, and did all he could to obstruct their progress. This justified the apostles in *turning to the Gentiles*, that this Jew was so malignant against them.

(1) This Elymas was a pretender *to the gift of prophecy, a sorcerer, a false-prophet*—one that would be taken for a divine, because he was skilled in the arts of divination.

(2) He was hanging on at court, *was with the deputy* of the country.

(3) He made it his business to withstand Barnabas and Saul, as the magicians of Egypt, in Pharaoh's court, *withstood* Moses and Aaron, 2 Tim. iii. 8. He set up himself to be a messenger from heaven, and denied that they were. And *thus he sought to turn away the deputy from the faith* (*v.* 8), to keep him from receiving the gospel, which he saw him inclined to do.

(4) Saul (who is here for the first time called Paul) fell upon him for this with a holy indignation. Now of Paul it is said,

[1] That he was *filled with the Holy Ghost* upon this occasion, filled with a holy zeal against a professed enemy of Christ, which

was one of the graces of the Holy Ghost. What Paul said did not come from any personal resentment, but from the strong impressions which the Holy Ghost made upon his spirit.

[2] He *set his eyes upon him*, to face him down, and to show a holy boldness, in opposition to his wicked impudence. He set his eyes upon him, as an indication that the eye of the heart-searching God was upon him, and saw through and through him.

[3] He gave him his true character, not in passion, but by the Holy Ghost, who knows men better than they know themselves, *v.* 10. He describes him to be, *First*, An agent for hell. *Secondly*, An adversary to heaven.

[4] He charged upon him his present crime, and expostulated with him upon it. Note, *First*, The ways of the Lord are right: they are all so, they are perfectly so. The ways of the Lord Jesus are right, the only right ways to heaven and happiness. *Secondly*, There are those who pervert these right ways, who not only wander out of these ways themselves but mislead others, and suggest to them unjust prejudices against these ways. *Thirdly*, Those who pervert the right ways of the Lord are commonly so hardened in it that, though the equity of those ways be set before them by the most powerful and commanding evidence, yet they will not cease to do it.

[5] He denounced the judgment of God upon him, in a present blindness (*v.* 11). This was designed both for the proof of his crime, as it was a miracle wrought to confirm the right ways of the Lord, and consequently to show the wickedness of him who would not cease to pervert them, as also for the punishment of his crime.

[6] This judgment was immediately executed. Let not him any more pretend to be a guide to the deputy's conscience who is himself struck blind.

3. Notwithstanding all the endeavours of Elymas *to turn away the deputy from the faith*, he was brought to believe, and this miracle, wrought upon the magician himself, contributed to it.

III. Their departure from the island of Cyprus. When they had done what they had to do, 1. They quitted the country, and *went to Perga.* 2. Then John *Mark quitted them, and returned to Jerusalem*, without the consent of Paul and Barnabas; either he did not like the work, or he wanted to go and see his mother. It was his fault, and we shall hear of it again.

PAUL PREACHES (*vv.* 14–41)

The next place we find them in is another Antioch, said to be in Pisidia, to distinguish it from that Antioch in Syria from which they were sent out. Pisidia was a province of the Lesser Asia, bordering upon Pamphylia; this Antioch, it is likely, was the metropolis of it. Abundance of Jews lived there, and to them *the gospel was to be first preached*; and Paul's sermon to them is what we have in these verses, which, it is likely, is the substance of what was preached by the apostles generally to the Jews in all places. We have here,

I. The appearance which Paul

and Barnabas made in a religious assembly of the Jews at Antioch, *v.* 14.

II. The invitation given them to preach. 1. The usual service of the synagogue was performed (*v.* 15). 2. When that was done, they were asked by *the rulers of the synagogue* to give them a sermon (*v.* 15). It is likely Paul did *often preach in the synagogue,* when he was not thus invited to it by the rulers of the synagogues; for he often preached *with much contention,* 1 Thess. ii. 2. But these were more noble, more generous, than the rulers of the synagogues generally were.

III. The sermon Paul preached in the synagogue of the Jews, at the invitation of the rulers of the synagogue. Every thing is touched in this sermon that might be proper either to convince the judgment or insinuate into the affections of the Jews, to prevail with them to receive and embrace Christ as the promised Messiah.

1. He owns them to be God's favourite people, whom he had taken into special relation to himself, and for whom he had done great things.

(1) That *the God of the whole earth* was, in a particular manner, *the God of this people Israel.*

(2) That he had *chosen their fathers* to be his friends: Abraham was called *the friend of God.*

(3) That he had *exalted that people,* and put a great deal of honour upon them, had advanced them into a people, and raised them from nothing, *when they dwelt as strangers in the land of Egypt,* and had nothing in them to recommend them to the divine favour. They

ought to remember this, and to infer hence that God was no debtor to them.

(4) That he had *with a high hand brought them out of Egypt,* where they were not only strangers, but captives, had delivered them at the expense of a great many miracles, both of mercy to them and judgment on their oppressors.

(5) That *he had suffered their manners forty years in the wilderness, v.* 18. Let not the Jews insist too much upon the privileges of their peculiarity, for they have forfeited them a thousand times.

(6) That he had put them in possession of the land of Canaan (*v.* 19). This was a signal favour of God to them, and he owns that hereby a great honour was put upon them, from which he would not in the least derogate.

(7) That he had raised up men, inspired from heaven, to deliver them out of the hands of those that invaded their rights, and oppressed them after their settlement in Canaan, *vv.* 20, 21. At last, he made David their king, *v,* 22. *When God had removed Saul,* for his maladministration, *he raised up unto them David to be their king,* and made *a covenant of royalty with him, and with his seed.*

2. He gives them a full account of our Lord Jesus, passing from David to the Son of David, and shows that this Jesus is his promised Seed (*v.* 23): *Of this man's seed,* from that *root of Jesse,* from that *man after God's own heart, hath God, according to his promise, raised unto Israel a Saviour—Jesus,* who carries salvation in his name.

(1) How welcome should the

preaching of the gospel of Christ be to the Jews, and how should they embrace it, as *well worthy of all acceptation*. Now,

(2) Concerning this Jesus, he tells them,

[1] That John the Baptist was his harbinger and forerunner, that great man whom all acknowledged to be a prophet.

[2] That the rulers and people of the Jews, who should have welcomed him, and been his willing, forward, faithful subjects, were his persecutors and murderers. When the apostles preach Christ as *the Saviour*, they are so far from concealing his ignominious death, and drawing a veil over it, that they always *preach Christ crucified*, yea, and (though this added much to the reproach of his sufferings) crucified by his own people, by *those that dwelt in Jerusalem*, the holy city—the royal city, and *their rulers*, *v.* 27. So Paul saith here, *Because they knew not the voice of the prophets*, therefore *they have fulfilled them*, which implies that if they had understood them they would not have fulfilled them.

[3] That he *rose again from the dead*, and saw no corruption. This was the great truth that was to be preached; for it is the main pillar, by which the whole fabric of the gospel is supported, and therefore he insists largely upon this, and shows,

First, That he rose by consent. When he was imprisoned in the grave for our debt, he did not break prison, but had a fair and legal discharge from the arrest he was under (*v.* 30): *God raised him from the dead*. His enemies laid him in a sepulchre, with design he should always lay there; but God said, *No*; and it was soon seen whose purpose should stand, his or theirs.

Secondly, That there was sufficient proof of his having risen (*v.* 31): *He was seen many days*, by those that were most intimately acquainted with him; for they *came up with him from Galilee to Jerusalem*, were his constant attendants, and *they are his witnesses unto the people*.

Thirdly, That the resurrection of Christ was the performance of the promise made to the patriarchs; it was not only true news, but good news (*vv.* 32, 33).

Fourthly, That the resurrection of Christ was the great proof of his being the Son of God, and confirms what was written in the second Psalm, *Thou art my Son, this day have I begotten thee.* The reason why it was impossible he should be held by the bands of death was because he was the Son of God, and consequently had *life in himself*, which he could not lay down but with a design to resume it. When his eternal generation is spoken of, it is not improper to say, *This day have I begotten thee*; for *from everlasting to everlasting* is with God as it were one and the same eternal day. Yet it may also be accommodated to his resurrection, in a subordinate sense, "This day have I made it to appear that I have begotten thee, and this day have I begotten all that are given to thee;" for it is said (1 Pet. i. 3) that *the God and Father of our Lord Jesus Christ*, as our God and Father, *hath begotten us again to a lively hope, by the resurrection of Jesus Christ from the dead.*

Fifthly, That his being raised the third day, so as not to see corruption, and to a heavenly life, so as no more to return to corruption, that is, to the state of the dead, as others did who were raised to life, further confirms his being the Messiah promised.

(*a*) It could not be accomplished in David himself (*v*. 36), for *David, after he had served his own generation, by the will of God*, who raised him up to be what he was, *fell asleep, and was laid to his fathers, and saw corruption.* Here we have a short account of the life, death, and burial, of the patriarch David, and his continuance under the power of death. But,

(*b*) It was accomplished in the Lord Jesus (*v*. 37): *He whom God raised again saw no corruption*; for it was in him that the sure mercies were to be reserved for us. He rose the third day, and therefore did not see corruption then; and he rose to die no more, and therefore never did. Of him therefore the promise must be understood, and no other.

Having given them this account of the Lord Jesus, he comes to make application of it.

(*a*) In the midst of his discourse, to engage their attention, he had told his hearers that they were concerned in all this (*v*. 26): "*To you is the word of this salvation sent*, to you first. If you by your unbelief make it a word of rejection to you, you may thank yourselves; but it is sent to you for a word of salvation; if it be not so, it is your own fault."

(*b*) In the close of his discourse he applies what he had said concerning Christ to his hearers. He had told them a long story concerning *this Jesus*; now they would be ready to ask, What is all this to us? And he tells them plainly what it is to them.

[*a*] It will be their unspeakable advantage if they embrace Jesus Christ, and believe this word of salvation. It will relieve them where their greatest danger lies; and that is from the guilt of their sins. Note, 1. The great concern of sinners is to be justified, to be acquitted from guilt and accepted as righteous in God's sight. 2. Those who are truly justified are acquitted from all their guilt; for if any be left charged upon the sinner he is undone. 3. It was impossible for a sinner to be justified by the law of Moses. Not by his moral law, for we have all broken it, and are transgressing it daily, so that instead of justifying us it condemns us. Not by his remedial law, for it was not possible that the *blood of bulls and goats should take away sin*, should satisfy God's offended justice, or pacify the sinner's wounded conscience. It was but a ritual and typical institution. See Heb. ix. 9; x. 1, 4. 4. By Jesus Christ we obtain a complete justification; for by him a complete atonement was made for sin. 5. All that believe in Christ, that rely upon him and give up themselves to be ruled by him, are justified by him, and none but they. 6. What the law *could not do* for us, *in that it was weak*, that the gospel of Christ does; and therefore it was folly, out of a jealousy for the law of Moses and the honour of that institution, to con-

ceive a jealousy of the gospel of Christ and the designs of that more perfect institution.

[*b*] It is at their utmost peril if they reject the gospel of Christ, and turn their backs upon the offer now made them (*vv.* 40, 41). Now the prophecy referred to we have Hab. i. 5, where the destruction of the Jewish nation by the Chaldeans is foretold as an incredible unparalleled destruction; and this is here applied to the destruction that was coming upon that nation by the Romans, for their rejecting the gospel of Christ. Those that will not wonder and be saved shall wonder and perish.

GENTILES CONVERTED
(*vv.* 42–52)

The design of this story being to vindicate the apostles, especially Paul (as he doth himself at large, Rom. xi.), from the reflections of the Jews upon him for preaching the gospel to the Gentiles, it is here observed that he proceeded therein with all the caution imaginable, and upon due consideration, of which we have here an instance.

I. There were some of the Jews that were so incensed against the preaching of the gospel, not to the Gentiles, but to themselves, that they would not bear to hear it, but *went out of the synagogue* while Paul was preaching (*v.* 42), in contempt of him and his doctrine, and to the disturbance of the congregation.

II. The Gentiles were as willing to hear the gospel as those rude and ill-conditioned Jews were to get out of the hearing of it. They begged, 1. That the same offer

might be made to them that was made to the Jews. Paul in this sermon had brought the word of salvation to the Jews and proselytes, but had taken no notice of the Gentiles; and therefore they begged that forgiveness of sins through Christ might be preached to them, as it was to the Jews. The Jews' leavings, nay, loathings, were their longings. This justifies Paul in his preaching to them, that he was invited to it, as Peter was sent for to Cornelius.

III. There were some, nay, there were many, both of Jews and proselytes, that were wrought upon by the preaching of the gospel. 1. They submitted to the grace of God, and were admitted to the benefit and comfort of it, which is implied in their being exhorted to continue in it. 2. They were exhorted and encouraged to persevere herein: *Paul and Barnabas, speaking to them* with all the freedom and friendship imaginable, *persuaded them to continue in the grace of God*, to hold fast that which they had received, to continue in their belief of the gospel of grace, their dependence upon the Spirit of grace, and their attendance upon the means of grace.

IV. There was a cheerful attendance upon the preaching of the gospel the *next sabbath day* (*v.* 44): *Almost the whole city* (the generality of whom were Gentiles) *came together to hear the word of God*.

V. The Jews were enraged at this; and not only would not receive the gospel themselves, but were filled with indignation at those that crowded after it (*v.* 45). 1. They grudged the interest the apostles had in the people, were vexed to see the synagogue so full when they were going to preach. 2. They opposed the doctrine the apostles preached. They did it with the utmost spite and rage imaginable: they persisted in their contradiction, and nothing would silence them, they contradicted for contradiction-sake, and denied that which was most evident; and, when they could find no colour of objection, they broke out into ill language against Christ and his gospel, blaspheming him and it.

VI. The apostles hereupon solemnly and openly declare themselves discharged from their obligations to the Jews, and at liberty to bring the word of salvation to the Gentiles, even by the tacit consent of the Jews themselves. 1. They own that the Jews were entitled to the first offer: "*It was necessary that the word of God should first have been spoken to you*, to whom the promise was made, to you *of the lost sheep of the house of Israel*, to whom Christ reckoned himself first sent." 2. They charge them with the refusal of it: *You put it from you*; you will not accept of it; nay, you will not so much as bear the offer of it, but take it as an affront to you." 3. Upon this they ground their preaching the gospel to the uncircumcised: "Since you will not accept eternal life as it is offered, our way is plain, *Lo, we turn to the Gentiles*." 4. They justify themselves in this by a divine warrant (*v.* 47): "*For so hath the Lord commanded us*; the Lord Jesus gave us directions to witness to him in Jerusalem and Judea first, and after that *to the*

utmost part of the earth, to preach the gospel to *every creature*, to *disciple all nations*."

VII. The Gentiles cheerfully embraced that which the Jews scornfully rejected, *vv.* 48, 49. The Jews, the natural branches, were broken off, and the Gentiles, that were branches of the wild olive, were thereupon grafted in, *vv.* 17, 19. Now here we are told how the Gentiles welcomed this happy turn in their favour.

1. They took the comfort of it: *When they heard this they were glad.* It was good news to them that they might have admission into covenant and communion with God by a clearer, nearer, and better way than submitting to the ceremonial law, and being proselyted to the Jewish religion.

2. They gave God the praise of it: *They glorified the word of the Lord*; that is, Christ (so some), the essential Word; they entertained a profound veneration for him, and expressed the high thoughts they had of him. Or, rather, *the gospel*; the more they knew of it, the more they admired it.

3. Many of them became, not only professors of the Christian faith, but sincerely obedient to the faith: *As many as were ordained to eternal life believed.* (1) Those believed to whom God gave grace to believe, whom by a secret and mighty operation he brought into subjection to the gospel of Christ, and made willing in the day of his power. Those came to Christ whom the Father drew, and to whom the Spirit made the gospel call effectual. (2) God gave this grace to believe to all those among them who were

73

ordained to eternal life (for *whom he had predestinated, them he also called*, Rom. viii. 30); or, *as many as were disposed to eternal life*, as many as had a concern about their eternal state, and aimed to make sure of eternal life, believed in Christ, in whom God hath treasured up that life (1 John v. 11), and who is the only way to it; and it was the grace of God that wrought it in them.

4. When they believed they did what they could to spread the knowledge of Christ and his gospel among their neighbours (*v.* 49).

VIII. Paul and Barnabas, having sown the seeds of a Christian church there, quitted the place, and went to do the like elsewhere. Now here we are told,

1. How *the unbelieving Jews* expelled the apostles out of that country. They first turned their back upon them, and then *lifted up the heel against them* (*v.* 50). When *they could not resist the wisdom and spirit wherewith they spoke*, they had recourse to these brutish methods, the last refuge of an obstinate infidelity. Observe, (1) What method the Jews took to give them trouble: *They stirred up the devout and honourable women* against them. These, according to the genius of their sex, were zealous in their way, and bigoted; and it was easy, by false stories and misrepresentations, to incense them against the gospel of Christ, as if it had been destructive of all religion, of which really it is perfective. (2) How far they carried it, so far that *they expelled them out of their coasts*.

2. How the apostles abandoned

and rejected the unbelieving Jews (*v.* 51): *They shook off the dust of their feet against them*. Hereby, (1) They declared that they would have no more to do with them, would take nothing that was theirs; for *they sought not theirs, but them*. (2) They expressed their detestation of their infidelity, and that, though they were Jews by birth, yet, having rejected the gospel of Christ, they were in their eyes no better than heathen and profane. Thus they left a testimony behind them that they had had a fair offer made them of the grace of the gospel, which shall be proved against them in the day of judgment.

3. What frame they left the new converts in *at Antioch* (*v.* 52): *The disciples, when they saw with what courage and cheerfulness Paul and Barnabas not only bore the indignities that were done them, but went on with their work notwithstanding, they were in like manner inspired.*

CHAPTER FOURTEEN

AT ICONIUM (*vv.* 1–7)

In these verses we have,

I. The preaching of the gospel in Iconium, whither the apostles were forced to retire from Antioch.

II. The success of their preaching there: *They so spoke that a great multitude*, some hundreds perhaps, if not thousands, *both of the Jews and also of the Greeks*, that is the Gentiles, *believed*.

III. The opposition that their preaching met with there, and the trouble that was created them; lest they should be puffed up with the multitude of their converts, there was given them this thorn in the flesh. 1. Unbelieving Jews were the first spring of their trouble here, as elsewhere (*v.* 2): they *stirred up the Gentiles.* 2. Disaffected Gentiles, irritated by the unbelieving Jews, were likely to be the instruments of their trouble.

IV. Their continuance in their work there, notwithstanding this opposition, and God's owning them in it *v.* 3. We have here, 1. The apostles working for Christ, faithfully and diligently, according to the trust committed to them. The more they perceived the spite and rancour of the town against the new converts, the more they were animated to go on in their work, and the more needful they saw it to continue among them, *to confirm them in the faith, and to comfort them. They spoke boldly,* and were not afraid of giving offence to the unbelieving Jews. 2. Christ working with the apostles, according to his promise, *Lo, I am with you always.* When they went on in his name and strength, he failed not to give testimony to the word of his grace.

V. The division which this occasioned in the city (*v.* 4): *The multitude of the city was divided* into two parties, and both active and vigorous. Among the rulers and persons of rank, and among the common people, there were some that held with the unbelieving Jews, and others that held with the apostles. Barnabas is here reckoned an apostle, though not one of the twelve, nor called in the extraordinary manner that Paul was, because set apart by special designation of *the Holy Ghost to the service of the Gentiles.*

VI. The attempt made upon the apostles by their enemies. Their evil affection against them broke out at length into violent outrages, *v.* 5. Observe, 1. Who the plotters were: *Both the Gentiles and the Jews, with their rulers.* If the church's enemies can thus unite for its destruction, shall not its friends, laying aside all personal feuds, unite for its preservation? 2. What the plot was. Having now got *the rulers* on their side, they doubted not but to carry their point, and their design was *to use the apostles despitefully,* to expose them to disgrace, and then *to stone them,* to put them to death; and thus they hoped to sink their cause.

VII. The deliverance of the apostles out of the hands of those *wicked and unreasonable men, vv.* 6, 7. They got away to *Lystra and Derbe;* and there, 1. They found safety. 2. They found work, and this was what they went for. In times of persecution ministers may see cause to quit the spot, when yet they do not quit the work.

LAME MAN HEALED
(*vv.* 8–18)

In these verses we have.

I. A miraculous cure wrought by Paul at Lystra upon a cripple that had been lame from his birth, such a one as was miraculously cured by Peter and John, *ch.* iii. 2. That introduced the gospel among the Jews, this among the Gentiles; both that and this were designed to represent the impotency of all the children of men in spiritual things: they are lame from their birth, till

Lame Man Healed

the grace of God puts strength into them; for it was when we were yet *without strength* that *Christ died for the ungodly*, Rom. v. 6.

II. The impression which this cure made upon the people: they were amazed at it, had never seen nor heard the like, and fell into an ecstacy of wonder. We find here, 1. The people take them for gods (*v.* 11): *They lifted up their voices* with an air of triumph, saying in their own language (for it was the common people that said it), *in the speech of Lycaonia,* which was a dialect of the Greek, *The gods are come down to us in the likeness of men.* They carried this notion so far here that they pretended to tell which of their gods they were, according to the ideas their poets had given them of the gods (*v.* 12): *They called Barnabas Jupiter*; for, if they will have him to be a god, it is as easy to make him the prince of their gods as not. It is probable that he was the senior, and the more portly comely man, that had something of majesty in his countenance. And *Paul they called Mercury,* who was the messenger of the gods, that was sent on their errands; for Paul, though he had not the appearance that Barnabas had, was *the chief speaker,* and had a greater command of language, and perhaps appeared to have something mercurial in his temper and genius. 2. The priest thereupon prepares *to do sacrifice to them, v.* 13. They *brought oxen,* to be sacrificed *to them, and garlands,* with which to crown the sacrifices. These garlands were made up of flowers and ribbons; and they gilded the horns of the oxen they sacrificed.

III. Paul and Barnabas protest against this undue respect paid them, and with much ado prevent it. Observe,

1. The holy indignation which Paul and Barnabas conceived at this: *When they heard this, they rent their clothes.* We do not find that they rent their clothes when the people vilified them, and spoke of stoning them; they could bear this without disturbance: but when they deified them, and spoke of worshipping them, they could not bear it, but rent their clothes, as being more concerned for God's honour than their own.

2. The pains they took to prevent it.

(1) *They ran in among the people,* as soon as they heard of it, and would not so much as stay awhile to see what the people would do. Their running in, like servants, among the people, showed that they were far from looking upon themselves as gods, or taking state upon them; they did not stand still, expecting honours to be done them, but plainly declined them by thrusting themselves into the crowd.

(2) They reasoned with them, *crying out,* that all might hear, "*Sirs, why do you these things?* Why do you go about to make gods of us? It is the most absurd thing you can do; for,

[1] "Our nature will not admit it: *We also are men of like passions with you.*

[2] "Our doctrine is directly against it. Must we be added to the number of your gods whose business it is to abolish the gods you have? *We preach unto you that you should turn from these vanities unto*

the living God. If we should suffer this, we should confirm you in that which it is our business to convert you from." See here what they preached to the Gentiles.

First, That the gods which they and their fathers worshipped, and all the ceremonies of their worship of them, were *vanities,* idle things, unreasonable, unprofitable, which no rational account could be given of, nor any real advantage gained from.

Secondly, That the God to whom they would have them *turn* is *the living God.* They had hitherto worshipped dead images, that were utterly unable to help them (Isa. lxiv. 9), or (as they now attempted) dying men, that would soon be disabled to help them; but now they are persuaded to worship a living God, who has life in himself, and life for us, and lives for evermore.

Thirdly, That this God is the creator of the world, the fountain of all being and power.

Fourthly, That the world owed it to his patience that he had not destroyed them long ere this for their idolatry (*v.* 16). Note, 1. God's patience with us hitherto should *lead us to repentance,* and not encourage us to presume upon the continuance of it, while we continue to provoke him. 2. Our having done ill while we were in ignorance will not bear us out in doing ill when we are better taught.

Fifthly, That even when they were not under the direction and correction of the word of God, yet they might have known, and should have known, to do better by the works of God, *v.* 17. For there were other *witnesses* for God, sufficient

to inform them that he and he only is to be worshipped, and that to him they owed all their services from whom they received all their comforts, and therefore that they were guilty of the highest injustice and ingratitude imaginable, in alienating them from him. God, having *not left himself without witness,* has not left us without a guide, and so has left us without excuse; for whatever is a witness for God is a witness against us, if we give that glory to any other which is due to him only.

Lastly, The success of this prohibition which the apostles gave to *the people* (*v.* 18). Paul and Barnabas had cured a cripple, and therefore the people deified them, instead of glorifying God for giving them such power, which should make us very cautious that we do not give that honour to another, or take it to ourselves, which is due to God only.

RETURN TO ANTIOCH
(*vv.* 19–28)

We have here a further account of the services and sufferings of Paul and Barnabas.

I. How Paul was stoned and left for dead, but miraculously came to himself again, *vv.* 19, 20. Now observe here, 1. How the people were incensed against Paul. *There came certain Jews from Antioch,* hearing, it is likely, and vexed to hear, what respect was shown to Paul and Barnabas at Lystra; and they incensed the people against them, as factious, seditious, dangerous persons, not fit to be harboured. See how restless the rage of the Jews was against the gospel of Christ;

they could not bear that it should have footing any where. 2. To what degree they were incensed by these barbarous Jews: they were irritated to such a degree that the mob rose and *stoned Paul.* 3. How he was delivered by the power of God: When he was *drawn out of the city, the disciples stood round about him v.* 20. It seems there were some here at Lystra that became disciples, that found the mean between deifying the apostles and rejecting them; and even these new converts had courage to own Paul when he was thus run down, though they had reason enough to fear that the same that stoned him would stone them for owning him. They stood round about him, as a guard against the further outrage of the people — stood about him to see whether he were alive or dead; and all of a sudden *he rose up.* Though he was not dead, yet he was ill crushed and bruised, no doubt, and fainted away; so that it was not without a miracle that he came so soon to himself, and was so well as to be able to go into the city.

II. How they went on with their work, notwithstanding the opposition they met with. All the stones they threw at Paul could not beat him off from his work.

1. They went to break up and sow fresh ground at *Derbe.* Thither the next day *Paul and Barnabas departed,* a city not far off; there they preached the gospel, there they *taught many, v.* 21. Nothing is recorded that happened at Derbe.

2. They returned, and went over their work again, watering what they had sown. Let us see what they did,

(1) They *confirmed the souls of the disciples;* that is, they inculcated that upon them which was proper to confirm them, *v.* 22.

(2) *They exhorted them to continue in the faith;* or, as it may be read, *they encouraged them.* They told them it was both their duty and interest to persevere; to abide in the belief of Christ's being the Son of God, and the Saviour of the world.

(3) That which they insisted most upon was *that we must through much tribulation enter into the kingdom of God.* Not only *they* must, but *we* must; it must be counted upon that all who will go to heaven must expect tribulation and persecution in their way thither. But is this the way to *confirm the souls of the disciples,* and to engage them to *continue in the faith?* One would think it would rather shock them, and make them weary. No, as the matter is fairly stated and taken entire, it will help to confirm them, and fix them for Christ.

(4) *They ordained them elders,* or presbyters, *in every church.* Now at this second visit they settled them in some order, formed them into religious societies under the guidance of a settled ministry, and settled that distinction between those that are taught in the word and those that teach. These elders were *ordained.* The qualifications of such as were proposed or proposed themselves (whether the apostles or the people put them up) were judged of by the apostles, as most fit to judge; and they, having *devoted* themselves, were solemnly set *apart* to the work of the ministry, and bound to it.

(5) *By prayer* joined with *fasting*

they *commended them to the Lord, to the Lord Jesus, on whom they believed.*

3. They went on preaching the gospel in other places where they had been, but, as it should seem, had not made so many converts as that now at their return they could form them into churches; therefore thither they came to pursue and carry on conversion-work.

III. How they at length came back to Antioch in Syria, whence they had been sent forth upon this expedition. From Attalia they came by sea to Antioch, *v.* 26. And we are here told,

1. Why they came thither: because *thence they had been recommended to the grace of God.* The brethren having recommended them to the grace of God, for the work *which they fulfilled,* now that they had fulfilled it they thought they owed them an account of it, that they might help them by their praises, as they had been helped by their prayers.

2. What account they gave them of their work (*v.* 27). When they had called them together, they gave them an account of two things: (1) Of the tokens they had had of the divine presence with them in their labours: *They rehearsed all that God had done with them.* They did not tell what *they* had done (this would have savoured of vainglory), but what God had done with them and by them. (2) Of the fruit of their labours among the heathen. They told how *God had opened the door of faith unto the Gentiles;* had not only ordered them to be invited to the gospel feast, but had inclined the hearts of many of them to

accept the invitation. Thus the gospel was spread, and it shone more and more, and none was able to shut this door which God had opened; not all the powers of hell and earth.

3. How they disposed of themselves for the present: *There they abode a long time with the disciples* (*v.* 28), longer than perhaps at first they intended, not because they *feared their enemies,* but because they *loved their friends,* and were loth to part from them.

CHAPTER FIFTEEN

DISSENSION AT ANTIOCH
(*vv.* 1–5)

If ever there was a heaven upon earth, surely it was in the church at Antioch at this time, when there were so many excellent ministers there, and blessed Paul among them, building up that church in her most holy faith. But here we have their peace disturbed, and differences arising. Here is,

I. A new doctrine started among them, which occasioned this division, obliging the Gentile converts to submit to circumcision and the ceremonial law, *v.* 1.

1. The persons that urged this were *certain men who came down from Judea;* some think such as had been of the Pharisees (*v.* 5), or perhaps of those priests who were *obedient to the faith,* ch. vi. 7. They came from Judea, pretending perhaps to be sent by the apostles at Jerusalem, at least to be countenanced by them.

2. The position they laid down, the thesis they gave, was this, that except the Gentiles who turned

Christians were *circumcised after the manner of Moses*, and thereby bound themselves to all the observances of the ceremonial law, *they could not be saved*.

II. The opposition which Paul and Barnabas gave to this schismatical notion, which limited salvation to the Jews, now that Christ had opened the door of salvation to the Gentiles (*v.* 2): *They had no small dissension and disputation with them*. They would by no means yield to this doctrine, but appeared and argued publicly against it. 1. As faithful servants of Christ, they would not see his truths betrayed. They knew that Christ came to free us from the yoke of the ceremonial law, and to take down that wall of partition between Jews and Gentiles and unite them both in himself. 2. As spiritual fathers to the Gentile converts, they would not see their liberties encroached upon. They had told the Gentiles that if they believed in Jesus Christ they should be saved; and now to be told that this was not enough to save them, except they were circumcised and kept the law of Moses, would be a stumblingblock in their way; and therefore the apostles set themselves against it.

III. They determined that Paul and Barnabas, and some others of their number, should *go to Jerusalem to the apostles and elders*, concerning this doubt. Not that the church at Antioch had any doubt concerning it: they knew the liberty wherewith Christ had made them free; but they sent the case to Jerusalem, 1. Because those who taught this doctrine came from

Jerusalem, and pretended to have directions from the apostles there to urge circumcision upon the Gentile converts; it was therefore very proper to send to Jerusalem about it, to know if they had any such direction from the church there. 2. Because those who were taught this doctrine would be the better confirmed in their opposition to it, and in the less danger of being shocked and disturbed by it, if they were sure that *the apostles 'and elders at Jerusalem* (which was the Christian church that of all others retained the most affection to the law of Moses) were against it. 3. Because the apostles at Jerusalem were fittest to be consulted in a point not yet fully settled; and being most eminent for an infallible spirit, peculiar to them as apostles, their decision would be likely to end the controversy.

IV. Their journey to Jerusalem upon this errand, *v.* 3. They were men that would not lose time, and therefore visited the churches by the way; they passed through Phenice and Samaria, and as they went *declared the conversion of the Gentiles*, and what wonderful success the gospel had had among them, which *caused great joy to all the brethren*.

V. Their hearty welcome at Jerusalem, *v.* 4. 1. The good entertainment their friends gave them. 2. The good entertainment they gave their friends: They *declared all things that God had done with them*, gave them an account of the success of their ministry among the Gentiles, not what they had done, but *what God had done with them*, what he had by his grace in them enabled them to do, and what he had by his grace in their hearers enabled them to receive.

VI. The opposition they met with from the same party at Jerusalem, *v.* 5. When Barnabas and Paul gave an account of the multitude of the Gentiles, and of the great harvest of souls gathered in to Christ there, and all about them congratulated them upon it, *there rose up certain of the sect of the Pharisees,* who received the tidings very coldly, and, though they believed in Christ, yet were not satisfied in the admission of these converts, but thought it was needful to circumcise them.

COUNCIL OF JERUSALEM
(*vv.* 6–21)

We have here a council called, not by writ, but by consent, on this occasion (*v.* 6): *The apostles and presbyters came together, to consider of this matter.* Now here we have,

I. Peter's speech in this synod. He did not in the least pretend to any primacy or headship in this synod. When both sides had been heard, *Peter rose up,* and addressed himself to the assembly, *Men and brethren,* as did James afterwards, *v.* 13. And here,

1. He put them in mind of the call and commission he had some time ago *to preach the gospel to the Gentiles*; he wondered there should be any difficulty made of a matter already settled.

2. He puts them in mind how remarkably God owned him in preaching to the Gentiles, and gave testimony to their sincerity in embracing the Christian faith (*v.* 8).

3. He sharply reproves those teachers (some of whom, it is likely, were present) who went about to bring the Gentiles under the obligation of the law of Moses, *v.* 10. Here he shows that in this attempt, (1) They offered a very great affront to God: "You tempt him, by calling that in question which he has already settled and determined by no less an indication than that of the gift of the Holy Ghost; you do, in effect, ask, 'Did he know what he did? Or was he in earnest in it? Or will he abide by his own act?'" (2) They offered a very great wrong to the disciples: Christ came to proclaim *liberty to the captives,* and they go about to enslave those whom he has made free. See Neh. v. 8.

4. Whereas the Jewish teachers had urged that circumcision was necessary to salvation, Peter shows it was so far from being so that both Jews and Gentiles were to be saved purely *through the grace of our Lord Jesus Christ,* and in no other way (*v.* 11).

II. An account of what Barnabas and Paul said in this synod, which did not need to be related, for they only gave in a narrative of what was recorded in the foregoing chapters. Observe, 1. What account they gave; they declared, or opened in order, and with all the magnifying and affecting circumstances, what glorious miracles, what signs and wonders, *God had wrought among the Gentiles by them.* Thus God had honoured these apostles whom the Jewish teachers condemned, and had thus honoured the Gentiles whom they contemned. What need had they of any other advocate when God himself pleaded their cause? 2. What attention was given to them: *All the multitude* (who, though they had not votes, yet came together to hear what was said) *kept silence, and gave audience to Paul and Barnabas*; it should seem they took more notice of their narrative than they did of all the arguments that were offered.

III. The speech which James made to the synod. He let Paul and Barnabas say what they had to say, and then he made the application of it.

1. He addresses himself respectfully to those present: "*Men and brethren, hearken unto me.*"

2. He refers to what Peter had said concerning the conversion of the Gentiles (*v.* 14). James observes here, (1) That the *grace of God* was the origin of it; it was God *that visited the Gentiles*; and it was a kind visit. (2) That the glory of God was the end of it: it was *to take out of them a people for his name*, who should glorify him, and in whom he would be glorified.

3. He confirms this with a quotation out of the Old Testament: he could not prove the calling of the Gentiles by a vision, as Peter could, nor by miracles wrought by his hand, as Paul and Barnabas could, but he would prove that it was foretold in the Old Testament, and therefore it must be fulfilled, *v.* 15. *To this agree the words of the prophets*; most of the Old-Testament prophets spoke more or less of the calling in of the Gentiles, even Moses himself, Rom. x. 19. It was the general expectation of the pious Jews that the Messiah should be *a light to enlighten the Gentiles*

(Luke ii. 32): but James waives the more illustrious prophecies of this, and pitches upon one that seemed more obscure: *It is written*, Amos ix. 11, 12, where is foretold, (1) The setting up of the kingdom of the Messiah (*v.* 16): *I will raise up the tabernacle of David, that is fallen.* (2) The bringing in of the Gentiles as the effect and consequence of this (*v.* 17): *That the residue of men might seek after the Lord*; not the Jews only, who thought they had the monopoly of the tabernacle of David, but *the residue of men*, such as had hitherto been left out of the pale of the visible church. The uniting of *Jews and Gentiles in one body*, and all those things that were done in order to achieve it, which were here foretold, were, [1] What God did: *This was the Lord's doing*, whatever instruments were employed in it: and, [2] It was what God delighted in, and was well pleased with; for he is the God of the Gentiles, as well as the Jews, and it is his honour *to be rich in mercy to all that call upon him.*

4. He resolves it into the purpose and counsel of God (v. 18): *Known unto God are all his works from the beginning of the world.* He not only foretold the calling of the Gentiles many ages ago by the prophets (and therefore it ought not to be a surprise or stumbling-block to us), but he foresaw and foreordained it in his eternal counsels, which are unquestionably wise and unalterably firm.

5. He gives his advice what was to be done in the present case, as the matter now stood with reference *to the Gentiles* (v. 19): *My sentence is; I give it as my opinion*, or judg-

ment; not as having authority over the rest, but as being an adviser with them. Now his advice is,

(1) That circumcision and the observance of the ceremonial law be by no means imposed upon the Gentile converts; no, not so much as recommended nor mentioned to them.

(2) That yet it would be well that in some things, which gave most offence to the Jews, the Gentiles should comply with them. It will please the Jews (and, if a little thing will oblige them, better do so than cross them) if the Gentile converts abstain, [1] *From pollutions of idols, and from fornication*, which are two bad things, and always to be abstained from. [2] *From things strangled, and from blood*, which, though not evil in themselves, as the other two, nor designed to be always abstained from, as those were, had been forbidden by *the precepts of Noah* (Gen. ix. 4), before the giving of the law of Moses; and the Jews had a great dislike to them, and to all those that took a liberty to use them; and therefore, to avoid giving offence, let the Gentile converts abridge themselves of their liberty herein, 1 Cor. viii. 9, 13. Thus we must *become all things to all men.*

6. He gives a reason for his advice—that great respect ought to be shown to the Jews, for they have been so long accustomed to the solemn injunctions of the ceremonial law that they must be borne with, if they cannot presently come off from them (*v.* 21). We must therefore give them time, must meet them half-way; they must be borne

with awhile, and brought on gradually, and we must comply with them as far as we can without betraying our gospel liberty.

COUNCIL DECISIONS
(*vv.* 22–35)

We have here the result of the consultation that was held at Jerusalem about the imposing of the ceremonial law upon the Gentiles. Now observe here,

I. The choice of the delegates that were to be sent with Paul and Barnabas on this errand.

1. They thought fit *to send men of their own company to Antioch, with Paul and Barnabas, v.* 22. This was agreed to by *the apostles and elders, with the whole church*, who, it is likely, undertook to bear their charges, I Cor. ix. 7.

2. Those they sent were not inferior persons, who might serve to carry the letters, and attest the receipt of them from the apostles; but *they were chosen men, and chief men among the brethren*, men of eminent gifts, graces, and usefulness; for these are the things which denominate men chief among the brethren, and qualify them to be the messengers of the churches.

II. The drawing up of the letters, circular letters, that were to be sent to the churches, to notify the sense of the synod in this matter.

1. Here is a very condescending, obliging preamble to this decree, *v.* 23. There is nothing in it haughty or assuming.

2. Here is a just and severe rebuke to the judaizing teachers (*v.* 24). (1) They did a great deal of wrong to the apostles and ministers at Jerusalem, in pretending that they

had instructions from them to impose the ceremonial law upon the Gentiles, when there was no colour for such a pretension. (2) They did a great deal of wrong to the Gentile converts, in saying, *You must be circumcised, and must keep the law.* [1] It perplexed them: *"They have troubled you with words*, have occasioned disturbance and disquietment to you." [2] It endangered them; they *subverted* their souls, put them into disorder, and pulled down that which had been built up.

3. Here is an honourable testimony given of the messengers by whom these letters were sent (*vv.* 25, 26).

4. Here is the direction given what to require from the Gentile converts, where observe,

(1) The matter of the injunction, which is according to the advice given by James.

(2) The manner in which it is worded. [1] They express themselves with something of authority, that what they wrote might be received with respect, and deference paid to it. It is all sweetness and love and good humour, such as became the followers of him who, when he called us to take his yoke upon us, assured us we should find him *meek and lowly in heart.* The difference of the style of the true apostles from that of the false is very observable. Those that were for imposing the ceremonial laws were positive and imperious: *Except you keep it, you cannot be saved* (*v.* 1), you are excommunicated *ipso facto —at once, and delivered to Satan.* The apostles of Christ, who only recommend necessary things, are mild and gentle: *"From which if you*

keep yourselves, you will do well, and as becomes you. *Fare ye well*; we are hearty well-wishers to your honour and peace."

III. The delivering of the letters, and how the messengers disposed of themselves.

1. *When they were dismissed they then came to Antioch.*

2. As soon as they came to Antioch, *they gathered the multitude together, and delivered the epistle to them* (*vv.* 30, 31).

3. The people were wonderfully pleased with the orders that came from Jerusalem (*v.* 31): *They rejoiced for the consolation*; and a great consolation it was to the multitude, (1) That they were confirmed in their freedom from the yoke of the ceremonial law, and were not burdened with that, as those upstart teachers would have had them to be. It was a comfort to them to hear that the carnal ordinances were no longer imposed on them, which perplexed the conscience, but could not purify nor pacify it. (2) That those who troubled their minds with an attempt to force circumcision upon them were hereby for the present silenced and put to confusion, the fraud of their pretensions being now discovered. (3) That the Gentiles were hereby encouraged to receive the gospel, and those that had received it to adhere to it. (4) That the peace of the church was hereby restored, and that removed which threatened a division. All this was consolation which they rejoiced in, and blessed God for.

4. They got the strange ministers that came from Jerusalem to give

84

them each a sermon, and more, *v.* 32.

5. The dismissal of the Jerusalem ministers, *v.* 33. When they had *spent some time among them—having made some stay*, and having made it to good purpose, not having trifled away time, but having filled it up, they were let go in peace from the brethren at Antioch, to the apostles at Jerusalem, with all possible expressions of kindness and respect.

6. The continuance of Silas, notwithstanding, together with Paul and Barnabas, at Antioch. Antioch, being the chief city of Syria, it is probable there was a great resort of Gentiles thither from all parts upon one account or other, as there was of Jews to Jerusalem; so that in preaching there they did in effect preach to many nations, for they preached to those who would carry the report of what they preached to many nations, and thereby prepare them for the apostles' coming in person to preach to them.

DISPUTE OVER MARK
(*vv.* 36–41)

We have seen one unhappy difference among the brethren, which was of a public nature, brought to a good issue; but here we have a private quarrel between two ministers, no less men than Paul and Barnabas, not compromised indeed, yet ending well.

I. Here is a good proposal Paul made to Barnabas to go and review their work among the Gentiles and renew it, to take a circuit among the churches they had planted, and see what progress the gospel made among them.

II. The disagreement between Paul and Barnabas about an assistant; it was convenient to have a young man with them who should attend on them and minister to them, and be a witness of their *doctrine, manner of life, and patience*, and that should be fitted and trained up for further service, by being occasionally employed in the present service. Now, 1. Barnabas would have his nephew John, whose surname was Mark, to go along with them, *v.* 37. He determined to take him, because he was his relation, and, it is likely, was brought up under him, and he had a kindness for him, and was solicitous for his welfare. We should suspect ourselves of partiality, and guard against it in preferring our relations. 2. Paul opposed it (*v.* 38): *He thought not good to take him with them—he did not think him worthy* of the honour, nor fit for the service, who had *departed from them*, clandestinely as it should seem, without their knowledge, or wilfully, without their consent, from Pamphylia (*ch.* xiii. 13), and *went not with them to the work*.

III. The issue of this disagreement: it came to such a height that they separated upon it. Barnabas was peremptory that he would not go with Paul unless they took John Mark with them; Paul was as peremptory that he would not go if John did go with them. Neither would yield, and therefore there is no remedy but they must part. Now here is that which is very humbling, and just matter of lamentation, and yet very instructive. For we see, 1. That the best of men are but men, *subject to like passions* as we are, as

85

these two good men had expressly owned concerning themselves (*ch.* xiv. 15), and now it appeared too true. 2. That we are not to think it strange if there be differences among wise and good men; we were told before that such offences would come, and here is an instance of it. 3. That these differences often prevail so far as to occasion separations. Paul and Barnabas, who were not separated by the persecutions of the unbelieving Jews, nor the impositions of the believing Jews, were yet separated by an unhappy disagreement between themselves.

IV. The good that was brought out of this evil—meat out of the eater, and sweetness out of the strong. It was strange that even the sufferings of the apostles (as Phil. i. 12), but much more strange that even the quarrels of the apostles, should tend to the *furtherance of the gospel of Christ*; yet so it proved here. God would not permit such things to be, if he knew not how to make them to serve his own purposes. 1. More places are hereby visited. 2. More hands are hereby employed in the ministry of the gospel among the Gentiles; for, (1) John Mark, who had been an unfaithful hand, is not rejected, but is again made use of, against Paul's mind, and, for aught we know, proves a very useful and successful hand, though many think it was not the same with that Mark that wrote the gospel, and founded the church at Alexandria, and whom Peter calls his son, 1 Pet. v. 13. (2) Silas who was a new hand, and never yet employed in that work, nor intended to be, but to return to

the service of the church at Jerusalem, had not God changed his mind (*vv*. 33, 34), he is brought in, and engaged in that noble work.

V. We may further observe, 1. That the church at Antioch seem to countenance Paul in what he did. Barnabas sailed with his nephew to Cyprus, and no notice was taken of him, nor a recommendation given him. 2. That yet Paul afterwards seems to have had, though not upon second thoughts, yet upon further trial, a better opinion of John Mark than now he had; for he writes to Timothy (2 Tim iv. 11), *Take Mark and bring him with thee, for he is profitable to me for the ministry*; and he writes to the Colossians concerning Marcus, sister's son to Barnabas, that *if he came to them* they should *receive him*, bid him welcome, and employ him (Col. iv. 10).

CHAPTER SIXTEEN

PAUL ENLISTS TIMOTHY
(*vv*. 1–5)

Paul was a spiritual father, and as such a one we have him here adopting Timothy. Here is,

I. His taking Timothy into his acquaintance and under his tuition. And we are here accordingly told, 1. That he was a disciple, one that belonged to Christ, and was baptized, probably in his infancy, when his mother became a believer, as Lydia's household was baptized upon her believing, *v*. 15. Him, that was a disciple of Christ, Paul took to be his disciple, that he might further train him up in the knowledge and faith of Christ; he took him to be brought up for Christ.

2. That his mother was a Jewess originally, *but believed in Christ*; her name was *Eunice*, his grandmother's name was *Lois*. 3. That his father was a Greek, a Gentile. The marriage of a Jewish woman to a Gentile husband (though some would make a difference) was prohibited as much as the marriage of a Jewish man to a Gentile wife, Deut. vii. 3. Now because his father was a Greek he was not circumcised: for the entail of the covenant and the seal of it, as of other entails in that nation, went by the father, not by the mother. 4. That he had gained a very good character among the Christians. Not only those in the place where he was born, but those in the neighbouring cities, admired him, and spoke honourably of him. He had a name for good things with good people. 5. That Paul would have him *to go forth with him*, to accompany him, to give attendance on him, to receive instruction from him, and to join with him in the work of the gospel—to preach for him when there was occasion, and to be left behind in places where he had planted churches. 6. That Paul took him and circumcised him, or ordered it to be done. This was strange. Had not Paul opposed those with all his might that were for imposing circumcision upon the Gentile converts? Had he not at this time the decrees of the council at Jerusalem with him, which witnessed against it? He had, and yet circumcised Timothy, not, as those teachers designed in imposing circumcision, to oblige him to keep the ceremonial law, but only to render his ministry passable, and,

if it might be, acceptable among the Jews that abounded in those quarters. He knew Timothy was a man likely to do a great deal of good among them, being admirably qualified for the ministry, if they were not invincibly prejudiced against him; and therefore, that they might not shun him as one unclean, because uncircumcised, he took him and *circumcised him*. Thus *to the Jews he became as a Jew, that he might gain the Jews*, and *all things to all men, that he might gain some*. It is probable that it was at this time that Paul laid his hands on Timothy, for the conferring of the gift of the Holy Ghost upon him, 2 Tim. i. 6.

II. His confirming the churches which he had planted (*vv.* 4, 5): *He went through the cities* where he had *preached the word of the Lord*, as he intended (*ch.* xv. 36), to enquire into their state. And we are told,

1. That they delivered to them copies of the decrees of the Jerusalem synod.

2. That this was of very good service to them. (1) The churches were hereby *established in the faith*, v. 5. (2) They *increased in number daily*. Not a day passed but some or other gave up their names to Christ. And it is a joy to those who heartily wish well to the honour of Christ, and the welfare of the church and the souls of men, to see such an increase.

A MAN OF MACEDONIA
(*vv.* 6–15)

In these verses we have,

I. Paul's travels up and down to do good. 1. He and Silas his colleague went throughout Phrygia and the region of Galatia, where, it should seem, the gospel was already planted, but whether by Paul's hand or no is not mentioned; it is likely it was, for in his epistle to the Galatians he speaks of his *preaching the gospel to them at the first*, and how very acceptable he was among them, Gal. iv. 13–15. 2. They were forbidden at this time to preach the gospel in Asia (the country properly so called), because it did not need, other hands being at work there; or because the people were not yet prepared to receive it, as they were afterwards (*ch*. xix. 10), when *all those that dwelt in Asia heard the word of the Lord*; or, as Dr. Lightfoot suggests, because at this time Christ would employ Paul in a piece of new work, which was to preach the gospel to a Roman colony at Philippi, for hitherto the Gentiles to whom he had preached were Greeks. 3. They would have gone into Bithynia, but were not permitted: *the Spirit suffered them not*, *v*. 7. Observe, Though their judgment and inclination were to go into Bithynia, yet, having then extraordinary ways of knowing the mind of God, they were overruled by them, contrary to their own mind. We must now follow providence, and submit to the guidance of that pillar of cloud and fire; and, if this *suffer us not* to do what we assay to do, we ought to acquiesce, and believe it for the best. *The Spirit of Jesus* suffered them not; so many ancient copies read it. The servants of the Lord Jesus ought to be always under the check and conduct of the *Spirit of the Lord Jesus*, by whom he

governs men's minds. 4. They *passed by Mysia*, or passed *through it* (so some), sowing good seed, we may suppose, as they went along; and they came down to Troas, the city of Troy, so much talked of, or the country thereabouts. It should seem that at Troas Luke fell in with Paul, and joined himself to his company; for henceforward, for the most part, when he speaks of Paul's journeys, he puts himself into the number of his retinue, *we* went, *v*. 10.

II. Paul's particular call to Macedonia, that is, to Philippi, the chief city, inhabited mostly by Romans, as appears, *v*. 21. Here we have,

1. The vision Paul had, *v*. 9. Paul had many visions, sometimes to encourage, sometimes, as here, to direct him in his work. An angel appeared to him, to intimate to him that it was the will of Christ he should go to Macedonia. Now observe, (1) The person Paul saw. There stood by him *a man of Macedonia*, who by his habit or dialect seemed so to Paul, or who told him he was so. The angel, some think, assumed the shape of such a man; or, as others think, impressed upon Paul's fancy, when between asleep and awake, the image of such a man: he dreamt he saw such a one. (2) The invitation given him. This honest Macedonian *prayed him, saying, Come over into Macedonia, and help us*; that is, "Come and preach the gospel to us; let us have the benefit of thy labours."

2. The interpretation made of the vision (*v*. 10): They *gathered assuredly from this that the Lord had called them to preach the gospel*

there; and they were ready to go wherever God directed.

III. Paul's voyage to Macedonia hereupon: He *was not disobedient to the heavenly vision*, but followed this divine direction much more cheerfully, and with more satisfaction, than he would have followed any contrivance or inclination of his own.

IV. The cold entertainment which Paul and his companions met with at Philippi. 1. It is a good while before any notice at all is taken of him: *We were in that city abiding certain days*, probably at a public house and at their own charge, for they had no friend to invite them so much as to a meal's meat, till Lydia welcomed them. 2. When they have an opportunity of preaching it is in an obscure place, and to a mean and small auditory, *v.* 13. The place of this meeting is out of the city. It was a place *where prayer was wont to be made*; a chapel, or smaller synagogue. But I rather take it, as we read it, where prayer was appointed or accustomed to be. Those that worshipped the true God, and would not worship idols, met there to pray together, and, according to the description of the most ancient and universal devotion, *to call upon the name of the Lord*. Thither Paul and Silas and Luke went, and *sat down*, to instruct the congregation, that they might the better pray with them. They *spoke unto the women who resorted thither*, encouraged them in practising according to the light they had, and led them on further to the knowledge of Christ.

V. The conversion of *Lydia*, who

probably was the first that was wrought upon there to believe in Christ, though not the last. Observe,

1. Who this convert was that there is such particular notice taken of. Four things are recorded of her:

(1) Her name, *Lydia*.

(2) Her calling. She was *a seller of purple*, either of purple dye or of purple cloth or silk. Though she had a calling to mind, yet she was a worshipper of God, and found time to improve advantages for her soul.

(3) The place she was of—*of the city of Thyatira*, which was a great way from Philippi; there she was born and bred, but either married at Philippi, or brought by her trade to settle there. Providence brings Lydia to Philippi, to be under Paul's ministry, and there, where she met with it, she made a good use of it; so should we improve opportunities.

(4) Her religion before the Lord opened her heart. [1] She worshipped God according to the knowledge she had; she was one of the devout women. [2] She heard the apostles. Here, where prayer was made, when there was an opportunity, *the word was preached*; for hearing the word of God is a part of religious worship, and how can we expect God should hear our prayers if we will not hearken to his word? Those that worshipped God according to the light they had looked out for further light; we must improve *the day of small things*, but must not rest in it.

2. What the work was that was wrought upon her: *Whose heart the Lord opened*. Observe here, (1) The author of this work: it was *the Lord*,—the Lord Christ, to whom this judgment is committed,—

the Spirit of the Lord, who is the sanctifier. (2) The seat of this work; it is in the heart that the change is made, it is to the heart that this blessed turn is given; it was the heart of Lydia that was wrought upon. Conversion-work is heart-work; it is a *renewing of the heart, the inward man, the spirit of the mind.* (3) The nature of the work; she had not only her heart touched, but her heart opened.

3. What were the effects of this work on the heart. (1) She took great notice of the word of God. (2) She gave up her name to Jesus Christ, and took upon her the profession of his holy religion: *She was baptized,* and by this solemn rite was admitted a member of the church of Christ. (3) She was very kind to the ministers, and very desirous to be further instructed by them in *the things pertaining to the kingdom of God.*

AN EVIL SPIRIT (*vv.* 16–24)

Paul and his companions, though they were for some time buried in obscurity at Philippi, yet now begin to be taken notice of.

I. *A damsel that had a spirit of divination* caused them to be taken notice of, by proclaiming them to them to be the servants of God. Observe,

1. The account that is given of this damsel: She was actuated by an evil spirit, that dictated ambiguous answers to those who consulted her, which served to gratify their vain desire of knowing things to come, but often deceived them. This damsel *brought her masters much gain by soothsaying.*

2. The testimony which this

damsel gave to Paul and his companions. When she met with them she followed them, crying, *"These men are the servants of the most high God,* for *they show unto us the way of salvation."* How came this testimony from the mouth of one that had a spirit of divination? We may take it either, [1] As extorted from this spirit of divination for the honour of the gospel by the power of God; as the devil was forced to say of Christ (Mark i. 24): *I know thee who thou art, the Holy One of God.* Or, [2] As designed by the evil spirit, that subtle serpent, to the dishonour of the gospel; as if these divines were of the same fraternity with their diviners, because they were witnessed to by them, and then the people might as well adhere to those they had been used to.

II. Christ caused them to be taken notice of, by giving them power to cast the devil out of this damsel. Power went along with the word of Christ, before which Satan could not stand, but was forced to quit his hold, and in this case it was a strong hold: *He came out the same hour.*

III. The masters of the damsel that was dispossessed caused them to be taken notice of, by bringing them before the magistrates for doing it, and laying it to their charge as their crime. Observe here,

1. That which provoked them was, that, the damsel being restored to herself, *her masters saw that the hope of their gain was gone, v.* 19.

2. The course they took with them was to incense the higher powers against them, as men fit to be punished.

3. The charge they exhibited against them was that they were the troublers of the land, *v.* 20.

IV. The magistrates, by their proceedings against them, caused them to be taken notice of.

1. By countenancing the persecution they raised the mob upon them (*v.* 22): *The multitude rose up together against them*, and were ready to pull them to pieces.

2. By going on to an execution they further represented them as the vilest malefactors. The magistrates commanded that they should be whipped as vagabonds, by the lictors or beadles who attended the prætors, and carried rods with them for that purpose; this was one of those three times that Paul was beaten with rods, according to the Roman usage, which was not under the compassionate limitation of the number of stripes not to exceed forty, which was provided by the Jewish law. The judges made their commitment very strict: They *charged the jailer to keep them safely*, and have a very watchful eye upon them. *He put them into the inner prison*, the dungeon, into which none were usually put but condemned malefactors, dark at noon-day, damp and cold, dirty, it is likely, and every way offensive, like that into which Jeremiah was let down (Jer. xxxviii. 6); and, as if this were not enough, *he made their feet fast in the stocks*.

JAILER CONVERTED
(vv. 25–34)

We have here the designs of the persecutors of Paul and Silas baffled and broken.

I. The persecutors designed to dishearten and discourage the preachers of the gospel, and to make them sick of the cause and weary of their work; but here we find them both hearty and heartened.

1. They were themselves hearty, wonderfully hearty. (1) They prayed together, prayed to God to support them and comfort them in their afflictions. (2) *They sang praises to God.* They praised God; for we must *in every thing give thanks*. We never want matter for praise, if we do not want a heart. And what should put the heart of a child of God out of tune for this duty if a dungeon and a pair of stocks will not do it? (3) Notice is here taken of the circumstance that *the prisoners heard them.* If the prisoners did not hear them pray, yet *they heard them sing praises.* The prisoners were made to hear the prison-songs of Paul and Silas, that they might be prepared for the miraculous favour shown to them all for the sake of Paul and Silas, when *the prison-doors were thrown open.*

2. God heartened them wonderfully by his signal appearances for them, *v.* 26. (1) There was immediately a great earthquake; how far it extended we are not told, but it was such a violent shock in this place *that the very foundations of the prison were shaken.* (2) The prison-doors were thrown open, and the prisoners' fetters were knocked off: *Every man's bands were loosed.* As afterwards God gave to Paul all *those that were in the ship with him* (ch. xxvii. 24), so now he gave him all those that were in the prison with him.

II. It is probable that some of the prisoners, if not all, were converted. But it is only the conversion of the jailer that is recorded.

1. He is afraid he shall lose his life, and Paul makes him easy as to this care, *vv.* 27, 28. (1) He *awoke out of his sleep*. This waking him out of his sleep signified the awakening of his conscience out of its spiritual slumber. The call of the gospel is, *Awake, thou that sleepest* (Eph. v. 14). (2) He saw the prison-doors open, and supposed, as well he might, that the prisoners had fled; and then what would become of him? He knew the Roman law in that case, and it was executed not long ago upon the keepers out of whose hands Peter escaped, *ch.* xii. 19. (3) In his fright *he drew his sword*, and was going *to kill himself*, to prevent a more terrible death. (4) Paul stopped him from his proceeding against himself (*v.* 28): He *cried with a loud voice*, not only to make him hear, but to make him heed, *saying, Do not practise any evil to thyself; Do thyself no harm.*

2. He is afraid he shall lose his soul, and Paul makes him easy as to this care too. One concern leads him to another, and a much greater. Perhaps the heinousness of the sin he was running into helped to alarm him.

(1) Whatever was the cause, he was put into a great consternation. The Spirit of God, that was sent to convince, in order to his being a Comforter, struck a terror upon him, and startled him.

(2) In this consternation, he applied to Paul and Silas for relief. Observe, [1] How reverent and respectful his address to them is: *He called for a light*, because they were in the dark, and that they might see what a fright he was in; *he fell down before them*, as one amazed at the badness of his own condition, and ready to sink under the load of his terror because of it. He gave them a title of respect, *Sirs, lords, masters*; just now it was, *Rogues* and *villains*, and he was their master; but now, *Sirs, lords*, and they are his masters. [2] How serious his enquiry is: *What must I do to be saved? First*, His salvation is now his great concern, and lies nearest his heart, which before was the furthest thing from his thoughts. *Secondly*, He does not enquire concerning others, what they must do; but concerning himself, "What must I do?" *Thirdly*, He is convinced that something must be done, and done by him too, in order to achieve his salvation. *Fourthly*, He is willing to do any thing: "Tell me what I must do, and I am here ready to do it." *Fifthly*, He is inquisitive what he should do, is desirous to know what he should do, and asks those that were likely to tell him. *Sixthly*, He *brought them out*, to put this question to them, that their answer might not be by duress or compulsion, but that they might prescribe to him, though he was their keeper, with the same liberty as they did to others. He brings them out of the dungeon, in hopes they will bring him out of a much worse.

(3) They very readily directed him what he must do, *v.* 31. *Believe in the Lord Jesus Christ*. One would think they should have said, "Repent of thy abusing us, in the

first place." No, that is overlooked and easily passed by, if he will but believe in Christ. Here is the sum of the whole gospel, the covenant of grace in a few words: *Believe in the Lord Jesus Christ, and thou shalt be saved, and thy house.* Here is, [1] The happiness promised: *"Thou shalt be saved."* Though a great sinner, though a persecutor, yet thy heinous transgressions shall be all forgiven through the merits of Christ. [2] The condition required: *Believe in the Lord Jesus Christ.* We must admit the record that God hath given in his gospel concerning his Son, and assent to it as faithful, and well *worthy of all acceptation.* We must approve the method God has taken of reconciling the world to himself by a Mediator; and accept of Christ as he is offered to us, and give up ourselves to be ruled and taught and saved by him. This is the only way and a sure way to salvation. [3] The extension of this to his family: *Thou shalt be saved, and thy house;* that is, "God will be in Christ a God to thee and to thy seed, as he was to Abraham. Believe, and salvation shall *come to thy house,* as Luke xix. 9."

(4) They proceeded to instruct him and his family in the doctrine of Christ (v. 32): They *spoke unto him the word of the Lord.* He was, for aught that appears, an utter stranger to Christ, and therefore it is requisite he should be told who this Jesus is, that he may believe in him, John ix. 36.

(5) The jailer and his family were immediately baptized, and thereby took upon them the profession of Christianity, submitted to its laws,

and were admitted to its privileges, upon their declaring solemnly, as the eunuch did, that they believed that *Jesus Christ is the Son of God*: He was *baptized, he and all his, straightway.*

(6) The jailer was hereupon very respectful to Paul and Silas, as one that knew not how to make amends for the injury he had done to them, much less for the kindness he had received from them.

(7) The voice of rejoicing with that of salvation was heard in the jailer's house; never was such a truly merry night kept there before: *He rejoiced, believing in God, with all his house.*

THEY LEAVE PHILIPPI
(vv. 35–40)

In these verses we have,

I. Orders sent for the discharge of Paul and Silas out of prison *vv.* 35, 36.

II. Paul's insisting upon the breach of privilege which the magistrates had been guilty of, *v.* 37. It is probable that the magistrates had some intimation that they were Romans, and were made aware that their fury had carried them further than the law would bear them out; and that this was the reason why they gave orders for their discharge. Now observe,

1. Paul did not plead this before he was beaten, though it is probable that it might have prevented it, lest he should seem to be afraid of suffering for the truth which he had preached.

2. He did plead it afterwards, to put an honour upon his sufferings and upon the cause he suffered for, to let the world know that the

preachers of the gospel were not such despicable men as they were commonly looked upon to be, and that they merited better treatment. He insists upon it that they should make them an acknowledgment of their error, and give them a public discharge, to make it the more honourable, as they had done them a public disgrace, which made that the more disgraceful. It was not a point of honour that Paul stood thus stiffly upon, but a point of justice, and not to himself so much as to his cause.

III. The magistrates' submission, and the reversing of the judgment given against Paul and Silas, *vv.* 38, 39. 1. The magistrates were frightened when they were told (though it may be they knew it before) that Paul was a Roman. 2. They *came and besought them* not to take advantage of the law against them, but to overlook the illegality of what they had done and say no more of it: they *brought them out* of the prison, owning that they were wrongfully put into it, and desired them that they would peaceably and quietly *depart out of the city*.

IV. The departure of Paul and Silas from Philippi, *v.* 40. Paul and Silas had an extraordinary call to Philippi; and yet, when they have come thither, they see little of the fruit of their labours, and are soon driven thence. Yet they did not come in vain. Though the beginnings here were *small, the latter end greatly increased*; now they laid the foundation of a church at Philippi, which became very eminent, had its bishops and deacons, and people that were more generous

to Paul than any other church, as appears by his epistle to the Philippians, *ch.* i. 1; iv. 25. Let not ministers be discouraged, though they see not the fruit of their labours at once; the seed sown seems to be lost under the clods, but it shall come up again in a plentiful harvest in due time.

CHAPTER SEVENTEEN

PAUL AT THESSALONICA
(*vv.* 1–8)

Paul's two epistles to the Thessalonians, the first two he wrote by inspiration, give such a shining character of that church, that we cannot but be glad here in the history to meet with an account of the first founding of the church there.

I. Here is Paul's coming to Thessalonica, which was the chief city of this country, called at this day *Salonech*, in the Turkish dominions.

II. His preaching to the Jews first, in their synagogue at Thessalonica. He found a synagogue of the Jews there (*v.* 1), which intimates that one reason why he passed through those other cities mentioned, and did not continue long in them, was because there were no synagogues in them. But, finding one in Thessalonica, by it he made his entry. 1. It was always his manner to begin with the Jews, to make them the first offer of the gospel, and not to turn to the Gentiles till they had refused it, that their mouths might be stopped from clamouring against him because he preached to the Gentiles. 2. He met them in their synagogue on the sabbath day, in their place and at their time of meeting, and thus he would pay respect to both. 3. He *reasoned with them out of the scriptures.* They agreed with him to receive the scriptures of the Old Testament: so far they were of a mind. But they received the scripture, and therefore thought they had reason to reject Christ; Paul received the scripture, and therefore saw great reason to embrace Christ. 4. He continued to do this *three sabbath days* successively. If he could not convince them the first sabbath, he would try the second and the third; for *precept must be upon precept, and line upon line.* 5. The drift and scope of his preaching and arguing was to prove that *Jesus is the Christ;* this was that which he opened and alleged, *v.* 3. He showed them, (1) That it was necessary the Messiah should *suffer, and die, and rise again,* that the Old-Testament prophecies concerning the Messiah made it necessary he should. (2) That Jesus is the Messiah.

III. The success of his preaching there, *v.* 4. 1. Some of the Jews believed, notwithstanding their rooted prejudices against Christ and his gospel, and they *consorted with Paul and Silas.* 2. Many more of the devout Greeks, and of the chief women, embraced the gospel. These were proselytes of the gate, the *godly among the Gentiles* (so the Jews called them), such as, though they did not submit to the law of Moses, yet renounced idolatry and immorality, worshipped the true God only, and did no man any wrong.

IV. The trouble that was given to Paul and Silas at Thessalonica. Observe,

1. Who were the authors of their trouble: the *Jews who believed not, who were moved with envy, v.* 5. The Jews were in all places the most inveterate enemies to the Christians, especially to those Jews that turned Christians, against whom they had a particular spleen, as deserters.

2. Who were the instruments of the trouble: the Jews made use of *certain lewd persons of the baser sort.* All wise and sober people looked upon them with respect, and valued them, and none would appear against them but such as were the scum of the city, a company of vile men, that were given to all manner of wickedness.

3. In what method they proceeded against them. (1) They *set the city in an uproar,* made a noise to put people in a fright, and then every body ran to see what the matter was; they began a riot, and then the mob was up presently. (2) They *assaulted the house of Jason,* where the apostles lodged, with a design *to bring them out to the people,* whom they had incensed and enraged against them, and by whom they hoped to see them pulled to pieces. (3) When they could not get the apostles into their hands, then they fall upon an honest citizen of their own, who entertained the apostles in his house, his name *Jason,* a converted Jew, and drew him out with some others of the brethren to the rulers of the city. (4) They accused them to the rulers, and represented them as dangerous persons, not fit to be tolerated. [1] That they were enemies to the public peace, and threw every thing into disorder

wherever they came: *Those that have turned the world upside down are come hither also*. In one sense it is true that wherever the gospel comes in its power to any place, to any soul, it works such a change there, gives such a wide change to the stream, so directly contrary to what it was, that it may be said to turn the world upside down in that place, in that soul. But in the sense in which they meant it it is utterly false: they would have it thought that the preachers of the gospel were incendiaries and mischief makers wherever they came, that they sowed discord among relations, set neighbours together by the ears, obstructed commerce, and inverted all order and regularity. [2] That they were enemies to the established government, and disaffected to that, and their principles and practices were destructive to monarchy and inconsistent with the constitution of the state (*v*. 7).

4. The great uneasiness which this gave to the city (*v*. 8). They had no ill opinion of the apostles or their doctrine, could not apprehend any danger to the state from them, and therefore were willing to connive at them; but, if they be represented to them by the prosecutors as enemies to Cæsar, they will be obliged to take cognizance of them, and to suppress them, for fear of the government, and this troubled them.

5. The issue of this troublesome affair. The magistrates here were not so easily incensed against the apostles as the magistrates at Philippi were, but were more considerate and of better temper; so they *took security of Jason and the*

other, bound them to their good behaviour; and perhaps they gave bond for Paul and Silas, that they should be forthcoming when they were called for, if any thing should afterwards appear against them.

THE NOBLE BEREANS
(*vv*. 10–15)

In these verses we have,

I. Paul and Silas removing to Berea, and employed in preaching the gospel there, *v*. 10.

II. The good character of the Jews in Berea (*v*. 11): *These were more noble than those in Thessalonica*.

1. They had a freer thought, and lay more open to conviction, were willing to hear reason, and admit the force of it, and to subscribe to that which appeared to them to be truth, though it was contrary to their former sentiments. This was more noble.

2. They had a better temper, were not so sour, and morose, and ill-conditioned towards all that were not of their mind. They neither prejudged the cause, nor were moved with envy at the managers of it, as the Jews at Thessalonica were, but very generously gave both it and them a fair hearing, without passion or partiality; for, (1) *They received the word with all readiness of mind*; they were very willing to hear it, presently apprehended the meaning of it, and did not shut their eyes against the light. (2) *They searched the scriptures daily whether those things were so*. Their readiness of mind to receive the word was not such as that they took things upon trust, swallowed

them upon an implicit faith: no; but since Paul reasoned out of the scriptures, and referred them to the Old Testament for the proof of what he said, they had recourse to their Bibles, turned to the places to which he referred them, read the context, considered the scope and drift of them, compared them with other places of scripture, examined whether Paul's inferences from them were natural and genuine and his arguments upon them cogent, and determined accordingly. Those that rightly study the scriptures, and *meditate therein day and night*, have their minds filled with noble thoughts, fixed to noble principles, and formed for noble aims and designs. *These are more noble.*

III. The good effect of the preaching of the gospel at Berea: it had the desired success; the people's hearts being prepared, a great deal of work was done suddenly, *v.* 12.

IV. The persecution that was raised against Paul and Silas at Berea, which forced Paul thence. 1. *The Jews at Thessalonica* were the mischief-makers at *Berea.* Thus we read before that the Jews of Antioch and Iconium came to Lystra on purpose to incense the people against the apostles, *ch.* xiv. 19. 2. This occasioned Paul's removal to Athens. By seeking to extinguish this divine fire which Christ had already kindled, they did but spread it the further and the faster. He went out from Berea, in that road which went to the sea, that the Jews, if they enquired after him, might think he had gone to a great distance; but he went by land to Athens, in which there was no culpable dissimulation at all.

PAUL AT ATHENS (*vv.* 16–21)

A scholar that has acquaintance, and is in love, with the learning of the ancients, would think he should be very happy if he were where Paul now was, at Athens, in the midst of the various sects of philosophers, and would have a great many curious questions to ask them, for the explication of the remains we have of the Athenian learning; but Paul, though bred a scholar, and an ingenious active man, does not make this any of his business at Athens. He has other work to mind: it is not the improving of himself in their philosophy that he aims at, he has learned to call it a vain thing, and is above it (Col. ii. 8); his business is, in God's name, to correct their disorders in religion, and *to turn them from the service of idols*, and of Satan in them, to the *service of the true and living God* in Christ.

I. Here is the impression which the abominable ignorance and superstition of the Athenians made upon Paul's spirit, *v.* 16. Observe, 1. The account here given of that city: it was *wholly given to idolatry.* This agrees with the account which the heathen writers give of it, that there were more idols in Athens than there were in all Greece besides put together, and that they had twice as many sacred feasts as others had. 2. The disturbance which the sight of this gave to Paul. Paul was not willing to appear publicly till Silas and Timothy came to him, that out of the mouth of two or three witnesses the word might be established; but in the mean time *his spirit was stirred within him.* He was filled with concern for the glory of God, which he saw given to idols, and with compassion to the souls of men, which he saw thus enslaved to Satan, *and led captive by him at his will.*

II. The testimony that he bore against their idolatry, and his endeavours to bring them to the knowledge of the truth. 1. *He went to the synagogue of the Jews,* who, though enemies to Christianity, were free from idolatry, and joined with them in that among them which was good, and took the opportunity given him there of disputing for Christ, *v.* 17. 2. He entered into conversation with all that came in his way about matters of religion: *In the market,* in the exchange, or place of commerce, *he disputed daily,* as he had occasion, *with those that met with him,* or that he happened to fall into company with, that were heathen, and never came to the Jews' synagogue. The zealous advocates for the cause of Christ will be ready to plead it in all companies, as occasion offers.

III. The enquiries which some of the philosophers made concerning Paul's doctrine. Observe,

1. Who they were the encountered him, that entered into discourse with him, and opposed him. (1) *The Epicureans,* who *thought God altogether such a one as themselves,* an idle inactive being, that minded nothing, nor put any difference between good and evil. (2) *The Stoics,* who thought themselves altogether as good as God, and indulged themselves as much in the pride of life as the Epicureans did in the lusts of the flesh and of the

eye; they made their virtuous man to be no way inferior to God himself, nay to be superior.

2. What their different sentiments were of him; such there were as there were of Christ, *v.* 18. (1) *Some called him a babbler,* and thought he spoke, without any design, whatever came uppermost, as men of crazed imaginations do: (2) *Others* called him *a setter forth of strange gods,* and thought he spoke with design to make himself considerable by that means. And, if he had strange gods to set forth, he could not bring them to a better market than to Athens. From his first coming among them he ever and anon harped upon these two strings which are indeed the principal doctrines of Christianity—Christ and a future state—Christ our way, and heaven our end; and, though he did not call these gods, yet they thought he meant to make them so. Jesus they took for a new god, and the resurrection, for a new goddess.

3. The proposal they made to give him a free, full, fair, and public hearing, *vv.* 19, 20. (1) They look upon it as strange and surprising, and very different from the philosophy that had for many ages been taught and professed at Athens. (2) They desired to know more of it, only because it was new and strange. (3) The place they brought him to for him to make this public declaration of his doctrine; it was *to Areopagus,* the same word that is translated (*v.* 22) *Mars' Hill;* it was the townhouse, or guildhall of their city, where the magistrates met upon public business, and the courts of justice were kept; and it

was as the theatre in the university, or the schools, where learned men met to communicate their notions.

4. The general character of the people of that city given upon this occasion (*v.* 21): *All the Athenians spent their time in nothing else but either to tell or to hear some new thing*, which comes in as the reason why they were inquisitive concerning Paul's doctrine, not because it was *good*, but because it was *new*.

PAUL'S SERMONS AT ATHENS (*vv.* 22–31)

We have here St. Paul's sermon at Athens.

I. He lays down this, as the scope of his discourse, that he aimed to bring them to *the knowledge of the only living and true God*, as the sole and proper object of their adoration. Now,

1. He shows them that they needed to be instructed herein; for they had lost the knowledge of the true God that made them, in the worship of false gods that they had made. *I perceive that in all things you are too superstitious*. He uses a word which among them was taken in a good sense: *You are every way more than ordinarily religious*, so some read it; *you are very devout in your way.*

2. He shows them that they themselves had given a fair occasion for the declaring of this one true God to them, by *setting up an altar*, *To the unknown God*, which intimated an acknowledgment that there was a God who was yet to them *an unknown God*; and it is sad to think that at Athens, a place which was supposed to have the monopoly of wisdom, the true God

was an unknown God, the only God that was unknown. (1) He tells them that the God he preached to them was one that they did already worship, and therefore he was not a setter forth of new or strange gods: "As you have a dependence upon him, so he has had some kind of homage from you." (2) He was one whom they ignorantly worshipped, which was a reproach to them, who were famous all the world over for their knowledge.

II. He confirms his doctrine of one living and true God, by his works of creation and providence. Now Paul here sets himself, in the first place, to reform the philosophy of the Athenians (he corrects the mistakes of that), and to give them right notions of *the one only living and true God*, and then to carry the matter further than they ever attempted for the reforming of their worship, and the bringing them off from their polytheism and idolatry. Observe what glorious things Paul here says of that God whom he served, and would have them to serve.

1. *He is the God that made the world, and all things therein; the Father almighty, the Creator of heaven and earth.* This was admitted by many of the philosophers; but those of Aristotle's school denied it, and maintained "that the world was from eternity, and every thing always was what now it is." Those of the school of Epicurus fancied "that the world was made by a fortuitous concourse of atoms, which, having been in perpetual motion, at length accidently jumped into this frame." Against both

these Paul here maintains that God by the operations of an infinite power, according to the contrivance of an infinite wisdom, in the beginning of time made the world and all things therein, the origin of which was owing, not as they fancied to an eternal matter, but to an eternal mind.

2. He is therefore *Lord of heaven and earth*, that is, he is their rightful owner, proprietor, and possessor.

3. He is, in a particular manner, the Creator of men, of all men (*v.* 26): *He made of one blood all nations of men.* He made the first man, he makes every man, is the former of every man's body and the Father of every man's spirit. He made them all of one blood, of one and the same nature; *he fashions their heart alike. He hath made them to dwell on all the face of the earth.* He made them not to live in one place, but to be dispersed over all the earth; one nation therefore ought not to look with contempt upon another, as the Greeks did upon all other nations; for those on all the face of the earth are of the same blood.

4. That he is the great benefactor of the whole creation (*v.* 25): *He giveth to all life, and breath, and all things.* He not only *breathed into the first man the breath of life*, but still breathes it into every man.

5. That he is the sovereign disposer of all the affairs of the children of men, according to the counsel of his will (*v.* 26).

6. That *he is not far from every one of us*, *v.* 27. He is every where present, has his eye upon us at all times, and knows us better than we know ourselves.

7. That *in him we live, and move, and have our being*, *v.* 28. (1) *In him we live*; that is, the continuance of our lives is owing to him and the constant influence of his providence. (2) *In him we move*; it is by his providence that our souls move and our thoughts run to and fro. (3) *In him we have our being*; not only from him we had it at first, but in him we have it still.

8. That upon the whole matter we are *God's offspring*; he is *our Father that begat us* (Deut. xxxii. 6, 18), and he hath *nourished and brought us up as children*, Isa. i. 2. The apostle here quotes a saying of one of the Greek poets, Aratus, a native of Cilicia, Paul's countryman, who, in his *Phenomena*, in the beginning of his book, speaking of the heathen *Jupiter*, that is, in the poetical dialect, the supreme *God*, says this of him, *for we are also his offspring.*

III. From all these great truths concerning God, he infers the absurdity of their idolatry, as the prophets of old had done. If this be so, 1. Then God cannot be represented by an image. 2. Then *he dwells not in temples made with hands*, *v.* 24. He is not invited to any temple men can build for him, nor confined to any. 3. Then he is *not worshipped*, he is *not served*, or *ministered unto, with men's hands, as though he needed any thing*, *v.* 25. He that made all, and maintains all, cannot be benefited by any of our services, nor needs them. 4. Then it concerns us all to enquire after God (*v.* 27): *That they should seek the Lord*, that is, fear and worship him in a right manner. Therefore God has kept the children of men in a constant dependence upon him for life and all the comforts of life, that he might keep them under constant obligations to him.

IV. He proceeds to call them all to repent of their idolatries, and to turn from them, *vv.* 30, 31. This is the practical part of Paul's sermon before the university; having declared God to them (*v.* 23), he properly presses upon them *repentance towards God*, and would also have taught them *faith towards our Lord Jesus Christ*, if they had had the patience to hear him. Observe,

1. The conduct of God towards the Gentile world before the gospel came among them: *The times of this ignorance God winked at.* (1) They were times of great ignorance. Human learning flourished more than ever in the Gentile world just before Christ's time; but in the things of God they were grossly ignorant. (2) These times of ignorance God winked at. Understand it, [1] As an act of divine justice. God despised or neglected these times of ignorance, and did not send them his gospel, as now he does. Or rather, [2] As an act of divine patience and forbearance. He winked at these times; he did not restrain them from these idolatries by sending prophets to them, as he did to Israel; he did not punish them in their idolatries, as he did Israel; but gave them the gifts of his providence, *ch.* xiv. 16, 17.

2. The charge God gave to the Gentile world by the gospel, which he now sent among them: *He now commandeth all men every where to repent*—to change their mind and

their way, to be ashamed of their folly and to act more wisely, to break off the worship of idols and bind themselves to the worship of the true God.

3. The great reason to enforce this command, taken from the judgment to come. God commands us to repent, *because he hath appointed a day in which he will judge the world in righteousness* (*v.* 31), and has now under the gospel made a clearer discovery of a state of retribution in the other world than ever before. God will judge the world *by that man whom he hath ordained*, who can be no other than the Lord Jesus, to whom all judgment is committed. God's raising Christ from the dead is the great proof of his being appointed and ordained the Judge of quick and dead. His raising him from the dead was the beginning of his exaltation, his judging the world will be the perfection of it; and he that begins will make an end.

REACTIONS (*vv.* 32–34)

We have here a short account of the issue of Paul's preaching at Athens.

I. Few were the better: the gospel had as little success at Athens as anywhere; for the pride of the philosophers there, as of the Pharisees at Jerusalem, prejudiced them against the gospel of Christ. They heard him patiently till he came to speak of the resurrection of the dead (*v.* 32), and then some of them began to hiss him: they *mocked.*

II. Yet there were some that were wrought upon, *v.* 34. If some would not, others would. There were certain men that adhered to him, and believed. Two are particularly named; one was an eminent man, *Dionysius the Areopagite*, one of that high court or great council that sat in Areopagus, or Mars' Hill—a judge, a senator, one of those before whom Paul was summoned to appear; his judge becomes his convert. The *woman named Damaris* was, as some think, the wife of Dionysius; but, rather, some other person of quality; and, though there was not so great a harvest gathered in at Athens as there was at other places, yet, these few being wrought upon there, Paul had no reason to say he had *laboured in vain*.

CHAPTER EIGHTEEN
PAUL VISITS CORINTH
(vv. 1–6)

Corinth was the chief city of Achaia, now a province of the empire, a rich and splendid city. Now here we have,

I. Paul working for his living, *vv.* 2, 3. 1. Though he was bred a scholar, yet he was master of a handicraft trade. He was a tentmaker, an upholsterer. 2. Though he was entitled to a maintenance from the churches he had planted, and from the people to whom he preached, yet he worked at his calling to get bread, which is more to his praise who did not ask for supplies than to theirs who did not supply him unasked, knowing what straits he was reduced to. 3. Though he was himself a great apostle, yet he chose to work with

Aquila and Priscilla, because he found them to be very intelligent in the things of God, as appears afterwards (*v.* 26), and he owns that they had been his *helpers in Christ Jesus*, Rom. xvi. 3. Concerning this Aquila we are here told, (1) That he was a Jew, but born in Pontus, *v.* 2. (2) That he was lately come from Italy to Corinth. (3) That the reason of his leaving Italy was because by a late edict of the emperor Claudius Cæsar all Jews were banished from Rome; for the Jews were generally hated, and every occasion was taken to put hardship and disgrace upon them.

II. We have here Paul preaching to the Jews.

1. He *reasoned with them in the synagogue* publicly *every sabbath.* God invites us to come and reason with him (Isa. i. 18), and challenges sinners to *produce their cause*, and *bring forth their strong reasons*, Isa. xli. 21. Paul was a rational as well as a scriptural preacher.

2. *He persuaded them.* It denotes, (1) The urgency of his preaching. Or, (2) The good effect of his preaching. He persuaded them, that is, he prevailed with them; so some understand it.

3. He was yet more earnest in this matter when his fellow-labourers, his seconds, came up with him (*v.* 5).

III. We have him here abandoning the unbelieving Jews, and turning from them to the Gentiles, as he had done in other places, *v.* 6.

1. Many of the Jews, and indeed the most of them, persisted in their contradiction to the gospel of Christ, and would not yield to the strongest reasonings nor the most

102

winning persuasions; they *opposed themselves* and *blasphemed.*

2. Paul hereupon declared himself discharged from them, and left them to perish in their unbelief.

3. Having given them over, yet he does not give over his work. Though Israel be not gathered, Christ and his gospel shall be glorious.

PAUL ENCOURAGED
(*vv.* 7–11)

Here we are told,

I. That Paul changed his quarters. He departed out of the synagogue, being driven out by the perverseness of the unbelieving Jews, and he *entered into a certain man's house, named Justus, v.* 7. But observe the account of this man and his house. 1. The man was next door to a Jew; he was one that *worshipped God*; he was not an idolater, though he was a Gentile, but was a worshipper of the God of Israel, and him only, as Cornelius. 2. The house was next door to the synagogue, it *joined close to it,* which some perhaps might interpret as done with design to draw people from the synagogue to the meeting; but I rather think it was done in charity, to show that he would come as near to them as he could.

II. That Paul presently saw the good fruit of his labours, both among Jews and Gentiles. 1. *Crispus* a Jew, an eminent one, the *chief ruler of the synagogue, believed on the Lord Jesus, with all his house, v.* 8. 2. Many of the Corinthians, who were Gentiles (and some of them persons of bad character, as appears, 1 Cor. vi. 11, *such were some of you*), *hearing, believed, and were baptized.*

III. That Paul was encouraged by a vision to go on with his work at Corinth (*v.* 9). 1. He renewed his commission and charge to preach the gospel. 2. He assured him of his presence with him, which was sufficient to animate him, and put life and spirit into him. 3. He gave him a warrant of protection to save him harmless. 4. He gave him a prospect of success: "*For I have much people in this city.*" The Lord knows those that are his, yea, and those that shall be his; for it is by his work upon them that they become his, and *known unto him are all his works*. Let us not despair concerning any place, when even in Corinth Christ had *much people*.

IV. That upon this encouragement he made a long stay there (*v.* 11). 1. For the bringing in of those that were outside. The people Christ has at Corinth must be called in by degrees, some by one sermon, others by another; *we see not yet all things put under Christ.* 2. For the building up of those that were within. Those that are converted have still need to be *taught the word of God*, and particular need at Corinth to be taught it by Paul himself; for no sooner was the good seed sown in that field than the enemy came and sowed tares, the false apostles, those deceitful workers, of whom Paul in his epistles to the Corinthians complains so much.

PAUL BEFORE GALLIO
(*vv.* 12–17)

We have here an account of some disturbance given to Paul and his friends at Corinth, but no great harm done, nor much hindrance given to the work of Christ there.

I. Paul is accused by the Jews before the Roman governor, *vv.* 12, 13. The governor was *Gallio, deputy of Achaia*, that is, proconsul; for Achaia was a consular province of the empire. Now observe, 1. How rudely Paul is apprehended, and brought before Gallio; *The Jews made insurrection with one accord against Paul*. 2. How falsely Paul is accused before Gallio (*v.* 13): *This fellow persuades men to worship God contrary to the law*. They could not charge him with persuading men not to worship God at all, or to worship other gods (Deut. xiii. 2): but only to worship God in a way contrary to the law. The Romans allowed the Jews in their provinces the observance of their own law; and what then? Must those therefore be prosecuted as criminals who worship God in any other way?

II. Gallio, upon the first hearing, or rather without any hearing at all, dismisses the cause, and will not take any cognizance of it, *vv.* 14, 15. Observe,

1. He shows himself very ready to do the part of a judge in any matter that it was proper for him to take cognizance of. But,

2. He will by no means allow them to make a complaint to him of a thing that was not within his jurisdiction (*v.* 15): "*If it be a question of words and names, and of your law, look you to it*; end it among yourselves as you can, but *I will be no judge of such matters*; you shall neither burden my patience with the hearing of it, nor burden my conscience with giving

judgment upon it;" and therefore, when they were urgent and pressing to be heard, *he drove them from the judgment-seat* (*v.* 16), and ordered another cause to be called.

III. The abuse done to Sosthenes, and Gallio's unconcernedness in it, *v.* 17. 1. The parties put a great contempt upon the court, when *they took Sosthenes and beat him before the judgment-seat*. He is said be a *ruler of the synagogue*, either joint-ruler with Crispus (*v.* 8), or a ruler of one synagogue, as Crispus was of another. As for the Greeks that abused him, it is very probable that they were either Hellenist Jews, or Jewish Greeks, those that joined with the Jews in opposing the gospel (*vv.* 4, 6), and that the native Jews put them on to do it, thinking it would in them be less offensive. They were so enraged against Paul that they beat Sosthenes; and so enraged against Gallio, because he would not countenance the prosecution, that they beat him before the judgment-seat, whereby they did, in effect, tell him that they cared not for him; if he would not be their executioner, they would be their own judges. 2. The court put no less a contempt upon the cause, and the persons too. But *Gallio cared for none of these things*. If by this be meant that he cared not for the affronts of bad men, it was commendable. While he steadily adhered to the laws and rules of equity, he might despise their contempts; but, if it be meant (as I think it is) that he concerned not himself for the abuses done to good men, it carries his indifference too far, and gives us but an ill character of him.

PAUL AT EPHESUS AND JERUSALEM (*vv.* 18–23)

Here is,

I. Paul's departure from Corinth, *v.* 18. 1. He did not go away till some time after the trouble he met with there; from other places he had departed when the storm arose, but not from Corinth, because there it had no sooner risen than it fell again. 2. When he went, he took leave of the brethren solemnly. His farewell sermon would leave impressions upon them. 3. He took *with him Priscilla and Aquila*, because they had a mind to accompany him. 4. At Cenchrea, which was hard by Corinth, the port where those that went to sea from Corinth took ship, either Paul or Aquila (for the original does not determine which) had his head shaved, to discharge himself from the vow of a Nazarite. The Nazarite's head was to be shaved when either his consecration was accidentally polluted, in which case he must begin again, or *when the days of his separation were fulfilled* (Num. vi. 9; xiii. 18), which, we suppose, was the case here. Some throw it upon Aquila, who was a Jew (*v.* 2), and retained perhaps more of his Judaism than was convenient; but I see no harm in admitting it concerning Paul, for concerning him we must admit the same thing (*ch.* xxi. 24, 26), not only in compliance for a time with the Jews, to whom he *became as a Jew* (1 Cor. ix. 20), *that he might win upon them*, but because the vow of the Nazarites, though ceremonial, and as such ready to vanish away, had yet a great deal of moral and very pious

significance, and therefore was fit to die the last of all the Jewish ceremonies.

II. Paul's calling *at Ephesus*, which was the metropolis of the Lesser Asia, and a sea-port. The Jews at Ephesus were so far from driving Paul away that they courted his stay with them (*v.* 20): *They desired him to tarry longer with them*, to instruct them in the gospel of Christ. Paul would not stay with them now: *He consented not*; *but bade them farewell.* He had further to go; he *must by all means keep this feast at Jerusalem*; not that he thought himself bound in duty to it (he knew the laws of the feasts were no longer binding), but he had business at Jerusalem (whatever it was) which would be best done at the time of the feast, when there was a general rendezvous of all the Jews from all parts; which of the feasts it was we are not told, probably it was the passover, which was the most eminent.

III. Paul's visit to Jerusalem; a short visit it was, but it served as a token of respect to that truly mother-church. Paul thought it requisite to show himself among them, that they might not think his success among the Gentiles had made him think himself either above them or estranged from them, or that the honour God had put upon him made him unmindful of the honour he owed to them.

IV. His return through those countries where he had formerly preached the gospel. 1. *He went and spent some time in Antioch*, among his old friends there, whence he was first sent out to preach among the Gentiles, *ch.* xiii. 1. 2. *Thence he*

*went over the country of Galatia and
Phrygia in order,* where he had
preached the gospel, and planted
churches, which, though very briefly mentioned (*ch.* xvi. 6) was yet a
glorious work, as appears by Gal.
iv. 14, 15, where Paul speaks of his
preaching the gospel to the Galatians at the first, and their receiving
him *as an angel of God.*

APOLLOS THE JEW (*vv.* 24–28)

The sacred history leaves Paul
upon his travels, and goes here to
meet Apollos at Ephesus.

I. Here is an account of his
character, when he came to
Ephesus.

1. He was *a Jew, born at Alexandria* in Egypt, but of Jewish parents.

2. He was a man of excellent
good parts, and well fitted for
public service. He was *an eloquent
man, and mighty in the scriptures* of
the Old Testament, in the knowledge of which he was, as a Jew,
brought up.

3. He *was instructed in the way of
the Lord*; that is, he had some
acquaintance with the doctrine of
Christ, had obtained some general
notions of the gospel and the
principles of Christianity, *that
Jesus is the Christ,* and *that prophet
that should come into the world*; the
first notice of this would be readily
embraced by one that was so mighty
in the scripture as Apollos was, and
therefore understood the *signs of
the times.* He *was instructed,*
κατηχημένος — *he was catechised* (so
the word is), either by his parents or
by ministers; he was taught something of Christ and the way of
salvation by him.

4. Yet he *knew only the baptism of*

John; he was instructed in the
gospel of Christ as far as John's
ministry would carry him, and no
further. We cannot but think he
had heard of Christ's death and
resurrection, but he was not let into
the mystery of them, had not had
opportunity of conversing with any
of the apostles since the pouring
out of the Spirit; or he had himself
been baptized *only with the baptism
of John,* but he was not baptized
with the Holy Ghost, as the disciples were at the day of pentecost.

II. We have here the employment
and improvement of his gifts at
Ephesus.

1. He there made a very good use
of his gifts in public. He came,
probably, recommended to the
synagogue of the Jews as a fit man
to be a teacher there, and according
to the light he had, and *the
measure of the gift given to him,* he
was willing to be employed (*v.* 25):
*Being fervent in the Spirit, he spoke
and taught diligently the things of
the Lord.*

2. He there made a good increase
of his gifts in private, not so much
in study, as in conversation with
Aquila and Priscilla. They did not
take occasion from what they
observed of his deficiency either to
despise him themselves, or to dis-
parage him to others; did not call
him a young raw preacher, not fit
to come into a pulpit, but considered the disadvantages he had
laboured under, as knowing only
the baptism of John; and, having
themselves got great knowledge in
the truths of the gospel by their
long and intimate conversation
with Paul, they communicated what
they knew to him, and gave him a

clear, distinct, and methodical account of those things which before he had but confused notions of.

III. Here is his preferment to the service of the church of Corinth, which was a larger sphere of usefulness than Ephesus at present was. Paul was gone, was called away to other work, and now there was a fair occasion in this vacancy for Apollos to set in, who was fitted rather to water than to plant, to build up those that were within than to bring in those that were outside.

CHAPTER NINETEEN

PAUL AT EPHESUS (*vv.* 1–6)

Ephesus was a city of great note in Asia, famous for a temple built there to Diana, which was one of the wonders of the world: thither *Paul came to preach the gospel while Apollos was at Corinth* (*v.* 1). At his first coming, he met with some disciples there, who professed faith in Christ as the true Messiah, but were as yet in the first and lowest form in the school of Christ, under his usher John the Baptist. They were in number *about twelve* (*v.* 7). Observe here,

I. How Paul catechised them. He was told, probably by Aquila and Priscilla, that they were believers, that they did own Christ, and had given up their names to him; now Paul hereupon takes them under examination.

1. They did believe in the Son of God; but Paul enquires whether they had *received the Holy Ghost*, — whether they believed in the Spirit, whose operations on the minds of men, for conviction, conversion,

and comfort, were revealed some time after the doctrine of Jesus being the Christ, — whether they had been acquainted with, and had admitted, this revelation? This was not all; extraordinary gifts of the Holy Ghost were conferred upon the apostles and other disciples presently after Christ's ascension, which was frequently repeated upon occasion; had they participated in these gifts? "*Have you received the Holy Ghost since you believed?* Have you had that seal of the truth of Christ's doctrine in yourselves?"

2. They owned their ignorance in this matter. They spoke as if they expected it, and wondered they did not hear of it, and were ready to welcome the notice of it.

3. Paul enquired how they came to be baptized, if they knew nothing of the Holy Ghost; for, if they were baptized by any of Christ's ministers, they were instructed concerning the Holy Ghost, and were baptized in his name.

4. They own that they were baptized *unto John's baptism* — that is, as I take it, they were baptized in the name of John, not by John himself (he was far enough from any such thought), but by some weak, well-meaning disciple of his, that ignorantly kept up his name as the head of a party.

5. Paul explains to them the true intent and meaning of John's baptism, as principally referring to Jesus Christ, and so rectifies the mistake of those who had baptized them into the baptism of John, and had not directed them to look any further, but to rest in that.

6. When they were thus shown the error they were led into, they

107

thankfully accepted the discovery, and *were baptized in the name of the Lord Jesus*, *v*. 5. It does not therefore follow hence that there was not an agreement between John's baptism and Christ's, or that they were not for substance the same; much less does it follow that those who have been once baptized *in the name of the Father, Son, and Holy Ghost* (which is the appointed form of Christ's baptism), may be again baptized in the same name; for those that were here baptized *in the name of the Lord Jesus* had never been so baptized before.

II. How Paul conferred the extraordinary gifts of the Holy Ghost upon them, *v*. 6. 1. Paul solemnly *prayed to God* to give them those gifts, signified by his *laying his hands on them*, which was a gesture used in blessing by the patriarchs, especially in conveying the great trust of the promise, as Gen. xlviii. 14. 2. God granted the thing he prayed for: *The Holy Ghost came upon them* in a surprising overpowering manner, and *they spoke with tongues and prophesied*, as the apostles did and the first Gentile converts, *ch*. x. 44. Oh, what a wonderful change was here made on a sudden in these men! those that but just now had *not so much as heard that there was any Holy Ghost* are now themselves filled with the Holy Ghost; for the Spirit, like the wind, blows where and when he listeth.

MIRACLES BY PAUL (*vv*. 8–12)

Paul is here very busy at Ephesus to do good.

I. He begins, as usual, in the Jews' synagogue, and makes the first offer of the gospel to them, that he might gather in the *lost sheep of the house of Israel*, who were now scattered upon the mountains. Observe,

What success his preaching had among them. (1) There were some that were persuaded to believe in Christ; some think this is intimated in the word *persuading*—he prevailed with them. But, (2) Many continued in their infidelity, and were confirmed in their prejudices against Christianity. When Paul called on them before, and preached only some general things to them, they courted his stay among them (*ch*. xviii. 20); but now that he settled among them, and his word came more closely to their consciences, they were soon weary of him.

II. When he had carried the matter as far as it would go in the synagogue of the Jews, and found that their opposition grew more obstinate, he left the synagogue, because he could not safely, or rather because he could not comfortably and successfully, continue in communion with them. Now observe,

1. When Paul departed from the Jews he took the disciples with him, and *separated them, to save them from that untoward generation* (according to the charge Peter gave to his new converts, *ch*. ii. 40).

2. When Paul separated from the synagogue he set up a meeting of his own, he *disputed daily in the school of one Tyrannus*. He left the synagogue of the Jews, that he might go on with the more freedom in his work; still he disputed for Christ and Christianity, and was

ready to answer all opponents whatsoever in defence of them; and he had by this separation a double advantage. (1) That now his opportunities were more frequent. In the synagogue he could only preach every sabbath day (*ch.* xiii. 42), but now he disputed daily, he set up a lecture every day, and thus redeemed time. (2) That now they were more open. To the synagogue of the Jews none might come, nor could come, but Jews or proselytes; Gentiles were excluded; but, when he set up a meeting in the school of Tyrannus, both Jews and Greeks attended his ministry, *v.* 10.

3. Here he continued his labours for *two years*, read his lectures and disputed daily.

4. The gospel hereby spread far and near (*v.* 10): *All those that dwelt in Asia heard the word of the Lord Jesus*. The gospel is Christ's word, it is a word concerning Christ. This they heard, or at least heard of it. Some of all sects, some out of all parts both in city and country, embraced this gospel, and entertained it, and by them it was communicated to others; and so they all *heard the word of the Lord Jesus*, or might have heard it.

III. God confirmed Paul's doctrine by miracles, which awakened people's enquiries after it, fixed their affection to it, and engaged their belief of it, *vv.* 11, 12. 1. They were *special miracles*, God exerted powers that were not according to the common course of nature. 3. He not only cured the sick that were brought to him, or to whom he was brought, but *from his body were brought to the sick handkerchiefs or aprons*. Now was fulfilled

that word of Christ to his disciples, *Greater works than these shall you do*. We read of one that was cured by the touch of Christ's garment when it was upon him, and he perceived that *virtue went out of him*; but here were people cured by Paul's garments when they were taken from him.

EXORCISTS DEFEATED
(*vv.* 13–20)

I. Here is the confusion of some of Satan's servants, some *vagabond Jews*, that were *exorcists*, who made use of Christ's name profanely and wickedly in their diabolical enchantments, but were made to pay dearly for their presumption. Observe,

1. The general character of those who were guilty of this presumption. They were Jews, but *vagabond* Jews, were of the Jewish nation and religion, but went about from town to town to get money by conjuring.

2. A particular account of some at Ephesus that led this course of life and came thither in their travels; they were *seven sons of one Sceva, a Jew, and chief of the priests, v.* 14.

3. The profaneness they were guilty of: *They took upon them to call over evil spirits the name of the Lord Jesus*; not as those who had a veneration for Christ and a confidence in his name; but as those who were willing to try all methods to carry on their wicked trade.

4. The confusion they were put to in their impious operations. (1) The evil spirit gave them a sharp reply (*v.* 15): "*Jesus I know, and Paul I know; but who are you?* I know that Jesus has conquered principalities

and powers, and that Paul has authority in his name to cast out devils; but what power have you to command us in his name, or who gave you any such power?'' (2) *The man in whom the evil spirit was* gave them a warm reception, fell foul upon them, *leaped upon them* in the height of his frenzy and rage; so that *they fled out of the house*, not only *naked*, but *wounded*; their clothes pulled off their backs, and their heads broken. This is written for a warning to all those who name the name of Christ, but do not depart from iniquity.

5. The general notice that was taken of this, and the good impression it made upon many (*v.*17). God was glorified; *the name of the Lord Jesus*, by which his faithful servants cast out devils and cured diseases, without any resistance, *was the more magnified*; for now it appeared to be a name above every name.

II. Here is the conversion of others of Satan's servants, with the evidences of their conversion.

1. Those that had been guilty of wicked practices confessed them, *v.* 18. These confessions were not extorted from them, but were voluntary, for the ease of their consciences, upon which the late miracles had struck a terror.

2. Those that had conversed with wicked books burnt them (*v.* 19). It is taken for granted that they were convinced of the evil of these curious arts, and resolved to deal in them no longer; but they did not think this enough unless they burnt their books. (1) Thus they showed a holy indignation at the sins they had been guilty of. (2) Thus they showed their resolution

never to return to the use of those arts, and the books which related to them, again. (3) Thus they showed a contempt of the wealth of this world; for the price of the books was cast up, probably by those that persuaded them not to burn them, and it was found to be *fifty thousand pieces of silver*.

III. Here is a general account of the progress and success of the gospel in and about Ephesus (*v.* 20): *So mightily grew the word of God, and prevailed.*

RIOT AT EPHESUS (*vv.* 21–41)

I. Paul is here brought into some trouble at Ephesus, just when he is forecasting to go thence, and to cut out work for himself elsewhere. See here,

1. How he laid his purpose of going to other places, *vv.* 21, 22. Having spent above two years at Ephesus, (1) He designed a visit to the churches of Macedonia and Achaia, especially of Philippi and Corinth, the chief cities of those provinces, *v.* 21. There he had planted churches, and now is concerned to visit them. He *purposed in the spirit*, either in his own spirit, not communicating his purpose as yet, but keeping it to himself; or by the direction of the Holy Spirit, who was his guide in all his motions, and by whom he was led. (2) Thence he designed to go to Jerusalem, to visit the brethren there; and thence he intended to go to Rome; to see the Christians there, and to do them some service, Rom. i. 11. (3) He sent Timothy and Erastus into Macedonia, to give them notice of the visit he intended them, and to

get their collection ready for the poor saints at Jerusalem.

2. How he was seconded in his purpose, and obliged to pursue it by the troubles which at length he met with at Ephesus.

II. But in the trouble here related, he was worse frightened than hurt. Here is, ·

1. A great complaint against Paul and the other preachers of the gospel for drawing people off from the worship of Diana, and so spoiling the trade of the silversmiths that worked for Diana's temple.

(1) The complainant is Demetrius, a silversmith, a principal man, it is likely, of the trade, and one that would be thought to understand and consult the interests of it more than others of the company. Whether he worked in other sorts of plate or no we are not told; but the most advantageous branch of his trade was *making silver shrines for Diana*, v. 24.

(2) The persons he appeals to are not the magistrates, but the mob.

(3) His complaint and representation are very full. [1] He lays it down for a principle that the art and mystery of making silver shrines for the worshippers of Diana was very necessary to be supported and kept up (v. 25). [2] He charges it upon Paul that he had dissuaded men from worshipping idols. The words, as they are laid in the indictment, are, that he had asserted, *Those are no gods which are made with hands*, v. 26. [3] He reminds them of the danger which their trade was in of going to decay. Whatever touches this touches them in a sensible tender

part. [4] He pretends a mighty zeal for Diana, and a jealousy for her honour.

2. The popular resentment of this complaint. The charge was managed by a craftsman, and was framed to incense the common people, and it had the desired effect. *The whole city was full of confusion* —the common and natural effect of an intemperate zeal for a false religion.

3. The proceedings of the mob under the power of these resentments, and how far they were carried.

(1) They laid hands on some of Paul's companions, and hurried them into the theatre (v. 29). Those whom they seized were *Gaius and Aristarchus*, of both of whom we read elsewhere. *Gaius was of Derbe*, *ch.* xx. 4. *Aristarchus* is also there spoken of, and Col. iv. 10. They came with Paul *from Macedonia*, and this was their only crime, that they were Paul's companions in travel, both in services and sufferings.

(2) *Paul*, who had escaped being seized by them, when he perceived his friends in distress for his sake, *would have entered in unto the people*, to sacrifice himself, if there were no other remedy, rather than his friends should suffer upon his account; and it was an evidence of a generous spirit, and that he loved his neighbour as himself.

(3) He was persuaded from it by the kindness of his friends, who overruled him.

(4) The mob was in a perfect confusion (v. 32): *Some cried one thing and some another*, according as their fancies and passions, and

perhaps the reports they received, led them. For the truth was *the greater part knew not wherefore they had come together*.

(5) The Jews would have interested themselves in this tumult (in other places they had been the first movers of such riots) but now at Ephesus they had not interest enough to raise the mob, and yet, when it was raised, they had ill-will enough to set in with it (*v.* 33): *They drew Alexander out of the multitude*, called him out to speak on the behalf of the Jews against Paul and his companions.

(6) This occasioned the prosecutors to drop the prosecution of Paul's friends, and to turn it into acclamations in honour of their goddess (*v.* 34): *When they knew that he was a Jew*, and, as such, an enemy to the worship of Diana (for the Jews had now an implacable hatred to idols and idolatry), whatever he had to say for Paul or against him, they were resolved not to hear him, and therefore set the mob a shouting, "*Great is Diana of the Ephesians*".

4. The suppressing and dispersing of these rioters, by the prudence and vigilance of *the town-clerk*. With much ado he, at length, stilled the noise, so as to be heard, and then made a pacific speech to them, and gave us an instance of that of Solomon, *The words of wise men are heard in quiet more than the cry of him that rules among fools*, as Demetrius did. Eccl. ix. 17.

See here, [1] How the overruling providence of God preserves the public peace, by an unaccountable power over the spirits of men. [2] See how many ways God has of

protecting his people. Perhaps this town-clerk was no friend at all to Paul, nor to the gospel he preached, yet his human prudence is made to serve the divine purpose.

CHAPTER TWENTY

TO TROAS (*vv* 1–6)

These travels of Paul which are thus briefly related, if all in them had been recorded that was memorable and worthy to be written in letters of gold, *the world would not contain the books that would have been* written; and therefore we have only some general hints of occurrences, which therefore ought to be the more precious. Here is,

I. Paul's departure from Ephesus. He had tarried there longer than he had done at any one place since he had been ordained to the apostleship of the Gentiles; and now it was time to think of removing, for he must *preach in other cities also*.

II. His visitation of the Greek churches, which he had planted, and more than once watered, and which appear to have laid very near his heart.

III. The altering of his measures; for we cannot always stand to our purposes. Accidents unforeseen put us upon new counsels, which oblige us to purpose with a proviso. 1. *Paul was about to sail into Syria, to Antioch*, whence he was first sent out into the service of the Gentiles, and which therefore in his journeys he generally contrived to take in his way; but he changed his mind, and resolved *to return to Macedonia*, the same way he came. 2. The reason was because the Jews, expecting he would steer that course as usual, had way-laid him, designing to be the death of him.

IV. His companions in his travels when he went into Asia; they are here named, *v.* 4.

V. His coming to Troas, where he had appointed a general rendezvous of his friends. 1. They went before, and stayed for him at Troas (*v.* 5), designing to go along with him to Jerusalem, as Trophimus particularly did, *ch.* xxi. 29. 2. Paul made the best of his way thither; and, it should seem, Luke was now in company with him; for he says, *We sailed from Philippi* (*v.* 6), and the first time we find him in his company was here at Troas, *ch.* xvi. 11. *The days of unleavened bread* are mentioned only to describe the time, not to intimate that Paul kept the passover after the manner of the Jews.

A MIRACLE AT TROAS
(*vv.* 7–12)

We have here an account of what passed at Troas the last of the seven days that Paul stayed there.

I. There was a solemn religious assembly of the Christians that were there, according to their constant custom, and the custom of all the churches. They *came together upon the first day of the week*, which they called *the Lord's day* (Rev. i. 10), the Christian sabbath, celebrated to the honour of Christ and the Holy Spirit, in remembrance of the resurrection of Christ, and the pouring out of the Spirit, both on the first day of the week.

II. In this assembly Paul gave them a sermon, a long sermon, a farewell sermon, *v.* 7. 1. He gave them a sermon: he *preached to them*. Though they were disciples already, yet it was very necessary they should have the word of God preached to them, in order to their increase in knowledge and grace. 2. It was a farewell sermon, he being *ready to depart on the morrow*. 3. It was a very long sermon: He *continued his speech until midnight*; for he had a great deal to say, and knew not that ever he should have another opportunity of preaching to them.

III. *A young man* in the congregation, that slept at sermon, was killed by a fall *out of the window, but raised to life again*; his name signifies *one that had good fortune—Eutychus, bene fortunatus*; and he answered his name. Observe,

1. The infirmity with which he was overtaken. It is probable his parents brought him, though but a boy, to the assembly, out of a desire to have him well instructed in the things of God by such a preacher as Paul. The particular notice taken of his sleeping makes us willing to hope none of the rest slept, though it was sleeping time and after supper; but this youth fell fast asleep, he was *carried away with it* (so the word is), which intimates that he strove against it, but was overpowered by it, and at last sunk down with sleep.

2. The calamity with which he was seized herein: He *fell down from the third loft, and was taken up dead*.

3. The miraculous mercy shown him in his recovery *to life again*, *v.* 10. Various speculations, we may suppose, this ill accident had occasioned in the congregation, but

Paul puts an end to them all: "*Trouble not yourselves*, be not in any disorder about it, let it not put you into any hurry, *for his life is in him*; he is not dead, but sleepeth: lay him awhile upon a bed, and he will come to himself, for he is now alive.' Thus, when Christ raised Lazarus, he said, *Father, I thank thee that thou hast heard me*. (3) He returned to his work immediately after this interruption (*v*. 11): *He came up again* to the meeting, they broke bread together in a love-feast, which usually attended the eucharist, in token of their communion with each other, and for the confirmation of friendship among them; and *they talked a long while, even till break of day*. (4) Before they parted *they brought the young man alive* into the congregation, every one congratulating him upon his return to life from the dead, and *they were not a little comforted*, *v*. 12.

ON VOYAGE (*vv*. 13–16)

Paul is hastening towards Jerusalem, but strives to do all the good he can by the way. He had called at Troas, and done good there; and now he makes a sort of coasting voyage, the merchants would call it a trading voyage, going from place to place, and no doubt endeavouring to make every place he came to the better for him, as every good man should do.

I. He sent his companions by sea to Assos, but he himself was *minded to go afoot*, *v*. 13. That he might call on his friends by the way, and do good among them, either converting sinners or edifying saints; and in both he was

serving his great Master, and carrying on his great work.

II. At Assos he went on board with his friends. There they *took him in*; for by this time he had enough of his walk, and was willing to betake himself to the other way of travelling.

III. He made the best of his way to Jerusalem. He aimed to be there by the feast of pentecost because it was a time of concourse, which would give him an opportunity of propagating the gospel among the Jews and proselytes, who came from all parts to worship at the feast: and the feast of pentecost had been particularly made famous among the Christians by the pouring out of the Spirit.

FAREWELL TO EPHESUS
(*vv*. 17–35)

These elders, or presbyters, some think, were those twelve who received the Holy Ghost by Paul's hands, *ch*. xix. 6. But, besides these, it is probable that Timothy had ordained other elders there for the service of that church, and the country about; these Paul sent for, that he might instruct and encourage them to go on in the work to which they had laid their hands. And what instructions he gave to them they would give to the people under their charge.

I. He appeals to them concerning both his life and doctrine, all the time he had been in and about Ephesus (*v*. 18): "*You know after what manner I have been with you*, and how I have done the work of an apostle among you." He mentions this as a confirmation of his commission and consequently of the doctrine he had preached among them.

1. His spirit and conversation were excellent and exemplary; they knew after what manner he had been among them, and how he had had his conversation towards them, in simplicity and godly sincerity (2 Cor. i. 12), how holily, justly, and unblamably he behaved himself, and how gentle he was towards them, 1 Thess. ii. 7, 10.

2. His preaching was likewise such as it should be, *vv.* 20, 21. He came to Ephesus to preach the gospel of Christ among them, and he had been faithful both to them and to him that appointed him. He was a truly evangelical preacher. He did not preach philosophical notions, or matters of doubtful disputation, nor did he preach politics, or intermeddle at all with affairs of state or the civil government; but he preached faith and repentance, the two great gospel graces, the nature and necessity of them; these he urged upon all occasions.

II. He declares his expectation of sufferings and afflictions in his present journey to Jerusalem, *vv.* 22–24.

(1) Of holy courage and resolution in our work, notwithstanding the difficulties and oppositions we meet with in it; he saw them before him, but he made nothing of them. None of these things moved him. [1] They did not drive him off from his work; he did not tack about, and go back again, when he saw the storm rise, but went on resolutely, preaching there, where he knew how dearly it would cost him. [2] They did not deprive him of his comfort,

nor make him drive on heavily in his work. In the midst of troubles he was as one unconcerned.

(2) Of a holy contempt of life, and the continuance and comforts of it: *Neither count I my life dear to myself.* Life is sweet, and is naturally dear to us. *All that a man has will he give for his life*; but all that a man has, and life too, will he give who understands himself aright and his own interest, rather than lose the favour of God and hazard eternal life. Paul was of this mind.

(3) Of a holy concern to go through with the work of life, which should be much more our care than to secure either the outward comforts of it or the countenance of it. Two things this great and good man is in care about, and if he gain them it is no matter to him what becomes of life: [1] That he may be found faithful to the trust reposed in him, that he may *finish the ministry which he has received of the Lord Jesus*, may do the work which he was sent into the world about, or, rather, which he was sent into the church about. [2] That he may finish well. He cares not when the period of his life comes, nor how, be it ever so soon, ever so sudden, ever so sad, as to outward circumstances, so that he may but *finish his course with joy*.

III. Counting upon it that this was the last time they should see him, he appeals to their consciences concerning his integrity, and demands of them a testimony to it.

1. He tells them that he was now taking his last leave of them (*v.* 25).

2. He appeals to them concerning the faithful discharge of his ministry among them (*v.* 26): "*Where-*

fore, seeing my ministry is at an end with you, it concerns both you and me to reflect, and look back;" and, (1) He challenges them to prove him unfaithful, or to have said or done any thing by which he had made himself accessory to the ruin of any precious soul: *I am pure from the blood of all men*, the blood of souls. This plainly refers to that of the prophet (Ezek. xxxiii. 6), where the blood of him that perishes by the sword of the enemy is said to be required at the hand of the unfaithful watchman that did not give warning: 'You cannot say but I have given warning, and therefore no man's blood can be laid at my door." (2) He therefore leaves the blood of those that perish upon their own heads, because they had fair warning given them, but they would not take it. (3) He charges these ministers to look to it that they took care and pains, as he had done: "*I am pure from the blood of all men*, see that you keep yourselves so too."

3. He proves his own fidelity with this (*v.* 27): *For I have not shunned to declare unto you all the counsel of God.* (1) He had preached to them nothing but the counsel of God, and had not added any inventions of his own. (2) He had preached to them the whole counsel of God. As he had preached to them the gospel pure, so he had preached it to them entire. (3) He had not shunned to do it; had not wilfully nor designedly avoided the declaring of any part of the counsel of God.

IV. He charges them as ministers to be diligent and faithful in their work.

1. He commits the care of the

church at Ephesus, that is, the saints, the Christians that were there and thereabouts (Eph. i. 1), to them, who, though doubtless they were so numerous that they could not all meet in one place, but worshipped God in several congregations, under the conduct of several ministers, are yet called here *one flock*, because they not only agreed in one faith, as they did with all Christian churches, but in many instances they kept up communion one with another. To these elders or presbyters the apostle here, upon the actual foresight of his own final leaving them, commits the government of this church, and tells then that not he, but *the Holy Ghost, had made them overseers — bishops of the flock.*

2. He commanded them to mind the work to which they were called. Dignity calls for duty; if the Holy Ghost has made them *overseers of the flock*, that is, shepherds, they must be true to their trust. They must feed the church of God, must do all the parts of the shepherd's office, must lead the sheep of Christ into the green pastures, must lay meat before them, must do what they can to heal those that have no appetite to their meat, must feed them with wholesome doctrine, with a tender evangelical discipline, and must see that nothing is wanting that is necessary in order to their being nourished up to eternal life. They must watch (*v.* 31), as shepherds keep watch over their flocks by night, must be awake and watchful, must not give way to spiritual sloth and slumber, but must stir up themselves to their business and closely attend it.

116

3. He gives them several good reasons why they should mind the business of their ministry.

(1) Let them consider the interest of their Master, and his concern for the flock that was committed to their charge, *v.* 28. It is *the church which he has purchased with his own blood.*

(2) Let them consider the danger that the flock was in of being made a prey to its adversaries, *vv.* 29, 30. "If the flock be thus precious upon the account of its relation to God, and its redemption by Christ, then you are concerned to take heed both to yourselves and to it." Here are reasons for both. [1] *Take heed to the flock,* for wolves are abroad, that seek to devour (*v.* 29): *I know this, that after my departure grievous wolves shall enter in among you. First,* Some understand it of persecutors, that will inform against the Christians, and incense the magistrates against them, and will have no compassion on the flock. *Secondly,* It is rather to be understood of seducers and false teachers. Probably Paul has an eye to those of the circumcision, who preached up the ceremonial law; these he calls *grievous wolves,* for though they came in sheep's clothing, nay, in shepherd's clothing, they made mischief in the congregations of Christians, sowed discord among them, drew away many from the pure gospel of Christ, and did all they could to blemish and defame those that adhered to it. [2] *Take heed to yourselves,* for some shepherds will apostatize (*v.* 30). Some read it, *to draw away disciples after them*—those that are already disciples of Christ, draw them from him to follow them. But, though

there were some such seducers in the church of Ephesus, yet it should seem by Paul's Epistle to that church that that church was not so much infested with false teachers, at least not so much infected with their false doctrine, as some other churches were; but its peace and purity were preserved by the blessing of God on the pains and vigilance of these presbyters.

(3) Let them consider the great pains that Paul had taken in planting this church (*v.* 31): "*Remember that for the space of three years*" (for so long he had been preaching in Ephesus, and the parts adjacent) "*I ceased not to warn every one night and day with tears*; and be not you negligent in building upon that foundation which I was so diligent to lay."

V. He recommends them to divine direction and influence (*v.* 32). They were in care what would become of them, how they should go on in their work, break through their difficulties, and what provision would be made for them and their families. In answer to all these perplexities, Paul directs them to look up to God with an eye of faith, and beseeches God to look down on them with an eye of favour.

VI. He recommends himself to them as an example of indifference to this world, and to every thing in it, which, if they would walk in the same spirit and in the same steps, they would find to contribute greatly to their easy and comfortable passage through it. He had recommended them to God, and to the word of his grace, for spiritual blessings, which, without doubt, are the best blessings; but what shall they do for food for their families, an agreeable subsistence for themselves, and portions for their children? "As to these," Paul says, "do as I did;" and how was that? He here tells them,

1. That he never aimed at worldly wealth (*v.* 33).

2. That he had worked for his living, and taken a great deal of pains to get bread (*v.* 34). When he was to earn his bread, he did it by a manual occupation. Paul had a head and a tongue that he might have got money by, but they were these hands, saith he, *that ministered to my necessities.*

3. That even then, when he worked for the supply of his own necessities, yet he spared something out of what he got for the relief of others; for this he here obliges them to do (*v.* 35). The sentiment of the children of this world is contrary to this; they are afraid of giving. "This giving," they say, "undoes us all;" but they are in hope of getting. *Every one for his gain from his quarter,* Isa. lvi. 11. Clear gain is with them the most blessed thing that can be; but Christ tells us, *It is more blessed* (more excellent in itself, an evidence of a more excellent disposition of mind, and the way to a better blessedness at last) *to give than to receive.* It makes us more like to God, who gives to all, and receives from none; and to the Lord Jesus, *who went about doing good.* It is more blessed to give our pains than to receive pay for it, and what we should delight to do if the necessities of ourselves and families would admit it.

PAUL TAKES HIS LEAVE
(*vv.* 36–38)

After the parting sermon that Paul preached to the elders of Ephesus, which was very affecting, we have here the parting prayer and tears, which were yet more affecting; we can scarcely read the account here given of them, and meditate upon them with dry eyes.

I. They parted with prayer (*v.* 36): *And, when he had thus spoken, he kneeled down, and prayed with them all.* And, no doubt, it was a prayer every way suited to the present mournful occasion. He committed them to God in this prayer, prayed that he would not leave them, but continue his presence with them.

II. They parted with tears, abundance of tears, and most affectionate embraces, *vv.* 37, 38.

III. They *accompanied him unto the ship,* partly to show their respect for him (they would bring him on his way as far as they could), and partly that they might have a little more of his company and conversation. But this was a comfort to both sides, and soon turned this tide of passion, that the presence of Christ both went with him and stayed with them.

CHAPTER TWENTY-ONE
A WARNING FOR PAUL
(*vv.* 1–7)

We may observe here,

I. How much ado Paul had to get clear from Ephesus, intimated in the first words of the chapter, *after we had gotten from them,* that is, were drawn from them as by violence. It was a force put upon

both sides; Paul was loth to leave
them, and they were loth to part
with him, and yet there was no
remedy, but so it must be.

II. What a prosperous voyage
they had thence. Without any
difficulty, *they came with a straight
course*, by direct sailing, *to Coos*,
a famous Grecian island,—*the next
day to Rhodes*, talked of for the
Colossus there,—*thence to Patara*,
a famous port, the metropolis of
Lycia (*v*. 1); here they very happily
*found a ship sailing over into
Phenicia*, the very course they were
steering, *v*. 2. This ship that was
bound for Phenicia (that is, Tyre)
they took the convenience of, *went
on board, and set sail* for Tyre. In
this voyage *they discovered Cyprus*,
the island that Barnabas was of,
and which he took care of, and
therefore Paul did not visit it, but
we left it on the left hand (*v*. 3),
sailed upon the coast of *Syria, and*
at length *landed at Tyre*, that celebrated mart of the nations, so it
had been, but was now reduced;
yet something of a trade it had still,
*for there the ship was to unlade her
burden*, and did so.

III. The halt that Paul made at
Tyre.

1. *At Tyre he found disciples*,
some that had embraced the gospel,
and professed the Christian faith.

2 Paul, *finding those disciples at
Tyre, tarried there seven days*, they
urging him to stay with them as
long as he could.

3. The disciples at Tyre were
endowed with such gifts that they
could by the Spirit foretell the
troubles Paul would meet with at
Jerusalem; for *the Holy Ghost
witnessed it in every city, ch*. xx. 23.

Therefore they said to him, *by the
Spirit, that he should not go up*,
because they concluded it would be
most for the glory of God that he
should continue at liberty; and it
was not at all their fault to think
so, and consequently to dissuade
him; but it was their mistake, for
his trial would be for the glory of
God and the furtherance of the
gospel, and he knew it; and the
importunity that was used with
him, to dissuade him from it,
renders his pious and truly heroic
resolution the more illustrious.

4. The disciples of Tyre, though
they were none of Paul's converts,
yet showed a very great respect to
Paul, whose usefulness in the
church they had heard so much of
when he departed from Tyre.

5. They parted with prayer, as
Paul and the Ephesian elders had
done, *ch*. xx. 36. Thus Paul has
taught us by example, as well as
rule, to pray always, to pray without ceasing.

6. They parted at last (*v*. 6):*When
we had taken our leave one of
another*, with the most affectionate
embraces and expressions of love
and grief, *we took ship* to be gone,
and *they returned home again*, each
complaining that this is a parting
world.

IV. Their arrival at Ptolemais,
which was not far from Tyre (*v*. 7).
Paul begged leave to go ashore
there, *to salute the brethren,* to enquire of their state, and to testify
his good will to them.

A SECOND WARNING
(*vv*. 8–14)

We have here Paul and his company arrived at length at Cæsarea,

119

where he designed to make some stay, it being the place where the gospel was first preached to the Gentiles, and *the Holy Ghost fell upon them*, *ch.* x. 1, 44. Now here we are told,

I. Who it was that entertained Paul and his company *at Cæsarea*. He seldom had occasion to go to a public house, but, wherever he came, some friend or other took him in, and bade him welcome. Now at Cæsarea,

1. They were entertained by Philip the evangelist, whom we left at Cæsarea many years ago, after he had baptized the eunuch (*ch.* viii. 40), and there we now find him again.

2. This Philip *had four maiden daughters, who did prophesy, v.* 9. It intimates that they prophesied of Paul's troubles at Jerusalem, as others had done, and dissuaded him from going; or perhaps they prophesied for his comfort and encouragement, in reference to the difficulties that were before him. Here was a further accomplishment of that prophecy, Joel ii. 28, of such a plentiful pouring out of the Spirit upon all flesh that their *sons and their daughters should prophesy*, that is, foretell things to come.

II. A plain and full prediction of the sufferings of Paul, by a noted prophet, *vv.* 10, 11. *Agabus took Paul's girdle*, when he laid it by, or perhaps took it from about him, and with it *bound* first *his own hands, and then his own feet*, or perhaps bound his hands and feet together; this was designed both to confirm the prophecy (it was as sure to be done as if it were done already) and to affect those about him with

it, because that which we see usually makes a greater impression upon us than that which we only hear of. *Thus saith the Holy Ghost*, the Spirit of prophecy, *So shall the Jews at Jerusalem bind the man that owneth this girdle, and,* as they dealt with his Master (Matt. xx. 18, 19), *shall deliver him into the hands of the Gentiles,* as the Jews in other places had all along endeavoured to do, by accusing him to the Roman governors.

III. The great importunity which his friends used with him to dissuade him from going forward to Jerusalem, *v.* 12.

IV. The holy bravery and intrepidity with which Paul persisted in his resolution, *v.* 13.

1. He reproves them for dissuading him. Here is a quarrel of love on both sides, and very sincere and strong affections clashing with each other. They love him dearly, and therefore oppose his resolution; he loves them dearly, and therefore chides them for opposing it: *What mean you to weep and to break my heart?* They were an offence to him, as Peter was to Christ, when, in a like case, he said, *Master, spare thyself.* Their weeping about him *broke his heart*.

2. He repeats his resolution to go forward, notwithstanding. Now, (1) See how far his resolution extends: You are told that I must be bound at Jerusalem, and you would have me keep away for fear of this. I tell you, *I am ready not only to be bound, but,* if the will of God be so, *to die at Jerusalem;* not only to lose my liberty, but to lose my life." (2) See what it is that carries him out thus, that makes him willing

to suffer and die: it is *for the name of the Lord Jesus.* All that a man has will he give for his life; but life itself will Paul give for the service and honour of the name of Christ.

V. The patient acquiescence of his friends in his resolution, *v.* 14. 1. They submitted to the wisdom of a good man. They had carried the matter as far as they could with decency; but, "*when he would not be persuaded, we ceased* our importunity." They submitted to the will of a good God: *We ceased,* saying, *The will of the Lord be done.* They did not resolve his resolution into his stubbornness, but into his willingness to suffer, and God's will that he should.

PAUL ARRIVES AT JERUSALEM (*vv.* 15–26)

In these verses we have,

I. Paul's journey to Jerusalem from Cæsarea, and the company that went along with him.

II. Paul's welcome at Jerusalem. 1. Many of the brethren there *received him gladly, v.* 17. They *gladly received his word.* 2. They paid a visit to James and the elders of the church, at a church-meeting (*v.* 18). Paul saluted them all, paid his respects to them, enquired concerning their welfare, and gave them the right hand of fellowship.

III. The account they had from him of his ministry among the Gentiles, and their satisfaction in it. 1. He gave them a narrative of the success of the gospel in those countries where he had been employed, knowing it would be very acceptable to them to hear of the enlarging of Christ's kingdom. Observe how modestly he speaks, not what

things he had wrought (he was but the instrument), but what God had wrought by his ministry. It was *not I, but the grace of God which was with me.* He planted and watered, but God gave the increase. 2. Hence they took occasion to give praise to God (*v.* 20): *When they heard it, they glorified the Lord.* Paul ascribed it all to God, and to God they gave the praise of it.

IV. The request of James and the elders of the church at Jerusalem to Paul, or their advice rather, that he would gratify the believing Jews by showing some compliance with the ceremonial law, and appearing publicly in the temple to offer sacrifice, which was not a thing in itself sinful. It was dead, but not buried; dead, but not yet deadly. And, being not sinful, they thought it was a piece of prudence in Paul to conform thus far.

1. They desired him to take notice of the great numbers there were of the Jewish converts. The number of the names at first was but one hundred and twenty, yet now many thousands. Let none therefore despise the day of small things; for, though the beginning be small, God can make the latter end greatly to increase.

2. They informed him of a prevailing infirmity these believing Jews laboured under, of which they could not yet be cured: *They are all zealous of the law.* They believe in Christ as the true Messiah, they rest upon his righteousness and submit to his government; but they know the law of Moses was of God, they have found spiritual benefit in their attendance on the institutions of it, and therefore they can by no

means think of parting with it, no, nor of growing cold to it. This was a great weakness and mistake, to be so fond of the shadows when the substance was come, to keep their necks under a yoke of bondage when Christ had come to make them free. But see, (1) The power of education and long usage, and especially of a ceremonial law. (2) The charitable allowance that must be made in consideration of these. Their being zealous of the law was capable of a good construction, which charity would put upon it; and it was capable of a good excuse, considering what they were brought up in, and among whom they lived.

3. They gave him to understand that these Jews, who were so zealous of the law, were ill-affected to him, *v.* 21. Now, (1) It was true that Paul preached the abrogation of the law of Moses, taught them that it was impossible to be justified by it, and therefore we are not bound up any longer to the observance of it. But, (2) It was false that he taught them to forsake Moses; for the religion he preached tended not to destroy the law, but to fulfil it. He preached Christ (*the end of the law for righteousness*), and repentance and faith, in the exercise of which we are to make great use of the law.

4. They therefore desired Paul that he would by some public act, now that he had come to Jerusalem, make it appear that the charge against him was false, and that he did not teach people to forsake Moses and to break the customs of the Jewish church, for he himself retained the use of them.

(1) Now something must be done to satisfy them that Paul does not teach the people to forsake Moses, and they think it necessary, [1] For Paul's sake, that his reputation should be cleared. [2] For the people's sake, that they may not continue prejudiced against so good a man, nor lose the benefit of his ministry by those prejudices.

(2) They produce a fair opportunity which Paul might take to clear himself. *We have four men*, Jews who believe, of our own churches, and *they have a vow on them*, a vow of Nazariteship for a certain time; their time has now expired (*v.* 23), and they are to offer their offering according to the law, when they shave the head of their separation, a he-lamb for a burnt-offering, a ewe-lamb for a sin-offering, and a ram for a peace-offering, with other offerings appertinent to them, Num. vi. 13–20. Now Paul having so far of late complied with the law as to take upon him the vow of a Nazarite, and to signify the expiration of it by shaving his head at Cenchrea (*ch.* xviii. 18), according to the custom of those who lived at a distance from the temple, they desire him but to go a little further, and to join with these four in offering the sacrifices of a Nazarite. This, they think, will effectually stop the mouth of calumny, and every one will be convinced that the report was false, that Paul was not the man he was represented to be, did not teach the Jews to forsake Moses, but that he himself, being originally a Jew, walked orderly, and kept the law; and then all would be well.

5: They enter a protestation that this shall be no infringement at all of the decree lately made in favour of the Gentile converts, nor do they intend by this in the least to derogate from the liberty allowed them (*v.* 25).

V. Here is Paul's compliance with it. He was willing to gratify them in this matter. Though he would not be persuaded not to go to Jerusalem, yet, when he was there, he was persuaded to do as they there did, *v.* 26. Now it has been questioned whether James and the elders did well to give Paul this advice, and whether he did well to take it. 1. Some have blamed this occasional conformity of Paul's, as indulging the Jews too much in their adherence to the ceremonial law, and a discouragement of those who stood fast in the liberty wherewith Christ had made them free. But, 2. Others think the advice was prudent and good, and Paul's following it was justifiable enough, as the case stood. It was Paul's avowed principle, *To the Jews became I as a Jew, that I might gain the Jews,* 1 Cor. ix. 20. It is true, this compliance of Paul's sped ill to him, for this very thing by which he hoped to pacify the Jews did but provoke them, and bring him into trouble; yet this is not a sufficient ground to go upon in condemning it: Paul might do well, and yet suffer for it.

PAUL ARRESTED (*vv.* 27–40)

I. We have here Paul seized, and laid hold on.

1. He was seized in the temple, when he was there attending the days of his purifying, and the solemn services of those days, *v.* 27.

2. The informers against him were the Jews of Asia, not those of Jerusalem—the Jews of the dispersion, who knew him best, and who were most exasperated against him.

3. The method they took was to raise the mob, and to incense them against him.

4. The arguments wherewith they exasperated the people against him were popular, but very false and unjust. Note, The enemies of Christianity, since they could never prove it to be an ill thing, have been always very industrious, right or wrong, to put it into an ill name, and so run it down by outrage and outcry.

5. They charge upon him both bad doctrine and bad practice, and both against the Mosaic ritual.

(1) They charge upon him bad doctrine; not only that he holds corrupt opinions himself, but that he vents and publishes them.

(2) They charge upon him bad practices. He *has brought Gentiles also into the temple,* into the inner court of the temple, which none that were uncircumcised were admitted, under any pretence, to come into; there was written upon the wall that enclosed this inner court, in Greek and Latin, *It is a capital crime for strangers to enter.* —Joseph. *Antiq.* lib. xv. cap. 14. They had seen him with him in the city, and therefore they supposed that Paul had brought him with him into the temple, which was utterly false.

II. We have Paul in danger of being pulled in pieces by the rabble.

1. All the city was in an uproar,

v. 30. But God does not reckon himself at all honoured by those whose zeal for him transports them to such irregularities, and who, while they pretend to act for him, act in such a brutish barbarous manner.

2. They drew Paul out of the temple, and shut the doors between the outer and inner court of the temple, or perhaps the doors of the outer court. The officers of the temple shut the doors, either, [1] Lest Paul should find means to get back and take hold of the horns of the altar, and so protect himself by that sanctuary from their rage. Or rather, [2] Lest the crowd should by the running in of more to them be thrust back into the temple, and some outrage should be committed, to the profanation of that holy place.

3. They went about to kill him (*v.* 31), for they fell a beating him (*v.* 32), resolving to beat him to death by blows without number, a punishment which the Jewish doctors allowed in some cases (not at all to the credit of their nation), and called *the beating of the rebels*.

III. We have here Paul rescued out of the hands of his Jewish enemies by a Roman enemy.

IV. The provision which the chief captain made, with much ado, to bring Paul to speak for himself.

1. There was no knowing the sense of the people; for when the chief captain enquired concerning Paul, *some cried one thing, and some another*, among the multitude; so that it was impossible for the chief captain to know their mind, when really they knew not either one another's mind or their own, when every one pretended to give the sense of the whole body.

2. There was no quelling the rage and fury of the people; for when *the chief captain commanded that Paul should be carried into the castle*, the tower of Antonia, where the Roman soldiers kept garrison, near the temple, the soldiers themselves had much ado to get him safely thither out of the noise, the people were so violent (*v.* 35).

3. Paul at length begged leave of the chief captain to speak to him (*v.* 37).

4. The chief captain tells him what notion he had of him: *Canst thou speak Greek?* I am surprised to hear thee speak a learned language; for, *Art not thou that Egyptian who made an uproar?* The Jews made the uproar, and then would have it thought that Paul had given them occasion for it, by beginning first; for probably some of them whispered this in the ear of the chief captain. It seems, there had lately been an insurrection somewhere in that country, headed by an Egyptian, who took on him to be a prophet. The ringleader of this rebellion, it seems, had made his escape, and the chief captain concluded that one who lay under so great an odium as Paul seemed to lie under, and against whom there was so great an outcry, could not be a criminal of less figure than this Egyptian.

5. Paul rectifies his mistake concerning him, by informing him particularly what he was; not such a vagabond, a scoundrel, a rake, as that Egyptian, who could give no good account of himself. No: *I am a man who is a Jew* originally, and

no Egyptian—a Jew both by nation and religion; *I am of Tarsus, a city of Cilicia*, of honest parents and a liberal education (Tarsus was a university), and, besides that, *a citizen of no mean city*. Whether he means Tarsus or Rome is not certain; they were neither of them mean cities, and he was a freeman of both.

6. He humbly desired a permission from the chief captain, whose prisoner he now was, to speak to the people.

7. He obtained leave to plead his own cause, for he needed not to have counsel assigned him, when the Spirit of the Father was ready to dictate to him, Matt. x. 20. *The chief captain gave him license* (v. 40), so that now he could speak with a good grace, and with the more courage; he had, I will not say that favour, but that justice, done him by the chief captain, which he could not obtain from his countrymen the Jews; for they would not hear him, but the captain would, though it were but to satisfy his curiosity. This licence being obtained, (1) The people were attentive to hear. There he *beckoned with the hand unto the people*, made signs to them to be quiet and to have a little patience, for he had something to say to them; and so far he gained his point that every one cried hush to his neighbour, and there was made a profound silence. (2) Paul addressed himself to speak, well assured that he was serving the interest of Christ's kingdom as truly and effectually as if he had been preaching in the synagogue: he *spoke unto them in the Hebrew tongue*, that is, in their own vulgar tongue, which was the language of their country, to which he hereby owned not only an abiding relation, but an abiding respect.

CHAPTER TWENTY-TWO
PAUL GAINS A HEARING
(*vv.* 1–2)

Paul had, in the last verse of the foregoing chapter, gained a great point, by commanding so profound a silence after so loud a clamour. Now here observe,

I. With what an admirable composure and presence of mind he addresses himself to speak.

II. What respectful titles he gives even to those who thus abused him, and how humbly he craves their attention.

III. The language he spoke in, which recommended what he said to the auditory. *He spoke in the Hebrew tongue*, that is, the vulgar language of the Jews, which, at this time, was not the pure Old-Testament Hebrew, but the Syriac, a dialect of the Hebrew, or rather a corruption of it, as the Italian of the Latin.

PAUL'S DEFENCE
(*vv.* 3–21)

Paul here gives such an account of himself as might serve not only to satisfy the chief captain that he was not that Egyptian he took him to be, but the Jews also that he was not that enemy to their church and nation, to their law and temple, they took him to be, and that what he did in preaching Christ, and particularly in preaching him to the Gentiles, he did by a divine commission. He here gives them to understand,

I. What his extraction and education were. 1. That he was one of their own nation, *of the stock of Israel, of the seed of Abraham, a Hebrew of the Hebrews*, not of any obscure family, or a renegado of some other nation. 2. That he was born in a creditable reputable place, *in Tarsus, a city of Cilicia*, and was by his birth a freeman of that city. 3. That he had a learned and liberal education. He was not only a Jew, and a gentleman, but a scholar. 4. That he was in his early days a very forward and eminent professor of the Jews' religion; his studies and learning were all directed that way. So far was he from being principled in his youth with any disaffection to the religious usages of the Jews that there was not a young man among them who had a greater and more entire veneration for them than he had, was more strict in observing them himself, or more hot in enforcing them upon others.

II. What a fiery furious persecutor he had been of the Christian religion in the beginning of his time, *vv.* 4, 5. He mentions this to make it the more plainly and evidently to appear that the change which was wrought upon him, when he was converted to the Christian faith, was purely the effect of a divine power.

III. In what manner he was converted, and made what he now was. 1. He was as fully bent upon persecuting the Christians just before Christ arrested him as ever. He *made his journey, and was come nigh to Damascus* (*v.* 6), and had no other thought than to execute the cruel design he was sent upon. 2.

It was *a light from heaven* that first startled him, *a great light*, which *shone suddenly round about him*, and the Jews knew that God is light, and his angels angels of light, and that such a light as this shining at noon, and therefore exceeding that of the sun, must be from God. 3. It was a *voice from heaven* that first begat in him awful thoughts of Jesus Christ, of whom before he had had nothing but hateful spiteful thoughts. By which it appeared that this Jesus of Nazareth, whom they also were now persecuting, was one that spoke from heaven, and they knew it was dangerous resisting one that did so, Heb. xii. 25. 4. Lest it should be objected, "How came this light and voice to work such a change upon him, and not upon those that journeyed with him?" (though, it is very probable, it had a good effect upon them, and that they thereupon became Christians), he observes *that his fellow travellers saw indeed the light, and were afraid* they should be consumed with fire from heaven; but, though the light made them afraid, they heard not the voice of him that spoke to Paul, that is, they did not distinctly hear the words. 5. He assures them that when he was thus startled he referred himself entirely to a divine guidance; he did not hereupon presently cry out, "Well, I will be a Christian," but, "*What shall I do, Lord?* Let the same voice from heaven that has stopped me in the wrong way guide me into the right way, *v.* 10. 6. As a demonstration of the greatness of that light which fastened upon him, he tells them of the immediate effect it had upon his eye-sight (*v.* 11): *I could not see for the glory of that light*. Those that were with Paul had not the light so directly darted into their faces as Paul had into his, and therefore they were not blinded, as he was; yet, considering the issue, who would not rather have chosen his lot than theirs? They, having their sight, led *Paul by the hand into the city*.

IV. How he was confirmed in the change he had made, and further directed what he should do, by Ananias who lived at Damascus.

Observe, 1. The character here given of Ananias. He was not a man that was any way prejudiced against the Jewish nation or religion, but was himself *a devout man according to the law*; and he conducted himself so well that he had a *good report of all the Jews that dwelt at Damascus*.

2. The cure immediately wrought by him upon Paul's eyes, which miracle was to confirm Ananias's mission to Paul, and to ratify all that he should afterwards say to him.

3. The declaration which Ananias makes to him of the favour, the peculiar favour, which the Lord Jesus designed him above any other.

(1) In the present manifestation of himself to him (*v.* 14): *The God of our fathers has chosen thee*. This powerful call is the result of a particular choice. *This God of our fathers has chosen thee that thou shouldst*, [1] *Know his will*, the will of his precept that is to be done by thee, the will of his providence that is to be done concerning thee. He hath chosen thee that thou shouldst know it in a more peculiar manner; not of man nor by man, but

immediately by *the revelation of Christ*, Gal. i. 1, 12. [2] *That thou shouldst see that Just One, and shouldst hear the voice of his mouth*, and so shouldst know his will immediately from himself. This was what Paul was, in a particular manner, chosen to above others; it was a distinguishing favour, that he should see Christ here upon earth after his ascension into heaven.

(2) In the after-manifestation of himself by him to others (*v.* 15). He told them what God had done for his soul, to encourage them to hope that he would do something for their souls.

4. The counsel and encouragement he gave him to join himself to the Lord Jesus by baptism (*v.* 16): *Arise, and be baptized*.

V. How he was commissioned to go and preach the gospel to the Gentiles. This was the great thing for which they were so angry at him, and therefore it was requisite he should for this, in a special manner, produce a divine warrant; and here he does it. He tells them, 1. That he received his orders to do it when he was at prayer, begging of God to appoint him his work and to show him the course he should steer. Now as Paul's praying in the temple was an evidence, contrary to their malicious suggestion, that he had a veneration for the temple, though he did not make an idol of it as they did; so God's giving him this commission there in the temple was an evidence that the sending him to the Gentiles would be no prejudice to the temple, unless the Jews by their infidelity made it so. 2. He received it in a vision. He fell *into a trance*

(v. 17), his external senses, for the present, locked up; he was in an ecstasy, as when he was *caught up into the third heaven*, and was not at that time sensible whether he was *in the body or out of the body*. In this trance he saw Jesus Christ, not with the eyes of his body, as at his conversion, but represented to the eye of his mind (v. 18): *I saw him saying unto me.* 3. Before Christ gave him a commission to go to the Gentiles, he told him it was to no purpose for him to think of doing any good at Jerusalem; so that they must not blame him, but themselves, if he be sent to the Gentiles. 4. Paul, notwithstanding this, renewed his petition that he might be employed at Jerusalem, because they knew, better than any did, what he had been before his conversion, and therefore must ascribe so great a change in him to the power of almighty grace, and consequently give the greater regard to his testimony; thus he reasoned, both with himself and with the Lord, and thought he reasoned justly (vv. 19, 20). 5. Paul's petition for a warrant to preach the gospel at Jerusalem is overruled, and he has peremptory orders to go among the Gentiles (v. 21). It is God that appoints his labourers both their day and their place, and it is fit they should acquiesce in his appointment, though it may cross their own inclinations.

PAUL, THE FREEMAN
(vv. 22–30)

Paul was going on with this account of himself. But when he speaks of being sent to the Gentiles, though it was what Christ himself said to him, they cannot bear it, not so much as to hear the Gentiles named, such an enmity had they to them, and such a jealousy of them.

I. They interrupted him, by lifting up their voice, to put him into confusion, and that nobody might hear a word he said.

II. They clamoured against him as one that was unworthy of life, much more of liberty. Without weighing the arguments he had urged in his own defence, or offering to make any answer to them, they cried out with a confused noise, "*Away with such a fellow* as this *from the earth*, who pretends to have a commission to preach to the Gentiles; why, *it is not fit that he should live.*" He that was worthy of the greatest honours of life is condemned as not worthy of life itself.

III. They went stark mad against Paul, and against the chief captain for not killing him immediately at their request, or throwing him as a prey into their teeth, that they might devour him (v. 23).

IV. The chief captain took care for his safety, by ordering him to be brought into the castle, v. 24.

V. He ordered him the torture, to force from him a confession of some flagrant crimes which had provoked the people to such an uncommon violence against him.

VI. Paul pleaded his privilege as a Roman citizen, by which he was exempted from all trials and punishments of this nature (v. 25).

VII. The chief captain was surprised at this, and put into a fright. He had taken Paul to be a vagabond Egyptian, and wondered he could speak Greek (*ch.* xxi. 37), but is much more surprised now he finds that he is as good a gentleman as himself. Now, 1. The chief captain would be satisfied of the truth of this from his own mouth (*v.* 27): "*Tell me, art thou a Roman?*" 2. The chief captain very freely compares notes with him upon this matter, and it appears that the privilege Paul had as a Roman citizen was of the two more honourable than the colonel's; for the colonel owns that his was purchased. 3. This put an immediate stop to Paul's trouble. Those that were appointed to examine him by scourging quitted the spot; they *departed from him* (*v.* 29), lest they should run themselves into a snare. 4. The governor, the next day, brought Paul before the sanhedrim, *v.* 30. He first *loosed him from his bands,* and then summoned the chief priests and all their council to come together to take cognizance of Paul's case, for he found it to be a matter of religion, and therefore looked upon them to be the most proper judges of it. Gallio in this case discharged Paul; finding it to be a matter of their law, he drove the prosecutors from the judgment-seat (*ch.* xviii. 16), and would not concern himself at all in it: but this Roman, who was a military man, kept Paul in custody, and appealed from the rabble to the general assembly.

CHAPTER TWENTY-THREE
PAUL BEFORE THE COUNCIL
(*vv.* 1–5)

Here we have,

I. Paul's protestation of his own integrity. Whether the chief priest put any question to him, or the chief captain made any representation of his case to the court, we are not told; but Paul appeared here,

1. With a good courage. He was not at all put out of countenance upon his being brought before such an august assembly, for which in his youth he had conceived such a veneration; nor did he fear their calling him to an account about the letters they gave him to Damascus, to persecute the Christians there, though (for aught we know) this was the first time he had ever seen them since; but *he earnestly beheld the council.*

2. With a good conscience, and that gave him a good courage. He said, "*Men and brethren, I have lived in all good conscience before God unto this day.* I may be reproached, my heart does not reproach me, but witnesses for me."

II. The outrage of which Ananias the high priest was guilty: he *commanded those that stood by,* the beadles that attended the court, *to smite him on the mouth* (*v.* 2), to give him a dash on the teeth, either with a hand or with a rod. 1. The high priest was highly offended at Paul; some think, because he looked so boldly and earnestly at the council, as if he would face them down; others because he did not address himself particularly to him as president, with some title of honour and respect, but spoke freely and familiarly to them all, as men and brethren. 2. In his rage he ordered him to be smitten, so to put disgrace upon him, and to be smitten on the mouth, as having offended with his lips, and in token of his enjoining him silence.

III. The denunciation of the wrath of God against the high priest for this *wickedness in the place of judgment* (Eccl. iii. 16). Paul did not speak this in any sinful heat or passion, but in a holy zeal against the high priest's abuse of his power, and with something of a prophetic spirit, not at all with a spirit of revenge. 1. He gives him his due character: *Thou whited wall*; that is, thou hypocrite—a mud-wall, trash and dirt and rubbish underneath, but plastered over, or whitewashed. 2. He reads him his just doom: *"God shall smite thee."* 3. He assigns a good reason for that doom: "For *sittest thou* there as president in the supreme judicature of the church, pretending *to judge me after the law*, to convict and condemn me by the law, and yet *commandest me to be smitten* before any crime is proved upon me, which is *contrary to the law?"*

IV. The offence which was taken at this bold word of Paul's (*v.* 4): *Those that stood by said, Revilest thou God's high priest?*

V. The excuse that Paul made for what he had said, because he found it was a stumbling-block to his weak brethren, and might prejudice them against him in other things. He wished he had not done it; and though he did not beg the high priest's pardon, nor excuse it to him, yet he begs their pardon who took offence at it, because this was not a time to inform them better, nor to say what he could say to justify himself. 1. He

excuses it with this, that he did not consider when he said it to whom he spoke (*v* 5): *I wist not, brethren, that he was the high priest* I see not how we can with any probability think that Paul did not know him to be the high priest, for Paul had been seven days in the temple at the time of the feast, where he could not miss of seeing the high priest; and his telling him that *he sat to judge him after the law* shows that he knew who he was; but, says he, I did not consider it. Yet, 2. He takes care that what he had said should not be drawn into a precedent, to the weakening of the obligation of that law in the least: *For it is written*, and it remains a law in full force, *Thou shalt not speak evil of the ruler of thy people.*

PAUL DIVIDES THE OPPOSITION (*vv.* 6–11)

I. Paul's own prudence and ingenuity stand him in some stead, and contribute much to his escape. The honest policy Paul used here for his own preservation was to divide his judges, and to set them at variance one with another about him; and, by incensing one part of them more against him, to engage the contrary part for him.

1. The great council was made up of Sadducees and Pharisees, and Paul perceived it. Now these differed very much from one another, and yet they ordinarily agreed well enough to do the business of the council together. (1) The Pharisees were bigots, zealous for the ceremonies, not only those which God had appointed, but those which

were enjoined by the tradition of the elders. But at the same time they were very orthodox in the faith of the Jewish church concerning the world of spirits, the resurrection of the dead, and the life of the world to come. (2) The Sadducees were deists—no friends to the scripture, or divine revelation. The books of Moses they admitted as containing a good history and a good law, but had little regard to the other books of the Old Testament; see Matt. xxii. 23. The account here given of these Sadducees is, [1] That they *deny the resurrection*; not only the return of the body to life, but a future state of rewards and punishments. [2] That they denied the existence of angels and spirits, and allowed of no being but matter. They thought that God himself was corporeal, and had parts and members as we have.

2. In this matter of difference between the Pharisees and Sadducees Paul openly declared himself to be on the Pharisees' side against the Sadducees (*v.* 6). Though Paul preached against the traditions of the elders (as his Master had done), and therein opposed the Pharisees, yet he valued himself more upon his preaching the resurrection of the dead, and a future state, in which he concurred with the Pharisees.

3. This occasioned a division in the council. It is probable that the high priest sided with the Sadducees (as he had done *ch.* v. 17, and made it to appear by his rage at Paul, *v.* 2), which alarmed the Pharisees so much the more; but so it was, there arose a *dissension*

between the Pharisees and the Sadducees (*v.* 7), for this word of Paul's made the Sadducees more warm and the Pharisees more cool in the prosecution of him; so that *the multitude was divided.*

4. The Pharisees hereupon (would one think it?) took Paul's part (*v.* 9). Nay, they go further, "*If a spirit or an angel hath spoken to him* concerning Jesus, and put him upon preaching as he does, though we may not be so far satisfied as to give credit to him, yet we ought to be cautioned not to oppose him, *lest we be found fighting against God*;" as Gamaliel, who was himself a Pharisee, had argued, *ch.* v. 39.

II. The chief captain's care and conduct stand him in more stead. 1. See here Paul's danger. Between his friends and his enemies he had like to have been pulled to pieces. 2. His deliverance: *The chief captain ordered his soldiers to go down* from the upper wards, and *to take them by force from among them,* out of that apartment in *the temple* where he had ordered the council to meet, and *to bring him into the castle,* or tower of Antonia; for he saw he could make nothing of them towards the understanding of the merits of his cause.

III. Divine consolations stood him in most stead of all. Then did the Lord Jesus make him a kind visit, and, though at midnight, yet a very seasonable one (*v.* 11). 1. Christ bids him have a good heart upon it: "*Be of good cheer, Paul*; be not discouraged; let not what has happened sadden thee, nor let what may yet be before thee frighten thee." 2. It is a strange argument which he makes use of to encourage him: *As thou hast testified of me in Jerusalem, so must thou bear witness also at Rome.* One would think this was but cold comfort: "As thou hast undergone a great deal of trouble for me so thou must undergo a great deal more;" and yet this was designed to encourage him; for hereby he is given to understand, (1) That he had been serving Christ as a witness for him in what he had hitherto endured. It was for no fault that he was buffeted, and it was not his former persecuting of the church that was now remembered against him, however he might remember it against himself, but he was still going on with his work. (2) That he had not yet finished his testimony, nor was, by his imprisonment, laid aside as useless, but was only reserved for further service.

A PLOT AGAINST PAUL
(*vv.* 12–35)

We have here the story of a plot against the life of Paul; how it was laid, how it was discovered, and how it was defeated.

I. How this plot was laid. They found they could gain nothing by popular tumult, or legal process, and therefore have recourse to the barbarous method of assassination; they will come upon him suddenly, and stab him, if they can but get him within their reach. Now observe here,

1. Who they were that formed this conspiracy. They were *certain Jews* that had the utmost degree of indignation against him because he

was the apostle of the Gentiles, *v.* 12. *And they were more than forty* that were in the design, *v.* 13.

2. When the conspiracy was formed: *When it was day.* In the night Christ appeared to Paul to protect him, and, when it was day, here were forty men appearing against him to destroy him; they were not up so soon but Christ was up before them.

3. What the conspiracy was. These men *banded together* in a league, perhaps they called it a *holy* league; they engaged to stand by one another, and every one, to his power, to be aiding and assisting to murder Paul.

4. How firm they made it, as they thought, that none of them might fly off, upon conscience of the horror of the fact, at second thoughts: *They bound themselves under an anathema*, imprecating the heaviest curses upon themselves, their souls, bodies, and families, if they did not kill Paul, and so quickly *that they would not eat nor drink till they had done it.*

5. What method they took to bring it about. Having been all day employed in engaging one another to this wickedness, towards evening they come to the principal members of the great sanhedrim, and, though they might have concealed their mean design and yet might have moved them upon some other pretence to send for Paul, they are so confident of their approbation of this villainy, that they are not ashamed nor afraid to own to them *that they have bound themselves under a great curse*, without consulting the priests first whether they might lawfully do it *that they*

will eat nothing the next day *till they have killed Paul.* And yet, vile as the proposal was which was made to them (for aught that appears), the priests and elders consented to it, and at the first word, without boggling at it in the least, promised to gratify them.

II. How the plot was discovered. See here,

1. How it was discovered to Paul, *v.* 16. There was a youth that was related to Paul, *his sister's son,* whose mother probably lived in Jerusalem; and some how or other, we are not told how, *he heard of their lying in wait,* either overheard them talking of it among themselves, or got intelligence from some that were in the plot: and *he went into the castle,* probably, as he used to do, to attend on his uncle, and bring him what he wanted, which gave him a free access to him, and *he told Paul* what he heard.

2. How it was discovered to the chief captain by the young man that told it to Paul. This part of the story is related very particularly, perhaps because the penman was an eye-witness of the prudent and successful management of this affair, and remembered it with a great deal of pleasure.

III. How the plot was defeated: The chief captain resolves to send him away with all speed out of their reach.

1. He orders a considerable detachment of the Roman forces under his command to get ready *to go to Cæsarea* with all expedition, and to bring Paul thither to *Felix the governor,* where he might sooner expect to have justice done him than by the great sanhedrim at Jerusalem. See how justly God brought the Jewish nation under the Roman yoke, when such a party of the Roman army was necessary to restrain them from the most execrable villainies!

2. The chief captain orders, for the greater security of Paul, that he be taken away at *the third hour of the night,* which some understand of three hours after sun-set, that, it being now soon after *the feast of pentecost* (that is, in the midst of summer), they might have the cool of the night to march in. Others understand it of *three hours after midnight, in the third watch, about three in the morning,* that they might have the day before them, and might get out of Jerusalem before Paul's enemies were stirring, and so might prevent any popular tumult, and leave them to roar when they rose, like a lion disappointed of his prey.

3. *He writes a letter to Felix the governor* of this province, by which he discharges himself from any further care about Paul, and leaves the whole matter with Felix.

4. Paul was accordingly conducted to Cæsarea.

5. He was delivered into the hands of Felix, as his prisoner, *v.* 33. (1) He promises him a speedy trial (*v.* 35): "*I will hear thee when thine accusers have come,* and will have an ear open to both sides, as becomes a judge." (2) He ordered him into custody, that he should *be kept* a prisoner *in Herod's judgment-hall,* in some apartment belonging to that palace which was denominated from Herod the Great, who built it.

CHAPTER TWENTY-FOUR
THE CASE AGAINST PAUL
(*vv.* 1–9)

We must suppose *that Lysias, the chief captain*, when he had *sent away Paul to Cæsarea*, gave notice to the chief priests, and others that had appeared against Paul, that if they had any thing to accuse him of they must follow him to Cæsarea, and there they would find him, and a judge ready to hear them— thinking, perhaps, they would not have given themselves so much trouble; but what will not malice do?

I. We have here the cause followed against Paul, and it is vigorously carried on. 1. Here is no time lost, for they are ready for a hearing *after five days*; all other business is laid aside immediately, to prosecute Paul; so intent are evil men to do evil! 2. Those who had been his judges do themselves appear here as his prosecutors. *Ananias* himself *the high priest*, who had sat to judge him, now stands to inform against him. *The elders* attended him, to signify their concurrence with him, and to invigorate the prosecution; for they could not find any attorneys or solicitors that would follow it with so much violence as they desired.

II. We have here the cause pleaded against Paul. The prosecutors brought *with them a certain orator named Tertullus*, a Roman, skilled in the Roman law and language, and therefore fittest to be employed in a cause before *the Roman governor*, and most likely to gain favour. His speech (or at

least an abstract of it, for it appears, by Tully's orations, that the Roman lawyers, on such occasions, used to make long harangues) is here reported, and it is made up of flattery and falsehood; it calls evil good, and good evil.

1. One of the worst of men is here applauded as one of the best of benefactors, only because he was the judge. Felix is represented by the historians of his own nation, as well as by Josephus the Jew, as a very bad man, who, depending upon his interest in the court, allowed himself in all manner of wickedness, was a great oppressor, very cruel, and very covetous, patronising and protecting assassins.—Joseph. *Antiq.* lib. xx. cap. 6. And yet Tertullus here, in the name of the high priest and elders, and probably by particular directions from them and according to the instructions of his brief, compliments him, and extols him to the sky, as if he were so good a magistrate as never was the like.

2. One of the best of men is here accused as one of the worst of malefactors, only because he was the prisoner. Two things Tertullus here complains of to Felix, in the name of the high priest and the elders:

(1) That the peace of the nation was disturbed by Paul.

[1] Paul was a useful man, and a great blessing to his country, a man of exemplary candour and goodness, obliging to all, and provoking to none; and yet he is here called *a pestilent fellow* (*v.* 5).

[2] Paul was a peace-maker, was a preacher of that gospel which has a direct tendency to *slay all*

enmities, and to establish true and lasting peace; he lived peaceably and quietly himself, and taught others to do so too, and yet is here represented as *a mover of sedition among all the Jews throughout all the world.*

[3] Paul was a man of catholic charity, who did not affect to be singular, but made himself the servant of all for their good; and yet he is here charged as being a *ringleader of the sect of the Nazarenes*, a standard-bearer of that sect, so the word signifies. Now it was true that Paul was an active leading man in propagating Christianity. But, *First*, It was utterly false that this was a sect; he did not draw people to a party or private opinion, nor did he make his own opinions their rule. True Christianity establishes that which is of common concern to all mankind, published good-will to men, and shows us God in Christ reconciling the world to himself, and therefore cannot be thought to take its rise from such narrow opinions and private interests as sects owe their origin to. *Secondly*, It is invidiously called *the sect of the Nazarenes*, by which Christ was represented as of Nazareth, whence no good thing was expected to arise; whereas he was of Bethlehem, where the Messiah was to be born. *Thirdly*, It was false that Paul was the author or standard-bearer of this sect; for he did not draw people to himself, but to Christ—did not preach himself, but Christ Jesus.

[4] Paul had a veneration for the temple, as it was the place which God had chosen to put his name there, and had lately himself with reverence attended the temple-service; and yet it is here charged upon him that he went about to *profane the temple*, and that he designedly put contempt upon it, and violated the laws of it, *v.* 6. Their proof of this failed; for what they alleged as matter of fact was utterly false, and they knew it, *ch.* xxi. 29.

(2) That the course of justice against Paul was obstructed by the chief captain. [1] They pleaded that they *took him, and would have judged him according to their law.* [2] They reflected upon the chief captain as having done them an injury in rescuing Paul out of their hands; whereas he therein not only did him justice, but them the greatest kindness that could be, in preventing the guilt they were bringing upon themselves. [3] They referred the matter to Felix and his judgment, yet seeming uneasy that they were under a necessity of doing so, the chief captain having obliged them to it (*v.* 8).

III. The assent of the Jews to this charge which Tertullus exhibited (*v.* 9): *They confirmed it, saying that those things were so.*

PAUL'S DEFENCE (*vv.* 10–21)

We have here Paul's defence of himself, in answer to Tertullus's charge. And here,

I. He addressed himself very respectfully to the governor, and with a confidence that he would do him justice. Here are no such flattering compliments as Tertullus soothed him up with, but, which was more truly respectful, a profession that he *answered for himself cheerfully*, and with good assurance *before him*, looking upon him, though not as one that was his friend, yet as one that would be fair and impartial. He thus expresses his expectation that he would be so, to engage him to be so.

II. He denies the facts that he was charged with, upon which their character of him was grounded. Now he would have him to understand (and what he said he was ready, if required, to make out by witnesses),

1. That he came up to Jerusalem on purpose to worship God in peace and holiness, so far was he from any design to move sedition among the people, or to profane the temple. He came to keep up his communion with the Jews, not to put any affront upon them.

2. That it was but twelve days since he came up to Jerusalem, and he had been six days a prisoner; he was alone, and it could not be supposed that in so short a time he could do the mischief they charged upon him. And, as for what he had done in other countries, they knew nothing of it but by uncertain report, by which the matter was very unfairly represented.

3. That he had demeaned himself at Jerusalem very quietly and peaceably, and had made no manner of stir. If it had been true (as they alleged) that he was a *mover of sedition among all the Jews*, surely he would have been industrious to make a party at Jerusalem: but he did not do so. (1) He had nothing in him of a contradicting spirit, as the movers of sedition have; he had no disposition to quarrel or oppose. They never found him *dis-puting with any man*. (2) He had nothing in him of a turbulent spirit: "They never found me *raising up the people*, by incensing them against their governors in church or state or suggesting to them fears and jealousies concerning public affairs, nor by setting them at variance one with another or sowing discord among them."

4. That as to what they had charged him with, of moving sedition in other countries, he was wholly innocent, and they could not make good the charge (*v.* 13): *Neither can they prove the things whereof they now accuse me*.

III. He gives a fair and just account of himself, which does at once both clear him from crime and likewise intimate what was the true reason of their violence in prosecuting him.

1. He acknowledges himself to be one whom they looked upon as a heretic, and that was the reason of their spleen against him. I confess that *in the way which they call heresy*—or a *sect, so worship I the God of my fathers*.

2. He vindicates himself from this imputation. They call Paul a heretic, but he is not so; for,

(1) He *worships the God of his fathers*, and therefore is right in the object of his worship.

(2) He *believes all things which are written in the law and the prophets*, and therefore is right in the rule of his worship.

(3) He has his eye upon a future state, and is a believing expectant of that, and therefore is right in the end of his worship.

(4) His way of life is of a piece with his devotion (*v.* 16): *And*

herein do I exercise myself, to have always a conscience void of offence towards God and towards men. Prophets and their doctrine were to be tried by their fruits. Observe, [1] What was Paul's aim and desire: To *have a conscience void of offence.* Either, *First,* "A conscience not offending; not informing me wrong, nor flattering me, nor dealing deceitfully with me, nor in any thing misleading me." Or, *Secondly,* A conscience not offended; it is like Job's resolution, "*My heart shall not reproach me,*" that is, I will never give it any occasion to do so. [2] What was his care and endeavour, in pursuance of this: "I make it my constant business, and govern myself by this intention." [3] The extent of this care: *First,* To all times: *To have always a conscience void of offence,* always void of gross offence; for though Paul was conscious to himself that he *had not yet attained perfection,* and the evil that he would not do yet he did, yet he was *innocent from the great transgression. Secondly,* To all things: *Both towards God, and towards man.* His conscientious care extended itself to the whole of his duty, and he was afraid of breaking the law of love either to God or his neighbour. [4] The inducement to it: "Because I look for the resurrection of the dead and the life of the world to come, therefore I thus exercise myself." The consideration of the future state should engage us to be universally conscientious in our present state.

IV. Having made confession of his faith, he gives a plain and faithful account of his case, and of the wrong done him by his persecutors.

(1) It was very hard to accuse him as an *enemy to their nation,* when after long absence from Jerusalem he came to *bring alms to his nation,* money which (though he had need enough himself of it) he had collected among his friends, for the relief of the poor at Jerusalem. (2) It was very hard to accuse him of having profaned the temple when he brought offerings to the temple, and was himself at charges therein (*ch.* xxi. 24), and was found *purifying himself in the temple,* according to the law (*v.* 18), and that in a very quiet decent manner, *neither with multitude nor with tumult.*

2. In the council: "Since the Jews of Asia are not here to prove any thing upon me done amiss in the temple, let *these same* that are *here,* the high priest and the elders, say whether they have *found any evil doing in me,* or whether I was guilty of any misdemeanour *when I stood before the council,* when also they were ready to pull me in pieces, *v.* 20. When I was there, they could not take offence at any thing I said; for all I said was, *Touching the resurrection of the dead I am called in question by you this day* (*v.* 21), which gave no offence to any one but the Sadducees. This I hope was no crime, that I stuck to that which is the faith of the whole Jewish church, excepting those whom they themselves call heretics."

FELIX POSTPONES JUDGMENT (*vv.* 22–27)

We have here the result of Paul's trial before Felix, and what was the consequence of it.

I. Felix adjourned the cause, and took further time to consider of it (*v.* 22). Now, 1. It was a disappointment to the high priest and the elders that Paul was not condemned, or remitted to their judgment, which they wished for and expected. 2. It was an injury to Paul that he was not released. It is a wrong not only to deny justice, but to delay it.

II. He detained the prisoner in custody, and would not take bail for him; else here at Cæsarea Paul had friends enough that would gladly have been his security. The high priest and the elders grudged him his life, but Felix generously allows him a sort of liberty; for he had not those prejudices against him and his way that they had. He also gave orders that none of his friends should be hindered from coming to him; the centurion must not forbid any of his acquaintances from ministering to him; and a man's prison is as it were his own house, if he had but his friends about him.

III. He had frequent conversation with him afterwards in private, once particularly, not long after his public trial, *vv.* 24, 25. Observe.

1. With what design *Felix sent for Paul*. He had a mind to have some talk with him *concerning the faith in Christ*, the Christian religion: he had some knowledge of that way, but he desired to have an account of it from Paul, who was so celebrated a preacher of that faith, above the rest.

2. What the account was which Paul gave him of the Christian religion; by the idea he had of it, he expected to be amused with a mystical divinity, but, as Paul represents it to him, he is alarmed

with a practical divinity. Paul, being asked *concerning the faith in Christ, reasoned* (for Paul was always a rational preacher) concerning *righteousness, temperance, and judgment to come.* It is probable that he mentioned the peculiar doctrines of Christianity concerning the death and resurrection of the Lord Jesus, and his being *the Mediator between God and man*; but he hastened to his application, in which he designed to come home to the consciences of his hearers. Felix and Drusilla were such hardened sinners that it was not at all likely they should be brought to repentance by Paul's preaching, especially under such disadvantages; and yet Paul deals with them as one that did not despair of them.

3. What impressions Paul's discourse made upon this great but wicked man. Paul never trembled before him, but he was made to tremble before Paul. See here, (1) The power of the word of God, when it comes with commission; it is searching, it is startling, it can strike a terror into the heart of the most proud and daring sinner, by *setting his sins in order before him*, and showing him *the terrors of the Lord.* (2) The workings of natural conscience; when it is startled and awakened, it fills the soul with horror and amazement at its own deformity and danger.

4. How Felix struggled to get clear of these impressions, and to shake off the terror of his convictions; he did by them as he did by Paul's prosecutors (*v.* 25), *he deferred them*; he said, *Go thy way for this time, when I have a convenient season I will call for thee.*

Note, [1] Many lose all the benefit of their convictions for want of striking while the iron is hot. If Felix, now that he trembled, had but asked, as Paul and the jailer did when they trembled, *What shall I do?* he might have been brought to the faith of Christ, and have been a *Felix* indeed, *happy* for ever; but, by dropping his convictions now, he lost them for ever, and himself with them. [2] In the affairs of our souls, delays are dangerous; nothing is of more fatal consequence than men's putting off their conversion from time to time.

IV. After all, he detained him a prisoner, and left him so, when two years after he was removed from the government, *vv.* 26, 27.

CHAPTER TWENTY-FIVE

PAUL BEFORE FESTUS
(*vv.* 1–12)

We commonly say, "New lords, new laws, new customs;" but here was a new governor, and yet Paul had the same treatment from him that he had from the former, and no better. Festus, like Felix, is not so just to him as he should have been, for he does not release him; and yet not so unjust to him as the Jews would have had him to be, for he will not condemn him to die, nor expose him to their rage. Here is,

I. The pressing application which the high priest and other Jews used with the governor to persuade him to abandon Paul; for to send him to Jerusalem was in effect to abandon him.

II. The governor's resolution that

Paul shall take his trial at Cæsarea, where he now is, *vv.* 4, 5. See how he manages the prosecutors. 1. He will not do them the kindness to send for him to Jerusalem; no, he gave orders *that Paul should be kept at Cæsarea*. 2. Yet he will do them the justice to hear what they have to say against Paul, if they will go down to Cæsarea, and appear against him there.

III. Paul's trial before Festus. Festus stayed *at Jerusalem about ten days*, and then *went down to Cæsarea*, and the prosecutors, it is likely, in his retinue. Now here we have, 1. The court set, and the prisoner called to the bar. Festus *sat in the judgment-seat*, as he used to do when any cause was brought before him that was of consequence, and he *commanded Paul to be brought*, and to make his appearance, *v.* 6. 2. The prosecutors exhibiting their charges against the prisoner (*v.* 7): *The Jews stood round about*, which intimates that they were many. They charged him with high crimes and misdemeanors. 3. The prisoner's insisting upon his own vindication, *v.* 8. (1) He had not violated the law of the Jews, not taught any doctrine destructive of it. (2) He had not profaned the temple, nor put any contempt at all upon the temple-service; his helping to set up the gospel temple did not at all offend against that temple which was a type of it. (3) He had not offended against Cæsar, nor his government.

IV. Paul's appeal to the emperor, and the occasion of it. This gave the cause a new turn. Whether he had before designed it, or whether it was a sudden resolve upon the present provocation, does not appear; but God puts it into his heart to do it, for the bringing about of that which he had said to him, *that he must bear witness to Christ at Rome*, for there the emperor's court was, *ch.* xxiii. 11. We have here,

1. The proposal which Festus made to Paul to go and take his trial at Jerusalem, *v.* 9.

2. Paul's refusal to consent to it, and his reasons for it. He knew, if he were removed to Jerusalem, notwithstanding the utmost vigilance of the president, the Jews would find some means or other to be the death of him; and therefore desires to be excused, and pleads, (1) That, as a citizen of Rome, it was most proper for him to be tried, not only by the president, but in that which was properly his court, which sat at Cæsarea: *I stand at Cæsar's judgment-seat, where I ought to be judged*, in the city which is the metropolis of the province. (2) That, as a member of the Jewish nation, he had done nothing to make himself obnoxious to them. (3) That he was willing to abide by the rules of the law, and to let that take its course, *v.* 11.

3. His appealing to court. "*I appeal unto Cæsar*. Rather than be delivered to the Jews" (which Festus seems inclined to consent to) "let me be delivered to Nero."

V. The judgment given upon the whole matter. Paul is neither released nor condemned. 1. The president takes advice upon the matter: *He conferred with the council*—not with the council of the Jews, but with his own counsellors, who were always ready to assist the governor with their advice. 2. He determines to send him to Rome. Some think Paul meant not an appeal to Cæsar's person, but only to his court, the sentence of which he would abide by, rather than be remitted to the Jew's council, and that Festus might have chosen whether he would have sent him to Rome, or, at least, whether he would have joined issue with him upon the appeal. But it should seem, by what Agrippa said (*ch.* xxvi. 32), that *he might have been set at liberty if he had not appealed to Cæsar*—that, by the course of the Roman law, a Roman citizen might appeal at any time to a superior court, even to the supreme. Festus, therefore, either of choice or of course, comes to this resolution: *Hast thou appealed unto Cæsar? Unto Cæsar thou shalt go.*

PAUL BEFORE AGRIPPA
(*vv.* 13–27)

We have here the preparation that was made for another hearing of Paul before king Agrippa, not in order to his giving judgment upon him, but in order to his giving advice concerning him, or rather only to gratify his curiosity. Here is,

I. The kind and friendly visit which king Agrippa made to Festus, now upon his coming into the government in that province (*v.* 13). Observe,

1. Who the visitants were. (1) King Agrippa, the son of that Herod (surnamed *Agrippa*) who killed James the apostle, and was himself eaten of worms, and great grandson of Herod the Great, under whom Christ was born. (2)

Bernice came with him. She was his own sister, now a widow, the widow of his uncle Herod, king of Chalcis, after whose death she lived with this brother of hers, who was suspected to be too familiar with her, and, after she was a second time married to Polemon king of Cilicia, she got to be divorced from him, and returned to her brother king Agrippa.

2. What the design of this visit was: they *came to salute Festus*, to give him joy of his new promotion, and to wish him joy in it.

II. The account which Festus gave to king Agrippa of Paul and his case.

(1) He found him a prisoner when he came into the government of this province; and therefore could not of his own knowledge give an account of his cause from the beginning.

(2) That the Jewish sanhedrim were extremely set against him. These being great pretenders to religion, and therefore to be supposed men of honour and honesty, Festus thinks he ought to give credit to them; but Agrippa knows them better than he does, and therefore Festus desires his advice in this matter.

(3) That he had insisted upon the Roman law in favour of the prisoner, and would not condemn him unheard (*v.* 16).

(4) That he had brought him upon his trial, according to the duty of his place, *v.* 17. He called a great court on purpose for the trial of Paul, that the sentence might be definitive, and the cause ended.

(5) That he was extremely *disap-*

pointed in the charge they brought against him (*vv.* 18, 19): *When he accusers stood up against him,* and opened their indictment, *they brought no accusations of such things as I supposed.*

(6) That therefore he had proposed to Paul that the cause might be adjourned to the Jewish courts, as best able to take cognizance of an affair of this nature (*v.* 20).

(7) That Paul had chosen rather to remove his cause to Rome than to Jerusalem, as expecting fairer play from the emperor than from the priests.

III. The bringing of him before Agrippa, that he might have the hearing of his cause.

1. The king desired it (*v.* 22). Agrippa would not for all the world have gone to a meeting to hear Paul preach, any more than Herod to hear Jesus; and yet they are both glad to have them brought before them, only to satisfy their curiosity.

2. Festus granted it: *To-morrow thou shalt hear him.*

3. Great preparation was made for it (*v.* 23): *The next day* there was a great appearance *in the place of hearing,* Paul and his cause being much talked of, and the more for their being much talked against.

IV. The speech with which Festus introduced the cause, when the court, or rather the audience, was set, which is much to the same purport with the account he had just now given to Agrippa. He could not as yet write *any thing certain* concerning Paul; so confused were the informations that were given in against him, and so inconsistent, that Festus could make nothing at all of them. He therefore desired

Paul might thus be publicly examined, that he might be advised by them what to write.

PAUL'S ADDRESS TO AGRIPPA (vv. 1–11)

I. Paul addressed himself with a very particular respect to Agrippa, *vv.* 2, 3. He answered cheerfully before Felix, because he knew he had been *many years a judge to that nation*, ch. xxiv. 10. But his opinion of Agrippa goes further. Observe, 1. Being accused of the Jews, and having many base things laid to his charge, he is glad he has an opportunity of clearing himself; so far is he from imagining that his being an apostle exempted him from the jurisdiction of the civil powers. Magistracy is an ordinance of God, which we have all benefit by, and therefore must all be subject to. 2. Since he is forced to answer for himself, he is glad it is before king Agrippa, who, being himself a proselyte to the Jewish religion, understood all matters relating to it better than the other Roman governors did. 3. He therefore begs that he would *hear him patiently, with long suffering*. Paul designs a long discourse, and begs that Agrippa will hear him out, and not be weary.

II. He professes that though he was hated and branded as an apostate, yet he still adhered to all that good which he was first educated and trained up in; his religion was always built upon the *promise of God made unto the fathers*; and this he still built upon.

See here what his religion is. He has not indeed such a zeal for the ceremonial law as he had in his youth. The sacrifices and offerings appointed by that, he thinks, are superseded by the great sacrifice which they typified; ceremonial pollutions and purifications from them he makes no conscience of, and thinks the Levitical priesthood is honourably swallowed up in the priesthood of Christ; but for the main principles of his religion he is as zealous for them as ever, and more so, and resolves to live and die by them.

(1) His religion is built upon the *promise made of God unto the fathers*. It is built upon divine revelation, which he receives and believes, and ventures his soul upon; it is built upon divine grace, and that grace manifested and conveyed by promise. The promise of God is the guide and ground of his religion, the promise *made to the fathers*, which was more ancient than the ceremonial law, *that covenant which was confirmed before of God in Christ, and which the law, that was not till four hundred and thirty years after, could not disannul*, Gal. iii. 17. Christ and heaven are the two great doctrines of the gospel—that *God has given to us eternal life, and this life is in his Son.* Now these two are the matter of the *promise made unto the fathers*.

(2) His religion consists in the hopes of this promise. He places it not, as they did, in meats and drinks, and the observance of carnal ordinances. Paul had no confidence in the flesh, but in Christ; no expectation at all of great things in this world, but of greater things in the other world than any this

world can pretend to; he had his eye upon a future state.

Herein he concurred with all the pious Jews; his faith was not only according to the scripture, but according to the testimony of the church, which was a support to it. Now all the Israelites profess to believe in this promise, both of Christ and heaven, and hope to come to the benefits of them. They all hope for a Messiah to come, and we that are Christians hope in a Messiah already come; so that we all agree to build upon the same promise. They look for the *resurrection of the dead* and *the life of the world to come*, and this is what I look for.

This was what he was now suffering for—for preaching that doctrine which they themselves, if they did but understand themselves aright, must own.

(5) This was what he would persuade all that heard him cordially to embrace (v. 8): *Why should it be thought a thing incredible with you that God should raise the dead?* This seems to come in somewhat abruptly; but it is probable Paul said much more than is here recorded, and that he explained the *promise made to the fathers* to be the promise of the resurrection and eternal life, and proved that he was in the right way of pursuing his hope of that happiness because he believed in Christ who had *risen from the dead*, which was a pledge and earnest of that resurrection which the fathers hoped for.

III. He acknowledges that while he continued a Pharisee he was a bitter enemy to Christians and Christianity, and thought he ought

to be so, and continued so to the moment that Christ wrought that wonderful change in him. This he mentions,

1. To show that his becoming a Christian and a preacher was not the product and result of any previous disposition or inclination that way, or any gradual advance of thought in favour of the Christian doctrine; he did not reason himself into Christianity by a chain of arguments, but was brought into the highest degree of an assurance of it, immediately from the highest degree of prejudice against it, by which it appeared that he was made a Christian and a preacher by a supernatural power.

2. Perhaps he designs it for such an excuse of his prosecutors as Christ made for his, when he said, *They know not what they do.*

PAUL RELATES HIS CONVERSION
(vv. 12–23)

Paul here, by a plain and faithful narrative of matters of fact, makes it out to this august assembly that he had an immediate call from heaven to preach the gospel of Christ to the Gentile world, which was the thing that exasperated the Jews against him. He here shows,

I. That he was made a Christian by a divine power, notwithstanding all his prejudices against that way. Two things bring about this surprising change, a vision from heaven and a voice from heaven, which conveyed the knowledge of Christ to him by the two learning senses of seeing and hearing.

1. He saw a heavenly vision, the circumstances of which were such

143

that it could not be a _delusion,_ but it was without doubt a divine appearance.

2. He heard a heavenly voice, an articulate one, _speaking to him_; it is here said to be _in the Hebrew tongue_ (which was not taken notice of before), his native language, the language of his religion, to intimate to him that though he must be sent among the Gentiles, yet he must not forget that he was a Hebrew, nor make himself a stranger to the Hebrew language. In what Christ said to him we may observe, (1) That he called him by his name, and repeated it (_Saul, Saul_), which would surprise and startle him; and the more because he was now in a strange place, where he thought nobody knew him. (2) That he convinced him of sin, of that great sin which he was now in the commission of, the sin of persecuting the Christians, and showed him the absurdity of it. (3) That he interested himself in the sufferings of his followers: _Thou persecutest me_ (_v._ 14), and again, It is _Jesus whom thou persecutest, v._ 15. (4) That he checked him for his wilful resistance of those convictions: _It is hard for thee to kick against the pricks_, or goads, _as a bullock unaccustomed to the yoke._ (5) That, upon his enquiry, Christ made himself known to him. This convinced him that the doctrine of Jesus was divine and heavenly, and not only not to be opposed, but to be cordially embraced.

II. That he was made a minister by a divine authority: _That the same Jesus that appeared to him in that glorious light_ ordered him _to go and preach the gospel to the Gen-_

tiles; he did not run without sending, nor was he sent by men like himself, but by him whom the Father sent, John xx. 21. Observe,

1. The office to which Paul is appointed: he is made a minister, to attend on Christ, and act for him, as a witness—to give evidence in his cause, and attest the truth of his doctrine.

2. The matter of Paul's testimony: he must give an account to the world, (1) _Of the things which he had seen_, now at this time, must tell people of Christ's manifesting himself to him by the way, and what he said to him. (2) _Of those things in which he would appear to him._ Christ now settled a correspondence with Paul, which he designed afterwards to keep up, and only told him now that he should hear further from him.

3. The spiritual protection he was taken under, while he was thus employed as Christ's witness: all the powers of darkness could not prevail against him till he had finished his testimony (_v._ 17), _delivering thee from the people of the Jews and from the Gentiles._

4. The special commission given him to go among the Gentiles, and the errand upon which he is sent to them; it was some years after Paul's conversion before he was _sent to the Gentiles_, or (for aught that appears) knew any thing of his being designed for that purpose (see _ch._ xxii. 21); but at length he is ordered to steer his course that way.

There is a great happiness designed for the Gentiles by this work—_that they may receive forgiveness of sins, and inheritance among those who are sanctified_; they are turned from the darkness of sin to the light of holiness, from the slavery of Satan to the service of God; not that God may be a gainer by them, but that they may be gainers by him.

III. That he had discharged his ministry, pursuant to his commission, by divine aid, and under divine direction and protection. God, who called him to be an apostle, owned him in his apostolical work, and carried him on in it with enlargement and success.

1. God gave him a heart to comply with the call (v. 19): *I was not disobedient to the heavenly vision*, for any one would say he ought to be obedient to it.

2. God enabled him to go through a great deal of work, though in it he grappled with a great deal of difficulty, *v.* 20. He applied himself to the preaching of the gospel with all vigour.

3. His preaching was all practical. He showed them, declared it, demonstrated it, that they ought, (1) *To repent of their sins*, to be sorry for them and to confess them, and enter into covenant against them. (2) *To turn to God.* They must not only conceive an antipathy to sin, but they must come into a conformity to God—must not only turn from that which is evil, but turn to that which is good. (3) *To do works meet for repentance.* Those that profess repentance must practise it, must live a life of repentance, must in every thing carry it as becomes penitents. It is not enough to speak penitent words, but we must do works agreeable to those words.

4. The Jews had no quarrel with

him but upon this account, that he did all he could to persuade people to be religious, and to bring them to God by bringing them to Christ (v. 21): It was for these causes, and no other, *that the Jews caught me in the temple, and went about to kill me*; and let any one judge whether these were crimes worthy of death or of bonds.

5. He had no help but from heaven; supported and carried on by that, he went on in this great work (v. 22).

6. He preached no doctrine but what agreed with the scriptures of the Old Testament. These indeed were but what the prophets of the Old Testament had preached; but, besides these, he had preached Christ, and his death, and his resurrection, and this was what they quarrelled with him for, as appears by *ch.* xxv. 19, *that he affirmed Jesus to be alive:* "And so I did," says Paul, "and so I do, but therein also I say *no other than that which Moses and the prophets said should come*; and what greater honour can be done to them than to show that what they foretold is accomplished, and in the appointed season too—that what they said should come is come, and at the time they prefixed?" This also was foretold by the Old-Testament prophets, *that the Gentiles should be brought to the knowledge of God by the Messiah*; and what was there in all this that the Jews could justly be displeased at?

REACTION OF FESTUS
(vv. 24–32)

It was a thousand pities that he should be interrupted, as he is here, and that, being permitted to speak for himself (*v.* 1), he should not be permitted to say all he designed.

I. Festus, the Roman governor, is of opinion that the poor man is crazed. Now here observe,

1. What it was that Festus said of him (*v.* 24): *Much learning hath made thee mad*, thou hast cracked thy brains with studying. This he speaks, not so much in anger, as in scorn and contempt.

2. How Paul cleared himself from this invidious imputation. (1) He denies the charge, with due respect indeed to the governor, but with justice to himself, protesting that there was neither ground nor colour for it (*v.* 25). (2) He appeals to Agrippa concerning what he spoke (*v.* 26): *For the king knows of these things*, concerning Christ, and his death and resurrection, and the prophecies of the Old Testament, which had their accomplishment therein. *This thing was not done in a corner*; all the country rang of it; and any of the Jews present might have witnessed for him that they had heard it many a time from others, and therefore it was unreasonable to censure him as a distracted man for relating it, much more for speaking of the death and resurrection of Christ, which was so universally spoken of.

II. Agrippa is so far from thinking him a madman that he thinks he never heard a man argue more strongly, nor talk more to the purpose.

1. Paul applies himself closely to Agrippa's conscience. "*King Agrippa, believest thou the prophets?* Dost thou receive the scriptures of the Old Testament as a divine

revelation, and admit them as foretelling good things to come?" He does not stay for an answer, but, in compliment to Agrippa, takes it for granted: *I know that thou believest*; for every one knew that Agrippa professed the Jews' religion, as his fathers had done, and therefore both knew the writings of the prophets and gave credit to them.

2. Agrippa owns there was a great deal of reason in what Paul said (*v.* 28): *Almost thou persuadest me to be a Christian.* Some understand this as spoken ironically, and read it thus, *Wouldest thou in so little a time persuade me to be a Christian?* But, taking it so, it is an acknowledgment that Paul spoke very much to the purpose, and that, whatever others thought of it, to his mind there came a convincing power along with what he said. Others take it as spoken seriously, and as a confession that he was in a manner, or within a little, convinced that Christ was the Messiah; for he could not but own, and had many a time thought so within himself, that the prophecies of the Old Testament had had their accomplishment in him; and now that it is urged thus solemnly upon him he is ready to yield to the conviction, he begins to sound a parley, and to think of rendering. He is as near being persuaded to believe in Christ as Felix, when he trembled, was to leave his sins.

3. Paul, not being allowed time to pursue his argument, concludes with a compliment, or rather a pious wish that all his hearers were Christians, and this wish turned into a prayer.

III. They all agree that Paul is an

innocent man, and is wronged in his prosecution. 1. The court broke up with some precipitation (*v.* 30). The king himself found his own heart begin to yield, and durst not trust himself to hear more, but, like Felix, dismissed Paul for this time. 2. They all concurred in an opinion of Paul's innocence, *v.* 31. The court withdrew to consult of the matter; to know one another's minds upon it, and *they talked among themselves,* all to the same purport, *that this man does nothing worthy of death*—he is not a criminal that deserves to die; nay, he *does nothing worthy of bonds*—he is not a dangerous man, whom it is prudent to confine. 3. *Agrippa* gave his judgment *that he might have been set at liberty, if he had not himself appealed to Cæsar* (*v.* 32), but by that appeal he had put a bar in his own door. Some think that by the Roman law this was true. Others think that Agrippa and Festus, being unwilling to disoblige the Jews by setting him at liberty, made this serve for an excuse of their continuing him in custody, when they themselves knew they might have justified the discharging of him.

CHAPTER TWENTY-SEVEN

PAUL'S VOYAGE BEGINS
(*vv.* 1–11)

Here we are told,

I. How Paul was shipped off for Italy: a long voyage, but there is no remedy. He has appealed to Cæsar, and to Cæsar he must go. Now here we are told, 1. Whose custody he was committed to—to *one named Julius, a centurion of*

Augustus's band, as Cornelius was of the Italian band, or legion, *ch.* x. 1. 2. What vessel he embarked in: they. went on board a ship of Adramyttium (*v.* 2), a sea-port of Africa, whence this ship brought African goods, and, as it should seem, made a coasting voyage for Syria, where those goods came to a good market. 3. What company he had in this voyage, there were some prisoners who were committed to the custody of the same centurion, and who probably had appealed to Cæsar too, or were upon some other account removed to Rome, to be tried there, or to be examined as witnesses against some prisoners there. But he had also some of his friends with him, Luke particularly, the penman of this book, for he puts himself in all along, *We* sailed into Italy, and, *We* launched, *v.* 2.

II. What course they steered, and what places they touched at, which are particularly recorded for the confirming of the truth of the history to those who lived at that time, and could by their own knowledge tell of their being at such and such a place.

III. What advice Paul gave them with reference to that part of their voyage they had before them—it was to be content to winter where they were, and not to think of stirring till a better season of the year. 1. It was now a bad time for sailing; they had lost a deal of time while they were struggling with contrary winds. Sailing was now dangerous. 2. Paul put them in mind of it, and gave them notice of their danger (*v.* 10): "*I perceive*" (either by notice from God, or by observing their wilful resolution to

147

prosecute the voyage notwithstanding the peril of the season) "that *this voyage will be with hurt and damage*; you that have effects on board are likely to lose them, and it will be a miracle of mercy if our lives be given us for a prey." There were some good men in the ship, and many more bad men: but in things of this nature *all things come alike to all*, and *there is one event to the righteous and to the wicked.* If both be in the same ship, they both are in the same danger. 3. They would not be advised by Paul in this matter, *v.* 11. The centurion gave more regard to the opinion of the master and owner of the ship than to Paul's; for every man is to be credited in his own profession ordinarily: but such a man as Paul, who was so intimate with Heaven, was rather to be regarded in seafaring matters than the most celebrated sailors.

THE STORM BREAKS
(*vv.* 12–19)

In these verses we have,

I. The ship putting to sea again, and pursuing her voyage at first with a promising gale.

II. The ship in a storm presently, a dreadful storm. They looked at second causes, and took their measures from the favourable hints they gave, and imagined that because the south wind now blew softly it would always blow so; in confidence of this, they ventured to sea, but were soon made sensible of their folly in giving more credit to a smiling wind than to the word of God in Paul's mouth, by which they had fair warning given them of a storm. Observe,

1. What their danger and distress was, (1) There *arose against them a tempestuous wind,* which was not only contrary to them, and directly in their teeth, so that they could not get forward, but a violent wind, which raised the waves, like that which was sent forth in pursuit of Jonah, though Paul was following God, and going on in his duty, and not as Jonah running away from God and his duty. This wind the sailors called *Euroclydon,* a northeast wind, which upon those seas perhaps was observed to be in a particular manner troublesome and dangerous.

2. What means they used for their own relief: they betook themselves to all the poor shifts (for I can call them no better) that sailors in distress have recourse to.

3. The despair which at last they were brought to (*v.* 20): *All hope that we should be saved was then taken away.* The storm continued, and they saw no symptoms of its abatement; we have known very blustering weather to continue for some weeks. The means they had used were ineffectual, so that they were at their wits' end; and such was the consternation that this melancholy prospect put them into that they had no heart either to eat or drink. They had provision enough on board (*v.* 38), but such bondage were they under, through fear of death, that they could not admit the supports of life.

SHIPWRECK (*vv.* 21–44)

We have here the issue of the distress of Paul and his fellow-travellers; they escaped with their lives and that was all, and that was for Paul's sake. Now here we have,

I. The encouragement Paul gave them, by assuring them, in the name of God, that their lives should all be saved, even when, in human appearance, all hope that they should be saved was taken away.

1. He reproves them for not taking his advice, which was to stay where they were, in the road of Lasea (*v.* 8). Paul, before administering comfort, will first make them sensible of their sin in no hearkening to him, by upbraiding them with their rashness, and probably, when he tells them of their gaining harm and loss, he reflects upon what they promised themselves by proceeding on their voyage, that they should gain so much time, gain this and the other point: "But," says he, "you have gained nothing but harm and loss; how will you answer it?"

2. He assures them that though they should lose the ship yet they should none of them lose their lives. He tells them, (1) That they must count upon the loss of the ship. But, (2) *Not a life shall be lost.* This would be good news to those that were ready to die for fear of dying, and whose guilty consciences made death look very terrible to them.

3. He tells them what ground he had for this assurance, that it is not a banter upon them, to put them into humour, nor a human conjecture, he has a divine revelation for it, and is as confident of it as that God is true, being fully satisfied that he has his word for it. An angel of God appeared to him in the night, and told him that for his sake they should all be preserved

(*vv.* 23–25), which would double the mercy of their preservation, that they should have it not only by providence, but by promise, and as a particular favour to Paul. Now observe here,

(1) The solemn profession Paul makes of relation to God, the God from whom he had this favourable intelligence: It is he *whose I am, and whom I serve.*

(2) The account he gives of the vision he had: *There stood by me this night an angel of God*, a divine messenger who used formerly to bring him messages from heaven; he *stood by him*, visibly appeared to him, probably when he was awake upon his bed.

(3) The encouragements that were given him in the vision, *v.* 14. [1] He is forbidden to fear. Though all about him are at their wits' end, and lost in despair, yet, *Fear not, Paul;* fear not *their fear, nor be afraid*, Isa. viii. 12. [2] He is assured that for his part he shall come safely to Rome: *Thou must be brought before Cæsar.* [3] That for his sake all that were in the ship with him should be delivered too from perishing in this storm: *God hath given thee all those that sail with thee.*

4. He comforts them with the same comforts wherewith he himself was comforted (*v.* 25): "*Wherefore, Sirs, be of good cheer*, you shall see even this will end well; *for I believe God*, and depend upon his word, *that it shall be even as it was told me.*"

5. He gives them a sign, telling them particularly what this tempestuous voyage would issue in (*v.* 26).

149

II. Their coming at length to an anchor upon an unknown shore, *vv.* 27–29. 1. They had been a full fortnight in the storm, continually expecting death. 2. *About midnight the mariners apprehended that they drew near to some shore,* which confirmed what Paul had told them, that they must be driven upon some island. To try whether it was so or no, *they sounded,* in order to their finding the depth of the water, for the water would be shallower as they drew nearer to shore; by the first experiment *they found they drew twenty fathoms deep of water,* and by *the next fifteen fathoms,* which was a demonstration that they were near some shore. 3. They took the hint, and, fearing rocks near the shore, *they cast anchor, and wished for the day;* they durst not go forward for fear of rocks, and yet would not go back in hope of shelter, but they would wait for the morning, and heartily wished for it; who can blame them when the affair came to a crisis? When they had light, there was no land to be seen; now that there was land near them, they had no light to see it by; no marvel then they wished for day.

III. The defeating of the sailors' attempt to quit the ship; here was a new danger added to their distress, which they narrowly escaped. Observe, 1. The treacherous design of the seamen to leave the sinking ship. 2. Paul's discovery of it, and protestation against it, *v.* 31. *Except these abide in the ship, you cannot be saved.* 3. The effectual defeat of it by the soldiers, *v.* 32. It was no time to stand arguing the case with the seamen, and therefore they made

no more ado, *but cut the ropes of the boat.* And now the seamen, being forced to stay in the ship whether they would or no, are forced likewise to work for the safety of the ship as hard as they could, because if the rest perish they must perish with them.

IV. The new life which Paul put into the company, by cheerfully inviting them to take some refreshment, and by the repeated assurances he gave them that they should all of them have their lives given tehm for a prey. *He gave thanks to God in presence of them all.* We have reason to think he had often prayed with Luke and Aristarchus, and what others there were among them that were Christians, that they prayed daily together; but whether he had before this prayed with the whole company is not certain. Now *he gave thanks to God, in presence of them all,* that they were alive, and had been preserved hitherto, and that they had a promise that their lives should be preserved in the imminent peril now before them; he gave thanks for the provision they had, and begged a blessing upon it. He set them a good example: *When he had given thanks, he broke the bread* (it was sea-biscuit) and *he began to eat.* It had a happy influence upon them all (*v.* 36): *Then were they all of good cheer.* They then ventured to believe the message God sent them by Paul when they plainly perceived that Paul believed it himself, who was in the same common danger with them.

V. Their putting to shore, and the staving of the ship in the adventure. They made a shift among them *to run the ship aground*, in a shelf or bed of sand, as it should seem, or an isthmus, or neck of land, washed with the sea on both sides, and therefore two seas are said to meet upon it, and *there the forepart stuck fast*; and then, when it had no liberty to play, as a ship has when it rides at anchor, but remained immovable, *the hinder part* would soon be broken of course *by the violence of the waves*. Whether the seamen did not do their part, being angry that they were disappointed in their design to escape, and therefore wilfully ran the ship aground, or whether we may suppose that they did their utmost to save it, but God in his providence overruled, for the fulfilling of Paul's word, *that the ship must be lost* (*v.* 22), I cannot say; but this we are sure of *that God will confirm the word of his servants, and perform the counsel of his messengers*, Isa. xliv. 26. The ship, that had strangely weathered the storm in the vast ocean, where it had room to roll, is dashed to pieces when it sticks fast.

VI. A particular danger that Paul and the rest of the prisoners were in, besides their share in the common calamity, and their deliverance from it. 1. In this critical moment, when every man hung in doubt of his life, *the soldiers advised the killing of the prisoners* that were committed to their custody, and whom they were to give an account of, *lest any of them should swim out and escape, v.* 42. 2. The centurion, for Paul's sake, quashed this motion presently. Paul, who was his prisoner, had found favour with him, as Joseph with the captain of

the guard. Julius, though he despised Paul's advice (*v.* 11), yet afterwards saw a great deal of cause to respect him, and therefore, being *willing to save Paul*, he prevented the execution of that bloody project.

VII. The saving of the lives of all the persons in the ship, by the wonderful providence of God. When the ship broke under them, surely *there was but a step between them and death*; and yet infinite mercy interposed, and that step was not stepped. Here was an instance of the performance of a particular word of promise which God gave, that all the persons in this ship should be saved for Paul's sake.

CHAPTER TWENTY-EIGHT

PAUL ON MALTA (*vv.* 1–10)

Even stormy winds fulfil God's counsel, and an ill wind indeed it is that blows nobody any good; this ill wind blew good to the island of Melita; for it gave them Paul's company for three months, who was a blessing to every place he came to. Now here we have,

I. The kind reception which the inhabitants of this island gave to the distressed strangers that were shipwrecked on their coast (*v.* 2): *The barbarous people showed us no little kindness. They kindled a fire*, in some large hall or other, and *they received us every one*—made room for us about the fire, and bade us all welcome, without asking either what country we were of or what religion.

II. The further danger that Paul was in by a viper's fastening on his hand, and the unjust construction that the people put upon it. Paul is among strangers, and appears one of the meanest and most contemptible of the company, therefore God distinguishes him, and soon causes him to be taken notice of.

1. When the fire was to be made, and to be made bigger, that so great a company might all have the benefit of it, Paul was as busy as any of them in gathering sticks, *v.* 3.

2. The sticks being old dry rubbish, it happened there was a viper among them, that lay as dead till it came to the heat, and then revived, or lay quiet till it felt the fire, and then was provoked, and flew at him that unawares threw it into the fire, and *fastened upon his hand, v.* 3.

3. The barbarous people concluded that Paul, being a prisoner, was certainly a murderer, who had appealed to Rome, to escape justice in his own country, and that this viper was sent by divine justice to be the avenger of blood; or, if they were not aware that he was a prisoner, they supposed that he was in his flight; and *when they saw the venomous animal hang on his hand,* which it seems he could not, or would not, immediately throw off, but let it hang, they concluded, "*No doubt this man is a murderer,* has shed innocent blood, and therefore, *though he has escaped the sea, yet* divine *vengeance* pursues him, and fastens upon him now that he is pleasing himself with the thoughts of that escape, and will *not suffer him to live.*"

4. When he shook off the viper from his hand, yet they expected that divine vengeance would ratify the censure they had passed, and

that he would have swollen and burst, through the force of the poison, or *that he would have fallen down dead suddenly.*

III. Paul's deliverance from the danger, and the undue construction the people put upon this. The viper's fastening on his hand was a trial of his faith; and it was found to praise, and honour, and glory: for, 1. It does not appear that it put him into any fright or confusion at all. 2. He carelessly *shook off the viper into the fire,* without any difficulty, calling for help, or any means used to loosen its hold; and it is probable that it was consumed in the fire. 3. He was none the worse. Those that thought it would have been his death *looked a great while, but saw no harm at all come to him.* God hereby intended to make him remarkable among these barbarous people, and so to make way for the entertainment of the gospel among them. 4. They then magnified him as much as before they had vilified him: *They changed their minds, and said that he was a god*—an immortal god; for they thought it impossible that a mortal man should have a viper hang on his hand so long and be never the worse.

IV. The miraculous cure of an old gentleman that was ill of a fever, and of others that were otherwise diseased, by Paul. And, with these confirmations of the doctrine of Christ, no doubt there was a faithful publication of it.

V. The grateful acknowledgment which even these barbarous people made of the kindness Paul had done them, in preaching Christ unto them. They were civil to him, and to the other ministers that were with him, who, it is likely, were assisting to him in preaching among them, *v.* 10. They showed them all possible respect; they saw God honoured them, and therefore they justly thought themselves obliged to honour them, and thought nothing too much by which they might testify the esteem they had for them.

PAUL REACHES ROME
(*vv.* 11–16)

We have here the progress of Paul's voyage towards Rome, and his arrival there at length.

We have here,

I. Their leaving Malta. That island was a happy shelter to them, but it was not their home; when they are refreshed they must put to sea again.

II. Their landing in or about Italy, and the pursuing of their journey towards Rome. They came to Puteoli, a sea-port town not far from Naples, now called *Pozzolana.* The ship of Alexandria was bound for that port, and therefore there Paul, and the rest that were bound for Rome, were put ashore, and went the remainder of their way by land. At Puteoli they *found brethren,* Christians. Who brought the knowledge of Christ hither we are not told, but here it was, so wonderfully did the leaven of the gospel diffuse itself. God has many that serve and worship him in places where we little think he has. From Puteoli they went forward towards Rome; whether they travelled on foot, or whether they had beasts provided for them to ride on (as *ch.* xxiii. 24), does not appear; but

to Rome they must go, and this was their last stage.

III. The meeting which the Christians at Rome gave to Paul. It is probable that notice was sent to them by the Christians at Puteoli, as soon as ever Paul had come thither, how long he intended to stay there, and when he would set forward for Rome, which gave an opportunity for this interview. He finds there are those there who love and value him, and whom he may both converse with and consult with as his friends, which will take off much of the tediousness of his imprisonment, and the terror of his appearing before Nero. Note, It is an encouragement to those who are travelling towards heaven to meet with their fellow travellers, who are their *companions in the kingdom and datience of Jesus Christ.*

IV. The delivering of Paul into custody at Rome, *v.* 16. He is now come to his journey's end. And, 1. He is still a prisoner. He had longed to see Rome, but, when he comes there, he is delivered, with other prisoners, to the *captain of the guard,* and can see no more of Rome than he will permit him. 2. Yet he has some favour shown him. He is a prisoner, but not a close prisoner, not in the common jail: *Paul was suffered to dwell by himself,* in some convenient private lodgings which his friends there provided for him, and a soldier was appointed to be his guard, who, we hope, was civil to him, and let him take all the liberty that could be allowed to a prisoner, for he must be very ill-natured indeed that could be so to such a courteous obliging man as Paul. Paul, being suffered to dwell by himself, could the better enjoy himself, and his friends, and his God, than if he had been lodged with the other prisoners.

THE JEWS AT ROME
(vv. 17–22)

Paul, with a great deal of expense and hazard, is brought a prisoner to Rome, and when he has come nobody appears to prosecute him or lay any thing to his charge; but he must call his own cause; and here he represents it to the chief of the Jews at Rome. And here we are told,

I. What he said to them, and what account he gave them of his cause. Now, 1. He professes his own innocency, and that he had not given any just occasion to the Jews to bear him such an ill will as generally they did. 2. He modestly complains of the hard usage he had met with—that, though he had given no offence, yet *he was delivered prisoner from Jerusalem into the hands of the Romans.* 3. He declares the judgment of the Roman governors concerning him, *v.* 18. They examined him, enquired into his case, heard what was to be said against him, and what he had to say for himself. The chief captain examined him, so did Felix, and Festus, and Agrippa, and they could find no cause of death in him; nothing appeared to the contrary but that he was an honest, quiet, conscientious, good man, and therefore they would never gratify the Jews with a sentence of death upon him; but, on the contrary, would have let him go, and have let him go on in his work too, and

have given him no interruption, for they all heard him and liked his doctrine well enough. It was for the honour of Paul that those who most carefully examined his case acquitted him, and none condemned him but unheard, and such as were prejudiced against him. 4. He pleads the necessity he was under to remove himself and his cause to Rome; and that it was only in his own defence, and not with any design to recriminate, or exhibit a cross bill against the complainants, (*v.* 19). 5. He puts his sufferings upon the true footing, and gives them such an account of the reason of them as should engage them not only to join with his persecutors against him, but to concern themselves for him, and to do what they could on his behalf (*v.* 20). He carried the mark of his imprisonment about with him, and probably was chained to the soldier that kept him; and it was, (1) Because he preached that the Messiah was come, who was the hope of Israel, he whom Israel hoped for. (2) Because he preached that the resurrection of the dead would come. This also was the hope of Israel; so he had called it, *ch.* xxiii. 6; xxiv. 15; xxvi. 6, 7.

II. What was their reply. They own, 1. That they had nothing to say in particular against him; nor had any instructions to appear as his prosecutors before the emperor, either by letter or word of mouth (*v.* 21). 2. That they desired to know particularly concerning the doctrine he preached, and the religion he took so much pains to propagate in the face of so much opposition (*v.* 22).

PAUL AT ROME (vv. 23–29)

We have here a short account of a long conference which Paul had with the Jews at Rome about the Christian religion.

I. We are here told how Paul managed this conference in defence of the Christian religion. The Jews appointed the time, a day was set for this dispute, that all parties concerned might have sufficient notice, v. 23. Those Jews seemed well disposed to receive conviction, and yet it did not prove that they all were so. Now when the day came,

1. There were *many got together to Paul*. Though he was a prisoner, and could not come out to them, yet they were willing to come to him to his lodging.

2. He was very large and full in his discourse with them, seeking their conviction more than his own vindication.

3. He was very long; for he continued his discourse, and it should seem to have been a continued discourse, from *morning till evening*; perhaps it was a discourse eight or ten hours long.

II. What was the effect of his discourse. One would have thought that so good a cause as that of Christianity, and managed by such a skilful hand as Paul's could not but carry the day, and that all the hearers would have yielded to it presently; but it did not prove so. 1. *They did not agree among themselves*, v. 25. 2. *Some believed the things that were spoken, and some believed not*, v. 24. There was the disagreement. Such as this has always been the success of the gospel.

III. The awakening word which Paul said to them at parting.

1. "You will by the righteous judgment of God be sealed up under unbelief."

2. "Your unbelief will justify God in sending the gospel to the Gentile world, which is the thing you look upon with such a jealous eye (v. 28): therefore seeing you put the grace of God away from you, and will not submit to the power of divine truth and love, seeing you will not be converted and healed in the methods which divine wisdom has appointed, *therefore be it known unto you that the salvation of God is sent unto the Gentiles*, that salvation which was of the Jews only (John iv. 22), the offer of it is made to them, the means of it afforded to them, and they stand fairer for it than you do; it is sent to them, and they will hear it, and receive it, and be happy in it.

IV. The breaking up of the assembly, as it should seem, in some disorder. They departed, many of them with a resolution never to hear Paul preach again, nor trouble themselves with further enquiries about this matter.

EPILOGUE (vv. 30, 31)

We are here taking our leave of the history of blessed Paul; and therefore, since God saw it not fit that we should know any more of him, we should carefully take notice of every particular of the circumstances in which we must here leave them.

I. It cannot but be a trouble to us that we must leave him in bonds for Christ, nay, and that we have no prospect given us of his being set at liberty.

II. Yet it is a pleasure to us (for we are sure it was to him) that, though we leave him in bonds for Christ, yet we leave him at work for Christ, and this made his bonds easy that he was not by them bound out from serving God and doing good. His prison becomes a temple, a church, and then it is to him a palace. His hands are tied, but, thanks be to God, his mouth is not stopped; a faithful zealous minister can better bear any hardship than being silenced. Here is Paul a prisoner, and yet a preacher; he is bound, but the word of the Lord is not bound. When he wrote his epistle to the Romans, he said *he longed to see them, that he might impart into them some spiritual gift* (Rom. i. 11); he was glad *to see some of them* (*v.* 15), but it would not be half his joy unless he could impart to them some spiritual gift, which here he has an opportunity to do, and then he will not complain of his confinement. Observe,

1. To whom he preached: to all that had a mind to hear him, whether Jews of Gentiles.

2. What he preached. He does not fill their heads with curious speculations, nor with matters of state and politics, but he keeps to his text, minds his business as an apostle. Paul stuck still to his principle—to know and preach *nothing but Christ, and him crucified.*

Ministers, when in their preaching they are tempted to diverge from that which is their main business, should reduce themselves with this question, What does this concern the Lord Jesus Christ? What tendency has it to bring us to him, and to keep us walking in him? *For we preach not ourselves, but Christ.*

3. With what liberty he preached. (1) Divine grace gave him a liberty of spirit. He preached *with all confidence*, as one that was himself well assured of the truth of what he preached—that it was what he durst stand by; and of the worth of it—that it was what he durst suffer for. He was *not ashamed of the gospel of Christ.* (2) Divine Providence gave him a liberty of speech: *No man forbidding him*, giving him any check for what he did or laying any restraint upon him. The Jews that used to forbid him to speak to the Gentiles had no authority here; and the Roman government as yet took no cognizançe of the profession of Christianity as a crime. Though it was a very low and narrow sphere of opportunity that Paul was here placed in, compared with what he had been in, yet, such as it was, he was not molested nor disturbed in it. Though it was not a wide door that was opened to him, yet it was kept open, and no man was suffered to shut it; and it was to many an effectual door, so that there were saints even in Cæsar's household, Phil. iv. 22.

THE EPISTLE OF ST. PAUL TO THE

ROMANS

CHAPTER ONE
INTRODUCTION (vv. 1–7)

In this paragraph we have,

I. The person who writes the epistle described (*v. 1*): *Paul, a servant of Jesus Christ*; this is his title of honour, which he glories in. *Called to be an apostle.* Some think he alludes to his old name Saul, which signifies *one called for*, or *enquired after*: Christ sought him to make an apostle of him, Acts ix. 15. *Separated to the gospel of God.* The Pharisees had their name from separation, because they *separated themselves to the study of the law*; such a one Paul had formerly been; but now he had changed his studies, was a gospel Pharisee, separated by the counsel of God (Gal. i. 15), *separated from his mother's womb*, by an immediate direction of the Spirit, and a regular ordination according to that direction (Acts xiii. 2, 3), by a dedication of himself to this work. He was an entire devotee to the gospel of God, the gospel which has God for its author, the origin and extraction of it divine and heavenly.

II. Having mentioned the gospel of God, he digresses, to give us an encomium of it.

1. The antiquity of it. It was *promised before* (*v. 2*); it was no novel upstart doctrine, but of ancient standing in the promises and prophecies of the Old Testament.

2. The subject-matter of it: it is concerning Christ, *vv. 3, 4*. The prophets and apostles all bear witness to him; he is the true treasure hid in the field of the scriptures.

3. The fruit of it (*v. 5*): This apostleship was received *for obedience and faith*, that is, to bring people to that obedience; as Christ, so his ministers, received that they might give.

III. The persons to whom it is written (*v. 7*): *To all that are in Rome, beloved of God, called to be saints*; that is, to all the professing Christians that were in Rome, whether Jews or Gentiles originally, whether high or low, bond or free, learned or unlearned.

IV. The apostolical benediction (*v. 7*): *Grace to you and peace.* This is one of the tokens in every epistle; and it hath not only the affection of a good wish, but the authority of a blessing.

PAUL, THE DEBTOR (vv. 8–15)

We may here observe,

I. His thanksgiving for them (*v. 8*): *First, I thank my God.* In all our thanksgivings, it is good for us to eye God as our God; this makes every mercy sweet, when we can say of God, "He is mine in covenant."—*Through Jesus Christ*. All our duties and performances are pleasing to God only through Jesus Christ, praises as well as prayers.—*For you all*. We must express our love to our friends, not only by praying for them, but by praising God for them. *That your faith is spoken of*. Paul travelled up and down from place to place, and, wherever he came, he heard great commendations of the Christians at Rome, which he mentions, not to make them proud, but to quicken them to answer the general character people gave of them, and the general expectation people had from them. The faith of the Roman Christians came to be thus talked of, not only because it was excelling in itself, but because it was eminent and observable in its circumstances. Rome was a city upon a hill, every one took notice of what was done there.

II. His prayer for them, *v*. 9. From Paul's example here we may learn. 1. Constancy in prayer: *Always without ceasing*. He did himself observe the same rules he gave to others, Eph. vi. 18; 1 Thes. v. 17. 2. Charity in prayer: *I make mention of you*. Though he had no particular acquaintance with them, nor interest in them, yet he prayed for them; not only for all saints in general, but he made express mention of them. *God, whom I serve with my spirit*. Those that serve God with their spirits may, with a humble confidence, appeal to him; hypocrites who rest in bodily exercise cannot. His particular prayer, among many other petitions he put up for them, was that he might have an opportunity of paying them

a visit (*v*. 10): *Making request, if by any means*, &c.

III. His great desire to see them, with the reasons for it, *vv*. 11–15. He had heard so much of them that he had a great desire to be better acquainted with them. Fruitful Christians are as much the joy as barren professors are the grief of faithful ministers. Accordingly, he *often purposed to come, but was let hitherto* (*v*. 13), for man purposeth, but God disposeth. He was hindered by other business that took him off, by his care of other churches, whose affairs were pressing; and Paul was for doing that first, not which was most pleasant (then he would have gone to Rome), but which was most needful. Paul desired to visit these Romans,

1. That they might be edified (*v*. 11): *That I may impart unto you*. He received, that he might communicate.—*To the end you may be established*. Having commended their flourishing he here expresses his desire of their establishment, that as they grew upward in the branches they might grow downward in the root.

2. That he might be comforted, *v*. 12. What he heard of their flourishing in grace was so much a joy to him that it must needs be much more so to behold it. *By the mutual faith both of you and me*, that is, our mutual faithfulness and fidelity. Their edification would be his advantage, it would be fruit abounding to a good account.

3. That he might discharge his trust as the apostle of the Gentiles (*v*. 14): *I am a debtor*. (1) His receivings made him a debtor; for they were talents he was entrusted

with to trade for his Master's honour. (2) His office made him a debtor. He was a debtor as he was an apostle; he was called and sent to work, and had engaged to mind it. Accordingly, we find him paying his debt, both in his preaching and in his writing, doing good *both to Greeks and barbarians*, and suiting his discourse to the capacity of each. For these reasons he was ready, if he had an opportunity, *to preach the gospel at Rome, v.* 15.

THE POWER OF GOD
(*vv.* 16–18)

Paul here enters upon a large discourse of justification. He was ready to preach the gospel at Rome, though a place where the gospel was run down by those that called themselves the wits; *for*, saith he, *I am not ashamed of it, v.* 16. The reason of this bold profession, taken from the nature and excellency of the gospel, introduces his dissertation.

I. The proposition, *vv.* 16, 17. The excellency of the gospel lies in this, that it reveals to us,

1. The salvation of believers as the end: *It is the power of God unto salvation.* But, (1) *It is through the power of God*; without that power the gospel is but a dead letter. (2) It is to those, and those only, that believe. Believing interests us in the gospel salvation; to others it is hidden. The medicine prepared will not cure the patient if it be not taken.—*To the Jew first. The lost sheep of the house of Israel* had the first offer made them, both by Christ and his apostles.

2. The justification of believers

as the way (*v.* 17): *For therein*, that is, in this gospel, which Paul so much triumphs in, *is the righteousness of God revealed.* This evangelical righteousness, (1) Is called the *righteousness of God*; it is of God's appointing, of God's approving and accepting. (2) it is said to be *from faith to faith*, from the faithfulness of God revealing to the faith of man receiving (so some); from the faith of dependence upon God, and dealing with him immediately, as Adam before the fall, to the faith of dependence upon a Mediator, and so dealing with God (so others); from the first faith, by which we are put into a justified state, to after faith, by which we live, and are continued in that state. *The just shall live by faith. Just by faith*, there is faith justifying us; *live by faith*, there is faith maintaining us; and so *there is a righteousness from faith to faith.* Faith is all in all, both in the beginning and progress of a Christian life.

II. The proof of this proposition. Justification must be either by faith or works. It cannot be by works, which he proves at large by describing the works both of Jews and Gentiles; and therefore he concludes it must be by faith, *ch.* iii. 20, 28. Here is

1. The sinfulness of man described; he reduces it to two heads, *ungodliness and unrighteousness*; ungodliness against the laws of the first table, unrighteousness against those of the second.

2. The cause of that sinfulness, and that is, *holding the truth in unrighteousness.* An unrighteous wicked heart is the dungeon in

which many a good truth is detained and buried.

3. The displeasure of God against it: *The wrath of God is revealed from heaven.*

THE GENTILES (*vv.* 19–32)

In this last part of the chapter the apostle applies what he had said particularly to the Gentile world, in which we may observe,

I. This means and helps they had to come to the knowledge of God. Observe,

1. What discoveries they had: *That which may be known of God is manifest among them*; that is, there were some even among them that had the knowledge of God.

2. Whence they had these discoveries: *God hath shown it to them.* Those common natural notions which they had of God were imprinted upon their hearts by the God of nature himself, who is the *Father of lights.*

3. By what way and means these discoveries and notices which they had were confirmed and improved, namely, by the work of creation (*v.* 20): *For the invisible things of God,* &c.

(1) Observe what they knew: *The invisible things of him, even his eternal power and Godhead.* Though God be not the object of sense, yet he hath discovered and made known himself by those things that are sensible.

(2) How they knew it: *By the things that are made*, which could not make themselves, nor fall into such an exact order and harmony by any casual hits; and therefore must have been produced by some first cause or intelligent agent,

which first cause could be no other than an eternal powerful God. See Ps. xix. 1; Isa. xl. 26; Acts xvii. 24.

II. Their gross idolatry, notwithstanding these discoveries that God made to them of himself; described here, *vv.* 21–23, 25. Observe,

1. The inward cause of their idolatry, *vv.* 21, 22. They are therefore without excuse, in that they did know God, and from what they knew might easily infer that it was their duty to worship him, and him only.

2. The outward acts of their idolatry, *vv.* 23–25. (1) Making images of God (*v.* 23), by which, as much as in them lay, they *changed the glory of the incorruptible God.* Compare Ps. cvi. 20; Jer. ii. 11. They ascribed a deity to the most contemptible creatures, and by them represented God. (2) Giving divine honour to the creature: *Worshipped and served the creature, besides the Creator.* Or, *above* the Creator, paying more devout respect to their inferior deities, stars, heroes, demons, thinking the supreme God inaccessible, or above their worship.

III. The judgments of God upon them for this idolatry. Observe,

1. By whom they were given up. God gave them up, in a way of righteous judgment, as the just punishment of their idolatry—taking off the bridle of restraining grace—leaving them to themselves —letting them alone; for his grace is his own, he is debtor to no man, he may give or withhold his grace at pleasure.

2. To what they were given up.

(1) *To uncleanness and vile affections, vv.* 24, 26, 27. Those who

dishonoured God were given up to dishonour themselves. A man cannot be delivered up to a greater slavery than to be given up to his own lusts.

(2) To a reprobate mind in these abominations, *v.* 28.

[1] They *did not like to retain God in their knowledge*. The blindness of their understandings was caused by the wilful aversion of their wills and affections.

[2] Answerable to this wilfulness of theirs, in gainsaying the truth, God gave them over to a wilfulness in the grossest sins, here called a *reprobate mind*, a mind void of all sense and judgment to discern things that differ, so that they could not distinguish their right hand from their left in spiritual things.

First, Sins against the first table: *Haters of God.* Here is the devil in his own colours, sin appearing sin.

Secondly, Sins against the second table. These are especially mentioned, because in these things they had a clearer light. (2) They knew the penalty; so it is explained here: They knew *that those who commit such things were worthy of death,* eternal death; their own consciences could not but suggest this to them, and yet they ventured upon it.

Now lay all this together, and then say whether the Gentile world, lying under so much guilt and corruption, could be justified before God by any works of their own

CHAPTER TWO

GOD'S PERFECT JUSTICE
(*vv.* 1–16)

In the former chapter the apostle had represented the state of the Gentile world to be as bad and black as the Jews were ready enough to pronounce it. And now, designs to show that the state of the Jews was very bad too, and their sin in many respects more aggravated.

I. He arraigns them for their censoriousness and self-conceit (*v.* 1): *Thou art inexcusable, O man, whosoever thou art that judgest.* The Jews were generally a proud sort of people, that looked with a great deal of scorn and contempt upon the poor Gentiles, as not worthy to be set with the dogs of their flock; while in the mean time they were themselves as bad and immoral—though not idolaters, as the Gentiles, yet sacrilegious, *v.* 22. *Therefore thou art inexcusable.*

II. He asserts the invariable justice of the divine government *vv.* 2, 3. To drive home the conviction, he here shows what a righteous God that is with whom we have to do, and how just in his proceedings.

III. He draws up a charge against them (*vv.* 4, 5) consisting of two branches:

1. Slighting the goodness of God (*v.* 4), *the riches of his goodness.* This is especially applicable to the Jews, who had singular tokens of the divine favour. Means are mercies, and the more light we sin against the more love we sin against.

2. Provoking the wrath of God, *v.* 5. The rise of this provocation is a *hard and impenitent heart*; and the ruin of sinners is their walking after such a heart, being led by it.

IV. He describes the measures by which God proceeds in his judgment.

1. He will *render to every man according to his deeds* (*v.* 6), a truth often mentioned in scripture, to prove that the Judge of all the earth does right.

(1) In dispensing his favours; and this is mentioned twice here, both in *v.* 7 and *v.* 10. For he delights to show mercy.

(2) In dispensing his frowns (*vv.* 8, 9). Observe, [1] The objects of his frowns. In general those that do evil, more particularly described to be *such as are contentious and do not obey the truth.* Contentious against God. Every wilful sin is a quarrel with God, it is *striving with our Maker* (Isa. xlv. 9), the most desperate contention. [2] The products or instances of these frowns: *Indignation and wrath, tribulation and anguish.* These are the wages of sin. *Indignation and wrath* the causes—*tribulation and anguish* the necessary and unavoidable effects.

2. *There is no respect of persons with God, v.* 11. As to the spiritual state, there is a respect of persons; but not as to outward relation or condition. Jews and Gentiles stand upon the same level before God. This was Peter's remark upon the first taking down of the partition-wall (Acts x. 34), that God is no respecter of persons; and it is explained in the next words, that *in every nation he that fears God, and works righteousness, is accepted of him.*

V. He proves the equity of his proceedings with all, when he shall actually come to Judge them (*vv.* 12–16), upon this principle, that that which is the rule of man's obedience is the rule of God's judgment. Three degrees of light

are revealed to the children of men:

1. The light of nature. This the Gentiles have, and by this they shall be judged. They had that within them which approved and commended what was well done and which reproached them for what was done amiss. So that the guilty Gentiles are left without excuse. God is justified in condemning them. They cannot plead ignorance, and therefore are likely to perish if they have not something else to plead.

2. The light of the law. This the Jews had, and by this they shall be judged (*v.* 12). It was a great privilege that they had the law, but not a saving privilege, unless they lived up to the law they had, which it is certain the Jews did not, and therefore they had need of a righteousness wherein to appear before God.

3. The light of the gospel: and according to this those that enjoyed the gospel shall be judged (*v.* 16): *According to my gospel.* As many as are under that dispensation shall be judged according to that dispensation, Mark xvi. 16.

A TRUE JEW (*vv.* 17–29)

In the latter part of the chapter the apostle directs his discourse more closely to the Jews, and shows what sins they were guilty of, notwithstanding their profession and vain pretensions. He had said (*v.* 13) that not the hearers but the doers of the law are justified; and he here applies that great truth to the Jews. Observe,

I. He allows their profession (*vv.* 17–20) and specifies their particular pretensions and privileges in which they prided themselves, that they might see he did not condemn them out of ignorance of what they had to say for themselves; no, he knew the best of their cause.

1. They were a peculiar people, separated and distinguished from all others by their having the written law and the special presence of God among them.

2. They were a knowing people (v. 18). They did not only know the truth of God, but the will of God, that which he would have them do. The Jews, having the touchstone of the law ready at hand, were, or at least thought they were, able to distinguish, to cleave the hair in doubtful cases.

3. They were a teaching people, or at least thought themselves so (vv. 19, 20): *And art confident that thou thyself art a guide of the blind.* Apply it, (1) To the Jews in general. They thought themselves guides to the poor blind Gentiles that sat in darkness, were very proud of this, that whoever would have the knowledge of God must be beholden to them for it. (2) To their rabbis, and doctors, and leading men among them, who were especially those that judged others, v. 1.

II. He aggravates their provocations (vv. 21–24) from two things:

1. That they sinned against their knowledge and profession, did that themselves which they taught others to avoid: *Thou that teachest another, teachest thou not thyself?*

2. That they dishonoured God by their sin, vv. 23, 24. While God and his law were an honour to them, which they boasted of and prided themselves in, they were a dis-

honour to God and his law, by their sin.

III, He asserts the utter insufficiency of their profession to clear them from the guilt of these provocations (vv. 25–29). Further to illustrate this,

1. He shows that the uncircumcised Gentiles, if they live up to the light they have, stand upon the same level with the Jews; if *they keep the righteousness of the law* (v. 26), *fulfil the law* (v. 27); that is, by submitting sincerely to the conduct of natural light, perform the matter of the law.

2. He describes the true circumcision, vv. 28, 29. (1). It is *not that which is outward in the flesh and in the letter.* To be Abraham's children is to do the works of Abraham, John viii. 39, 40. (2) It is *that which is inward, of the heart, and in the spirit.* It is the heart that God looks at, the circumcising of the heart that renders us acceptable to him. See Deut. xxx. 6. This is *the circumcision that is not made with hands,* Col. ii. 11, 12. (3) The praise thereof, though it be *not of men,* who judge according to outward appearance, yet it is *of God,* that is, God himself will own and accept and crown this sincerity; for *he seeth not as man seeth.*

CHAPTER THREE
JEWS' ADVANTAGES
(vv. 1–18)

I. Here the apostle answers several objections, which might be made, to clear his way.

Object. 1. If Jew and Gentile stand so much upon the same level

Jews' Advantages

before God, *what advantage then hath the Jew?*

Answer. The door is open to the Gentiles as well as the Jews, but the Jews have a fairer way up to this door, by reason of their church-privileges, which are not to be undervalued, though many that have them perish eternally for not improving them. The Jews had the means of salvation, but they had not the monopoly of salvation.

Object 2. To what purpose were the oracles of God committed to them, when so many of them, notwithstanding these oracles, continued strangers to Christ, and enemies to his gospel? *Some did not believe, v.* 3.

Answer. It is very true that some, nay most of the present Jews, do not believe in Christ; *but shall their unbelief make the faith of God without effect?* The apostle startles at such a thought: *God forbid!* The infidelity and obstinacy of the Jews could not invalidate the overthrow those prophecies of the Messiah which were contained in the oracles committed to them. Christ will be glorious, *though Israel be not gathered,* Isa. xlix. 5. God's words shall be accomplished, his purposes performed, and all his ends answered, though there be a generation that by their unbelief go about to make God a liar. *Let God be true but every man a liar;* let us abide by this principle, that God is true to every word which he has spoken, and will let none of his oracles fall to the ground, though thereby we give the lie to man; better question and overthrow the credit of all the men in the world than doubt of the faithfulness of God.

Object. 3. Now it may be suggested, If all our sin be so far from overthrowing God's honour that it commends it, and his ends are secured, so that there is no harm done, it is not unjust for God to punish our sin and unbelief so severely?

Answer. God forbid; far be it from us to imagine such a thing. Suggestions that reflect dishonour upon God and his justice and holiness are rather to be startled at than parleyed with. The sin has never the less of malignity and demerit in it though God bring glory to himself out of it. It is only accidentally that sin commends God's righteousness. No thanks to the sinner for that, who intends no such thing.

Object. 4. The former objection is repeated and prosecuted (*vv* 7, 8). *Let us do evil that good may come* is oftener in the heart than in the mouth of sinners, so justifying themselves in their wicked ways.

Answer. He says no more by way of confutation but that, whatever they themselves may argue, the damnation of those is just. Those who deliberately do evil that good may come of it will be so far from escaping, under the shelter of that excuse, that it will rather justify their damnation, and render them the more inexcusable; for sinning upon such a surmise, and in such a confidence, argues a great deal both of the wit and of the will in the sin —a wicked will deliberately to choose the evil, and a wicked wit to palliate it with the pretence of good arising from it.

II. Paul, having removed these objections, next revives his assertion of the general guilt and corruption of mankind in common, both of Jews and Gentiles, vv. 9–18. They *are all under sin.* Under the guilt of sin: under it as under a sentence;—under it as under a bond, by which they are bound over to eternal ruin and damnation;—under it as under a burden (Ps. xxxviii. 4) that will sink them to the lowest hell: we are guilty before God, v. 19. He who, when he himself had made all, looked upon every thing that he had made, and behold all was very good, now that man had marred all, looked, and behold all was very bad. Let us take a view of the particulars. Observe,

1. That which is habitual, which is twofold:

(1) An habitual defect of every thing that is good. [1] *There is none righteous,* none that has an honest good principle of virtue, or is governed by such a principle, none that retains any thing of that image of God, consisting in righteousness, wherein man was created; *no, not one;* implying that, if there had been but one, God would have found him out. [2] *There is none that understandeth,* v. 11. The fault lies in the corruption of the understanding; that is blinded, depraved, perverted. [3] *None that seeketh after God,* that is, none that has any regard to God, any desire after him. [4] *They are together become unprofitable,* v. 12. Those that have forsaken God soon grow good for nothing, useless burdens of the earth. [5] *There is none that doeth good;* no, not a just man upon the earth, that doeth good, and sinneth not, Eccl. vii. 23.

(2) An habitual defection to every thing that is evil: *They are all gone out of the way.* No wonder that those miss the right way who do not seek after God, the highest end. God made man in the way, set him in right, but he hath forsaken it. The corruption of mankind is an apostasy.

2. That which is actual. And what good can be expected from such a degenerate race? He instances,

(1) In their words (vv. 13, 14), in three things particularly: [1] Cruelty: *Their throat is an open sepulchre,* ready to swallow up the poor and innocent. These passages are borrowed from Ps. v. 9 and cxl. 3. [2] Cheating: *With their tongues they have used deceit.* [3] Cursing: reflecting upon God, and blaspheming his holy name; wishing evil to their brethren: *Their mouth is full of cursing and bitterness.*

(2) In their ways (vv. 15–17): *Their feet are swift to shed blood;* that is, they are very industrious to compass any cruel design, ready to lay hold of all such opportunities.

(3) The root of all this we have: *There is no fear of God before their eyes,* v. 18. The fear of God is here put for all practical religion, which consists in an awful and serious regard to the word and will of God as our rule, to the honour and glory of God as our end.

SIN AND JUSTIFICATION
(vv. 19–31)

From all this Paul infers that it is in vain to look for justification by the works of the law, and that it is to be had only by faith, which is the point he has been all along proving, from *ch.* i. 17, and which he lays down (*v.* 28) as the summary of his discourse.

I. He argues from man's guiltiness, to show the folly of expecting justification by the works of the law. Now concerning the guiltiness of man,

1. He fastens it particularly upon the Jews; for they were the men that made their boast of the law, and set up for justification by it.

2. He extends it in general to all the world: *That all the world may become guilty before God. For all have sinned* (*v.* 23); all are sinners by nature, by practice, and *have come short of the glory of God—* have failed of that which is the chief end of man. *Come short,* as the archer comes short of the mark, as the runner comes short of the prize; so come short, as not only not to win, but to be great losers.

3. Further to drive us off from expecting justification by the law, he ascribes this conviction to the law (*v.* 20): *For by the law is the knowledge of sin.* That law which convicts and condemns us can never justify us.

II. He argues from God's glory to prove that justification must be expected only by faith in Christ's righteousness. There is no justification by the works of the law. Must guilty man then remain eternally under wrath? Is there no hope? Is the wound become incurable because of transgression? No, blessed be God, it is not (*vv.* 21, 22); there is another way laid open for us, *the righteousness of God without the law is manifested* now under the gospel.

1. Now concerning this righteousness of God observe, (1) That it is manifested. The gospel-way of justification is a high-way, a plain way, it is laid open for us. (2) It is *without the law.* Here he obviates the method of the judaizing Christians, who would needs join Christ and Moses together. (3) Yet *it is witnessed by the law and the prophets*; that is, there were types, and prophecies, and promises, in the Old Testament, that pointed at this. (4) It is by the *faith of Jesus Christ*, that faith which hath Jesus Christ for its object—an *anointed Saviour*, so Jesus Christ signifies. (5) It is *to all, and upon all, those that believe.* In this expression he inculcates that which he had been often harping upon, that Jews and Gentiles, if they believe, stand upon the same level, and are alike welcome to God through Christ; *for there is no difference.*

2. But now how is this for God's glory?

(1) It is for the glory of his grace (*v.* 24). It comes freely to us, but Christ bought it, and paid dearly for it, which yet is so ordered as not to derogate from the honour of free grace.

(2) It is for the glory of his justice and righteousness (*vv.* 25, 26): *Whom God hath set forth to be a propitiation*, &c. Note, [1] Jesus Christ is the great propitiation, or propitiatory sacrifice, typified by the *mercy-seat*, under the law. He is all in all in our reconciliation, not only the maker, but the matter of it—our priest, our sacrifice, our altar, our all. [2] *God hath set him forth* to be so. See Matt. iii. 17, and xvii. 5. [3] That *by faith in his blood*

166

we become interested in this propitiation. Christ is the propitiation; there is the healing plaster provided. Faith is the applying of this plaster to the wounded soul. [4] That all who by faith are interested in this propitiation have *the remission of their sins that are past. Through the forbearance of God.* Divine patience has kept us out of hell, that we might have space to repent, and get to heaven. [5] That God does in all this *declare his righteousness. First,* In the propitiation itself. Never was there such a demonstration of the justice and holiness of God as there was in the death of Christ. *Secondly,* In the pardon upon that propitiation; so it follows, by way of explanation: *That he might be just, and the justifier of him that believeth.* It would not comport with his justice to demand the debt of the principal when the surety has paid it and he has accepted that payment in full satisfaction. See I John i. 9.

(3) It is for God's glory; for boasting is thus excluded, *v.* 27. God will have the great work of the justification and salvation of sinners carried on from first to last in such a way as to exclude boasting, that no flesh may glory in his presence, 1 Cor. i. 29–31.

From all this he draws this conclusion (*v.* 28): *That a man is justified by faith without the deeds of the law.*

III. In the close of the chapter he shows the extent of this privilege of justification by faith, and that it is not the peculiar privilege of the Jews, but pertains to the Gentiles also; for he had said (*v.* 22) that there is no difference.

CHAPTER FOUR

THE CASE OF ABRAHAM
(*vv.* 1–8)

I. If he had been justified by works, room would have been left for boasting, which must for ever be excluded. If so, *he hath whereof to glory* (*v.* 2), which is not to be allowed. "But," might the Jews say, "was not his name made great (Gen. xii. 2), and then might not he glory?" Yes, but not before God; he might deserve well of men, but he could never merit of God.

II. It is expressly said that Abraham's faith was counted to him for righteousness. *What saith the scripture? v.* 3. It is mentioned in Genesis, upon occasion of a very signal and remarkable act of faith concerning the promised seed, and is the more observable in that it followed upon a grievous conflict he had had with unbelief; his faith was now a victorious faith, newly returned from the battle. It is not the perfect faith that is required to justification (there may be acceptable faith where there are remainders of unbelief), but the prevailing faith, the faith that has the upper hand of unbelief.

III. If he had been justified by works, the reward would have been *of debt, and not of grace,* which is not to be imagined. This is his argument (*vv,* 4, 5): Abraham's reward was God himself; so he had told him but just before (Gen. xv. 1), *I am thy exceeding great reward.* Now, if Abraham had merited this by the perfection of his obedience, it had not been an act of grace in God, but Abraham might have demanded it with as much confidence as ever any labourer in the vineyard demanded the penny he had earned. But this cannot be; it is impossible for man, much more guilty man, to make God a debtor to him, Rom. xi. 35.

IV. He further illustrates this by a passage out of the Psalms, where David speaks of the remission of sins, the prime branch of justification, as constituting the happiness and blessedness of a man, pronouncing blessed, not the man who has no sin, or none which deserved death (for then, while man is so sinful, and God so righteous, where would be the blessed man?) but *the man to whom the Lord imputeth not sin,* who though he cannot plead, Not guilty, pleads the act of indemnity, and his plea is allowed. It is quoted from Ps. xxxii. 1, 2.

ABRAHAM JUSTIFIED
(*vv.* 9–17)

St. Paul observes in this paragraph when and why Abraham was thus justified; for he has several things to remark upon that. It was before he was circumcised, and before the giving of the law; and there was a reason for both.

I. It was before he was circumcised, *v.* 10. Abraham was pardoned and accepted in uncircumcision, a circumstance which, as it might silence the fears of the poor uncircumcised Gentiles, so it might lower the pride and conceitedness of the Jews, who gloried in their circumcision, as if they had the monopoly of all happiness. Here are two reasons why Abraham was justified by faith in circumcision:

1. That circumcision might be *a seal of the righteousness of faith, v.*

11. The tenor of the covenants must first be settled before the seal can be annexed. Sealing supposes a previous bargain, which is confirmed and ratified by that ceremony.

2. *That he might be the father of all those that believe.* Abraham was the father of believers, because to him particularly the *magna charta* was renewed. (1) The father of believing Gentiles, *though they be not circumcised.* Zaccheus, a publican, if he believe, is reckoned a son of Abraham, Luke xix. 9. (2) The father of believing Jews, not merely as circumcised, and of the seed of Abraham according to the flesh, but because believers, because they *are not of the circumcision only* (that is, are not only circumcised), *but walk in the steps of that faith*—have not only the sign, but the thing signified—not only are of Abraham's family, but follow the example of Abraham's faith.

II. It was before the giving of the law, *vv.* 13–16. Now observe,

1. What that promise was—*that he should be the heir of the world,* that is, of the land of Canaan, the choicest spot of ground in the world,—or the father of many nations of the world, who sprang from him, besides the Israelites,—or the heir of the comforts of the life which now is.

2. How it was made to him: *Not through the law, but through the righteousness of faith. Not through the law,* for that was not yet given: but it was upon that believing which was counted to him for righteousness; it was upon his trusting God, in his leaving his own country when God commanded

him, Heb. xi. 8. Now, being by faith, it could not be by the law, which he proves by the opposition there is between them (*vv.* 14, 15).

3. Why the promise was made to him by faith; for three reasons, *v.* 16. (1) *That it might be by grace*, that grace might have the honour of it. (2) *That the promise might be sure.* The first covenant, being a covenant of works, was not sure. (3) *That it might be sure to all the seed.* If it had been *by the law*, it had been limited to the Jews, *to whom pertained the glory, and the covenants, and the giving of the law* (*ch.* ix. 4); but therefore it was by faith that Gentiles as well as Jews might become inteested in it, the spiritual as well as the natural seed of faithful Abraham.

ABRAHAM'S FAITH
(*vv.* 17–22)

Having observed when Abraham was justified by faith, and why, for the honour of Abraham, and for example to us who call him father, the apostle here describes and commends the faith of Abraham, where observe,

I. Whom he believed: *God who quickeneth.* It is God himself that faith fastens upon: *other foundation can no man lay.*

II. How he believed. 1. *Against hope, he believed in hope, v.* 18. There was a hope against him, a natural hope. All the arguments of sense, and reason, and experience, which in such cases usually beget and support hope, were against him; no second causes smiled upon him, nor in the least favoured his hope. But, against all those inducements to the contrary, he believed;

for he had a hope for him: *He believed in hope*, which arose, as his faith did, from the consideration of God's all-sufficiency. 2. *Being not weak in faith, he considered not his own body, v.* 19. It is mere weakness of faith that makes a man lie poring upon the difficulties and seeming impossibilities that lie in the way of a promise. Though it may seem to be the wisdom and policy of carnal reason, yet it is the weakness of faith, to look into the bottom of all the difficulties that arise against the promise. 3. *He staggered not at the promise of God through unbelief* (*v.* 20), and he therefore staggered not because he considered not the frowns and discouragements of second causes. Unbelief is at the bottom of all our staggerings at God's promises. It is not the promise that fails, but our faith that fails when we stagger. 4. He *was strong in faith, giving glory to God.* The strength of his faith appeared in the victory it won over his fears. And hereby he gave glory to God. 5. He was *fully persuaded that what God had promised he was able to perform.* Such was his full persuasion, and it was built on the omnipotence of God: *He was able.*

A UNIVERSAL TRUTH
(*vv.* 23–25)

In the close of the chapter, he applies all to us; and, having abundantly proved that Abraham was justified by faith, he here concludes that his justification was to be the pattern or sampler of ours: *It was not written for his sake alone.* The accounts we have of the Old-Testament saints were not intended for histories only, barely to inform and divert us, but for precedents to direct us, for examples (1 Cor. x. 11) for *our learning*, ch. xv. 4.

CHAPTER FIVE
JUSTIFIED BY FAITH
(*vv*. 1–5)

The precious benefits and privileges which flow from justification are exceedingly precious.

I. *We have peace with God*, *v*. 1. Justification takes away the guilt, and so makes way for peace. By faith we lay hold of God's arm and of his strength, and so are at peace, Isa. xxvii, 4, 5. There is more in this peace than barely a cessation of enmity, there is friendship and loving-kindness, for God is either the worst enemy or the best friend.

II. *We have access by faith into this grace wherein we stand*, *v*. 2. Now into this grace we have access, *an introduction*, which implies that we were not born in this state; we are *by nature children of wrath*, and *the carnal mind is enmity against God*; but we are brought into it. *By whom we have access by faith*. By Christ as the author and principal agent, by faith as the means of this access. *Wherein we stand*. Not only wherein we are, but wherein we stand, a posture that denotes our discharge from guilt; *we stand in the judgment* (Ps. i. 5), not cast, as convicted criminals, but our dignity and honour secured, not thrown to the ground, as abjects. The phrase denotes also our progress; while we stand, we are going. We must not lie down, as if we had already attained, but stand as those that are pressing forward, stand as

servants attending on Christ our master.

III. *We rejoice in hope of the glory of God*. Besides the happiness in hand, there is a happiness in hope, *the glory of God*, the glory which God will put upon the saints in heaven, glory which will consist in the vision and fruition of God.

IV. *We glory in tribulations also*. How come we to glory in tribulations? Why, because tribulations, by a chain of causes, greatly befriend hope, which he shows in the method of its influence. 1. *Tribulation worketh patience*, not in and of itself, but the powerful grace of God working in and with the tribulation. 2. *Patience experience*, *v*. 4. It works an experience of God, and the songs he gives in the night; the patient sufferers have the greatest experience of the divine consolations, which abound as afflictions abound. 3. *Experience hope*. Experience of God is a prop to our hope; he that hath delivered doth and will. Experience of ourselves helps to evidence our sincerity. 4. This *hope maketh not ashamed*; that is, it is a hope that will not deceive us. Nothing confounds more than disappointment. Sense of God's love to us will make us not ashamed, either of our hope in him or our sufferings for him.

THE SECOND ADAM
(*vv*. 6–21)

The apostle here describes the fountain and foundation of justification, laid in the death of the Lord Jesus.

I. The character we were under when Christ died for us.

1. *We were without strength* (*v*.

6), in a sad condition; and, which is worse, altogether unable to help ourselves out of that condition. God's time to help and save is when those that are to be saved are without strength, that his own power and grace may be the more magnified, Deut. xxxii. 36.

2. *He died for the ungodly*; not only helpless creatures, and therefore likely to perish, but guilty sinful creatures, and therefore deserving to perish. *While we were yet sinners*, implying that we were not to be always sinners, there should be a change wrought; for he died to save us, not in our sins, but from our sins; but we were yet sinners when he died for us. Nay, which is more, *we were enemies* (v. 10). And that for such as these Christ should die is such a mystery, such a paradox, such an unprecedented instance of love, that it may well be our business to eternity to adore and wonder at it.

II. The precious fruits of his death.

1. Justification and reconciliation are the first and primary fruit of the death of Christ: *We are justified by his blood* (v. 9), *reconciled by his death*, v. 10. Sin is pardoned, the sinner accepted as righteous, the quarrel taken up, the enmity slain, an end made of iniquity, and an everlasting righteousness brought in.

2. Hence results salvation from wrath: *Saved from wrath* (v. 9), *saved by his life*, v. 10. When that which hinders our salvation is taken away, the salvation must needs follow. Nay, the argument holds very strongly; if God justified and reconciled us when we were

enemies, and put himself to so much charge to do it, much more will he save us when we are justified and reconciled. He that has done the greater, which is of enemies to make us friends, will certainly do the less, which is when we are friends to use us friendly and to be kind to us.

3. All this produces, as a further privilege, our *joy in God*, v. 11. *And not only so*, there is more in it yet, a constant stream of favours; we not only go to heaven, but go to heaven triumphantly; not only get into the harbour, but come in with full sail: *We joy in God*, not only saved from his wrath, but solacing ourselves in his love. To *receive the atonement* is, (1) To give our consent to the atonement, approving of, and agreeing to, those methods which Infinite Wisdom has taken of saving a guilty world by the blood of a crucified Jesus, being willing and glad to be saved in a gospel way and upon gospel terms. (2) To take the comfort of the atonement, which is the fountain and the foundation of our joy in God.

III. The parallel that the apostle runs between the communication of sin and death by the first Adam and of righteousness and life by the second Adam (v. 12, to the end). Now, for the opening of this, observe,

1. A general truth laid down as the foundation of his discourse—that Adam was a type of Christ (v. 14): *Who is the figure of him that was to come.* Christ is therefore called the *last Adam*, 1 Cor. xv. 45. Compare v. 22.

2. A more particular explanation of the parallel, in which observe,

(1) How Adam, as a public person, communicated sin and death to all his posterity (*v.* 12): *By one man sin entered.* [1] By him *sin entered.* When God pronounced all very good (Gen. i. 31) there was no sin in the world; it was when Adam ate forbidden fruit that sin made its entry. Now Adam acted thus as a public person, by the sovereign ordination and appointment of God, and yet that founded upon a natural necessity; for God, as the author of nature, had made this the law of nature, that man should beget in his own likeness, and so the other creatures. In Adam therefore, as in a common receptacle, the whole nature of man was reposited, from him to flow down in a channel to his posterity; for all mankind are made *of one blood* (Acts xvii. 26). Adam therefore sinning and falling, the nature became guilty and corrupt, and is so derived. Thus in him all have sinned. [2] *Death by sin*, for death is the wages of sin. Sin, when it is finished, brings forth death. When sin came, of course death came with it. Death is here put for all that misery which is the due desert of sin, temporal, spiritual, eternal death. *Death reigned, v.* 14. He speaks of death as a mighty prince, and his monarchy the most absolute, universal, and lasting monarchy. None are exempted from its sceptre; it is a monarchy that will survive all other earthly rule, authority, and power, for it is the last enemy, 1 Cor. xv. 26.

Further, to clear this, he shows that sin did not commence with the law of Moses, but was *in the world until*, or *before*, that law; therefore that law of Moses is not the only rule of life, for there was a rule, and that rule was transgressed, before the law was given. It likewise intimates that we cannot be justified by our obedience to the law of Moses, any more than we were condemned by and for our disobedience to it.

(2) How, in correspondence to this, Christ, as a public person, communicates righteousness and life to all true believers, who are his spiritual seed. Observe,

[1] Wherein the resemblance holds. This is laid down most fully, *vv.* 18, 19.

First, By the offence and disobedience of one many were made sinners, and judgment came upon all men to condemnation.

Secondly, In like manner, *by the righteousness and obedience of one* (and that one is Jesus Christ, the second Adam), *are many made righteous,* and so the *free gift comes upon all.* It is observable how the apostle inculcates this truth, and repeats it again and again, as a truth of very great consequence. Here observe, 1. The nature of Christ's righteousness, how it is brought in; it is by his obedience. The disobedience of the first Adam ruined us, the obedience of the second Adam saves us. 2. The fruit of it. (1) There is a *free gift come upon all men*, that is, it is made and offered promiscuously to all. (2) *Many shall be made righteous—*many compared with one, or as many as belong to the election of grace, which, though but a few as they are scattered up and down in the world, yet will be a great many when they come all together.

[2] Wherein the communication of grace and love by Christ goes beyond the communication of guilt and wrath by Adam; and this he shows, *vv.* 15–17. His expressions are a little intricate, but this he seems to intend: *First*, If guilt and wrath be communicated, much more shall grace and love; for it is agreeable to the idea we have of the divine goodness to suppose that he should be more ready to save upon an imputed righteousness than to condemn upon an imputed guilt. *Secondly*, If there was so much power and efficacy, as it seems there was, in the sin of a man, who was of the earth, earthy, to condemn us, much more are there power and efficacy in the righteousness and grace of Christ, who is the Lord from heaven, to justify and save us.

IV. In the last two verses the apostle seems to anticipate an objection which is expressed, Gal. iii. 19, *Wherefore then serveth the law?* Answer, 1. *The law entered that the offence might abound*. Not to make sin to abound the more in itself, otherwise than as sin takes occasion by the commandment, but to discover the abounding sinfulness of it. 2. *That grace might much more abound*—that the terrors of the law might make gospel-comforts so much the sweeter.

CHAPTER SIX

FREEDOM FROM SIN
(*vv.* 1–23)

The apostle is very full in pressing the necessity of holiness in this chapter, which may be reduced to two heads: His exhortations to holiness, which show the nature of it; and his motives or arguments to enforce those exhortations, which show the necessity of it.

I. For the first, we may hence observe the nature of sanctification, what it is, and wherein it consists. In general it has two things in it, mortification and vivification—dying to sin and living to righteousness, elsewhere expressed by putting off the old man and putting on the new, ceasing to do evil and learning to do well.

1. Mortification, putting off the old man; several ways this is expressed. (1) We must *live no longer in sin* (*v.* 2), we must not be as we have been nor do as we have done. The time past of our life must suffice, 1 Peter iv. 3. Though there are none that live without sin, yet, blessed be God, there are those that do not live in sin, do not live in it as their element, do not make a trade of it: this is to be sanctified. (2) *The body of sin must be destroyed*, *v.* 6. The corruption that dwelleth in us is the body of sin, consisting of many parts and members, as a body. This is the root to which the axe must be laid. (3) *We must be dead indeed unto sin*, *v.* 11. As the death of the oppressor is a release, so much more is the death of the oppressed, Job iii. 17, 18. Death makes a mighty change; such a change doth sanctification make in the soul, it cuts off all correspondence with sin. (4) *Sin must not reign in our mortal bodies that we should obey it*, *v.* 12. Though sin may remain as an outlaw, though it may oppress as a tyrant, yet let it not reign as a king. (5) We must not *yield our members as instruments of un-*

righteousness, *v.* 13. The members of the body are made use of by the corrupt nature as tools, by which the wills of the flesh are fulfilled; but we must not consent to that abuse.

2. Vivification, or living to righteousness; and what is that? (1) It is to *walk in newness of life*, *v.* 4. Newness of life supposes newness of heart, for out of the heart are the issues of life, and there is no way to make the stream sweet but by making the spring so. (2) Is is to be *alive unto God through Jesus Christ our Lord*, *v.* 11. The love of God reigning in the heart is the life of the soul towards God. (3) It is to *yield ourselves to God, as those that are alive from the dead*, *v.* 13. The very life and being of holiness lie in the dedication of ourselves to the Lord, giving our own selves to the Lord, 2 Cor. viii. 5. (4) It is to yield *our members as instruments of righteousness to God*. The members of our bodies, when withdrawn from the service of sin, are not to lie idle, but to be made use of in the service of God.

II. The motives or arguments here used to show the necessity of sanctification.

1. He argues from our sacramental conformity to Jesus Christ. Our baptism, with the design and intention of it, carries in it a great reason why we should die to sin, and live to righteousness. Thus we must improve our baptism as a bridle of restraint to keep us in from sin, as a spur of constraint to quicken us to duty. Observe this reasoning.

(1) In general, we are *dead to sin*, that is, in profession and in obliga-

tion. Our baptism signifies our cutting off from the kingdom of sin. We profess to have no more to do with sin. All this is in vain if we persist in sin; we contradict a profession, violate an obligation, return to that to which we were dead, like walking ghosts, than which nothing is more unbecoming and absurd. For (*v.* 7) *he that is dead is freed from sin*; that is, he that is dead to it is freed from the rule and dominion of it, as the servant that is dead is freed from his master, Job iii. 19.

(2) In particular, being *baptized into Jesus Christ, we were baptized into his death*, *v.* 3. Baptism binds us to Christ, it binds us apprentice to Christ as our teacher, it is our allegiance to Christ as our sovereign.

[1] Our conformity to the death of Christ obliges us to die unto sin; thereby we know the *fellowship of his sufferings*, Phil. iii. 10. *First, Our old man is crucified with him*, *v.* 6. The death of the cross was a slow death; the body, after it was nailed to the cross, gave many a throe and many a struggle: but it was a sure death, long in expiring, but expired at last; such is the mortification of sin in believers. *Secondly*, We are dead with Christ, *v.* 8. Christ was obedient to death: when he died, we might be said to die with him, as our dying to sin is an act of conformity both to the design and to the example of Christ's dying for sin. Baptism signifies and seals our union with Christ, our engrafting into Christ; so that we are dead with him, and engaged to have no more to do with sin than he had. *Thirdly, We are buried with him by*

baptism, *v.* 4. Our conformity is complete. We are in profession quite cut off from all commerce and communion with sin, as those that are buried are quite cut off from all the world; not only not of the living, but no more among the living, have nothing more to do with them. Thus must we be, as Christ was, separate from sin and sinners.

[2] Our conformity to the resurrection of Christ obliges us to rise again to newness of life. This is *the power of his resurrection* which Paul was so desirous to know, Phil. iii. 10.

2. He argues from the precious promises and privileges of the new covenant, *v.* 14. God's promises to us are more powerful and effectual for the mortifying of sin than our promises to God. Sin may struggle in a believer, and may create him a great deal of trouble, but it shall not have dominion; it may vex him, but shall not rule over him.

3. He argues from the evidence that this will be of our state, making for us, or against us (*v.* 16): *To whom you yield yourselves servants to obey, his servants you are.* All the children of men are either the servants of God, or the servants of sin; these are the two families. Now, if we would know to which of these families we belong, we must enquire to which of these masters we yield obedience.

4. He argues from their former sinfulness, *vv.* 17–21, where we may observe,

(1) What they had been and done formerly. We have need to be often reminded of our former state. Paul frequently remembers it con-cerning himself, and those to whom he writes.

(2) How the blessed change was made, and wherein it did consist.

[1] *You have obeyed from the heart that form of doctrine which was delivered to you, v.* 17. This describes conversion, what it is; it is our conformity to, and compliance with, the gospel which was delivered to us by Christ and his ministers.

[2] *Being made free from sin, you became servants of righteousness* (*v.* 18), *servants to God, v.* 22. Conversion is, *First*, A freedom from the service of sin; it is the shaking off of that yoke, resolving to have no more to do with it. *Secondly*, A resignation of ourselves to the service of God and righteousness, to God as our master, to righteousness as our work.

(3) What apprehensions they now had of their former work and way. He appeals to themselves (*v.* 21), whether they had not found the service of sin, [1] An unfruitful service. The present pleasure and profit of sin do not deserve to be called fruit; they are but chaff, ploughing iniquity, sowing vanity, and reaping the same. [2] It is an unbecoming service; it is that of which we *are now ashamed* — ashamed of the folly, ashamed of the filth, of it.

5. He argues from the end of all these things. (1) The end of sin is death (*v.* 21): *The end of those things is death.* Though the way may seem pleasant and inviting, yet the end is dismal: at the last it bites; it will be bitterness in the latter end. *The wages of sin is death, v.* 23. (2) If the fruit be unto

holiness, if there be an active principle of true and growing grace the end will be everlasting life—a, very happy end!—Though the way be up-hill, though it be narrow, and thorny, and beset, yet everlasting life at the end of it is sure. So, *v.* 23, *The gift of God is eternal life.* The death is the wages of sin, it comes by desert; but the life is a gift it comes by favour. Sinners merit hell, but saints do not merit heaven. And this gift is *through Jesus Christ our Lord.* It is Christ that purchased it, prepared it, prepares us for it, preserves us to it; he is *the Alpha and Omega,* All in all in our salvation.

CHAPTER SEVEN
NOT UNDER LAW
(*vv.* 1–6)

Among other arguments used in the foregoing chapter to persuade us against sin, and to holiness, this was one (*v.* 14), that *we are not under the law*; and this argument is here further insisted upon and explained (*v.* 6): *Ve are delivered from the law.* What is meant by this? And how is it an argument why sin should not reign over us, and why we should walk in newness of life? 1. We are delivered from that power of the law which curses and condemns us for the sin committed by us. The sentence of the law against us is vacated and reversed, by the death of Christ, to all true believers. The law saith, *The soul that sins shall die*; but we are delivered from the law. 2. We are delivered from that power of the law which irritates and provokes the sin that dwelleth in us.

This the apostle seems especially to refer to (*v.* 5): *The motions of sins which were by the law.* The law, by commanding, forbidding, threatening, corrupt and fallen man, but offering no grace to cure and strengthen, did but stir up the corruption.

The difference between a law-state and a gospel-state he had before illustrated by the similitude of rising to a new life, and serving a new master; now here he speaks of it under the similitude of being married to a new husband.

I. Our first marriage was to the law, which, according to the law of marriage, was to continue only during the life of the law. The law of marriage is binding till the death of one of the parties, no matter which, and no longer. The death of either discharges both. Thus were we married to the law (*v.* 5): *When we were in the flesh*, that is, in a carnal state, under the reigning power of sin and corruption—in the flesh as in our element—then *the motions of sins which were by the law did work in our members*, we were carried down the stream of sin, and the law was but as an imperfect dam, which made the stream to swell the higher, and rage the more. Our desire was towards sin, as that of the wife towards her husband, and sin ruled over us. And this continues during life, while the law is alive to us, and we are alive to the law.

II. Our second marriage is to Christ: and how comes this about? Why,

1. We are freed, by death, from our obligation to the law as a covenant, as the wife is from her

obligation to her husband, *v.* 3. This resemblance is not very close, nor needed it to be. *You are become dead to the law, v.* 4.

2. We are married to Christ. The day of our believing is the day of our espousals to the Lord Jesus. We enter upon a life of dependence on him and duty to him: *Married to another, even to him who is raised from the dead,* a periphrasis of Christ very pertinent here; for as our dying to sin and the law is in conformity to the death of Christ, and the crucifying of his body, so our devotedness to Christ in newness of life is in conformity to the resurrection of Christ. We are married to the raised exalted Jesus, a very honourable marriage. Compare 2 Cor. xi. 2; Eph. v. 29. Now we are thus married to Christ, (1) *That we should bring forth fruit unto God, v.* 4. As our old marriage to sin produced fruit unto death, so our second marriage to Christ produces fruit unto God, fruits of righteousness. (2) *That we should serve in newness of spirit, and not in the oldness of the letter, v.* 6. Being married to a new husband, we must change our way. Still we must serve, but it is a service that is perfect freedom, whereas the service of sin was a perfect drudgery. We are under the dispensation of the Spirit, and therefore must be spiritual, and serve in the spirit. Compare with this 2 Cor. iii. 3, 6, &c.

THE LAW IS GOOD
(*vv.* 7–14)

To what he had said in the former paragraph, the apostle here raises an objection, which he answers

very fully: *What shall we say then? Is the law sin?* Observe in particular,

I. The great excellency of the law in itself. Far be it from Paul to reflect upon the law; no, he speaks honourably of it. 1. It is *holy, just, and good, v.* 12. The law in general is so, and every particular commandment is so. Laws are as the law-makers are. God, the great lawgiver, is holy, just, and good, therefore his law must needs be so. 2. *The law is spiritual* (*v.* 14), not only in regard to the effect of it, as it is a means of making us spiritual, but in regard to the extent of it; it reaches our spirits, it lays a restraint upon, and gives a direction to, the motions of the inward man; *it is a discerner of the thoughts and intents of the heart,* Heb. iv. 12.

II. The great advantage that he had found by the law. 1. It was discovering: *I had not known sin but by the law, v.* 7. As that which is straight discovers that which is crooked, as the looking-glass shows us our natural face with all its spots and deformities, so there is no way of coming to that knowledge of sin which is necessary to repentance, and consequently to peace and pardon, but by comparing our hearts and lives with the law. Particularly he came to the knowledge of the sinfulness of lust by the law of the tenth commandment. By lust he means sin dwelling in us, sin in its first motions and workings, the corrupt principle. This he came to know when the law said, *Thou shalt not covet.* The law spoke in other language than the scribes and Pharisees made it to speak in; it spoke in the spiritual sense and meaning of it. 2. It was humbling (*v.* 9): *I was alive.* He thought himself in a very good condition; he was alive in his own opinion and apprehension, very secure and confident of the goodness of his state. He had the letter of the law, but he had not the spiritual meaning of it—the shell, but not the kernel. He had the law in his hand and in his head, but he had it not in his heart; the notion of it, but not the power of it. *But when the commandment came,* came in the power of it (not to his eyes only, but to his heart), *sin revived,* as the dust in a room rises (that is, appears) when the sun-shine is let into it. Paul then saw that in sin which he had never seen before: sin in its consequences, sin with death at the heels of it, sin and the curse entailed upon it. "Thus sin revived, and then I died; I lost that good opinion which I had had of myself, and came to be of another mind." Of this excellent use is the law; it is a lamp and a light; it converts the soul, opens the eyes, prepares the way of the Lord in the desert, rends the rocks, levels the mountains, makes ready a people prepared for the Lord.

III. The ill use that his corrupt nature made of the law notwithstanding. 1. *Sin, taking occasion by the commandment, wrought in me all manner of concupiscence, v.* 8. The restraint of the law actually provoked him to sin. *Without the law sin was dead,* as a snake in winter, which the sunbeams of the law quicken and irritate. 2. It *deceived me.* Sin puts a cheat upon the sinner, and it is a fatal cheat, *v.* 11. *By it* (by the commandment) *slew me.*

There being in the law no such express threatening against sinful lustings, sin, that is, his own corrupt nature, took occasion thence to promise him impunity, and to say, as the serpent to our first parents, *You shall not surely die.* Thus it deceived and slew him. 3. It *wrought death in me by that which is good, v.* 13. That which works concupiscence works death for sin bringeth forth death. Now in this sin appears sin. The worst thing that sin does, and most like itself, is the perverting of the law, and taking occasion from it to be so much the more malignant. Thus the commandment, which was ordained to life, was intended as a guide in the way to comfort and happiness, proved unto death, through the corruption of nature, *v.* 10.

THE INNER CONFLICT
(*vv.* 14–25)

Here is a description of the conflict between grace and corruption in the heart, between the law of God and the law of sin. And it is applicable two ways: 1. To the struggles that are in a convinced soul, but yet unregenerate, in the person of whom it is supposed, by some, that Paul speaks. 2. To the struggles that are in a renewed sanctified soul, but yet in a state of imperfection; as others apprehend. And a great controversy there is of which of these we are to understand the apostle here.

I. Apply it to the struggles that are felt in a convinced soul, that is yet in a state of sin, knows his Lord's will, but does it not, approves the things that are more excellent, being instructed out of the law, and yet lives in the constant breach of it, *ch.* ii. 17–23. Though he has that within him that witnesses against the sin he commits, and it is not without a great deal of reluctancy that he does commit it, the superior faculties striving against it, natural conscience warning against it before it is committed and smiting for it afterwards, yet the man continues a slave to his reigning lusts. It is not thus with every unregenerate man, but with those only that are convinced by the law, but not changed by the gospel. The law may discover sin, and convince of sin, but it cannot conquer and subdue sin, witness the predominancy of sin in many that are under very strong legal convictions. It discovers the defilement, but will not wash it off.

II. It seems rather to be understood of the struggles that are maintained between grace and corruption in sanctified souls. That there are remainders of indwelling corruption, even where there is a living principle of grace, is past dispute; that this corruption is daily breaking forth in sins of infirmity (such as are consistent with a state of grace) is no less certain. If we say that we have no sin, we deceive ourselves, 1 John, i. 8, 10. That true grace strives against these sins and corruptions, does not allow of them, hates them, mourns over them as a burden, groans under them as a burden, is likewise certain (Gal. v. 17). These are the truths which, I think, are contained in this discourse of the apostle. Understanding it thus, we may observe here,

1. What he complains of—the remainder of indwelling corruptions, which he here speaks of, to show that the law is insufficient to justify even a regenerate man, that the best man in the world hath enough in him to condemn him, if God should deal with him according to the law. Observe the particulars of this complaint. (1) *I am carnal, sold under sin*, *v.* 14. He speaks of the Corinthians as carnal, 1 Cor. iii. 1. Even where there is spiritual life there are remainders of carnal affections. (2) *What I would, that I do not; but what I hate, that do I*, *v.* 15. And to the same purport, *vv.* 19, 21, *When I would do good, evil is present with me.* Such was the strength of corruptions, that he could not attain that perfection in holiness which he desired and breathed after. (3) *In me, that is in my flesh, dwelleth no good*, *v.* 18. As the new nature, as far as that goes, cannot commit sin (1 John iii. 9), so the flesh, the old nature, as far as that goes, cannot perform a good duty. How should it? For the flesh serveth the law of sin (*v.* 25), it is under the conduct and government of that law; and, while it is so, it is not likely to do any good. The corrupt nature is elsewhere called flesh (Gen. vi. 3, John iii. 6); and, though there may be good things dwelling in those that have this flesh, yet, as far as the flesh goes, there is no good, the flesh is not a subject capable of any good. (4) *I see another law in my members warring against the law of my mind*, *v.* 23. The corrupt and sinful inclination is here compared to a law, because it controlled and checked him in his good motions. It is said to be seated in

his members, because, Christ having set up his throne in his heart, it was only the rebellious members of the body that were the instruments of sin. (5) His general complaint we have *v.* 24, *O wretched man that I am! who shall deliver me from the body of this death?* The thing he complains of is a body of death; either the body of flesh, which is a mortal dying body (while we carry this body about with us, we shall be troubled with corruption; when we are dead, we shall be freed from sin, and not before), or the body of sin, the old man, the corrupt nature, which tends to death, that is, to the ruin of the soul. This made him cry out, *O wretched man that I am!* A man that had learned in every state to be content yet complains thus of his corrupt nature. *Who shall deliver me?* The remainders of indwelling sin are a very grievous burden to a gracious soul.

2. What he comforts himself with. The case was sad, but there were some allays. Three things comforted him:

(1) That his conscience witnessed for him that he had a good principle ruling and prevailing in him, notwithstanding. [1] *I consent unto the law that it is good, v.* 16. Here is the approbation of the judgment. Wherever there is grace there is not only a dread of the severity of the law, but a consent to the goodness of the law. [2] *I delight in the law of God after the inward man, v.* 22. All that are savingly regenerate or born again do truly delight in the law of God, delight to know it, to do it—cheerfully submit to the authority of it, and take a com-

placency in that submission, never better pleased than when heart and life are in the strictest conformity to the law and will of God. *After the inward man.* The new man is called the *inner man* (Eph. iii. 16), the *hidden man of the heart*, 1 Pet. iii. 4. Paul, as far as he was sanctified, had a delight in the law of God. [3] *With the mind I myself serve the law of God, v.* 52. It is not enough to consent to the law, and to delight in the law, but we must serve the law; our souls must be entirely delivered up into the obedience of it. Thus it was with Paul's mind.

(2) That the fault lay in that corruption of his nature which he did really bewail and strive against: *It is no more I that do it, but sin that dwelleth in me.* This he mentions twice (*vv.* 17, 20), not as an excuse for the guilt of his sin (it is enough to condemn us, if we were under the law, that the sin which does the evil dwelleth in us), but as a salvo for his evidences, that he might not sink in despair, but take comfort from the covenant of grace, which accepts the willingness of the spirit, and has provided pardon for the weakness of the flesh.

(3) His great comfort lay in Jesus Christ (*v.* 25): *I thank God, through Jesus Christ our Lord.* In the midst of his complaints he breaks out into praises. *Who shall deliver me?* says he (*v.* 24), as one at a loss for help. At length he finds an all-sufficient friend, even Jesus Christ. If it were not for Christ, this iniquity that dwells in us would certainly be our ruin. He is our advocate with the Father, and

through him God pities, and spares, and pardons, and lays not our iniquities to our charge.

CHAPTER EIGHT

THE SPIRIT OF LIFE
(vv. 1–9)

I. The apostle here begins with one signal privilege of true Christians, and describes the character of those to whom it belongs: *There is therefore now no condemnation to those that are in Christ Jesus*, v. 1. 1. It is the unspeakable privilege and comfort of all those that are in Christ Jesus that there is therefore now no condemnation to them. He does not say, "There is no accusation against them," for this there is; but the accusation is thrown out, and the indictment quashed. Now this arises from their being in Christ Jesus; by virtue of their union with him through faith they are thus secured. They are in Christ Jesus, as in their city of refuge, and so are protected from the avenger of blood. 2. It is the undoubted character of all those who are so in Christ Jesus as to be freed from condemnation that *they walk not after the flesh but after the Spirit*. Observe, The character is given from their walk, not from any one particular act, but from their course and way.

II. This great truth, thus laid down, he illustrates in the following verses; and shows how we come by this great privilege, and how we may answer this character.

1. How comes it about?

(1) The law could not do it, v. 3. It could neither justify nor sanctify, neither free us from the guilt nor

from the power of sin, having not the promises either of pardon or grace. The law made nothing perfect: *It was weak*.

(2) *The law of the Spirit of life in Christ Jesus* does it, v. 2. The covenant of grace made with us in Christ is a treasury of merit and grace, and thence we receive pardon and a new nature, *are freed from the law of sin and death*, that is, both from the guilt and power of sin—from the course of the law, and the dominion of the flesh. We are under another covenant, another master, another husband, under the *law of the Spirit*, the law that gives the Spirit, spiritual life to qualify us for eternal. Observe, [1] How Christ appeared *In the likeness of sinful flesh*. Not sinful, for he was holy, harmless, undefiled; but in the likeness of that flesh which was sinful. [2] What was done by this appearance of his: Sin *was condemned*, that is, God did therein more than ever manifest his hatred of sin; and not only so, but for all that are Christ's both the damning and the domineering power of sin is broken and taken out of the way. [3] The happy effect of this upon us (v. 4): *That the righteousness of the law might be fulfilled in us*. Both in our justification and in our sanctification, the righteousness of the law is fulfilled. Now,

2. Observe how we may answer to this character, v. 5, &c.

(1) By looking to our minds. The man is as the mind is. The mind is the forge of thoughts. *As he thinketh in his heart, so is he*, Prov. xxiii. 7. Now, to caution us against this carnal-mindedness, he

shows the great misery and malignity of it, and compares it with the unspeakable excellency and comfort of spiritual-mindedness. [1] It is death, *v.* 6. It is spiritual death, the certain way to eternal death. [2] It is enmity to God (*v.* 7), and this is worse than the former. The former speaks the carnal sinner a dead man, which is bad; but this speaks him a devil of a man. It is not only an enemy, but enmity itself. Hence he infers (*v.* 8), *Those that are in the flesh cannot please God.* We may know our state and character,

(2) By enquiring whether we have the Spirit of God and Christ, or not (*v.* 9): *You are not in the flesh, but in the Spirit.* This expresses states and conditions of the soul vastly different. All the saints have flesh and spirit in them; but to be in the flesh and to be in the Spirit are contrary. It denotes our being overcome and subdued by one of these principles. As we say, A man is *in love*, or *in drink*, that is, overcome by it. Now the great question is whether we are in the flesh or in the Spirit; and how may we come to know it? Why, by enquiring whether the Spirit of God dwell in us. The Spirit dwelling in us is the best evidence of our being in the Spirit, for the indwelling is mutual (1 John iv. 16): *Dwelleth in God, and God in him.*

THE LIFEGIVING SPIRIT
(*vv.* 10–16)

In these verses the apostle represents two more excellent benefits, which belong to true believers.

I. Life. Now we are here told what becomes of the bodies and souls of those in whom Christ is.

1. We cannot say but that *the body is dead*; it is a frail, mortal, dying body, and it will be dead shortly; it is a house of clay, whose foundation is in the dust.

2. But the spirit, the precious soul, that is life; it is now spiritually alive, nay, it is life. Grace in the soul is its new nature; the life of the saint lies in the soul, while the life of the sinner goes no further than the body. When the body dies, and returns to the dust, *the spirit is life*; not only living and immortal, but swallowed up of life.

3. There is a life reserved too for the poor body at last: *He shall also quicken your mortal bodies, v.* 11. Two great assurances of the resurrection of the body are mentioned: (1) The resurrection of Christ: *he that raised up Christ from the dead shall also quicken.* Christ rose as the head, and first-fruits, and forerunner of all the saints, 1 Cor. xv. 20. (2) The indwelling of the Spirit. The same Spirit that raiseth the soul now will raise the body shortly: *By his Spirit that dwelleth in you.* Hence the apostle by the way infers how much it is our duty to walk not after the flesh, but after the Spirit, *vv.* 12, 13. Let not our life be after the wills and motions of the flesh. Two motives he mentions here: [1] We are not debtors to the flesh, neither by relation, gratitude, nor any other bond or obligation. [2] Consider the consequences, what will be at the end of the way. Here are life and death, blessing and cursing, set before us. *If you live after the flesh, you shall die*; that is, die eternally. But, on the other hand, *You shall live*, live and be happy to eternity; that is

the true life: *If you through the Spirit mortify the deeds of the body.*

II. The *Spirit of adoption* is another privilege belonging to those that are in Christ Jesus, *vv.* 14–16.

1. All that are Christ's are taken into the relation of children to God, *v.* 14. *They are the sons of God,* received into the number of God's children by adoption, owned and loved by him as his children.

2. And those that are the sons of God have the Spirit,

(1) To work in them the disposition of children.

[1] *You have not received the spirit of bondage again to fear, v.* 15. Understand it, *First,* Of that spirit of bondage which the Old-Testament church was under, by reason of the darkness and terror of that dispensation. The veil signified bondage, 2 Cor. iii. 15. Compare *v.* 17. *Secondly,* Of that spirit of bondage which many of the saints themselves were under at their conversion, under the convictions of sin and wrath set home by the Spirit; as those in Acts ii. 37, the jailer (Acts xvi. 30), Paul, Acts ix. 6. Then the Spirit himself was to the saints a spirit of bondage: "But," says the apostle, "with you this is over."

[2] But you *have received the Spirit of adoption.* Men may give a charter of adoption; but it is God's prerogative, when he adopts, to give a spirit of adoption—the nature of children. *Whereby we cry, Abba, Father.* Now, the Spirit teaches us in prayer to come to God as a Father, with a holy humble confidence, emboldening the soul in that duty.

(2) To witness to the relation of children, *v.* 16. The former is the work of the Spirit as a Sanctifier; this as a Comforter. *Beareth witness with our spirit.* The Spirit witnesses to none the privileges of children who have not the nature and disposition of children.

THE REDEMPTION OF THE BODY (*vv.* 17–25)

In these words the apostle describes a fourth illustrious branch of the happiness of believers, namely, a title to the future glory. 1. *Heirs of God.* The Lord himself is the portion of the saints' inheritance (Ps. xvi. 5), a goodly heritage, *v.* 6. 2. *Joint-heirs with Christ.* Christ, as Mediator, is said to be the heir of all things (Heb. i. 2), and true believers, by virtue of their union with him, *shall inherit all things,* Rev. xxi. 7. Now this future glory is further spoken of as the reward of present sufferings and as the accomplishment of present hopes.

I. As the reward of the saints' present sufferings; and it is a rich reward: *If so be that we suffer with him* (*v.* 17), or *forasmuch as we suffer with him.* See the gains of suffering for Christ; though we may be losers for him, we shall not, we cannot, be losers by him in the end. This gospel is filled with the assurances of. Now, that suffering saints may have strong supports and consolations from their hopes of heaven, he holds the balance (*v.* 18), in a comparison between the two, which is observable. 1. In one scale he puts the *sufferings of this present time.* The sufferings of the saints are but sufferings of this present time, strike no deeper than the things of time, last no longer than the present time (2 Cor. iv. 17), light affliction, and but for a moment. 2. In the other scale he puts the glory, and finds that a weight, an exceeding and eternal weight: *Glory that shall be revealed.* In our present state we come short, not only in the enjoyment, but in the knowledge of that glory (1 Cor. ii. 9; 1 John iii. 2): it shall be revealed. It surpasses all that we have yet seen and known. 3. He concludes the sufferings *not worthy to be compared with the glory.* They cannot merit that glory; and, if suffering for Christ will not merit, much less will doing.

II. As the accomplishment of the saints' present hopes and expectations, *v.* 19, &c. Now he observes an expectation of this glory,

1. In the creatures *vv.* 19–22. That must needs be a great, a transcendent glory, which all the creatures are so earnestly expecting and longing for. The sense of the apostle in these four verses we may take in the following observations: (1) That there is a present vanity to which the creature, by reason of the sin of man, is made subject, *v.* 20. *Under the bondage of corruption, v.* 21. There is an impurity, deformity, and infirmity, which the creature has contracted by the fall of man. They are thus captivated, not for any sin of their own, which they had committed, but for man's sin: *By reason of him who hath subjected the same.* (2) That the creatures *groan and travail in pain* together under this vanity and corruption, *v.* 22. It is a figurative expression. (3) That the creature, that is now thus burdened, shall,

at the time of the restitution of all things, be *delivered from this bondage into the glorious liberty of the children of God (v.* 21)—they shall no more be subject to vanity and corruption, and the other fruits of the curse; but, on the contrary, this lower world shall be renewed: when there will be new heavens there will be a new earth (2 Pet. iii. 13; Rev. xxi. 1). (4) That the creature doth therefore earnestly expect and wait for the *manifestation of the children of God, v.* 19. Observe, At the second coming of Christ there will be a manifestation of children of God. Now the saints are God's hidden ones, the wheat seems lost in a heap of chaff; but then they shall be manifested. It does not yet appear what we shall be (1 John iii. 2), but then the glory shall be revealed.

2. In the saints, who are new creatures, *vv.* 23–25. Observe, (1) The grounds of this expectation in the saints. It is our having received *the first-fruits of the Spirit,* which both quickens our desires and encourages our hopes, and both ways raises our expectations. *We groan within ourselves,* which denotes the strength and secrecy of these desires. (2) The object of this expectation. What is it we are thus desiring and waiting for? What would we have? *The adoption, to wit, the redemption of our body.* The resurrection is here called *the redemption of the body.* It shall then be rescued from the power of death and the grave, and the bondage of corruption; and, though a vile body, yet it shall be refined and beautified, and made like that glorious body of Christ, Phil. iii.

21; 1 Cor. xv. 42. This is called *the adoption*. (3) The agreeableness of this to our present state, *vv.* 24, 25. Our happiness is not in present possession: *We are saved by hope*.

THE SPIRIT INTERCEDES
(*vv.* 26–28)

The apostle here suggests two privileges more to which true Christians are entitled:

I. The help of the Spirit in prayer. Now observe,

1. Our weakness in prayer: *We know not what we should pray for as we ought*. If so great a saint as Paul knew not what to pray for, what little reason have we to go forth about that duty in our own strength!

2. The assistances which the Spirit gives us in that duty. He *helps our infirmities*, meant especially for our praying infirmities, which most easily beset us in that duty, against which the Spirit helps. The Spirit in the word helps; many rules and promises there are in the word for our help. The Spirit in the heart helps, dwelling in us, working in us, as a Spirit of grace and supplication. Why, the *Spirit itself makes intercession for us*, dictates our requests, indites our petitions, draws up our plea for us. Christ intercedes for us in heaven, the Spirit intercedes for us in our hearts. Now this intercession which the Spirit makes is, (1) *With groanings that cannot be uttered*. There may be praying in the Spirit where there is not a word spoken; as Moses prayed (Exod. xiv. 15), and Hannah, 1 Sam. i. 13. (2) *According to the will of God, v.*

27. The Spirit in the heart never contradicts the Spirit in the word.

3. The sure success of these intercessions: *He that searches the heart knoweth what is the mind of the Spirit, v.* 27. He knows what we have need of before we ask, Matt. vi. 8. He knows what is the mind of his own Spirit in us.

II. The concurrence of all providences for the good of those that are Christ's, *v.* 28. Observe here.

1. The character of the saints, who are interested in this privilege; they are here described by such properties as are common to all that are truly sanctified. (1) *They love God*. (2) *They are the called according to his purpose*, effectually called according to the eternal purpose.

2. The privilege of the saints, that *all things work together for good to them*, that is, all the providences of God that concern them. All that God performs he performs for them, Ps. lvii. 2. Either directly or indirectly, every providence has a tendency to the spiritual good of those that love God, breaking them off from sin, bringing them nearer to God, weaning them from the world, fitting them for heaven.

PREDESTINATION (*vv.* 29, 30)

The apostle, having reckoned up so many ingredients of the happiness of true believers, comes here to represent the ground of them all, which he lays in predestination. There are four links of it:

I. *Whom he did foreknow he also did predestinate to be conformed to the image of his Son*. All that God designed for glory and happiness as the end he decreed to grace and holiness as the way. Not, whom he did foreknow to be holy those he predestinated to be so. The counsels and decrees of God do not truckle to the frail and fickle will of men; no, God's foreknowledge of the saints is the same with that everlasing love wherewith he is said to have loved them, Jer. xxxi. 3. God's knowing his people is the same with his owning them, Ps. i. 6; John x. 14; 2 Tim. ii. 19. See *ch*. xi. 2.

II. *Whom he did predestinate those he also called*, not only with the external call (so many are called that were not chosen, Matt. xx. 16; xxii. 14), but with the internal and effectual call. The former comes to the ear only, but this to the heart. All that God did from eternity predestinate to grace and glory he does, in the fulness of time, effectually call.

III. *Whom he called those he also justified*. All that are effectually called are justified, absolved from guilt, and accepted as righteous through Jesus Christ.

IV. *Whom he justified those he also glorified*. The power of corruption being broken in effectual calling, and the guilt of sin removed in justification, all that which hinders is taken out of the way, and nothing can come between that soul and glory.

THE BELIEVER'S TRIUMPH
(*vv.* 31–39)

The apostle closes this excellent discourse upon the privileges of believers with a holy triumph, in the name of all the saints. More particularly.

I. We have supplies ready in all our wants (*v.* 32): *He that spared*, & c. Who can be against us, to strip us, to deprive us of our comforts? 1. Observe what God has done for us, on which our hopes are built: *He spared not his own Son*. When he was to undertake our salvation, the Father was willing to part with him, did not think him too precious a gift to bestow for the salvation of poor souls. 2. What we may therefore expect he will do: He will *with him freely give us all things*. Can it be imagined that he should do the greater and not do the less? that he should give so great a gift for us when we were enemies, and should deny us any good thing, now that through him we are friends and children?

II. We have an answer ready to all accusations and a security against all condemnations (*vv.* 33, 34): *Who shall lay any thing?* Doth the law accuse them? Do their own consciences accuse them? Is the devil, the accuser of the brethren, accusing them before our God day and night? This is enough to answer all those accusations, *It is God that justifieth*. It is by virtue of our interest in Christ, our relation to him, and our union with him, that we are thus secured. 1. His death: *It is Christ that died*. By the merit of his death he paid our debt; and the surety's payment is a good plea to an action of debt. It is Christ, an able all-sufficient Saviour. 2. His resurrection: *Yea, rather, that has risen again*. This is a much greater encouragement, for it is a convincing evidence that divine justice was satisfied by the merit of his death. 3. His sitting at the right hand of God: He is *even at the right hand of*

God—a further evidence that he has done his work, and a mighty encouragement to us in reference to all accusations, that we have a friend, such a friend, in court. 4. The intercession which he makes there. He is there, not unconcerned about us, not forgetful of us, but *making intercession*. He is agent for us there, an advocate for us, to answer all accusations, to put in our plea, and to prosecute it with effect, to appear for us and to present our petitions.

III. We have good assurance of our preservation and continuance in this blessed state, *v.* 35, to the end. We have here from the apostle,

1. A daring challenge to all the enemies of the saints to separate them, if they could, from the love of Christ. *Who shall?* None shall, *vv.* 35–37. Observe here,

(1) The present calamities of Christ's beloved ones supposed. Can a case be supposed more black and dismal? It is illustrated (*v.* 36) by a passage quoted from Ps. xlix. 22, *For thy sake we are killed all the day long*, which intimates that we are not to think strange, no not concerning the fiery bloody trial.

(2) The inability of all these things to separate us from the love of Christ. Shall they, can they, do it? No, by no means. All this will not cut the bond of love and friendship that is between Christ and true believers.

(3) The triumph of believers in this (*v.* 37): *Nay, in all these things we are more than conquerors.*

[1] We are conquerors: though killed all the day long, yet conquerors. A strange way of conquering,

but it was Christ's way; thus he triumphed over principalities and powers in his cross.

[2] We are more than conquerors. In our patiently bearing these trials we are not only conquerors, but more than conquerors, that is, triumphers.

[3] It is only *through Christ that loved us*, the merit of his death taking the sting out of all these troubles, the Spirit of his grace strengthening us, and enabling us to bear them with holy courage and constancy, and coming in with special comforts and supports. Thus we are conquerors, not in our own strength, but in the grace that is in Christ Jesus.

2. A direct and positive conclusion of the whole matter: *For I am persuaded*, *vv.* 38, 39. It denotes a full, and strong, and affectionate persuasion, arising from the experience of the strength and sweetness of the divine love. And here he enumerates all those things which might be supposed likely to separate between Christ and believers, and concludes that it could not be done.

CHAPTER NINE

THE ISRAELITES (*vv.* 1–5)

We have here the apostle's solemn profession of a great concern for the nation and people of the Jews—that he was heartily troubled that so many of them were enemies to the gospel, and out of the way of salvation.

I. He asserts it with a solemn protestation (*v.* 1): *I say the truth in Christ,* "I speak it as a Christian."

II. He backs it with a very

serious imprecation, which he was ready to make, out of love to the Jews. He would be willing to undergo the greatest misery to do them good.

III. He gives us the reason of this affection and concern.

1. Because of their relation to them: *My brethren, my kinsmen, according to the flesh.* We ought to be in a special manner concerned for the spiritual good of our relations, our brethren and kinsmen.

2. Especially because of their relation to God (vv. 4, 5): *Who are Israelites*, the seed of Abraham, God's friend, and of Jacob his chosen, taken into the covenant of peculiarity, dignified and distinguished by visible church-privileges, many of which are here mentioned.

THE PROMISE STANDS
(vv. 6–13)

Now the difficulty is to reconcile the rejection of the unbelieving Jews with the word of God's promise, and the external tokens of the divine favour, which had been conferred upon them.

In this paragraph the apostle explains the true meaning and intention of the promise. When we mistake the word, and misunderstand the promise, no marvel if we are ready to quarrel with God about the accomplishment; and therefore the sense of this must first be duly stated. Now he here makes it out that, when God said he would be *a God to Abraham, and to his seed* (which was the famous promise made unto the fathers), he did not mean it of all his seed according to

the flesh, as if it were a necessary concomitant of the blood of Abraham; but that he intended it with a limitation only to such and such. And as from the beginning it was appropriated to Isaac and not to Ishmael, to Jacob and not to Esau, and yet for all this the word of God was not made of no effect; so now the same promise is appropriated to believing Jews that embrace Christ and Christianity, and, though it throws off multitudes that refuse Christ, yet the promise is not therefore defeated and invalidated, any more than it was by the typical rejection of Ishmael and Esau.

GOD IS SOVEREIGN
(vv. 14–24)

Now this part of his discourse is in answer to two objections.

I. It might be objected, *Is there unrighteousness with God?* If God, in dealing with the children of men, do thus, in an arbitrary manner, choose some and refuse others, may it not be suspected that there is unrighteousness with him? This the apostle startles at the thought of: *God forbid!* He denies the consequences, and proves the denial.

1. In respect of those to whom he shows mercy, vv. 15, 16. He quotes that scripture to show God's sovereignty in dispensing his favours (Exod. xxxiii. 19): *I will be gracious to whom I will be gracious.* God is a competent judge, even in his own case. Whatsoever God does, or is resolved to do, is both by the one and the other proved to be just.

2. In respect of those who perish, v. 17. God's sovereignty, manifested

in the ruin of sinners, is here discovered in the instance of Pharaoh; it is quoted from Exod. ix. 16,

II. It might be objected, *Why doth he yet find fault? For who hath resisted his will? v.* 19. If God, while he gives effectual grace to some, denies it to others, why doth he find fault with those to whom he denies it? If he hath rejected the Jews, and hid from their eyes the things that belong to their peace, why doth he find fault with them for their blindness? This objection he answers at large,

1. By reproving the objector (*v.* 20): *Nay but, O man.* This is not an objection fit to be made by the creature against his Creator, by man against God.

2. By resolving all into the divine sovereignty. We are the thing formed, and he is the former; and it does not become us to challenge or arraign his wisdom in ordering and disposing of us into this or that shape of figure. The rude and unformed mass of matter hath no right to this or that form, but is shaped at the pleasure of him that formeth it. God's sovereignty over us is fitly illustrated by the power that the potter hath over the clay; compare Jer. xviii. 6, where, by a like comparison, God asserts his dominion over the nation of the Jews, when he was about to magnify his justice in their destruction by Nebuchadnezzar.

THE REMNANT (*vv.* 25–29)

Now he shows how this, which was so uneasy to them, was spoken of in the scripture.

I. By the prophet Hosea, who speaks of the taking in of a great many of the Gentiles, Hos. ii. 23 and Hos. i. 10.

II. By the prophet Isaiah, who speaks of the casting off of many of the Jews, in two places:

1. One is Isa. x. 22, 23, which speaks of the saving of a remnant, that is, but a remnant, which, though in the prophecy it seems to refer to the preservation of a remnant from the destruction and desolation that were coming upon them by Sennacherib and his army, yet is to be understood as looking further, and sufficiently proves that it is no strange thing for God to abandon to ruin a great many of the seed of Abraham, and yet maintain his word of promise to Abraham in full force and virtue.

2. Another is quoted from Isa. i. 9, where the prophet is showing how in a time of general calamity and destruction God would preserve a seed. This is to the same purport with the former; and the scope of it is to show that it was no strange thing for God to leave the greatest part of the people of the Jews to ruin, and to reserve to himself only a small remnant: so he had done formerly, as appears by their own prophets; and they must not wonder if he did so now.

THE STUMBLING STONE (*vv.* 30–33)

The apostle comes here at last to fix the true reason of the reception of the Gentiles, and the rejection of the Jews. There was a difference in the way of their seeking, and therefore there was that different success, though still it was the free grace of God that made them differ.

I. Concerning the Gentiles observe, 1. How they had been alienated from righteousness: they followed not after it; they knew not their guilt and misery, and therefore were not at all solicitous to procure a remedy. In their conversion preventing grace was greatly magnified: God was *found of those that sought him not*, Isa. lxv. 1. 2. How they attained to righteousness, notwithstanding: *By faith;* not by being proselyted to the Jewish religion, and submitting to the ceremonial law, but by embracing Christ, and believing in Christ, and submitting to the gospel.

II. Concerning the Jews observe, 1. How they missed their end: they *followed after the law of righteousness* (*v.* 31)—they talked much of justification and holiness, seemed very ambitious of being the people of God and the favourites of heaven, but they did not attain to it, that is, the greatest part of them did not. 2. How they mistook their way, which was the cause of their missing the end, *vv.* 32, 33. They sought, but not in the right way, not in the humbling way, not in the instituted appointed way. *Not by faith.* But still there is a remnant that do believe on him; and they *shall not be ashamed*, that is, their hopes and expectations of justification by him shall not be disappointed, as theirs are who expect it by the law. So that, upon the whole, the unbelieving Jews have no reason to quarrel with God for rejecting them; they had a fair offer of righteousness, and life, and salvation, made to them upon gospel terms, which they did not like, and would not come up to; and

therefore, if they perish, they may thank themselves—their blood is upon their own heads.

CHAPTER TEN
THE JEWS' MISTAKE
(*vv.* 1–11)

The scope of the apostle in this part of the chapter is to show the vast difference between the righteousness of the law and the righteousness of faith, and the great pre-eminence of the righteousness of faith above that of the law; that he might induce and persuade the Jews to believe in Christ, aggravate the folly of sin and those that refused, and justify God in the rejection of such refusers.

I. Paul here professes his good affection to the Jews, with the reason of it (*vv.* 1, 2), where he gives them a good wish, and a good witness.

I bear them record that they have a zeal of God. Their opposition to the gospel is from a principle of respect to the law, which they know to have come from God. There is such a thing as a blind misguided zeal: such was that of the Jews, who, when they hated Christ's people and ministers, and cast them out, said, *Let the Lord be glorified* (Isa. lxvi. 5); nay, they killed them, and thought they did God good service, John xvi. 2.

II. He here shows the fatal mistake that the unbelieving Jews were guilty of, which was their ruin. Their zeal was *not according to knowledge*. This he shows further, *v.* 3, where we may observe,

1. The nature of their unbelief. They *have not submitted themselves*

to the righteousness of God, that is, they have not yielded to gospel-terms, nor accepted the tender of justification by faith in Christ, which is made in the gospel.

2. The causes of their unbelief, and these are two: (1) Ignorance of God's righteousness. They did not understand, and believe, and consider, the strict justice of God, in hating and punishing sin, and demanding satisfaction. (2) A proud conceit of their own righteousness: *Going about to establish their own*—a righteousness of their own devising, and of their own working out, by the merit of their works, and by their observance of the ceremonial law.

III. He here shows the folly of that mistake, and what an unreasonable thing it was for them to be seeking justification by the works of the law, now that Christ had come, and had brought in an everlasting righteousness; considering,

1. The subserviency of the law to the gospel (*v.* 4): *Christ is the end of the law for righteousness*. The design of the law was to lead people to Christ.

2. The excellency of the gospel above the law. This he proves by showing the different constitution of these two.

(1) What is the righteousness which is of the law? This he shows, *v.* 5. The tenour of it is, *Do, and live*. The doing supposed must be perfect and sinless, without the least breach or violation. Now, was it not extreme folly in the Jews to adhere so closely to this way of justification and salvation, which was in itself so hard, and by the corruption of nature now become

impossible, when there was a new and a living way opened?

(2) What is that righteousness which is of faith, *v.* 6, &c. This he describes in the words of Moses, in Deuteronomy xxx. 11–14, and shows,

[1] That it is not at all hard or difficult. The way of justification and salvation has in it no such depths or knots as may discourage us, no insuperable difficulties attending it; but, as was foretold, it is a high-way, Isa. xxxv. 8.

[2] But it is very plain and easy: *The word is nigh thee*. When we speak of looking upon Christ, and receiving Christ, and feeding upon Christ, it is not Christ in heaven, nor Christ in the deep, that we mean; but Christ in the promise, Christ exhibited to us, and offered, in the word. Christ is nigh thee, for the word is nigh thee: nigh thee indeed: it is *in thy mouth, and in thy heart*; there is no difficulty in understanding, believing, and owning it. Now what is this word faith We have the tenour of it, *vv.* 9, 10, the sum of the gospel, which is plain and easy enough. Observe,

First, What is promised to us: *Thou shalt be saved*.

Secondly, Upon what terms.

a. Two things are required as conditions of salvation: (*a*) *Confessing the Lord Jesus*—openly professing relation to him and dependence on him, as our prince and Saviour. (*b*) *Believing in the heart that God raised him from the dead*. The profession of faith with the mouth, if there be not the power of it in the heart, is but a mockery.

b. This is further illustrated (*v.* 10), and the order inverted, because there must first be faith in the heart before there can be an acceptable confession with the mouth. (*a*) Concerning faith: It is *with the heart that man believeth*, which implies more than an assent of the understanding, and takes in the consent of the will, an inward, hearty, sincere, and strong consent. (*b*) Concerning profession: It is with *the mouth that confession is made*—confession to God in prayer and praise (*ch.* xv. 6), confession to men by owning the ways of God before others, especially when we are called to it in a day of persecution. So that we have here a brief summary of the terms of salvation, and they are very reasonable; in short this, that we must devote, dedicate, and give up, to God, our souls and our bodies—our souls in believing with the heart, and our bodies in confessing with the mouth. This do, and thou shalt live. For this (*v* 11) he quotes Isa. xxviii. 16, *Whosoever believeth on him shall not be ashamed*.

PREACHING THE GOSPEL
(*vv.* 12–21)

In Jesus Christ there is neither Greek nor Jew, Col. iii. 11. *There is no difference*. For the proof of this he urges two arguments:

I. That God is the same to all: *The same Lord over all is rich unto all*. There is not one God to the Jews who is more kind, and another to the Gentiles who is less kind; but he is the same to all, a common father to all mankind.

II. That the promise is the same to all (*v.* 13): *Whoever shall call*—one as well as another, without exception. For the further illustration of this he observes,

1. How necessary it was that the gospel should be preached to the Gentiles, *vv.* 14, 15. This was what the Jews were so angry with Paul for, that he was the apostle of the Gentiles, and preached the gospel to them. Now he shows how needful it was to bring them within the reach of the forementioned promise, an interest in which they should not envy any of their fellow-creatures. (1) *They cannot call on him in whom they have not believed*. (2) *They cannot believe in him of whom they have not heard*. Some way or other the divine revelation must be made known to us, before we can receive it and assent to it; it is not born with us. (3) *They cannot hear without a preacher;* how should they? Somebody must tell them what they are to believe. (4) *They cannot preach except they be sent*, except they be both commissioned and in some measure qualified for their preaching work.

2. How welcome the gospel ought to be to those to whom it was preached, because it showed the way to salvation, *v.* 15. For this he quotes Isa. lii. 7.

3. He answers an objection against all this, which might be taken from the little success which the gospel had in many places (*v.* 16): *But they have not all obeyed the gospel*. All the Jews have not, all the Gentiles have not; far the greater part of both remain in unbelief and disobedience. In answer to this,

(1) He shows that the word preached is the ordinary means of working faith (*v.* 17): though many

that hear do not believe, yet those that believe have first heard. *Faith cometh by hearing*. It is the summary of what he had said before, *v. 14*.

(2) That those who would not believe the report of the gospel, yet, having heard it, were thereby left inexcusable, and may thank themselves for their own ruin, *v. 18, to the end*.

Many that will not accept of a good proposal will yet acknowledge that they have nothing to say against it: but the Jews who believed not rested not there, but contradicted and blasphemed. God's patience with them was a very great aggravation of their disobedience, and rendered it the more exceedingly sinful; as their disobedience advanced the honour of God's patience and rendered it the more exceedingly gracious. It is a wonder of mercy in God that his goodness is not overcome by man's badness; and it is a wonder of wickedness in man that his badness is not overcome by God's goodness.

CHAPTER ELEVEN

THE FUTURE OF THE JEWS
(*vv. 1–32*)

The apostle proposes here a plausible objection, which might be urged against the divine conduct in casting off the Jewish nation (*v. 1*): "*Hath God cast away his people?* Is the rejection total and final?"

I. The Jews, it is true, were many of them cast off, but not all. The supposition of this he introduces with a *God forbid*. He will by no means endure such a suggestion.

God had made a distinction between some of them and others.

1. There was a chosen remnant of believing Jews, that obtained righteousness and life by faith in Jesus Christ, *vv. 1–7*. Now,

(1) He shows that he himself was one of them.

(2) He suggests that as in Elijah's time, so now, this chosen remnant was really more and greater than one would think it was, which intimates likewise that it is no new nor unusual thing for God's grace and favour to Israel to be limited and confined to a remnant of that people; for so it was in Elijah's time. They were the persons whom God had in his eye in the counsels of his love; they are the election; they are God's choice. Such was the favour of God to the chosen remnant. But,

2. *The rest were blinded, v. 7*. Some are chosen and called, and the call is made effectual. But others are left to perish in their unbelief; nay, they are made worse by that which should have made them better. The gospel, which to those that believed was the savour of life unto life, to the unbelieving was the savour of death unto death. The same sun softens wax and hardens clay. Blindness and hardness are expressive of the same senselessness and stupidity of spirit. They shut their eyes, and would not see; this was their sin: and then God, in a way of righteous judgment, blinded their eyes, that they could not see; this was their punishment.

II. Another thing which qualified this doctrine of the rejection of the Jews was that though they were cast off and unchurched, yet the Gentiles were taken in (*v.* 11–14), which he applies by way of caution to the Gentiles, *vv.* 17–22.

1. The rejection of the Jews made room for the reception of the Gentiles. The Jews' leavings were a feast for the poor Gentiles (*v.* 11).

2. The use that the apostle makes of this doctrine concerning the substitution of the Gentiles in the room of the Jews.

(1) As a kinsman to the Jews, here is a word of excitement and exhortation to them, to stir them up to receive and embrace the gospel-offer. This God intended in his favour to the Gentiles, to provoke the Jews to jealousy (*v.* 11), and Paul endeavours to enforce it accordingly (*v.* 14): *If by any means I might provoke to emulation those who are my flesh.*

(2) As an apostle to the Gentiles, here is a word of caution for them: "*I speak to you Gentiles.* You believing Romans, you hear what riches of salvation are come to you by the fall of the Jews, but take heed lest you do any thing to forfeit it." Now two things he exhorts the Gentiles to, with reference to the rejected Jews:

[1] To have a respect for the Jews, notwithstanding, and to desire their conversion.

[2] To take heed to themselves, lest they should stumble and fall, as the Jews had done, *vv.* 17–22.

III. Another thing that qualifies this doctrine of the Jews' rejection is that, though for the present they are cast off, yet the rejection is not final; but, when the fulness of time is come, they will be taken in again. They are not cast off for ever, but

mercy is remembered in the midst of wrath. The Jews shall continue in blindness, till God hath performed his whole work among the Gentiles, and then their turn will come next to be remembered. This was the purpose and ordination of God, for wise and holy ends; things should not be ripe for the Jews' conversion till the church was replenished with the Gentiles, that it might appear that God's taking them again was not because he had need of them, but of his own free grace.

THE WISDOM OF GOD
(*vv.* 33–36)

Here the apostle does with great affection and awe adore,

1. The secrecy of the divine counsels: *O the depth!* in these proceedings towards the Jews and Gentiles; or, in general, the whole mystery of the gospel, which we cannot fully comprehend.

II. The sovereignty of the divine counsels. In all these things God acts as a free agent, does what he will, because he will, and gives not account of any of his matters (Job xxiii. 13; xxxiii. 13), and yet there is no unrighteousness with him.

CHAPTER TWELVE
REASONABLE SERVICE
(*vv.* 1–21)

We may observe here the apostle's exhortations,

I. Concerning our duty to God, We see what is godliness.

1. It is to surrender ourselves to God, and so to lay a good foundation. We must first give our own selves unto the Lord, 2 Cor. viii. 5.

This is here pressed as the spring of all duty and obedience, *vv.* 1, 2. Man consists of body and soul, Gen. ii. 7; Eccl. xii. 7.

The mind must be renewed for God. This is pressed (*v.* 2): "*Be you transformed by the renewing of your mind;* see to it that there be a saving change wrought in you, and that it be carried on." Conversion and sanctification are the renewing of the mind, a change not of the substance, but of the qualities of the soul.

[1] What is the great enemy to this renewing, which we must avoid; and that is, conformity to this world: *Be not conformed to this world.* All the disciples and followers of the Lord Jesus must be nonconformists to this world. We must not conform to the things of the world; they are mutable, and the fashion of them is passing away.

[2] What is the great effect of this renewing, which we must labour after: *That you may prove what is that good, and acceptable, and perfect will of God.* By the will of God here we are to understand his revealed will concerning our duty, what the Lord our God requires of us. *First,* The will of God is *good, and acceptable, and perfect;* three excellent properties of a law. It is good (Mic. vi. 8); it is exactly consonant to the eternal reason of good and evil. It is good in itself. It is good for us. It is acceptable, it is pleasing to God; that and that only is so which is prescribed by him. The only way to attain his favour as the end is to conform to his will as the rule. It is perfect, to which nothing can be added. *Secondly,* That it concerns Christians to

prove what is that will of God which is good, and acceptable, and perfect; that is, to know it with judgment and approbation, to know it experimentally, to know the excellency of the will of God by the experience of a conformity to it.

2. When this is done, to serve him in all manner of gospel obedience. Some hints of this we have here (*vv.* 11, 12), *Serving the Lord.* How? (1) We must make a business of it, and not be slothful in that business. *Not slothful in business.* There is the business of the world, that of our particular calling, in which we must not be slothful, 1 Thess, iv. 11. But this seems to be meant of the business of serving the Lord, our Father's business, Luke ii. 49. (2) We must be *fervent in spirit, serving the Lord.* God must be served with the spirit (*ch.* i. 9; John iv. 24), under the influences of the Holy Spirit. And there must be fervency in the spirit—a holy zeal, and warmth, and ardency of affection in all we do, as those that love God not only with the heart and soul, but with all our hearts and with all our souls. (3) *Rejoicing in hope.* God is worshipped and honoured by our hope and trust in him, especially when we rejoice in that hope, take a complacency in that confidence, which argues a great assurance of the reality and a great esteem of the excellency of the good hoped for. (4) *Patient in tribulation.* Thus also God is served, not only by working for him when he calls us to work, but by sitting still quietly when he calls us to suffer. (5) *Continuing instant in prayer.* It signifies both fervency and perseverance in prayer. We

should not be cold in the duty, nor soon weary of it, Luke xviii. 1; 1 Thess. v. 17; Eph. vi. 18; Col. iv. 2. This is our duty which immediately respects God.

II. Concerning our duty which respects ourselves; this is sobriety.

1. A sober opinion of ourselves, *v*. 3. Pride is a sin that is bred in the bone of all of us, and we have therefore each of us need to be cautioned and armed against it. Now the reasons why we must have such a sober opinion of ourselves, our own abilities and attainments, are these:

(1) Because whatever we have that is good, *God hath dealt* it to us; every good and perfect gift *comes from above*, James i. 17. What have we that we have not received? And, if we have received it, why then do we boast? 1 Cor. iv. 7.

(2) Because God deals out his gifts in a certain measure: According to *the measure of faith*. Now faith, and other spiritual gifts with it, are dealt by measure, according as Infinite Wisdom sees meet for us. Christ had the Spirit given him without measure, John iii. 34. But the saints have it by measure; see Eph. iv. 7.

(3) Because God has dealt out gifts to others as well as to us: *Dealt to every man*. This reasoning he illustrates by a comparison taken from the members of the natural body (as 1 Cor. xii. 12; Eph. iv. 16): *As we have many members in one body*, &c. *vv.* 4, 5. We stand in relation one to another; we are engaged to do all the good we can one to another, and to act in conjunction for the common benefit. See this illustrated at large, 1 Cor. xii. 14, &c. Therefore we must not be puffed up with a conceit of our own attainments, because, whatever we have, as we received it, so we received it not for ourselves, but for the good of others.

2. A sober use of the gifts that God hath given us. As we must not on the one hand be proud of our talents so on the other hand we must not bury them. *Having then gifts*. The following induction of particulars supplies the sense of this general. *Having gifts*, let us use them. Authority and ability for the ministerial work are the gift of God. —*Gifts differing*. There were in the primitive church extraordinary gifts of tongues, of discerning, of healing; but he speaks here of those that are ordinary. Compare 1 Cor. xii. 4; 1 Tim. iv. 14; 1 Pet. iv. 10. Seven particular gifts he specifies (*vv.* 6–8), which seem to be meant of so many distinct offices, used by the prudential constitution of many of the primitive churches, especially the larger. There are two general ones here expressed by prophesying and ministering, the former the work of the bishops, the latter the work of the deacons, which were the only two standing officers, Phil. i. 1.

(1) *Prophecy*. *Whether prophecy, let us prophesy according to the proportion of faith*. It is not meant of the extraordinary gifts of foretelling things to come, but the ordinary office of preaching the word: so *prophesying* is taken, 1 Cor. xiv. 1–3, &c.; xi. 4; 1 Thess. v. 20.

(2) *Ministry*. If a man hath *the office of a deacon*, or assistant to the

pastor and teacher, let him use that office well. Particularly, [1] *He that giveth, let him do it with simplicity* Those church-officers that were the stewards of the church's alms, collected money, and distributed it according as the necessities of the poor were. Let them do it *liberally* and faithfully. Some understand it in general of all almsgiving: He that hath wherewithal, let him give, and give plentifully and liberally; so the word is translated, 2 Cor. viii. 2; ix. 13. God loves a cheerful bountiful giver. [2] *He that ruleth with diligence.* The word denotes both care and industry to discover what is amiss, to reduce those that go astray, to reprove and admonish those that have fallen, to keep the church pure. [3] *He that showeth mercy with cheerfulness.* A pleasing countenance in acts of mercy is a great relief and comfort to the miserable; when they see it is not done grudgingly and unwillingly, but with pleasant looks and gentle words, and all possible indications of readiness and alacrity.

III. Concerning that part of our duty which respects our brethren, of which we have many instances, in brief exhortations. Now all our duty towards one another is summed up in one word, and that a sweet word, *love*. More particularly, there is a love owing to our friends, and to our enemies. He specifies both.

1. To our friends. He that hath friends must show himself friendly. There is a mutual love that Christians owe, and must pay.

(1) An affectionate love (*v.* 10): *Be kindly affectioned one to another, with brotherly love*—it signifies not only love, but a readiness and inclination to love, the most genuine and free affection, kindness flowing out as from a spring.

(2) A respectful love: *In honour preferring one another.* Instead of contending for superiority, let us be forward to give to others the pre-eminence. This is explained, Phil. ii. 3, *Let each esteem other better than themselves.*

(3) A liberal love (*v.* 13): *Distributing to the necessities of saints.* It is but a mock love which rests in the verbal expressions of kindness and respect, while the wants of our brethren call for real supplies, and it is in the power of our hands to furnish them. We must be ready, as we have ability and opportunity, to relieve any that are in want; but we are in a special manner bound to communicate to the saints. There is a common love owing to our fellow-creatures, but a special love owing to our fellow christians (Gal. vi. 10), *Especially to those who are of the household of faith.* He mentions another branch of this bountiful love: *Given to hospitality.* Those who have houses of their own should be ready to entertain those who go about doing good, or who, for fear of persecution, are forced to wander for shelter.

(4) A sympathizing love (*v.* 15): *Rejoice with those that do rejoice, and weep with those that weep.* Where there is a mutual love between the members of the mystical body, there will be such a fellow-feeling. See 1 Cor. xii. 26. True love will interest us in the sorrows and joys of one another, and teach us to make them our own.

(5) A united love: "*Be of the same mind one towards another* (v. 16), endeavour to be all one, not affecting to clash, and contradict, and thwart one another; but keep the unity of the Spirit in the bond of peace, Phil. ii. 2; iii. 15. 16; 1 Cor. i. 10.

(6) A condescending love: *Mind not high things, but condescend to men of low estate, v.* 16. True love cannot be without lowliness, Eph. iv. 1, 2; Phil. ii. 3. *Condescend;* that is, suit yourselves to them, stoop to them, stoop to them for their good; as Paul, 1 Cor. ix. 19, &c. Some think the original word is a metaphor taken from travellers, when those that are stronger and swifter of foot say for those that are weak and slow, make a halt, and take them with them; thus must Christians be tender towards their fellow travellers. We are members one of another, depend upon one another, are obliged to one another; and therefore, *Be not wise by yourselves*, remembering it is the merchandise of wisdom that we profess; now merchandise consists in commerce, receiving and returning.

(7) A love that engages us, as much as lies in us, *to live peaceably with all men, v.* 18. Observe how the exhortation is limited. It is not expressed so as to oblige us to impossibilities: *If it be possible, as much as lies in you.* Thus Heb. xii. 14, *Follow peace.* Eph. iv. 3, *Endeavouring to keep.* Study the things that make for peace. — *If it be possible.* It is not possible to preserve the peace when we cannot do it without offending God and wounding conscience.

2. To our enemies. Since men

became enemies to God, they have been found very apt to be enemies one to another. Now Christianity teaches us how to behave towards our enemies; and in this instruction it quite differs from all other rules and methods, which generally aim at victory and dominion; but this at inward peace and satisfaction. Whoever are our enemies, that wish us ill and seek to do us ill, our rule is to do them no hurt, but all the good we can.

(1) To do them no hurt (v. 17): *Recompense to no man evil for evil*, for that is a brutish recompence, and befitting only those animals which are not conscious either of any being above them or of any state before them. To the same purport, v. 19, *Dearly beloved, avenge not yourselves.* Would you pacify a brother offended? Call him dearly beloved. Such a soft word, fitly spoken, may be effectual to turn away wrath. *Avenge not yourselves;* that is, when any body has done you any ill turn, do not desire nor endeavour to bring the like mischief or inconvenience upon him. This is a hard lesson to corrupt nature; and therefore he subjoins, [1] A remedy against it: *Rather give place unto wrath.* Not to our own wrath; to give place to this is to give place to the devil, Eph. iv. 26, 27. We must resist, and stifle, and smother, and suppress this; but, *First,* To the wrath of our enemy. "Give place to it, that is, be of a yielding temper." When others are angry, let us be calm; this is a remedy against revenge, and seems to be the genuine sense. But, *Secondly,* Many apply it to the wrath of God: "Give place to this,

make room for him to take the throne of judgment, and let him alone to deal with thine adversary." [2] A reason against it: *For it is written, Vengeance is mine*. We find it written, Deut. xxxii. 35. God is the sovereign King, the righteous Judge, and to him it belongs to administer justice.

[2] We must not only not do hurt to our enemies, but our religion goes higher, and teaches us to do them all the good we can. It is a command peculiar to Christianity, and which does highly commend it: *Love your enemies*, Matt. v. 44. We are here taught to show that love to them both in word and deed.

[1] In word: *Bless those who persecute you*, *v*. 14. It has been the common lot of God's people to be persecuted, either with a powerful hand or with a spiteful tongue. Now we are here taught to bless those that so persecute us.

[2] In deed (*v*. 20). It is said of archbishop Cranmer that the way for a man to make him his friend was to do him an ill turn. The precept is quoted from Prov. xxv. 21, 22; so that, high as it seems to be, the Old Testament was not a stranger to it. *Thou shalt heap coals of fire on his head;* that is, "Thou shalt either," 1. "Melt him into repentance and friendship, and mollify his spirit towards thee" or 2. "It will aggravate his condemnation, and make his malice against thee the more inexcusable. Thou wilt hereby hasten upon him the tokens of God's wrath and vengeance." Not that this must be our intention in showing him kindness, but, for our encouragement, such will be the effect. (1) *Be not over-come of evil*. He that cannot quietly bear an injury is perfectly conquered by it. (2) *But overcome evil with good*, with the good of patience and forbearance, nay, and of kindness and beneficence to those that wrong you.

3. To conclude, there remain two exhortations yet untouched, which are general, and which recommend all the rest as good in themselves, and of good report.

(1) As good in themselves (*v*. 9): *Abhor that which is evil, cleave to that which is good*. God hath shown us what is good: these Christian duties are enjoined; and that is evil which is opposite to them.

(2) As of good report (*v*. 17): "*Provide things honest in the sight of all men;* that is, not only do, but study and forecast and take care to do, that which is amiable and creditable, and recommends religion to all with whom you converse." See Phil. iv. 8.

CHAPTER THIRTEEN
CHRISTIANS AND THE STATE (*vv*. 1–6)

We are here taught to conduct ourselves towards magistrates, and those that are in authority over us, called here the *higher powers*. Observe,

I. The duty enjoined: *Let every soul be subject*. Not that our consciences are to be subjected to the will of any man. It is God's prerogative to make laws immediately to bind conscience, and we must render to God the things that are God's. But it intimates that our subjection must be free and voluntary, sincere and hearty. "They are *higher powers*; be content they should be so, and submit to them accordingly." Now there was good reason for the pressing of this duty of subjection to civil magistrates, 1. Because of the reproach which the Christian religion lay under in the world, as an enemy to public peace, order, and government, as a sect that turned the world upside down, and the embracers of it as enemies to Cæsar, and the more because the leaders were Galileans—an old slander. 2. Because of the temptation which the Christians lay under to be otherwise affected to civil magistrates, some of them being originally Jews, and so leavened with a principle that it was unmeet for any of the seed of Abraham to be subject to one of another nation—their king just be of their brethren, Deut. xvii. 15. Besides, the civil powers were persecuting powers; the body of the law was against them.

II. The reasons to enforce this duty. Why must we be subject?

1. For *wrath's* sake. Because of the danger we run ourselves into by resistance. Magistrates bear the sword, and to oppose them is to hazard all that is dear to us in this world; for it is to no purpose to contend with him that bears the sword. This is a good argument, but it is low for a Christian.

2. We must be subject, *not only for wrath, but for conscience' sake*. Now to oblige conscience to this subjection he argues, *vv.* 1–4, 6.

(1) From the institution of magistracy: *There is no power but of God.* God as the ruler and governor of the world hath appointed the ordinance of magistracy, so that all civil power is derived from him as from its original, and he hath by his providence put the administration into those hands, whatever they are that have it. By him kings reign, Prov. viii. By him kings reign, Prov. viii. Hence it follows (*v.* 2) that whosoever *resisteth the power resisteth the ordinance of God.* Magistrates are therefore called gods (Ps. lxxxii. 6), because they bear the image of God's authority. And those who spurn at their power reflect upon God himself. Magistrates are here again and again called God's ministers. He is the *minister of God, v.* 4, 6. Magistrates are in a more peculiar manner God's servants; the dignity they have calls for duty. Though they are lords to us, they are servants to God, have work to do for him, and an account to render to him.

(2) From the intention of magistracy: *Rulers are not a terror to good works, but to the evil*, &c. Magistracy was designed to be,

[1] A terror to evil works and evil workers. They bear the sword; not only the sword of war, but the sword of justice. Hence it appears that laws with penalties for the lawless and disobedient (1 Tim. i. 9) must be constituted in Christian nations, and are agreeable with, and not contradictory to, the gospel.

[2] A praise to those that do well. Those that keep in the way of their duty shall have the commendation and protection of the civil powers, to their credit and comfort. Never did sovereign prince pervert the

ends of government as Nero did, and yet to him Paul appealed, and under him had the protection of the law and the inferior magistrates more than once. Better a bad government than none at all.

(3) From our interest in it: "He is *the minister of God to thee for good.* Thou hast the benefit and advantage of the government, and therefore must do what thou can'st to preserve it, and nothing to disturb it." Protection draws allegiance.

PAYING TAXES (*vv.* 7–10)

We are here taught a lesson of justice and charity.

I. Of justice (*v.* 7): *Render therefore all their dues,* especially to magistrates, for this refers to what goes before; and likewise to all with whom we have to do. He specifies, 1. Due taxes: *Tribute to whom tribute is due, custom to whom custom.* Many, who in other things seem to be just, yet make no conscience of this, but pass it off with a false ill-favoured maxim, that it is no sin to cheat the state, directly contrary to Paul's rule, *Tribute to whom tribute is due.* 2. Due respect: *Fear to whom fear, honour to whom honour.* This sums up the duty which we owe not only to magistrates, but to all superiors, parents, masters, all that are over us in the Lord, according to the fifth commandment; *Honour thy father and mother.*

II. Of charity: *Owe no man any thing; you do owe* no man any thing; so some read it: "Whatever you owe to any relation, or to any with whom you have to do, it is

eminently summed up and included in this debt of love. But to *love one another*, this is a debt that must be always in the paying, and yet always owing." Love is a debt. The law of God and the interest of mankind make it so. Now, to prove that love is the fulfilling of the law, he gives us, 1. An induction of particular precepts, *v.* 9. He specifies the last five of the ten commandments, which he observes to be all summed up in this royal law, *Thou shalt love thy neighbour as thyself*—with an *as* of quality, not of equality—"with the same sincerity that thou lovest thyself, though not in the same measure and degree." 2. A general rule concerning the nature of brotherly love: *Love worketh no ill* (*v.* 10)—he that walks in love, that is actuated and governed by a principle of love, *worketh no ill*; he neither practises nor contrives any ill *to his neighbour*, to any one that he has any thing to do with. Love is a living active principle of obedience to the whole law. The whole law is written in the heart, if the law of love be there.

TIME TO AWAKE
(*vv.* 11–14)

We are here taught a lesson of sobriety and godliness in ourselves.

I. When to awake: *Now it is high time to awake* (*v.* 11), to awake out of the sleep of sin (for a sinful condition is a sleeping condition), out of the sleep of carnal security, sloth and negligence, out of the sleep of spiritual death, and out of the sleep of spiritual deadness; both the wise and foolish virgins slumbered and slept, Matt. xxv. 5. Considering, 1. The time we are cast into: *Knowing the time.* Consider what time of day it is with us, and you will see it is high time to awake. It is gospel time, it is the accepted time, it is working time; it is a time when more is expected than was in the times of that ignorance which God winked at, when people sat in darkness. It is high time to awake; for the sun has been up a great while, and shines in our faces. Have we this light to sleep in? See 1 Thess. v. 5, 6. 2. The salvation we are upon the brink of: *Now is our salvation nearer than when we believed*—than when we first believed, and so took upon us the profession of Christianity.

II. How to dress ourselves. This is the next care, when we are awake and up. Observe then,

1. What we must put off; put off our night-clothes, which it is a shame to appear abroad in: *Cast off the works of darkness.* Sinful works are works of darkness; they come from the darkness of ignorance and mistake, they covet the darkness of privacy and concealment, and they end in the darkness of hell and destruction.

2. "What we must put on." (1) *Put on the armour of light.* Christians are soldiers in the midst of enemies, and their life a warfare, therefore their array must be armour, that they may stand upon their defence—the *armour of God,* to which we are directed, Eph. vi. 13, &c. (2) *Put on the Lord Jesus Christ, v. 14.* This stands in opposition to a great many base lusts, mentioned *v.* 13. *Rioting and drunkenness* must be cast off: one

would think it should follow, but "Put on sobriety, temperance, chastity," the opposite virtues: no, "*Put on Christ,* this includes all. Put him on as Lord to rule you, as Jesus to save you, and in both as Christ, anointed and appointed by the Father to this ruling saving work.

III. How to walk. When we are up and dressed, we are not to sit still in an affected closeness and privacy. What have we good clothes for, but to appear abroad in them?—*Let us walk.* Christianity teaches us how to walk so as to please God, whose eye is upon us: 1 Thess. iv. 1 *Walk honestly as in the day.* Compare Eph. v. 8, *Walk as children of light.*

IV. What provision to make (*v.* 14): *Make not provision for the flesh.* Be not anxious about the body. The necessities of the body must be considered, but the lusts of it must not be gratified. Natural desires must be answered, but wanton appetites must be checked and denied.

CHAPTER FOURTEEN

AVOIDING DIVISION
(*vv.* 1–23)

We have in this chapter,

I. An account of the unhappy contention which had broken out in the Christian church.

1. There was a difference among them about the distinction of meats and days; these are the two things specified. The case was this: The members of the Christian church at Rome were some of them originally Gentiles, and others of them Jews.

Now those that had been Jews were trained up in the observance of the ceremonial appointments touching meats and days. This, which had been bred in the bone with them, could hardly be got out of the flesh even after they turned Christians. While other Christians that understood themselves better, and knew their Christian liberty, made no such difference. (1) Concerning meats (*v.* 2): *One believeth that he may eat all things*—he is well satisfied that the ceremonial distinction of meats into clean and unclean is no longer in force, but that every creature of God is good, and nothing to be refused; nothing *unclean of itself, v.* 14. On the other hand, *another, who is weak*, is dissatisfied in this point, is not clear in his Christian liberty, but rather inclines to think that the meats forbidden by the law remain still unclean; and therefore, to keep at a distance from them, he will eat no flesh at all, but *eateth herbs*, contenting himself with only the fruits of the earth. (2) Concerning days, *v.* 5. Those who thought themselves still under some kind of obligation by the ceremonial law esteemed *one day above another*—kept up a respect to the times of the passover, pentecost, new moons, and fast of tabernacles. Those who knew that all these things were abolished and done away by Christ's coming esteemed every day alike.

2. It was not so much the difference itself that did the mischief as the mismanagement of the difference, making it a bone of contention. Well, this was the disease, and we see it remaining in the church to this day; the like differences, in like manner mismanaged, are still the disturbers of the church's peace. But,

II. We have proper directions and suggestions laid down for allaying this contention, and preventing the ill consequences of it. Let us observe the rules he gives, some to the strong and some to the weak, and some to both, for they are interwoven; and reduce the reasons to their proper rules.

1. Those who are weak must be *received but not to doubtful disputations, v.* 1. Take this for a general rule; spend your zeal in those things wherein you and all the people of God are agreed, and do not dispute about matters that are doubtful.

2. Those who are strong must by no means despise the weak; nor those who are weak judge the strong, *v.* 3. This is levelled directly against the fault of each party. It is seldom that any such contention exists but there is a fault on both sides, and both must mend. He argues against both these jointly: we must not despise nor judge our brethren.

(1) Because God hath received them; and we reflect upon him if we reject those whom he hath received.

(2) Because they are servants to their own master (*v.* 4): *Who art thou that judgest another man's servant?* We reckon it a piece of ill manners to meddle with other people's servants, and to find fault with them and censure them. Weak and strong Christians are indeed our brethren, but they are not our servants.

[3] Because both the one and the other, if they be true believers, and are right in the main, have an eye to God, and do approve themselves to God in what they do, *v.* 6. Observe his description of true Christians, taken from their end and aim (*vv.* 7, 8), and the ground of it, *v.* 9.

[1] Our end and aim: not self, but the Lord. As the particular end specifies the action, so the general scope and tendency specify the state. If we would know what way we walk in, we must enquire what end we walk towards. *First,* Not to self. We have learned to deny ourselves; this was our first lesson: *None of us liveth to himself. Secondly,* But *to the Lord* (*v.* 8), to the Lord Christ, to whom all power and judgment are committed, and in whose name we are taught, as Christians, to do every thing we do (Col. iii. 17), with an eye to the will of Christ as our rule, to the glory of Christ as our end, Phil. i. 21. This is true Christianity, which makes Christ all in all. So that, *whether we live or die, we are the Lord's,* devoted to him, depending on him, designed and designing for him.

[2] The ground of this, *v.* 9. It is grounded upon Christ's absolute sovereignty and dominion, which were the fruit and end of his death and resurrection. *To this end he both died, and rose, and revived* (he, having risen, entered upon a heavenly life, the glory which he had before) *that he might be Lord both of dead and living*—that he might be universal monarch, Lord of all (Acts x. 36), all the animate and inanimate creatures; for he is head over all things to the church.

(4) Because both the one and the other must shortly give an account, *vv.* 10–12. A believing regard to the judgment of the great day would silence all these rash judgings: *Why dost thou* that art weak *judge thy brother* that is strong? And *why dost thou* that art strong *set at nought thy brother* that is weak? Why is all this clashing, and contradicting, and censuring, among Christians? *We shall all stand before the judgment-seat of Christ,* 2 Cor. v. 10.

(5) Because the stress of Christianity is not to be laid upon these things, nor are they at all essential to religion, either on the one side or on the other. This is his reason (*vv.* 17, 18), which is reducible to this branch of exhortation. Why should you spend your zeal either for or against those things which are so minute and inconsiderable in religion?

3. Another rule here given is this, that in these doubtful things every one not only may, but must, walk according to the light that God hath given him. This is laid down *v.* 5, *Let every man be fully persuaded in his own mind.* To this purport he argues, *vv.* 14 and 23, which two verses explain this, and give us a rule not to act against the dictates,

(1) Of a mistaken conscience, *v.* 14. If a thing be indifferent, so that it is not in itself a sin not to do it, if we really think it a sin to do it it is to us a sin, though not to others, because we act against our consciences, though mistaken and misinformed.

(2) Nor must we act against the dictates of a doubting conscience. In those indifferent things were we are sure it is no sin not to do, and yet are not clear that it is lawful to do them, we must not do them while we continue under those doubts; for he *that doubteth is damned if he eat* (v. 23), that is, it turns into sin to him. *He is condemned* of his own conscience, because he *eateth not of faith*, because he does that which he is not fully persuaded he may lawfully do.

4. Another rule here prescribed is to those who are clear in these matters, and know their Christian liberty, yet to take heed of using it so as to give offence to a weak brother. This is laid down v. 13, *Let us not judge one another any more*. We must take heed of saying or doing any thing which may occasion our brother to stumble or fall; the one signifies a less, the other a greater degree of mischief and offence—that which may be an occasion,

(1) Of grief to our brother. Christians should take heed of grieving one another, and of saddening the hearts of Christ's little ones. See Matt. xviii. 6, 10.

(2) Of guilt to our brother. The former is a *stumbling-block*, that gives our brother a great shake, and is a hindrance and discouragement to him; but this is an *occasion to fall*. It is a generous piece of self-denial, for which we have Paul's example (1 Cor. viii. 13), *If meat make my brother to offend*; he does not say, *I will eat no meat*, that is to destroy himself; but *I will eat no flesh*, that is to deny himself, *while*

the world stands. This is to be extended to all such indifferent things whereby thy brother stumbleth, or is offended, is involved either in sin or in trouble: or *is made weak*—his graces weakened, his comforts weakened, his resolutions weakened. Observe the motives to enforce this caution.

[1] Consider the royal law of Christian love and charity, which is hereby broken (v. 15).

[2] Consider the design of Christ's death: *Destroy not him with thy meat for whom Christ died*, v. 15. Thou pleadest that it is thy own meat, and thou mayest do what thou wilt with it; but remember that, though the meat is thine, the brother offended by it is Christ's, and a part of his purchase.

[3] Consider the work of God (v. 20): "*For meat destroy not the work of God*—the work of grace, particularly the work of faith in thy brother's soul."

[4] Consider the evil of giving offence, and what an abuse it is of our Christian liberty. He grants that *all things indeed are pure*. We may lawfully eat flesh, even those meats which were prohibited by the ceremonial law; but, if we abuse this liberty, it turns into sin to us: *It is evil to him that eats with offence*.

5. There is one rule more laid down here; and it is general: *Let us therefore follow after the things which make for peace, and things wherewith one may edify another*, v. 19. Here is the sum of our duty towards our brethren. None so strong but they may be edified; none so weak but may edify; and, while we edify others, we benefit ourselves.

CHAPTER FIFTEEN

THE CHRISTIAN'S DUTY
(*vv.* 1–4)

The apostle here lays down two precepts, with reasons to enforce them, showing the duty of the strong Christian to consider and condescend to the weakest.

I. We must *bear the infirmities of the weak. v.* 1. We all have our infirmities; but the weak are more subject to them than others—the weak in knowledge or grace, the bruised reed and the smoking flax. We must consider these; not trample upon them, but encourage them, and bear with their infirmities.

II. We must not please ourselves, but our neighbour, *vv.*1, 2.

1. Christians must not please themselves. We must not make it our business to gratify all the little appetites and desires of our own heart; it is good for us to cross ourselves sometimes, and then we shall the better bear others crossing of us.

2. Christians must please their brethren. How amiable and comfortable a society would the church of Christ be if Christians would study to please one another, as now we see them commonly industrious to cross, and thwart, and contradict one another?—*Please his neighbour,* not in every thing, it is not an unlimited rule; but *for his good,* especially for the good of his soul: not please him by serving his wicked wills, and humouring him in a sinful way, or consenting to his enticements, or suffering sin upon him; this is a base way of pleasing our neighbour to the ruin of his soul: if we thus please men, we are not the servants of Christ; but please him for his good; not for our own secular good, or to make a prey of him, but for his spiritual good. Observe,

(1) That Christ pleased not himself. His whole life was a self-denying self-displeasing life. He bore the *infirmities of the weak,* Heb. iv. 15.

(2) That herein the scripture was fulfilled: *As it is written, The reproaches of those that reproached thee fell on me.* This is quoted out of Ps. lxix. It is quoted to show that Christ was so far from pleasing himself that he did in the highest degree displease himself. He preferred our benefit before his own ease and pleasure.

(3) That therefore we must go and do likewise: *For whatsoever things were written aforetime were written for our learning.* [1] That which is written of Christ, concerning his self-denial and sufferings, is *written for our learning*; he hath left us an example. [2] That which is written in the scriptures of the Old Testament in the general is written for our learning. What David had said in his own person Paul had just now applied to Christ. Now lest this should look like a straining of the scripture, he gives us this excellent rule in general, that all the scriptures of the Old Testament (much more those of the New) were written for our learning, and are not to be looked upon as of private interpretation. *That we through patience and comfort of the scriptures might have hope.* That hope which hath eternal life for its object is here proposed as the end of scripture-learning. The scripture

was written that we might know what to hope for from God, and upon what grounds, and in what way. This should recommend the scripture to us that it is a special friend to Christian hope. Now the way of attaining this hope is *through patience and comfort of the scripture*. The more patience we exercise under troubles the more hopefully we may look through our troubles; nothing more destructive to hope than impatience. And the *comfort of the scriptures*, that comfort which springs from the word of God (that is the surest and sweetest comfort) is likewise a great stay to hope, as it is an earnest in hand of the good hoped for.

CHRISTIAN UNITY (*vv.* 5, 6)

The apostle, having delivered two exhortations, before he proceeds to more, intermixes here a prayer for the success of what he had said. Faithful ministers water their preaching with their prayers, because, whoever sows the seed, it is God that gives the increase. We can but speak to the ear; it is God's prerogative to speak to the heart. Observe,

I. The title he gives to God: *The God of patience and consolation*, who is both the author and the foundation of all the patience and consolation of the saints, from whom it springs and on whom it is built.

II. The mercy he begs of God: *Grant you to be like-minded one towards another, according to Christ Jesus*. 1. The foundation of Christian love and peace is laid in like-mindedness, a consent in judgment

as far as you have attained, or at least a concord and agreement in affection. 2. This like-mindedness must be *according to Christ Jesus*, according to the precept of Christ, the royal law of love, according to the pattern and example of Christ, which he had propounded to them for their imitation, *v.* 3.

III. The end of his desire: that God may be glorified, *v.* 6. The unity of Christians glorifies *God as the Father of our Lord Jesus Christ*, because it is a kind of counter-part or representation of the oneness that is between the Father and the Son.

THE DESTINY OF THE GENTILES
(*vv.* 7–12)

The apostle here returns to his exhortation to Christians. What he says here (*v.* 7) is to the same purport with the former; but the repetition shows how much the apostle's heart was upon it. Those that have received Christ by faith must receive all Christians by brotherly love. Now the reason why Christians must receive one another is taken, as before, from the condescending love of Christ to us: *As Christ also received us, to the glory of God*.

I. Christ hath received us to the glory of God. The end of our reception by Christ is that we might glorify God in this world, and be glorified with him in that to come.

II. We must receive one another to the glory of God. This must be our great end in all our actions, that God may be glorified; and nothing more conduces to this than the mutual love and kindness of those that profess religion; compare *v.* 6, *That you may with one mind and one mouth glorify God.*

1. He received the Jews, *v.* 8. Let not any think hardly or scornfully therefore of those that were originally Jews, and still, through weakness, retain some savour of their old Judaism; for, (1) Jesus Christ was a *minister of the circumcision.* (2) He was so for the truth of God. That which he preached to them was the truth; for he came into the world to bear witness to the truth, John xviii. 37. And he is himself the truth, John xiv. 6.

2. He received the Gentiles likewise. This he shows, *vv.* 9–12.

(1) Observe Christ's favour to the Gentiles, in taking them in to praise God—the work of the church on earth and the wages of that in heaven. One design of Christ was that the Gentiles likewise might be converted, that they might be one with the Jews in Christ's mystical body. A good reason why they should not think the worse of any Christian for his having been formerly a Gentile; for Christ has received him.

(2) The fulfilling of the scriptures in this. The favour of God to the Gentiles was not only mercy, but truth. Though there were not promises directly given to them, as to the fathers of the Jews, yet there were many prophecies concerning them, which related to the calling of them, and the embodying of them in the church, some of which he mentions because it was a thing that the Jews were hardly persuaded to believe.

A PRAYER (*v.* 13)

Here is another prayer directed to God, as the God of hope; and it is, as the former (*vv.* 5, 6), for spiritual blessings: these are the best blessings, and to be first and chiefly prayed for.

I. Observe how he addresses himself to God, as the *God of hope.* It is good in prayer to fasten upon those names, titles, and attributes of God, which are most suitable to the errand we come upon, and will best serve to encourage our faith concerning it.

II. What he asks of God, not for himself, but for them.

1. *That they might be filled with all joy and peace in believing.* Joy and peace are two of those things in which the kingdom of God consists, *ch.* xiv. 17. Joy in God, peace of conscience, both arising from a sense of our justification; see *ch.* v. 1, 2.

2. That they might *abound in hope through the power of the Holy Ghost.* The joy and peace of believers arise chiefly from their hopes. What is laid out upon them is but little, compared with what is laid up for them; therefore the more hope they have the more joy and peace they have.

PAUL'S APOSTOLIC MINISTRY I (*vv.* 14–16)

Here, I. He commends these Christians with the highest characters that could be. 1. That they *were full of goodness*; therefore the more likely to take in good part what he had written, and to account it a kindness; and not only so, but to comply with it, and to put it in practice, especially that which relates to their union and to the healing of their differences. A good understanding of one another, and a good will to one another, would soon put an end to strife. 2. *Filled with all knowledge.* Goodness and knowledge together! A very rare and an excellent conjunction; the head and the heart of the new man. 3. *Able to admonish one another.* To this there is a further gift requisite, even the gift of utterance. Those that have goodness and knowledge should communicate what they have for the use and benefit of others. Would to God that all the Lord's people were prophets. But that which is every body's work is nobody's work; and therefore,

II. He clears himself from the suspicion of intermeddling needlessly with that which did not belong to him, *v.* 15. But then consider,

1. He did it only as their remembrancer:*As putting you in mind.*

2. He did it as the apostle of the Gentiles. It was in pursuance of his office: *Because of the grace* (that is, the *apostleship, ch.* i. 5) *given to me of God,* to be the minister *of Jesus Christ to the Gentiles, v.* 16. Observe here, (1) Whose minister he was: the *minister of Jesus Christ,* 1 Cor. iv. 1. He is our Master; his we are, and him we serve. (2) To whom: to the Gentiles. So God had appointed him, Acts xxii. 21. So Peter and he had agreed, Gal. ii. 7–9. (3) What he ministered: the *gospel of God;—ministering as about holy things* (so the word signifies), executing the office of a Christian priest, more spiritual, and therefore more excellent, than the

Levitical priesthood. (4) For what end: *that the offering up* (or sacrificing) *of the Gentiles might be acceptable*—that God might have the glory which would redound to his name by the conversion of the Gentiles. And it is an acceptable offering, *being sanctified by the Holy Ghost.* Paul preached to them, and dealt with them; but that which made them sacrifices to God was their sanctification; and this was not his work, but the work of the Holy Ghost. None are acceptably offered to God but those that are sanctified: unholy things can never be pleasing to the holy God.

PAUL'S APOSTOLIC MINISTRY II (*vv.* 17–21)

The apostle here gives some account of himself and of his own affairs.

I. His unwearied diligence and industry in his work. He was one that laboured *more abundantly than they all.*

1. He preached in many places: *From Jerusalem,* whence the law went forth as a lamp that shineth, and *round about unto Illyricum,* many hundred miles distant from Jerusalem. We have in the book of the Acts an account of Paul's travels. Now it might be suspected that if Paul undertook so much work, surely he did it by the halves. "No," says he, "*I have fully preached the Gospel of Christ*— have given them a full account of the truth and terms of the gospel, have not shunned to declare the whole counsel of God (Acts xx. 27), have kept back nothing that was necessary for them to know."

2. He preached in places that had

not heard the gospel before, *vv.* 20, 21. He broke up the fallow ground, laid the first stone in many places, and introduced Christianity where nothing had reigned for many ages but idolatry and witchcraft, and all sorts of diabolism. He was in care not to *build upon another man's foundation*, lest he should thereby disprove his apostleship, and give occasion to those who sought occasion to reflect upon him. He quotes a scripture for this out of Isa. lii. 15, *To whom he was not spoken of, they shall see.*

II. The great and wonderful success that he had in his work: It was effectual to *make the Gentiles obedient*. The design of the gospel is to bring people to be *obedient*; it is not only a truth to be believed, but a law to be obeyed. It is the Spirit's operation that makes the difference. Paul himself, as great a preacher as he was, with all his mighty signs and wonders, could not make one soul obedient further than the power of the Spirit of God accompanied his labours.

PAUL'S APOSTOLIC MINISTRY III (*vv.* 22–29)

St. Paul here declares his purpose to come and see the Christians at Rome.

I. He excuses it that he never came yet. Observe how careful Paul was to keep in with his friends, and to prevent or anticipate any exceptions against him; not as one that lorded it over God's heritage.

II. He promised to come and see them shortly, *vv.* 23, 24, 29. *Having no more place in these parts*, namely, in Greece, where he then was. The whole of that country

being more or less leavened with the savour of the gospel, churches being planted in the most considerable towns and pastors settled to carry on the work which Paul had begun, he had little more to do there. Observe,

1. How he forecasted his intended visit. His project was to see them in his way to Spain. It appears by this that Paul intended a journey into Spain, to plant Christianity there. Observe his prudence. It is wisdom for every one of us to order our affairs so that we may do the most work in the least time. Observe how doubtfully he speaks: *I trust to see you:* not, "I am resolved I will," but, "I hope I shall." we must purpose all our purposes and make all our promises in like manner with a submission to the divine providence; not boasting ourselves of to-morrow, because we know not what a day may bring forth, Prov. xxvii. 1; James iv. 13–15.

2. What he expected in his intended visit. (1) What he expected from them. He expected they would bring him on his way towards Spain. (2) What he expected in them: to *be somewhat filled with their company*. That which Paul desired was their company and conversation. The good company of the saints is very desirable and delightful. (3) What he expected from God with them, *v.* 29. He expected to come *in the fulness of the blessing of the gospel of Christ*. When ministers are fully prepared to give out, and people fully prepared to receive, this blessing, both are happy. Many have the gospel who have not the blessing of the gospel, and so they have it in vain.

The gospel, and so they have it in vain. The gospel will not profit, unless God bless it to us; and it is our duty to wait upon him for that blessing, and for the fulness of it.

III. He gives them a good reason why he could not come and see them now, because he had other business upon his hands, which required his attendance, upon which he must first make a journey to Jerusalem, *vv.* 25–28. He gives a particular account of it, to show that the excuse was real. He was going to Jerusalem, as the messenger of the church's charity to the poor saints there. Ministering to the saints is good work, and is not below the greatest apostles. This Paul had undertaken, and therefore he resolves to go through with it, before he fell upon other work (*v.* 28): *When I have sealed to them this fruit.* He calls the alms *fruit*, for it is one of the fruits of righteousness; it sprang from a root of grace in the givers, and redounded to the benefit and comfort of the receivers. And his sealing it intimates his great care about it, that what was given might be kept entire, and not embezzled, but disposed of according to the design of the givers.

A REQUEST FOR PRAYER
(*vv.* 30–33)

Here we have, I. St. Paul's desire of a share in the prayers of the Romans for him, expressed very earnestly, *vv.* 30–32.

1. Observe why they must pray for him. (1) "*For the Lord Jesus Christ's sake.* He is my Master, I am going about his work, and his glory is interested in the success of

it: if you have any regard to Jesus Christ, and to his cause and kingdom, pray for me. You love Christ, and own Christ; for his sake then do me this kindness." (2) "*For the love of the Spirit.* As a proof and instance of that love which the Spirit works in the hearts of believers one to another, pray for me; as a fruit of that communion which we have one with another by the Spirit though we never saw one another."

2. How they must pray for him: *That you strive together.* (1) That *you strive in prayer.* We must put forth all that is within us in that duty; pray with fixedness, faith, and fervency; wrestle with God, as Jacob did. (2) That you strive together with me. When he begged their prayers for him, he did not intend thereby to excuse his praying for himself. Those who beg the prayers of others must not neglect to pray for themselves.

3. What they must beg of God for him. He mentions particulars; for, in praying both for ourselves and for our friends, it is good to be particular. (1) The dangers which he was exposed to: *That I may be delivered from those that do not believe in Judea.* (2) His services: *Pray that my service which I have for Juersalem may be accepted of the saints.* Why, was there any danger that it would not be accepted? Can money be otherwise than acceptable to the poor? Yes, there was some ground of suspicion in this case; for Paul was the apostle of the Gentiles, and as the unbelieving Jews looked spitefully at him, which was their wickedness, so those that believed were shy of him upon that

account, which was their weakness. (3) His journey to them. To engage their prayers for him, he interests them in his concerns (v. 32): *That I may come unto you with joy*.

II. Here is another prayer of the apostle for them (v. 33): *Now the God of peace be with you all, Amen*. The Lord of hosts, the God of battle, is the God of peace, the author and lover of peace. Those who are united in the blessing of God should be united in affection one to another.

CHAPTER SIXTEEN

PERSONAL GREETINGS
(vv. 1–16)

Such remembrances as these are usual in letters between friends; and yet Paul, by the savouriness of his expressions, sanctifies these common compliments.

I. Here is the recommendation of a friend, by whom (as some think) this epistle was sent—one *Phebe*, vv. 1, 2. It should seem that she was a person of quality and estate, who had business which called her to Rome, where she was a stranger; and therefore Paul recommends her to the acquaintance of the Christians there: an expression of his true friendship to her. Paul was as well skilled in the art of obliging as most men. True religion, rightly received, never made any man uncivil. Courtesy and Christianity agree well together.

II. Here are commendations to some particular friends among those to whom he wrote, more than in any other of the epistles. Though the care of all the churches came upon Paul daily, enough to distract

an ordinary head, yet he could retain the remembrance of so many; and his heart was so full of love and affection as to send salutations to each of them with particular characters of them, and expressions of love to them and concern for them. *Greet* them, *salute* them. "Let them know that I remember them, and love them, and wish them well."

Lastly, He concludes with the recommendation of them to the love and embraces one of another: *Salute one another with a holy kiss*. Mutual salutations, as they express love, so they increase and strengthen love, and endear Christians one to another: therefore Paul here encourages the use of them, and only directs that they may be holy—a chaste kiss, in opposition to that which is wanton and lascivious; a sincere kiss, in opposition to that which is treacherous and dissembling, as Judas's, when he betrayed Christ with a kiss. He adds, in the close, a general salutation to them all, in the name of the churches of Christ (v. 16): "*The churches of Christ salute you*; that is, the churches which I am with, and which I am accustomed to visit personally, as knit together in the bonds of the common Christianity, desire me to testify their affection to you and good wishes for you." This is one way of maintaining the communion of saints.

SOME WARNINGS
(vv. 17–20)

The apostle having endeavoured by his endearing salutations to unite them together, it was not improper to subjoin a caution to take heed of those whose principles and practices were destructive to Christian love. And we may observe,

I. The caution itself, which is given in the most obliging manner that could be: *I beseech you, brethren.* He teaches them, 1. To see their danger: *Mark those who cause divisions and offences.* Our Master had himself foretold that divisions and offences would come, but had entailed a woe on those by whom they come (Matt. xviii. 7), and against such we are here cautioned. 2. To shun it: "*Avoid them.* Shun all unnecessary communion and communication with them, lest you be leavened and infected by them. Do not strike in with any dividing interests, nor embrace any of those principles or practices which are destructive to Christian love and charity, or to the truth which is according to godliness.— *Their word will eat as doth a canker.*"

II. The reasons to enforce this caution.

1. Because of the pernicious policy of these seducers, *v.* 18. The worse they are, the more need we have to watch against them. Now observe his description of them, in two things: (1) The master they serve: not *our Lord Jesus Christ.* Though they call themselves Christians, they do not serve Christ; do not aim at his glory, promote his interest, nor do his will, whatever they pretend. But they *serve their own belly*—their carnal, sensual, secular interests. (2) The method they take to compass their design: *By good words and fair speeches they deceive the hearts of the simple.*

2. Because of the peril we are in,

through our proneness and aptness to be inveigled and ensnard by them. And, (1) These seducing teachers would be the more apt to assault them. The devil and his agents have a particular spite against flourishing churches and flourishing souls. (2) They were in danger from these seducers. This Paul suggests with a great deal of modesty and tenderness; not as one suspicious of them, but as one solicitous for them: "Your *obedience has come abroad unto all men*; we grant this and rejoice in it: *I am glad therefore on your behalf.*" Thus does he insinuate their commendation, the better to make way for the caution. A holy jealousy of our friends may very well comport with a holy joy in them. "You think yourselves a very happy people, and so do I too: but for all that you must not be secure: *I would have you wise unto that which is good, and simple concerning evil.* You are a willing good-natured people, but you had best take heed of being imposed upon by those seducers."

3. Because of the promise of God, that we shall have victory at last, which is given to quicken and encourage, not to supersede, our watchful cares and vigorous endeavours. It is a very sweet promise (*v.* 20): *The God of peace shall bruise Satan under your feet.* When Satan seems to have prevailed, and we are ready to give up all for lost, then will the God of peace cut the work short in righteousness. If the grace of Christ be with us, who can be against us so as to prevail? *Be strong therefore in the grace which is in Christ Jesus.* Paul, not only as a

friend, but as a minister and an apostle, who had received grace for grace, thus with authority blesses them with this blessing, and repeats it, *v.* 24.

MORE GREETINGS
(*vv.* 21–24)

As the apostle had before sent his own salutations to many of this church, and that of the churches round him to them all, he here adds an affectionate remembrance of them from some particular persons who were now with him, the better to promote acquaintance and fellowship among distant saints, and that the subscribing of these worthy names, known to them, might the more recommend this epistle. He mentions, 1. Some that were his particular friends, and probably known to the Roman Christians: *Timotheus my work-fellow.* Paul sometimes calls Timothy his son, as an inferior; but here he styles him his work-fellow, as one equal with him, such a respect does he put upon him: and *Lucius,* probably Lucius of Cyrene, a noted man in the church of Antioch (Acts xiii. 1), as Jason was at Thessalonica, where he suffered for entertaining Paul (Acts xvii. 5, 6): and *Sosipater,* supposed to be the same with Sopater of Berea, mentioned Acts xx. 4. These Paul calls his kinsmen; not only more largely, as they were Jews, but as they were in blood or affinity nearly allied to him. It seems, Paul was of a good family, that he met with so many of his kindred in several places. It is a very great comfort to see the holiness and usefulness of our kindred.

2. One that was Paul's amanuensis (*v.* 22): *I Tertius, who wrote this epistle.* Paul made use of a scribe, not out of state nor idleness, but because he wrote a bad hand, which was not very legible, which he excuses, when he writes to the Galatians with his own hand (Gal. vi. 11).

FINAL PRAYER (*vv.* 25–27)

Here the apostle solemnly closes his epistle with a magnificent ascription of glory to the blessed God, as one that terminated all in the praise and glory of God, and studied to return all to him, seeing all is of him and from him. He does, as it were, breathe out his soul to these Romans in the praise of God, choosing to make that the end of his epistle which he made the end of his life. Observe here,

I. A description of the gospel of God, which comes in in a parenthesis; having occasion to speak of it as the means by which the power of God establishes souls, and the rule of that establishment: *To establish you according to my gospel.* Paul calls it his gospel, because he was the preacher of it and because he did so much glory in it.

1. It is the *preaching of Jesus Christ.* Christ was the preacher of it himself; it began to be spoken by the Lord, Heb. ii. 3. We preach not ourselves, says Paul, but Christ Jesus the Lord. That which establishes souls is the plain preaching of Jesus Christ.

2. *It is the revelation of the mystery which was kept secret since the world began, and by the scriptures of the prophets made known.*

The subject-matter of the gospel is a mystery. Our redemption and salvation by Jesus Christ, in the foundation, method, and fruits of it, are, without controversy, a great mystery of godliness, 1 Tim. iii. 16. And yet, blessed be God, there is as much of this mystery made plain as will suffice to bring us to heaven, if we do not wilfully neglect so great salvation.

II. A doxology to that God whose gospel it is, ascribing glory to him for ever (*v.* 27), acknowledging that he is a glorious God, and adoring him accordingly, with the most awful affections, desiring and longing to be at this work with the holy angels, where we shall be doing it to eternity. This is praising God, ascribing glory to him for ever.

CORINTHIANS

CHAPTER ONE
PREFACE (vv. 1–9)

We have here the apostle's preface to his whole epistle, in which we may take notice,

I. Of the inscription, in which, according to the custom of writing letters then, the name of the person by whom it was written and the persons to whom it was written are both inserted. The persons to whom this epistle was directed were *the church of God that was at Corinth, sanctified in Christ Jesus, and called to be saints*. All Christians are thus far sanctified in Christ Jesus, that they are by baptism dedicated and devoted to him, they are under strict obligations to be holy, and they make profession of real sanctity. If they be not truly holy, it is their own fault and reproach.

II. Of the apostolical benediction. *Grace be to you, and peace, from God our Father, and from the Lord Jesus Christ.* An apostle of the prince of peace must be a messenger and minister of peace.

III. Of the apostle's thanksgiving to God on their behalf. Paul begins most of his epistles with thanksgiving to God for his friends and prayer for them. He gives thanks, 1. For their conversion to the faith of Christ: *For the grace which was given you through Jesus Christ, v.*

4. 2. For the abundance of their spiritual gifts. This the church of Corinth was famous for. They did not come behind any of the churches in any gift, *v.* 7. He specifies *utterance and knowledge, v.* 5. Where God has given these two gifts, he has given great capacity for usefulness. Many have the flower of utterance that have not the root of knowledge, and their converse is barren. Many have the treasure of knowledge, and lack utterance to employ it for the good of others, and then it is in a manner wrapped up in a napkin. But, where God gives both, a man is qualified for eminent usefulness.

IV. Of the encouraging hopes the apostle had of them for the time to come, founded on the power and love of Christ, and the faithfulness of God, *vv.* 8, 9. He who had begun a good work in them, and carried it on thus far, would not leave is unfinished.

PARTY SPIRIT (vv. 10–13)

Here the apostle enters on his subject.

I. He exhorts them to unity and brotherly love, and reproves them for their divisions. He had received an account from some that wished them well of some unhappy differences among them.

II. He hints at the origin of these contentions. Pride lay at the bottom, and this made them factious. *Only of pride cometh contention*, Prov. xiii. 10. They quarrelled about their ministers. Paul and Apollos were both faithful ministers of Jesus Christ, and helpers of their faith and joy: but those who were disposed to be contentious broke into parties, and set their ministers at the head of their several factions: some cried up Paul, perhaps as the most sublime and spiritual teacher; others cried up Apollos, perhaps as the most eloquent speaker; some Cephas, or Peter, perhaps for the authority of his age, or because he was the apostle of the circumcision; and some were for none of them, but Christ only. So liable are the best things in the world to be corrupted, and the gospel and its institutions, which are at perfect harmony with themselves and one another, to be made the engines of variance, discord, and contention.

III. He expostulates with them upon their discord and quarrels: "*Is Christ divided?*" No, there is but one Christ, and therefore Christians should be of one heart. Ministers, however instrumental they are of good to us, are not to be put in Christ's stead. And happy were it for the churches if there were no name of distinction among them, as Christ is not divided.

TRUE WISDOM (*vv.* 14–31)

Here the apostle gives an account of his ministry among them. He thanks God he had baptized but a few among them, *Crispus*, who had been a ruler of a synagogue at Corinth (Acts xviii. 8), *Gaius, and*

the household of Stephanas, besides whom, he says, he did not remember that he had baptized any. But how was this a proper matter for thankfulness? He is not to be understood in such a sense as if he were thankful for not having baptized at all, but for not having done it in present circumstances, lest it should have had this very bad construction put upon it—that he had baptized in his own name, made disciples for himself, or set himself up as the head of a sect.

We have here,

I. The manner in which Paul preached the gospel, and the cross of Christ: *Not with the wisdom of words* (*v.* 17), *the enticing words of man's wisdom* (*ch.* ii. 4), the flourish of oratory, or the accuracies of philosophical language, upon which the Greeks so much prided themselves, and which seem to have been the peculiar recommendations of some of the heads of the faction in this church that most opposed this apostle. He did not preach the gospel in this manner, lest *the cross of Christ should be of no effect*, lest the success should be ascribed to the force of art, and not of truth; not to the plain doctrine of a crucified Jesus, but to the powerful oratory of those who spread it, and hereby the honour of the cross be diminished or eclipsed.

II. We have the different effects of this preaching: To those who perish it is foolishness, *but to those who are saved it is the power of God*, *v.* 18. *It is to the Jews a stumbling-block, and to the Greeks foolishness; but unto those who are called, both Jews and Greeks, Christ the power of God and the wisdom of*

God, *vv*. 23, 24. 1. Christ crucified is a stumbling-block to the Jews. They could not get over it. They despised him, and looked upon him as execrable, because he was hanged on a tree, and because he did not gratify them with a sign to their mind, though his divine power shone out in innumerable miracles. The Jews require a sign, *v*. 22. See Matt. xii. 38. 2. He was to the Greeks foolishness. They laughed at the story of a crucified Saviour, and despised the apostles' way of telling it. They sought for wisdom. They were men of wit and reading, men that had cultivated arts and sciences, and had, for some ages, been in a manner the very mint of knowledge and learning. There was nothing in the plain doctrine of the cross to suit their taste, nor humour their vanity, nor gratify a curious and wrangling temper: they entertained it therefore with scorn and contempt. 3. To those who are called and saved *he is the wisdom of God, and the power of God*. Those who are called and sanctified, who receive the gospel, and are enlightened by the Spirit of God, discern more glorious discoveries of God's wisdom and power in the doctrine of Christ crucified than in all his other works.

III. We have here the triumphs of the cross over human wisdom, according to the ancient prophecy (Isa. xxix. 14). All the valued learning of this world was confounded, baffled, and eclipsed, by the Christian revelation and the glorious triumphs of the cross. The heathen politicians and philosophers, the Jewish rabbis and doctors, the curious searchers into the secrets of nature, were all baffled. All the boasted science of the heathen world did not, could not, effectually bring home the world to God.

1. The thing preached was foolishness in the eyes of worldly-wise men. Our living through one who died, our being blessed by one who was made a curse, our being justified by one who was himself condemned, was all folly and inconsistency to men blinded with self-conceit and wedded to their own prejudices and the boasted discoveries of their reason and philosophy.

2. The manner of preaching the gospel was foolishness to them too. None of the famous men for wisdom or eloquence were employed to plant the church or propagate the gospel. A few fishermen were called out, and sent upon this errand. But God seeth not as man seeth. He hath chosen the foolish things of the world, the weak things of the world, the base and despicable things of the world, men of mean birth, of low rank, of no liberal education, to be the preachers of the gospel and planters of the church.

IV. We have an account how admirably all is fitted, 1. To beat down the pride and vanity of men. The gospel dispensation is a contrivance to humble man. But, 2. It is as admirably fitted to glorify God. Though the ministers were poor and unlearned, and the converts generally of the meanest rank, yet the hand of the Lord went along with the preachers, and was mighty in the hearts of the hearers;

and Jesus Christ was made both to ministers and Christians what was truly great and honourable. He is made of God to us *wisdom, righteousness, sanctification, and redemption* (*v.* 30): all we need, or can desire. Man is humbled, and God glorified and exalted, by the whole scheme.

CHAPTER TWO

PAUL AT CORINTH
(*vv.* 1–5)

In this passage the apostle pursues his design, and reminds the Corinthians how he acted when he first preached the gospel among them.

I. As to the matter or subject he tells us (*v.* 2), *He determined to know nothing among them but Jesus Christ and him crucified*—to make a show of no other knowledge than this, to preach nothing, to discover the knowledge of nothing, but Jesus Christ, and him crucified.

II. The manner wherein he preached Christ is here also observable. 1. Negatively. *He came not among them with excellency of speech or wisdom, v.* 1. *His speech and preaching were not with enticing words of man's wisdom, v.* 4. Neither his speech, nor the wisdom he taught, savoured of human skill: he learnt both in another school. Divine wisdom needed not to be set off with such human ornaments. 2. Positively. He came among them *declaring the testimony of God, v.* 1. He published a divine revelation; and there he left the matter. *He was also among them in weakness and fear, and in much trembling;* and yet *his speech and preaching were in demonstration of the Spirit*

and of power, v. 3, 4. He acted in his office with much modesty, concern, and care. He behaved with great humility among them; not as one grown vain with the honour and authority conferred on him, but as one concerned to approve himself faithful, and fearful of himself, lest he should mismanage in his trust. But, though Paul managed with this modesty and concern, yet he spoke with authority: *In the demonstration of the Spirit and of power*. He preached the truths of Christ in their native dress, with plainness of speech.

III. Here is the end mentioned for which he preached Christ crucified in this manner: *That your faith should not stand in the wisdom of man, but the power of God* (*v.* 5)—that they might not be drawn by human motives, nor overcome by mere human arguments, lest it should be said that either rhetoric or logic had made them Christians. But, when nothing but Christ crucified was plainly preached, the success must be entirely attributed to a divine power accompanying the word. Their faith must be founded, not on human wisdom, but divine evidence and operation. The gospel was so preached that God might appear and be glorified in all.

THE SPIRIT AS INTERPRETER
(*vv.* 6–16)

In this part of the chapter the apostle shows them that though he had not come to them with the excellency of human wisdom, with any of the boasted knowledge and literature of the Jews or Greeks, yet he had communicated to them a treasure of the truest and the highest wisdom: *We speak wisdom among those who are perfect* (v. 6), among those who are well instructed in Christianity, and come to some maturity in the things of God. Now, concerning this wisdom, observe,

I. The rise and origin of it: *It was ordained of God, before the world, to our glory*, v. 7. It was ordained of God; he had determined long ago to reveal and make it known, from many ages past, from the beginning, nay, from eternity; and that to our glory, *the glory of us*, either us apostles or us Christians.

II. The ignorance of the great men of the world about it: *Which none of the princes of this world knew* (v. 8), the principal men in authority and power, or in wisdom and learning.

III. It is such wisdom as could not have been discovered without a revelation, according to what the prophet Isaiah says (Isa. lxiv. 4), *Eye hath not seen, nor ear heard, nor have entered into the heart of man the things which God hath prepared for those that love him—for him that waiteth for him*, that waiteth for his mercy, so the LXX. It was a testimony of love to God in the Jewish believers to live in expectation of the accomplishment of evangelical promises. Waiting upon God is an evidence of love to him. *Lo, this is our God, we have waited for him*, Isa. xxv. 9.

IV. We here see by whom this wisdom is discovered to us: *God hath revealed them to us by his Spirit*, v. 10. The scripture is given by inspiration of God. *Holy men spoke of old as they were moved by*

the Holy Ghost, 2 Pet. i. 21. And the apostles spoke by inspiration of the same Spirit, as he taught them, and gave their utterance. Here is a proof of the divine authority of the holy scriptures.

V. We see here in what manner this wisdom was taught or communicated: *Which things we speak, not in the words which man's wisdom teaches, but which the Holy Ghost teaches*, v. 13. They had received the wisdom they taught, not from the wise men of the world, not from their own enquiry nor invention, but from the Spirit of God. Nor did they put a human dress on it, but plainly declared the doctrine of Christ, in terms also taught them by the Holy Spirit. The language of the Spirit of God is the most proper to convey his meaning.

VI. We have an account how this wisdom is received.

1. *The natural man receiveth not the things of God, for they are foolishness to him, neither can he know them, because they are spiritually discerned*, v. 14. The *natural man, the animal man*. Revelation is not with him a principle of science; he looks upon it as delirium and dotage, the extravagant thought of some deluded dreamer. It is no way to wisdom among the famous masters of the world; and for that reason he can have no knowledge of things revealed, because they are only spiritually discerned, or made known by the revelation of the Spirit, which is a principle of science or knowledge that he will not admit.

2. *But he that is spiritual judgeth all things, yet he himself is judged*, or discerned, *of no man*, v. 15. He does

not lose the power of reasoning, nor renounce the principles of it, by founding his faith and religion on revelation. But *he himself is judged of no man*—can be judged, so as to be confuted, by no man; nor can any man who is not spiritual (see *ch.* xiv. 37), or not founding his faith on a divine revelation, discern or judge whether what he speaks be true or divine, or not. In short, he who founds all his knowledge upon principles of science, and the mere light of reason, can never be a judge of the truth or falsehood of what is received by revelation. *For who hath known the mind of the Lord, that he may instruct him* (*v.* 16), that is, the *spiritual man?* He only is the person to whom God immediately communicates the knowledge of his will. And who can inform or instruct him in the mind of God who is so immediately under the conduct of his own Spirit? Very few have known any thing of the mind of God by a natural power. *But*, adds the apostle, *we have the mind of Christ*: and the mind of Christ is the mind of God. He is God, and the principal messenger and prophet of God. And the apostles were empowered by his Spirit to make known his mind to us. And in the holy scriptures the mind of Christ, and the mind of God in Christ, are fully revealed to us.

CHAPTER THREE
SPIRITUAL INFANTS
(*vv.* 1–4)

Here, I. Paul blames the Corinthians for their weakness and nonproficiency. The apostle tells *them*

he could not speak to them as unto spiritual men, *but as unto carnal* men, *as to babes in Christ*, *v.* 1. They were still mere babes in Christ. They had received some of the first principles of Christianity, but had not grown up to maturity of understanding in them, or of faith and holiness; and yet it is plain, from several passages in this epistle, that the Corinthians were very proud of their wisdom and knowledge. The apostle assigns their little proficiency in the knowledge of Christianity as a reason why he had communicated no more of the deep things of it to them. They could not bear such food, they needed to be fed with milk, not with meat, *v.* 2.

II. He blames them for their carnality, and mentions their contention and discord about their ministers as evidence of it: *For you are yet carnal; for whereas there are among you envyings, and strifes, and divisions, are you not carnal, and walk as men?* *v.* 3. They had mutual emulations, and quarrels, and factions among them, upon the account of their ministers, *while one said, I am of Paul; and another, I am of Apollos*, *v.* 4. These were proofs of their being carnal, that fleshly interest and affections too much swayed them.

WORKERS TOGETHER
(*vv.* 5–10)

Here the apostle instructs them how to cure this failing, and rectify what was amiss among them upon this head,

I. By reminding them that the ministers about whom they contended were but ministers: *Who then is Paul, and who is Apollos, but ministers by whom you believed? Even as the Lord gave to every man, v. 5.* They are but ministers, mere instruments used by the God of all grace. *Paul had planted and Apollos had watered, v. 6.* Both were useful, one for one purpose, the other for another. Note, The success of the ministry must be derived from the divine blessing: *Neither he that planteth is any thing, nor he that watereth, but God who giveth the increase, v. 7.* Even apostolical ministers are nothing of themselves, can do nothing with efficacy and success unless God give the increase.

II. By representing to them the unanimity of Christ's ministers: *He that planteth and he that watereth are one (v. 8),* employed by one Master, entrusted with the same revelation, busied in one work, and engaged in one design—in harmony with one another, however they may be set in opposition to each other by factious party-makers. They have their different gifts from one and the same Spirit, for the very same purposes; and they heartily carry on the same design. Planters and waterers are but fellow-labourers in the same work. They are working together with God, in promoting the purposes of his glory, and the salvation of precious souls; and he who knows their work will take care they do not labour in vain.

THE TRUE FOUNDATION
(vv. 11–15)

Here the apostle informs us what foundation he had laid at the bottom of all his labours among them—*even Jesus Christ, the chief corner-stone,* Eph. ii. 20. Upon this foundation all the faithful ministers of Christ build. Upon this rock all Christians found their hopes. Those that build their hopes of heaven on any other foundation build upon the sand. *Other foundation can no man lay besides what is laid—even Jesus Christ.* But of those that hold the foundation, and embrace the general doctrine of Christ's being the mediator between God and man, there are two sorts:

I. Some build upon this foundation *gold, silver, and precious stones (v.* 12), namely, those who receive and propagate the pure truths of the gospel, who hold nothing but the *truth as it is in Jesus,* and preach nothing else. This is building well upon a good foundation.

II. Others *build wood, hay, and stubble,* on this foundation; that is, though they adhere to the foundation, they depart from the mind of Christ in many particulars, substitute their own fancies and inventions in the room of his doctrines and institutions, and build upon the good foundation what will not abide the test when the day of trial shall come, and the fire must make it manifest, as wood, hay, and stubble, will not bear the trial by fire, but must be consumed in it. There is a time coming when a discovery will be made of what men have built on this foundation: *Every man's work shall be made manifest.* In that day, 1. Some men's works will *abide the trial*—will be found standard. It will appear that they not only held the foundation, but that they built regularly and well upon it—that they laid on proper materials, and in due form and order. 2. There are others *whose works shall be burnt* (v. 15), whose corrupt opinions and doctrines, or vain inventions and usages in the worship of God, shall be discovered, disowned, and rejected, in that day—shall be first manifested to be corrupt, and then disapproved of God and rejected. He shall be saved, *yet so as by fire*, saved out of the fire. He himself shall be snatched out of that flame which will consume his work. This intimates that it will be difficult for those that corrupt and deprave Christianity to be saved. God will have no mercy on their works, though he may pluck them as brands out of the burning.

THE TEMPLE OF GOD
(vv. 16, 17)

Here the apostle resumes his argument and exhortation, founding it on his former allusion, *You are God's building*, v. 9, and here, *Know you not that you are the temple of God, and the Spirit of God dwelleth in you? If any man defile* (corrupt and destroy) *the temple of God, him shall God destroy* (the same word is in the original in both clauses); *for the temple of God is holy, which temple you are*. It may be undersood of the church of Corinth collectively, or of every single believer among them; Christian churches are temples of God. He dwells among them by his Holy Spirit. *They are built together for a habitation of God through the Spirit*, Eph. ii. 22. Every Christian is a living temple of the living God. God dwelt in the Jewish temple, took possession of it, and resided in it, by that glorious cloud that

was the token of his presence with that people. So Christ by his Spirit dwells in all true believers. If we are the temples of God, we must do nothing that shall alienate ourselves from him, or corrupt and pollute ourselves, and thereby unfit ourselves for his use; and we must hearken to no doctrine nor doctor that would seduce us to any such practices.

THE WORLD'S WISDOM
(vv. 18-20)

Here he prescribes humility, and a modest opinion of themselves, for the remedy of the irregularities in the church of Corinth, the divisions and contests among them: "*Let no man deceive himself, v. 18.* Do not be led away from the truth and simplicity of the gospel by pretenders to science and eloquence, by a show of deep learning, or a flourish of words, by rabbis, orators, or philosophers." But *he who seems to be wise must become a fool that he may be wise*. He just be aware of his own ignorance, and lament it; he must distrust his own understanding, and not lean on it. The thoughts of the wisest men in the world have a great mixture of vanity, of weakness and folly, in them; and before God their wisest and best thoughts are very vanity, compared, I mean, with his thoughts of things. And should not all this teach us modesty, diffidence in ourselves, and a deference to the wisdom of God, make us thankful for his revelations, and willing to be taught of God, and not be led away by specious pretences to human wisdom and skill, from the simplicity of Christ, or a regard to his heavenly doctrine? Note, He who would be wise indeed must learn of God, and not set his own wisdom up in competition with God's.

GLORYING IN MEN (*vv.* 21–23)

Here the apostle founds an exhortation against over-valuing their teachers on what he had just said, and on the consideration that they had an equal interest in all their ministers: *Therefore let no man glory in men* (*v.* 21)—forget that their ministers are men, or pay that defence to them that is due only to God. All faithful ministers are serving one Lord and pursuing one purpose. They were appointed of Christ, for the common benefit of the church: "*Paul, and Apollos, and Cephas, are all yours.* One is not to be set up against another, but all are to be valued and used for your own spritual benefit." Upon this occasion also he gives in an inventory of the church's possessions, the spiritual riches of a true believer: "*All is yours*—ministers of all ranks, ordinary and extra-ordinary. Nay, the world itself is yours." Not that saints are proprietors of the world, but it stands for their sake, they have as much of it as Infinite Wisdom sees to be fit for them, and they have all they have with the divine blessing. But it must be remembered, at the same time, *that we are Christ's,* the subjects of his kingdom, his property. He is Lord over us, and we must own his dominion, and cheerfully submit to his command and yield themselves to his pleasure, if we would have all things minister to our advantage. All things are ours, upon no other ground than

our being Christ's. *And Christ is God's.* He is the Christ of God, anointed of God, and commissioned by him, to bear the office of a Mediator, and to act therein for the purposes of his glory.

CHAPTER FOUR

APOSTOLIC STEWARDSHIP (*vv.* 1–6)

Here, I. The apostle challenges the respect due to him on account of his character and office, in which many among them had at least very much failed: *Let a man so account of us as of the ministers of Christ, and stewards of the mysteries of God* (*v.* 1), though possibly others might have valued them too highly, by setting him up as the head of a party, and professing to be his disciples. In our opinion of ministers, as well as all other things, we should be careful to avoid extremes. They did not set up for master, but they deserved respect and esteem in this honourable service. Especially,

II. When they did their duty in it, and approved themselves faithful: *It is required in stewards that a man be found faithful* (*v.* 2), trustworthy. They must be true to the interest of their Lord, and consult his honour.

III. The apostle takes occasion hence to caution the Corinthians against censoriousness—the forward and severe judging of others: *Therefore judge nothing before the time, until the Lord come, v.* 5. There is a time coming when *the Lord will bring to light the hidden things of darkness, and make manifest the counsels of the hearts—*

deeds of darkness that are now done in secret, and all the secret inclinations, purposes, and intentions, of the hidden man of the heart. *The day shall declare it.* The Judge will bring these things to light. The Lord Jesus Christ will manifest the counsels of the heart, of all hearts.

IV. The apostle here lets us into the reason why he had used his own name and that of Apollos in this discourse of his. He had done *it in a figure,* and *he had done it for their sakes.* He chose rather to mention his own name, and the name of a faithful fellow-labourer, than the names of any heads of factions among them, that hereby he might avoid what would provoke, and so procure for his advice the greater regard.

FOOLS FOR CHRIST (*vv.* 7–13)

I. Paul cautions them against pride and self-conceit by this consideration, that all the distinction made among them was owing to God: *Who maketh thee to differ? And what hast thou that thou didst not receive? v.* 7. Here the apostle turns his discourse to the ministers who set themselves at the head of these factions, and did but too much encourage and abet the people in those feuds. What had they to glory in, when all their peculiar gifts were from God? They had received them, and could not glory in them as their own, without wronging God.

II. He presses the duty of humility upon them by a very smart irony, or at least reproves them for their pride and self-

conceit: "*You are full, you are rich, you have reigned as kings without us.*" See how apt pride is to over-rate benefits and overlook the benefactor, so swell upon its possessions and forget from whom they come; nay, it is apt to behold them in a magnifying-glass: "*You have reigned as kings,*" says the apostle, "that is, in your own conceit; and *I would to God you did reign, that we also might reign with you.* I wish you had as much of the true glory of a Christian church upon you as you arrogate to yourselves. I should come in then for a share of the honour: *I should reign with you;* I should not be overlooked by you as now I am, but valued and regarded as a minister of Christ, and a very useful instrument among you."

III. He comes to set forth his own circumstances and those of the other apostles, and compares them with theirs. 1. To set forth the case of the apostles: *For I think it hath pleased God to set forth us the apostles last, as it were appointed to death. For we are made a spectacle to the world, and to angels, and to men.* Paul and his fellow-apostles were exposed to great hardships. Never were any men in this world so hunted and worried. They carried their lives in their hands: *God hath set forth us the apostles last, as it were appointed to death, v.* 9. The general meaning is that the apostles were exposed to continual danger of death, and that of the worst kinds, in the faithful discharge of their office. God had set them forth, brought them into view, as the Roman emperors brought their combatants into the arena, the place of show, though not for the same purposes. They did it to please the populace, and humour their own vanity, and sometimes a much worse principle. The apostles were shown to manifest the power of divine grace, to confirm the truth of their mission and doctrine, and to propagate religion in the world. 2. He compares his own case with that of the Corinthians: *"We are fools for Christ's sake, but you are wise in Christ; we are weak, but you are strong; you are honourable, but we are despised, v.* 10. *We are fools for Christ's sake*; such in common account, and we are well content to be so accounted. We can pass for fools in the world, and be despised as such, so that the wisdom of God and the honour of the gospel may by this means be secured and displayed." *"But you are wise in Christ.* You have the fame of being wise and learned Christians, and you do not a little value yourselves upon it." The Corinthians may think themselves, and be esteemed by others, as wiser and stronger men in Christ than the apostles themselves. But O! how gross is the mistake!

IV. He enters into some particularities of their sufferings: *Even to this present hour*; that is, after all the service we have been doing among you and other churches, *we hunger and thirst, and are naked, and are buffeted, and have no certain dwelling-place, and labour, working with our own hands, vv.* 11, 12. Nay, they were *made as the filth of the world, and the off-scouring of all things, v.* 13. They were forced to labour with their own hands to get subsistence, and had so much, and

so much greater, business to mind, that they could not attend enough to this, to get a comfortable livelihood, but were exposed to hunger, thirst, and nakedness—many times wanted meat, and drink, and clothes. They were driven about the world, without having any fixed abode, any stated habitation. Poor circumstances indeed, for the prime ministers of our Saviour's kingdom to have no house nor home, and to be destitute of food and raiment! But yet no poorer than his who had not *where to lay his head*, Luke ix. 58. They were the common-sewer into which all the reproaches of the world were to be poured. To be the off-scouring of any thing is bad, but what is it to be the off-scouring of all things! How much did the apostles resemble their Master, *and fill up that which was behind of his afflictions, for his body's sake, which is the church!* Col. i. 24.

V. We have here the apostles' behaviour under all; and the return they made for this maltreatment: *Being reviled, we bless; being persecuted, we suffer it; being defamed, we entreat, vv.* 12, 13. They returned blessings for reproaches, and entreaties and kind exhortations for the rudest slanders and defamation, and were patient under the sharpest persecutions.

THEIR SPIRITUAL FATHER
(*vv.* 14–16)

Here Paul challenges their regard to him as their father. He tells them, 1. That what he had written was not for their reproach, but admonition; not with the gall of an enemy, but the bowels of a father (*v.* 14): *I* write not to shame you, but as my beloved children I warn you. 2. He shows them upon what foundation he claimed paternal relation to them, and called them his sons. They might have other pedagogues or instructors, but he was their father; *for in Christ Jesus he had begotten them by the gospel, v. 15.* They were made Christians by his ministry. 3. We have here the special advice he urges on them: *Wherefore I beseech you be you followers of me, v. 16.* This he elsewhere explains and limits (*ch.* xi. 1): "*Be you followers of me, as I also am of Christ.* Follow me as far as I follow Christ."

PAUL'S AUTHORITY
(*vv.* 17–21)

Here, I. He tells them of his having sent Timothy to them, *to bring them into remembrance of his ways in Christ, as he taught every where in every church (v.* 17)—to remind them of his ways in Christ, to refresh their memory as to his preaching and practice, what he taught, and how he lived among them.

II. He rebukes the vanity of those who imagined he would not come to them, by letting them know this was his purpose, though he had sent Timothy: "*I will come to you shortly,* though some of you are so vain as to think I will not." But he adds, *if the Lord will.* It seems, as to the common events of life, apostles knew no more than other men, nor were they in these points under inspiration.

III. He lets them know what would follow upon his coming to

them: *I will know, not the speech of those that are puffed up, but the power, v.* 19. He would bring the great pretenders among them to a trial, would know what they were, not by their rhetoric or philosophy, but by the authority and efficacy of what they taught, whether they could confirm it by miraculous operations, and whether it was accompanied with divine influences and saving effects on the minds of men. For, adds he, *the kingdom of God is not in word, but in power.*

IV. He puts it to their choice how he should come among them, *whether with a rod or in love and the spirit of meekness (v.* 21); that is, according as they were they would find him. If they continued perverse among themselves and with him, it would be necessary to come with a rod. But this is far from being desirable, if it may be prevented. And therefore the apostle adds that it was in their own option whether he should come with a rod or in a quite different disposition and manner: *Or in love and the spirit of meekness.*

CHAPTER FIVE
SIN IN THE CHURCH
(*vv.* 1–6)

Here the apostle states the case; and,

I. Lets them know what was the common or general report concerning them, that one of their community was guilty of fornication, *v.* 1. This was not a common instance of fornication, but *such as was not so much as named among the Gentiles, that a man should have his father's wife*—either marry her while his father was alive, or keep her as his concubine, either when he was dead or while he was alive. Yet such a horrible wickedness was committed by one in the church of Corinth, and, as is probable, a leader of one of the factions among them, a principal man.

II. He greatly blames them for their own conduct hereupon: *They were puffed up* (v. 2), *they gloried,* 1. Perhaps on account of this very scandalous person. He might be a man of great eloquence, of deep science, and for this reason very greatly esteemed, and followed, and cried up, by many among them. They were proud that they had such a leader. Instead of mourning for his fall, and their own reproach upon his account, and renouncing him and removing him from the society, they continued to applaud him and pride themselves in him. Or else, 2. It may intimate to us that some of the opposite party were puffed up. They were proud of their own standing, and trampled upon him that fell.

III. We have the apostle's direction to them how they should now proceed with this scandalous sinner. He would have him excommunicated and delivered to Satan (*vv.* 3–5); *as absent in body, yet present in spirit, he had judged already as if he had been present*; that is, he had, by revelation and the miraculous gift of discerning vouchsafed him by the Spirit, as perfect a knowledge of the case, and had hereupon come to the following determination, not without special authority from the Holy Spirit. He says this to let them know that, though he was at a distance, he did not pass an unrighteous sentence, nor judge without having as full cognizance of the case as if he had been on the spot. Paul had judged that *he should be delivered to Satan* (v. 5), and this was to be done *in the name of Christ*, with the power of Christ, and in a full assembly, where the apostle would be also present in spirit, or by his spiritual gift of discerning at a distance. Some think that this is to be understood of a mere ordinary excommunication, and that delivering him to Satan for the destruction of the flesh is only meant of disowning him, and casting him out of the church, that by this means he might be brought to repentance, and his flesh might be mortified. Others think the apostle is not to be understood of mere excommunication, but of a miraculous power or authority they had of delivering a scandalous sinner into the power of Satan, to have bodily diseases inflicted, and to be tormented by him with bodily pains, which is the meaning of the *destruction of the flesh*. In this sense the destruction of the flesh has been a happy occasion of the salvation of the spirit. It is probable that this was a mixed case.

IV. He hints the danger of contagion from this example: *Your glorying is not good. Know you not that a little leaven leaveneth the whole lump?* The bad example of a man in rank and reputation is very mischievous, spreads the contagion far and wide. It did so, probably, in this very church and case: see 2 Cor. xii. 21.

CHRIST, OUR PASSOVER
(*vv.* 7, 8)

Here the apostle exhorts them to purity, by purging out the old leaven. In this observe,

I. The advice itself, addressed either, 1. To the church in general; and so purging out the old leaven, that they might be a new lump, refers to the *putting away from themselves that wicked person, v.* 13. Or, 2. To each particular member of the church. And so it implies that they should purge themselves from all impurity of heart and life, especially from this kind of wickedness, to which the Corinthians were addicted to a proverb.

II. The reason with which this advice is enforced: *For Christ our passover is sacrificed for us, v.* 7. This is the great doctrine of the gospel. The Jews, after they had killed the passover, kept the feast of unleavened bread. So must we; not for seven days only, but all our days. We should die with our Saviour to sin, be planted into the likeness of his death by mortifying sin, and into the likeness of his resurrection by rising again to newness of life, and that internal and external. We must have new hearts and new lives.

SHUN BAD COMPANY
(*vv.* 9–13)

Here the apostle advises them to shun the company and converse of scandalous members. Consider,

I. The advice itself: *I wrote to you in a letter not to company with fornicators, v.* 9. Some think this was an epistle written to them before, which is lost. Some think it is to be understood of this very epistle, that he had written this advice before he had full information of their whole case, but thought it needful now to be more particular. And therefore on this occasion he tells them that if any man called a brother, any one professing Christianity, and being a member of a Christian church, were *a fornicator, or covetous, or an idolator, or a railer,* that they should not *keep company with him, nor so much as eat with such a one.*

II. How he limits this advice. He does not forbid Christians the like commerce with scandalously wicked heathens. He does not forbid their eating nor conversing with the *fornicators of this world,* &c. They know no better. They profess no better. Note, Christians may and ought to testify more respect to loose worldlings than to loose Christians.

III. The reason of this limitation is here assigned. It is impossible the one should be avoided. Christians must have gone out of the world to avoid the company of loose heathens. But this was impossible, as long as they had business in the world. While they are minding their duty, and doing their proper business, God can and will preserve them from contagion. But the dread of sin wears off by familiar converse with wicked Christians. Our own safety and preservation are a reason of this difference. But, besides, heathens were such as Christians had nothing to do to judge and censure, and avoid upon a censure passed; for *they are without* (*v.* 12), and must be left to *God's judgment, v.* 13. But, as to members of the church, they are within, are professedly bound by the laws and rules of Christianity, and not only liable to the judgment of God, but to the censures of those who are set over them, and the fellow-members of the same body, when they transgress those rules. Every Christian is bound to judge them unfit for communion and familiar converse.

IV. How he applies the argument to the case before him: "*Therefore put away from among yourselves that wicked person,*" *v.* 13.

CHAPTER SIX

GOING TO LAW (*vv.* 1–8)

Here the apostle reproves them for going to law with one another before heathen judges for little matters; and therein blames all *vexatious law-suits*, concerning which observe,

I. The fault he blames them for: it was going to law. Not but that *the law is good, if a man use it lawfully*. But, 1. *Brother went to law with brother* (*v.* 6), one member of the church with another. The near relation could not preserve peace and good understanding. The bonds of fraternal love were broken through. 2. They brought the matter before the heathen magistrates: *they went to law before the unjust, not before the saints* (*v.* 1), brought the controversy before unbelievers (*v.* 6), and did not compose it among themselves, Christians and saints, at least in profession. This tended much to the reproach of Christianity.

II. He lays before them the aggravations of their fault: *Do you*

not know that the saints shall judge the world (*v.* 2), shall judge angels? *v.* 3. And are they unworthy *to judge the smallest matters, the things of this life?* It was a dishonour to their Christian character, a forgetting of their real dignity, as saints, for them to carry little matters, about the things of life, before heathen magistrates.

III. He puts them on a method to remedy this fault. And this twofold: 1. By referring it to some to make it up: "*Is it so that there is no wise man among you, no one able to judge between his brethren? v.* 5. 2. By suffering wrong rather than taking this method to right themselves: *It is utterly a fault among you to go to law in this matter*: it is always a fault of one side to go to law, except in a case where the title is indeed dubious, and there is a friendly agreement of both parties to refer it to the judgment of those learned in the law to decide it. And this is referring it, rather than contending about it, which is the thing the apostle here seems chiefly to condemn: *Should you not rather take wrong, rather suffer yourselves to be defrauded?*

EVILS TO BE AVOIDED
(*vv.* 9–11)

Here he takes occasion to warn them against many heinous evils, to which they had been formerly addicted.

1. He puts it to them as a plain truth, of which they could not be ignorant, that such sinners should not inherit the kingdom of God.

II. Yet he warns them against deceiving themselves: *Be not deceived*. Those who cannot but know the fore-mentioned truth are but too apt not to attend to it. Men are very much inclined to flatter themselves that *God is such a one as themselves*, and that they may live in sin and yet die in Christ, may lead the life of the devil's children and yet go to heaven with the children of God. But this is all a gross cheat.

III. He puts them in mind what a change the gospel and grace of God had made in them: *Such were some of you* (v. 11), such notorious sinners as he had been reckoning up.

FORNICATION (vv. 12–20)

The twelfth verse and former part of the thirteenth seem to relate to that early dispute among Christians about the distinction of meats, and yet to be prefatory to the caution that follows against fornication. The connection seems plain enough if we attend to the famous determination of the apostles, Acts xv., where the prohibition of certain foods was joined with that of fornication. Now some among the Corinthians seem to have imagined that they were as much at liberty in the point of fornication as of meats, especially because it was not a sin condemned by the laws of their country. They were ready to say, even in the case of fornication, *All things are lawful for me*. This pernicious conceit Paul here sets himself to oppose.

I. The body is not for fornication, but for the Lord. This is the first argument he uses against this sin, for which the heathen inhabitants of Corinth were infamous, and the converts to Christianity retained too favourable an opinion of it. It is making things to cross their intention and use. The *body is not for fornication*; it was never formed for any such purpose, *but for the Lord*, for the service and honour of God. And *the Lord is for the body*, that is, as some think, Christ is to be Lord of the body, to have property in it and dominion over it, having assumed a body and been made to partake of our nature, that he might be head of his church, and head over all things, Heb. ii. 5, 18.

II. Some understand this last passage, *The Lord is for the body*, thus: He is for its resurrection and glorification, according to what follows, *v.* 14, which is a second argument against this sin, the honour intended to be put on our bodies: *God hath both raised up our Lord, and will raise us up by his power* (v. 14), by the power of him who *shall change our vile body, and make it like to his glorious body by that power whereby he is able to subdue all things to himself*, Phil. iii. 21. It is an honour done to the body that Jesus Christ was raised from the dead: and it will be an honour to our bodies that they will be raised. Let us not abuse those bodies by sin, and make them vile, which, if they be kept pure, shall, notwithstanding their present vileness, be made like to *Christ's glorious body*.

III. A third argument is the honour already put on them: *Know you not that your bodies are the members of Christ? v.* 15. If the soul be united to Christ by faith, the whole man is become a member of his mystical body. *But now*, says the

231

apostle, *shall I take the members of Christ, and make them the members of a harlot? God forbid.* Or, *take away* the members of Christ? Would not this be a gross abuse, and the most notorious injury? Would it not be dishonouring Christ, and dishonouring ourselves to the very last degree? What, make Christ's members the members of a harlot, prostitute them to so vile a purpose! The thought is to be abhorred. God forbid. *Know you not that he who is joined to a harlot is one body* with hers? *For two,* says he, *shall be one flesh. But he who is joined to the Lord is one spirit,* vv. 16, 17. Now shall one in so close a union with Christ as to be one spirit with him yet be so united to a harlot as to become one flesh with her? Were not this a vile attempt to make a union between Christ and harlots? And can a greater indignity be offered to him or ourselves? Can any thing be more inconsistent with our profession or relation?

IV. A fourth argument is that it is a sin against our own bodies. *Every sin that a man does is without the body; he that committeth fornication sinneth against his own body* (v. 18); every sin, that is, every other sin, every external act of sin besides, is outside the body. Nor does it give the power of the body to another person. This sin is in a peculiar manner styled uncleanness, especially in a Christian. He sins against his own body; he defiles it, he degrades it, making it one with the body of that vile creature with whom he sins. He casts vile reproach on what his Redeemer has dignified to the last degree by taking it into union with himself.

V. The fifth argument against this sin is that the bodies of Christians are *the temples of the Holy Ghost which is in them, and which they have of God,* v. 19. He that is joined to Christ is one spirit. He is yielded up to him, is consecrated thereby, and set apart for his use, and is hereupon possessed, and occupied, and inhabited, by his Holy Spirit. And shall we desecrate his temple, defile it, prostitute it, and offer it up to the use and service of a harlot? Horrid sacrilege!

VI. The apostle argues from the obligation we are under *to glorify God both with our body and spirit, which are his,* v. 20. He made both, he bought both, and therefore both belong to him and should be used and employed for him, and therefore should not be defiled, alienated from him, and prostituted by us. No, they must be kept as vessels fitted for our Master's use.

CHAPTER SEVEN

RULES ABOUT MARRIAGE I
(vv. 1–9)

The apostle comes now, as a faithful and skilful casuist, to answer some cases of conscience which the Corinthians had proposed to him. He tells them in general,

I. That it was good, in that juncture of time at least, to abstain from marriage altogether: *It is good for a man not to touch a woman* (not to take her to wife). Yet,

II. He informs them that marriage, and the comforts and satisfactions of that state, are by divine wisdom prescribed for preventing fornication (*v.* 2). To avoid these, *Let every man*, says he, *have his own wife, and every woman her own husband*; that is, marry, and confine themselves to their own mates. And, when they are married, let each render the other *due benevolence* (*v.* 3), render conjugal duty, which is owing to each other. For, as the apostle argues (*v.* 4), in the married state neither person has power of his own body, but has delivered it into the power of the other, the wife hers into the power of the husband, the husband his into the power of the wife.

III. The apostle limits what he had said about *every man's having his own wife*, &c. (*v.* 2): *I speak this by permission, not of command*. He did not lay it as an injunction upon every man to marry without exception. Any man might marry. No law of God prohibited the thing. But, on the other hand, no law bound a man to marry so that he sinned if he did not; I mean, unless his circumstances required it for preventing the lust of uncleanness. No, he *could wish all men were as himself* (*v.* 7), that is, single, and capable of living continently in that state. There were several conveniences in it, which at that season, if not at others, made it more eligible in itself. Paul could wish all men were as himself, but *all men cannot receive such a saying, save those to whom it is given*, Matt. xix. 11.

IV. He sums up his sense on this head (*vv.* 9, 10): *I say therefore to the unmarried and widows*, to those in a state of virginity or widowhood, *It is good for them if they abide even as I*. There are many conveniences, and especially at this juncture, in a single state, to render it preferable to a married one. It is convenient therefore *that the unmarried abide as I*, which plainly implies that Paul was at that time unmarried. *But, if they cannot contain, let them marry; for it is better to marry than to burn*. This is God's remedy for lust. The fire may be quenched by the means he has appointed. And marriage, with all its inconveniences, is much better than to burn with impure and lustful desires. *Marriage is honourable in all;* but it is a duty in those who cannot contain nor conquer those inclinations.

RULES ABOUT MARRIAGE II (*vv.* 10–16)

In this paragraph the apostle gives them direction in a case which must be very frequent in that age of the world, especially among the Jewish converts; I mean whether they were to live with heathen relatives in a married state. Concerning this matter the apostle here gives direction. And,

I. In general, he tells them that marriage, by Christ's command, is for life; and therefore those who are married must not think of separation. The wife *must not depart from the husband* (*v.* 10), nor the *husband put away his wife*, *v.* 11. This *I command*, says the apostle; *yet not I, but the Lord*.

II. He brings the general advice home to the case of such as had an unbelieving mate (*v.* 12): *But to the rest speak I, not the Lord;* that is, the Lord had not so expressly spoken to this case as to the former divorce. But, having thus prefaced his advice, we may attend,

1. To the advice itself, which is that if an unbelieving husband or wife were pleased to dwell with a Christian relative, the other should not separate. The believer is not by faith in Christ loosed from matrimonial bonds to an unbeliever, but is at once bound and made apt to be a better relative. But, though a believing wife or husband should not separate from an unbelieving mate, yet, if the unbelieving relative desert the believer, and no means can reconcile to a cohabitation, in such *a case a brother or sister is not in bondage* (v. 15), not bound servilely to follow or cleave to the malicious deserter, or not bound to live unmarried after all proper means for reconciliation have been tried, at least if the deserter contract another marriage or be guilty of adultery, which was a very easy supposition, because a very common instance among the heathen inhabitants of Corinth.

2. We have here the reasons of this advice. (1) Because the relation or state is sanctified by the holiness of either party: *For the unbelieving husband is sanctified by the wife, and the unbelieving wife by the husband* (v. 14), or *hath been sanctified*. The relation itself, and the conjugal use of each other, are sanctified to the believer. He is sanctified for the wife's sake. She is sanctified for the husband's sake. Both are one flesh. He is to be reputed clean who is one flesh with her that is holy, and *vice versa*: *Else were your children unclean, but*

now are they holy (v. 14), that is, they would be heathen, out of the pale of the church and covenant of God. They would not be of the holy seed (as the Jews are called, Isa. vi. 13), but common and unclean, in the same sense as heathens in general were styled in the apostle's vision, Acts x. 28. (2) Another reason is that *God hath called Christians to peace*, v. 15. The Christian religion obliges us to act peaceably in all relations, natural and civil. (3) A third reason is that it is possible for the believing relative to be an instrument of the other's salvation (v. 16): *What knowest thou, O wife, whether thou shalt save thy husband?* Note, It is the plain duty of those in so near a relation to seek the salvation of those to whom they are related.

CHRISTIAN CONTENTMENT
(vv. 17-24)

Here the apostle takes occasion to advise them to continue in the state and condition in which Christianity found them, and in which they became converts to it. And here,

I. He lays down this rule in general—*as God hath distributed to every one*. Note, Our states and circumstances in this world are distributions of divine Providence.

II. He specifies particular cases; as, 1. That of circumcision. *Is any man called being circumcised? Let him not be uncircumcised. Is any man called being uncircumcised? Let him not be circumcised.* 2. That of servitude and freedom. It was common in that age of the world for many to be in a state of slavery, bought and sold for money, and so the property of those who purchased them. "Now," says the apostle, *"art thou called being a servant? Care not for it.* Be not over-solicitous about it. It is not inconsistent with thy duty, profession, or hopes, as a Christian. *Yet, if thou mayest be made free, use it rather," v.* 21.

III. He sums up his advice: *Let every man wherein he is called abide therein with God, v.* 24. This is to be understood of the state wherein a man is converted to Christianity. No man should make his faith or religion an argument to break through any natural or civil obligations. He should quietly and comfortably abide in the condition in which he is; and this he may well do, when he may abide therein with God.

ADVICE FOR SPINSTERS
(*vv.* 25–35)

The apostle here resumes his discourse, and gives directions to virgins how to act, concerning which we may take notice,

I. Of the manner wherein he introduces them: *"Now concerning virgins I have no commandment of the Lord, v.* 25. I have no express and universal law delivered by the Lord himself concerning celibacy; but *I give my judgment, as one who hath obtained mercy of the Lord to be faithful,"* namely, in the apostleship.

II. The determination he gives, which, considering the present distress, was that a state of celibacy was preferable: *It is good for a man so to be,* that is, *to be single. I suppose,* says the apostle, or it is my opinion. It is worded with modesty,

but delivered, notwithstanding, with apostolical authority.

III. Notwithstanding he thus determines, he is very careful to satisfy them that he does not condemn marriage in the gross, nor declare it unlawful. And therefore, though he says, "If thou *art loosed from a wife* (in a single state, whether bachelor or widower, virgin or widow) *do not seek a wife,* do not hastily change conditions;" yet he adds, *"If thou art bound to a wife, do not seek to be loosed.* It is thy duty to continue in the married relation, and do the duties of it." Marrying is not in itself a sin, but marrying at that time was likely to bring inconvenience upon them, and add to the calamities of the times; and therefore he thought it advisable and expedient that such as could contain should refrain from it.

IV. He takes this occasion to give general rules to all Christians to carry themselves with a holy indifference towards the world, and every thing in it. 1. *As to relations:* Those *that had wives must be as though they had none*; that is, they must not set their hearts too much on the comforts of the relation; they must be as though they had none. 2. As to afflictions: *Those that weep must be as though they wept not*; that is, we must not be dejected too much with any of our afflictions, nor indulge ourselves in the sorrow of the world, but keep up a holy joy in God in the midst of all our troubles, so that even in sorrow the heart may be joyful, and the end of our grief may be gladness. 3. As to worldly enjoyments: *Those that rejoice should be as though they rejoiced not*; that is, they should not take too great a complacency in any of their comforts. 4. As to worldly traffic and employment: *Those that buy must be as though they possessed not*. Those that prosper in trade, increase in wealth, and purchase estates, should hold these possessions as though they held them not. It is but setting their hearts on that which is not (Prov. xxiii. 5) to do otherwise. 5. As to all worldly concerns: *Those that use this world as not abusing it*, v. 31. The world may be used, but must not be abused. It is abused when it is not used to those purposes for which it is given, to honour God and do good to men.

V. He enforces these advices with two reasons: 1. *The time is short*, v. 29. We have but little time to continue in this world; but a short season for possessing and enjoying worldly things. Possess what you must shortly leave without suffering yourselves to be possessed by it. 2. *The fashion of this world passeth away* (v. 31), the habit, figure, appearance, of the world, passeth away. It is daily changing countenance. It is in a continual flux. All is show, nothing solid in it; and it is transient show too, and will quickly be gone. How proper and powerful an argument is this to enforce the former advice! How irrational is it to be affected with the images, the fading and transient images, of a dream!

VI. He presses his general advice by warning them against the embarrassment of worldly cares: *But I would have you without carefulness*, v. 32. Indeed to be careless is

a fault; a wise concern about worldly interests is a duty; but to be careful, full of care, to have an anxious and perplexing care about them, is a sin. Now the married state at that time (if not at all times) did bring most worldly care along with it. *He that is married careth for the things of the world, that he may please his wife*, v. 33. *And she that is married careth for the things of the world, how she may please her husband*. But the unmarried man and woman mind the things of the Lord, that they may please the Lord, and be holy both in body and spirit, vv. 32, 34. Not but the married person may be holy both in body and spirit too. Celibacy is not in itself a state of greater purity and sanctity than marriage; but the unmarried would be able to make religion more their business at that juncture, because they would have less distraction from worldly cares.

ACT WISELY (vv. 36–38)

In this passage the apostle is commonly supposed to give advice about the disposal of children in marriage, upon the principle of his former determination. In this view the general meaning is plain. If a man has determined in himself to keep his daughter a virgin, and stands to this determination, and is under no necessity to dispose of her in marriage, but is at liberty, with her consent, to pursue his purpose, he does well in keeping her a virgin. In short, he that gives her in marriage does well; but he that keeps her single, if she can be easy and innocent in such a state, does what is better; that is, more convenient for her in the present state of things, if not at all times and seasons."

But I think the apostle is here continuing his former discourse, and advising unmarried persons, who are at their own disposal, what to do. The general meaning of the apostle is the same, that it was no sin to marry, if a man thought there was a necessity upon him, to avoid popular reproach, much less to avoid the hurrying fervours of lust. But he that was in his own power, stood firm in his purpose, and found himself under no necessity to marry, would, at that season, and in the circumstances of Christians at that time, at least, make a choice every way most for his own conveniency, ease, and advantage, as to his spiritual concerns.

WIDOWS (*vv.* 39, 40)

The whole is here closed up with advice to widows: *As long as the husband liveth the wife is bound by the law*, confined to one husband, and bound to continue and cohabit with him. *But, the husband being dead, she is at liberty to marry whom she will.* There is no limitation by God's law to be married only for such a number of times. It is certain, from this passage, that second marriages are not unlawful. But the apostle asserts she has such a liberty, when her husband is dead, only with a limitation that *she marry in the Lord.* In our choice of relations, and change of conditions, we should always have an eye to God. *But she is happier*, says the apostle, *if she so abide* (that is, continue a widow) *in my judgment;*

and I think I have the Spirit of God, v. 40. At this juncture, at least, if not ordinarily, it will be much more for the peace and quiet of such, and give them less hindrance in the service of God, to continue unmarried. And this, he tells them, was by inspiration of the Spirit.

CHAPTER EIGHT

THINGS OFFERED TO IDOLS
(*vv.* 1–3)

The apostle comes here to the case of things that had been offered to idols, concerning which some of them sought satisfaction. For the better understanding of it, it must be observed that it was a custom among the heathens to make feasts on their sacrifices, and not only to eat themselves, but invite their friends to partake with them. These were usually kept in the temple, where the sacrifice was offered (*v.* 10), and, if any thing was left when the feast ended, it was usual to carry away a portion to their friends; what remained, after all, belonged to the priests, who sometimes sold it in the markets. See *ch.* x. 25. In this circumstance of things, while Christians lived among idolaters, had many relations and friends that were such, with whom they must keep up acquaintance and maintain good neighbourhood, and therefore have occasion to eat at their tables, what should they do if any thing that had been sacrificed should be set before them? What, if they should be invited to feast with them in their temples? It seems as if some of the Corinthians had imbibed an opinion that even this might be done, because they knew an idol was nothing in the world, *v.* 4.

IDOLS ARE NOTHING
(*vv.* 4–6)

In this passage he shows the vanity of idols: *As to the eating of things that have been sacrificed to idols, we know that an idol is nothing in the world*; or, there is no idol in the world; or, an idol can do nothing in the world; for the form of expression in the original is elliptical. The meaning in the general is, that heathen idols have no divinity in them; and therefore in the Old Testament they are commonly called *lies* and *vanities*, or *lying vanities*. All their divinity and mediation were imaginary. For, 1. *To us there is but one God*, says the apostle, *the Father, of whom are all things, and we in or for him*. We Christians are better informed; we well know there is but one God, the fountain of being, the author of all things, maker, preserver, and governor of the whole world, of whom and for whom are all things. 2. There is to us but one Lord, one Mediator between God and men, even Jesus Christ. Not many mediators, as the heathen imagined, but one only, by whom all things were created and do consist, and to whom all our hope and happiness are owing—the man Christ Jesus; but a man in personal union with the divine Word, or God the Son. This very man hath God made both Lord and Christ, Acts ii. 36.

ABUSE OF LIBERTY
(*vv.* 7–13)

The apostle, having granted, and indeed confirmed, the opinion of some among the Corinthians, that idols were nothing. He does not indeed here so much insist upon the unlawfulness of the thing in itself as the mischief such freedom might do to weaker Christians, persons that had not the same measure of knowledge with these pretenders. And here,

I. He informs them that every Christian man, at that time, was not so fully convinced and persuaded that an idol was nothing. Note, We should be careful to do nothing that may occasion weak Christians to defile their consciences.

II. He tells them that mere eating and drinking had nothing in them virtuous nor criminal, nothing that could make them better nor worse, pleasing nor displeasing to God.

III. He cautions them against abusing their liberty, the liberty they thought they had in this matter. For that they mistook this matter, and had no allowance to sit at meat in the idol's temple, seems plain from *ch.* x. 20, &c. But the apostle argues here that, even upon the supposition that they had such power, they must be cautious how they use it; it might be a *stumbling-block to the weak* (*v.* 9), it might occasion their falling into idolatrous actions, perhaps their falling off from Christianity and revolting again to heathenism.

IV. He enforces all with his own example (*v.* 13): *Wherefore if meat make my brother to offend I will eat no flesh while the world standeth, lest I make my brother to offend*. He does not say that he will never eat more. This were to destroy himself, and to commit a heinous sin, to prevent the sin and fall of a brother. Such evil must not be done that good may come of it. But, though it was necessary to eat, it was not necessary to eat flesh. And therefore, rather than occasion sin in a brother, he would abstain from it as long as he lived.

CHAPTER NINE
THE APOSTLE'S RIGHTS
(vv. 1–14)

Having asserted his apostolical authority (*vv.* 1, 2) Paul proceeds to claim the rights belonging to his office, especially that of being maintained by it.

I. These he states, *vv.* 3–6. "*My answer to those that do examine me* (that is, enquire into my authority, or the reasons of my conduct, if I am an apostle) is this: *Have we not power to eat and drink* (*v.* 4), or a right to maintenance? *Have we not power to lead about a sister, a wife, as well as other apostles, and the brethren of the Lord, and Cephas*; and, not only to be maintained ourselves, but have them maintained also?* Though Paul was at that time single, he had a right to take a wife when he pleased, and to lead her about with him, and expect a maintenance for her, as well as himself, from the churches. In short, the apostle here claims a maintenance from the churches, both for him and his. This was due from them, and what he might claim.

II. He proceeds, by several arguments, to prove his claim. 1. From the common practice and expectations of mankind. Those who addict and give themselves up to any way

of business in the world expect to live out of it. 2. He argues it out of the Jewish law: *Say I these things as a man? Or saith not the law the same also? v.* 8. God had therein ordered that the ox should not be muzzled while he was treading out the corn, nor hindered from eating while he was preparing the corn for man's use, and treading it out of the ear. *Those who plough should plough in hope; and those who thresh in hope should be partakers of their hope, v.* 10. The law saith this about oxen for our sakes. 3. He argues from common equity: *If we have sown unto you spiritual things, is it a great thing if we shall reap your carnal things?* What they had sown was much better than they expected to reap. They had taught them the way to eternal life, and laboured heartily to put them in possession of it. It was no great matter, surely, while they were giving themselves up to this work, to expect a support of their own temporal life. 4. He argues from the maintenance they afforded others: *"If others are partakers of this power over you, are not we rather?* You allow others this maintenance, and confess their claim just; but who has so just a claim as I from the church of Corinth? Who has given greater evidence of the apostolical mission? Who has laboured so much for your good, or done like service among you?" 5. He argues from the old Jewish establishment: "*Do you not know that those who minister about holy things live of the things of the temple, and those who wait at the altar are partakers with the altar? v.* 13. And, if the Jewish priesthood was maintained out of the holy things that were then offered, shall not Christ's ministers have a maintenance out of their ministry? He asserts it to be the institution of Christ: "*Even so hath the Lord ordained that those who preach the gospel should live of the gospel* (v. 14), should have a right to a maintenance, though not bound to demand it, and insist upon it."

A PRIVILEGE WAIVED
(*vv.* 15–18)

Here he tells them that he had, notwithstanding, waived his privilege, and lays down his reason for doing it.

I. He tells them that he had neglected to claim his right in times past: *I have used none of these things*, v. 15. Nor did he write this to make his claim now. Though he here asserts his right, yet he does not claim his due; but denies himself for their sakes, and the gospel.

II. We have the reason assigned of his exercising this self-denial. He would not have his glorying made void: *It were better for him to die than that any man should make his glorying void*, v. 15. It was a singular pleasure to him to preach the gospel without making it burdensome; and he was resolved that among them he would not lose this satisfaction.

III. He shows that this self-denial was more honourable in itself, and yielded him much more content and comfort, than his preaching did: "*Though I preach the gospel, I have nothing whereof to glory; for necessity is laid upon me; yea, woe is unto me, if I preach not the gospel*, v. 16. It is my charge, my business;

it is the work for which I am constituted an apostle, *ch.* i. 17. This is a duty expressly bound upon me. It is not in any degree a matter of liberty. *Necessity is upon me.* I am false and unfaithful to my trust, I break a plain and express command, and *woe be to me, if I do not preach the gospel*." Note, It is a high attainment in religion to renounce our own rights for the good of others; this will entitle to a peculiar reward from God. For,

IV. The apostle here informs us that doing our duty with a willing mind will meet with a gracious recompence from God: *If I do this thing*, that is, either preach the gospel or take no maintenance, *willingly, I have a reward*. Indeed, it is willing service only that is capable of reward from God. It is not the bare doing of any duty, but the doing of it heartily (that is, willingly and cheerfully) that God has promised to reward.

V. The apostle sums up the argument, by laying before them the encouraging hope he had of a large recompense for his remarkable self-denial: *What is my reward then? v.* 18. What is it I expect a recompence from God for? *That when I preach the gospel I may make it without charge, that I abuse not my power in the gospel.*

ALL THINGS TO ALL MEN
(*vv.* 19–23)

The apostle takes occasion from what he had before discoursed to mention some other instances of his self-denial and parting with his liberty for the benefit of others.

I. He asserts his liberty (*v.* 19): *Though I be free from all men.* He was free-born, a citizen of Rome. He made himself a servant, that they might be made free.

II. He specifies some particulars wherein he made himself a servant to all. He accommodated himself to all sorts of people. 1. *To the Jews, and those under the law, he became a Jew*, and as under the law, to gain them. Though he looked on the ceremonial law as a yoke taken off by Christ, yet in many instances he submitted to it, that he might work upon the Jews, remove their prejudices, prevail with them to hear the gospel, and win them over to Christ. 2. *To those that are without the law as without law* that is, to the Gentiles, whether converted to the Christian faith or not. In innocent things he could comply with people's usages or humours for their advantage. He would reason with the philosophers in their own way. And, as to converted Gentiles, he behaved among them as one that was not under the bondage of the Jewish laws, but as one who was bound by the laws of Christ. 3. *To the weak he became as weak, that he might gain the weak, v.* 22. He was willing to make the best of them. He did not despise nor judge them, but became as one of them, forbore to use his liberty for their sake, and was careful to lay no stumbling-block in their way.

III. He assigns his reason for acting in this manner (*v.* 23): *This I do for the gospel's sake, and that I may be partaker thereof with you*; that is, for the honour of Christ, whose the gospel is, and for the salvation of souls, for which it was designed.

THE CHRISTIAN RACE
(*vv.* 24–27)

In these verses the apostle hints at the great encouragement he had to act in this manner. He had a glorious prize, an incorruptible crown, in view. Upon this head he compares himself to the racers and combatants in the Isthmian games, an allusion well known to the Corinthians, because they were celebrated in their neighbourhood: "*Know you not that those who run in a race run all, but one obtaineth the prize? v.* 24. All run at your games, but only one gets the race and wins the crown." And here,

I. He excites them to their duty: "*So run that you may obtain.* It is quite otherwise in the Christian race than in your races; only one wins the prize in them. You may all run so as to obtain."

II. He directs them in their course, by setting more fully to view his own example, still carrying on the allusion. 1. Those that ran in their games were kept to a set diet: "*Every man that strives for the mastery is temperate in all things, v.* 23." They do not indulge themselves, but restrain themselves from the food they eat and so from the liberties they use on other occasions. 2. They were not only temperate, but inured themselves to hardships. Christians must fight, not as those that beat the air, but must strive against their enemies with all their might. One enemy the apostle here mentions, namely, the body; this must be kept under, beaten black and blue, as the combatants were in these Grecian games, and thereby brought into subjection. By the body we are to understand fleshly appetites and inclinations.

III. The apostle presses this advice on the Corinthians by proper arguments drawn from the same contenders. 1. They take pains, and undergo all those hardships, *to obtain a corruptible crown* (*v.* 25), *but we an incorruptible.* Those who conquered in these games were crowned only with the withering leaves or boughs of trees, of olive, bays, or laurel. But Christians have an incorruptible crown in view, a crown of glory that never fadeth away, an inheritance incorruptible, reserved in heaven for them. 2. The racers in these games run at uncertainty. All run, but one receives the prize, *v.* 24. Every racer, therefore, is at a great uncertainty whether he shall win it or no. But the Christian racer is at no such uncertainty. Every one may run here so as to obtain; but then he must run within the lines, he must keep to the path of duty prescribed, which, some think, is the meaning of *running not as uncertainly, v.* 26. He who keeps within the limits prescribed, and keeps on in his race, will never miss his crown, though others may get theirs before him. 3. He sets before himself and them the danger of yielding to fleshly inclinations, and pampering the body and its lusts and appetites: *I keep my body under, lest that by any means, when I have preached to others, I myself should be a cast-away* (*v.* 27), *rejected, disapproved.* one to whom *the judge* or *umpire* of the race, will not decree the crown. The allusion to the games runs through the whole sentence.

CHAPTER TEN

WARNINGS (*vv.* 1–5)

In order to dissuade the Corinthians from communion with idolaters, and security in any sinful course, he sets before them the example of the Jews, the church under the Old Testament. They enjoyed great privileges, but, having been guilty of heinous provocations, they fell under very grievous punishments. In these verses he reckons up their privileges, which, in the main, were the same with ours.

I. He prefaces this discourse with a note of regard: "*Moreover, brethren, I would not that you should be ignorant.*" I would not have you without the knowledge of this matter; it is a thing worthy both of your knowledge and attention.

II. He specifies some of their privileges. He begins, 1 With their deliverance from Egypt. They were very dear to God, and much in his favour, when he would work such miracles for their deliverance, and take them so immediately under his guidance and protection. 2. They had sacraments like ours. (1) *They were all baptized unto Moses in the cloud, and in the sea* (*v.* 2), or into Moses, that is, brought under obligation to Moses's law and covenant, as we are by baptism under the Christian law and covenant. It was to them a typical baptism. (2) *They did all eat of the same spiritual meat, and drink of the same spiritual drink,* that we do. The manna on which they fed was a type of Christ crucified, the bread which came down from heaven, which whoso eateth shall live for ever. Their drink was a stream fetched from a rock which followed them in all their journeyings in the wilderness; and this rock was Christ, that is, in type and figure. These were great privileges. One would think that this should have saved them; that all who ate of that spiritual meat and drank of that spiritual drink, should have been holy and acceptable to God. Yet was it otherwise: *With many of them God was not well pleased; for they were overthrown in the wilderness, v.* 5. Note, Men may enjoy many and great spiritual privileges in this world, and yet come short of eternal life.

TEMPTATIONS (*vv.* 6–14)

The apostle, having recited their privileges, proceeds here to an account of their faults and punishments, their sins and plagues, which are left upon record for an example to us, a warning against the like sins, if we would escape the like punishments. We must not do as they did, lest we suffer as they suffered.

I. Several of their sins are specified as cautions to us; as, 1. We should shun inordinate desires after carnal objects: *Not lust after evil things, as they lusted, v.* 6. God fed them with manna, but they must have flesh, Num. xi. 4. They had food for their supply, but, not content with this, they asked *meat for their lusts,* Ps. cvi. 14. Carnal desires get head by indulgence, and therefore should be observed and checked in their first rise. 2. He warns against idolatry (*v.* 7): *Neither be you idolaters, as were some of them; as it is written, The*

people sat down to eat and drink, and rose up to play. The sin of the golden calf is referred to, Exod. xxxii. 6. 3. He cautions against fornication, a sin to which the inhabitants of Corinth were in a peculiar manner addicted. 4. He warns us against *tempting Christ (as some of them tempted, and were destroyed of serpents, v.* 9), or provoking him to jealousy, *v.* 22. He was with the church in the wilderness; he was the angel of the covenant, who went before them. 5. He warns against murmuring: *Neither murmur you as some of them also murmured, and were destroyed of the destroyer (v.* 10), by a destroying angel, an executioner of divine vengeance. They quarrelled with God, and murmured against Moses his minister, when any difficulties pressed them.

II. The apostle subjoins to these particular cautions a more general one (*v.* 11): *All these things happened to them for ensamp'es, and were written for our admonition.* Not only the laws and ordinances of the Jews, but the providences of God towards them, were typical. Their sins against God, and backslidings from him, were typical of the infidelity of many under the gospel. God's judgments on them were types of spiritual judgments now. Upon this hint the apostle grounds a caution (*v.* 12): *Let him that thinketh he standeth take heed lest he fall.* Note, The harms sustained by others should be cautions to us.

III. But to this word of caution he adds a word of comfort, *v.* 13. Though it is displeasing to God for us to presume, it is not pleasing to him for us to despair. For, 1.

"*No temptation*," says the apostle, "*hath yet taken you, but such as is common to man*." Note, The trials of common Christians are but common trials: others have the like burdens and the like temptations; what they bear up under, and break through, we may also. 2. *God is faithful.* Though Satan be a deceiver, God is true. Men may be false, and the world may be false; but God is faithful, and our strength and security are in him. 3. He is wise as well as faithful, and will proportion our burden to our strength. *He will not suffer us to be tempted above what we are able.* He knows what we can bear, and what we can bear up against; and he will, in his wise providence, either proportion our temptations to our strength or make us able to grapple with them.

IV. And upon this argument he grounds another caution against idolatry: *Wherefore, my dearly beloved, flee from idolatry.* Note, We have all the encouragement in the world to flee sin and prove faithful to God. We cannot fall by a temptation if we cleave fast to him.

RULES FOR COMMUNION
(*vv.* 15–22)

In this passage the apostle urges the general caution against idolatry, in the particular case of eating the heathen sacrifices as such, and out of any religious respect to the idol to whom they were sacrificed.

I. He prefaces his argument with an appeal to their own reason and judgment: "*I speak to wise men, judge you what I say, v. 15.* You are great pretenders to wis-

dom, to close reasoning and argument; I can leave it with your own reason and conscience whether I do not argue justly."

II. He lays down his argument from the Lord's supper: *The cup which we bless, is it not the communion of the blood of Christ? The bread which we break, is it not the communion of the body of Christ?* Is not this sacred rite an instrument of communion with God? Do we not therein profess to be in friendship, and to have fellowship, with him? Is it not a token whereby we professedly hold communion with Christ, whose body was broken, and blood shed, to procure remission of our sins, and the favour of God? And can we be in alliance with Christ, or friendship with God, without being devoted to him? In short, the Lord's supper is a feast on the sacrificed body and blood of our Lord. And to eat of the feast is to partake of the sacrifice, and so to be his guests to whom the sacrifice was offered, and this in token of friendship with him. *Because the bread is one, we, being many, are one body, for we are made partakers of one bread*, or loaf (*v.* 17), which I think is thus more truly rendered: "By partaking of one broken loaf, the emblem of our Saviour's broken body, who is the only true bread that came down from heaven, we coalesce into one body, become members of him and one another." Those who truly partake by faith have this communion with Christ, and one another; and those who eat the outward elements make profession of having this communion, of belonging to God and the blessed fraternity of his people and worshippers. This is the true meaning of this holy rite.

III. He confirms this from the Jewish worship and customs: *Behold Israel after the flesh: are not those who eat of the sacrifices partakers of the altar,* that is, of the sacrifice offered upon it? Those who were admitted to eat of the offerings were reckoned to partake of the sacrifice itself, as made for them, and to be sanctified thereby; and therefore surely to worship God, and be in alliance or covenant with him, even the God of Israel, to whom the sacrifice was made: this was a symbol or token of holding communion with him.

IV. He applies this to the argument against feasting with idolaters on their sacrifices, and to prove those that do so idolaters. This he does, 1. By following the principle on which they would argue it to be lawful, namely, that an idol was nothing. Many of them were nothing at all, none of them had any divinity in them. Now the apostle allows that the food was not changed as to its nature, was as fit to be eaten as common food, where it was set before any who knew not of its having been offered to an idol. But, 2. He proves that the eating of it as a part of a heathen sacrifice was, (1) A partaking with them in their idolatry. *It was having fellowship with devils,* because what the Gentiles sacrificed they sacrificed to devils. (2) It was a virtual renouncing of Christianity: *You cannot drink the cup of the Lord, and the cup of devils: you cannot be partakers of the Lord's table, and the table of devils, v. 21.*

To partake of this Christian feast was to have communion with Christ: to partake of the feasts made in honour of the heathen idols, and made of things sacrificed to them, was to have communion with devils. Now this was to compound contraries; it was by no means consistent.

V. He warns them, upon the whole, against such idolatry, by signifying to them that God is a jealous God (*v.* 22): *Do we provoke the Lord to jealousy? Are we stronger than he?* It is very probable that many among the Corinthians made light of being at these heathen feasts, and thought there was no harm in it. But the apostle bids them beware.

LAW AND CONSCIENCE
(*vv.* 23–33)

In this passage the apostle shows in what instances, notwithstanding, Christians might lawfully eat what had been sacrificed to idols. But,

I. He gives a caution against abusing our liberty in lawful things. That may be lawful which is not expedient, which will not edify.

II. He tells them that what was *sold in the shambles they might eat without asking questions.* The priest's share of heathen sacrifices was thus frequently offered for sale, after it had been offered in the temple. Now the apostle tells them they need not be so scrupulous as to ask the butcher in the market whether the meat he sold had been offered to an idol? It was there sold as common food, and as such might be bought and used; *for the earth is the Lord's, and the fulness thereof* (*v*. 26), and the fruit and products of the earth were designed by him, the great proprietor, for the use and subsistence of mankind, and more especially of his own children and servants.

III. He adds that if they were invited by any heathen acquaintances to a feast, *they might go, and eat what was set before them, without asking questions* (*v*. 27), *nay, though* they knew things sacrificed to idols were served up at such entertainments, as well as sold in the shambles. Note, The apostle does not prohibit their going to a feast upon the invitation of those that believed not. There is a civility owing even to infidels and heathens. Christianity does by no means bind us up from the common offices of humanity, nor allow us an uncourteous behaviour to any of our own kind, however they may differ from us in religious sentiments or practices. And when Christians were invited to feast with infidels they were not to ask needless questions about the food set before them, but eat without scruple.

IV. Yet, even at such an entertainment, he adds, if any should say it was a thing that had been offered to idols, they should refrain: *Eat not, for his sake that showed it, and for conscience' sake.* Whether it were the master of the feast or any of the guests, whether it were spoken in the hearing of all or whispered in the ear, they should refrain for his sake who suggested this to them, whether he were an infidel or an infirm Christian; and for conscience' sake, out of regard to conscience, that they might show a regard to it in themselves, and keep up a regard to it in others.

V. He urges them to refrain where they will give offence, while yet he allows it lawful to eat what was set before them as common food, though it had been offered in sacrifice.

VI. The apostle takes occasion from this discourse to lay down a general rule for Christians' conduct, and apply it to this particular case (*vv*. 31, 32), namely, that in eating and drinking, and in all we do, we should aim at the glory of God, at pleasing and honouring him. This is the fundamental principle of practical godliness. Our own humour and appetite must not determine our practice, but the honour of God and the good and edification of the church. We should not so much consult our own pleasure and interest as the advancement of the kingdom of God among men.

VII. He presses all upon them by his own example: *Even as I please all men* (or study to do it) *in all things* (that I lawfully can), *not seeking my own profit, but that of many, that they may be saved, v. 33.*

CHAPTER ELEVEN

REDRESS OF GRIEVANCES
(*vv*. 1–16)

Paul, having answered the cases put to him, proceeds in this chapter to the redress of grievances. He reprehends and reforms an indecency among them, of which the women were more especially guilty, concerning which observe,

I. How he prefaces it. He begins

with a commendation of what was praiseworthy in them (*v.* 2): *I praise you, that you remember me in all things, and keep the ordinances as I delivered them to you.*

II. How he lays the foundation for his reprehension by asserting the superiority of the man over the woman: *I would have you know that the head of every man is Christ, and the head of the woman is the man, and the head of Christ is God.* Christ, in his mediatorial character and glorified humanity, is at the head of mankind. And as God is the head of Christ, and Christ the head of the whole human kind, so the man is the head of the two sexes: not indeed with such dominion as Christ has over the kind or God has over the man Christ Jesus; but a superiority and headship he has, and the woman should be in subjection and not assume or usurp the man's place. This is the situation in which God has placed her; and for that reason she should have a mind suited to her rank, and not do any thing that looks like an affectation of changing places. Something like this the women of the church of Corinth seem to have been guilty of, who were under inspiration, and prayed and prophesied even in their assemblies, *v.* 5. It is indeed an apostolical canon, that the women *should keep silence in the churches* (*ch.* xiv. 34; 1 Tim. ii. 12), which some understand without limitation, as if a woman under inspiration also must keep silence, which seems very well to agree with the connection of the apostle's discourse, *ch.* xiv. Others with a limitation: though a woman might not

from her own abilities pretend to teach, or so much as question and debate any thing in the church, yet when under inspiration the case was altered, she had liberty to speak. Or, though she might not preach even by inspiration (because teaching is the business of a superior), yet she might pray or utter hymns by inspiration, even in the public assembly. She did not show any affectation of superiority over the man by such acts of public worship. It is plain the apostle does not in this place prohibit the thing, but reprehend the manner of doing it.

III. The thing he reprehends is the woman's praying or prophesying uncovered, or the man's doing either covered *vv.* 4, 5. To understand this, it must be observed that it was a signification either of shame or subjection for persons to be veiled, or covered, in the eastern countries, contrary to the custom of ours, where the being bareheaded betokens subjection, and being covered superiority and dominion. And this will help us the better to understand.

IV. The reasons on which he grounds his reprehension. *The man that prays or prophesies with his head covered dishonoureth his head,* namely, Christ, the head of every man (*v.* 3), by appearing in a habit unsuitable to the rank in which God has placed him. *The woman,* on the other hand, *who prays or prophesies with her head uncovered dishonoureth her head,* namely, the man, *v.* 3. She appears in the dress of her superior, and throws off the token of her subjection. It was doing a thing which, in that age of the world, betokened superiority, and therefore a tacit claim of what did not belong to them but the other sex. Note, The sexes should not affect to change places.

V. He thinks fit to guard his argument with a caution lest the inference be carried too far (*vv.* 11, 12): *Nevertheless, neither is the man without the woman, nor the woman without the man in the Lord.* They were made for one another. *It is not good for him to be alone* (Gen. ii. 18), and therefore was a· woman made, and made for the man; and the man was intended to be a comfort, and help, and defence, to the woman, though not so directly and immediately made for her. They were made to be a mutual comfort and blessing, not one a slave and the other a tyrant.

VI. He sums up all by referring those who were contentious to the usages and customs of the churches, *v.* 16. Custom is in a great measure the rule of decency. And the common practice of the churches is what he would have them govern themselves by.

REVERENCE AT WORSHIP
(*vv.* 17–22)

In this passage the apostle sharply rebukes them for much greater disorders than the former, in their partaking of the Lord's supper, which was commonly done in the first ages, as the ancients tell us, with a love-feast annexed, which gave occasion to the scandalous disorders which the apostle here reprehends, concerning which observe,

I. The manner in which he introduces his charge: "*Now in this that*

I declare to you I praise you not, v. 17." I cannot commend, but must blame and condemn you.

II. He enters upon his charge against them in more particulars than one. 1. He tells them that, upon coming together, they fell into *divisions, schisms.* 2. He charges them not only with discord and division, but with scandalous disorder: *For in eating every one taketh before the other his own supper; and one is hungry, and another is drunken, v.* 21. Heathens used to drink plentifully at their feasts upon their sacrifices. Many of the wealthier Corinthians seem to have taken the same liberty at the Lord's table, or at least at their *love-feasts,* that were annexed to the supper. They would not stay for one another; the rich despised the poor, and ate and drank up the provisions they themselves brought, before the poor were allowed to partake; and thus some wanted, while others had more than enough. This was profaning a sacred institution, and corrupting a divine ordinance, to the last degree.

III. The apostle lays the blame of this conduct closely on them, 1. By telling them that their conduct perfectly destroyed the purpose and use of such an institution: *This is not to eat the Lord's supper, v.* 20. Thus to eat the outward elements was not to eat Christ's body. 2. Their conduct carried in it a contempt of God's house, or of the church, *v.* 22. If they had a mind to feast, they might do it at home in their own houses; but to come to the Lord's table, and quarrel, and keep the poor from their share of the provision there made for them as well as the rich, was such an abuse of the ordinance, and such a contempt of the poorer members of the church more especially, as merited a very sharp rebuke.

THE PURPOSE OF THE LORD'S SUPPER
(*vv.* 23–34)

To rectify these gross corruptions and irregularities, the apostle sets the sacred institution here to view. This should be the rule in the reformation of all abuses.

I. He tells us how he came by the knowledge of it. He was not among the apostles at the first institution; but *he had received from the Lord what he delivered to them, v.* 23. He had the knowledge of this matter by revelation from Christ: and what he had received he communicated, without varying from the truth a tittle, without adding or diminishing.

II. He gives us a more particular account of the institution than we meet with elsewhere. We have here an account,

1. Of the author—our Lord Jesus Christ. The king of the church only has power to institute sacraments.

2. The time of the institution: *It was the very night wherein he was betrayed*; just as he was entering on his sufferings which are therein to be commemorated.

3. The institution itself. Our Saviour took bread, and when he had given thanks, or *blessed* (as it is in Matt. xxvi. 26), *he broke, and said, Take, eat; this is my body, broken for you; this do in remembrance of me. And in like manner he took the cup, when he had supped,* saying, *This cup is the New Testament in my blood; this do, as oft as you drink it, in remembrance of me, vv.* 24, 25. Here observe,

(1) The materials of this sacrament; both, [1] As to the visible signs: these are bread and the cup. [2] The things signified by these outward signs: they are Christ's body and blood, his body broken, his blood shed, together with all the benefits which flow from his death and sacrifice: *it is the New Testament in his blood.*

(2) We have here the sacramental actions, the manner in which the materials of the sacrament are to be used. [1] Our Saviour's actions, which are taking the bread and cup, giving thanks, breaking the bread, and giving about both the one and the other. [2] The actions of the communicants, which were to take the bread and eat, to take the cup and drink, and both in remembrance of Christ.

(3) We have here an account of the ends of this institution. [1] It was appointed to be done *in remembrance of Christ*, to keep fresh in our minds an ancient favour, his dying for us, as well as to remember an absent friend, even Christ interceding for us, in virtue of his death, at God's right hand. [2] It was *to show forth Christ's death*, to declare and publish it. It is not barely in remembrance of Christ, of what he has done and suffered, that this ordinance was instituted; but to commemorate, to celebrate, his glorious condescension and grace in our redemption. We set it in view of our own faith, for our own comfort and quickening: and we own before the world, by this very

service, that we are the disciples of Christ, who trust in him alone for salvation and acceptance with God.

(4) It is moreover hinted here, concerning this ordinance, [1] That it should be frequent: *As often as you eat this bread*, &c. [2] That it must be perpetual. It is to be celebrated *till the Lord shall come*; till he shall come the second time, without sin, for the salvation of those that believe, and to judge the world.

III. He lays before the Corinthians the danger of receiving unworthily, of prostituting this institution as they did, and using it to the purposes of feasting and faction. 1. It is great guilt which such contract. They shall *be guilty of the body and blood of the Lord* (*v.* 27), of violating this sacred institution, of despising his body and blood. 2. It is a great hazard which they run: *They eat and drink judgment to themselves*, *v.* 29. They provoke God, and are likely to bring down punishment on themselves. The Corinthians came to the Lord's table as to a common feast, *not discerning the Lord's body*—not making a difference or distinction between that and common food, but setting both on a level.

IV. He points out the duty of those who would come to the Lord's table. 1. In general: *Let a man examine himself* (*v.* 28), try and approve himself. Let him consider the sacred intention of this holy ordinance, its nature, and use, and compare his own views in attending on it and his disposition of mind for it; and, when he has approved himself to his own conscience in the

sight of God, then let him attend. 2. The duty of those who were yet unpunished for their profanation of this ordinance: *If we would judge ourselves, we should not be judged*, *v.* 31. If we would thoroughly search and explore ourselves, and condemn and correct what we find amiss, we should prevent divine judgments.

V. He closes all with a caution against the irregularities of which they were guilty (*vv.* 33, 34), charging them to avoid all indecency at the Lord's table. Holy things are to be used in a holy manner, or else they are profaned. What else was amiss in this matter, he tells them, he would rectify when he came to them.

CHAPTER TWELVE

SPIRITUAL GIFTS (*vv.* 1–11)

The apostle comes now to treat of spiritual gifts, which abounded in the church of Corinth, but were greatly abused.

I. The apostle tells them he would not have them ignorant either of their original or use.

II. He puts them in mind of the sad state out of which they had been recovered: *You were Gentiles, carried away to dumb idols, even as you were led*, *v.* 2. While they were so, they could have no pretensions to be spiritual men, nor to have spiritual gifts. If they well understood their former condition, they could not but know that all true spiritual gifts were from God. Now concerning this observe, 1. Their former character: they *were Gentiles*. Not God's peculiar people, but of the nations whom he had in a manner abandoned. 2. The conduct they were under: *Carried away to these dumb idols, even as you were led.* They were hurried upon the grossest idolatry, the worship even of stocks and stones, through the force of a vain imagination, and the fraud of their priests practising on their ignorance, for, whatever were the sentiments of their philosophers, this was the practice of the herd.

III. He shows them how they might discern those gifts that were from the Spirit of God, true spiritual gifts: *No man, speaking by the Spirit, calls Jesus accursed.* Now the apostle tells them none could act under the influence, nor by the power, of the Spirit of God, who disowned and blasphemed Christ: for the Spirit of God bore uncontrollable witness to Christ by prophecy, miracles, his resurrection from the dead, the success of his doctrine among men, and its effect upon them; and could never so far contradict itself as to declare him accursed. And on the other hand *no man could say Jesus was the Lord* (that is, live by this faith, and work miracles to prove it), *but it must be by the Holy Ghost.* To own this truth before men, and maintain it to the death, and live under the influence of it, could not be done without the sanctification of the Holy Ghost. He adds,

IV. These spiritual gifts, though proceeding from the same Spirit, are yet various. They have one author and original, but are themselves of various kinds. A free cause may produce variety of effects; and the same giver may bestow various

gifts, *v.* 4. However different they may be in themselves, in this they agree; all are from God. And several of the kinds are here specified, *vv.* 8–10. Different persons had their distinct gifts, some one, some another, all from and by the same Spirit. To one was given the *word of wisdom*; that is, say some, a knowledge of the mysteries of the gospel, and ability to explain them, an exact understanding of the design, nature, and doctrines, of the Christian religion. Some confine this word of wisdom to the revelations made to and by the apostles. — *To another the word of knowledge, by the same Spirit*; that is, say some, the knowledge of mysteries (*ch.* ii. 13): wrapped up in the prophecies, types, and histories of the Old Testament: say others, a skill and readiness to give advice and counsel in perplexed cases. — *To another faith, by the same Spirit*; that is, the faith of miracles, or a faith in the divine power and promise, whereby they were enabled to work miracles; or an extraordinary impulse from above, whereby they were enabled to trust God in any emergency, and go on in the way of their duty, and own and profess the truths of Christ, whatever was the difficulty or danger. — *To another the gift of healing, by the same Spirit*; that is, healing the sick, either by laying on of hands, or anointing with oil, or with a bare word. — *To another the working of miracles*; the efficacies of powers, such as raising the dead, restoring the blind to sight, giving speech to the dumb, hearing to the deaf, and the use of limbs to the lame. — *To another prophecy*, that is, ability to foretell future events, which is the more usual sense of prophecy; or to explain scripture by a peculiar gift of the Spirit. See *ch*. xiv. 24.—*To another the discerning of Spirits*, power to distinguish between true and false prophets, or to discern the real and internal qualifications of any person for an office, or to discover the inward workings of the mind by the Holy Ghost, as Peter did those of Ananias, Acts v. 3.—*To another divers kinds of tongues*, or ability to speak languages by inspiration.—*To another the interpretation of tongues*, or ability to render foreign languages readily and properly into their own. With such variety of spiritual gifts were the first ministers and churches blessed.

V. The end for which these gifts were bestowed: *The manifestation of the Spirit is given to every man to profit withal, v.* 7. The Spirit was manifested by the exercise of these gifts; his influence and interest appeared in them. But they were not distributed for the mere honour and advantage of those who had them, but for the benefit of the church, to edify the body, and spread and advance the gospel.

VI. The measure and proportion in which they are given: *All these worketh one and the same Spirit, dividing to every man as he will.* It is according to the sovereign pleasure of the donor. What more free than a gift? And shall not the Spirit of God do what he will with his own?

THE UNITY OF THE BODY
(*vv.* 12–26)

The apostle here makes out the truth of what was above asserted,

and puts the gifted men among the Corinthians in mind of their duty, by comparing the church of Christ to a human body.

I. By telling us that one body may have many members, and that the many members of the same body make but one body (*v.* 12): *As the body is one, and hath many members, and all the members of that one body, being many, are one body, so also is Christ*; that is, Christ mystical, as divines commonly speak. Christ and his church making one body, as head and members, this body is made up of many parts or members, yet but one body; for all the members are *baptized into the same body, and made to drink of the same Spirit, v.* 13.

II. Each member has its particular form, place, and use. 1. The meanest member makes a part of the body. The foot and ear are less useful, perhaps, than the hand and eye; but because one is not a hand, and the other an eye, shall they say, therefore, that they do not belong to the body? *vv.* 15, 16. So every member of the body mystical cannot have the same place and office; but what then? 2. There must be a distinction of members in the body: *Were the whole body eye, where were the hearing? Were the whole ear, where were the smelling? v.* 17. *If all were one member, where were the body? v.* 19. *They are many members*, and for that reason must have distinction among them, *and yet are but one body, v.* 20. Variety in the members of the body contributes to the beauty of it. So it is for the beauty and good appearance of the church that there should be diversity of gifts and offices in it. 3. The disposal of members in a natural body, and their situation, are as God pleases: *But now hath God set the members, every one of them, in the body, as it hath pleased him*, v. 18. We may plainly perceive the divine wisdom in the distribution of the members; but it was made according to the counsel of his will; he distinguished and distributed them as he pleased. So is it also in the members of Christ's body: they are chosen out to such stations, and endued with such gifts, as God pleases. 4. All the members of the body are, in some respect, useful and necessary to each other: (*vv.* 21, 22); God has so fitted and tempered them together that they are all necessary to one another, and to the whole body; there is no part redundant and unnecessary. None should despise and envy another, seeing God has made the distinction between them as he pleased, yet so as to keep them all in some degree of mutual dependence, and make them valuable to each other, and concerned for each other, because of their mutual usefulness. 5. Such is the man's concern for his whole body that *on the less honourable members more abundant honour is bestowed, and our uncomely parts have more abundant comeliness*. Those parts which are not fit, like the rest, to be exposed to view, which are either deformed or shameful, we most carefully clothe and cover; whereas the comely parts have no such need. So should the members of Christ's body behave towards their fellow-members: instead of despising them, or

reproaching them, for their infirmities, they should endeavour to cover and conceal them, and put the best face upon them that they can. 6. Divine wisdom has contrived and ordered things in this manner that the members of the body should not be schismatics, divided from each other and acting upon separate interests, but well affected to each other, tenderly concerned for each other, having a fellow-feeling of each other's griefs and a communion in each other's pleasures and joys, *vv.* 25, 26.

VARIETY IN THE BODY
(*vv.* 27–31)

I. Here the apostle sums up the argument, and applies this similitude to the church of Christ, concerning which observe,

1. The relation wherein Christians stand to Christ and one another. The church, or whole collective body of Christians, in all ages, is his body. Every Christian is a member of his body, and every other Christian stands related to him as a fellow-member (*v.* 27): *Now you are the body of Christ, and members in particular*, or particular members.

2. The variety of offices instituted by Christ, and gifts or favours dispensed by him (*v.* 28). Concerning all these observe, (1) The plenteous variety of these gifts and offices. What a multitude are they! A good God was free in his communications to the primitive church; he was no niggard of his benefits and favours. (2) Observe the order of these offices and gifts. They are here placed in their proper ranks.

Those of most value have the first place. What holds the last and lowest rank in this enumeration is diversity of tongues. It is by itself the most useless and insignificant of all these gifts. Healing diseases, relieving the poor, helping the sick, have their use: but how vain a thing is it to speak languages, if a man does it merely to amuse or boast himself! This may indeed raise the admiration, but cannot promote the edification, of the hearers, nor do them any good. And yet it is manifest from *ch*. xiv. that the Corinthians valued themselves exceedingly on this gift. (3) The various distribution of these gifts, not all to one, nor to every one alike. All members and officers had not the same rank in the church, nor the same endowments (*vv*. 29, 30). We must be content with our own rank and share, if they be lower and less than those of others. We must not be conceited of ourselves, and despise others, if we are in the higher rank and have greater gifts.

II. He closes this chapter with an advice (as the generality read it) and a hint. 1. An advice to covet the best gifts, either the most valuable in themselves or the most serviceable to others; and these are, in truth, most valuable in themselves, though men may be apt to esteem those most that will raise their fame and esteem highest. 2. By giving them the hint of a more excellent way, namely, of charity, of mutual love and good-will. This was the only right way to quiet and cement them, and make their gifts turn to the advantage and edification of the church.

CHAPTER THIRTEEN

THE VALUE OF LOVE
(*vv*. 1–3)

Here the apostle shows what more excellent way he meant, or had in view, in the close of the former chapter, namely, *charity*, or, as it is commonly elsewhere rendered, *love*. Without this the most glorious gifts are nothing, of no account to us, of no esteem in the sight of God. He specifies, 1. The gift of tongues. Could a man speak all the languages on earth, and that with the greatest propriety, elegance, and fluency, could he talk like an angel, and yet be without charity, it would be all empty noise, mere unharmonious and useless sound, that would neither profit nor delight. 2. Prophecy, and the understanding of mysteries, and all knowledge. This without charity is as nothing, *v*. 2. It is not great knowledge that God sets a value upon, but true and hearty devotion and love. 3. Miraculous faith, the faith of miracles, or the faith by which persons were enabled to work miracles. The most wonder-working faith, to which nothing is in a manner impossible, is itself nothing without charity. 4. The outward acts of charity: *Bestowing his goods to feed the poor, v*. 3. Should all a man has be laid out in this manner, if he had no charity, it would profit him nothing. Our doing good to others will do none to us, if it be not well done, namely, from a principle of devotion and charity, love to God, and good-will to men. 5. Even sufferings, and even those of the most grievous kind: *If we give our bodies to be burnt, without*

254

charity, it profiteth nothing, v. 3. Should we sacrifice our lives for the faith of the gospel, and be burnt to death in maintenance of its truth, this will stand us in no stead without charity, unless we be animated to these sufferings by a principle of true devotion to God, and sincere love to his church and people, and good-will to mankind.

THE QUALITY OF LOVE
(*vv.* 4–7)

The apostle gives us in these verses some of the properties and effects of charity. As,

I. *It is long suffering.* It can endure evil, and injury, and provocation, without being filled with resentment, indignation, or revenge.

II. *It is kind.* It is benign, bountiful; it is courteous and obliging. *The law of kindness is in her lips;* her heart is large, and her hand open. She is ready to show favours and to do good.

III. Charity suppresses envy: *It envieth not;* it is not grieved at the good of others; neither at their gifts nor at their good qualities, their honours nor their estates. If we love our neighbour we shall be so far from envying his welfare, or being displeased with it, that we shall share in it and rejoice at it.

IV. Charity subdues pride and vain-glory: *It vaunteth not itself, is not puffed up,* is not bloated with self-conceit, does not swell upon its acquisitions, nor arrogate to itself that honour, or power, or respect, which does not belong to it.

V. Charity is careful not to pass the bounds of decency; *it behaveth*

not unseemly; it does nothing indecorous, nothing that in the common account of men is base or vile.

VI. Charity is an utter enemy to selfishness: *Seeketh not its own,* does not inordinately desire nor seek its own praise, or honour, or profit, or pleasure. It often neglects its own for the sake of others; prefers their welfare, and satisfaction, and advantage, to its own.

VII. It tempers and restrains the passions, *is not exasperated.* It corrects a sharpness of temper, sweetens and softens the mind, so that it does not suddenly conceive, nor long continue, a vehement passion.

VIII. Charity *thinks no evil.* It cherishes no malice, nor gives way to revenge; so some understand it. It does not suspect evil of others, *it does not reason out* evil, charge guilt upon them by inference and *innuendo*, when nothing of this sort appears open.

IX. The matter of its joy and pleasure is here suggested: 1. Negatively: *It rejoiceth not in iniquity.* It takes no pleasure in doing injury or hurt to any. 2. Affirmatively: *It rejoiceth in the truth,* is glad of the success of the gospel, commonly called *the truth,* by way of emphasis, in the New Testament; and rejoices to see men moulded into an evangelical temper by it, and made good.

X. *It beareth all things, it endureth all things.* Some read the first, *covers all things.* So the original also signifies. *Charity will cover a multitude of sins,* 1 Pet. iv. 8. It will draw a veil over them, as far as it can consistently with duty· Or, it *beareth all things,*—will pass by and put up with injuries, without indulging anger or cherishing revenge, will be patient upon provocation, and long patient, holds firm, though it be much shocked, and borne hard upon; sustains all manner of injury and ill usage, and bears up under it.

XI. Charity believes and hopes well of others: *Believeth all things; hopeth all things.* Indeed charity does by no means destroy prudence, and, out of mere simplicity and silliness, believe every word, Prov. xiv. 15. Wisdom may dwell with love, and charity be cautious. But it is apt to believe well of all, to entertain a good opinion of them when there is no appearance to the contrary; nay, to believe well when there may be some dark appearances, if the evidence of ill be not clear.

LOVE NEVER ENDS (*vv.* 8–13)

Here the apostle goes on to commend charity, and show how much it is preferable to the gifts on which the Corinthians were so apt to pride themselves, to the utter neglect, and almost extinction, of charity. This he makes out,

I. From its longer continuance and duration: *Charity never faileth.* It is a permanent and perpetual grace, lasting as eternity; whereas the extraordinary gifts on which the Corinthians valued themselves were of short continuance. *Prophecy must fail*, that is, either the prediction of things to come (which is its most common sense) or the interpretation of scripture by immediate inspiration. *Tongues will cease*, that is, the miraculous power of speaking languages without learning them. There will be but one langu-

age in heaven. There is no confusion of tongues in the region of perfect tranquillity. And *knowledge will vanish away*. Not that, in the perfect state above, holy and happy souls shall be unknowing, ignorant: it is a very poor happiness that can consist with utter ignorance. The apostle is plainly speaking of miraculous gifts, and therefore of knowledge to be had out of the common way (see *ch.* xiv. 6), a knowledge of mysteries supernaturally communicated. Such knowledge was to vanish away.

II. He hints that these gifts are adapted only to a state of imperfection: *We know in part, and we prophesy in part, v.* 9. Our best knowledge and our greatest abilities are at present like our condition, narrow and temporary.

III. He takes occasion hence to show how much better it will be with the church hereafter than it can be here. A state of perfection is in view (*v.* 10): *When that which is perfect shall come, then that which is in part shall be done away.* When the end is once attained, the means will of course be abolished. There will be no need of tongues, and prophecy, and inspired knowledge, in a future life, because then the church will be in a state of perfection, complete both in knowledge and holiness. The difference between these two states is here pointed at in two particulars: 1. The present state is a state of childhood, the future that of manhood: *When I was a child, I spoke as a child* (that is, as some think, spoke with tongues), *I understood as a child; I thought*, or reasoned, *as a child; but, when I became a man, I put away childish things.* Such is the difference between earth and heaven. 2. Things are all dark and confused now, in comparison of what they will be hereafter: *Now we see through a glass darkly (in a riddle), then face to face; now we know in part, but then we shall know as we are known.* God is to be seen *face to face*; and we *are to know him* as *we are known by him*; not indeed as perfectly, but in some sense in the same manner.

IV. To sum up the excellences of charity, he prefers it not only to gifts, but to other graces, to faith and hope (*v.* 13): *And now abide faith, hope, and charity; but the greatest of these is charity.* True grace is much more excellent than any spiritual gifts whatever. And faith, hope, and love, are the three principal graces, of which charity is the chief, being the end to which the other two are but means. When faith and hope are at an end, true charity will burn for ever with the brightest flame.

CHAPTER FOURTEEN

SPEAKING IN TONGUES
(*vv.* 1–5)

The apostle, in the foregoing chapter, had himself preferred, and advised the Corinthians to prefer, Christian charity to all spiritual gifts. Here he teaches them, among spiritual gifts, which they should prefer, and by what rules they should make comparison. He begins the chapter,

I. With an exhortation to charity (*v.* 1): *Follow after charity,* pursue it. It is an exhortation to obtain charity, to get this excellent disposition of mind upon any terms, whatever pains or prayers it may cost.

II. He directs them with spiritual gift to prefer, from a principle of charity: "*Desire spiritual gifts, but rather that you may prophesy,* or chiefly that you may prophesy." Note, Gifts are fit objects of our desire and pursuit, in subordination to grace and charity. That should be sought first and with the greatest earnestness which is most worth.

III. He assigns the reasons of this preference. And it is remarkable here that he only compares prophesying with speaking with tongues. It seems, this was the gift on which the Corinthians principally valued themselves. This was more ostentatious than the plain interpretation of scripture, more fit to gratify pride, but less fit to pursue the purposes of Christian charity; it would not equally edify nor do good to the souls of men. For, 1. He that spoke with tongues must wholly speak between God and himself; for, whatever mysteries might be communicated in his language, none of his own countrymen could understand them, because they did not understand the language, *v.* 2. 2. He that speaks with tongues may edify himself, *v.* 4. He may understand and be affected with what he speaks; and so every minister should; and he that is most edified himself is in the disposition and fitness to do good to others by what he speaks; but he that speaks with tongues, or language unknown, can only edify himself; others can reap no benefit from his speech. 3. Indeed, no gift is to be despised, but the best gifts are to be preferred. *I could wish*, says the apostle, *that you all spoke with tongues, but rather that you prophesied, v.* 5. Every gift of God is a favour from God, and may be improved for his glory, and as such is to be valued and thankfully received; but then those are to be most valued that are most useful. *Greater is he that prophesieth than he that speaketh with tongues, unless he interpret, that the church may receive edifying, v.* 5. Greater is he who interprets scripture to edify the church than he who speaks tongues to recommend himself. And what other end he who spoke with tongues could have, unless he interpreted what he spoke, is not easy to say.

THE NECESSITY OF INTERPRETATION (*vv.* 6–14)

An apostle, with all his furniture, could not edify, unless he spoke to the capacity of his hearers.

I. He illustrates this by several allusions. 1. To a pipe and a harp playing always in one tone. Of what use can this be to those who are dancing? If there be no distinction of sounds, how should they order their steps or motions? Unintelligible language is like piping or harping without distinction of sounds. 2. To a trumpet giving an *uncertain sound*, a sound not manifest; either not the proper sound for the purpose, or not distinct enough to be discerned from every other sound. 3. He compares the speaking in an unknown tongue to the gibberish of barbarians. There are, as he says (*v.* 10), many kinds of voices in the world, none of

which is without its proper signification. But whatever proper signification the words of any language may have in themselves, and to those who understand them, they are perfect gibberish to men of another language, who understand them not. In this case, speaker and hearers are barbarians to each other (*v.* 11), they talk and hear only sounds without sense. To speak in the church in an unknown tongue is to talk gibberish; it is to play the barbarian; it is to confound the audience, instead of instructing them; and for this reason is utterly vain and unprofitable.

II. Having thus established his point, in the two next verses he applies it, 1. By advising them to be chiefly desirous of those gifts that were most for the church's edification, *v.* 12. This is the great rule he gives, which, 2. He applies to the matter in hand, that, if they did speak a foreign language, they should beg of God the gift of interpreting it, *v.* 13. That these were different gifts, see *ch.* xii. 10. 3. He enforces this advice with a proper reason, that, if *he prayed in an unknown tongue, his spirit might pray*, that is, a spiritual gift might be exercised in prayer, or his own mind might be devoutly engaged, *but his understanding would be unfruitful* (*v.* 14), that is, the sense and meaning of his words would be unfruitful, he would not be understood, nor therefore would others join with him in his devotions.

PRAYING WITH UNDERSTANDING (*vv.* 15–20)

The apostle here sums up the argument hitherto, and,

I. Directs them how they should sing and pray in public (*v.* 15): *What is it then? I will pray with the spirit, and I will pray with the understanding also. I will sing with the spirit,* &c. He does not forbid their praying or singing under a divine *afflatus,* or when they were inspired for this purpose, or had such a spiritual gift communicated to them; but he would have them perform both so as to be understood by others, that others might join with them.

II. He enforces the argument with several reasons.

1. That otherwise the unlearned could not say Amen to their prayers or thanksgivings, could not join in the worship, for they did not understand it, *v.* 16.

2. He alleges his own example, to make the greater impression, concerning which observe, (1) That he did not come behind any of them in this spiritual gift: "*I thank my God, I speak with tongues more than you all* (*v.* 18); not only more than any single person among you, but more than all together." Yet, (2) He had rather *speak five words with understanding,* that is, so as to be understood, and instruct and edify others, *than ten thousand words in an unknown tongue, v.* 19.

3. He adds a plain intimation that the fondness then discovered for this gift was but too plain an indication of the immaturity of their judgment: *Brethren, be not children in understanding; in malice be you children, but in understanding be men, v.* 20. Children are apt to be struck with novelty and strange appearances. They are taken with an outward show, without enquir-

ing into the true nature and worth of things. Do not you act like them, and prefer noise and show to worth and substance; show a greater ripeness of judgment, and act a more manly part; be like children in nothing but an innocent and inoffensive disposition.

THE VALUE OF PROPHECY
(*vv.* 21–25)

In this passage the apostle pursues the argument, and reasons from other topics; as,

I. Tongues, as the Corinthians used them, were rather a token of judgment from God than mercy to any people (*v.* 21): *In the law* (that is, the Old Testament) *it is written, With men of other tongues and other lips will I speak to this people; and yet for all this will they not hear me, saith the Lord,* Isa. xxviii. 11. Compare Deut. xxviii. 46, 49.

II. Tongues were rather a sign to unbelievers than to believers, *v.* 22. They were a spiritual gift, intended for the conviction and conversion of infidels, that they might be brought into the Christian church; but converts were to be built up in Christianity by profitable instructions in their own language.

III. The credit and reputation of their assemblies among unbelievers required them to prefer prophesying before speaking with tongues. For, 1. If, when they were all assembled for Christian worship, their ministers, or all employed in public worship, should talk unintelligible language, and infidels should drop in, they would conclude them to be mad, to be no better than a parcel of wild fanatics. Who in their right senses could carry on religious worship in such a manner? Or what sort of religion is that which leaves out sense and understanding? But, on the other hand, 2. If, instead of speaking with tongues, those who minister plainly interpret scripture, or preach, in language intelligible and proper, the great truths and rules of the gospel, a heathen or unlearned person, coming in, will probably be convinced, and become a convert to Christianity (*vv.* 24, 25).

RULES FOR GATHERINGS
(*vv.* 26–33)

In this passage the apostle reproves them for their disorder, and endeavours to correct and regulate their conduct for the future.

I. He blames them for the confusion they introduced into the assembly, by ostentation of their gifts (*v.* 26).

II. He corrects their faults, and lays down some regulations for their future conduct. 1. As to speaking in an unknown tongue, he orders that no more than two or three should do it at one meeting, and this not altogether, but successively, one after another. And even this was not to be done unless there were some one to interpret (*vv.* 27, 28), some other interpreter besides himself, who spoke; for to speak in an unknown tongue what he himself was afterwards to interpret could only be for ostentation. But, if there were none to interpret, he was to be silent in the church, and only exercise his gift between God and himself (*v.* 28), that is (as I think) in private, at home; for all who are present at public worship should join in it, and not be at their

private devotions in public assemblies. 2. As to prophesying he orders, (1) That two or three only should speak at one meeting (*v.* 20), and this successively, not all at once; and that the other should examine and judge what he delivered, that is, discern and determine concerning it, whether it were of divine inspiration or not. (2) He orders that, if any assistant prophet had a revelation, while another was prophesying, the other should hold his peace, be silent (*v.* 30), before the inspired assistant uttered his revelation. *That all might prophesy, one by one,* or one after another, which might easily be if he who was afterwards inspired forbore to deliver his new revelation till the former prophet had finished what he had to say. And, to confirm this sense, the apostle quickly adds, *The spirits of the prophets are subject to the prophets* (*v.* 33); that is, the spiritual gifts they have leave them still possessed of their reason, and capable of using their own judgment in the exercise of them. The man inspired by the Spirit of God may still act the man, and observe the rules of natural order and decency in delivering his revelations.

III. The apostle gives the reasons of these regulations. As, 1. That they would be for the church's benefit, their instruction and consolation. It is that *all may learn, and all may be comforted or exhorted,* that the prophets were to speak in the orderly manner the apostle advises. 2. He tells them, *God is not the God of confusion, but of peace and good order, v.* 33. Therefore divine inspiration should by no means throw Christian assemblies into confusion, and break through all rules of common decency. 3. He adds that things were thus orderly managed in all the other churches: *As in all the churches of the saints* (v. 33); they kept to these rules in the exercise of their spiritual gifts, which was a manifest proof that the church of Corinth might observe the same regulations.

WOMEN IN CHURCH
(vv. 34, 35)

Here the apostle, 1. Enjoins silence on their women in public assemblies, and to such a degree that they must not ask questions for their own information in the church, but ask their husbands at home. They were not ordinarily to teach, nor so much as to debate and ask questions in the church, but learn in silence there; and, if difficulties occurred, *ask their own husbands at home.* 2. We have here the reason of this injunction: It is God's law and commandment that they should be under obedience (v. 34); they are placed in subordination to the man, and it is a shame for them to do any thing that looks like an affectation of changing ranks, which speaking in public seemed to imply, at least in that age, and among that people, as would public teaching much more: so that the apostle concludes it was a shame for women to speak in the church, in the assembly.

DECENTLY AND IN ORDER
(vv. 36–40)

In these verses the apostle closes his argument, 1. With a just rebuke of the Corinthians for their extravagant pride and self-conceit: they so managed with their spiritual gifts as no church did like them; they behaved in a manner by themselves, and would not easily endure control nor regulation. 2. He lets them know that what he said to them was the command of God; nor durst any true prophet, any one really inspired, deny it (v. 37): "*If any man think himself a prophet, or spiritual, let him acknowledge,* &c., nay, let him be tried by this very rule. If he will not own what I deliver on this head to be the will of Christ, he himself never had the Spirit of Christ. 3. He sums up all in two general advices: (1) That though they should not despise the gift of tongues, nor altogether disuse it, under the regulations mentioned, yet they should prefer prophesying. This is indeed the scope of the whole argument. It was to be preferred to the other, because it was the more useful gift. (2) He charges them to let all things be done decently and in order (v. 40), that is, that they should avoid every thing that was manifestly indecent and disorderly.

CHAPTER FIFTEEN
THE GOSPEL MESSAGE
(vv. 1–11)

It is the apostle's business in this chapter to assert and establish the doctrine of the resurrection of the dead, which some of the Corinthians flatly denied, v. 12. He begins with an epitome or summary of the gospel, what he had preached among them, namely, the death and resurrection of Christ. Upon this foundation the doctrine of the resurrection of the dead is built. Now concerning the gospel observe,

I. What a stress he lays upon it (*vv.* 1, 2): *Moreover, brethren, I declare unto you the gospel which I preached to you.* 1. It was what he constantly preached. Truth is in its own nature invariable; and the infallible teachers of divine truth could never be at variance with themselves or one another. 2. It was what they had received; they had been convinced of the faith, believed it in their hearts, or at least made profession of doing so with their mouths. 3. It was that alone by which they could hope for salvation (*v.* 2), for there is *no salvation in any other name; no name given under heaven by which we may be saved, but by the name of Christ.* And there is no salvation in his name, but upon supposition of his death and resurrection. Now concerning these saving truths observe, (1) They must be retained in mind, they must be held fast (so the word is translated, Heb. x. 23): *Let us hold fast the profession of our faith.* They will not save us, if we do not attend to them, and yield to their power, and continue to do so to the end. (2) We believe in vain, unless we continue and persevere in the faith of the gospel. And in vain is it to profess Christianity, or our faith in Christ, if we deny the resurrection.

II. Observe what this gospel is, on which the apostle lays such stress. That Christ died for our sins, and was buried, and rose again.

III. Observe how this truth is confirmed,

1. By Old-Testament predictions. He died for our sins, according to the scriptures; he was buried, and rose from the dead, according to the scriptures, according to the scripture-prophecies, and scripture-types. Such prophecies as Ps. xvi. 10; Isa. liii. 4–6; Dan. ix. 26, 27; Hos. vi. 2.

2. By the testimony of many eye-witnesses, who saw Christ after he had risen from the dead. He reckons up five several appearances, beside that to himself. He *was seen of Cephas, or Peter, then of the twelve*, called so, though Judas was no longer among them, because this was their usual number; then he was *seen of above five hundred brethren at once*, many of whom were living when the apostle wrote this epistle, though some had fallen asleep. This was in Galilee, Matt. xxviii. 10. After that, he was seen of James singly, and then by all the apostles when he was taken up into heaven. This was on mount Olivet, Luke xxiv. 50. Compare Acts i. 2, 5–7. Even Paul himself was last of all favoured with the sight of him. It was one of the peculiar offices of an apostle to be a witness of our Saviour's resurrection (Luke xxiv. 48); and, when Paul was called to the apostolical office, he was made an evidence of this sort; the Lord Jesus appeared to him by the way to Damascus, Acts ix. 17. Having mentioned this favour, Paul takes occasion from it to make a humble digression concerning himself. He was highly favoured of God, but he always endeavoured to keep up a mean opinion of himself, and to express it.

After this digression, the apostle

returns to his argument, and tells them (*v.* 11) that he not only preached the same gospel himself at all times, and in all places, but that all the apostles preached the same: *Whether it were they or I, so we preached, and so you believed.* All the apostles agreed in this testimony; all Christians agree in the belief of it. By this faith they live. In this faith they die.

THE NECESSITY OF THE RESURRECTION (*vv.* 12–19)

Having confirmed the truth of our Saviour's resurrection, the apostle goes on to refute those among the Corinthians who said there would be none: *If Christ be preached that he rose from the dead, how say some among you that there is no resurrection of the dead? v.* 12. It seems from this passage, and the course of the argument, there were some among the Corinthians who thought the resurrection an impossibility. This was a common sentiment among the heathens. But against this the apostle produces an incontestable fact, namely, the resurrection of Christ; and he goes on to argue against them from the absurdities that must follow from their principle. As,

I. *If there be* (can be) *no resurrection of the dead, then Christ has not risen* (*v.* 13); and again, "*If the dead rise not,* cannot be raised or recovered to life, *then is Christ not raised,*" *v.* 16.

II. It would follow hereupon that the preaching and faith of the gospel would be vain: *If Christ be not risen, then is our preaching vain, and your faith vain, v.* 14. This

supposition admitted, would destroy the principal evidence of Christianity; and so, 1. Make preaching vain. If Christ be not raised, the gospel is a jest; it is chaff and emptiness. 2. This supposition would make the faith of Christians vain, as well as the labours of ministers: *If Christ be not raised, your faith is vain; you are yet in your sins* (*v.* 17), yet under the guilt and condemnation of sin, because it is through his death and sacrifice for sin alone that forgiveness is to be had.

III. Another absurdity following from this supposition is that *those who have fallen asleep in Christ have perished.* If there be no resurrection, they cannot rise, and therefore are lost, even those who have died in the Christian faith, and for it. And this,

IV. Would infer that Christ's ministers and servants were *of all men most miserable*, as having *hope in him in this life only* (*v.* 19), which is another absurdity that would follow from asserting no resurrection. Their condition who hope in Christ would be worse than that of other men. Note, It were a gross absurdity in a Christian to admit the supposition of no resurrection or future state. It would leave no hope beyond this world, and would frequently make his condition the worst in the world.

THE LAST ENEMY (*vv.* 20–34)

In this passage the apostle establishes the truth of the resurrection of the dead, the holy dead, the dead in Christ,

I. On the resurrection of Christ.

1. Because he is indeed *the first-fruits of those that slept*, v. 20. The whole body of Christ, all that are by faith united to him, are by his resurrection assured of their own. As he has risen, they shall rise; just as the lump is holy because the first-fruits are so. He has not risen merely for himself, but as head of the body, the church; and *those that sleep in him God will bring with him*, 1 Thess. iv. 14. This is the first argument used by the apostle in confirmation of the truth; and it is,

2. Illustrated by a parallel between the first and second Adam. For, since by man came death, it was every way proper that by man should come deliverance from it, or, which is all one, a resurrection, v. 21. All who die die through the sin of Adam; all who are raised, in the sense of the apostle, rise through the merit and power of Christ. But the meaning is not that, as all men died in Adam, so all men, without exception, shall be made alive in Christ; for the scope of the apostle's argument restrains the general meaning. Christ rose as the first-fruits; therefore *those that are Christ's* (v. 23) shall rise too. Hence it will not follow that all men without exception shall rise too.

3. Before he leaves the argument he states that there will be an order observed in their resurrection. What that precisely will be we are nowhere told, but in the general only here that there will be order observed.

II. He argues from the continuance of the mediatorial kingdom till all Christ's enemies are destroyed, the last of which is death, vv. 24–26.

1. This argument implies in it all these particulars: (1) That our Saviour rose from the dead to have all power put into his hands, and have and administer a kingdom, as Mediator. (3) That it is not to have an end till all opposing power be put down, and all enemies brought to his feet, vv. 24, 25. (4) That, among other enemies, death must be destroyed (v. 26) or abolished; its powers over its members must be disannulled. Thus far the apostle is express; but he leaves us to make the inference that therefore the saints must rise, else death and the grave would have power over them, nor would our Saviour's kingly power prevail against the last enemy of his people and annul its power.

2. The apostle drops several hints in the course of it which it will be proper to notice: as, (1) That our Saviour, as man and mediator between God and man, has a delegated royalty, a kingdom given: *All things are put under him, he excepted that did put all things under him*, v. 27. (2) That this delegated royalty must at length be *delivered up to the Father*, from whom it was received (v. 24); for it is a power received for particular ends and purposes, a power to govern and protect his church till all the members of it be gathered in, and the enemies of it for ever subdued and destroyed (vv. 25, 26), and when these ends shall be obtained the power and authority will not need to be continued. (3) The Redeemer shall certainly reign till the last enemy of his people be destroyed, till death itself be abolished, till his saints revive and

recover perfect life, never to be in fear and danger of dying any more. (4) When this is done, *and all things are put under his feet, then shall the Son become subject to him that put all things under him, that God may be all in all, v.* 28. The meaning of this I take to be that then the man Christ Jesus, who hath appeared in so much majesty during the whole administration of his kingdom, shall appear upon giving it up to be a subject of the Father.

III. He argues for the resurrection, from the case of those who were baptized for the dead (*v.* 29). But what is this baptism for the dead? It is as easy an explication of the phrase as any I have met with, and as pertinent to the argument, to suppose *the dead* to mean some among the Corinthians, who had been taken off by the hand of God. We read that *many were sickly among them, and many slept* (*ch.* xi. 30), because of their disorderly behaviour at the Lord's table. These executions might terrify some into Christianity; as the miraculous earthquake did the jailer, Acts xvi. 29, 30, &c. Persons baptized on such an occasion might be properly said to be baptized for the dead, that is, on their account. "Now," says he, "what shall they do, and why were they baptized, if the dead rise not? You have a general persuasion that these men have done right, and acted wisely, and as they ought, on this occasion; but why, if the dead rise not, seeing they may perhaps hasten their death, by provoking a jealous God, and have no hopes beyond it?" But whether this be the meaning, or whatever else be, doubtless

the apostle's argument was good and intelligible to the Corinthians. And his next is as plain to us.

IV. He argues from the absurdity of his own conduct and that of other Christians upon this supposition,

1. It would be a foolish thing for them to run so many hazards (*v.* 30): "*Why stand we in jeopardy every hour?*" Note, Christianity were a foolish profession if it proposed no hopes beyond this life, at least in such hazardous times as attended the first profession of it; it required men to risk all the blessings and comforts of this life, and to face and endure all the evils of it, without any future prospects.

2. It would be a much wiser thing to take the comforts of this life: *Let us eat and drink, for to-morrow we die* (*v.* 32); let us turn epicures. Thus this sentence means in the prophet, Isa. xxii. 13. Let us even live like beasts, if we must die like them. This would be a wiser course, if there were no resurrection, no after-life or state, than to abandon all the pleasures of life, and offer and expose ourselves to all the miseries of life, and live in continual peril of perishing by savage rage and cruelty.

V. The apostle closes his argument with a caution, exhortation, and reproof. 1. A caution against the dangerous conversation of bad men, men of loose lives and principles: *Be not deceived*, says he; *evil communications corrupt good manners, v.* 33. Possibly, some of those who said that there was no resurrection of the dead were men of loose lives, and endeavoured to countenance their vicious practices by so corrupt a principle; and had that speech often in their mouths, *Let us eat and drink, for to-morrow we die.* 2. Here is an exhortation to break off their sins, and rouse themselves, and lead a more holy and righteous life (*v.* 34): *Awake to righteousness,* or *awake righteously, and sin not,* or sin no more. The disbelief of a future state destroys all virtue and piety. 3. Here is a reproof, and a sharp one, to some at least among them: *Some of you have not the knowledge of God; I speak this to your shame.* Note, It is a shame in Christians not to have the knowledge of God. Note, Real atheism lies at the bottom of men's disbelief of a future state. Those who own a God and a providence, and observe how unequal the distributions of the present life are, and how frequently the best men fare worst, can hardly doubt an after state, where every thing will be set to rights.

THE RESURRECTION OF THE BODY (*vv.* 35–50)

The apostle comes now to answer a plausible and principal objection against the doctrine of the resurrection of the dead, concerning which observe the proposal of the objection: *Some man will say, How are the dead raised up? And with what body do they come? v.* 35. The objection is plainly two-fold. *How are they raised up?* that is, "By what means?" The other part of the objection is about the quality of their bodies, who shall rise: "*With what body will they come?* Will it be with the same body, with like shape, and form, and stature, and members, and qualities, or various?" The former objection is that of those who opposed the doctrine, the latter the enquiry of curious doubters.

I. To the former the apostle replies by telling them this was to be brought about by divine power, that very power which they had all observed to do something very like it, year after year, in the death and revival of the corn; and therefore it was an argument of great weakness and stupidity to doubt whether the resurrection of the dead might not be effected by the same power: *Thou fool! that which thou sowest is not quickened unless it die, v.* 36. It must first corrupt, before it will quicken and spring up. It not only sprouts after it is dead, but it must die that it may live. And why should any be so foolish as to imagine that the man once dead cannot be made to live again, by the same power which every year brings the dead grain to life? This is the substance of the apostle's answer to the first question.

II. But he is longer in replying to the second enquiry.

1. He begins by observing that there is a change made in the grain that is sown: It is *not that body which shall be* that is sown, but *bare grain,* of wheat or barley, &c.; but God gives it such a body as he will, and in such way as he will, only so as to distinguish the kinds from each other.

2. He proceeds hence to observe that there is a great deal of variety among other bodies, as there is among plants.

3. To speak directly to the point: *So also,* says he, *is the resurrection*

of the dead; so (as the plant growing out of the putrefied grain), so as no longer to be a terrestrial but a celestial body, and varying in glory from the other dead, who are raised, as one star does from another. But he specifies some particulars: as, (1) *It is sown in corruption, it is raised in incorruption.* Our bodies, which are sown, are corruptible, liable to putrefy and moulder, and crumble to dust; but, when we rise, they will be out of the power of the grave, and never more be liable to corruption. (2) *It is sown in dishonour, it is raised in glory.* Ours is at present a vile body, Phil. iii. 21. But at the resurrection a glory will be put upon it; it will be made like the glorious body of our Saviour. (3) *It is sown in weakness, it is raised in power.* It is laid in the earth, a poor helpless thing. But when we arise our bodies will have heavenly life and vigour infused into them. (4) *It is sown a natural*, or *animal* body, a body fitted to the low condition and sensitive pleasures and enjoyments of this life, which are all gross in comparison of the heavenly state and enjoyments. But when we rise it will be quite otherwise; our body will rise spiritual.

4. He illustrates this by a comparison of the first and second Adam: *There is an animal body*, says he, *and there is a spiritual body*; and then goes into the comparison in several instances. As surely therefore as we have had natural bodies, we shall have spiritual ones. The dead in Christ shall not only rise, but shall rise thus gloriously changed.

5. He sums up this argument by assigning the reason of this change (v. 50): *Now this I say that flesh and blood cannot inherit the kingdom of God; nor doth corruption inherit incorruption.* The natural body is flesh and blood; and, as such, it is of a corruptible frame and form, liable to dissolution, to rot and moulder. But no such thing shall inherit the heavenly regions; for this were for corruption to inherit incorruption, which is little better than a contradiction in terms. The heavenly inheritance is incorruptible, and never fadeth away, 1 Pet. i. 4.

DEATH DEFEATED
(*vv.* 51–58)

To confirm what he had said of this change,

I. He here tells them what had been concealed from or unknown to them till then—that all the saints would not die, but all would be changed. Those that are alive at our Lord's coming will be caught up into the clouds, without dying, 1 Thess. iv. 11. But it is plain from this passage that it will not be without changing from corruption to incorruption. The frame of their living bodies shall be thus altered, as well as those that are dead; and this *in a moment, in the twinkling of an eye, v.* 52.

II. He assigns the reason of this change (*v.* 53): *For this corruptible must put on incorruption, and this mortal must put on immortality.* How otherwise could the man be a fit inhabitant of the incorruptible regions, or be fitted to possess the eternal inheritance? How can that which is corruptible and mortal enjoy what is incorruptible, permanent, and immortal?

III. He lets us know what will follow upon this change of the living and dead in Christ: *Then shall be brought to pass that saying, Death is swallowed up in victory*; or, *He will swallow up death in victory*, Isa. xxv. 8. For *mortality shall be then swallowed up of life* (2 Cor. v. 4), and death perfectly subdued and conquered, and saints for ever delivered from its power. And upon this destruction of death will they break out into a song of triumph.

1. They will glory over death as a vanquished enemy, and insult this great and terrible destroyer: *"O death! where is thy sting?"*

2. The foundation for this triumph is here intimated, (1) In the account given whence death had its power to hurt: *The sting of death is sin*. Sin unpardoned, and nothing else, can keep any under his power. And the *strength of sin is the law*; it is the divine threatening against the transgressors of the law, the curse there denounced, that gives power to sin. Note, Sin is the parent of death, and gives it all its hurtful power. (2) In the account given of the victory saints obtain over it through Jesus Christ, *v.* 56. *The sting of death is sin*; but Christ, by dying, has taken out this sting. He has made atonement for sin; he has obtained remission of it. It may hiss therefore, but it cannot hurt. (3) If this triumph of the saints over death should issue in thanksgiving to God: *Thanks be to God, who giveth us the victory through Christ Jesus, our Lord, v.* 57. The way to sanctify all our joy

is to make it tributary to the praise of God. Note, How many springs of joy to the saints and thanksgiving to God are opened by the death and resurrection, the sufferings and conquests, of our Redeemer!

In verse 58 we have the improvement of the whole argument, in an exhortation, enforced by a motive resulting plainly from it. 1. That they should be steadfast—firm, fixed in the faith of the gospel, that gospel which he had preached and they had received. 2. He exhorts them to be *immovable*, namely, in their expectation of this great privilege of being raised incorruptible and immortal. Christians should not be moved away from this hope of the gospel (Col. i. 23), this glorious and blessed hope. 3. He exhorts them *to abound in the work of the Lord*, and that *always*, in the Lord's service, in obeying the Lord's commands. They should be diligent and persevering herein, and going on towards perfection; they should be continually making advances in true piety, and ready and apt for every good work. The most cheerful duty, the greatest diligence, the most constant perseverance, become those who have such glorious hopes.

II. The motive resulting from the former discourse is that their *labour shall not be in vain in the Lord*; nay, they know it shall not. They have the best grounds in the world to build upon: they have all the assurance that can rationally be expected: as surely as Christ is risen, they shall rise; and Christ is as surely risen as the scriptures are true, and the word of God.

CHAPTER SIXTEEN

THE COLLECTION (*vv.* 1–4)

In this chapter Paul begins with directing them about a charitable collection on a particular occasion, the distresses and poverty of Christians in Judea, which at this time were extraordinary, partly through the general calamities of that nation and partly through the particular sufferings to which they were exposed. Now concerning this observe,

I. How he introduces his direction. It was not a peculiar service which he required of them; he had given similar *orders to the churches of Galatia, v.* 1. He desired them only to conform to the same rules which he had given to other churches on a similar occasion.

II. The direction itself, concerning which observe,

1. The manner in which the collection was to be made: *Every one was to lay by in store* (*v.* 2), have a treasury, or fund, with himself, for this purpose. The meaning is that he should lay by as he could spare from time to time, and by this means make up a sum for this charitable purpose.

2. Here is the measure in which they are to lay by: *As God hath prospered them*; as he has been prospered, namely, by divine Providence, as God has been pleased to bless and succeed his labours and business. The more they had, through God's blessing, gained by their business or labour, their traffic or work, the more they were to lay by.

3. Here is the time when this is to be done: *The first day of the*

week, the Lord's day, the Christian holiday, when public assemblies were held and public worship was celebrated, and the Christian institutions and mysteries (as the ancients called them) were attended upon; then let every one lay by him.

4. We have here the disposal of the collections thus made: the apostle would have every thing ready against he came, and therefore gave direction as before: *That there be no gatherings when I come, v.* 2. But, when he came, as to the disposal of it, he would leave it much to themselves. The charity was theirs, and it was fit they should dispose of it in their own way, so it answered its end, and was applied to the right use.

PAUL'S PLANS (*vv.* 5–9)

In this passage the apostle notifies and explains his purpose of visiting them, concerning which, observe, 1. His purpose: he intended to pass out of Asia, where he now was (*vide vv.* 8, 19) and to go through Macedonia into Achaia, where Corinth was, and to stay some time with them, and perhaps the winter, *vv.* 5, 6. 2. His excuse for not seeing them now, because it would be *only by the way* (*v.* 7), *it would only be a transient visit*. He would not see them because he could not stay with them. Such a visit would give neither him nor them any satisfaction or advantage. 3. We have the limitation of this purpose: *I trust to tarry awhile with you, if the Lord permit, v.* 7. Though the apostles wrote under inspiration, they did not know thereby how God would dispose of them. But, 5. We have the reason given for his staying at

Ephesus for the present: *Because a great door, and effectual, was opened to him, and there were many adversaries, v.* 9. A great door and effectual was opened to him; many were prepared to receive the gospel at Ephesus, and God gave him great success among them; he had brought over many to Christ, and he had great hope of bringing over many more. For this reason he determined to stay awhile at Ephesus. And there were many adversaries, because a great door, and an effectual, was opened. Note, Great success in the work of the gospel commonly creates many enemies.

TIMOTHY AND APOLLOS
(*vv.* 10–12)

In this passage,

I. He recommends Timothy to them, in several particulars. As, 1. He bids them take care that he should *be among them without fear, v.* 10. Timothy was sent by the apostle to correct the abuses which had crept in among them; and not only to direct, but to blame, and censure, and reprove, those who were culpable. They should not fly out into resentment at his reproof. 2. He warns them against despising him, *v.* 11. He was but a young man, and alone, as Œcumenius observes. He had no one to back him, and his own youthful face and years commanded but little reverence; and therefore the great pretenders to wisdom among them might be apt to entertain contemptuous thoughts of him. "Now," says the apostle, "guard against this." 3. He tells them they should give him all due encourage-

ment, use him well while he was with them; and, as an evidence of this, they should send him away in friendship, and well prepared for his journey back again to Paul.

II. He assigns the reasons why they should behave thus towards Timothy. 1. Because he was employed in the same work as Paul, and acted in it by the same authority, *v.* 10. 2. Another reason is implied; as they were to esteem him for his work's sake, so also for Paul's sake, who had sent him to Corinth; not of his own errand indeed, but to work the work of the Lord.

III. He informs them of Apollos's purpose to see them. 1. He himself had greatly desired him to come to them, *v.* 12. 2. Apollos could not be prevailed on for the present to come, but would at a more convenient season. Perhaps their feuds and factions might render the present season improper.

RESPECT YOUR LEADERS
(*vv.* 13–18)

In this passage the apostle gives,

I. Some general advices; as, 1. That they should watch (*v.* 13), be wakeful and upon their guard. A Christian is always in danger, and therefore should ever be on the watch; but the danger is greater at some times and under some circumstances. 2. He advises them to *stand fast in the faith,* to keep their ground, adhere to the revelation of God, and not give it up for the wisdom of the world, nor suffer it to be corrupted by it—stand for the faith of the gospel, and maintain it even to death; and stand in it, so as to abide in the profession of it, and feel and yield to its influence. 3.

He advises them to act like men, and be strong. Note, Christians should be manly and firm in all their contests with their enemies, in defending their faith, and maintaining their integrity. 4. He advises them to do every thing in charity, *v.* 14. Our zeal and constancy must be consistent with charity.

II. Some particular directions how they should behave towards some that had been eminently serviceable to the cause of Christ among them (*vv.* 15–18).

FINAL GREETINGS
(*vv.* 19–24)

The apostle closes his epistle,

I. With salutations to the church of Corinth, first from those of Asia, from *Priscilla* and *Aquila* (who seem to have been at this time inhabitants of Ephesus, *vid.* Acts xviii. 26), *with the church in their house* (*v.* 19), and from *all the brethren* (*v.* 20) at Ephesus, where, it is highly probable at least, he then was. All these saluted the church at Corinth, by Paul. Note, Christianity does by no means destroy civility and good manners.

II. With a very solemn warning to them: *If any man love not the Lord Jesus Christ, let him be Anathema, Maran-atha, v.* 22. We sometimes need words of threatening, that we may fear. Here observe, 1. The person described, who is liable to this doom: *He that loveth not the Lord Jesus Christ.* But, 2. We have here the doom of the person described: "*Let him be Anathema, Maran-atha,* lie under the heaviest and most dreadful

curse. Let him be separated from the people of God, from the favour of God, and delivered up to his final, irrevocable, and inexorable vengeance." *Maran-atha* is a Syriac phrase, and signifies *The Lord cometh.* That very Lord whom they do not love, to whom they are inwardly and really disaffected whatever outward profession they make, is coming to execute judgment. And to be exposed to his wrath, to be divided to his left hand, to be condemned by him, how dreadful!

III. With his good wishes for them and expressions of good-will to them. 1. With his good wishes: *The grace of our Lord Jesus Christ be with you, v.* 23. The grace of our Lord Jesus Christ comprehends in it all that is good, for time or eternity. To wish our friends may have this grace with them is wishing them the utmost good. And this we should wish all our friends and brethren in Christ. 2. With the declaration of his love to them in Christ Jesus: *My love be with you all, in Christ Jesus, Amen, v.* 24. He had dealt very plainly with them in this epistle, and told them of their faults with just severity; but, to show that he was not transported with passion, he parts with them in love, makes solemn profession of his love to them, nay, to them all in Christ Jesus, that is, for Christ's sake. He tells them that his heart was with them, that he truly loved them; but lest this, after all, should be deemed flattery and insinuation, he adds that his affection was the result of his religion, and would be guided by the rules of it.

CORINTHIANS

CHAPTER ONE
INTRODUCTION (*vv.* 1, 2)

This is the introduction to this epistle, in which we have,

I. The inscription; and therein, 1. The person from whom it was sent, namely, Paul, who calls himself *an apostle of Jesus Christ by the will of God.* The apostleship itself was ordained by Jesus Christ, according to the will of God; and Paul was called to it by Jesus Christ, according to the will of God. He joins Timothy with himself in writing this epistle. 2. The persons to whom this epistle was sent, namely, *the church of God at Corinth*: and not only to them, but also *to all the saints in all Achaia,* that is, to all the Christians who lived in the region round about.

II. The salutation or apostolical benediction, which is the same as in his former epistle; and therein the apostle desires the two great and comprehensive blessings, grace and peace, for those Corinthians.

GOD'S GOODNESS
(*vv.* 3–6)

After the foregoing preface, the apostle begins with the narrative of God's goodness to him and his fellow-labourers in their manifold tribulations, which he speaks of by way of thanksgiving to God, and to advance the divine glory (*vv.*

3–6); and it is fit that in all things, and in the first place, God be glorified. Note, (1) What favours God bestows on us are intended not only to make us cheerful ourselves, but also that we may be useful to others (*v.* 4). (2) If we do imitate the faith and patience of good men in their afflictions, we may hope to partake of their consolations here and their salvation hereafter (*vv.* 5, 6).

PAUL'S TROUBLES
(*vv.* 7–11)

In these verses the apostle speaks for the encouragement and edification of the Corinthians; and tells them (*v.* 7) of his persuasion or stedfast hope that they should receive benefit by the troubles he and his companions in labour and travel had met with, that their faith should not be weakened, but their consolations increased. In order to this he tells them, 1. What their sufferings had been (*v.* 8): *We would not have you ignorant of our trouble.* It was convenient for the churches to know what were the sufferings of their ministers. 2. What they did in their distress: *They trusted in God.* And they were brought to this extremity in order *that they should not trust in themselves but in God, v.* 9. 3. What the deliverance was that they had obtained. God had delivered them, and did still deliver them, *v.* 10. *Having obtained help of God, they continued to that day,* Acts xxvi. 22. 4. What use they made of this deliverance: *We trust that he will yet deliver us* (*v.* 10), that God will deliver to the end, and *preserve to his heavenly kingdom.* 5. What was desired of the Corinthians upon this account: *That they would help together by prayer for them* (*v.* 11), by social prayer, agreeing and joining together in prayer on their behalf.

THEIR INTEGRITY
(*vv.* 12–14)

Here,

I. Paul appeals to the testimony of conscience with rejoicing (*v.* 12), in which observe, 1. The witness appealed to, namely, conscience, which is instead of a thousand witnesses. This is God's deputy in the soul, and the voice of conscience is the voice of God. 2. The testimony this witness gave. And here take notice, Conscience witnessed, (1) Concerning their conversation, their constant course and tenor of life: by that we may judge of ourselves, and not by this or that single act. (2) Concerning the nature or manner of their way of life; that it was in simplicity and godly sincerity. (3) Concerning the principle they acted from in all their conversation, both in the world and towards these Corinthians; and that was not fleshly wisdom, nor carnal politics and worldly views, but it was the grace of God, a vital gracious principle in their hearts, that cometh from God, and tendeth to God.

II. He appeals to the knowledge of the Corinthians with hope and confidence, *vv.* 13, 14. Their behaviour did in part fall under the observation of the Corinthians; and these knew how they behaved themselves, *how holily, and justly, and unblamably.*

THEIR CONSISTENCY
(*vv.* 15–24)

The apostle here vindicates himself from the imputation of levity and inconstancy, in that he did not hold his purpose of coming to them at Corinth. Now, for his justification,

I. He avers the sincerity of his intention (*vv.* 15–17), and he does this in confidence of their good opinion of him, and that they would believe him, when he assured them he *was minded,* or did really intend, *to come* to them, and that with the design, not that he might receive, but that they might receive a *second benefit,* that is, a further advantage by his ministry.

II. He would not have the Corinthians to infer that his gospel was false or uncertain, nor that it was contradictory in itself, nor unto truth, *vv.* 18, 19. For if it had been so, that he had been fickle in his purposes, or even false in the promises he made of coming to them, yet it would not follow that the gospel preached not only by him, but also by others in full agreement with him, was either false or doubtful. For *God is true,* and *the Son of God, Jesus Christ,* is true. Jesus Christ, whom the apostle preached, is not *yea* and *nay,* but in him was *yea* (*v.* 19), nothing but infallible truth. And the promises of God in Christ are not yea and nay, but yea and amen, *v.* 20. There is an inviolable constancy and unquestionable sincerity and certainty in all the parts of the gospel of Christ.

III. The apostle gives a good reason why he did not come to Corinth, as was expected, *v.* 23. It was that he might spare them. They ought therefore to own his kindness and tenderness.

CHAPTER TWO
PAUL'S ANGUISH
(*vv.* 1–4)

In these verses, 1. The apostle proceeds in giving an account of the reason why he did not come to Corinth, as was expected; namely, because he was unwilling to grieve them, or be grieved by them, *vv.* 1, 2. 2. He tells them it was to the same intent that he wrote his former epistle, *vv.* 3, 4. He had *written with tears, that they might know his abundant love to them.*

ATTITUDES TOWARDS THE OFFENDER (*vv.* 5–11)

In these verses the apostle treats concerning the incestuous person who had been excommunicated, which seems to be one principal cause of his writing this epistle. Here observe, 1. He tells them that the crime of that person had grieved him *in part*; and that he was grieved also with a part of them, who, notwithstanding this scandal had been found among them, were *puffed up and had not mourned,* 1 Cor. v. 2. However, he was unwilling to lay too heavy a charge upon the whole church, especially seeing they had cleared

themselves in that matter by observing the directions he had formerly given them. 2. He tells them that the punishment which had been inflicted upon this offender was sufficient, *v.* 6. The desired effect was obtained, for the man was humbled, and they had shown the proof of their obedience to his directions. 3. He therefore directs them, with all speed, to restore the excommunicated person, or to receive him again to their communion, *vv.* 7, 8. 4. He uses several weighty arguments to persuade them to do thus. (1) The case of the penitent called for this; for he was in danger of being *swallowed up with over-much sorrow,* *v.* 7. (2) They had shown obedience to his directions in passing a censure upon the offender and now he would have them comply with his desire to restore him, *v.* 9. (3) He mentions his readiness to forgive this penitent, and concur with them in this matter. (4) He gives another weighty reason (*v.* 11): *Lest Satan get an advantage against us.* Not only was there danger lest Satan should get an advantage against the penitent, by driving him to despair; but against the churches also, and the apostles or ministers of Christ, by representing them as too rigid and severe.

PAUL'S TRAVELS
(*vv.* 12–17)

After these directions concerning the excommunicated person the apostle makes a long digression, to give the Corinthians an account of his travels and labours for the furtherance of the gospel, and what success he had therein, declaring at

the same time how much he was
concerned for them in their affairs,
how he *had no rest in his spirit*,
when he found not Titus at Troas
(*v.* 13), as he expected, from whom
he hoped to have understood more
perfectly how it fared with them.
And we find afterwards (*ch.* vii.
5–7) that when the apostle had
come into Macedonia he was
comforted by the coming of Titus,
and the information he gave him
concerning them. So that we may
look upon all that we read from
this second chapter, *v*, 12, to *ch.*
vii. 5, as a kind of parenthesis.
Here observe,

I. The different success of the
gospel, and its different effects upon
several sorts of persons to whom it
is preached. The success is different;
for some are saved by it, while
others perish under it. Nor is this
to be wondered at, considering the
different effects the gospel has. For,
(1) Unto some it is a *savour of
death unto death*. Those who are
willingly ignorant, and wilfully
obstinate, disrelish the gospel, as
men dislike an ill savour, and therefore they are blinded and hardened
by it: it stirs up their corruptions,
and exasperates their spirits. (2)
Unto others the gospel is a *savour
of life unto life*. To humble and
gracious souls the preaching of the
word is most delightful and
profitable.

II. The awful impressions this
matter made upon the mind of the
apostle, and should also make upon
our spirits: *Who is sufficient for
these things?* *v.* 16. Who is able to
perform such a difficult work, that
requires so much skill and industry? The work is great and our

strength is small; yea, of ourselves
we have no strength at all; *all our
sufficiency is of God.*

III. The comfort which the
apostle had under this serious consideration, (1) Because faithful
ministers shall be accepted of God,
whatever their success be. (2) Because his conscience witnessed to his
faithfulness, *v.* 17. Though many
did corrupt the word of God, yet
the apostle's conscience witnessed
to his fidelity.

CHAPTER THREE

HUMAN LETTERS
(*vv.* 1–5)

In these verses,

I. The apostle makes an apology
for seeming to commend himself.
And he tells them, 1. That he
neither needed nor desired any
verbal commendation to them, nor
letters testimonial from them, as
some others did, meaning the false
apostles or teachers, *v.* 1. 2. The
Corinthians themselves were his
real commendation, and a good
testimonial for him, that God was
with him of a truth, that he was
sent of God: *You are our epistle*,
v. 2.

II. The apostle is careful not to
assume too much to himself, but
to ascribe all the praise to God.
Therefore, 1. He says they were the
epistle of Christ, *v.* 3. This epistle
was not written with *ink, but with
the Spirit of the living God*; nor was
it written in *tables of stone*, as the
law of God given to Moses, but
on the *heart*; and that heart not a
stony one, but a heart of flesh,
upon the *fleshy tables of the heart*,
that is, upon hearts that are softened

and renewed by divine grace. 2. He utterly disclaims the taking of any praise to themselves, and ascribes all the glory to God: "*We are not sufficient of ourselves*," v. 5.

A MORE GLORIOUS MINISTRY (*vv.* 6–11)

Here the apostle makes a comparison, between the Old Testament and the New, the law of Moses and the gospel of Jesus Christ, and values himself and his fellow-labourers by this, that *they were able ministers of the New Testament*, that God had made them so, *v.* 6. This he does in answer to the accusations of false teachers, who magnify greatly the law of Moses.

I. He distinguishes between the letter and the spirit even of the New Testament, *v.* 6. As able ministers of the New Testament, they were ministers not merely of the letter, to read the written word, or to preach the letter of the gospel only, but they were ministers of the Spirit also; the Spirit of God did accompany their ministrations.

II. He shows the difference between the Old Testament and the New, and the excellency of the gospel above the law. For, 1. The Old-Testament dispensation was the *ministration of death* (*v.* 7), whereas that of the New Testament is the *ministration of life*. 2. The law was the *ministration of condemnation*, for that condemned and cursed every one who *continued not in all things written therein to do them*; but the gospel is the *ministration of righteousness*: therein the righteousness of God by faith is revealed. 3. The law is done away,

but the gospel does and shall *remain*, v. 11.

THE VEIL (*vv.* 12–18)

In these verses the apostle draws two inferences from what he had said about the Old and New Testament:

I. Concerning the duty of the ministers of the gospel to use great plainness or clearness of speech. They ought not, like Moses, to put a veil upon their faces, or obscure and darken those things which they should make plain.

II. Concerning the privilege and advantage of those who enjoy the gospel, above those who lived under the law. For, 1. Those who lived under the legal dispensation had their minds blinded (*v.* 14), and there was a *veil upon their hearts*, *v.* 15. Nevertheless, the apostle tells us, there is a time coming when this *veil also shall be taken away*, and *when it* (the body of that people) *shall turn to the Lord*, *v.* 16. Or, when any particular person is converted to God, then the veil of ignorance is taken away; the blindness of the mind, and the hardness of the heart, are cured. 2. The condition of those who enjoy and believe the gospel is much more happy. For, (1) They have liberty: *Where the Spirit of the Lord is*, and where he worketh, as he does under the gospel-dispensation, *there is liberty* (*v.* 17), freedom from the yoke of the ceremonial law, and from the servitude of corruption; liberty of access to God, and freedom of speech in prayer. (2) They have *light*; for with *open face we behold the glory of the Lord*, *v.* 18. The

Israelites saw the glory of God in a cloud, which was dark and dreadful; but Christians see the glory of the Lord as in a glass, more clearly and comfortably.

CHAPTER FOUR
TRUE MINISTRY (*vv.* 1–7)

The apostle had, in the foregoing chapter, been *magnifying his office*, upon the consideration of the excellency or glory of that gospel about which he did officiate; and now in this chapter his design is to vindicate their ministry from the accusation of false teachers.

I. Two things in general we have an account of: Their constancy and sincerity in their work and labour, concerning which observe, 1. Their constancy and perseverance in their work are declared. 2. Their sincerity in their work is avouched (*v.* 2) in several expressions: *We have renounced the hidden things of dishonesty.* They had no base and wicked designs covered with fair and specious pretences of something that was good. Nor did they in their preaching *handle the word of God deceitfully*; but, as he said before, they used *great plainness of speech*, and did not make their ministry serve a turn, or truckle to base designs. And all this they did *as in the sight of God*, desirous thus to commend themselves to God, and to the consciences of men, by their undisguised sincerity.

II. An objection is obviated, which might be thus formed: "If it be thus, how then does it come to pass, that the gospel is hid, and proves ineffectual, as to some who hear it?" To which the apostle answers by showing that this was not the fault of the gospel, nor of the preachers thereof. But the true reasons of this are, 1. *Those are lost souls* to whom the gospel is hid, or is ineffectual, *v.* 3. 2. *The god of this world hath blinded their minds*, *v.* 4. They are under the influence and power of the devil, who is here called *the god of this world*, and elsewhere *the prince of this world*. The design of the devil is to keep men in ignorance; and, when he cannot keep the light of the gospel out of the world, he makes it his great business to keep it out of the hearts of men.

III. A proof of their integrity is given, *v.* 5. They made it their business to preach Christ, and not themselves: *We preach not ourselves.* Self was not the matter nor the end of the apostles' preaching: they did not give their own notions and private opinions, nor their passions and prejudices, for the word and will of God; nor did they seek themselves, to advance their own secular interest or glory. But they *preached Christ Jesus the Lord*; and thus it did become them and behove them to do, as being Christ's servants. And there was good reason, 1. Why they should preach Christ. For by gospel light we have the *knowledge of the glory of God*, which shines in the *face of Jesus Christ*, *v.* 6. And the light of this *Sun of righteousness* is more glorious than that light which God commanded to shine out of darkness. 2. Why they should not preach themselves: because they were but earthen vessels, things of little or no worth or value. And

God has so ordered it that the weaker the vessels are the stronger his power may appear to be, that the treasure itself should be valued the more.

SUFFERING AND SUPPORT
(*vv*. 8–18)

In these verses the apostle gives an account of their courage and patience under all their sufferings, where observe,

I. How their sufferings, and patience under them, are declared, *vv*. 8–12. The apostles were great sufferers; therein they followed their Master: Christ had told them *that in the world they should have tribulation*, and so they had; yet they met with wonderful support, great relief, and many allays of their sorrows. Still they were preserved, and kept their heads above water. Note, Whatever condition the children of God may be in, in this world, they have a "*but not*" to comfort themselves with; their case sometimes is bad, very bad, but not so bad as it might be. The apostle speaks of their sufferings as constant, and as a counterpart of the sufferings of Christ, *v*. 10. So great were the sufferings of the apostles that, in comparison with them, other Christians were, even at this time, in prosperous circumstances: *Death worketh in us; but life in you, v*. 12.

II. What it was that kept them from sinking and fainting under their sufferings, *vv*. 13–18.

1. Faith kept them from fainting: *We have the same spirit of faith* (*v*. 13), that faith which is of the operation of the Spirit; the same faith by which the saints of old did and suffered such great things.

2. Hope of the resurrection kept them from sinking, *v*. 14. They knew that Christ was raised, and that his resurrection was an earnest and assurance of theirs.

3. The consideration of the glory of God and the benefit of the church, by means of their sufferings, kept them from fainting, *v*. 15. Their sufferings were for the church's advantage (*ch*. i. 6), and thus did redound to God's glory.

4. The thoughts of the advantage their souls would reap by the sufferings of their bodies kept them from fainting: *Though our outward man perish, our inward man is renewed day by day, v*. 16. Here note, (1) We have every one of us an outward and an inward man, a body and a soul. (2) If the outward man perish, there is no remedy, it must and will be so, it was made to perish. (3) It is our happiness if the decays of the outward man do contribute to the renewing of the inward man.

5. The prospect of eternal life and happiness kept them from fainting, and was a mighty support and comfort. As to this observe, (1) The apostle and his fellow-sufferers saw their afflictions working towards heaven, and that they would end at last (*v*. 17), whereupon they weighed things aright in the balance of the sanctuary; they did as it were put the heavenly glory in one scale and their earthly sufferings in the other; and, pondering things in their thoughts, they found afflictions to be light, and the glory of heaven to be *a far more exceeding weight*. (2) Their faith enabled them to make this right

judgment of things: *We look not at the things which are seen, but at the things which are not seen,* v. 18. It is by faith that we see God, who is invisible (Heb. xi. 27), and by this we look to an unseen heaven and hell, and faith is the *evidence of things not seen.*

CHAPTER FIVE
HEREAFTER (vv. 1–11)

The apostle in these verses pursues the argument of the former chapter, concerning the grounds of their courage and patience under afflictions. And,

I. He mentions their expectation, and desire, and assurance, of eternal happiness after death, vv. 1–5. Observe particularly,

1. The believer's expectation of eternal happiness after death, v. 1. Note, [1] That the body, this earthly house, is but a tabernacle, that must be dissolved shortly; and then the body will return to dust as it was. [2] When this comes to pass, then comes the house not made with hands. The spirit returns to God who gave it; and such as have walked with God here shall dwell with God for ever.

2. The believer's earnest desire after this future blessedness, which is expressed by this word, *groan,* which denotes, (1) A groaning of sorrow under a heavy load; so believers groan under the burden of life. The body of flesh is a heavy burden, the calamities of life are a heavy load. (2) There is a groaning of desire after the happiness of another life; and thus believers groan: *Earnestly desiring to be clothed upon our house which is*

from heaven (v. 2), to obtain a blessed immortality, *that mortality might be swallowed up of life* (v. 4), *that being found clothed, we may not be naked* (v. 3).

3. The believer's assurance of his interest in this future blessedness, on a double account: (1) From the experience of the grace of God, in preparing and making him meet for this blessedness. (2) The *earnest of the Spirit* gave them this assurance: for an earnest is part of payment, and secures the full payment.

II. The apostle deduces an inference for the comfort of believers in their present state and condition in this world, vv. 6–8. True Christians, if they duly considered the prospect faith gives them of another world, and the good reasons of their hope of blessedness after death, would be comforted under the troubles of life, and supported in the hour of death.

III. He proceeds to deduce an inference to excite and quicken himself and others to duty, vv. 9–11. Here observe, 1. What it was that the apostle was thus ambitious of—*acceptance with God.* This they coveted as the greatest favour and the highest honour: it was the summit of their ambition. 2. What further quickening motives they had to excite their diligence, from the consideration of the judgment to come, vv. 10, 11. The apostle calls this awful judgment *the terror of the Lord* (v. 11), and, by the consideration thereof, was excited to persuade men to repent, and live a holy life, that, when Christ shall appear, they may appear before him comfortably.

CONSTRAINT OF LOVE
(vv. 12–15)

Here observe, I. The apostle makes an apology for seeming to commend himself and his fellow-labourers (v. 13), and tells them, 1. It was not to commend themselves, nor for their own sakes, that he had spoken of their fidelity and diligence in the former verses; nor was he willing to suspect their good opinion of him. But, 2. The true reason was this, to put an argument in their mouths wherewith to answer his accusers, who made vain boastings, and gloried in appearances only.

II. He gives good reasons for their great zeal and diligence. The apostle tells them, 1. It was for the glory of God, and the good of the church, that he was thus zealous and industrious. For, 2. *The love of Christ constrained them,* v. 14. They were under the sweetest and strongest constraints to do what they did.

AMBASSADORS FOR CHRIST
(vv 16–21)

In these verses the apostle mentions two things that are necessary for our living to Christ, both of which are the consequences of Christ's dying for us; namely, regeneration and reconciliation.

I. Regeneration, which consists of two things; namely, 1. Weanedness from the world: *"Henceforth we know no man after the flesh,"* v. 16. *Yea, though we have known Christ after the flesh, yet,* says the apostle, *we know him no more.* It is questioned whether Paul had seen Christ in the flesh. However, the rest of the apostles had, and so might some among those he was now writing to. However, he would not have them value themselves upon that account; for even the bodily presence of Christ is not to be desired nor doted upon by his disciples. We must live upon his spiritual presence, and the comfort it affords. 2. A thorough change of the heart: *For if any man be in Christ,* if any man be a Christian indeed, and will approve himself such, *he is,* or he must be, *a new creature,* v. 17. Some read it, *Let him be a new creature.*

II. Reconciliation, which is here spoken of under a double notion:

1. As an unquestionable privilege, vv. 18, 19. Reconciliation supposes a quarrel, or breach of friendship; and sin has made a breach, it has broken the friendship between God and man. Yet, behold, there may be a reconciliation; the offended Majesty of heaven is willing to be reconciled.

2. Reconciliation is here spoken of as our indispensable duty, v. 20. As God is willing to be reconciled to us, we ought to be reconciled to God. Faithful ministers are Christ's ambassadors, sent to treat with sinners on peace and reconciliation: they come in God's name, with his entreaties, and act in Christ's stead, doing the very thing he did when he was upon this earth, and what he wills to be done now that he is in heaven. And for our encouragement so to do the apostle subjoins what should be well known and duly considered by us (v. 21), namely (1) The purity of the Mediator: *He knew no sin.* (2) The sacrifice he offered: *He was made*

sin; not a sinner, but *sin*, that is, a sin-offering, a sacrifice for sin. (3) The end and design of all this: that *we might be made the righteousness of God in him*, might be justified freely by the grace of God through the redemption which is in Christ Jesus.

CHAPTER SIX

WORKERS WITH GOD
(vv. 1–10)

In these verses we have an account of the apostle's general errand and exhortation to all to whom he preached in every place where he came, with the several arguments and methods he used. Observe,

I. The errand or exhortation itself, namely, to comply with the gospel offers of reconciliation—that, being favoured with the gospel, they would not receive this *grace of God in vain, v.* 1.

II. The arguments and method which the apostle used. And here he tells them,

1. The present time is the only proper season to accept of the grace that is offered, and improve that grace which is afforded: Now *is the accepted time.* NOW *is the day of salvation, v.* 2.

2. What caution they used not to give offence that might hinder the success of their preaching: *Giving no offence in any thing, v.* 3. He was careful, in all his words and actions, not to give offence, or occasion of guilt or grief.

3. Their constant aim and endeavour in all things to approve themselves faithful, as became the ministers of God, *v.* 4. (1) By much patience in afflictions. (2) By

acting from good principles. The apostle went by a good principle in all he did, and tells them what his principles were (*vv.* 6, 7); namely, pureness; and there is no piety without purity. (3) By a due temper and behaviour under all the variety of conditions in this world, *vv.* 8–10. They were despised as poor, upon the account of their poverty in this world; and yet they made many rich, by preaching the unsearchable riches of Christ. Such a paradox is a Christian's life, and through such a variety of conditions and reports lies our way to heaven; and we should be careful in all these things to approve ourselves to God.

NO COMPROMISE (vv. 11–18)

The apostle proceeds to address himself more particularly to the Corinthians, and cautions them against mingling with unbelievers. Here observe,

I. How the caution is introduced with a profession of the most tender affection to them, *even like that of a father to his children, vv.* 11–13.

II. The caution or exhortation itself, not to mingle with unbelievers, not to be *unequally yoked* with them, *v.* 14. Either,

1. In stated relations. Those relations that are our choice must be chosen by rule; and it is good for those who are themselves the children of God to join with those who are so likewise; for there is more danger that the bad will damage the good than hope that the good will benefit the bad.

2. In common conversation. We should not yoke ourselves in friendship and acquaintance with wicked men and unbelievers. Though we

cannot wholly avoid seeing, and hearing, and being with such, yet we should never choose them for our bosom-friends.

3. Much less should we join in religious communion with them. The apostle gives several good reasons against this corrupt mixture. (1) It is a very great absurdity, *vv.* 14, 15. It is an unequal yoking of things together that will not agree together. (2) It is a dishonour to the Christian's profession (*v.* 16); for Christians are by profession, and should be in reality, the *temples of the living God*—dedicated to, and employed for, the service of God. Now there can be no agreement between *the temple of God and idols.* Idols are rivals with God for his honour, and God is a jealous God, and will not give his glory to another. (3) There is a great deal of danger in communicating with unbelievers and idolaters, danger of being defiled and of being rejected; therefore the exhortation is (*v.* 17) *to come out from among them,* and keep at a due distance, *to be separate.* (4) It is base ingratitude to God for all the favours he has bestowed upon believers and promised to them, *v.* 18.

CHAPTER SEVEN

PROGRESSIVE HOLINESS
(*vv.* 1–4)

These verses contain a double exhortation:

I. To make a progress in holiness, or *to perfect holiness in the fear of God, v.* 1. The promises of God are strong inducements to sanctification, in both the branches thereof; namely, 1. The dying unto sin, or

mortifying our lusts and corruptions: we must *cleanse ourselves from all filthiness of flesh and spirit.* 2. The living unto righteousness and holiness. If we hope God is our Father, we must endeavour to be *partakers of his holiness,* to be holy as he is holy, and perfect as our Father in heaven is perfect.

II. To show a due regard to the ministers of the gospel: *Receive us, v.* 2. If the ministers of the gospel are thought contemptible because of their office, there is danger lest the gospel itself be contemned also. He tells them, 1. He had done nothing to forfeit their esteem and good-will, but was cautious not to do any thing to deserve their ill-will (*v.* 2). 2. He did not herein reflect upon them for want of affection to him, *vv.* 3, 4. So tenderly and cautiously did the apostle deal with the Corinthians, among whom there were some who would be glad of any occasion to reproach him, and prejudice the minds of others against him.

GODLY SORROW (*vv.* 5–11)

There seems to be a connection between *ch.* ii. 13 (where the apostle said he had no rest in his spirit when he found not Titus at Troas) and the fifth verse of this chapter: and so great was his affection to the Corinthians, and his concern about their behaviour in relation to the incestuous person, that, in his further travels, he still had no rest till he heard from them. And now he tells them,

I. How he was distressed, *v.* 5. He was troubled when he did not meet with Titus and, besides this, they met with other troubles, with incessant storms of persecutions; there were *fightings without*, or continual contentions with, and opposition from, Jews and Gentiles; and there were *fears within*, and great concern for such as had embraced the Christian faith, lest they should be corrupted or seduced, and give scandal to others, or be scandalized.

II. How he was comforted, *vv.* 6, 7. Here observe, 1. The very coming of Titus was some comfort to him. It was matter of joy to see him, whom he long desired and expected to meet with.

III. How greatly he rejoiced at their repentance, and the evidences thereof. The apostle was sorry that he had grieved them, but now he rejoiced, when he found they had *sorrowed to repentance, v.* 9. Their sorrow in itself was not the cause of his rejoicing; but the nature of it, and the effect of it (*repentance unto salvation, v.* 10), made him rejoice. Observe here,

1. The antecedent of true repentance is godly sorrow; this worketh repentance. It is not repentance itself, but it is a good preparative to repentance, and in some sense the cause that produces repentance.

2. The happy fruits and consequences of true repentance are mentioned (*v.* 11); and those *fruits that are meet for repentance* are the best evidences of it. Where the heart is changed, the life and actions will be changed too.

BOASTING COME TRUE
(*vv.* 12–16)

In these verses the apostle endeavours to comfort the Corinthians, upon whom his admonitions had had such good effect. And in order thereto, 1. He tells them he had a good design in his former epistle, which might be thought severe, *v.* 12. It was not chiefly *for his cause that did the wrong*, not only for his benefit, much less merely that he should be punished; nor was it merely *for his cause that suffered wrong*, namely, the injured father, and that he might have what satisfaction could be given him; but it was also to manifest his great and sincere concern and *care for them*, for the whole church, lest that should suffer by letting such a crime, and the scandal thereof, remain among them without due remark and resentment. 2. He acquaints them with the joy of Titus as well as of himself upon the account of their repentance and good behaviour. 3. He concludes this whole matter with expressing the entire confidence he had in them.

CHAPTER EIGHT
THE GENEROUS MACEDONIANS
(*vv.* 1–6)

Observe here,

I. The apostle takes occasion from the good example of the churches of Macedonia, that is, of Philippi, Thessalonica, Berea, and others in the region of Macedonia, to exhort the Corinthians and the Christians in Achaia to the good work of charity. And,

1. He acquaints them with their great liberality, which he calls *the grace of God bestowed on the churches, v.* 1. Some think the words should be rendered, *the gift of God given in or by the churches.*

He certainly means the charitable gifts of these churches, which are called the grace or gifts of God.

2. He commends the charity of the Macedonians, and sets it forth with good advantage. He tells them, (1) They were but in a low condition, and themselves in distress, yet they contributed to the relief of others. (2) They gave very largely, with *the riches of liberality* (*v.* 2), that is, as liberally as if they had been rich. It was a large contribution they made, all things considered; it was *according to*, yea *beyond, their power* (*v.* 3), as much as could well be expected from them, if not more. (3) They were very ready and forward to this good work. *They were willing of themselves* (*v.* 3), and were so far from needing that Paul should urge and press them with many arguments that they *prayed him with much entreaty to receive the gift, v.* 4. (4) Their charity was founded in true piety, and this was the great commendation of it. They performed this good work in a right method: *First they gave themselves to the Lord, and then* they gave unto us their contributions, *by the will of God* (*v.* 5), that is, according as it was the will of God they should do, or to be disposed of as the will of God should be, and for his glory.

II. The apostle tells them that Titus was desired to go and make a collection among them (*v.* 6), and Titus, he knew, would be an acceptable person to them.

MOTIVES FOR GIVING
(*vv.* 7–15)

In these verses the apostle uses several cogent arguments to stir up the Corinthians to this good work of charity.

I. He urges upon them the consideration of their eminence in other gifts and graces, and would have them excel in this of charity also, *v.* 7. Great address and much holy art are here used by the apostle.

II. Another argument is taken from the consideration of the grace of our Lord Jesus Christ. He was born in poor circumstances, lived a poor life, and died in poverty; and this was for our sakes, that we thereby might be made rich, rich in the love and favour of God, rich in the blessings and promises of the new covenant, rich in the hopes of eternal life, being heirs of the kingdom. This is a good reason why we should be charitable to the poor out of what we have, because we ourselves live upon the charity of the Lord Jesus Christ.

III. Another argument is taken from their good purposes, and their forwardness to begin this good work. As to this he tells them, 1. It was expedient for them to perform what they purposed, and finish what they had begun, *vv.* 10, 11. For, 2. This would be acceptable to God. *This willing mind is accepted* (*v.* 12), when accompanied with sincere endeavours. When men purpose that which is good, and endeavour, according to their ability, to perform also, God will accept of what they have, or can do, and not reject them for what they have not, and what is not in their power to do.

IV. Another argument is taken from the discrimination which the divine Providence makes in the distribution of the things of this world, and the mutability of human affairs, *vv.* 13–15. The force of the arguing seems to be this: It is the will of God that, by our mutually supplying one another, there should *be some sort of equality*; not an *absolute* equality indeed, or such a levelling as would destroy property, for in such a case there could be no exercise of charity. But as in works of charity there should be an equitable proportion observed, that the burden should not lie too heavy on some, while others are wholly eased, so all should think themselves concerned to supply those who are in want. Note, Such is the condition of men in this world that we mutually depend on one another, and should help one another.

PAUL'S MESSENGERS
(*vv.* 16–24)

In these verses the apostle commends the brethren who were sent to them to collect their charity; and, as it were, gives them letters credential, that, if they *were enquired after* (*v.* 23), if any should be inquisitive or suspicious concerning them, it might be known who they were and how safely they might be trusted.

I. He commends Titus, 1. For his earnest care and great concern of heart for them, and desire in all things to promote their welfare. 2. For his readiness to this present service.

II. He commends another brother, who was sent with Titus. It is generally thought that this was Luke. He is commended, 1. As a

man whose *praise was in the gospel through all the churches*, *v.* 18. His ministerial services of several kinds were well known, and he had approved himself praiseworthy in what he had done. 2. As one chosen of the churches (*v.* 19) and joined with the apostle in his ministration.

III. He commends also another brother who was joined with the two former in this affair. This brother is thought to be Apollos.

IV. He concludes this point with a general good character of them all (*v.* 23), as *fellow-labourers with him* for their welfare; as the *messengers of the churches*; as the *glory of Christ*, who were to him for a name and a praise, who brought glory to Christ as instruments and had obtained honour from Christ to be counted faithful and employed in his service.

CHAPTER NINE
BE GENEROUS! (*vv.* 1–5)

In these verses the apostle speaks very respectfully to the Corinthians, and with great skill; and, while he seems to excuse his urging them so earnestly to charity, still presses them thereto, and shows how much his heart was set upon this matter.

I. He tells them it was needless to press them with further arguments to afford relief to their poor brethren (*v.* 1), being satisfied he had said enough already to prevail with those of whom he had so good an opinion. Note, Christians should consult the reputation of their profession, and endeavour to *adorn the doctrine of God our Saviour*.

GOD'S GIFT (*vv.* 6–15)

Here we have,

I. Proper directions to be observed about the right and acceptable manner of bestowing charity; and it is of great concernment that we not only do what is required, but do it as is commanded. Now, as to the manner in which the apostle would have the Corinthians give, observe, 1. It should be bountifully; this was intimated, *v.* 5, that a liberal contribution was expected, a matter of bounty, not what savoured of covetousness; and he offers to their consideration that men who expect a good return at harvest are not wont to pinch and spare in sowing their seed, for the return is usually proportionable to what they sow, *v.* 6. 2. It should be deliberately. *Every man, according as he purposes in his heart, v.* 7. Works of charity, like other good works, should be done with thought and design. 3. It should be freely, whatever we give, be it more or less: *Not grudgingly, nor of necessity,* but cheerfully, *v.* 7.

II. Good encouragement to perform this work of charity in the manner directed. Here the apostle tells the Corinthians,

1. They themselves would be no losers by what they gave in charity. For, (1) God loveth a cheerful giver (*v.* 7), and what may not those hope to receive who are the objects of the divine love? (2) God is able to make our charity redound to our advantage, *v.* 8. (3) The apostle puts up a prayer to God in their behalf that they might be gainers, and not losers, *vv.* 10, 11.

2. While they would be no losers, the poor distressed saints would be gainers; for this service would *supply their wants, v.* 12.

3. This would redound to the praise and glory of God. Many thanksgivings would be given to God on this account, by the apostle, and by those who were employed in this ministration, *v.* 11.

4. Those whose wants were supplied would make the best return they were able, by sending up many prayers to God for those who had relieved them, *v.* 14.

Lastly, The apostle concludes this whole matter with this doxology, *Thanks be to God for his unspeakable gift, v.* 15. It should seem that he means Jesus Christ, who is indeed the unspeakable gift of God unto this world, a gift we have all reason to be very thankful for.

CHAPTER TEN

THE CHRISTIAN'S WEAPONS
(*vv.* 1–6)

Here we may observe,

I. The mild and humble manner in which the blessed apostle addresses the Corinthians. 1. He addresses them in a very mild and humble manner: *I Paul myself beseech you, v.* 1.

2. He is desirous that no occasion may be given to use severity, *v.* 2. Hereupon,

II. He asserts the power of his preaching and his power to punish offenders.

1. The power of his preaching, *vv.* 3, 5. Here observe, (1) The work of the ministry is a warfare, not *after the flesh* indeed, for it is a spiritual warfare, with spiritual

enemies and for spiritual purposes. (2) The doctrines of the gospel and discipline of the church are the weapons of this warfare; and these are not carnal: outward force, therefore, is not the method of the gospel, but strong persuasions, by the power of truth and the meekness of wisdom.

2. The apostle's power to punish offenders (and that in an extraordinary manner) is asserted in *v.* 6. The apostle speaks not of personal revenge, but of punishing disobedience to the gospel, and disorderly walking among church-members by inflicting church-censures.

PAUL'S BODILY PRESENCE
(*vv.* 7–11)

In these verses the apostle proceeds to reason the case with the Corinthians, in opposition to those who despised him, judged him, and spoke hardly of him: "*Do you,*" says he, "*look on things after the outward appearance?*" *v.* 7. In outward appearance, Paul was mean and despicable with some; he did not make a figure, as perhaps some of his competitors might do: but this was a false rule to make a judgment by. It should seem that some boasted mighty things of themselves, and made a fair show. But there are often false appearances. A man may seem to be learned who has not learned Christ, and appear virtuous when he has not a principle of grace in his heart. However, the apostle asserts two things of himself:

I. His relation to Christ: *If any man trust to himself that he is Christ's, even so are we Christ's,* *v.* 7.

II. His authority from Christ as an apostle. This he had mentioned before (*v.* 6), and now he tells them that he might speak of it again, and that with some sort of boasting, seeing it was a truth, that the *Lord had given it to him,* and it was more than his adversaries could justly pretend to.

SELF-COMMENDATION NO VIRTUE
(*vv.* 12–18)

In these verses observe,

I. The apostle refuses to justify himself, or to act by such rules as the false apostles did, *v.* 12.

II. He fixes a better rule for his conduct, namely, *not to boast of things without his measure,* which was the measure *God had distributed* to him, *v.* 13. His meaning is, either that he would not boast of more gifts or graces, or power and authority, than God had really bestowed on him; or, rather, that he would not act beyond his commission as to persons or things, nor go beyond the line prescribed to him, which he plainly intimates the false apostles did, while they *boasted of other men's labours.* The apostle's resolution was to keep within his own province, and that compass of ground which God had marked out for him.

III. He acted according to this rule: *We stretch not ourselves beyond our measure,* *v.* 14.

IV. He declares his success in observing this rule. His hope was that their faith was increased, and that others beyond them, even in the remoter parts of Achaia, would embrace the gospel also; and in all this he exceeded not his commission, nor acted in another man's line.

V. He seems to check himself in this matter, as if he had spoken too much in his own praise. 1. *He that glorieth should glory in the Lord, v. 17.* 2. *Not he that commendeth himself is approved, but he whom the Lord commendeth, v. 18.*

CHAPTER ELEVEN

GODLY JEALOUSY (vv. 1–4)

Here we may observe, 1. The apology the apostle makes for going about to commend himself. It is no pleasure to a good man to speak well of himself, yet in some cases it is lawful, namely, when it is for the advantage of others, or for our own necessary vindication; as thus it was here. For, 2. We have the reasons for what the apostle did. (1) To preserve the Corinthians from being corrupted by the insinuations of the false apostles, *vv.* 2, 3. (2) To vindicate himself against the false apostles, forasmuch as they could not pretend they had another Jesus, or another Spirit, or another gospel, to preach to them, *v.* 4.

FALSE APOSTLES (vv. 5–15)

After the foregoing preface to what he was about to say, the apostle in these verses mentions,

1. His equality with the other apostles—that *he was not a whit behind the very chief of the apostles, v.* 5. The apostleship, as an office, was equal in all the apostles; but

the apostles, like other Christians, differed one from another.

II. His equality with the false apostles in this particular—the preaching of the gospel unto them freely, without wages. This the apostle largely insists on, and shows that, as they could not but own him to be a minister of Christ, so they ought to acknowledge he had been a good friend to them. For, 1. He had preached the gospel to them freely, *vv.* 7–10. He says he himself had *taken wages of other churches* (*v.* 8), so that he had a right to have asked and received from them: yet he waived his right, and chose rather to abase himself, by working with his hands in the trade of tent-making to maintain himself, than be burdensome to them, that they might *be exalted,* or encouraged to receive the gospel, which they had so cheaply. 2. He informs them of the reason of this his conduct among them. It was not because *he did not love them* (*v.* 11), but it was to avoid offence, that *he might cut off occasion from those that desired occasion.* He would not give occasion for any to accuse him of worldly designs in preaching the gospel.

III. The false apostles are charged *as deceitful workers* (*v.* 13), and that upon this account, because they would *transform themselves* into the likeness of the apostles of Christ, and, though they were the ministers of Satan, would seem to be the *ministers of righteousness.* But it follows, *Their end is according to their works* (*v.* 15); the end will discover them to be deceitful workers, and their work will end in ruin and destruction.

THE RELUCTANT BOASTER I (*vv.* 16–21)

Here we have a further excuse that the apostle makes for what he was about to say in his own vindication. 1. He would not have them think he was guilty of folly, in saying what he said to vindicate himself: *Let no man think me a fool*, *v.* 16. Ordinarily, indeed, it is unbecoming a wise man to be much and often speaking in his own praise. Boasting of ourselves is usually not only a sign of a proud mind, but a mark of folly also. However, says the apostle, yet *as a fool receive me*; that is, if you count it folly in me to *boast a little*, yet give due regard to what I shall say. 2. He mentions a caution, to prevent the abuse of what he should say, telling them that what he spoke, *he did not speak after the Lord*, *v.* 17. He would not have them think that boasting of ourselves, or glorying in what we have, is a thing commanded by the Lord in general unto Christians. 3. He gives a good reason why they should suffer him to boast a little; namely, because they suffered others to do so who had less reason. *You suffer fools gladly, seeing you yourselves are wise* (*v.* 19), may be ironical, and then the meaning is this: "Notwithstanding all your wisdom, you willingly suffer yourselves to be *brought into bondage* under the Jewish yoke, or suffer others to tyrannize over you."

THE RELUCTANT BOASTER (*vv.* 22–33)

Here the apostle gives a large account of his own qualifications, labours, and sufferings (not out of pride or vain-glory, but to the honour of God, who had enabled him to do and suffer so much for the cause of Christ). Observe,

I. He mentions the privileges of his birth (*v.* 22), which were equal to any they could pretend to.

II. He makes mention also of his apostleship, that he was more than an ordinary minister of Christ, *v.* 23.

III. He chiefly insists upon this, that he had been an extraordinary sufferer for Christ; and this was what he gloried in, or rather he gloried in the grace of God that had enabled him to be more *abundant in labours*, and to endure very great sufferings, such as *stripes above measure*, *frequent imprisonments*, and *often* the dangers of *death*, *v.* 23.

CHAPTER TWELVE

THORN IN THE FLESH (*vv.* 1–10)

Here we may observe,

I. The narrative the apostle gives of the favours God had shown him, and the honour he had done him; for doubtless he himself is the man in Christ of whom he speaks. Concerning this we may take notice, 1. Of the honour itself which was done to the apostle: he was *caught up into the third heaven*, *v.* 2. The apostle does not mention what he saw in the third heaven or paradise, but tells us that *he heard unspeakable words*, such as it is not possible for a man to utter—such are the sublimity of the matter and our unacquaintedness with the language of the upper world: nor was it lawful to utter those words, because, while we are here in this world, we have a more sure word of prophecy than such visions and revelations. 2 Pet. i. 19. 2. The modest and humble manner in which the apostle mentions this matter is observable. One would be apt to think that one who had had such visions and revelations as these would have boasted greatly of them; but, says he, *It is not expedient for me doubtless to glory*, v. 1.

II. The apostle gives an account of the methods God took to keep him humble, and to prevent his *being lifted up above measure*; and this he speaks of to balance the account that was given before of the visions and revelations he had had. Here observe,

1. The apostle was pained with a thorn in the flesh, and buffeted with a messenger of Satan, *v.* 7. We are much in the dark what this was, whether some great trouble or some great temptation. Some think it was an acute bodily pain or sickness; others think it was the indignities done him by the false apostles, and the opposition he met with from them, particularly on the account of his speech, which was contemptible.

2. The design of this was to keep the apostle humble: *Lest he should be exalted above measure*, v. 7. If God love us, he will hide pride from us, and keep us from being exalted above measure; and spiritual burdens are ordered, to cure spiritual pride. This thorn in the flesh is said to be a messenger of Satan, which he did not send with a good design, but, on the contrary, with ill intentions, to discourage the apostle (who had been

so highly favoured of God) and hinder him in his work. But God designed this for good, and he overruled it for good, and made this messenger of Satan to be so far from being a hindrance that it was a help to the apostle.

3. The apostle prayed earnestly to God for the removal of this sore grievance.

4. We have an account of the answer given to the apostle's prayer, that, although the trouble was not removed, yet an equivalent should be granted: *My grace is sufficient for thee*. Note, (1) Though God accepts the prayer of faith, yet he does not always answer it in the letter; as he sometimes grants in wrath, so he sometimes denies in love. (2) When God does not remove our troubles and temptations, yet, if he gives us grace sufficient for us, we have no reason to complain, nor to say that he deals ill by us.

III. Here is the use which the apostle makes of this dispensation: *He gloried in his infirmities* (*v.* 9), and took pleasure in them, *v.* 10. And the reason of his glory and joy on account of these things was this —they were fair opportunities for Christ to manifest the power and sufficiency of his grace resting upon him, by which he had so much experience of the strength of divine grace that he could say, *When I am weak then am I strong*. This is a Christian paradox: when we are weak in ourselves, then we are strong in the grace of our Lord Jesus Christ.

APOSTOLIC SIGNS (*vv.* 11–21)

In these verses the apostle addresses

himself to the Corinthians two ways:

I. He blames them for what was faulty in them; namely, that they had not stood up in his defence as they ought to have done, and so made it the more needful for him to insist so much on his own vindication. They in a manner compelled him to commend himself, who *ought to have been commended of them, v.* 11.

II. He gives a large account of his behaviour and kind intentions towards them, in which we may observe the character of a faithful minister of the gospel. 1. He was not willing to be burdensome to them, nor did he seek theirs, but them. 2. He would gladly spend and be spent for them (*v.* 15); that is, he was willing to take pains and to suffer loss for their good. 3. He did not abate in his love to them, notwithstanding their unkindness and ingratitude to him. 4. He was careful not only that he himself should not be burdensome, but that none he employed should. This seems to be the meaning of what we read, *vv.* 16–18. 5. He was a man who did all things for edifying, *v.* 19. This was his great aim and design, to do good, to lay the foundation well, and then with care and diligence to build the superstructure. 6. He would not shrink from his duty for fear of displeasing them, though he was so careful to make himself easy to them. 7. He was grieved at the apprehension that he should find scandalous sins among them not duly repented of. This, he tells them, would be the cause of great humiliation and lamentation.

CHAPTER THIRTEEN

OBSTINACY REPROVED
(*vv.* 1–6)

In these verses observe,

I. The apostle threatens to be severe against obstinate sinners when he should come to Corinth, having now sent to them a first and second epistle, with proper admonitions and exhortations, in order to reform what was amiss among them. Concerning this we may notice, 1. The caution with which he proceeded in his censures: he was not hasty in using severity, but gave a first and second admonition. 2. The threatening itself: *That if* (or when) *he came again* (in person) *he would not spare* obstinate sinners, and such as were impenitent, in their scandalous enormities. He would not spare such, but would inflict church-censures upon them, which are thought to have been accompanied in those early times with visible and extraordinary tokens of divine displeasure.

II. The apostle assigns a reason why he would be thus severe, namely, for *a proof of Christ's speaking in him*, which they *sought after, v.* 3. *Examine yourselves*, &c. Hereby he intimates that, if they could prove their own Christianity, this would be a proof of his apostleship; for if they were in the faith, if Jesus Christ was in them, this was a proof that Christ spoke in him, because it was by his ministry that they did believe.

AIM AT PERFECTION
(*vv.* 7–10)

Here we have,

I. The apostle's prayer to God

on the behalf of the Corinthians, that they might *do no evil, v.* 7. We are more concerned to pray that we may not do evil than that we may not suffer evil.

II. The reasons why the apostle put up this prayer to God on behalf of the Corinthians. Observe, he tells them, 1. It was not so much for his own personal reputation as for the honour of religion: "*Not that we should appear approved, but that you should do that which is honest*, or decent, and for the credit of religion, though we should be reproached and vilified, and accounted as reprobates," *v.* 7. 2. Another reason was this: that they might be free from all blame and censure when he should come to them. This is intimated in *v.* 8, *We can do nothing against the truth, but for the truth. "We are glad,"* says he (*v.* 9), "*when we are weak and you are strong*; that is, that we have no power to censure those who are strong in faith and fruitful in good works." For, 3. He desired their perfection (*v.* 9); that

is, that they might be sincere, and aim at perfection (sincerity is our gospel-perfection), or else he wished there might be a thorough reformation among them.

A LAST WORD (*vv.* 11–14)

Thus the apostle concludes this epistle with,

I. A valediction. He gives them a parting farewell, and takes his leave of them for the present, with hearty good wishes for their spiritual welfare.

II. The apostolical benediction (*v.* 14): *The grace of the Lord Jesus Christ, and the love of God, and the communion of the Holy Ghost, be with you all.* Thus the apostle concludes his epistle, and thus it is usual and proper to dismiss worshipping assemblies. This plainly proves the doctrine of the gospel, and is an acknowledgment that Father, Son, and Spirit, are three distinct persons, yet but one God; and herein the same, that they are the fountain of all blessings to men.

GALATIANS

CHAPTER ONE

INTRODUCTION (*vv.* 1–5)

In these verses we have the preface or introduction to the epistle, where observe,

I. The person or persons from whom this epistle is sent—from Paul *an apostle, &c., and all the brethren that were with him.*

II. To whom this epistle is sent— *to the churches of Galatia.* There were several churches at that time in the country, and it should seem that all of them were more or less corrupted through the arts of those seducers who had crept in among them; and therefore Paul, on whom *came daily the care of all the churches,* being deeply affected with their state, and concerned for their recovery to the faith and establishment in it, writes this epistle to them. He directs it to all of them, as being all more or less concerned in the matter of it; and he gives them the name of *churches,* though they had done enough to forfeit it, for corrupt churches are never allowed to be churches: no doubt there were some among them who still continued in the faith, and he was not without hope that others might be recovered to it.

III. The apostolical benediction, *v.* 3. Herein the apostle, and the brethren who were with him, wish these churches *grace and peace from God the Father, and from the Lord Jesus Christ.* This is the usual blessing wherewith he blesses the churches in the name of the Lord— *grace and peace.* Having mentioned the Lord Jesus Christ, he cannot pass without enlarging upon his love; and therefore adds (*v.* 4), *Who gave himself for our sins, that he might deliver, &c.* Jesus Christ gave himself for our sins, as a great sacrifice to make atonement for us; this the justice of God required, and to this he freely submitted for our sakes. One great end hereof was *to deliver us from this present evil world*; not only to redeem us from the wrath of God, and the curse of the law, but also to recover us from the corruption that is in the world.

ANOTHER GOSPEL (*vv.* 6–9)

Here the apostle comes to the body of the epistle; and he begins it with a more general reproof of these churches for their unsteadiness in the faith, which he afterwards, in some following parts of it, enlarges more upon. Here we may observe,

I. How much he was concerned at their defection: *I marvel, &c.* It filled him at once with the greatest surprise and sorrow. Their sin and folly were that they did not hold fast the doctrine of Christianity as it had been preached to them, but suffered themselves to be removed from the purity and simplicity of it.

They were removed to *another gospel, which yet was not another*. Thus the apostle represents the doctrine of these judaizing teachers; he calls it another gospel, because it opened a different way of justification and salvation from that which was revealed in the gospel, namely, by works, and not by faith in Christ. And yet he adds, "*Which is not another*—you will find it to be no gospel at all—not really another gospel, but the perverting of the gospel of Christ, and the overturning of the foundations of that"—whereby he intimates that those who go about to establish any other way to heaven than what the gospel of Christ has revealed are guilty of a gross perversion of it, and in the issue will find themselves wretchedly mistaken.

II. How confident he was that the gospel he had preached to them was the only true gospel. He was so fully persuaded of this that he pronounced an anathema upon those who pretended to preach any other gospel (*v.* 8), and, to let them see that this did not proceed from any rashness or intemperate zeal in him, he repeated it, *v.* 9.

PAUL'S TESTIMONY
(*vv.* 10–24)

Paul here sets himself to prove the divinity both of his mission and doctrine, that thereby he might wipe off the aspersions which his enemies had cast upon him, and recover these Christians into a better opinion of the gospel he had preached to them. This he gives sufficient evidence of,

I. From the scope and design of his ministry, which was *not to persuade men, but God,* &c. The meaning of this may be either that in his preaching the gospel he did not act in obedience to men, but God, who had called him to this work and office; or that his aim therein was to bring persons to the obedience, not of men, but of God.

II. From the manner wherein he received the gospel which he preached to them, concerning which he assures them (*vv.* 11,12) that he had it not by information from others, but by revelation from heaven. This he was concerned to make out, to prove himself an apostle: and to this purpose,

1. He tells them what his education was, and what, accordingly, his conversation in time past had been, *vv.* 13, 14. Particularly, he acquaints them that he had been brought up in the Jewish religion, and *that he had profited in it above many his equals of his own nation*—that *he had been exceedingly zealous of the traditions of the elders. He had beyond measure persecuted the church of God, and wasted it.*

2. In how wonderful a manner he was turned from the error of his ways, brought to the knowledge and faith of Christ, and appointed to the office of an apostle, *vv.* 15, 16. This was not done in an ordinary way, nor by ordinary means, but in an extraordinary manner; for, (1) God had *separated him hereunto from his mother's womb*: the change that was wrought in him was in pursuance of a divine purpose concerning him, whereby he was appointed to be a Christian and an apostle, before he came into the world, or had done either good or

evil. (2) He was *called by his grace*. All who are savingly converted are called by the grace of God; their conversion is the effect of his good pleasure concerning them, and is effected by his power and grace in them. (3) He had Christ *revealed in him*. He was not only revealed to him, but in him. It pleased God *to reveal his Son in him*, to bring him to the knowledge of Christ and his gospel by special and immediate revelation. And, (4) It was with this design, that he should preach him among the heathen; not only that he should embrace him himself, but preach him to others; so that he was both a Christian and an apostle by revelation.

3. He acquaints them how he behaved himself hereupon, from *v*. 16, to the end. Being thus called to this work and office, *he conferred not with flesh and blood*. This may be taken more generally, and so we may learn from it that, when God calls us by his grace, we must not consult flesh and blood. But the meaning of it here is that he did not consult men; he did not apply to any others for their advice and direction; *neither did he go up to Jerusalem, to those that were apostles before him*, as though he needed to be approved by them, or to receive any further instructions or authority from them: but, instead of that, he steered another course, and *went into Arabia*, either as a place of retirement proper for receiving further divine revelations, or in order to preach the gospel there among the Gentiles, being appointed to be the apostle of the Gentiles; and thence *he returned again to Damascus*, where he had

first begun his ministry, and whence he had with difficulty escaped the rage of his enemies, Acts ix. It was not till *three years after* his conversion that *he went up to Jerusalem, to see Peter*; and when he did so he made but a very short stay with him, no more than *fifteen days*; nor, while he was there, did he go much into conversation; for *others of the apostles he saw none, but James, the Lord's brother*. So that it could not well be pretended that he was indebted to any other either for his knowledge of the gospel or his authority to preach it; but it appeared that both his qualifications for, and his call to, the apostolic office were extraordinary and divine. After this he acquaints them that *he came into the regions of Syria and Cilicia*: having made this short visit to Peter, he returns to his work again. He had no communication at that time with the *churches of Christ in Judea*, they had not so much as *seen his face; but, having heard that he who persecuted them in times past now preached the faith which he once destroyed, they glorified God* because of him; thanksgivings were rendered by many unto God on that behalf; the very report of this mighty change in him, as it filled them with joy, so it excited them to give glory to God on the account of it.

CHAPTER TWO

PAUL AT JERUSALEM

(*vv*. 1–10)

In these verses Paul informs us of another journey which he took to Jerusalem, and of what passed between him and the other apostles there, *vv.* 1–10. Here he acquaints us,

I. With some circumstances relating to this his journey thither. As particularly, 1. With the time of it: that it was not till *fourteen years* after the former (mentioned *ch.* i. 18), or, as others choose to understand it, from his conversion, or from the death of Christ.

II. He gives us an account of his behaviour while he was at Jerusalem, which was such as made it appear that he was not in the least inferior to the other apostles, but that both his authority and qualifications were every way equal to theirs. He particularly acquaints us,

1. That *he there communicated the gospel to them, which he preached among the Gentiles, but privately,* &c. Here we may observe both the faithfulness and prudence of our great apostle. (1) His faithfulness in giving them a free and fair account of the doctrine which he had all along preached among the Gentiles, and was still resolved to preach—that of pure Christianity, free from all mixtures of Judaism. And yet, (2) He uses prudence and caution herein, for fear of giving offence.

2. That in his practice he firmly adhered to the doctrine which he had preached. Paul was a man of resolution, and would adhere to his principles; and therefore, though he had Titus with him, who was a Greek, yet he would not suffer him to be circumcised, because he would not betray the doctrine of Christ, as he had preached it to the Gentiles. It does not appear that the apostles at all insisted upon

this; for, though they connived at the use of circumcision among the Jewish converts, yet they were not for imposing it upon the Gentiles. But there were others who did, whom the apostle here calls *false brethren,* and concerning whom he informs us that they were *unawares brought in,* that is, into the church, or into their company, and that they came only to *spy out their liberty which they had in Christ Jesus,* or to see whether Paul would stand up in defence of that freedom from the ceremonial law which he had taught as the doctrine of the gospel, and represented as the privilege of those who embraced the Christian religion. Their design herein was *to bring them into bondage,* which they would have effected could they have gained the point they aimed at.

3. That, though he conversed with the other apostles, yet he did not receive any addition to his knowledge or authority from them, *v.* 6.

4. That the issue of this conversation was that the other apostles were fully convinced of his divine mission and authority, and accordingly acknowledged him as their fellow-apostle, *vv.* 7–10.

CRUCIFIED WITH CHRIST
(*vv.* 11–21)

I. To give the greater weight to what he had already said, and more fully to fortify them against the insinuations of the judaizing teachers, he acquaints them with another interview which he had with the apostle Peter at Antioch, and what passed between them there, *vv.* 11–14.

Peter and the other apostles had both acknowledged Paul's commission and approved his doctrine, and they parted very good friends. But in this Paul finds himself obliged to oppose Peter, for *he was to be blamed*. Here we may observe,

1. Peter's fault. When he came among the Gentile churches, he complied with them, and did eat with them, though they were not circumcised, agreeably to the instructions which were given in particular to him (Acts x.), when he was warned by the heavenly vision *to call nothing common or unclean*. But, when there came some Jewish Christians from Jerusalem, he grew more shy of the Gentiles, only to humour those of the circumcision and for fear of giving them offence, which doubtless was to the great grief and discouragement of the Gentile churches. Then *he withdrew, and separated himself*. His fault herein had a bad influence upon others, for *the other Jews also dissembled with him*. And (would you think it?) Barnabas himself, one of the apostles of the Gentiles, and one who had been instrumental in planting and watering the churches of the Gentiles, *was carried away with their dissimulation*.

2. The rebuke which Paul gave him for his fault. Notwithstanding Peter's character, yet, when he observes him thus behaving himself to the great prejudice both of the truth of the gospel and the peace of the church, he is not afraid to reprove him for it.

II. Paul having thus established his character and office, and sufficiently shown that he was not inferior to any of the apostles, no, not to Peter himself, from the account of the reproof he gave him he takes occasion to speak of that great fundamental doctrine of the gospel—That justification is only by faith in Christ, and not by the works of the law. Now concerning this Paul aquaints us,

1. With the practice of the Jewish Christians themselves. If it would be wrong in us who are Jews by nature to return to the law, and expect justification by it, would it not be much more so to require this of the Gentiles, who were never subject to it, since *by the works of the law no flesh shall be justified?* To give the greater weight to this he adds (*v.* 17), "*But if, while we seek to be justified by Christ, we ourselves also are found sinners, is Christ the minister of sin?*" If, while we seek justification by Christ alone, and teach others to do so, we ourselves are found giving countenance or indulgence to sin, or rather are accounted sinners of the Gentiles, and such as it is not fit to have communion with, unless we also observe the law of Moses, *is Christ the minister of sin?* Will it not follow that he is so, if he engage us to receive a doctrine that gives liberty to sin? Thus does the apostle argue for the great doctrine of justification by faith without the works of the law from the principles and practice of the Jewish Christians themselves, and from the consequences that would attend their departure from it, whence it appeared that Peter and the other Jews were much in the wrong in refusing to communicate with the Gentile Christians, and endeavour-

ing to bring them under the bondage of the law.

2. He acquaints us what his own judgment and practice were. (1) That he was dead to the law. (2) That, as he was dead to the law, so he was alive unto God through Jesus Christ (*v.* 20): *I am crucified with Christ*, &c. And here in his own person he gives us an excellent description of the mysterious life of a believer. [1] He is crucified, and yet he lives; the old man is crucified (Rom. vi. 6), but the new man is living; he is dead to the world, and dead to the law, and yet alive to God and Christ; sin is mortified, and grace quickened. [2] *He lives, and yet not he.* This is strange: *I live, and yet not I*; he lives in the exercise of grace; he has the comforts and the triumphs of grace; and yet that grace is not from himself, but from another. Believers see themselves living in a state of dependence. [3] *He is crucified with Christ*, and yet *Christ lives in him*; This results from his mystical union with Christ, by means of which he is interested in the death of Christ, so as by virtue of that to die unto sin; and yet interested in the life of Christ, so as by virtue of that to live unto God. [4] *He lives in the flesh*, and yet *lives by faith*; to outward appearance he lives as other people do, his natural life is supported as others are; yet he has a higher and nobler principle that supports and actuates him, that of faith in Christ, and especially as eyeing the wonders of his love in giving himself for him.

Lastly, The apostle concludes this discourse with acquainting us that by the doctrine of justification

by faith in Christ, without the works of the law (which he asserted, and others opposed), he avoided two great difficulties, which the contrary opinion was loaded with: 1. *That he did not frustrate the grace of God*, which the doctrine of justification by the works of the law did; for, as he argues (Rom. xi. 6), *If it be of works, it is no more of grace.* 2. That he did not frustrate the death of Christ; whereas, *if righteousness come by* the law, then it must follow *that Christ has died in vain*; for, if we look for salvation by the law of Moses, then we render the death of Christ needless: for to what purpose should he be appointed to die, if we might have been saved without it?

CHAPTER THREE

GOING ON IN FAITH
(*vv.* 1–5)

The apostle is here dealing with those who, having embraced the faith of Christ, still continued to seek for justification by the works of the law.

He reproves them, and the reproof is very close and warm: he calls them *foolish Galatians, v.* 1. Several things proved and aggravated the folly of these Christians.

1. *Jesus Christ had been evidently set forth as crucified among them*; that is, they had had the doctrine of the cross preached to them, and the sacrament of the Lord's supper administered among them, in both which Christ crucified had been set before them.

2. He appeals to the experiences they had had of the working of the

Spirit upon their souls (*v.* 2); he puts them in mind that, upon their becoming Christians, *they had received the Spirit*, that many of them at least had been made partakers not only of the sanctifying influences, but of the miraculous gifts, of the Holy Spirit. To convince them of the folly of their departing from this doctrine, he desires to know how they came by these gifts and graces: Was it *by the works of the law*, that is, the preaching of the necessity of these in order to justification? Or was it by the *hearing of faith*, that is, the preaching of the doctrine of faith in Christ as the only way of justification?

3. He calls upon them to consider their past and present conduct, and thence to judge whether they were not acting very weakly and unreasonably (*vv.* 3, 4): he tells them that *they had begun in the Spirit*, but now were seeking *to be made perfect by the flesh*.

4. He puts them in mind that they had had ministers among them (and particularly himself) who came with a divine seal and commission; for they had *ministered the Spirit to them, and wrought miracles among them*: and he appeals to them whether they did it *by the works of the law or by the hearing of faith*.

THE EXAMPLE OF ABRAHAM (*vv.* 6–18)

The apostle having reproved the Galatians for not obeying the truth, and endeavoured to impress them with a sense of their folly herein, in these verses he largely proves the doctrine which he had reproved them for rejecting, namely, that of justification by faith without the works of the law. This he does several ways.

I. From the example of Abraham's justification. This argument the apostle uses, Rom. iv. *Abraham believed God, and that was accounted to him for righteousness* (*v.* 6); that is, his faith fastened upon the word and promise of God, and upon his believing he was owned and accepted of God as a righteous man: as on this account he is represented as the father of the faithful, so the apostle would have us to know *that those who are of faith are the children of Abraham* (*v.* 7).

II. He shows that we cannot be justified but by faith fastening on the gospel, because the law condemns us. A strange method it was which Christ took to redeem us from the curse of the law; it was *by his being himself made a curse for us*. Being made sin for us, he was made a curse for us. Hence it appeared that it was not by putting themselves under the law, but by faith in Christ, that they became the people of God and heirs of the promise.

III. To prove that justification is by faith, and not by the works of the law, the apostle alleges the express testimony of the Old Testament, *v.* 11. The place referred to is Habak. ii. 4, where it is said, *The just shall live by faith*; it is again quoted, Rom. i. 17, and Heb. x. 38. The design of it is to show that those only are just or righteous who do truly live, who are freed from death and wrath, and restored into a state of life in the favour of God; and that it is only through faith that persons become righteous, and as such obtain this life and happiness

—that they are accepted of God, and enabled to live to him now, and are entitled to an eternal life in the enjoyment of him hereafter.

IV. To this purpose the apostle urges the stability of the covenant which God made with Abraham, which was not vacated nor disannulled by the giving of the law to Moses, *vv.* 15, &c. Faith had the precedence of the law, for Abraham was justified by faith. It was a promise that he built upon, and promises are the proper objects of faith.

THE LAW'S PURPOSE
(*vv.* 19–22)

It might be asked, "If that promise be sufficient for salvation, wherefore then serveth the law? Or, Why did God give the law by Moses?" To this he answers,

I. The law *was added because of transgressions, v.* 19. The Israelites, though they were chosen to be God's people, were sinners as well as others, and therefore the law was given to convince them of their sin, and of their obnoxiousness to the divine displeasure on the account of it; *for by the law is the knowledge of sin* (Rom. iii. 20), and *the law entered that sin might abound*, Rom. v. 20.

The apostle adds that the law was given for this purpose *till the seed should come to whom the promise was made*; that is, either till Christ should come (the principal seed referred to in the promise, as he had before shown), or till the gospel dispensation should take place, when Jews and Gentiles, without distinction, should, upon believing, become the seed of Abraham.

As a further proof that the law was not designed to vacate the promise, the apostle adds, *It was ordained by angels in the hand of a mediator.* Whereas the promise was given immediately by God himself, the law was given *by the ministry of angels, and the hand of a mediator.* Hence it appeared that the law could not be designed to set aside the promise; for (*v.* 20), *A mediator is not a mediator of one,* of one party only; *but God is one,* but one party in the promise or covenant made with Abraham: and therefore it is not to be supposed that by a transaction which passed only between him and the nation of the Jews he should make void a promise which he had long before made to Abraham and all his spiritual seed, whether Jews or Gentiles.

II. The law was given to convince men of the necessity of a Saviour. *For the scripture hath concluded all under sin* (*v.* 22), or declared that all, both Jew and Gentile, are in a state of guilt, and therefore unable to attain to righteousness and justification by the works of the law.

III. The law was designed for *a schoolmaster, to bring men to Christ, v.* 24. It was their schoolmaster, to instruct and govern them in their state of minority to lead and conduct them to Christ (as children were wont to be led to school by those servants who had the care of them; that they might be more fully instructed by him as their schoolmaster, in the true way of justification and salvation, which is only by faith in him, and of which he was appointed to give the fullest and clearest discoveries.

Having shown for what intent the law was given, in the close of the chapter he acquaints us with our privilege by Christ, where he particularly declares,

(1) That *we are the children of God by faith in Christ Jesus, v. 26.* And here we may observe, [1] The great and excellent privilege which real Christians enjoy under the gospel: *They are the children of God.* [2] How they come to obtain this privilege, and that is *by faith in Christ Jesus.* And this faith in Christ, whereby they became the children of God, he reminds us (*v.* 27), was what they professed in baptism; for he adds, *As many of you as have been baptized into Christ have put on Christ.*

(2) That this privilege of being the children of God, and of being by baptism devoted to Christ, is now enjoyed in common by all real Christians. The law indeed made a difference between Jew and Greek, giving the Jews on many accounts the pre-eminence. But it is not so now; they all stand on the same level, *and are all one in Christ Jesus*: All who sincerely believe on Christ, of what nation, or sex, or condition, soever they be, are accepted of him, and become the children of God through faith in him.

(3) That, *being Christ's, we are Abraham's seed, and heirs according to the promise.* Their judaizing teachers would have them believe that they must be circumcised and keep the law of Moses, or they could not be saved: "No," says the apostle, "there is no need of that; for *if you be Christ's,* if you sincerely believe on him, who is the promised seed, in whom all the nations of the earth were to be blessed, you therefore become the true *seed of Abraham,* the father of the faithful, and as such *are heirs according to the promise,* and consequently are entitled to the great blessings and privileges of it."

CHAPTER FOUR

SONS OF GOD (*vv.* 1–7)

Here,

I. He acquaints us with the state of the Old-Testament church: it was like a child under age, and it was used accordingly, being kept in a state of darkness and bondage, in comparison of the greater light and liberty which we enjoy under the gospel.

II. He acquaints us with the much happier state of Christians under the gospel-dispensation, *vv.* 4–7. *When the fulness of time had come,* the time appointed of the Father, when he would put an end to the legal dispensation, and set up another and a better in the room of it, *he sent forth his Son,* &c. The person who was employed to introduce this new dispensation was no other than the Son of God himself, the only-begotten of the Father, who, as he had been prophesied of and promised from the foundation of the world, so in due time he was manifested for this purpose. He, in pursuance of the great design he had undertaken, submitted to be *made of a woman*—there is his incarnation; and to be *made under the law*—there is his subjection. He who was truly God for our sakes became man; and he who was Lord of all consented to come into a state of subjection and to take upon him the form of a servant; and one great end of all this was *to redeem those that were under the law*—to save us from that intolerable yoke and to appoint gospel ordinances more rational and easy. For he was sent to redeem us, *that we might receive the adoption of sons*—that we might no longer be accounted and treated as servants, but as sons grown up to maturity, who are allowed greater freedoms, and admitted to larger privileges, than while they were under tutors and governors. Now, under the gospel, particular believers receive the adoption; and, as an earnest and evidence of it, they have together therewith the Spirit of adoption, putting them upon the duty of prayer, and enabling them in prayer to eye God as a Father (*v.* 6). From what the apostle says in these verses, we may observe,

1. The wonders of divine love and mercy towards us.

2. The great and invaluable advantages which Christians enjoy under the gospel; for, (1) We receive *the adoption of sons*. Whence note, It is the great privilege which believers have through Christ that they are adopted children of the God of heaven. (2) We receive *the Spirit of adoption*. All who are received into the number partake of the nature of the children of God; for he will have all his children to resemble him.

BACK TO BONDAGE?
(*vv.* 8–11)

In these verses the apostle puts them in mind of what they were before their conversion to the faith of Christ, and what a blessed change their conversion had made upon them; and thence endeavours to convince them of their great weakness in hearkening to those who would bring them under the bondage of the law of Moses.

I. He reminds them of their past state and behaviour, and what they were before the gospel was preached to them. Then *they knew not God*; for *they did service to those which by nature were no gods*, they were employed in a great number of superstitious and idolatrous services.

II. He calls upon them to consider the happy change that was made in them by the preaching of the gospel among them. Now *they had known God or rather were known of God*; this happy change in their state, whereby they were turned from idols to the living God, and through Christ had received the adoption of sons, was not owing to themselves, but to him.

III. Hence he infers the unreasonableness and madness of their suffering themselves to be brought again into a state of bondage. What they suffered themselves to be brought into bondage to were but *weak and beggarly elements*, such things as had no power in them to cleanse the soul, nor to afford any solid satisfaction to the mind. And therefore their weakness and folly were the more aggravated, in submitting to them, and in symbolizing with the Jews in observing their various festivals, here signified by *days, and months, and times, and years.*

IV. Hereupon he expresses his fears concerning them, *lest he had bestowed on them labour in vain.*

THEIR REJECTION OF PAUL
(*vv.* 12–16)

That these Christians might be the more ashamed of their defection from the truth of the gospel which Paul had preached to them, he here reminds them of the great affection they formerly had for him and his ministry, and puts them upon considering how very unsuitable their present behaviour was to what they then professed. And here we may observe,

I. How affectionately he addresses himself to them.

II. How he magnifies their former affection to him, that hereby they might be the more ashamed of their present behaviour towards him.

III. How earnestly he expostulates with them hereupon: *Where is then,* says he, *the blessedness you spoke of?* What has become of that pleasure they used to take in communion with God, and in the company of his servants? The more to impress upon them a just shame of their present conduct, he again asks (*v.* 16), "*Am I become your enemy, because I tell you the truth?*"

SLAVERY OR FREEDOM?
(*vv.* 17–31)

He here gives them the character of those false teachers who made it their business to draw them away from it, which if they would attend to, they might soon see how little reason they had to hearken to them: whatever opinion they might have of them, he tells them they were designing men, who were aiming to set up themselves, and who, under their specious pretences, were more consulting their

own interest than theirs (*vv.* 17, 18). They were too ready to account him their enemy, but he assures them that he was their friend; nay, not only so, but that he had the feelings of a parent towards them. He calls them *his children,* as he justly might, since he had been the instrument of their conversion to the Christian faith. *He travailed in birth for them* (*v.* 19): and the great thing which he was in so much pain about, and which he was so earnestly desirous of, was not so much that they might affect him as *that Christ might be formed in them,* that they might become Christians indeed, and be more confirmed and established in the faith of the gospel.

In verses 21–31 the apostle illustrates the difference between believers who rested in Christ only and those judaizers who trusted in the law, by a comparison taken from the story of Isaac and Ishmael. 1. Here he represents the different state and condition of these two sons of Abraham—that the one, Ishmael, *was by a bond-maid,* and the other, Isaac, *by a free-woman*; and that whereas the former *was born after the flesh,* or by the ordinary course of nature, the other *was by promise,* when in the course of nature there was no reason to expect that Sarah should have a son. 2. He acquaints them with the meaning and design of this history, or the use which he intended to make of it (*vv.* 24–27): *These things,* says he, *are an allegory,* wherein, besides the literal and historical sense of the words, the Spirit of God might design to signify something further to us, and that was, That these two, Agar and Sarah, *are the two covenants*, or were intended to typify and prefigure the two different dispensations of the covenant. The former, Agar, represented that which was given from mount Sinai, and *which gendereth to bondage*; that is, it justly represents the present state of the Jews, who, continuing in their infidelity and adhering to that covenant, are still in bondage with their children. But the other, Sarah, was intended to prefigure Jerusalem which is above, or the state of Christians under the new and better dispensation of the covenant, which is free both from the curse of the moral and the bondage of the ceremonial law, and *is the mother of us all*—a state into which all, both Jews and Gentiles, are admitted, upon their believing in Christ. 3. He applies the history thus explained to the present case (*v.* 28): *Now we, brethren*, says he, *as Isaac was, are the children of the promise*. We Christians, who have accepted Christ, and rely upon him, and look for justification and salvation by him alone, as hereby we become the spiritual, though we are not the natural, seed of Abraham, so we are entitled to the promised inheritance and interested in the blessings of it.

CHAPTER FIVE
CIRCUMCISION (*vv.* 1–12)

It is our duty to *stand fast in this liberty*, constantly and faithfully to adhere to the gospel and to the liberty of it, and not to suffer ourselves, upon any consideration, *to be again entangled in the yoke of bondage*, nor persuaded to return back to the law of Moses. This is the general caution or exhortation, which in the following verses the apostle enforces by several reasons or arguments. As,

I. That their submitting to circumcision, and depending on the works of the law for righteousness, were an implicit contradiction of their faith as Christians and a forfeiture of all their advantages by Jesus Christ, *vv.* 2–4.

II. To persuade them to stedfastness in the doctrine and liberty of the gospel, he sets before them his own example, and that of other Jews who had embraced the Christian religion, and acquaints them what their hopes were, namely, That *through the Spirit they were waiting for the hope of righteousness by faith*. Here we may observe, 1. What it is that Christians are waiting for: it is *the hope of righteousness*, by which we are chiefly to understand the happiness of the other world. 2. How they hope to obtain this happiness, namely, by faith, that is, in our Lord Jesus Christ, not by the works of the law, or any thing they can do to deserve it, but only by faith, receiving and relying upon him as the Lord our righteousness. And, 3. Whence it is that they are thus waiting for the hope of righteousness: it is *through the Spirit*. Herein they act under the direction and influence of the Holy Spirit.

III. He argues from the nature and design of the Christian institution, which was to abolish the difference between Jew and Gentile, and to establish faith in Christ as the way of our acceptance with

God. He tells them (*v.* 6) that *in Christ Jesus*, or under the gospel dispensation, *neither circumcision availeth any thing nor uncircumcision.* Christ, who is *the end of the law*, having come, now it was neither here nor there whether a man were circumcised or uncircumcised; he was neither the better for the one nor the worse for the other, nor would either the one or the other recommend him to God.

IV. To recover them from their backslidings, and engage them to greater stedfastness for the future, he puts them in mind of their good beginnings, and calls upon them to consider whence it was that they were so much altered from what they had been, *v.* 7.

1. He tells them that *they did run well*, at their first setting out in Christianity. Therefore,

2. He asks them, and calls upon them to ask themselves, *Who did hinder you?* He very well knew who they were, and what it was that hindered them; but he would have them to put the question to themselves, and seriously consider whether they had any good reason to hearken to those who gave them this disturbance, and whether what they offered was sufficient to justify them in their present conduct.

V. He argues for their stedfastness in the faith and liberty of the gospel from the ill rise of that persuasion whereby they were drawn away from it (*v.* 8): *This persuasion*, says he, *cometh not of him that calleth you.* The opinion or persuasion of which the apostle here speaks was no doubt that of the necessity of their being circumcised, and keeping the law of Moses, or of their mixing the works of the law with faith in Christ, in the business of justification.

VI. The danger there was of the spreading of this infection, and the ill influence it might have upon others, are a further argument which the apostle urges against their complying with their false teachers in what they would impose on them. *A little leaven leaveneth the whole lump* — the whole lump of Christianity may be tainted and corrupted by one such erroneous principle.

VII. That he might conciliate the greater regard to what he had said, he expresses the hopes he had concerning them (*v.* 10): *I have confidence in you*, says he, *through the Lord, that you will be none otherwise minded.* Herein he teaches us that we ought to hope the best even of those concerning whom we have cause to fear the worst.

VIII. Their judaizing teachers had misrepresented him, that they might the more easily gain their ends upon them. When he says (*v.* 11), *And I brethren, if I yet preach circumcision*, it plainly appears that they had reported him to have done so, and that they had made use of this as an argument to prevail with the Galatians to submit to it. To prove the injustice of that charge upon him, he offers such arguments as, if they would allow themselves to consider, could not fail to convince them of it. 1. If he would have preached circumcision, he might have avoided persecution. 2. If he had yielded to the Jews herein, *then would the offence of the cross have ceased.* They would not have taken so much offence against the doctrine of Christianity as they did, nor would he and others have been exposed to so much suffering on the account of it as they were.

FLESH AND SPIRIT (*vv.* 13–25)

In the latter part of this chapter the apostle comes to exhort these Christians to serious practical godliness, as the best antidote against the snares of the false teachers. Two things especially he presses upon them:

I. That they should not strive with one another, but love one another. *But*, says he, if instead of serving one another in love, and therein fulfilling the law of God, *you bite and devour one another, take heed that you be not consumed one of another*. If, instead of acting like men and Christians, they would behave themselves more like brute beasts, in tearing and rending one another, they could expect nothing as the consequence of it, but that they would be consumed one of another; and therefore they had the greatest reason not to indulge themselves in such quarrels and animosities.

II. That they should all strive against sin. To excite Christians hereunto, and to assist them herein, the apostle shows,

1. That there is in every one a struggle between the flesh and the spirit (*v.* 17).

2. That it is our duty and interest in this struggle to side with the better part, to side with our convictions against our corruptions and with our graces against our lusts. This the apostle represents as

our duty, and directs us to the most effectual means of success in it.

3. The apostle specifies the works of the flesh, which must be watched against and mortified, and the fruits of the Spirit, which must be cherished and brought forth (*vv.* 19, &c.); and by specifying particulars he further illustrates what he is here upon. (1) He begins with *the works of the flesh*, which, as they are many, so they are manifest. The particulars he specifies are of various sorts; some are sins against the seventh commandment, such as *adultery, fornication, uncleanness, lasciviousness*, by which are meant not only the gross acts of these sins, but all such thoughts, and words, and actions, as have a tendency towards the great transgression. Some are sins against the first and second commandments, as *idolatry* and *witchcraft*. Others are sins against our neighbour, and contrary to the royal law of brotherly love, such as *hatred, variance, emulations, wrath, strife*, which too often occasion *seditions, heresies, envyings*, and sometimes break out into *murders*, not only of the names and reputation, but even of the very lives, of our fellow-creatures. Others are sins against ourselves, such as *drunkenness and revellings*. These are sins which undoubtedly shut men out of heaven, unless they be first *washed and sanctified, and justified in the name of our Lord Jesus, and by the Spirit of our God*, 1 Cor. vi. 11. (2) He specifies the fruits of the Spirit, or the renewed nature, which as Christians we are concerned to bring forth, *vv.* 22, 23. He particularly recommends to us, *love*, to

God especially, and to one another for his sake,—*joy*, by which may be understood cheerfulness in conversation with our friends, or rather a constant delight in God,—*peace*, with God and conscience, or a peaceableness of temper and behaviour towards others,—*long-suffering*, patience to defer anger, and a contentedness to bear injuries,—*gentleness*, such a sweetness of temper, and especially towards our inferiors, as disposes us to be affable and courteous, and easy to be entreated when any have wronged us,—*goodness* (kindness, beneficence), which shows itself in a readiness to do good to all as we have opportunity,—*faith*, fidelity, justice, and honesty, in what we profess and promise to others,—*meekness*, wherewith to govern our passions and resentments, so as not to be easily provoked, and, when we are so, to be soon pacified,—and *temperance*, in meat and drink, and other enjoyments of life, so as not to be excessive and immoderate in the use of them. Concerning these things, or those in whom these fruits of the Spirit are found, the apostle says, *There is no law against them*, to condemn and punish them. *And those that are Christ's*, says he, *have crucified the flesh with the affections and lusts*. Our Christianity obliges us not only to die unto sin, but to live unto righteousness; not only to oppose the works of the flesh, but to bring forth the fruits of the Spirit too.

4. The apostle concludes this chapter with a caution against pride and envy, *v.* 26. Note, (1) The glory which comes from men is vain-glory, which, instead of being

desirous of, we should be dead to. (2) An undue regard to the approbation and applause of men is one great ground of the unhappy strifes and contentions that exist among Christians.

CHAPTER SIX

GOD IS NOT MOCKED
(*vv.* 1–10)

I. We are here taught to deal tenderly with those who are overtaken in a fault, *v.* 1. He puts a common case: *If a man be overtaken in a fault*, that is, be brought to sin by the surprise of temptation. *Those who are spiritual*, by whom is meant, not only the ministers (as if none but they were to be called spiritual persons), but other Christians too, especially those of the higher form in Christianity; these must *restore such a one with the spirit of meekness. Considering thyself, lest thou also be tempted.* We ought to deal very tenderly with those who are overtaken in sin, because we none of us know but it may some time or other be our own case.

II. We are here directed *to bear one another's burdens*, *v.* 2. To excite us hereunto, the apostle adds, by way of motive, that so we shall *fulfil the law of Christ*. This is to act agreeably to the law of his precept, which is the law of love, and obliges us to a mutual forbearance and forgiveness, to sympathy with and compassion towards each other; and it would also be agreeable to his pattern and example, which have the force of a law to us.

III. We are advised every one to test his own work, *v.* 4. By our own work is chiefly meant our own actions or behaviour. These the apostle directs us to prove, that is, seriously and impartially to examine them by the rule of God's word, to see whether or no they are agreeable to it, and therefore such as God and conscience do approve. That we may be persuaded to this necessary and profitable duty of proving our own work, the apostle urges two considerations very proper for this purpose:

1. This is the way to *have rejoicing in ourselves alone*. If we set ourselves in good earnest to *prove our own work*, and, upon the trial, can approve ourselves to God, as to our sincerity and uprightness towards him, then may we expect to have comfort and peace in our own souls, having the testimony of our own consciences for us (as 2 Cor. i. 12), and this, he intimates, would be a much better ground of joy and satisfaction than to be able to rejoice *in another*.

2. The other argument which the apostle uses to press upon us this duty of proving our own work is that every man shall bear his own burden (*v.* 5), the meaning of which is that at the great day every one shall be reckoned with according as his behaviour here has been.

IV. Christians are here exhorted to be free and liberal in maintaining their ministers (*v.* 6): *Let him that is taught in the word communicate to him that teacheth, in all good things.*

V. Here is a caution to take heed of mocking God, or of deceiving ourselves, by imagining that he can be imposed upon by mere pretensions or professions (*v.* 7): *Be not deceived, God is not mocked.* Our present time is seed-time: in the other world there will be a great harvest; and, as the husbandman reaps in the harvest according as he sows in the seedness, so we shall reap then as we sow now. And he further informs us (*v.* 8) that, as there are two sorts of seedness, sowing to the flesh and sowing to the Spirit, so accordingly will the reckoning be hereafter: *If we sow to the flesh, we shall of the flesh reap corruption.* If we sow the wind, we shall reap the whirlwind.

VI. Here is a further caution given us, *not to be weary in well doing*, *v.* 9. As we should not excuse ourselves from any part of our duty, so neither should be grow weary in it.

VII. Here is an exhortation to all Christians to do good in their places (*v.* 10): *As we have therefore an opportunity*, &c. It is not enough that we be good ourselves, but we must do good to others, if we would approve ourselves to be Christians indeed.

FINAL APPEAL (*vv.* 11–18)

The apostle, having at large established the doctrine of the gospel, and endeavoured to persuade these Christians to a behaviour agreeable to it, seems as if he intended here to have put an end to the epistle, especially when he had acquainted them that, as a particular mark of his respect for them, he had written this large letter with his own hand. But such is his affection to them that he cannot break off till he has once again given them the true character of those teachers.

I. He gives them the true character of those teachers who were industrious to seduce them, in several particulars. As, 1. They were men who *desired to make a fair show in the flesh*, *v.* 12. 2. They were men who were afraid of suffering, for they constrained the Gentile Christians to be circumcised, *only lest they should suffer persecution for the cross of Christ*. And, 3. Another part of their character was that they were men of a party spirit, and who had no further zeal for the law than as it subserved their carnal and selfish designs; for they desired to have these Christians circumcised, *that they might glory in their flesh* (*v.* 13).

II. He acquaints us, on the other hand, with his own temper and behaviour, or makes profession of his own faith, hope, and joy; particularly,

1. That his principal glory was in the cross of Christ: *God forbid*, says he, *that I should glory, save in the cross of our Lord Jesus Christ*, *v.* 14.

2. That he was dead to the world. By Christ, or by the cross of Christ, *the world was crucified to him, and he to the world*; he had experienced the power and virtue

of it in weaning him from the world, and this was one great reason of his glorying in it.

3. That he did not lay the stress of his religion on one side or the other of the contesting interests, but on sound Christianity, *v.* 15. Here he instructs us both wherein real religion does not and wherein it does consist. It does not consist in circumcision or uncircumcision, in our being in this or the other denomination of Christians; but it consists in our being new creatures; not in having a new name, or putting on a new face, but in our being renewed in the spirit of our minds and having Christ formed in us. *And as many as walk according to this rule peace be upon them, and mercy upon the Israel of God*, by whom he means all sincere Christians, whether Jews or Gentiles.

4. That he had cheerfully suffered persecution for the sake of Christ and Christianity, *v.* 17.

III. The apostle, having now finished what he intended to write for the conviction and recovery of the churches of Galatia, concludes the epistle with his apostolical benediction, *v.* 18.

EPHESIANS

CHAPTER ONE

INTRODUCTION (vv. 1, 2)

Here is, 1. The title St. Paul takes to himself, as belonging to him— *Paul, an apostle of Jesus Christ*, &c. 2. The persons to whom this epistle is sent: *To the saints who are at Ephesus*, that is, to the Christians who were members of the church at Ephesus, the metropolis of Asia.

CHOSEN IN CHRIST (vv. 3–14)

He begins with thanksgivings and praise, and enlarges with a great deal of fluency and copiousness of affection upon the exceedingly great and precious benefits which we enjoy by Jesus Christ.

I. In general he blesses God for *spiritual blessings*, v. 3, where he styles him *the God and Father of our Lord Jesus Christ*.

II. The particular spiritual blessings with which we are blessed in Christ, and for which we ought to bless God, are (many of them) here enumerated and enlarged upon. 1. Election and predestination, which are the secret springs whence the others flow, vv. 4, 5, 11. We have here the date of this act of love: it was *before the foundation of the world*; not only before God's people had a being, but before the world had a beginning; for they were chosen in the counsel of God from all eternity. *All is of God, and*

from him, and through him, and therefore all must be to him, and centre in his praise. 2. The next spiritual blessing the apostle takes notice of is acceptance with God through Jesus Christ: *Wherein*, or by which grace, *he hath made us accepted in the beloved*, v. 6. Jesus Christ is the beloved of his Father (Matt. iii. 17), as well as of angels and saints. It is our great privilege to be accepted of God, which implies his love to us and his taking us under his care and into his family. 3. Remission of sins, and redemption through the blood of Jesus, v. 7. No remission without redemption. It was by reason of sin that we were captivated, and we cannot be released from our captivity but by the remission of our sins. This redemption we have in Christ, and this remission through his blood. 4. Another privilege which the apostle here blesses God for is divine revelation—that God hath *made known to us the mystery of his will* (v. 9), that is, so much of his good-will to men, which had been concealed for a long time, and is still concealed from so great a part of the world: this we owe to Christ, who, having lain in the bosom of the Father from eternity, came to declare his will to the children of men. 5. Union in and with Christ is a great privilege, a spiritual blessing, and the foundation of many others. *He gathers together in one and all things in Christ, v.* 10. All the lines of divine revelation meet in Christ; all religion centres in him. 6. The eternal inheritance is the great blessing with which we are blessed in Christ: *In whom also we have obtained an inheritance, v.* 11. Heaven is the inheritance, the happiness of which is a sufficient portion for a soul: it is conveyed in the way of an inheritance, being the gift of a Father to his children. *If children, then heirs.* 7. The seal and earnest of the Spirit are of the number of these blessings. We are said to be *sealed with that Holy Spirit of promise, v.* 13. The earnest is part of payment, and it secures the full sum: so is the gift of the Holy Ghost; all his influences and operations, both as a sanctifier and a comforter, are heaven begun, glory in the seed and bud.

THE LORDSHIP OF CHRIST
(vv. 15–23)

We have come to the last part of this chapter, which consists of Paul's earnest prayer to God in behalf of these Ephesians. The graces and comforts of the Spirit are communicated to the soul by the enlightening of the understanding. In this way he gains and keeps possession. Observe,

I. Whence this knowledge must come from *the God of our Lord Jesus Christ, v.* 17. The Lord *is a God of knowledge,* and there is no sound saving knowledge but what comes from him. This knowledge is first in the understanding. He prays that *the eyes of their understanding may be enlightened, v.* 18.

II. What it is that he more particularly desires they should grow in the knowledge of. 1. *The hope of his calling, v.* 18. Christianity is our calling. God has called us to it, and on that account it is said to be his calling. There is a hope in this calling; for those who deal with God deal upon trust. And it is a desirable thing to know what this hope of our calling is. 2. *The riches of the glory of his inheritance in the saints.* Besides the heavenly inheritance prepared for the saints, there is a present inheritance in the saints; for grace is glory begun, and holiness is happiness in the bud. 3. *The exceeding greatness of God's power towards those who believe, v.* 19. The practical belief of the all-sufficiency of God, and of the omnipotence of divine grace, is absolutely necessary to a close and steady walking with him. Many understand the apostle here as speaking of that *exceeding greatness of power* which God will exert for raising the bodies of believers to eternal life, even the same *mighty power which he wrought in Christ when he raised him,* &c. And how desirable a thing must it be to become at length acquainted with that power, by being raised out of the grave thereby unto eternal life!

Having said something of Christ and his resurrection, the apostle digresses a little from the subject he is upon to make some further honourable mention of the Lord Jesus and his exaltation. He sits at the Father's *right hand in the heavenly places,* &c. *vv.* 20, 21. Jesus Christ is advanced above all, and he is set in authority over all, they being made subject to him. All the glory of the upper world, and all the powers of both worlds, are entirely devoted to him. The Father *hath put all things under his feet* (*v.* 22), according to the promise, Ps. cx. 1. Jesus Christ filleth all in all; he supplies all defects in all his members, filling them with his Spirit, and even with *the fulness of God*, ch. iii. 19. And yet the church is said to be his fulness, because Christ as Mediator would not be complete if he had not a church. How could he be a king if he had not a kingdom? This therefore comes in to the honour of Christ, *as Mediator, that the church is his fulness.*

CHAPTER TWO
LIFE FROM DEATH (*vv.* 1–3)

The miserable condition of the Ephesians by nature is here in part described. Observe, 1. Unregenerate souls are dead in trespasses and sins. Sin is the death of the soul. 2. A state of sin is a state of conformity to this world, *v.* 2. 3. We are by nature bond-slaves to sin and Satan. Those who walk in trespasses and sins, and according to the course of this world, walk *according to the prince of the power of the air*. The devil, or the prince of devils, is thus described. See Matt. xii. 24, 26. 4. We are by nature drudges to the flesh, and to our corrupt affections, *v.* 3. 5. We are *by nature the children of wrath, even as others*. All men, being naturally children of disobedience, are also by nature children of wrath: God is angry with the wicked every day.

SAVED BY GRACE (*vv.* 4–10)

Here the apostle begins his account of the glorious change that was wrought in them by converting grace, where observe,

I. By whom, and in what manner, it was brought about and effected. 1. Negatively: *Not of yourselves, v.* 8. Our faith, our conversion, and our eternal salvation, are not the mere product of any natural abilities, nor of any merit of our own. 2. Positively: *But God, who is rich in mercy*, &c. *v.* 4. God himself is the author of this great and happy change, and his great love is the spring and fontal cause of it; hence he resolved to show mercy. And then *by grace you are saved* (*v.* 5), and *by grace are you saved through faith — it is the gift of* God, *v.* 8. The grace that saves them is the free undeserved goodness and favour of God; and he saves them, not *by the works of the law*, but through faith in Christ Jesus, by means of which they come to partake of the great blessings of the gospel. Observe,

II. Wherein this change consists, in several particulars, answering to the misery of our natural state, some of which are enumerated in this section, and others are mentioned below. 1. We who were dead are quickened (*v.* 5), we are saved from the death of sin and have a principle of spiritual life implanted in us. 2. We who were buried are raised up, *v.* 6. When he raised Christ from the dead, he did in effect raise up all believers together with him, he being their common head.

III. Observe what is the great

design and aim of God in producing and effecting this change: And this, 1. With respect to others: *That in the ages to come he might show, &c.* (*v.* 7), that he might give a specimen and proof of his great goodness and mercy, for the encouragement of sinners in future time. 2. With respect to the regenerated sinners themselves: *For we are his workmanship, created in Christ Jesus unto good works, &c. v.* 10. It appears that all is of grace, because all our spiritual advantages are from God. *We are his workmanship;* he means in respect of the new creation; not only as men, but as saints. The new man is a new creature; and God is its Creator. *Unto good works, &c.* The apostle having before ascribed this change to divine grace in exclusion of works, lest he should seem thereby to discourage good works, he here observes that though the change is to be ascribed to nothing of that nature (*for we are the workmanship of God*), yet God, in his new creation, has designed and prepared us for good works: *Created unto good works,* with a design that we should be fruitful in them.

ALIENS WELCOMED
(*vv.* 11–13)

In these verses the apostle proceeds in his account of the miserable condition of these Ephesians by nature. "*At that time,* while you were Gentiles, and in an unconverted state, you were," 1. "In a Christless condition, without the knowledge of the Messiah, and without any saving interest in him or relation to him." 2. *Aliens from the commonwealth of Israel;* they

did not belong to Christ's church, and had no communion with it, that being confined to the Israelitish nation. 3. *They are strangers from the covenants of promise.* The covenant of grace has ever been the same for substance, though, having undergone various additions and improvements in the several ages of the church, it is called covenants; and the covenants of promise, because it is made up of promises, and particularly contains the great promise of the Messiah, and of eternal life through him. Now the Ephesians, in their gentilism, were strangers to this covenant, having never had any information nor overture of it; and all unregenerate sinners are strangers to it, as they have no interest in it. 4. They had no hope, that is, beyond this life— no well-grounded hope in God, no hope of spiritual and eternal blessings.

The apostle proceeds (*v.* 13) further to illustrate the happy change that was made in their state: *But now, in Christ Jesus, you who sometimes were far off, &c.* They were far off from Christ, from his church, from the promises, from the Christian hope, and from God himself. They were brought home to God, received into the church, taken into the covenant, and possessed of all other privileges consequent upon these.

CHRIST THE RECONCILER
(*vv.* 14–22)

Between the Jews and the Gentiles there had been a great enmity; so there is between God and every unregenerate man. Now Jesus Christ is our peace, *v.* 14. He made peace by the sacrifice of himself; and came to reconcile, 1. Jews and Gentiles to each other. He *made both one*, by reconciling these two divisions of men, who were wont to malign, to hate, and to reproach each other before. He *broke down the middle wall of partition*, the ceremonial law, that made the great feud, and was the badge of the Jews' peculiarity, called *the partition-wall* by way of allusion to the partition in the temple, which separated the court of the Gentiles from that into which the Jews only had liberty to enter. Thus *he abolished in his flesh the enmity*, v. 15. 2. There is an enmity between God and sinners, whether Jews or Gentiles; and Christ came to slay that enmity, and to reconcile them both to God, v. 16. Sin breeds a quarrel between God and men. Christ came to take up the quarrel, and to bring it to an end, by reconciling both Jew and Gentile, now collected and gathered into one body, to a provoked and an offended God: and this *by the cross*, or by the sacrifice of himself upon the cross, *having slain the enmity thereby*. He, being slain or sacrificed, slew the enmity that there was between God and poor sinners. Now the effect of this peace is the free access which both Jews and Gentiles have unto God (v. 18): *For through him*, in his name and by virtue of his mediation, *we both have access* or admission into the presence of God, who has become the common reconciled Father of both. The Ephesians, upon their conversion, having such an access to God, as well as the Jews, and by the same Spirit, the apostle tells

them, *Now therefore you are no more strangers and foreigners*, v. 19. In v. 20 the church is compared to a building. The apostles and prophets are *the foundation* of that building. They may be so called in a secondary sense, Christ himself being the primary foundation; but we are rather to understand it of the doctrine delivered by the prophets of the Old Testament and the apostles of the New. It follows, *Jesus Christ himself being the chief corner-stone*. In him both Jews and Gentiles meet, and constitute one church; and Christ supports the building by his strength: *In whom all the building, fitly framed together*, &c. v. 21.

CHAPTER THREE

THE WISDOM OF GOD
(vv. 1–12)

Here we have the account which Paul gives the Ephesians concerning himself, as he was appointed by God the apostle of the Gentiles.

I. We may observe that he acquaints them with the tribulations and sufferings which he endured in the discharge of that office, v. 1.

II. The apostle informs them of God's appointing him to the office, and eminently fitting and qualifying him for it, by a special revelation that he made unto him. 1. God appointed him to the office: *If you have heard of the dispensation of the grace of God, which is given me to you-ward*, v. 2. 2. As God appointed him to the office, so he eminently qualified him for it, by a special revelation that he made unto him. He makes mention both of the mystery that was revealed and of the revelation of it. (1) The mystery revealed is *that the Gentiles should be fellow-heirs, and of the same body, and partakers of his promise in Christ, by the gospel* (v. 6). (2) Of the revelation of this truth he speaks, *vv.* 3–5. Here we may observe that the coalition of Jews and Gentiles in the gospel church was a mystery, a great mystery, what was designed in the counsel of God before all worlds, but what could not be fully understood for many ages, till the accomplishment expounded the prophecies of it. And it is called the mystery of Christ because it was revealed by him (Gal. i. 12), and because it relates so very much to him.

III. The apostle informs them how he was employed in this office, and that with respect to the Gentiles, and to all men.

1. With respect to the Gentiles, he *preached* to them *the unsearchable riches of Christ, v.* 8. Observe, in this verse, how humbly he speaks of himself, and how highly he speaks of Jesus Christ. (1) How humbly he speaks of himself: *I am less than the least of all saints.* (2) How highly he speaks of Jesus Christ: *The unsearchable riches of Christ.* And they are unsearchable riches, which we cannot find the bottom of, which human sagacity could never have discovered, and men could no otherwise attain to the knowledge of them but by revelation.

2. With respect to all men, *v.* 9. His business and employment were *to make all men see* (to publish and make known to the whole world) *what is the fellowship of the mystery* (that the Gentiles who have hitherto been strangers to the church, shall be admitted into communion with it) *which from the beginning of the world hath been hid in God* (kept secret in his purpose), *who created all things by Jesus Christ.* And this is *according to the eternal purpose which he purposed in Christ Jesus our Lord, v.* 11: the whole of what he has done in the great affair of man's redemption being in pursuance of his eternal decree about that matter. The apostle, having mentioned our Lord Jesus Christ, subjoins concerning him, *In whom we have boldness and access with confidence by the faith of him* (v. 12). We may come with humble boldness to hear from God, knowing that the terror of the curse is done away; and we may expect to hear from him good words and comfortable. We may have access with confidence to speak to God, knowing that we have such a Mediator between God and us, and such an Advocate with the Father.

THE LOVE OF CHRIST
(*vv.* 14–21)

We now come to the second part of this chapter, which contains Paul's devout and affectionate prayer to God for his beloved Ephesians. Observe,

I. To whom he prays—to God, as *the Father of our Lord Jesus Christ*, of which see *ch.* i. 3.

II. His outward posture in prayer, which was humble and reverent: *I bow my knees.*

III. What the apostle asks of God for these his friends—spiritual blessings, which are the best blessings, and the most earnestly to be sought and prayed for by every one of us, both for ourselves and for our friends. 1. Spiritual strength for the work and duty to which they were called, and in which they were employed. 2. The indwelling of Christ in their hearts, *v.* 17. Christ is said to dwell in his people, as he is always present with them by his gracious influences and operations. 3. The fixing of pious and devout affections in the soul: *That you being rooted and grounded in love,* stedfastly fixed in your love to God, the Father of our Lord Jesus Christ, and to all the saints, the beloved of our Lord Jesus Christ. In order to do this he prays, 4. For their experimental acquaintance with the love of Jesus Christ. The more intimate acquaintance we have with Christ's love to us, the more our love will be drawn out to him, and to those who are his, for his sake. 5. He prays that they may *be filled with all the fulness of God.* We are not to understand it of his fulness as God in himself, but of his fulness as a God in covenant with us, as a God to his people: such a fulness as God is ready to bestow, who is willing to fill them all to the utmost of their capacity, and that with all those gifts and graces which he sees they need.

The apostle closes the chapter with a doxology, *vv.* 20, 21. It is proper to conclude our prayers with praises.

CHAPTER FOUR

EXHORTATIONS (*vv.* 1–16)

This is a general exhortation to walk as becomes our Christian profession. We have here the petition of a poor prisoner, one of Christ's prisoners: "*I therefore, the prisoner of the Lord, beseech you,* &c." Observe, Christians ought to accommodate themselves to the gospel by which they are called, and to the glory to which they are called; both are their vocation.

There follows an exhortation to mutual love, unity, and concord, with the proper means and motives to promote them. Observe,

I. The means of unity: *Lowliness and meekness, long-suffering, and forbearing one another in love, v.* 2. By lowliness we are to understand humility, entertaining mean thoughts of ourselves, which is opposed to pride. By *meekness,* that excellent disposition of soul which makes men unwilling to provoke others, and not easily to be provoked or offended with their infirmities; and it is opposed to angry resentments and peevishness. *Long-suffering* implies a patient bearing of injuries, without seeking revenge. *Forbearing one another in love* signifies bearing their infirmities out of a principle of love, and so as not to cease to love them on the account of these.

II. The nature of that unity which the apostle prescribes: it is *the unity of the Spirit, v.* 3. This unity of heart and affection may be said to be of the Spirit of God; it is wrought by him, and is one of the fruits of the Spirit. This we should endeavour to keep. *Endeavouring* is a gospel word. We must do our utmost.

III. The motives proper to promote this Christian unity and concord. The apostle urges several, to persuade us thereto.

1. Consider how many unities there are that are the joy and glory of our Christian profession. There should be one heart; for *there is one body, and one Spirit*, v. 4. Two hearts in one body would be monstrous. *Even as you are called in one hope of your calling.* Hope is here put for its object, the thing hoped for, the heavenly inheritance, to the hope of which we are called. All Christians are called to the same hope of eternal life. There is one Christ that they all hope in, and one heaven that they are all hoping for; and therefore they should be of one heart. *One Lord* (*v.* 5), that is, Christ, the head of the church, to whom, by God's appointment, all Christians are immediately subject. *One faith*, that is, the gospel, containing the doctrine of the Christian faith. *One baptism*, by which we profess our faith, being baptized in the name of the Father, Son, and Holy Ghost; and so the same sacramental covenant, whereby we engage ourselves to the Lord Christ. *One God and Father of all*, v. 6. One God, who owns all the true members of the church for his children; for he is the Father of all such by special relation, as he is the Father of all men by creation.

2. Consider the variety of gifts that Christ has bestowed among Christians: *But unto every one of us is given grace according to the measure of the gift of Christ.* David prophesied of the ascension of Christ; and the apostle descants upon it here, and in the three following verses. *When he ascended up on high.* Christ, when he ascended into heaven, as a triumphant conqueror, *led captivity captive.* It is a phrase used in the Old Testament to signify a conquest over enemies, especially over such as formerly had led others captive; see Judges v. 12. *And he gave gifts unto men*: in the psalm it is, *He received gifts for men.* He received for them, that he might give to them, a large measure of gifts and graces; particularly, he enriched his disciples with the gift of the Holy Ghost. He descended to the earth in his incarnation. He descended into the earth in his burial, *that he might fill all things*, all the members of his church, with gifts and graces suitable to their several conditions and stations. Observe, Our Lord humbled himself first, and then he was exalted. *He gave some apostles*, &c. *v.* 11. The gift of the ministry is the fruit of Christ's ascension. And ministers have their various gifts, which are all given them by the Lord Jesus. The officers which Christ gave to his church were of two sorts—*extraordinary* ones advanced to a higher office in the church: such were *apostles*, *prophets*, and *evangelists*. The apostles were chief. The prophets seem to have been such as expounded the writings of the Old Testament, and foretold things to come. The evangelists were ordained persons (2 Tim. i. 6) whom the apostles took for their companions in travel (Gal. ii. 1), and sent them out to settle and establish such churches as the apostles themselves had planted (Acts xix. 22), and, not being fixed to any particular place, they were to continue till recalled, 2 Tim. iv. 9.

and then there are *ordinary* ministers, employed in a lower and narrower sphere; as *pastors* and *teachers.* Some take these two names to signify one office, implying the duties of ruling and teaching belonging to it. We see here that it is Christ's prerogative to appoint what officers and offices he pleases in his church.

3. The gifts of Christ were intended for the good of his church, and in order to advance his kingdom and interest among men. All are *for the perfecting of the saints* (*v.* 12); that is, according to the import of the original, to bring into an orderly spiritual state and frame those who had been as it were dislocated and disjointed by sin, and then to strengthen, confirm, and advance them therein, that so each, in his proper place and function, might contribute to the good of the whole. All are designed to prepare us for heaven: *Till we all come*, &c., *v.* 13. *Unto a perfect man*, to our full growth of gifts and graces, free from those childish infirmities that we are subject to in the present world. — *Unto the measure of the stature of the fulness of Christ*, so as to be Christians of a full maturity and ripeness in all the graces derived from Christ's fulness. The apostle further shows, in the following verses, what was God's design in his sacred institutions, and what effect they ought to have upon us. As, (1) *That we henceforth be no more children*, &c. (*v.* 14); that is, that we may be no longer children in knowledge, weak in the faith, and inconstant in our judgments, easily yielding to every temptation. (2) That we should *speak the truth in*

love (*v.* 15), or follow the truth in love, or be sincere in love to our fellow-christians. (3) That we should *grow up into Christ in all things*. Into Christ, so as to be more deeply rooted in him. In all things; in knowledge, love, faith, and all the parts of the new man. We should grow up towards maturity, which is opposed to being children. (4) We should be assisting and helpful one to another, as members of the same body, *v.* 16. Observe, Particular Christians receive their gifts and graces from Christ for the sake and benefit of the whole body. *Unto the edifying of itself in love.* We may understand this two ways: Either that all the members of the church may attain to a greater measure of love to Christ and to one another; or that they are moved to act in the manner mentioned from love to Christ and to one another.

PURITY AND HOLINESS
(*vv.* 17–32)

The apostle having gone through his exhortation to mutual love, unity, and concord, in the foregoing verses, there follows in these an exhortation to Christian purity and holiness of heart and life, and that both more general (*vv.* 17–24) and in several particular instances, *vv.* 25–32. Consider,

I. The more general exhortation to purity and holiness of heart and life.

II. The apostle proceeds to some things more particular. 1. Take heed of lying, and be ever careful to speak the truth (*v.* 25). 2. "Take heed of anger and ungoverned passions. *Be you angry, and sin not*," *v.* 26. This is borrowed from the LXX. translation of Ps. iv. 4, where we render it, *Stand in awe, and sin not*. Here is an easy concession; for as such we should consider it, rather than as a command. 3. We are here warned against the sin of stealing, the breach of the eighth commandment, and advised to honest industry and to beneficence: *Let him that stole steal no more, v.* 28. It is a caution against all manner of wrong-doing, by force or fraud. 4. We are here warned against corrupt communication; and directed to that which is useful and edifying, *v.* 29. The great use of speech is to edify those with whom we converse. 5. Here is another caution against wrath and anger, with further advice to mutual love and kindly dispositions towards each other, *vv.* 31, 32. By *bitterness*, *wrath*, and *anger*, are meant violent inward resentment and displeasure against others: and, by *clamour*, big words, loud threatenings, and other intemperate speeches, by which bitterness, wrath, and anger, vent themselves. The contrary to all this follows: *Be you kind one to another*. This implies the principle of love in the heart, and the outward expression of it, in an affable, humble, courteous behaviour. *Tender-hearted*; that is, merciful, and having a tender sense of the distresses and sufferings of others, so as to be quickly moved to compassion and pity. *Forgiving one another*. Occasions of difference will happen among Christ's disciples; and therefore they must be placable, and ready to forgive, therein resembling God himself, who *for Christ's sake hath*

forgiven them, and that more than they can forgive one another.

In the midst of these exhortations and cautions the apostle interposes that general one, *And grieve not the Holy Spirit of God, v.* 30. By looking to what precedes, and to what follows, we may see what it is that grieves the Spirit of God. It is a good reason why we should not grieve him that *by him we are sealed unto the day of redemption*. There is to be a day of redemption; the body is to be redeemed from the power of the grave at the resurrection-day, and then God's people will be delivered from all the effects of sin, as well as from all sin and misery, which they are not till rescued out of the grave: and then their full and complete happiness commences.

CHAPTER FIVE

CHILDREN OF LIGHT
(*vv.* 1–20)

Here we have the exhortation to mutual love, or to Christian charity. And those only are God's dear children who imitate him in these. It follows, *And walk in love, v.* 2. This godlike grace should conduct and influence our whole conversation, which is meant by walking in it. *As Christ also hath loved us.* Here the apostle directs us to the example of Christ, whom Christians are obliged to imitate, and in whom we have an instance of the most free and generous love that ever was, that great love wherewith he hath loved us.

I. To fortify us against the sins of uncleanness, &c., the apostle urges

319

several arguments, and prescribes several remedies, in what follows,

1. He urges several arguments, As, (1) Consider that these are sins which shut persons out of heaven: *For this you know*, &c., *v.* 5. They knew it, being informed of it by the Christian religion. (2) These sins bring the wrath of God upon those who are guilty of them: "*Let no man deceive you with vain words*, &c.," *v.* 6. *Be not you therefore partakers with them*, *v.* 7. "Do not partake with them in their sins, that you may not share in their punishment." We partake with other men in their sins, not only when we live in the same sinful manner that they do, and consent and comply with their temptations and solicitations to sin, but when we encourage them in their sins, prompt them to sin, and do not prevent and hinder them, as far as it may be in our power to do so. (3) Consider what obligations Christians are under to live at another rate than such sinners do: *For you were sometimes darkness, but now*, &c., *v.* 8. Sinners, like men in the dark, are going they know not whither, and doing they know not what. But the grace of God had produced a mighty change in their souls: *Now are you light in the Lord*, savingly enlightened by the word and the Spirit of God. *Now*, upon your believing in Christ, and your receiving the gospel. *Walk as children of light*.

2. The apostle prescribes some remedies against them. As, (1) If we would not be entangled by the lusts of the flesh, we must bring forth *the fruits of the Spirit*, *v.* 9. (2) We must have no fellowship with sin nor sinners, *v.* 11. Sinful works are works of darkness: they come from the darkness of ignorance, they seek the darkness of concealment, and they lead to the darkness of hell. We must therefore *have no fellowship* with these unfruitful works; as we must not practise them ourselves, so we must not countenance others in the practice of them. But, rather than have fellowship with them, we must *reprove them*, implying that if we do not reprove the sins of others we have fellowship with them. One reason given is, *For it is a shame even to speak of those things*, &c., *v.* 12. They are so filthy and abominable that it is a shame to mention them, except in a way of reproof, much more must it be a shame to have any fellowship with them. Christ, by his ministers, who preach the everlasting gospel, is continually calling upon sinners to this effect: *Awake, thou that sleepest, and arise from the dead*. When God calls upon them to awake, and to arise, his meaning is that they would break off their sins by repentance, and enter on a course of holy obedience, and he encourages them to essay and do their utmost that way, by that gracious promise, *And Christ shall give thee light*; or *Christ shall enlighten thee*, or *shall shine upon thee*. (3) Another remedy against sin is circumspection, care, or caution (*v.* 15): *See then*, &c. This may be understood either with respect to what immediately precedes, or else we have here another remedy or rather preservative from the before-mentioned sins; and this I take to be the design of the apostle, it being im-

possible to maintain purity and holiness of heart and life without great circumspection and care. It follows, *redeeming the time* (v. 16), literally, *buying the opportunity*. It is a metaphor taken from merchants and traders who diligently observe and improve the seasons for merchandise and trade. It is a great part of Christian wisdom to redeem the time. The reason given is *because the days are evil*, either by reason of the wickedness of those who dwell in them, or rather "as they are troublesome and dangerous times to you who live in them."

II. In the three following verses the apostle warns against some other particular sins, and urges some other duties. 1. He warns against the sin of drunkenness: *And be not drunk with wine*, v. 18. 2. Instead of being filled with wine, he exhorts them to *be filled with the Spirit*. Those who are full of drink are not likely to be full of the Spirit; and therefore this duty is opposed to the former sin. The meaning of the exhortation is that men should labour for a plentiful measure of the graces of the Spirit, that would fill their souls with great joy, strength, and courage, which things sensual men expect their wine should inspire them with. 3. To sing unto the Lord, v. 19. Drunkards are wont to sing obscene and profane songs. The heathens, in their Bacchanalia, used to sing hymns to Bacchus, whom they called the god of wine. Thus they expressed their joy; but the joy of Christians should express itself in songs of praise to their God. In these they should *speak to themselves* in their assemblies and meetings together, for mutual edification. 4. Thanksgiving is another duty that the apostle exhorts to, v. 20. We are appointed to sing psalms, &c., for the expression of our thankfulness to God; but, though we are not always singing, we should be *always giving thanks*; that is, we should never want a disposition for this duty, as we never want matter for it.

HUSBANDS AND WIVES
(vv. 21–33)

Here the apostle begins his exhortation to the discharge of relative duties. As a general foundation for these duties, he lays down that rule v. 21. There is a mutual submission that Christians owe one to another, condescending to bear one another's burdens: not advancing themselves above others, nor domineering over one another and giving laws to one another.

I. The duty prescribed to wives is submission to their husbands in the Lord (v. 22), which submission includes the honouring and obeying of them, and that from a principle of love to them. They must do this in compliance with God's authority, who has commanded it, which is doing it *as unto the Lord*. There is a resemblance of Christ's authority over the church in that superiority and headship which God has appointed to the husband. The apostle adds, *and he is the Saviour of the body*. Christ's authority is exercised over the church for the saving of her from evil, and the supplying of her with every thing good for her. In like manner should the husband be employed for the protection and comfort of his spouse; and therefore she should the more cheerfully submit herself unto him. So it follows, *Therefore as the church is subject unto Christ* (v. 24), with cheerfulness, with fidelity, with humility, *so let the wives be to their own husbands in every thing* — in every thing to which their authority justly extends itself, in every thing lawful and consistent with duty to God.

II. The duty of husbands (on the other hand), is to love their wives (v. 25); for without this they would abuse their superiority and headship, and, wherever this prevails as it ought to do, it will infer the other duties of the relation, it being a special and peculiar affection that is required in her behalf. The love of Christ to the church is proposed as an example of this, which love of his is a sincere, a pure, an ardent, and a constant affection, and that notwithstanding the imperfections and failures that she is guilty of. The greatness of his love to the church appeared in his giving himself unto the death for it. *For this cause* (because they are one, as Christ and his church are one) *shall a man leave his father and mother*; the apostle refers to the words of Adam, when Eve was given to him for a meet help, Gen. ii. 24. *And they two shall be one flesh*, that is, by virtue of the matrimonial bond. *This is a great mystery*, v. 32. Those words of Adam, just mentioned by the apostle, are spoken literally of marriage; but they have also a hidden mystical sense in them, relating to the union between Christ and his church, of which the conjugal union between Adam and the mother of us all was a type: though not instituted or appointed by God to signify this, yet it was a kind of natural type, as having a resemblance to it: *I speak concerning Christ and the church*.

After this, the apostle concludes this part of his discourse with a brief summary of the duty of husbands and wives, v. 33. "*Nevertheless* (though there be such a secret mystical sense, yet the plain literal sense concerns you) *let every one of you in particular so love his wife even as himself*, with such a sincere, peculiar, singular, and prevailing affection as that is which he bears to himself. *And the wife see that she reverence her husband*." Reverence consists of love and esteem, which produce a care to please, and of fear, which awakens a caution lest just offence be given. That the wife thus reverence her husband is the will of God and the law of the relation.

CHAPTER SIX

DUTIES OF CHILDREN
(vv. 1–9)

Here we have further directions concerning relative duties, in which the apostle is very particular.

I. The great duty of children is to obey their parents (v. 1), parents being the instruments of their being, God and nature having given them an authority to command, in subserviency to God.

II. The duty of parents: *And you fathers*, v. 4. Or, you parents, 1. "*Do not provoke your children to wrath*. Though God has given you power, you must not abuse that power, remembering that your children are, in a particular manner, pieces of yourselves, and therefore ought to be governed with great tenderness and love." 2. "*Bring them up* well, *in the nurture and admonition of the Lord*, in the discipline of proper and of compassionate correction, and in the knowledge of that duty which God requires of them and by which they may become better acquainted with him."

III. The duty of servants. This also is summed up in one word, which is, *obedience*. He is largest on this article, as knowing there was the greatest need of it. These servants were generally slaves. Civil servitude is not inconsistent with Christian liberty. Those may be the Lord's freemen who are slaves to men.

IV. The duty of masters: "*And you masters, do the same things unto them* (v. 9); that is, act after the same manner. Be just to them, as you expect they should be to you: show the like good-will and concern for them, and be careful herein to approve yourselves to God."

THE ARMOUR OF GOD
(vv. 10–18)

Here is a general exhortation to constancy in our Christian course, and to courage in our Christian warfare.

I. They must see that they be stout-hearted. This is prescribed here: *Be strong in the Lord*, &c. Be strong in the Lord, either in his cause and for his sake or rather in his strength. We have no sufficient strength of our own.

II. They must be well armed:

"*Put on the whole armour of God*" (v. 11). This the apostle enlarges upon here, and shows,

1. What our danger is, and what need we have to put on this whole armour, considering what sort of enemies we have to deal with—the devil and all the powers of darkness: *For we wrestle not against flesh and blood*, &c. v. 12. (1) We have to do with a subtle enemy, an enemy who uses wiles and stratagems, as v. 11. (2) He is a powerful enemy: *Principalities*, and *powers*, and *rulers*. They are numerous, they are vigorous; and rule in those heathen nations which are yet in darkness. (3) They are spiritual enemies: *Spiritual wickedness in high places*, or wicked spirits, as some translate it.

2. What our duty is: to take and put on the whole armour of God, and then to stand our ground, and withstand our enemies.

(1) We must *withstand*, v. 13. We must not yield to the devil's allurements and assaults, but oppose them.

(2) We must stand our ground: *And, having done all, to stand*. We must resolve, by God's grace, not to yield to Satan. Resist him, and he will flee. If we give back, he will get ground.

(3) We must stand armed; and this is here most enlarged upon. Here is a Christian in complete armour: and the armour is divine. [1] Truth or sincerity is our girdle, v. 14. God desires truth, that is, sincerity, in the inward parts. [2] Righteousness must be our breast-plate. The breast-plate secures the vitals, shelters the heart. The righteousness of Christ imput-

ed to us is our breast-plate against the arrows of divine wrath. [3] Resolution must be as the greaves to our legs: *And their feet shod with the preparation of the gospel of peace, v.* 15. *The preparation of the gospel of peace* signifies a prepared and resolved frame of heart, to adhere to the gospel and abide by it, which will enable us to walk with a steady pace in the way of religion, notwithstanding the difficulties and dangers that may be in it. [4] Faith must be our shield: *Above all,* or chiefly, *taking the shield of faith, v.* 16. This is more necessary than any of them. Faith is all in all to us in an hour of temptation. The devil is here called *the wicked one.* He is wicked himself, and he endeavours to make us wicked. His temptations are called *darts,* because of their swift and undiscerned flight, and the deep wounds that they give to the soul; *fiery darts,* by way of allusion to the poisonous darts which were wont to inflame the parts which were wounded with them, and therefore were so called, as the serpents with poisonous stings are called fiery serpents. Faith is the shield with which we must quench these fiery darts, wherein we should receive them, and so render them ineffectual, that they may not hit us, or at least that they may not hurt us. [5] Salvation must be our helmet (*v.* 17); that is, *hope,* which has salvation for its object; so 1 Thess. v. 8. The helmet secures the head. A good hope of salvation, well founded and well built, will both purify the soul and keep it from being defiled by Satan, and it will comfort the soul and keep it from being troubled

and tormented by Satan. [6] The word of God is the sword of the Spirit. The sword is a very necessary and useful part of a soldier's furniture. It is called *the sword of the Spirit,* because it is of the Spirit's inditing and he renders it efficacious and powerful, and *sharper than a two-edged sword.* [7] Prayer must buckle on all the other parts of our Christian armour, *v.* 18. We must join prayer with all these graces, for our defence against these spiritual enemies, imploring help and assistance of God, as the case requires: and we must pray always. And we must pray *with supplication,* not for ourselves only, but *for all saints*; for we are members one of another.

CONCLUSION (*vv.* 19–24)

Here, I. He desires their prayers for him, *v.* 19. Having mentioned *supplication for all saints,* he puts himself into the number. We must pray for all saints, and particularly for God's faithful ministers. Observe what it is he would have them pray for in his behalf: "*That utterance may be given unto me*; that I may be enlarged from my present restraints, and so have liberty to propagate the faith of Christ; that I may have ability to express myself in a suitable and becoming manner; *and that I may open my mouth boldly,* that is, that I may deliver the whole counsel of God, without any base fear, shame, or partiality." *To make known the mystery of the gospel.* The whole gospel was a mystery, till made known by divine revelation; and it is the work of Christ's ministers to publish it. Having thus desired their prayers,

II. He recommends Tychicus unto them, *vv.* 21, 22. He was a sincere Christian, and so a brother in Christ: he was a faithful minister in the work of Christ, and he was very dear to Paul, which makes Paul's love to these Christian Ephesians the more observable, in that he should now part with so

good and dear a friend for their sakes.

III. He concludes with his good wishes and prayers for them, and not for them only, but for all the brethren, *vv.* 23, 24. His usual benediction was, *Grace and peace*; here it is, *Peace be to the brethren, and love with faith.*

THE EPISTLE OF ST. PAUL TO THE

PHILIPPIANS

CHAPTER ONE
GREETINGS AND THANKS
(vv. 1–11)

We have here the inscription and benediction. Observe,

I. The persons writing the epistle —*Paul and Timothy*.

II. The persons to whom it is directed. 1. To *all the saints in Christ who are at Philippi*. 2. It is directed to the ministers, or church-officers—*with the bishops and deacons*, the bishops or elders, in the first place, whose office it was to teach and rule, and the deacons, or overseers of the poor, who took care of the outward business of the house of God.

III. Here is the apostolical benediction: *Grace be unto you, and peace, from God our Father, and from the Lord Jesus Christ, v. 2*. This is the same, almost word for word, in all the epistles.

The apostle proceeds after the inscription and benediction to thanksgiving for the saints at Philippi. He tells them what it was he thanked God for, upon their account. Observe here,

IV. Paul remembered them: he bore them much in his thoughts; and though they were out of sight, and he was at a distance from them, yet they were not out of his mind.

V. He remembered them with joy. At Philippi he was maltreated; there he was scourged and put into the stocks, and for the present saw little of the fruit of his labour; and yet he remembers Philippi with joy.

VI. He remembered them in prayer: *Always in every prayer of mine for you all, v. 4*. The best remembrance of our friends is to remember them at the throne of grace.

VII. He thanked God upon every joyful remembrance of them.

VIII. As in our prayers, so in our thanksgiving, we must eye God as our God: *I thank my God*. But what is the matter of this thanksgiving? 1. He gives thanks to God for the comfort he had in them: for *your fellowship in the gospel, from the first day until now, v. 5*. 2. For the confidence he had concerning them (*v. 6*): *Being confident of this very thing*, &c. *That he who has begun a good work in you will perform it unto the day of Jesus Christ*. He who hath planted Christianity in the world will preserve it as long as the world stands. Christ will have a church till the mystery of God shall be finished and the mystical body completed.

IX. The apostle expresses the ardent affection he had for them, and his concern for their spiritual welfare: *I have you in my heart, v. 7*.

326

He loved them as his own soul, and they lay near his heart. He thought much of them, and was in care about them. Having them in his heart, he longed after them; either he longed to see them, longed to hear from them, or he longed for their spiritual welfare and their increase and improvement in knowledge and grace. For this he appeals to God: *God is my record.* It was an inward disposition of mind that he expressed towards them, to the sincerity of which God only was witness, and therefore to him he appeals. "Whether you know it or not, or are sensible of it, God, who knows the heart, knows it."

X. He prayed, 1. That they might be a loving people, and that good affections might abound among them: *That your love might abound yet more and more.* He means it of their love to God, and one another, and all men. 2. That they might be a knowing and judicious people: that love might abound *in knowledge and in all judgment.* 3. That they might be a discerning people. This would be the effect of their knowledge and judgment: *That you may approve the things which are excellent* (*v.* 10). 4. That they might be an honest upright-hearted people: *That you may be sincere.* 5. That they might be an inoffensive people: that you may be *without offence until the day of Christ*; not apt to take offence; and very careful not to give offence to God or their brethren, to *live in all good conscience before God* (Acts xxiii. 1). 6. That they might be a fruitful useful people (*v.* 11): *Being filled with the fruits of righteousness,* &c.

PRISON AND PRAISE
(*vv.* 12–20)

Paul was now a prisoner at Rome; this might be a stumbling-block to those who had received the gospel by his ministry. Now to take off the offence of the cross, he expounds this dark and hard chapter of his sufferings, and makes it very easy and intelligible, and reconcilable to the wisdom and goodness of God who employed him.

I. He suffered by the sworn enemies of the gospel, who laid him in prison, and aimed at taking away his life; but they should not be stumbled at this, for good was brought out of it, and it tended to the furtherance of the gospel (*v.* 12). But how was this?

1. It alarmed those who were outside (*v.* 13): "*My bonds in Christ,* or for Christ, *are manifest in all the palace and in all other places.*"

2. It emboldened those who were within. As his enemies were startled at his sufferings, so his friends were encouraged by them. *Many of the brethren in the Lord waxing confident by my bonds, v.* 14.

II. He suffered from false friends as well as from enemies (*vv.* 15, 16): *Some preach Christ even of envy and strife. The one preach Christ of contention, not sincerely.* However, there were others who were animated by Paul's sufferings to preach Christ the more vigorously: *Some also of good will, and love.*

III. It is very affecting to see how easy he was in the midst of all: *Notwithstanding every way, whether in pretence or in truth, Christ is preached; and I therein do rejoice, yea, and I will rejoice, v.* 18. Note, The preaching of Christ is the joy of all who wish well to his kingdom among men. Two things made the apostle rejoice in the preaching of the gospel:

1. Because it tended to the salvation of the souls of men: *I know that this shall turn to my salvation, v.* 19.

2. Because it would turn to the glory of Christ, *v.* 20, where he takes occasion to mention his own entire devotedness to the service and honour of Christ.

LIVING OR DYING (*vv.* 21–26)

We have here an account of the life and death of blessed Paul: his life was Christ, and his death was gain. Observe, 1. It is the undoubted character of every good Christian that to him to live is Christ. 2. All those to whom to live is Christ to them to die *will be gain*: it is great gain, a present gain, everlasting gain. It might be thought, if death were gain to him, he would be weary of life, and impatient for death. No, says he,

I. *If I live in the flesh, this is the fruit of my labour* (*v.* 22), that is, Christ is. He reckoned his labour well bestowed, if he could be instrumental to advance the honour and interest of the kingdom of Christ in the world. Here we have him reasoning with himself upon the matter.

1. His inclination was for death (*v.* 23).

2. His judgment was rather to live awhile longer in this world, for the service of the church (*v.* 24):

Nevertheless to abide in the flesh is more needful for you.

II. *And, having this confidence, I know that I shall abide and continue with you all for your furtherance and joy of faith, v.* 25. Observe here, 1. What a great confidence Paul had in the divine Providence, that it would order all for the best to him. 2. Whatsoever is best for the church, we may be sure God will do. 3. Observe what ministers are continued for: *For our furtherance and joy of faith*, our further advancement in holiness and comfort. 4. What promotes our *faith and joy of faith* is very much for our furtherance in the way to heaven.

III. *That your rejoicing may be more abundant in Jesus Christ for me, by my coming to you again, v.* 26. They rejoiced in the hope of seeing him, and enjoying his further labours among them.

CHRISTIAN BEHAVIOUR (*vv.* 27–30)

The apostle concludes the chapter with two exhortations:

I. He exhorts them to strictness of behaviour (*v.* 27): *Only let your conversation be as becometh the gospel of Christ.* Observe, Those who profess the gospel of Christ should behave as becomes the gospel, or in a suitableness and agreeableness to it.

II. He exhorts them to courage and constancy in suffering: *And in nothing terrified by your adversaries, v.* 28. Our great care must be to keep close to our profession, and be constant to it: whatever oppositions we meet with, we must not be frightened at them, considering that the condition of the persecuted is much better and more desirable than the condition of the persecutors; for persecuting is an *evident token of perdition. For to you it is given on the behalf of Christ not only to believe, but also to suffer for his name, v.* 29. Here are two precious gifts given, and both on the behalf of Christ: 1. To believe in him. 2. To suffer for the sake of Christ is a valuable gift too: it is a great honour and a great advantage; for we may be very serviceable to the glory of God, which is the end of our creation, and encourage and confirm the faith of others.

CHAPTER TWO

THE HUMILITY OF CHRIST
(*vv.* 1–11)

The apostle proceeds in this chapter where he left off in the last, with further exhortations to Christian duties. Here we may observe,

I. The great gospel precept pressed upon us; that is, to love one another. This is the law of Christ's kingdom, the lesson of his school, the livery of his family. This he represents (*v.* 2) by being *likeminded, having the same love, being of one accord, of one mind*.

2. He proposes some means to promote it. (1) *Do nothing through strife and vain glory, v.* 3. There is no greater enemy to Christian love than pride and passion. (2) We must *esteem others in lowliness of mind better than ourselves*. (3) We must interest ourselves in the concerns of others, not in a way of curiosity and censoriousness, or as *busy-bodies in other men's matters*, but in Christian love and sympathy. A selfish spirit is destructive of Christian love.

II. Here is a gospel pattern proposed to our imitation, and that is the example of our Lord Jesus Christ: *Let this mind be in you which was also in Christ Jesus, v.* 5. Observe, Christians must be of Christ's mind. Now what was the mind of Christ? He was eminently humble, and this is what we are peculiarly to learn of him.

1. Here are the two natures of Christ: his divine nature and his human nature. (1) Here is his divine nature: *Who being in the form of God* (*v.* 6), partaking of the divine nature, as the eternal and only begotten Son of God. *He thought it no robbery to be equal with God*; did not think himself guilty of any invasion of what did not belong to him, or assuming another's right. He said, *I and my Father are one*, John x. 30. (2) His human nature: He was *made in the likeness of men*, and *found in fashion as a man*. He was really and truly man, *took part of our flesh and blood*, appeared in the nature and habit of man. And he voluntarily assumed human nature; it was his own act, and by his own consent. Herein he *emptied himself*, divested himself of the honours and glories of the upper world, and of his former appearance, to clothe himself with the rags of human nature. *He was in all things like to us*, Heb. ii. 17.

2. Here are his two estates, of humiliation and exaltation. (1) His estate of humiliation. He not only took upon him the likeness and fashion of a man, but the *form of a servant*, that is, a man of mean

estate. But the lowest step of his humiliation was his dying the death of the cross. *He became obedient to death, even the death of the cross*, a cursed, painful, and shameful death,—a death accursed by the law. Such was the condescension of the blessed Jesus. (2) His exaltation: *Wherefore God also hath highly exalted him*. His exaltation was the reward of his humiliation. Because he humbled himself, God exalted him; and he *highly exalted him*, raised him to an exceeding height. He exalted his whole person, the human nature as well as the divine; for he is spoken of as being in the form of God as well as in the fashion of man. His exaltation here is made to consist in honour and power. In honour; so *he had a name above every name*, a title of dignity above all the creatures, men and angels. And in power: *Every knee must bow to him*. The whole creation must be in subjection to him: *things in heaven, and things in earth, and things under the earth*, the inhabitants of heaven and earth, the living and the dead. *At the name of Jesus*; not at the sound of the word, but the authority of Jesus; all should pay a solemn homage. And that *every tongue should confess that Jesus Christ is Lord*—every nation and language should publicly own the universal empire of the exalted Redeemer, and that *all power in heaven and earth is given to him*, Matt. xxviii. 18.

GOD WORKING IN US
(*vv*. 12, 13)

I. He exhorts them to diligence and seriousness in the Christian course: *Work out your own salvation*. Observe, It concerns us above all things to secure the welfare of our souls: whatever becomes of other things, let us take care of our best interests. We are required to *work out our salvation*. The word signifies *working thoroughly* at a thing, and taking *true pains*. He adds, *With fear and trembling*, that is, with great care and circumspection.

II. He urges this from the consideration of their readiness always to obey the gospel. They were not merely awed by the apostle's presence, but did it even *much more in his absence*. "And because *it is God who worketh in you*, do you work out your salvation. Work, for he worketh." It should encourage us to do our utmost, because our *labour shall not be in vain*.

THE WORD OF LIFE
(*vv*. 14–18)

The apostle exhorts them in these verses to adorn their Christian profession by a suitable temper and behaviour, in several instances. 1. By a cheerful obedience to the commands of God (*v*. 14). 2. By peaceableness and love one to another. 3. By blameless behaviour towards all men (*v*. 15). *Among whom you shine as lights in the world*. Christ is the light of the world, and good Christians are lights in the world. They must shine as well as be sincere.—*Holding forth the word of life*, *v*. 16. The gospel is called the word of life because it reveals and proposes to us eternal life through Jesus Christ. *Life and immortality are brought to light by the gospel*, 2 Tim. i. 10. He would have them think his pains well bestowed, and that *he had not run in vain, nor laboured in vain.*

If I be offered, or *poured* out as the wine of the *drink-offerings,* 2 Tim. iv. 6, *I am now ready to be offered.* He could rejoice to seal his doctrine with his blood (*v.* 18): *For the same cause also do you joy and rejoice with me.* It is the will of God that good Christians should be much in rejoicing.

TWO GOOD MINISTERS
(*vv.* 19–30)

Paul takes particular notice of two good ministers; for though he was himself a great apostle, and *laboured more abundantly than they all,* yet he took all occasions to speak with respect of those who were far his inferiors.

I. He speaks of Timothy, whom he intended to send to the Philippians, that he might have an account of their state. Timothy was a man who had been tried, and had made *full proof of his ministry* (2 Tim. iv. 5), and was faithful in all that befell him. All the churches with whom he had acquaintance knew the proof of him.

II. Concerning Epaphroditus, whom he calls *his brother, and companion in labour, and fellow-soldier,* his Christian brother, to whom he bore a tender affection, — his companion in the work and sufferings of the gospel, who submitted to the same labours and hardships with himself, — and their messenger, one who was sent by them to him, probably to consult him about some affairs relating to their church, or to bring a present from them for his relief for he adds,

and *who ministered to my wants.* Observe, (1) Those who truly love Christ, and are hearty in the interests of his kingdom, will think it very well worth their while to hazard their health and life to do him service, and promote the edification of his church. (2) They were to receive him with joy, as newly recovered from sickness. It is an endearing consideration to have our mercies restored to us after danger of removal, and should make them the more valued and improved. What is given us in answer to prayer should be received with great thankfulness and joy.

A WARNING (*vv.* 1–3)

I. He exhorts them to *rejoice in the Lord* (*v.* 1), to rest satisfied in the interest they had in him and the benefit they hoped for by him.

II. He cautions them to take heed of those false teachers: *To write the same thing to you to me indeed is not grievous, but for you it is safe*; that is, the same things which I have already preached to you; as if he had said, "What has been presented to your ears shall be presented to your eyes: what I have spoken formerly shall now be written; to show that I am still of the same mind."

III. He describes true Christians, who are indeed the circumcision, the spiritual circumcision, the peculiar people of God, who are in covenant with him, as the Old-Testament Israelites were. Here are three characters: 1. They worshipped in the spirit, in opposition to the carnal ordinances of the Old

Testament, which consist in meats, and drinks, and divers washings, &c. 2. They *rejoice in Christ Jesus*, and not in the peculiar privileges of the Jewish church, or what answers to them in the Christian church—mere outward enjoyments and performances. 3. They have no *confidence in the flesh*, in those carnal ordinances and outward performances.

PAUL, THE EXAMPLE
(*vv.* 4–8)

The apostle here proposes himself for an example of trusting in Christ only, and not in his privileges as an Israelite.

I. He shows what he had to boast of as a Jew and a Pharisee. But,

II. The apostle tells us here how little account he made of these, in comparison of his interest in Christ and his expectations from him: *But what things were gain to me those have I counted loss for Christ* (*v.* 7); that is, those things which he had counted gain while he was a Pharisee, and which he had before reckoned up, *these he counted loss for Christ*. The apostle explains himself. 1. He tells us what it was that he was ambitious of and reached after: it was the knowledge of Christ Jesus his Lord, a believing experimental acquaintance with Christ as Lord; not a merely notional and speculative, but a practical and efficacious knowledge of him. 2. He shows how he had quitted his privileges as a Jew and a Pharisee. He had spoken before of *those things*, his Jewish privileges: here he speaks of *all things*, all worldly enjoyments and mere out-

ward privileges whatsoever, things of a like kind or any other kind which could stand in competition with Christ for the throne in his heart, or pretend to merit and desert. Nay, he not only counted them loss, but dung, *offals* thrown to dogs; they are not only less valuable than Christ, but in the highest degree contemptible, when they come in competition with him.

PRESSING TO THE MARK
(*vv.* 9–14)

We have heard what the apostle renounced; let us now see what he laid hold on, and resolved to cleave to, namely, Christ and heaven. He had his heart on these two great peculiarities of the Christian religion.

I. The apostle had his heart upon Christ as his righteousness. This is illustrated in several instances. 1. He desired to win Christ; and an unspeakable gainer he would reckon himself if he had but an interest in Christ and his righteousness, and if Christ became his Lord and his Saviour. 2. That he *might be found in him* (*v.* 9). There is a righteousness provided for us in Jesus Christ, and it is a complete and perfect righteousness. Observe, The apostle was as ambitious of being sanctified as he was of being justified. 4. That he might be conformable unto him, and this also is meant of his sanctification. We are then made conformable to his death when we die to sin, as Christ died for sin, when we are crucified with Christ, the flesh and affections of it mortified, and the *world is crucified to us*, and *we to the world, by virtue of the cross of*

Christ. This is our conformity to his death.

II. The apostle had his heart upon heaven as his happiness: *If by any means I might attain to the resurrection of the dead, v.* 11.

1. The happiness of heaven is here called the resurrection of the dead, because, though the souls of the faithful, when they depart, are immediately with Christ, yet their happiness will not be complete till the general resurrection of the dead at the last day.

2. This joyful resurrection the apostle pressed towards. He was willing to do any thing, or suffer any thing, that he might attain that resurrection. Observe,

(1) He looks upon himself to be in a state of imperfection and trial: *Not as though I had already attained, or were already perfect, v.* 12.

(2) What the apostle's actings were under this conviction. Considering that he had not already attained, and had not apprehended, he pressed forward (*v.* 12). He adds further (*v.* 13): *This one thing I do* (this was his great care and concern), *forgetting those things which are behind, and reaching forth to those things which are before.* There is a sinful forgetting of past sins and past mercies, which ought to be remembered for the exercise of constant repentance and thankfulness to God. But Paul forgot the things which were behind so as not to be content with present measures of grace: he was still for having more and more.

(3) The apostle's aim in these actings: *I press towards the mark, for the prize of the high calling of God in Christ Jesus,. v.* 14. He

pressed towards the mark. As he who runs a race never takes up short of the end, but is still making forwards as fast as he can, so those who have heaven in their eye must still be pressing forward to it in holy desires and hopes, and constant endeavours and preparations. Heaven is called here the mark, because it is that which every good Christian has in his eye; as the archer has his eye fixed upon the mark he designs to hit. *For the prize of the high calling.* Observe, A Christian's calling is a high calling: it is from heaven, as its original; and it is to heaven in its tendency.

TRANSFORMATION
(*vv.* 15–21)

We see here how he was minded; let us be like-minded, and set our hearts upon Christ and heaven, as he did. 1. He shows that this was the thing wherein all good Christians were agreed, to make Christ all in all, and set their hearts upon another world. 2. That this is a good reason why Christians who differ in smaller matters should yet bear with one another, because they are agreed in the main matter.

Paul then closes the chapter with warnings and exhortations.

I. He warns them against following the examples of seducers and evil teachers (*vv.* 18, 19): *Many walk, of whom I have told you often, and now tell you weeping, that they are the enemies of the cross of Christ.* Observe,

1. There are many called by Christ's name who are enemies to Christ's cross, and the design and intention of it.

2. He gives us the characters of

those who were the enemies of the cross of Christ. (1) Whose God is their belly. They minded nothing but their sensual appetites. (2) They glory in their shame. They not only sinned, but boasted of it and gloried in that of which they ought to have been ashamed. (3) They mind earthly things. Christ came by his cross to *crucify the world to us and us to the world*; and those who mind earthly things act directly contrary to the cross of Christ, and this great design of it. (4) Whose end is destruction. Their way seems pleasant, but death and hell are at the end of it.

II. He proposes himself and his brethren for an example, in opposition to these evil examples: *Brethren, be followers together of me, and mark those who walk as you have us for an example*, v. 17. Mark them out for your pattern. He explains himself (v. 20) by their regard to Christ and heaven: *For our conversation is in heaven.*

1. Because we look for the Saviour from heaven (v. 20).

2. Because at the second coming of Christ we expect to be happy and glorified there. There is a glory reserved for the bodies of the saints, which they will be instated in at the resurrection. Observe, (1) The example of this change, and that is, the glorious body of Christ; when he was transfigured upon the mount, *his face did shine as the sun, and his raiment was white as the light*, Matt. xvii. 2. (2) The power by which this change will be wrought: *According to the working whereby he is able even to subdue all things unto himself.* There is an efficacy of power, an *exceeding*

greatness of power, and the *working of mighty power*, Eph. i. 19.

CHAPTER FOUR

THE PEACE OF GOD (*vv.* 1–9)

The apostle begins the chapter with exhortations to divers Christian duties.

I. To stedfastness in our Christian profession, v. 1. Observe here,

1. The compellations are very endearing: *My brethren, dearly beloved and longed for, my joy and crown*; and again, *My dearly beloved.*

2. The exhortation itself: *So stand fast in the Lord.* Being in Christ, they must stand fast in him, be even and steady in their walk with him, and close and constant unto the end.

II. He exhorts them to unanimity and mutual assistance (*vv.* 2, 3): *I beseech Euodias and Syntyche that they be of the same mind in the Lord.* This is directed to some particular persons. Then he exhorts to mutual assistance (*v.* 3), and this exhortation he directs to particular persons: *I entreat thee also, true yoke-fellow.* Who this person was whom he calls true yoke-fellow is uncertain. Some think Epaphroditus, who is supposed to have been one of the pastors of the church of the Philippians.

III. He exhorts to holy joy and delight in God: *Rejoice in the Lord always, and again I say, Rejoice, v.* 4. All our joy must terminate in God; and our thoughts of God must be delightful thoughts.

IV. We are here exhorted to candour and gentleness, and good temper towards our brethren: "*Let* your moderation be known to all men, v. 5. The reason is, *the Lord is at hand.* The consideration of our Master's approach, and our final account, should keep us from smiting our fellow-servants, support us under present sufferings, and moderate our affections to outward good.

V. Here is a caution against disquieting perplexing care (*v.* 6): *Be careful for nothing*: the same expression with that Matt. vi: 25, *Take no thought for your life*; that is, avoid anxious care and distracting thought in the wants and difficulties of life.

VI. As a sovereign antidote against perplexing care he recommends to us constant prayer: *In every thing by prayer and supplication, with thanksgiving, let your requests be made known to God.* Not that God needs to be told either our wants or desires; for he knows them better than we can tell him: but he will know them from us, and have us show our regards and concern, express our value of the mercy and sense of our dependence on him. 4. The effect of this will be the *peace of God keeping our hearts, v.* 7. The *peace of God*, that is, the comfortable sense of our reconciliation to God and interest in his favour, and the hope of the heavenly blessedness, and enjoyment of God hereafter, *which passeth all understanding*, is a greater good than can be sufficiently valued or duly expressed.

VII. We are exhorted to get and keep a good name, a name for good things with God and good men: *Whatsoever things are true and honest (v.* 8), *just and pure,* —

agreeable to the rules of justice and righteousness in all our dealings with men, and without the impurity or mixture of sin. Whatsoever things are *lovely and of good report*, that is, amiable; that will render us beloved, and make us well spoken of, as well as well thought of, by others. *If there is any virtue, if there is any praise* — any thing really virtuous of any kind and worthy of commendation.

In these things he proposes himself to them for an example (*v.* 9). Observe, Paul's doctrine and life were of a piece.

ALL NEEDS MET (vv. 10–19)

In these verses we have the thankful grateful acknowledgment which the apostle makes of the kindness of the Philippians in sending him a present for his support, now that he was a prisoner at Rome. And here,

I. He takes occasion to acknowledge their former kindnesses to him, and to make mention of them, *vv.* 15, 16.

II. He excuses their neglect of late. It seems, for some time they had not sent to enquire after him, or sent him any present; but *now at last their care of him flourished again (v.* 10), like a tree in the spring, which seemed all the winter to be quite dead.

III. He commends their present liberality: *Notwithstanding, you have well done that you did communicate with my affliction, v.* 14.

IV. He takes care to obviate the bad use some might make of his taking so much notice of what was sent him. It did not proceed either from discontent and distrust (*v.* 11) or from covetousness and love of the world, *v.* 12. 1. It did not come from discontent, or distrust of Providence: *Not that I speak in respect of want* (*v.* 11); not in respect of any want he felt, nor of any want he feared. *For I have learned, in whatsoever state I am, therewith to be content.* He had learnt to be content; and that was the lesson he had as much need to learn as most men, considering the hardships and sufferings with which he was exercised. *I know both how to be abased and I know how to abound, v.* 12. This is a special act of grace, to accommodate ourselves to every condition of life, and carry an equal temper of mind through all the varieties of our state. But how must we learn it? *I can do all things through Christ who strengthens me, v.* 13. We have need of strength from Christ, to enable us to perform not only those duties which are purely Christian, but even those which are the fruit of moral virtue. 2. It did not come from covetousness, or an affection to worldly wealth: "*Not because I desired a gift* (*v.* 17); that is, I welcome your kindness, not because it adds to my enjoyments, but because it adds to your account." They sent him a small token, and he desired no more; he was not solicitous for a present superfluity, or a future supply.

V. The apostle assures them that God did accept, and would recompense, their kindness to him. 1. He did accept it: *It is an odour of a sweet smell, a sacrifice acceptable, well-pleasing to God.* Not a sacrifice of atonement, for none makes atonement for sin but Christ; but a sacrifice of acknowledgment, and *well-pleasing to God.* 2. He would recompense it: *But my God shall supply all your wants according to his riches in glory by Christ Jesus, v.* 19. He does as it were draw a bill upon the exchequer in heaven, and leaves it to God to make them amends for the kindness they had shown him.

CONCLUSION (*vv.* 20–23)

The apostle concludes the epistle in these verses,

1. With praises to God: *Now unto God and our Father be glory for ever and ever, Amen, v.* 20.

2. With salutations to his friends at Philippi.

3. He sends salutations from those who were at Rome. *Chiefly those who are of Cæsar's household*; the Christian converts who belonged to the emperor's court. Observe, There were saints in Cæsar's household. Though Paul was imprisoned at Rome, for preaching the gospel, by the emperor's command, yet there were some Christians in his own family.

4. The apostolical benediction, as usual.

THE EPISTLE OF ST. PAUL TO THE

COLOSSIANS

CHAPTER ONE

INTRODUCTION (vv. 1–8)

After the usual greetings, Paul proceeds to the body of the epistle, and begins with thanksgiving to God for what he had heard concerning them, though he had no personal acquaintance with them, and knew their state and character only by the reports of others.

I. He gave thanks to God for them, that they had embraced the gospel of Christ, and given proofs of their fidelity to him. Observe, 1. What he gives thanks to God for —for the graces of God in them, which were evidences of the grace of God towards them.

II. Having blessed God for these graces, he blesses God for the means of grace which they enjoyed: *Wherein you heard before in the word of the truth of the gospel.* They had heard in the word of the truth of the gospel concerning this *hope laid up for them in heaven.* Observe, 1. The gospel is the word of truth, and what we may safely venture our immortal souls upon. 2. It is a great mercy to hear this word of truth; for the great thing we learn from it is the happiness of heaven.

III. He takes this occasion to mention the minister by whom they believed (vv. 7, 8): *As you also learned of Epaphras, our dear fellow-servant, who is for you a faithful minister of Christ.* He mentions him with great respect, to engage their love to him.

HIS PRAYER (vv. 9–11)

The apostle proceeds in these verses to pray for them. Observe what it is that he begs of God for them,

I. That they might be knowing intelligent Christians: *filled with the knowledge of his will, in all wisdom and spiritual understanding.*

II. That their behaviour might be good. Good knowledge without a good life will not profit. Our understanding is then a spiritual understanding when we exemplify it in our way of living. Good words will not do without good works.

III. That they might be strengthened: *Strengthened with all might, according to his glorious power* (v. 11), fortified against the temptations of Satan and furnished for all their duty. The word of God is the means of it, by which he conveys it; and it must be fetched in by prayer. The special use of this strength was for suffering work: *That you may be strengthened unto all patience and long-suffering with joyfulness.* He prays not only that they may be *supported* under their troubles, but *strengthened* for them: the reason is there is work to be done even when we are suffering.

CHRIST IN YOU (*vv.* 12–29)

Here is a summary of the doctrine of the gospel concerning the great work of our redemption by Christ. The order and connection of the apostle's discourse may be considered in the following manner:

I. He speaks concerning the operations of the Spirit of grace upon us. We must give thanks for them, because by these we are qualified for an interest in the mediation of the Son: *Giving thanks to the Father*, &c. *vv.* 12, 13. Now what is it which is wrought for us in the application of redemption? 1. "He hath *delivered us from the power of darkness, v.* 13." They are *called out of darkness*, 1 Pet. ii. 9. 2. "He hath *translated us into the kingdom of his dear Son.*" Those were made willing subjects of Christ who were the slaves of Satan. 3. "He hath not only done this, but hath *made us meet to partake of the inheritance of the saints in light, v.* 12. He hath prepared us for the eternal happiness of heaven, as the Israelites divided the promised land by lot; and has given us the earnest and assurance of it.

II. Concerning the person of the Redeemer, Glorious things are here said of him; for blessed Paul was full of Christ, and took all occasions to speak honourably of him. He speaks of him distinctly as God, and as Mediator. 1. As God he speaks of him, *vv.* 15–17. (1) He is the *image of the invisible God*. Not as man was made *in the image of God* (Gen. i. 27), in his natural faculties and dominion over the creatures: no, he is the *express*

image of his person, Heb. i. 3. (2) He is the *first-born of every creature*. Not that he is himself a creature. It signifies his dominion over all things, as the first-born in a family is heir and lord of all, so he is the *heir of all things*, Heb. i. 2. (3) He is so far from being himself a creature that he is the Creator: *For by him were all things created, which are in heaven and earth, visible and invisible, v.* 16. (4) He *was before all things*. He not only had a being before he was born of the virgin, but he had a being before all time. (5) *By him all things consist.* They not only subsist in their beings, but consist in their order and dependences. He not only created them all at first, but it is by the word of his power that they are still upheld, Heb. i. 3.

2. The apostle next shows what he is as Mediator, *vv.* 18, 19. (1) He is the *head of the body the church*. (2) He is the *beginning, the first-born from the dead*, the principle of our resurrection, as well as the first-born himself. All our hopes and joys take their rise from him who is the author of our salvation. (3) He hath in *all things the pre-eminence*. It was the will of the Father that he should have *all power in heaven and earth*, that he might be preferred above angels and all the powers in heaven. He has the pre-eminence in the hearts of his people above the world and the flesh; and by giving him the pre-eminence we comply with the Father's will, That *all men should honour the Son even as they honour the Father*, John v. 23. (4) All fulness dwells in him, and it pleased the Father it should do so (*v.* 19); a

fulness of merit and righteousness, of strength and grace.

III. Concerning the work of redemption.

1. Wherein it consists. It is made to lie in two things: (1) In the remission of sin: *In whom we have redemption, even the forgiveness of sins, v.* 14. It was sin which sold us, sin which enslaved us: if we are redeemed, we must be redeemed from sin; and this is by forgiveness, or remitting the obligation to punishment. (2) In reconciliation to God. God by him *reconciled all things to himself, v.* 20. He is the Mediator of reconciliation, who procures peace as well as pardon for sinners.

2. How the redemption is procured: *it is through his blood* (*v.* 14); he has *made peace through the blood of his cross* (*v.* 20), and it is *in the body of his flesh through death, v.* 22. It was the *blood which made an atonement, for the blood is the life; and without the shedding of blood there is no remission,* Heb. ix. 22.

IV. Concerning the preaching of this redemption. Here observe,

1. To whom it was preached: *To every creature under heaven* (*v.* 23), that is, it was ordered to be preached to every creature, Mark xvi. 15.

2. By whom it was preached: *Whereof I am made a minister.* Paul was a great apostle; but he looks upon it as the highest of his titles of honour to be a minister of the gospel of Jesus Christ.

3. The gospel which was preached. We have an account of this: *Even the mystery which hath been hid from ages, and from generations,* *but is now made manifest to his saints, vv.* 26, 27. The meanest saint under the gospel understands more than the greatest prophets under the law. And what is this mystery? It is the riches of God's glory among the Gentiles, the breaking down of the partition-wall between the Jew and Gentile, and preaching the gospel to the Gentile world, and making those partakers of the privileges of the gospel state who before lay in ignorance and idolatry.

4. The duty of those who are interested in this redemption: *If you continue in the faith, grounded and settled, and be not moved away from the hope of the gospel which you have heard, v.* 23. We must continue in the faith grounded and settled, and not be moved away from the hope of the gospel; that is, we must be so well fixed in our minds as not to be moved from it by any temptations.

CHAPTER TWO

THE TREASURES OF CHRIST
(*vv.* 1–3)

We may observe here the great concern which Paul had for these Colossians and the other churches which he had not any personal knowledge of.

I. What was it that the apostle desired for them? *That their hearts may be comforted, being knit together in love,* &c., *v.* 2. It was their spiritual welfare about which he was solicitous.

1. *To understand the mystery,* either what was before concealed, but is now made known concerning the Father and Christ, or the

mystery before mentioned, of calling the Gentiles into the Christian church. This is what we should labour after, and then the soul prospers.

2. When our faith grows to a full assurance, or a well-settled judgment, upon their proper evidence, of the great truths of the gospel. This is called the *riches of the full assurance of understanding*.

3. *That their hearts might be comforted.* The soul prospers when it is filled with joy and peace (Rom. xv. 13), and has a satisfaction within which all the troubles without cannot disturb, and is able to joy in the Lord when all other comforts fail, Hab. iii. 17, 18.

4. *Being knit together in love.* Holy love knits the hearts of Christians one to another; and faith and love both contribute to our comfort.

II. His concern for them is repeated (v. 5): *Though I am absent in the flesh, yet am I with you in the spirit, joying, and beholding your order, and the stedfastness of your faith in Christ.*

WALKING IN CHRIST
(vv. 4–12)

The apostle cautions the Colossians against deceivers (v. 4). Observe,

I. A sovereign antidote against seducers (vv. 6, 7): *As you have therefore received Christ Jesus the Lord, so walk you in him, rooted and built up*, &c. Here note, 1. All Christians have, in profession at least, *received Jesus Christ the Lord*, consented to him, taken him for ours in every relation and every capacity, and for all the purposes and uses of them. 2. The great concern of those who have received Christ is *to walk in him*—to make their practices conformable to their principles and their behaviour agreeable to their engagements. 3. The more closely we walk with Christ the more we are *rooted and established in the faith.* If we walk in him, we shall be rooted in him; and the more firmly we are rooted in him the more closely we shall walk in him.

II. The fair warning given us of our danger: *Beware lest any man spoil you through philosophy and vain deceit, after the tradition of men, after the rudiments of the world, and not after Christ, v. 8.* There is a philosophy which is vain and deceitful, which is prejudicial to religion, and sets up the wisdom of man in competition with the wisdom of God, and while it pleases men's fancies ruins their faith. Those who pin their faith on other men's sleeves, and walk in the way of the world, have turned away from following after Christ.

Now here the apostle shows,

1. That we have in Christ the substance of all the shadows of the ceremonial law; for example, (1) Had they then the Shechinah, or special presence of God, called the glory, from the visible token of it? So have we now in Jesus Christ (v. 9). The fulness of the Godhead dwells in Christ really, and not figuratively; for he is both God and man. (2) Had they circumcision, which was the seal of the covenant? In Christ we are *circumcised with the circumcision made without hands* (v. 11), by the work of regeneration in us, which is the spiritual or Christian circumcision.

2. We have communion with Christ in his whole undertaking (*v.* 12): *Buried with him in baptism, wherein also you have risen with him.* The thing signified by our baptism is that we are buried with Christ, as baptism is the seal of the covenant and an obligation to our dying to sin; and that we are raised with Christ, as it is a seal and obligation to our living to righteousness, or newness of life.

CHRISTIAN PRIVILEGES
(*vv.* 13–15)

The apostle here represents the privileges we Christians have above the Jews, which are very great.

I. Christ's death is our life: *And you, being dead in your sins and the uncircumcision of your flesh, hath he quickened together with him, v.* 13. A state of sin is a state of spiritual death. Those who are in sin are dead in sin. Now through Christ we, who were dead in sins, are quickened. Christ's death was the death of our sins; Christ's resurrection is the quickening of our souls.

II. Through him we have the remission of sin: *Having forgiven you all the trespasses.* This is our quickening. The pardon of the crime is the life of the criminal.

III. Whatever was in force against us is taken out of the way. He has obtained for us a legal discharge from the *hand-writing of ordinances, which was against us* (*v.* 14), which may be understood, 1. Of that obligation to punishment in which consists the guilt of sin. Or rather, 2. It must be understood of the ceremonial law, the *hand-writing of ordinances,* which was a yoke to the

Jews and a partition-wall to the Gentiles. The Lord Jesus *took it out of the way, nailed it to his cross*; that is, disannulled the obligation of it, that all might see and be satisfied that it was no more binding.

IV. He has obtained a glorious victory for us over the powers of darkness: *And, having spoiled principalities and powers, he made a show of them openly, triumphing over them in it, v.* 15. The devil and all the powers of hell were conquered and disarmed by the dying Redeemer. He *spoiled them,* broke the devil's power, and conquered and disabled him, and *made a show of them openly*—exposed them to public shame, and made a show of them to angels and men.

WILL-WORSHIP (*vv.* 16–23)

The apostle concludes the chapter with exhortations to proper duty, which he infers from the foregoing discourse.

I. Here is a caution to take heed of judaizing teachers, or those who would impose upon Christians the yoke of the ceremonial law: *Let no man therefore judge you in meat nor in drink,* &c. *v.* 16.

II. He cautions them to take heed of those who would introduce the worship of angels as mediators between God and them, as the Gentile philosophers did: *Let no man beguile you of your reward, in a voluntary humility and worshipping of angels, v.* 18. It is the highest disparagement to Christ, who is the head of the church, for any of the members of it to make use of any intercessors with God but him.

III. He takes occasion hence to

warn them again: *"Wherefore, if you be dead with Christ from the rudiments of the world, why, as though living in the world, are you subject to ordinances? v.* 20. If as Christians you are dead to the observances of the ceremonial law, why are you subject to them? Such observances as, *Touch not, taste not, handle not," vv.* 21, 22. — *Which things have indeed a show of wisdom in will-worship and humility.* They thought themselves wiser than their neighbours, in observing the law of Moses together with the gospel of Christ, that they might be sure in the one, at least, to be in the right; but, alas! it was but a show of wisdom, a mere invention and pretence.

THE RISEN LIFE (*vv.* 1–4)

The apostle, having described our privileges by Christ in the former part of the epistle, and our discharge from the yoke of the ceremonial law, comes here to press upon us our duty as inferred thence.

I. He explains this duty (*v.* 2): *Set your affections on things above, not on things on the earth.* Observe, To seek heavenly things is to set our affections upon them, to love them and let our desires be towards them.

II. He assigns three reasons for this, *vv.* 3, 4.

1. That we are dead; that is, to present things, and as our portion. We are so in profession and obligation; for we are *buried with Christ, and planted into the likeness of his death.*

2. Our true life lies in the other world: *You are dead, and your life is hid with Christ in God, v.* 3. The new man has its livelihood thence. It is born and nourished from above; and the perfection of its life is reserved for that state. It is *hid with Christ:* not hid from us only, in point of secrecy, but hid for us, denoting security.

3. Because at the second coming of Christ we hope for the perfection of our happiness. If we live a life of Christian purity and devotion now, *when Christ, who is our life, shall appear, we shall also appear with him in glory, v.* 4.

PUTTING SIN TO DEATH
(*vv.* 5–7)

The apostle exhorts the Colossians to the mortification of sin, the great hindrance to seeking the things which are above. He specifies,

I. The lusts of the flesh, for which they were before so very remarkable.

II. The love of the world: *And covetousness, which is idolatry;* that is, an inordinate love of present good and outward enjoyments, which proceeds from too high a value in the mind. He proceeds to show how necessary it is to mortify sins, *v.* 6, 7. 1. Because, if we do not kill them, they will kill us: *For which things' sake the wrath of God cometh on the children of disobedience, v.* 6. 2. We should mortify these sins because they have lived in us: *In which you also walked some time, when you lived in them, v.* 7.

PUT OFF EVIL (*vv.* 8–11)

As we are to mortify inordinate appetites, so we are to mortify inordinate passions (*v.* 8): *But now you also put off all these, anger, wrath, malice*; for these are contrary to the design of the gospel, as well as grosser impurities; and, though they are more spiritual wickedness, have not less malignity in them. Seeing *you have put off the old man with his deeds, and have put on the new man, v.* 10. Those who have put off the old man have put it off with its deeds; and those who have put on the new man must put on all its deeds — not only espouse good principles but act them in a good way of life. The new man is said to be *renewed in knowledge*, because an ignorant soul cannot be a good soul. Without knowledge the heart cannot be good, Prov. xix. 2. In the privilege and duty of sanctification *there is neither Greek nor Jew, circumcision nor uncircumcision, Barbarian, Scythian, bond nor free, v.* 11. There is now no difference arising from different country or different condition and circumstance of life: it is as much the duty of the one as of the other to be holy, and as much the privilege of the one as of the other to receive from God the grace to be so.

PUT ON GOOD
(*vv.* 12–17)

The apostle proceeds to exhort to mutual love and compassion.

I. The argument here used to enforce the exhortation is very affecting: *Put on, as the elect of God, holy and beloved.* (1) Compassion towards the miserable: *Bowels of mercy*, the tenderest mercies. Those who owe so much to mercy ought to be merciful to all who are proper objects of mercy. (2) *Kindness* towards our friends, and those who love us. (3) *Humbleness of mind*, in submission to those above us, and condescension to those below us. (4) *Meekness* towards those who have provoked us, or been any way injurious to us. (5) *Long-suffering* towards those who continue to provoke us. (6) Mutual forbearance, in consideration of the infirmities and deficiencies under which we all labour: *Forbearing one another.* (7) A readiness to forgive injuries: *Forgiving one another, if any man have a quarrel against any.*

II. In order to do all this, we are exhorted here to several things: 1. To clothe ourselves with love (*v.* 14): *Above all things put on charity: over all things.* Let this be the upper garment, the robe, the livery, the mark of our dignity and distinction. 2. To submit ourselves to the government of the *peace of God* (*v.* 15): *Let the peace of God rule in your hearts.* "Let this peace *rule in your heart* — prevail and govern there, or as an umpire decide all matters of difference among you." — *To which you are called in one body.* We are called to this peace, to peace with God as our privilege and peace with our brethren as our duty. 3. To let the *word of Christ dwell in us richly, v.* 16. The gospel is the word of Christ, which has come to us; but that is not enough, it must dwell in us, or *keep house*, not as a servant in a family, who is under another's control, but as a master, who has a right to prescribe to and direct all under his roof. 4. We must *admonish one another in psalms and hymns.*

Observe, Singing of psalms is a gospel ordinance — the Psalms of David, and spiritual hymns and odes, collected out of the scripture, and suited to special occasions. But, when we sing psalms, we make no melody unless we sing with grace in our hearts. 5. All must be done in the name of Christ (*v.* 17): *And whatsoever you do in word or deed, do all in the name of the Lord Jesus*, according to his command and in compliance with his authority, by strength derived from him, with an eye to his glory, and depending upon his merit for the acceptance of what is good and the pardon of what is amiss, *Giving thanks to God and the Father by him.*

FAMILY DUTIES (*vv.* 18–25)

The apostle concludes the chapter with exhortations to relative duties, as before in the epistle to the Ephesians.

I. He begins with the duties of wives and husbands (*v.* 18): *Wives, submit yourselves unto your own husbands, as it is fit in the Lord.* Submission is the duty of wives. It is agreeable to the order of nature and the reason of things, as well as the appointment and will of God. On the other hand, *husbands must love their wives, and not be bitter against them, v.* 19. They must love them with tender and faithful affection, as Christ loved the church, and as their own bodies, and even as themselves (Eph. v. 25, 28, 33), with a love peculiar to the nearest relation and the greatest comfort and blessing of life.

II. The duties of children and parents: *Children, obey your parents in all things, for this is well-pleasing unto the Lord, v.* 20. They must be willing to do all their lawful commands, and be at their direction and disposal; as those who have a natural right and are fitter to direct them than themselves. And parents must be tender, as well as children obedient (*v.* 21): "*Fathers, provoke not your children to anger, lest they be discouraged.*" The bad temper and example of imprudent parents often prove a great hindrance to their children and a stumbling-block in their way; see Eph. vi. 4.

III. Servants and masters: *Servants, obey your masters in all things according to the flesh, v.* 22. Servants must do the duty of the relation in which they stand, and obey their master's commands in *all things* which are consistent with their duty to God their heavenly Master. *Not with eye-service, as men-pleasers* — not only when their master's eye is upon them, but when they are from under their master's eye. "And *whatsoever you do, do it heartily* (*v.* 23), with diligence, not idly and slothfully:" or, "Do it cheerfully, not discontented at the providence of God which put you in that relation."— *As to the Lord, and not as to men.* It sanctifies a servant's work when it is done as unto God — with an eye to his glory, and in obedience to his command, and not merely as unto men, or with regard to them only.

CHAPTER FOUR

MASTERS (*v.* 1)

The apostle proceeds with the duty of masters to their servants, which might have been joined to the foregoing chapter, and is a part of that discourse. Here observe, 1. Justice is required of them: *Give unto your servants that which is just and equal* (v. 1), not strict justice, but equity and kindness. 2. A good reason for this regard: "*Knowing that you also have a Master in heaven.*" Deal with your servants as you expect God should deal with you, and as those who believe they must give an account.

ADVICE FOR CHRISTIANS
(vv. 2–6)

If this be considered as connected with the foregoing verse, then we may observe that it is part of the duty which masters owe their servants to pray with them, and to pray daily with them, or *continue in prayer.* — *With thanksgiving*, or solemn acknowledgment of the mercies received. Thanksgiving must have a part in every prayer. — *Withal praying also for us, v.* 3. The people must pray particularly for their ministers, and bear them upon their hearts at all times at the throne of grace. *That God would open to us a door of utterance*, that is, either afford opportunity to preach the gospel (so he says, *a great door and effectual is opened to me*, 1 Cor. xvi. 9), or else give me ability and courage, and enable me with freedom and faithfulness; so Eph. vi. 19.

The apostle exhorts them further to a prudent and decent conduct towards all those with whom they conversed, towards the heathen world, or those out of the Christian church among whom they lived (v. 5): *Walk in wisdom towards those who are without.* "*Let your speech be always with grace, v.* 6." Let all your discourse be as becomes Christians, suitable to your profession — savoury, discreet, seasonable. Though it be not always of grace, it must be always with grace; and, though the matter of our discourse be that which is common, yet it must be in a Christian manner: *seasoned with salt.* Grace is the salt which seasons our discourse, makes it savoury, and keeps it from corrupting. *That you may know how to answer every man.* One answer is proper for one man, and another for another man Prov. xxvi. 4, 5. We have need of a great deal of wisdom and grace.

SUNDRY GREETINGS
(vv. 7–18)

In the close of this epistle the apostle does several of his friends the honour to leave their names upon record, with some testimony of his respect, which will be spoken of wherever the gospel comes, and last to the end of the world.

I. Concerning Tychicus, v. 7. By him this epistle was sent.

II. Concerning Onesimus (v. 9): *With Onesimus, a faithful and beloved brother, who is one of you.* He was sent back from Rome along with Tychicus. This was he whom Paul had begotten in his bonds, Philem. 10.

III. *Aristarchus, a fellow-prisoner.* Those who join in services and sufferings whould be thereby engaged to one another in holy love.

IV. *Marcus, sister's son to Barnabas.* This is supposed to be the same who wrote the gospel which bears his name.

V. Here is one who is called *Jesus*, which is the Greek name for the Hebrew *Joshua*.

VI. *Epaphras* (*v.* 12), the same with *Epaphroditus*. He is *one of you*, one of your church; *he salutes you*, or sends his service to you, and his best affections and wishes.

VII. *Luke* is another here mentioned, whom he calls the *beloved physician*. This is he who wrote the Gospel and Acts, and was Paul's companion.

VIII. *Demas*. Whether this was written before the second epistle to Timothy or after is not certain. There we read (2 Tim. iv. 10), *Demas hath forsaken me, having loved this present world*.

IX. The *brethren in Laodicea* are here mentioned, as living in the neighbourhood of Colosse: and Paul sends salutations to them, and orders that this epistle should be read in the church of the Laodiceans (*v.* 16).

X. *Nymphas* is mentioned (*v.* 15) as one who lived at Colosse, and had a church in his house; that is, either a religious family, where the several parts of worship were daily performed; or some part of the congregation met there, when they had no public places of worship allowed, and they were forced to assemble in private houses for fear of their enemies.

XI. Concerning *Archippus*, who was one of their ministers at Colosse.

XII. Concerning himself (*v.* 18): *The salutation of me Paul. Remember my bonds*. He had a scribe to write all the rest of the epistle, but these words he wrote with his own hand: *Remember my bonds*.

THE FIRST EPISTLE OF ST. PAUL TO THE

THESSALONIANS

CHAPTER ONE

INTRODUCTION AND THANKS (vv. 1–5)

In this introduction we have,

I. The inscription, where we have,
1. The persons from whom this epistle came, or by whom it was written. Paul was the inspired apostle and writer of this epistle.
2. The persons to whom this epistle is written, namely, the church of the Thessalonians, the converted Jews in Thessalonica.

II. The salutation or apostolical benediction.

III. The apostle then begins with thanksgiving to God. The apostle gave thanks not only for those who were his most intimate friends, or most eminently favoured of God, but for them all.

II. He joined prayer with his praise or thanksgiving. Note, As there is much that we ought to be thankful for on the behalf of ourselves and our friends, so there is much occasion of constant prayer for further supplies of good.

III. He mentions the particulars for which he was so thankful to God; namely,
1. The saving benefits bestowed on them.
2. He also takes notice, (1) Of the object and efficient cause of these graces, namely, our Lord Jesus Christ. (2) Of the sincerity of them:

being in the *sight of God even our Father*. (3) He mentions the fountain whence these graces flow, namely, God's electing love: *Knowing, brethren beloved, your election of God*, v. 4. Thus he runs up these streams to the fountain, and that was God's eternal election.

3. Another ground or reason of the apostle's thanksgiving is the success of his ministry among them. He was thankful on his own account as well as theirs, that he had not laboured in vain. Their *faith was the evidence of things not seen*; and the Thessalonians thus knew what manner of men the apostle and his fellow-labourers were among them, and what they did for their sake, and with what good success.

EVIDENCES OF THEIR FAITH (vv. 6–10)

In these words we have the evidence of the apostle's success among the Thessalonians, which was notorious and famous in several places. For,

I. They were careful in their holy conversation to imitate the good examples of the apostles and ministers of Christ, v. 6.

II. Their zeal prevailed to such a degree that they were themselves examples to all about them, vv. 7, 8. The word of the Lord, or its wonderful effects upon the Thessalonians, sounded, or was famous and well known, in the regions round about that city, and *in every place*. The effects of their faith were famous. (1) They quitted their idolatry; they turned from their idols, and abandoned all the false worship they had been educated in. (2) They gave themselves up to God, to the living and true God, and devoted themselves to his service. (3) They set themselves to wait for the Son of God from heaven, *v.* 10.

CHAPTER TWO
STRAIGHT TALKING
(*vv.* 1–6)

Here we have an account of Paul's manner of preaching, and his comfortable reflection upon his entrance in among the Thessalonians. He had no sinister or worldly design in his preaching, which he puts them in mind to have been,

I. With courage and resolution: *We were bold in our God to speak unto you the gospel of God, v.* 2.

II. With great simplicity and godly sincerity: *Our exhortation was not of deceit, nor of uncleanness, nor in guile, v.* 3. The apostle not only asserts his sincerity, but subjoins the reasons and evidences thereof. The reasons are contained, *v.* 4.

1. They were stewards, *put in trust* with the gospel: and it is required of a steward that he be faithful.

2. Their design was to please God and not men. God is a God of truth, and requires truth in the inward parts; and, if sincerity be wanting, all that we do cannot please God.

3. They acted under the consider-

ation of God's omniscience, as in the sight of him who *tries our hearts*. This is indeed the great motive to sincerity, to consider that God not only seeth all that we do, but knoweth our thoughts afar off, and searcheth the heart. The evidences of the apostle's sincerity follow; and they are these: (1) He avoided flattery: *Neither at any time used we flattering words, as you know, v.* 5. (2) He avoided covetousness. He did not make the ministry *a cloak,* or a covering, for *covetousness, as God was witness, v.* 5. His design was not to enrich himself by preaching the gospel. (3) He avoided ambition and vain-glory: *Nor of men sought we glory, neither of you nor yet of others, v.* 6.

PAUL'S WAY OF LIFE
(*vv.* 7–12)

In these words the apostle reminds the Thessalonians of the manner of his conversation among them. And,

I. He mentions the gentleness of their behaviour: *We were gentle among you, v.* 7.

II. He mentions their faithful discharge of the work and office of the ministry, *vv.* 11, 12. Concerning this also he could appeal to them as witnesses.

THE EFFECTIVE WORD
OF GOD (*vv.* 13–16)

Here observe, I. The apostle makes mention of the success of his ministry among these Thessalonians (*v.* 13), which is expressed,

1. By the manner of their receiving the word of God: *When you received the word of God, which you heard of us, you received it, not as the word of men, but (as it is in*

truth) the word of God. Such was the word the apostles preached by divine inspiration, and such is that which is left upon record, written in the scriptures by divine inspiration; and such is that word which in our days is preached, being either contained, or evidently founded on, or deduced from, these sacred oracles.

2. By the wonderful operation of this word they received: *It effectually worketh in those that believe, v.* 13. Those who by faith receive the word find it profitable. *It does good to those that walk uprightly,* and by its wonderful effects evidences itself to be the word of God.

II. He mentions the good effects which his successful preaching had,

1. Upon himself and fellow-labourers. It was a constant cause of thankfulness: *For this cause thank we God without ceasing, v.* 13.

2. Upon them. The word wrought effectually in them, not only to be examples unto others in faith and good works (which he had mentioned before), but also in constancy and patience under sufferings and trials for the sake of the gospel: *You became followers of the churches of God, and have suffered like things as they have done* (*v.* 14), and with like courage and constancy, with like patience and hope. The apostle mentions the sufferings of the churches of God, which *in Judea were in Christ Jesus.* Those in Judea first heard the gospel, and they first suffered for it: for the Jews were the most bitter enemies Christianity had, and were especially enraged against their countrymen who embraced Christianity. In every city where the

apostles went to preach the gospel the Jews stirred up the inhabitants against them. They were the ring-leaders of persecution in all places. They had *an implacable enmity to the Gentiles,* and envied them the offers of the gospel: *Forbidding the apostles to speak to the Gentiles, that they might be saved.* The means of salvation had long been confined to the Jews. And they were envious against the Gentiles, and angry that they should be admitted to share in the means of salvation. For the sake of these things *wrath has come upon them to the uttermost*; that is, wrath was determined against them, and would soon overtake them. It was not many years after this that Jerusalem was destroyed, and the Jewish nation cut off by the Romans.

CROWN OF JOY (*vv.* 17–20)

In these words the apostle apologizes for his absence. Here observe,

1. He tells them they were involuntarily forced from them: *We, brethren, were taken from you, v.* 17.
2. Though he was absent in body, yet he was present in heart. 3. Even his bodily absence was but for a short time, the time of an hour. 4. He earnestly desired and endeavoured to see them again: *We endeavoured more abundantly to see your face with great desire, v.* 17.
5. He tells them that Satan hindered his return (*v.* 18), that is, either some enemy or enemies, or the great enemy of mankind. 6. He assures them of his affection and high esteem for them, though he was not able, as yet, to be present with them according to his desire.

The apostle here puts the Thessalonians in mind that though he could not come to them as yet, and though he should never be able to come to them, yet our Lord Jesus Christ will come, nothing shall hindred this. And further, when he shall come, all must appear in his presence, or before him.

CHAPTER THREE

TIMOTHY SENT TO THESSALONICA
(*vv.* 1–5)

In these words the apostle gives an account of his sending Timothy to the Thessalonians. Observe,

I. The character he gives of Timothy (*v.* 2): *We sent Timotheus, our brother.* He calls him also a minister of God. He calls him also his fellow-labourer in the gospel of Christ.

II. The end and design why Paul sent Timothy: *To establish you and to comfort you concerning your faith, v.* 2. Paul had converted them to the Christian faith, and now he was desirous that they might be confirmed and comforted, that they might be confirmed in the choice they had made of the Christian religion, and be comforted in the profession and practice of it.

III. The motive inducing Paul to send Timothy for this end, namely, a godly fear or jealousy, lest they should be moved from the faith of Christ, *v.* 3.

1. He apprehended there was danger, and feared the consequence.

(1) There was danger, [1] By reason of *affliction* and persecution for the sake of the gospel, *v.* 3. [2] By reason of the tempter's subtlety and malice.

(2) The consequence the apostle

feared was lest his labour should be in vain.

2. To prevent this danger, with its bad consequence, the apostle tells them what care he took in sending Timothy, (1) To put them in mind of what he had told them before concerning suffering tribulation (*v.* 4), he says (*v.* 3), *We are appointed thereunto,* that is, unto afflictions. So is the will and purpose of God that *through many afflictions we must enter into his kingdom.* Their troubles and persecutions did not come by chance, not merely from the wrath and malice of the enemies of religion, but by the *appointment of God.* (2) To know their faith, that so he might inform the apostles whether they remained stedfast under all their sufferings, whether their faith failed or not, because, if their faith did not fail, they would be able to stand their ground against the tempter and all his temptations: their faith would be a *shield, to defend them against all the fiery darts of the wicked,* Eph. vi. 16.

STAND FAST (*vv.* 6–10)

Here we have Paul's great satisfaction upon the return of Timothy with good tidings from the Thessalonians, in which we may observe,

I. The good report Timothy made concerning them, *v.* 6. *Concerning their faith,* that is, concerning their stedfastness in the faith, that they were not shaken in mind, nor turned aside from the profession of the gospel. *Their love* also continued; their love to the gospel, and the ministers of the gospel.

II. The great comfort and satisfaction the apostle had in this good

350

report concerning them (*vv.* 7, 8): *Therefore, brethren, we were comforted in all our affliction and distress.*

III. The effects of this were thankfulness and prayer to God on their behalf. Observe, 1. How thankful the apostle was, *v.* 9. He was full of joy, and full of praise and thanksgiving. 2. He prayed for them night and day (*v.* 10), evening and morning, or very frequently, in the midst of the business of the day or slumber of the night lifting up his heart to God in prayer. Thus we should pray always. And Paul's prayer was fervent prayer. He prayed exceedingly, and was earnest in his supplication.

ABOUNDING IN LOVE
(*vv.* 11–13)

In these words we have the earnest prayer of the apostle. Observe,

I. Whom he prays to, namely, God and Christ. Prayer is a part of religious worship, and all religious worship is due unto God only.

II. What he prays for, with respect to himself and his fellow-labourers, and on behalf of the Thessalonians

1. He prays that himself and fellow-labourers might have a prosperous journey to them by the will of God, that their way might be directed to them, *v.* 11.

2. He prays for the prosperity of the Thessalonians. Whether he should have an opportunity of coming to them or not, yet he earnestly prayed for the prosperity of their souls. (1) That they might increase and abound in love (*v.* 12), in love to one another and in love to all men. (2) That they might be established unblamable in holiness,

v. 13. This spiritual benefit is mentioned as an effect of increasing and abounding love: *To the end that he* (the Lord) *may establish your hearts.*

CHAPTER IV
ABOUNDING IN HOLINESS
(*vv.* 1–8)

Here we have,

I. An exhortation to abound in holiness, to *abound more and more* in that which is good, *vv.* 1, 2. We may observe,

1. The manner in which the exhortation is given—very affectionately.

2. The matter of his exhortation —that they would abound more and more in holy walking, or excel in those things that are good, in good works.

3. The arguments with which the apostle enforces his exhortation. (1) They had been informed of their duty. They knew their Master's will, and could not plead ignorance as an excuse. (2) Another argument is that the apostle taught and exhorted them in the name, or by the authority, of the Lord Jesus Christ. He was Christ's minister and ambassador, declaring to them what was the will and command of the Lord Jesus. (3) Another argument is this. Herein they would please God. Holy walking is most pleasing to the holy God, *who is glorious in holiness*. (4) The rule according to which they ought to walk and act—*the commandments they had given them by the Lord Jesus Christ.*

II. A caution against uncleanness, this being a sin directly contrary to sanctification, or that holy walking to which he so earnestly exhorts them. This caution is expressed, and also enforced by many arguments.

1. It is expressed in these words: *That you should abstain from fornication* (v. 3), by which we are to understand all uncleanness whatsoever, either in a married or unmarried state.

2. There are several arguments to enforce this caution. As, (1) This branch of sanctification in particular is the will of God, *v.* 3. It is the will of God in general that we should be holy, because *he that called us is holy*, and because we are *chosen unto salvation through the sanctification of the Spirit*. (2) This will be greatly for our honour: so much is plainly implied, *v.* 4. Whereas the contrary will be a great dishonour. (3) To indulge the lust of concupiscence is to live and act like heathens. (4) The sin of uncleanness, especially adultery, is a great piece of injustice that God will be the avenger of; so we may understand those words, *That no man go beyond or defraud his brother* (v. 6) *in any matter*—in *this* matter of which the apostle is speaking, in the preceding and following verses, namely, the sin of uncleanness. (5) The sin of uncleanness is contrary to the nature and design of our Christian calling: *For God hath called us not unto uncleanness, but unto holiness*, v. 7. (6) The contempt therefore of God's law and gospel is the contempt of God himself: *He that despises despises God, not man* only.

HONEST WORK (*vv.* 9–12)

In these words the apostle mentions the great duties,

I. Of brotherly love. This he exhorts them to increase in yet more and more.

II. Of quietness and industry in their callings. Observe, 1. The apostle exhorts to these duties: that they should *study to be quiet*, v. 11. It is the most desirable thing to have a calm and quiet temper, and to be of a peaceable and quiet behaviour. It follows, *Do your own business*. Those who are busy-bodies, meddling in other men's matters, generally have but little quiet in their own minds and cause great disturbances among their neighbours; at least they seldom mind the other exhortation, to be diligent in their own calling, *to work with their own hands*; and yet this was what the apostle commanded them, and what is required of us also. Christianity does not discharge us from the work and duty of our particular callings, but teaches us to be diligent therein. 2. The exhortation is enforced with a double argument; namely, (1) So we shall live creditably. Thus we shall walk honestly, or decently and creditably, towards those that are without, *v.* 12. (2) We shall live comfortably, and have lack of nothing, *v.* 12. Such as are diligent in their own business live comfortably and have lack of nothing. They earn their own bread, and have the greatest pleasure in so doing.

THE CHRISTIAN DEAD
(*vv.* 13–18)

In these words the apostle comforts the Thessalonians who mourned for the death of their relations and friends that died in the Lord.

Yet we must not be immoderate in our sorrows, because,

I. This looks as if we had no hope, *v.* 13. This hope is more than enough to balance all our griefs upon account of any of the crosses of the present time.

II. This is an effect of ignorance concerning those who are dead, *v.* 13. There are some things concerning those especially who die in the Lord that we need not, and ought not, to be ignorant of; and, if these things be really understood and duly considered, they will be sufficient to allay our sorrow concerning them.

1. They sleep in Jesus. They are asleep, *v.* 13. They have *fallen asleep in Christ*, 1 Cor. xv. 18. Death does not annihilate them. It is but a sleep to them. It is their rest, and undisturbed rest. Their souls are in his presence, and their dust is under his care and power; so that they are not lost, nor are they losers, but great gainers by death, and their removal out of this world is into a better.

2. They shall be raised up from the dead, and awakened out of their sleep, for *God will bring them with him, v.* 14. The doctrine of the resurrection and the second coming of Christ is a great antidote against the fear of death and inordinate sorrow for the death of our Christian friends; and this doctrine we have a full assurance of, because we *believe that Jesus died and rose again, v.* 14.

3. Their state and condition shall be glorious and happy at the second coming of Christ. This the apostle informs the Thessalonians of *by the word of the Lord* (*v.* 15), by divine

revelation from the Lord Jesus. By this word of the Lord we know, (1) That the Lord Jesus will come down from heaven in all the pomp and power of the upper world (*v.* 16): *The Lord himself shall descend from heaven with a shout.* For, (2) The dead shall be raised: *The dead in Christ shall rise first* (*v.* 16), before those who are *found alive at Christ's coming shall be changed*; and so it appears that those who shall then *be found alive shall not prevent those that are asleep, v.* 15. The first care of the Redeemer in that day will be about his dead saints; he will raise them before the great change passes on those that shall be found alive: so that those who did not sleep in death will have no greater privilege or joy at that day than those who fell asleep in Jesus. (3) Those that shall be found alive will then be changed. They shall *be caught up together with them in the clouds, to meet the Lord in the air, v.* 17. At, or immediately before, this rapture into the clouds, those who are alive will undergo a mighty change, which will be equivalent to dying. This change is so mysterious that we cannot comprehend it: we know little or nothing of it, 1 Cor. xv. 51. Only, in the general, *this mortal must put on immortality*, and these bodies will be made fit to inherit the kingdom of God, which flesh and blood in its present state are not capable of. And those who are raised, and thus changed, shall meet together in the clouds, and there meet with their Lord. (4) Here is the bliss of the saints at that day: they shall *be ever with the Lord, v.* 17. It will be some part of their felicity that all the saints shall meet together, and remain together for ever; but the principal happiness of heaven is this, *to be with the Lord*, to see him, live with him, and enjoy him, for ever. And the apostle would have us *comfort one another with these words*, v. 18.

CHAPTER FIVE

THE DAY OF THE LORD
(vv. 1–5)

In these words observe,

I. The apostle tells the Thessalonians it was needless or useless to enquire about the particular time of Christ's coming: *Of the times and seasons you need not that I write unto you*, v. 1. The thing is certain that Christ will come, and there is a certain time appointed for his coming; but there was no need that the apostle should write about this, and therefore he had no revelation given him.

II. He tells them that the coming of Christ would be sudden, and a great surprise to most men, *v*. 2.

III. He tells them how terrible Christ's coming would be to the ungodly, *v*. 3. It will be to their destruction in that day of the Lord. 1. It will be sudden. It will overtake them, and fall upon them, in the midst of their carnal security and jollity, when they say in their hearts, *Peace and safety*. 2. It will be unavoidable destruction too: *They shall not escape*; they shall in no wise escape.

IV. He tells them how comfortable this day will be to the righteous, *vv*. 4, 5. They are not in darkness; they are the children of the light, &c. This was the happy condition of the Thessalonians as it is of all true Christians. They were not in a state of sin and ignorance as the heathen world. They were *some time darkness, but were made light in the Lord*. They were favoured with the divine revelation of things that are unseen and eternal, particularly concerning the coming of Christ, and the consequences thereof.

WATCH AND BE SOBER
(vv. 6–10)

On what had been said, the apostle grounds seasonable exhortations to several needful duties.

I. To watchfulness and sobriety, *v*. 6. 1. Then *let us not sleep as do others, but let us watch*; we must not be secure and careless, nor indulge spiritual sloth and idleness.

II. To be well armed as well as watchful: to put on the whole armour of God. 1. We must live by faith, and this will keep us watchful and sober. 2. We must get a heart inflamed with love; and this also will be our defence. 3. We must make salvation our hope, and should have a lively hope of it. This good hope, through grace, of eternal life, will be as a helmet to defend the head. Our hopes are to be grounded, (1) Upon God's appointment: because *God hath not appointed us to wrath, but to obtain salvation*, *v*. 9. (2) Upon Christ's merit and grace, and that salvation is by our Lord Jesus Christ, who died for us. Our salvation therefore is owing to, and our hopes of it are grounded on, Christ's atonement as well as God's appointment.

SOME WARNINGS (*vv.* 11–15)

In these words the apostle exhorts the Thessalonians to several duties.

I. Towards those who were nearly related one to another. Such should comfort themselves, or exhort one another, and edify one another, *v.* 11.

II. He shows them their duty towards their ministers, *vv.* 12, 13. The apostle here exhorts them to observe,

1. How the ministers of the gospel are described by the work of their office. (1) Ministers must labour among their people, labour with diligence, and unto weariness (so the word in the original imports); *they must labour in the word and doctrine,* 1 Tim. v. 17. And, (2) Ministers are to rule their people also, so the word is rendered, 1 Tim. v. 17. They must rule, not with rigour, but with love. (3) They must also admonish the people, and that not only publicly, but privately, as there may be occasion.

2. What the duty of the people is towards their ministers. There is a mutual duty between ministers and people. If ministers should labour among the people, then, (1) The people must know them. As the shepherd should know his flock, so the sheep must know their shepherd. (2) They must esteem their ministers highly in love; they should greatly value the office of the ministry, honour and love the persons or their ministers, and show their esteem and affection in all proper ways, and this for their work's sake.

III. He gives various other exhortations touching the duty Christians owe to one another. 1. *To be at peace among themselves, v.* 13. Ministers and people should avoid everything that tends to alienate their affections one from another. 2. *To warn the unruly, v.* 14. Such should be put in mind of what they should do, and be reproved for doing otherwise. 3. *To comfort the feeble-minded, v.* 14. By these are intended the timorous and faint-hearted, or such as are dejected and of a sorrowful spirit. 4. *To support the weak, v.* 14. Some are not well able to perform their work, nor bear up under their burdens; we should therefore support them, help their infirmities, and lift at one end of the burden, and so help to bear it. 5. *To be patient towards all men, v.* 14. We must bear and forbear. We must not be high in our expectations and demands, nor harsh in our resentments, nor hard in our impositions, but endeavour to make the best we can of every thing, and think the best we can of every body. 6. *Not to render evil for evil to any man, v.* 15. If others do us an injury, this will not justify us in returning it, in doing the same, or the like, or any other injury to them. 7. *Ever to follow that which is good, v.* 15. In general, we must study to do what is our duty, and pleasing to God, in all circumstances, whether men do us good turns or ill turns; whatever men do to us, we must do good to others.

INSTRUCTIONS (*vv.* 16–28)

Here we have divers short exhortations, that will not burden our memories, but will be of great use to direct the motions of our hearts and lives. 1. *Rejoice evermore, v.* 16. This must be understood of spiritual joy; for if we rejoice in God, we may do that evermore. 2. *Pray without ceasing, v.* 17. Note, The way to rejoice evermore is to pray without ceasing. We should rejoice more if we prayed more. 3. *In every thing give thanks, v.* 18. If we pray without ceasing, we shall not want matter for thanksgiving *in every thing.* 4. *Quench not the Spirit* (*v.* 19), for it is this Spirit of grace and supplication that helpeth our infirmities, that assisteth us in our prayers and thanksgivings. 5. *Despise not prophesyings* (*v.* 20); for, if we neglect the means of grace, we forfeit the Spirit of grace. By *prophesyings* here we are to understand the preaching of the word, the interpreting and applying of the scriptures. 6. *Prove all things, but hold fast that which is good, v.* 21. This is a needful caution, to test all things; for, though we must put a value on preaching, we must not take things upon trust from the preacher, but try them by the law and the testimony. 7. *Abstain from all appearance of evil, v.* 22. This is a good means to prevent our being deceived with false doctrines, or unsettled in our faith; for our Saviour has told us (John vii. 17), *If*

a man will do his will, he shall know of the doctrine whether it be of God. Corrupt affections indulged in the heart, and evil practices allowed of in the life, will greatly tend to promote fatal errors in the mind.

In *vv.* 23–28, which conclude this epistle, observe,

I. Paul's prayer for them, *v.* 23. He had told them, in the beginning of this epistle, that he always made mention of them in his prayers; and, now that he is writing to them, he lifts up his heart to God in prayer for them.

II. His comfortable assurance that God would hear his prayer: *Faithful is he who calleth you, who will also do it, v.* 24.

III. His request of their prayers: *Brethren, pray for us, v.* 25. We should pray for one another; and brethren should thus express brotherly love.

IV. His salutation: *Greet all the brethren with a holy kiss, v.* 26. Thus the apostle sends a friendly salutation from himself.

V. His solemn charge for the reading of this epistle, *v.* 27. This is not only an exhortation, but an adjuration by the Lord.

VI. The apostolical benediction that is usual in other epistles; *v.* 28.

THESSALONIANS

CHAPTER ONE
GREETINGS (vv. 1–4)

Here we have,

I. The introduction (vv. 1, 2) in the same words as in the former epistle.

II. The apostle's expression of the high esteem he had for them.

1. How his esteem of them is expressed. (1) He glorified God on their behalf: *We are bound to thank God always for you, brethren, as it is meet, v.* 3. (2) He also *glories in them before the churches of God, v.* 4. The apostle never flattered his friends, but he took pleasure in commending them, and speaking well of them, to the glory of God and for the excitement and encouragement of others.

2. For what he esteemed them and thanked God; namely, the increase of their faith, and love, and patience. The matter of the apostle's thanksgiving and glorifying on behalf of the Thessalonians was, (1) That their faith grew exceedingly, *v.* 3. (2) Their charity abounded (*v.* 3), their love to God and man. (3) Their patience as well as faith increased in all their persecutions and tribulations.

GOD'S VENGEANCE (vv. 5–10)

I. He tells them of the present happiness and advantage of their sufferings, *v.* 5. Their faith being thus tried, and patience exercised, they were improved by their sufferings, insomuch that they were *counted worthy of the kingdom of God.*

II. He tells them next of the future recompense that shall be given to persecutore and persecuted.

1. In this future recompense there will be, (1) A punishment inflicted on persecutors: God will *recompense tribulation to those that trouble you, v.* 6. (2) A reward for those that are persecuted: God will recompense their trouble with rest, *v.* 7. There is a rest that remains for the people of God, a rest from sin and sorrow.

2. Concerning this future recompence we are further to observe,

(1) The certainty of it, proved by the righteousness and justice of God: *It is a righteous thing with God (v.* 6) to render to every man according to his works.

(2) The time when this righteous recompense shall be made: *When the Lord Jesus shall be revealed from heaven, v.* 7. As,

[1] That the Lord Jesus will in that day appear from heaven.

[2] He will be revealed with his mighty angels (*v.* 7), or the angels of his power. They will summon the criminals to his tribunal, and gather in the elect, and be employed in executing his sentence.

[3] He will come in flaming fire,

v. 8. A fire goeth before him, which shall consume his enemies.

[4] The effects of this appearance will be terrible to some and joyful to others.

First, They will be terrible to some; for he will then take vengeance on the wicked. 1. On those that sinned against the principles of natural religion, and rebelled against the light of nature, *that knew not God* (*v.* 8), though the invisible things of him are manifested in the things that are seen. 2. On those that rebel against the light of revelation, that *obey not the gospel of our Lord Jesus Christ.* And this is the condemnation, that light is come into the world, and men love darkness rather than light. Their punishment will be no less than destruction, not of their being, but of their bliss; not that of the body alone, but both as to body and soul. This destruction shall come from the *presence of the Lord,* that is, immediately from God himself.

Secondly, It will be a joyful day to some, even to the saints, to those that believe and obey the gospel. In that bright and blessed day, 1. Christ Jesus will be glorified and admired by his saints. 2. Christ will be glorified and admired in them.

THE WORK OF FAITH
(*vv.* 11, 12)

In these verses the apostle again tells the Thessalonians of his earnest and constant prayer for them. Observe,

I. What the apostle prayer for, *v.* 11. 1. That God would begin his good work of grace in them; so we may understand this expression: *That our God would count you* (or,

as it might be read, *make you*) *worthy of this calling.* 2. That God would carry on the good work that is begun, and *fulfil all the good pleasure of his goodness.* The good pleasure of God denotes his gracious purposes towards his people, which flow from his goodness, and are full of goodness towards them; and it is thence that all good comes to us.

II. Why the apostle prayed for these things (*v.* 12); *That the name of the Lord Jesus may be glorified*; this is the end we should aim at in every thing we do and desire, that God and Christ in all things may be glorified.

CHAPTER TWO

THE COMING OF CHRIST
(*vv.* 1–12)

From *vv.* 1–3 it appears that some among the Thessalonians had mistaken the apostle's meaning, in what he had written in his former epistle about the coming of Christ, by thinking that it was near at hand, —that Christ was just ready to appear and come to judgment. Or, it may be, some among them pretended that they had the knowledge of this by particular revelation from the Spirit, or from some words they had heard from the apostle, when he was with them, or some letter he had written or they pretended he had written to them or some other person: and hereupon the apostle is careful to rectify this mistake, and to prevent the spreading of this error.

The apostle confutes the error against which he had cautioned them, and gives the reasons why they should not expect the coming of Christ as just at hand. There were several events previous to the second coming of Christ; in particular, he tells them there would be

I. A general apostasy, *there would come a falling away first, v.* 3. And let us observe that no sooner was Christianity planted and rooted in the world than there began to be a defection in the Christian church.

II. A revelation of that man of sin, that is (*v.* 3), antichrist would take his rise from this general apostasy. The apostle afterwards speaks of the revelation of that wicked one (*v.* 8), intimating the discovery which should be made of his wickedness; here he seems to speak of his rise, which should be occasioned by the general apostasy he had mentioned, and to intimate that all sorts of false doctrines and corruptions should centre in him.

The apostle further describes the reign and rule of this man of sin (*vv.* 9–11). Here we are to observe, (1) The manner of his coming, or ruling, and working: in general, that it is after the example of Satan, the grand enemy of souls, the great adversary of God and man. (2) The persons are described who are his willing subjects, or most likely to become such, *v.* 10. They are such as *love not the truth that they may be saved.* And of these persons it is said that they perish or are lost; they are in a lost condition, and in danger to be lost for ever. For,

6. We have the *sin and ruin of the subjects* of antichrist's kingdom declared, *vv.* 11, 12. (1) Their sin is this: *They believed not the truth, but had pleasure in unrighteousness.*

(2) Their ruin is thus expressed: *God shall send them strong delusions, to believe a lie.* Thus he will punish men for their unbelief, and for their dislike of the truth and love to sin and wickedness; not that God is the author of sin, but in righteousness he sometimes withdraws his grace from such sinners as are here mentioned.

HOLD THE TRADITIONS
(*vv.* 13–17)

Here observe, I. The consolation the Thessalonians might take against the terrors of this apostasy, *vv.* 13, 14. For they were chosen to salvation, and called to the obtaining of glory. This preservation of the saints is owing,

1. To the stability of the election of grace, *v.* 13. Therefore were they beloved of the Lord, because God had chosen them from the beginning.

2. To the efficacy of the gospel call, *v.* 14. As they were chosen to salvation, so they were called thereunto by the gospel. Whom he did predestinate those he also called, Rom. viii. 30. Hereupon there follows,

II. An exhortation to stedfastness and perseverance: *Therefore, brethren, stand fast, v.* 15. The Thessalonians are exhorted to stedfastness in their Christian profession, to *hold fast the traditions which they had been taught,* or the doctrine of the gospel, which had been delivered by the apostle, by word or epistle.

III. In *vv.* 16, 17 we have the apostle's earnest prayer for them, in which observe,

1. To whom he prays: *Our Lord*

Jesus Christ himself, and God, even our Father. We may and should direct our prayers, not only to God the Father, through the mediation of our Lord Jesus Christ, but also *to our Lord Jesus himself*; and should pray in his name unto God, not only as his Father but as our Father in and through him.

2. From what he takes encouragement in his prayer—from the consideration of what God had already done for him and them.

3. What it is that he asks of God for them—that *he would comfort their hearts, and establish them in every good word and work, v.* 17. We must be established in every good word and work, in the word of truth and the work of righteousness: Christ must be honoured by our good works and good words.

CHAPTER THREE

CHRISTIAN CONFIDENCE
(vv. 1–5)

In these words observe,

I. The apostle desires the prayers of his friends: *Finally, brethren, pray for us, v.* 1. He always remembered them in his prayers and would not have them forget him and his fellow-labourers, but bear them on their hearts at the throne of grace. Observe, further, what they are desired and directed to pray for; namely, (1) For the success of the gospel ministry: *That the word of the Lord may have free course, and be glorified, v.* 1. He desired that the word of the Lord might run (so it is in the original), that it might get ground, that the interest of religion in the world might go forward and not backward, and not only go

forward, but go apace. (2) For the safety of gospel ministers. He asks their prayers, not for preferment, but for preservation: *That we may be delivered from unreasonable and wicked men, v.* 2.

II. He encourages them to trust in God. We should not only pray to God for his grace, but also place our trust and confidence in his grace, and humbly expect what we pray for, *vv.* 3, 4.

III. He makes a short prayer for them, *v.* 5. It is a prayer for spiritual blessings. Two things of the greatest importance the apostle prays for: 1. That their hearts may be brought into the love of God, to be in love with God as the most excellent and amiable Being, the best of all beings. 2. That a *patient waiting for Christ* may be joined with this love of God. There is no true love of God without faith in Jesus Christ.

DISORDERLY CONDUCT
(vv. 6–15)

Observe,

I. That which was amiss among the Thessalonians, which is expressed,

1. More generally. There were some who *walked disorderly, not after the tradition they received* from the apostle, *v.* 6. They did not live regularly, nor govern themselves according to the rules of Christianity, nor agreeably to their profession of religion.

2. In particular, there were among them some *idle persons and busybodies, v.* 11. (1) There were some among them who were idle, *not working at all*, or doing nothing. It is probable that these persons had a

notion (by misunderstanding some passages in the former epistle) concerning the near approach of the coming of Christ, which served them for a pretence to leave off the work of their callings, and live in idleness. (2) There were busy-bodies among them: and it should seem, by the connection, that the same persons who were idle were busy-bodies also.

II. The good laws which were occasioned by these evil manners, concerning which we may take notice,

1. Whose laws they are: they are commands of the apostles of our Lord, given in the name of their Lord and ours, that is, the commands of our Lord himself. *We command you, brethren, in the name of the Lord Jesus Christ, v.* 6. Again, *We command and exhort you by our Lord Jesus Christ, v.* 12.

2. What the good laws and rules are.

(1) His commands and directions to the whole church regard, [I] Their behaviour towards the disorderly persons who were among them, which is thus expressed

(*v.* 6), to *withdraw themselves from such,* and afterwards to *mark that man, and have no company with him, that he may be ashamed; yet not to count him as an enemy, but to admonish him as a brother.* [2] Their general conduct and behaviour ought to be according to the good example the apostle and those who were with him had given them: *Yourselves know how you ought to follow us, v.* 7.

(2) He commands and directs those that lived idle lives to reform, and set themselves to their business. It was a proverbial speech among the Jews, *He who does not labour does not deserve to eat.*

(3) He exhorts *those that did well not* to be *weary in well-doing* (*v.* 13); as if he had said, "Go on and prosper. It will be time enough to rest when you come to heaven, that *everlasting rest which remains for the people of God.*"

BLESSING (*vv.* 16–18)

In this conclusion of the epistle we have the apostle's benediction and prayers for these Thessalonians.

THE FIRST EPISTLE OF ST. PAUL TO

TIMOTHY

CHAPTER ONE
INSCRIPTION (*vv.* 1–4)

Here is, I. The inscription of the epistle, from whom it is sent: *Paul an apostle of Jesus Christ*, constituted an apostle *by the commandment of God our Saviour, and Lord Jesus Christ*. He calls Timothy his own son, because he had been an instrument of his conversion, and because he had been a son that served him, served with him in the gospel, Phil. ii. 22.

II. The benediction is, *grace, mercy, and peace, from God our Father*.

III. Paul tells Timothy what was the end of his appointing him to this office: *I besought thee to abide at Ephesus*. Though he might assume an authority to command him, yet for love's sake he chose rather to beseech him. Observe, 1. Ministers must not only be charged to preach the true doctrine of the gospel, but charged to preach no other doctrine. 2. In the times of the apostles there were attempts made to corrupt Christianity, otherwise this charge to Timothy might have been spared. 3. He must not only see to it that he did not preach any other doctrine, but he must charge others that they might not add any thing of their own to the gospel, or take any thing from it, but that they preach it pure and uncorrupt.

THOSE WHO DEVIATE
(*vv.* 5–11)

Here the apostle instructs Timothy how to guard against the judaizing teachers, or others who mingled fables and endless genealogies with the gospel.

I. He shows the end and uses of the law: it is intended to promote love, *for love is the fulfilling of the law*, Rom. xiii. 10.

1. *The end of the commandment is charity*, or love, Rom. xiii. 8. The main scope and drift of the divine law are to engage us to the love of God and one another. Now some who set up for teachers of the law swerved from the very end of the commandment: they set up for disputers, but their disputes proved vain jangling; they set up for teachers, but they pretended to teach others what they themselves did not understand.

2. The use of the law (*v.* 8): *The law is good, if a man use it lawfully*. The abuse which some have made of the law does not take away the use of it; but when a divine appointment has been abused, call it back to its right use and take away the abuses, for the law is still very useful as a rule of life. It is the grace of God that changes men's hearts; but the terrors of the law may be of use to tie their hands and restrain their tongues. In this black roll of

sinners, he particularly mentions breaches of the second table, duties which we owe to our neighbour.

II. He shows the glory and grace of the gospel. Paul's epithets are expressive and significant; and frequently every one is a sentence: as here (*v.* 11), *According to the glorious gospel of the blessed God.* Paul reckoned it a great honour put upon him, and a great favour done him, that this glorious gospel was committed to his trust; that is, the preaching of it, for the framing of it is not committed to any man or company of men in the world. The settling of the terms of salvation in the gospel of Christ is God's own work; but the publishing of it to the world is committed to the apostles and ministers.

MINISTRY AND MERCY
(*vv.* 12–17)

Here the apostle, I. Returns thanks to Jesus Christ for putting him into the ministry. Observe, 1. It is Christ's work to put men into the ministry, Acts xxvi. 16, 17. He *counted me faithful*; and none are counted faithful but those whom he makes so.

II. The more to magnify the grace of Christ in putting him into the ministry, he gives an account of his conversion.

1. What he was before his conversion: *A blasphemer, a persecutor, and injurious.*

2. The great favour of God to him: *But I obtained mercy.*

(1) If Paul had persecuted the Christians wilfully, knowing them to be the people of God, for aught I know he had been guilty of the

unpardonable sin; but, because he did it ignorantly and in unbelief, he obtained mercy.

(2) Here he takes notice of the abundant grace of Jesus Christ, *v.* 14. *This is a faithful saying,* &c. Here we have the sum of the whole gospel, *that Jesus Christ came into the world.* His errand into the world was to seek and find, and so save, *those that were lost,* Luke xix. 10. The ratification of this is *that it is a faithful saying, and worthy of all acceptation.* It is good news, worthy of all acceptation; and yet not too good to be true, for it is a faithful saying. In the close of the verse Paul applies it to himself: *Of whom I am chief.* Paul was a sinner of the first rank; so he acknowledges himself to have been, for he breathed out threatenings and slaughter against the disciples of the Lord, &c., Acts ix. 1, 2.

(3) The mercy which Paul found with God, notwithstanding his great wickedness before his conversion, he speaks of,

[1] For the encouragement of others to repent and believe (*v.* 16).

[2] He mentions it to the glory of God, having spoken of the mercy he had found with God, he could not go on with his letter without inserting a thankful acknowledgment of God's goodness to him: *Now unto the King eternal, immortal, invisible, the only wise God, be honour and glory for ever and ever. Amen.*

HOLD THE FAITH (*vv.* 18–20)

Here is the charge he gives to Timothy to proceed in his work with resolution, *v.* 18. Observe, 1. The ministry is a warfare, it is a good warfare against sin and Satan: and under the banner of the Lord Jesus, who is the Captain of our salvation (Heb. ii. 10), and in his cause, and against his enemies, ministers are in a particular manner engaged. 2. Ministers must war this good warfare, must execute their office diligently and courageously, notwithstanding oppositions and discouragements. 3. The prophecies which went before concerning Timothy are here mentioned as a motive to stir him up to a vigorous and conscientious discharge of his duty; so the good hopes that others have entertained concerning us should excite us to our duty: *That thou by them mightest war a good warfare.* 4. We must hold both faith and a good conscience: *Holding faith and a good conscience, v.* 19. Those that put away a good conscience will soon make shipwreck of faith. As for those who had made shipwreck of the faith, he specifies two, *Hymeneus and Alexander,* who had made a profession of the Christian religion, but had quitted that profession; and Paul had delivered them to Satan.

CHAPTER TWO

DIRECTIONS FOR PRAYER
(*vv.* 1–8)

Here is, I. A charge given to Christians to pray for all men in general, and particularly for all in authority. We must pray for them, and we must give thanks for them, pray for their welfare and for the welfare of their kingdoms, and therefore must not plot against them, that in the peace thereof we may have peace, and give thanks

for them and for the benefit we have under their government, that *we may lead a quiet and peaceable life in all godliness and honesty.*

II. As a reason why we should in our prayers concern ourselves for all men, he shows God's love to mankind in general, *v.* 4.

1. One reason why all men are to be prayed for is because there is one God, and that God bears a good will to all mankind. There is one God (*v.* 5), and one only, there is no other, there can be no other, for there can be but one infinite. This one God *will have all men to be saved*; he desires not the death and destruction of any (Ezek. xxxiii. 11), but the welfare and salvation of all. Not that he has decreed the salvation of all, for then all men would be saved; but he has a good will to the salvation of all, and none perish but by their own fault, Matt. xxiii. 37.

2. There is one Mediator, and that Mediator gave himself a ransom for all. *He gave himself a ransom.* Observe, The death of Christ was a ransom, a counterprice. We deserved to have died. Christ died for us, to save us from death and hell. He died to work out a common salvation: to do this, he put himself into the office of Mediator between God and man. A mediator supposes a controversy. Sin had made a quarrel between us and God; Jesus Christ is a Mediator who undertakes to make peace, to bring God and man together.

III. A direction how to pray, *v.* 8. 1. *Pray every where.* We must pray in our closets, pray in our families, pray at our meals, pray when we are on journeys, and pray in the solemn assemblies, whether more public or private. 2. It is the will of God that in prayer we should lift up holy hands: *Lifting up holy hands*, or pure hands, pure from the pollution of sin, washed in the fountain opened for sin and uncleanness. 3. We must pray in charity: *Without wrath*, or malice, or anger at any person. 4. We must pray in faith *without doubting* (Jam. i. 6), or, as some read it, *without disputing*, and then it falls under the head of charity.

THE ROLE OF WOMEN
(vv. 9–15)

I. Here is a charge, that women who profess the Christian religion should be modest, sober, silent, and submissive, as becomes their place. 1. They must be very modest in their apparel, not affecting gaudiness, gaiety, or costliness. 2. Women must learn the principles of their religion, learn Christ, learn the scriptures; they must not think that their sex excuses them from that learning which is necessary to salvation. 3. They must be silent, submissive, and subject, and not usurp authority. The reason given is because *Adam was first formed, then Eve* out of him, to denote her subordination to him and dependence upon him; and that she was made for him, to be a help-meet for him.

II. Here observe, Women are to profess godliness as well as men; for they are baptized, and thereby stand engaged to exercise themselves to godliness; and, to their honour be it spoken, many of them were eminent professors of Christianity in the days of the apostles,

as the book of Acts will inform us. *Notwithstanding she shall be saved*, &c. Though in sorrow, yet she shall bring forth, and be a living mother of living children; with this proviso, that they continue in faith, and charity, and holiness with sobriety: and women, under the circumstance of child-bearing should by faith lay hold of this promise for their support in the needful time.

CHAPTER THREE
QUALIFICATIONS FOR LEADERSHIP (vv. 1–7)

Here we have the character of a gospel minister, whose office it is to preside in a particular congregation of Christians. Observe,

I. The ministry is a work. However the office of a bishop may be now thought a good preferment, then it was thought a good work. 1. The office of a scripture-bishop is an office of divine appointment, and not of human invention. 2. This office of a Christian bishop is a work, which requires diligence and application. 3. It is a good work, a work of the greatest importance, and designed for the greatest good. 4. There ought to be an earnest desire of the office in those who would be put into it; if a man desire, he should earnestly desire it for the prospect he has of bringing greater glory to God, and of doing the greatest good to the souls of men by this means.

II. To discharge this office, this work, the workman must be duly qualified. 1. A minister must be blameless, he must not lie under any scandal. 2. He must be the husband of one wife. 3. He must be vigilant and watchful against Satan, that subtle enemy; he must watch over himself, and the souls of those who are committed to his charge, of whom having taken the *oversight*, he must improve all opportunities of doing them good. 4. He must be sober, temperate, moderate in all his actions, and in the use of all creature-comforts. 5. He must be of good behaviour, composed and solid, and not light, vain, and frothy. 6. He must be given to hospitality. 7. Apt to teach. Therefor this is a preaching bishop whom Paul describes, one who is both able and willing to communicate to others the knowledge which God has given him. 8. No drunkard: *Not given to wine*. 9. No striker; one who is not quarrelsome, nor apt to use violence to any, but does every thing with mildness, love, and gentleness. 10. One who is not greedy of filthy lucre, who is dead to the wealth of this world. 11. He must be patient, and not a brawler, of a mild disposition. 12. Not covetous. Covetousness is bad in any, but it is worst in a minister, whose calling leads him to converse so much with another world. 13. He must be one who keeps his family in good order: *That rules well his own house. For, if a man know not how to rule his own house, how shall he take care of the church of God.* 14. He must not be a novice, not one newly brought to the Christian religion: the more ignorant men are the more proud they are: *Lest, being lifted up with pride, he fall into the condemnation of the devil.* 15. He must be of good reputation among his neighbours.

DEACONS (*vv.* 8–13)

We have here the character of deacons: these had the care of the temporal concerns of the church, that is, the maintenance of the ministers and provision for the poor: they served tables, while the ministers or bishops gave themselves only to the ministry of the word and prayer, Acts vi. 2, 4. They must be *grave*. Gravity becomes all Christians, but especially those who are in office in the church. *Not double-tongued*; that will say one thing to one and another thing to another, according as their interest leads them: a double tongue comes from a double heart; flatterers and slanderers are double-tongued. *Not given to much wine*; for this is a great disparagement to any man, especially to a Christian, and one in office, unfits men for business, opens the door to many temptations. *Not greedy of filthy lucre*; this would especially be bad in the deacons, who were entrusted with the church's money, and, if they were covetous and greedy of filthy lucre, would be tempted to embezzle it, and convert that to their own use which was intended for the public service. *Holding the mystery of faith in a pure conscience*, v. 9. The practical love of truth is the most powerful preservative from error and delusion. Their wives likewise must have a good character (*v.* 11). And the reason why the deacons must be thus qualified is (*v.* 13) because, though the office of a deacon be of an inferior degree, yet it is a step towards the higher degree; and those who had served tables well the church might see cause afterwards to discharge from that service, and prefer to serve in preaching the word and in prayer.

GROUND OF TRUTH
(*vv.* 14–16)

He concludes the chapter with a particular direction to Timothy. Observe,

I. Those who are employed in the house of God must see to it that they behave themselves well, lest they bring reproach upon the house of God, and that worthy name by which they are called.

II. It is the great support of the church that it is the church of the living *God*, the true God in opposition to false gods, dumb and dead idols.

1. As the church of God, it is *the pillar and ground of truth*; that is, either, (1) The church itself is the pillar and ground of truth. The church holds forth the scripture and the doctrine of Christ, as the pillar to which a proclamation is affixed holds forth the proclamation. (2) Others understand it of Timothy. He, not he himself only, but he as an evangelist, he and other faithful ministers, are the pillars and ground of truth; it is their business to maintain, hold up, and publish, the truths of Christ in the church.

2. But what is the truth which the churches and ministers are the pillars and grounds of? Observe,

(1) Christianity is a mystery, a mystery that could not have been found out by reason or the light of nature, and which cannot be comprehended by reason, because it is above reason, though not contrary thereto. It is a mystery, not of philosophy or speculation; but of godliness, designed to promote godliness; and herein it exceeds all the mysteries of the Gentiles. But,

(2) What is the mystery of godliness? It is Christ; and here are six things concerning Christ, which make up the mystery of godliness. [1] That he is God manifest in the flesh: *God was manifest in the flesh*. This proves that he is God, the eternal Word, that was made flesh and was manifest in the flesh. [2] He is *justified in the Spirit*. That is, it was made to appear that his sacrifice was accepted, and so he rose again for our justification, as he was delivered for our offences, Rom. iv. 25. He was put to death in the flesh, but quickened by the Spirit, 1 Pet. iii. 18. [3] He was *seen of angels*. They worshipped him (Heb. i. 6); they attended his incarnation, his temptation, his agony, his death, his resurrection, his ascension. [4] He is *preached unto the Gentiles*. This is a great part of the mystery of godliness, that Christ was offered to the Gentiles a Redeemer and Saviour. [5] That he was *believed on in the world*, so that he was not preached in vain. [6] He was *received up into glory*, in his ascension. This indeed was before he was believed on in the world; but it is put last, because it was the crown of his exaltation.

CHAPTER FOUR

APOSTASY FORETOLD
(*vv.* 1–5)

We have here a prophecy of the apostasy of the latter times, which he had spoken of as a thing expected and taken for granted among Christians, 2 Thess. ii.

I. The prophecies concerning antichrist, as well as the prophecies concerning Christ, came from the Spirit. The Spirit in both spoke expressly of a general apostasy from the faith of Christ and the pure worship of God. This should come in the *latter times*, during the Christian dispensation, for these are called the latter days; in the following ages of the church, for the mystery of iniquity now began to work. *Some shall depart from the faith*, or there shall be an apostasy from the faith. Some, not all; for in the worst of times God will have a remnant, according to the election of grace. *Giving heed to seducing spirits*, men who pretended to the Spirit, but were not really guided by the Spirit. Now here observe,

(1) It will be done by hypocrisy of those that speak lies, the agents and emissaries of Satan, who promote these delusions by lies and forgeries and pretended miracles, *v.* 2. This respects also the hypocrisy of those who have *their consciences seared with a red-hot iron*, who are perfectly lost to the very first principles of virtue and moral honesty. (2) Another part of their character is that they forbid to marry, and speak very reproachfully of marriage, though an ordinance of God; and that they command *to abstain from meats*, and place religion in such abstinence at certain times and seasons, only to exercise a tyranny over the consciences of men.

II. Having mentioned their hypocritical fastings, the apostle takes occasion to lay down the doctrine

of the Christian liberty, which we enjoy under the gospel, of using God's good creatures, — that, whereas under the law there was a distinction of meats between clean and unclean (such sorts of flesh they might eat, and such they might not eat), all this is now taken away; and we are to call nothing common or unclean, Acts x. 15.

AN EXAMPLE TO THE BELIEVERS (*vv.* 6-16)

I. Godliness is here pressed upon him and others: *Refuse profane and old wives' sayings, vv.* 7, 8. The Jewish traditions, which some people fill their heads with, have nothing to do with them. *But exercise thyself rather unto godliness*; that is, mind practical religion. Those who would be godly must exercise themselves unto godliness; it requires a constant exercise. The reason is taken from the gain of godliness; *bodily exercise profits little*, or for a little time. Abstinence from meats and marriage, and the like, though they pass for acts of mortification and self-denial, yet profit little, they turn to little account.

II. The encouragement which we have to proceed in the ways of godliness. Here is another of Paul's faithful sayings, worthy of all acceptation—that all our labours and losses in the service of God and the work of religion will be abundantly recompensed, so that though we lose for Christ we shall not lose by him. *Therefore we labour and suffer reproach, because we trust in the living God, v.* 10.

God is the general Saviour of all

men, as he has put them into a savable state; but he is in a particular manner the Saviour of true believers; there is then a general and a special redemption.

III. He concludes the chapter with an exhortation to Timothy,

1. To *command and teach these things* that he had now been teaching him.

2. To conduct himself with that gravity and prudence which might gain him respect, notwithstanding his youth.

3. To confirm his doctrine by a good example: *Be thou an example of the believers*, &c. Observe, Those who teach by their doctrine must teach by their life, else they pull down with one hand what they build up with the other: they must be examples both *in word and conversation*.

4. He charges him to study hard: *Till I come give attendance to reading, to exhortation, to doctrine, to meditation upon these things*, *v*. 13. Though Timothy had extraordinary gifts, yet he must use ordinary means.

5. He charges him to beware of negligence: *Neglect not the gift that is in thee*, *v*. 14. The gifts of God will wither if they be neglected. It was an extraordinary gift that we read of elsewhere as being conferred on him by the laying on of Paul's hands, but he was invested in the office of the ministry by the laying on of the hands of the presbytery.

6. Having this work committed to him, he must *give himself wholly* to it: "Be wholly in those things, *that thy profiting may appear.*" He was a wise knowing man, and yet must still be profiting, and make it

appear that he improved in knowledge.

7. He presses it upon him to be very cautious: "*Take heed to thyself and to the doctrine*, consider what thou preachest; *continue in them*, in the truths that thou hast received; and this will be the way to *save thyself, and those that hear thee.*"

CHAPTER FIVE

HANDLING PEOPLE (*vv*. 1–16)

Here the apostle gives rules to Timothy, and in him to other ministers, in reproving. A great difference is to be made in our reproofs, according to the age, quality, and other circumstances, of the persons rebuked; thus, an elder in age or office must be entreated as a father; *on some have compassion, making a difference*, Jude 22. The younger must be rebuked as brethren, with love and tenderness; The elder women must be reproved, when there is occasion, as mothers. The younger women must be reproved, but reproved as *sisters, with all purity*.

In *vv*. 3–16 directions are given concerning the taking of widows into the number of those who were employed by the church and had maintenance from the church.

I. It is appointed that those widows only should be relieved by the charity of the church who were pious and devout, and not wanton widows that *lived in pleasure*, *vv*. 5, 6. She is to be reckoned a widow indeed, and fit to be maintained at the church's charge, who, being *desolate, trusteth in God*.

II. Another rule he gives is that the church should not be charged with the maintenance of those widows who had relations of their own that were able to maintain them.

III. He gives directions concerning the characters of the widows that were to be taken into the number to receive the church's charity: not under sixty years old, nor any who have divorced their husbands or been divorced from them and have married again; she must have been *the wife of one man*, such as had been a housekeeper, had a good name for hospitality and charity, *well reported of for good works*. Here are instances of such good works as are proper to be done by good wives: *If she have brought up children. If she have lodged strangers*, and *washed the saints' feet*; if she have been ready to give entertainment to good Christians and good ministers, when they were in their travels for the spreading of the gospel.

IV. He cautions them to take heed of admitting into the number those who are likely to be no credit to them (*v.* 11): *The younger widows refuse*; they will be weary of their employments in the church, and of living by rule, as they must do; so they *will marry, and cast off their first faith*. Besides, the apostle here advises the younger widows to marry (*v.* 14), which he would not if hereby they must have broken their vows.

SUPPORTING THE MINISTRY (*vv.* 17–25)

Here are directions,

I. Concerning the supporting of ministers. Care must be taken that they be honourably maintained

(*v.* 17). Here we have, 1. The work of ministers; it consists principally in two things: ruling well and labouring in the word and doctrine. This was the main business of elders or presbyters in the days of the apostles. 2. The honour due to those who were not idle, but laborious in this work; they were worthy of double honour, esteem, and maintenance. He quotes a scripture to confirm this command concerning the maintenance of ministers that we might think foreign; but it intimates what a significancy there was in many of the laws of Moses, and particularly in this, *Thou shalt not muzzle the ox that treads out the corn*, Deut. xxv. 4. The beasts that were employed in treading out the corn (for that way they took instead of threshing it) were allowed to feed while they did the work, so that the more work they did the more food they had; therefore let the elders that labour in the word and doctrine be well provided for; *for the labourer is worthy of his reward* (Matt. x. 10).

II. Concerning the accusation of ministers (*v.* 19): *Against an elder receive not an accusation, but before two or three witnesses*. Here is the scripture-method of proceeding against an elder, when accused of any crime. Observe, (1) Public scandalous sinners must be rebuked publicly: as their sin has been public, and committed before many, or at least come to the hearing of all, so their reproof must be public, and before all. (2) Public rebuke is designed for the good of others, that they may fear, as well as for the good of the party rebuked.

III. Concerning the ordination of ministers (*v.* 22): *Lay hands suddenly on no man*; it seems to be meant of the ordaining of men to the office of the ministry, which ought not to be done rashly and inconsiderately, and before due trial made of their gifts and graces, their abilities and qualifications for it.

IV. Concerning absolution, to which *vv.* 24, 25, seem to refer: *Some men's sins are open beforehand, going before to judgment, and some follow after,* &c. Observe, Ministers have need of a great deal of wisdom, to know how to accommodate themselves to the variety of offences and offenders that they have occasion to deal with. Some men's sins are so plain and obvious, and not found by secret search, that there is no dispute concerning the bringing of them under the censures of the church; they *go before to judgment,* to lead them to censure.—*Others they follow after*; that is, their wickedness does not presently appear, nor till after a due search has been made concerning it.

V. Concerning Timothy himself. 1. Here is a charge to him to be careful of his office; and a solemn charge it is: *I charge thee before God, as thou wilt answer it to God before the holy and elect angels, observe these things without partiality, v.* 21. 2. He charges him to take care of his health: *Drink no longer water,* &c. It seems, Timothy was a mortified man to the pleasures of sense; he drank water, and he was a man of no strong constitution of body, and for this reason Paul advises him to use wine for the

helping of his stomach and the recruiting of his nature.

CHAPTER SIX

DUTY OF SERVANTS
(*vv.* 1–5)

I. Here is the duty of servants. They must respect their masters, *count them worthy of all honour* (because they are their masters), of all the respect, observance, compliance, and obedience, that are justly expected from servants to their masters. Or suppose the master were a Christian, and a believer, and the servant a believer too, would not this excuse him, because *in Christ there is neither bond nor free?* No, by no means, for Jesus Christ did not come to dissolve the bond of civil relation, but to strengthen it: *Those that have believing masters, let them not despise them because they are brethren.* Timothy is appointed to *teach and exhort these things.* Ministers must preach not only the general duties of all, but the duties of particular relations.

II. Paul here warns Timothy to withdraw from those who corrupted the doctrine of Christ, and made it the subject of strife, debate, and controversy. But he that does not consent to the words of Christ *is proud (v.* 4) and contentious, ignorant, and does a great deal of mischief to the church, knowing nothing. When men are not content with the words of the Lord Jesus Christ, and the doctrine which is according to godliness, but will frame notions of their own and impose them, and that too in their own words, which man's wisdom teaches, and not in the words which the Holy Ghost teaches (1 Cor. ii. 13), they sow the seeds of all mischief in the church. Hence come *perverse disputings of men of corrupt minds* (v. 5), disputes that are all subtlety, and no solidity. From such as these Timothy is warned to withdraw himself.

CONTENTMENT (*vv.* 6–12)

From the mention of the abuse which some put upon religion, making it to serve their secular advantages, the apostle,

I. Takes occasion to show the excellency of contentment and the evil of covetousness.

1. The excellency of contentment, *vv.* 6–8.

(1) The truth he lays down is that *godliness with contentment is great gain.* Godliness is itself great gain, it is profitable to all things; and, wherever there is true godliness, there will be contentment; but those that have arrived at the highest pitch of contentment with their godliness are certainly the easiest happiest people in this world.

(2) The reason he gives for it is, *For we brought nothing with us into this world, and it is certain we can carry nothing out, v.* 7. This is a reason why we should be content with a little. [1] Because we can challenge nothing as a debt that is due to us, for we came naked into the world. [2] We shall carry nothing with us out of this world. Why should we not be content with a little, because, how much soever we have, we must leave it behind us? Eccl. v. 15, 16.

(3) Hence he infers, *having food and raiment, let us be therewith content, v.* 8. Observe, If God give us the necessary supports of life, we ought to be content therewith, though we have not the ornaments and delights of it.

2. The evil of covetousness. *Those that will be rich* (that set their hearts upon the wealth of this world, and are resolved, right or wrong, they will have it) *fall into temptation and a snare, v.* 9. It is not said, those that are rich, but those that will be rich, that is, that place their happiness in worldly wealth, that covet it inordinately, and are eager and violent in the pursuit of it.

(2) The apostle affirms that *the love of money is the root of all evil, v.* 10. Observe, [1] What is the root of all evil; the love of money; people may have money, and yet not love it; but, if they love it inordinately, it will push them on to all evil. [2] Covetous persons will quit the faith, if that be the way to get money: *Which while some coveted after, they have erred from the faith.*

II. Hence he takes occasion to caution Timothy, and to counsel him to keep in the way of God and his duty, and particularly to fulfil the trust reposed in him as a minister. He addresses himself to him as *a man of God.* 1. He charges Timothy to take heed of the love of money, which had been so pernicious to many: *Flee these things.* 2. To arm him against the love of the world, he directs him to follow that which is good. *Follow after righteousness, godliness, faith, love, patience, meekness.* 3. He exhorts him to do the part of a soldier: *Fight the good fight of faith.* Note,

Those who will get to heaven must fight their way thither. There must be a conflict with corruption and temptations, and the opposition of the powers of darkness. Observe, It is a good fight, it is a good cause, and it will have a good issue. It is the fight of faith; we do not war after the flesh, for the weapons of our warfare are not carnal, 2 Cor. x. 3, 4. 4. He exhorts him to *lay hold on eternal life*. Observe, (1) Eternal life is the crown proposed to us, for our encouragement to war, and to fight the good fight of faith, the good warfare. (2) This we must lay hold on, as those that are afraid of coming short of it and losing it.

SOLEMN CHARGES
(*vv.* 13–21)

The apostle here charges Timothy *to keep this commandment* (that is, the whole work of his ministry, all the trust reposed in him, all the service expected from him) *without spot, unrebukable*; he must conduct himself so in his ministry that he might not lay himself open to any blame nor incur any blemish. What are the motives to move him to this?

I. He gives him a solemn charge: *I give thee charge in the sight of God that thou do this*. He charges him as he will answer it at the great day to that God whose eyes are upon us all, who sees what we are and what we do. Observe, Christ died not only as a sacrifice, but as a martyr; and he witnessed a good confession when he was arraigned before Pilate (John xviii. 36, 37).

II. He reminds him of the confession that he himself had made: *Thou hast professed a good profes-*

sion before many witnesses (*v.* 12), namely, when he was ordained by the laying on of the hands of the presbytery.

III. He reminds him of Christ's second coming. Keep it with an eye to his second coming, when we must all give an account of the talents we have been entrusted with," Luke xvi. 2. Observe,

1. Concerning Christ and God the Father the apostle here speaks great things. (1) That God is the only Potentate; the powers of earthly princes are all derived from him, and depend upon him. (2) He is the blessed and the only Potentate, infinitely happy, and nothing can in the least impair his happiness. (3) He is King of kings, and Lord of lords. (4) He only has immortality. He only is immortal in himself, and has immortality as he is the fountain of it, for the immortality of angels and spirits is derived from him. (5) He dwells in inaccessible light, *light which no man can approach unto*: no man can get to heaven but those whom he is pleased to bring thither, and admit into his kingdom. (6) He is invisible: *Whom no man hath seen, nor can see*. It is impossible that mortal eyes should bear the brightness of the divine glory. No man can see God and live.

2. Having mentioned these glorious attributes, he concludes with a doxology: *To him be honour and power everlasting. Amen.* God having all power and honour to himself, it is our duty to ascribe all power and honour to him.

IV. The apostle adds, by way of postscript, a lesson for rich people, *vv.* 17–19.

1. Timothy must charge those that are rich to beware of the temptations, and improve the opportunities, of their prosperous estate.

2. Hence we may observe, (1) Ministers must not be afraid of the rich; be they ever so rich, they must speak to them, and charge them. (2) They must caution them against pride, and vain confidence in their riches. (3) This is the way for the rich to lay up in store for themselves for the time to come, that they may lay hold on eternal life. 3. That science which opposes the truth of the gospel is falsely so called, it is not true science, for if it were it would approve of the gospel and consent to it (*v.* 20). Those who are so fond of such science are in great danger of erring concerning the faith; those who are for advancing reason above faith are in danger of leaving faith.

V. Our apostle concludes with a solemn prayer and benediction: *Grace be with thee. Amen.*

TIMOTHY

CHAPTER ONE
GREETINGS (*vv.* 1–5)

Here is, I. The inscription of the epistle. He calls Timothy his *beloved son.* Paul felt the warmest affection for him both because he had been an instrument of his conversion and because as a son with his father he had served with him in the gospel.

II. Paul's thanksgiving to God for Timothy's faith and holiness: he thanks God that he remembered Timothy in his prayers. He thanks God that Timothy kept up the religion of his ancestors, *v.* 5. Observe, The entail of religion descended upon Timothy by the mother's side; he had a good mother, and a good grandmother: they believed, though his father did not, Acts xvi. 1. It is a comfortable thing when children imitate the faith and holiness of their godly parents, and tread in their steps, 3 John 4.

HOLD FAST (*vv.* 6–14)

Here is an exhortation and excitation of Timothy to his duty (*v.* 6): *I put thee in remembrance.*

I. He exhorts him to stir *up the gift of God* that was *in him.* Stir it up as fire under the embers. It is meant of all the gifts and graces that God had given him, to qualify him for the work of an evangelist.

Observe, 1. The great hindrance of usefulness in the increase of our gifts is slavish fear. Paul therefore warns Timothy against this: *God hath not given us the spirit of fear,* v. 7. God hath delivered us from the spirit of fear, and hath given us the spirit *of power, and of love, and of a sound mind.* The spirit of power, or of courage and resolution to encounter difficulties and dangers; the spirit of love to God, which will carry us through the opposition we may meet with; the spirit of love to God will set us above the fear of man, and all the hurt that man can do us; and the spirit of a sound mind, or quietness of mind, a peaceable enjoyment of ourselves. 2. The spirit God gives to his ministers is not a fearful, but a courageous spirit; it is a spirit of power, for they speak in his name who has all power, both in heaven and earth; and it is a spirit of love, for love to God and the souls of men must inflame ministers in all their service; and it is a spirit of a sound mind, for they speak the words of truth and soberness.

II. He exhorts him to count upon afflictions, and get ready for them. Observe,

1. The gospel of Christ is what we have none of us reason to be ashamed of. We must not be ashamed of those who are suffering for the gospel of Christ. *Be partaker*

375

of the afflictions of the gospel;" or, as it may be read, *Do thou suffer with the gospel*.

2. Mentioning God and the gospel, he takes notice what great things God has done for us by the gospel, *vv*. 9, 10. To encourage him to suffer, he urges two considerations:

(1) The nature of that gospel which he was called to suffer for, and the glorious and gracious designs and purposes of it. It is usual with Paul, when he mentions Christ, and the gospel of Christ, to digress from his subject, and enlarge upon them; so full was he of that which is all our salvation, and ought to be all our desire. Let us value the gospel more than ever, as it is that whereby life and immortality are brought to light, for herein it has the pre-eminence above all former discoveries.

(2) Consider the example of blessed Paul, *vv*. 11, 12. He was appointed to teach the Gentiles. He thought it a cause worth suffering for, and why should not Timothy think so too? No man needs to be afraid nor ashamed to suffer for the cause of the gospel: *I am not ashamed*, says Paul, *for I know whom I have believed, and am persuaded that he is able to keep that which I have committed unto him against that day*. There is a day coming, and it will be a very solemn and awful day, when we must give an account of our stewardship (Luke xvi. 2), give an account of our souls: now, if by an active obedient faith we commit it to Jesus Christ, we may be sure he is able to keep it, and it shall be forthcoming to our comfort in that day.

III. He exhorts him to *hold fast the form of sound words*, *v*. 13. Adhere to it in opposition to all heresies and false doctrine, which corrupt the Christian faith. Hold that fast *which thou hast heard of me*. But how must it be held fast? *In faith and love*; that is, we must assent to it as *a faithful saying*, and bid it welcome as *worthy of all acceptation*. Faith and love must go together; it is not enough to believe the sound words, and to give an assent to them, but we must love them, believe their truth and love their goodness, and we must propagate the form of sound words in love; speaking the truth in love, Eph. iv. 15. To the same purport is that (*v*. 14), *That good thing which was committed unto thee keep by the Holy Ghost, which dwelleth in us*. That good thing was the form of sound words, the Christian doctrine, which was committed to Timothy in his baptism and education as he was a Christian, and in his ordination as he was a minister.

APOSTASY AND LOYALTY
(*vv*. 15–18)

Having (*vv*. 13, 14) exhorted Timothy to hold fast,

I. He mentions the apostasy of many from the doctrine of Christ, *v*. 15. He does not say that they had turned away from the doctrine of Christ (though it should seem they had) but they had turned away from him, and disowned him in the time of his distress.

II. He mentions the constancy of one that adhered to him, namely, Onesiphorus: *For he often refreshed me, and was not ashamed of my chain*, *v.* 16. He repays him with his prayers: *The Lord give mercy to Onesiphorus*.

III. He prays for Onesiphorus himself, as well as for his house: *That he may find mercy in that day*, in the day of death and of judgment, when Christ will account all the good offices done to his poor members as done to himself.

CHAPTER TWO
PERSEVERANCE (*vv.* 1–7)

Here Paul encourages Timothy to constancy and perseverance in his work: *Be strong in the grace that is in Christ Jesus*, *v.* 1. Observe,

I. Timothy must count upon sufferings, even unto blood, and therefore he must train up others to succeed him in the ministry of the gospel, *v.* 2. Two things he must have an eye to in ordaining ministers: Their fidelity or integrity ("Commit them to *faithful men*"), and also their ministerial ability. They must not only be knowing themselves, but be able to teach others also, and be apt to teach. Here we have, 1. The things Timothy was to commit to others—what he had heard of the apostle among many witnesses; he must not deliver any thing besides, and what Paul delivered to him and others he had received of the Lord Jesus Christ. 2. He was to commit them as a trust, as a sacred deposit, which they were to keep, and to transmit pure and uncorrupt unto others. 3. Those to whom he was to commit these things must be faithful, that is, trusty men, and who were skilful to teach others.

II. He must *endure hardness* (*v.* 3): *Thou therefore*, &c. 1. All Christians, but especially ministers, *are soldiers of Jesus Christ*. 2. The soldiers of Jesus Christ must approve themselves good soldiers, faithful to their captain, resolute in his cause. 3. Those who would approve themselves good soldiers of Jesus Christ must endure hardness; that is, we must expect it and count upon it in this world.

III. He must not entangle himself in the affairs of this world, *v.* 4. A soldier, when he has enlisted, leaves his calling, and all the business of it, that he may attend his captain's orders. If we have given up ourselves to be Christ's soldiers, we must sit loose to this world.

IV. He must see to it that in carrying on the spiritual warfare he went by rule, that he observed the laws of war (*v.* 5): *If a man strive for masteries, yet is he not crowned, except he strive lawfully*. We are striving for mastery, to get the mastery of our lusts and corruptions, to excel in that which is good, but we cannot expect the prize unless we observe the laws. In doing that which is good we must take care that we do it in a right manner, that our good may not be evil spoken of.

V. He must be willing to wait for a recompense (*v.* 6): *The husbandman that laboureth must be first partaker of the fruits*. Or, as it should be read, *The husbandman labouring first must partake of the fruits*, as appears by comparing it with Jam. v. 7. If we would be partakers of the fruits, we must labour; if we would gain the prize, we must run the race.

CHRIST'S FAITHFULNESS
(vv. 8–13)

I. To encourage Timothy in suffering, the apostle puts him in mind of the resurrection of Christ (v. 8). The incarnation and resurrection of Jesus Christ, heartily believed and rightly considered, will support a Christian under all sufferings in the present life.

II. Another thing to encourage him in suffering was that he had Paul for an example.

Good ministers may and should encourage themselves in the hardest services and the hardest sufferings, with this, that God will certainly bring good to his church, and benefit to his elect, out of them.

III. Another thing with which he encourages Timothy is the prospect of a future state.

1. Those who faithfully adhere to Christ and to his truths and ways, whatever it cost them, will certainly have the advantage of it in another world: *If we be dead with him, we shall live with him*, v. 11.

2. It is at our peril if we prove unfaithful to him: *If we deny him, he also will deny us.* If we deny him before man, he will deny us before his Father, Matt. x. 33. If we be faithful to Christ, he will certainly be faithful to us. If we be false to him, he will be faithful to his threatenings: *he cannot deny himself*, cannot recede from any word that he hath spoken, for he is yea, and amen, the faithful witness.

WARNINGS AGAINST ERROR (vv. 14–18)

Having thus encouraged Timothy to suffer, he comes in the next place to direct him in his work.

I. He must make it his business to edify those who were under his charge, *to put them in remembrance* of those things which they did already know. — *Study to show thyself approved unto God*, v. 15. Ministers must be workmen; they have work to do, and they must take pains in it. And what is their work? It is *rightly to divide the word of truth.* Not to invent a new gospel, but rightly to divide the gospel that is committed to their trust.

II. He must take heed of that which would be a hindrance to him in his work, v. 16. He must take heed of error: *Shun profane and vain babblings.* Upon this occasion the apostle mentions some who had lately advanced erroneous doctrines: *Hymeneus and Philetus.* They have *erred concerning the truth*, or concerning one of the fundamental articles of the Christian religion, which is truth. The resurrection of the dead is one of the great doctrines of Christ. Now see the subtlety of the serpent and the serpent's seed. They did not deny the resurrection (for that had been boldly and avowedly to confront the word of Christ), but they put a corrupt interpretation upon that true doctrine, saying that the resurrection was past already, that what Christ spoke concerning the resurrection was *to be understood mystically* and by way of allegory, that it must be meant of a spiritual resurrection only. It is true, there is a spiritual resurrection, but to infer thence that there will not be a true and real resurrection of the body at the last day is to dash one truth of

Christ in pieces against another. By this they *overthrow the faith of some*.

GOOD VESSELS (*vv.* 19–21)

Here we see what we may comfort ourselves with, in reference to this, and the little errors and heresies that both infect and infest the church, and do mischief.

I. It may be a great comfort to us that the unbelief of men cannot make the promise of God of no effect. The prophets and apostles, that is, the doctrines of the Old and New Testament, are still firm; and they have a seal with two mottoes upon it, one on the one side, and the other one the other, as is usual in a broad seal. 1. One expresses our comfort—that *the Lord knows those that are his*, and those that are not; knows them, that is, he owns them, so knows them that he will never lose them. 2. Another declares our duty—that every one who names the name of Christ must depart from iniquity. Those who would have the comfort of the privilege must make conscience of the duty.

II. Another thing that may comfort us is that though there are some whose faith is overthrown, yet there are others who keep their integrity, and hold it fast (*v.* 20). Now we should see to it that we be vessels of honour: we must *purge ourselves from these corrupt opinions*, that we may be sanctified for our Master's use.

THINGS TO AVOID (*vv.* 22–26)

I. Paul here exhorts Timothy to beware of *youthful lusts*, *v.* 22.

Though he was a holy good man, very much mortified to the world, yet Paul thought it necessary to caution him against youthful lusts. He prescribes an excellent remedy against youthful lusts: *Follow righteousness, faith, charity, peace*, &c.

II. He cautions him against contention, and, to prevent this (*v.* 23), against *foolish and unlearned questions*, that tend to no benefit, strifes of words. Those who advanced them, and doted upon them, thought themselves wise and learned; but Paul calls them foolish and unlearned. The mischief of these is that they *gender strifes*, that they breed debates and quarrels among Christians and ministers.—*The servant of the Lord must not strive, v.* 24. Nothing worse becomes the servant of the Lord Jesus, who himself did not strive nor cry (Matt. xii. 19). The servant of the Lord must be *gentle to all men*, and thereby show that he is himself subject to the commanding power of that holy religion which he is employed in preaching and propagating.—*Apt to teach.* Those are unapt to teach who are apt to strive, and are fierce and froward. Ministers must have in their eyes, in instructing those who oppose themselves, their recovery: *If God, peradventure, will give them repentance to the acknowledging of the truth.*

CHAPTER THREE

REPROBATES (*vv.* 1–9)

1. Timothy must know that in the *last days* (*v.* 1), in gospel times, there would *come perilous times*. These would be difficult times,

wherein it would be difficult for a man to keep a good conscience.

II. Paul tells Timothy what would be the occasion of making these times perilous, or what shall be the marks and signs whereby these times may be known, *vv.* 2, &c. 1. Self-love will make the times perilous. Men love to gratify their own lusts, and make provision for them, more than to please God and to do their duty. 2. Covetousness. Observe, Self-love brings in a long train of sins and mischiefs. When men are lovers of themselves, no good can be expected from them, as all good may be expected from those who love God with all their hearts. 3. Pride and vain-glory. The times are perilous when men, being proud of themselves, are *boasters and blasphemers*. 4. When children are disobedient to their parents, they make the times perilous; for what wickedness will those stick at who will be abusive to their own parents and rebel against them? 5. Unthankfulness and unholiness make the times perilous, and these two commonly go together. 6. The times are perilous when men will not be held by the bonds either of nature or common honesty, when they are *without natural affection*, and *truce-breakers*, *v.* 3. 7. The times are perilous when men are *false accusers* one of another, having no regard to the good name of others, or to the religious obligations of an oath, but thinking themselves at liberty to say and do what they please, Ps. xii. 4. 8. When men have no government of themselves and their own appetites, they are soon fired, upon the least provocation. 9. When that which is good

and ought to be honoured is generally despised and looked upon with contempt. 10. When men are generally treacherous, wilful, and haughty, the times are perilous (*v.* 4)—when men are *traitors, heady, high-minded*. 11. When men are generally *lovers of pleasure more than lovers of God*. When there are more epicures than true Christians, then the times are bad indeed. 12. When, notwithstanding all this, they *have the form of godliness* (*v.* 5), are called by the Christian name, baptized into the Christian faith, and make a show of religion; but, how plausible soever their form of godliness is, they deny the power of it.

III. Here Paul warns Timothy to take heed of certain seducers, not only that he might not be drawn away by them himself, but that he might arm those who were under his charge against their seduction. Though the spirit of error may be let loose for a time, God has it in a chain. Satan can deceive the nations and the churches no further and no longer than God will permit him: *Their folly shall be manifest*, it shall appear that they are impostors, and every man shall abandon them.

THE INSPIRED SCRIPTURES
(*vv.* 10–17)

Here the apostle, to confirm Timothy in that way wherein he walked,

I. Sets before him his own example, which Timothy had been an eye-witness of, having long attended Paul (*v.* 10): *Thou hast fully known my doctrine*. The more fully we know the doctrine of

Christ and the apostles, the more closely we shall cleave to it; the reason why many sit loose to it is because they do not fully know it.

II. He warns Timothy of the fatal end of seducers, as a reason why he should stick closely to the truth as it is in Jesus: *But evil men and·seducers shall wax worse and worse,* &c. v. 13.

III. He directs him to keep close to a good education, and particularly to what he had learned out of the holy scriptures (*vv.* 14, 15): *Continue thou in the things which thou hast learned.*

1. It is a great happiness to know the certainty of the things wherein we have been instructed (Luke i. 4); not only to know what the truths are, but to know that they are of undoubted certainty, for certainty in religion is of great importance and advantage: *Knowing,* (1) "That thou hast had good teachers. Consider of *whom thou hast learned them.*" (2) Knowing especially the firm foundation upon which thou has built, namely, that of the scripture (*v.* 15): *That from a child thou hast known the holy scriptures.*

2. Those who would acquaint themselves with the things of God, and be assured of them, must know the holy scriptures, for these are the summary of divine revelation.

3. It is a great happiness to know the holy scriptures from our childhood; and children should betimes get the knowledge of the scriptures.

4. The scriptures we are to know are the holy scriptures; they come from the holy God, were delivered by holy men, contain holy precepts, treat of holy things, and were designed to make us holy and to

lead us in the way of holiness to happiness. Now here observe,

(1) What is the excellency of the scripture. It is *given by inspiration of God* (*v.* 16), and therefore is his word. It is a divine revelation, which we may depend upon as infallibly true. The same Spirit that breathed reason into us breathes revelation among us.

(2) What use it will be of to us. [1] *It is able to make us wise to salvation*; that is, it is a sure guide in our way to eternal life. [2] It is *profitable* to us for all the purposes of the Christian life, *for doctrine, for reproof, for correction, for instruction in righteousness.* It answers all the ends of divine revelation. It instructs us in that which is true, reproves us for that which is amiss, directs us in that which is good. [3] *That the man of God may be perfect, v.* 17. The Christian, the minister, is the man of God. That which finishes a man of God in this world is the scripture. By it we are *thoroughly furnished for every good work.* There is that in the scripture which suits every case.

(3) On the whole we here see, [1] That the scripture has various uses, and answers divers ends and purposes: *It is profitable for doctrine, for reproof, for correction* of all errors in judgment and practice, and *for instruction in righteousness.* [2] The scripture is a perfect rule of faith and practice, and was designed for the man of God, the minister as well as the Christian who is devoted to God, for it is *profitable for doctrine,* &c. [3] If we consult the scripture, which was given by inspiration of God, and

follow its directions, we shall be made men of God, *perfect, and thoroughly furnished to every good work*.

CHAPTER FOUR

PAUL'S CHARGE (*vv*. 1–8)

Observe, I. How awfully this charge is introduced (*v*. 1): *I charge thee before God, and the Lord Jesus Christ, who shall judge the quick and the dead at his appearing and his kingdom*. Observe, The best of men have need to be awed into the discharge of their duty.

II. What is the matter of the charge, *vv*. 2–5. He is charged,

1. To *preach the word*. This is ministers' business; a dispensation is committed to them.

2. To urge what he preached, and to press it with all earnestness upon his hearers: "*Be instant in season and out of season, reprove, rebuke, exhort*." We must do it in season, that is, let slip no opportunity; and do it out of season, that is, not shift off the duty, under pretence that it is out of season.

3. He must tell people of their faults: "*Reprove them, rebuke them*."

4. He must direct, encourage, and quicken those who began well. "*Exhort them* (persuade them to hold on, and endure to the end) and this *with all long-suffering and doctrine*." (1) He must do it very patiently: *With all long-suffering*. (2) He must do it rationally, not with passion, but *with doctrine*.

5. He must *watch in all things*. "Seek an opportunity of doing them a kindness; let no fair occasion slip, through thy negligence.

6. He must count upon afflictions, and endure them, make the best of them.

7. He must remember his office, and discharge its duties: *Do the work of an evangelist*. The office of the evangelist was, as the apostles' deputies, to water the churches that they planted. They were not settled pastors, but for some time resided in, and presided over, the churches that the apostles had planted, till they were settled under a standing ministry. This was Timothy's work.

8. He must fulfil his ministry: *Make full proof of it*. It was a great trust that was reposed in him, and therefore he must answer it, and perform all the parts of his office with a diligence and care.

III. The reasons to enforce the charge.

1. Because errors and heresies were likely to creep into the church, by which the minds of many professing Christians would be corrupted (*vv*. 3, 4): "*For the time will come when they will not endure sound doctrine*." They will *turn away their ears from the truth*; they will grow weary of the old plain gospel of Christ, and then they will be greedy of fables, and take pleasure in them, and God will give them up to those strong delusions, because they received not the truth in the love of it, 2 Thess. ii. 11, 12.

2. Because Paul for his part had almost done his work: *Do thou make full proof of thy ministry, for I am now ready to be offered*, *v*. 6. Observe,

[1] With what pleasure he speaks of dying. He calls it his departure; though it is probable that he fore-

saw he must die a violent bloody death, yet he calls it his departure, or his release.

[2] With what pleasure he looks back upon the life he had lived (v. 7): *I have fought a good fight, I have finished my course*, &c. He did not fear death, because he had the testimony of his conscience that by the grace of God he had in some measure answered the ends of living.

[3] With what pleasure he looks forward to the life he was to live hereafter (v. 8): *Henceforth there is laid up for me a crown of righteousness*, &c. He had lost for Christ, but he was sure he should not lose by him, Phil. iii. 8.

DIRECTIONS (vv. 9–15)

Here are particular matters which Paul mentions to Timothy, now at the closing of the epistle. 1. He bids him hasten to him, if possible (v. 9): *Do thy diligence to come shortly to me*. Paul wanted Timothy's company and help; and the reason he gives is because several had left him (v. 10); one from an ill principle, namely, *Demas*, who abides under an ill name for it: *Demas hath forsaken me, having loved this present world*. *Crescens* had gone one way and *Titus* another way. *Luke* however remained with Paul (vv. 11, 12), and was not this enough? Paul did not think it so; he loved the company of his friends. 2. He speaks respectfully concerning *Mark*: *He is profitable to me for the ministry*. It is supposed that this Mark was he about whom Paul and Barnabas had contended, Acts xv. 39. By this it appears that Paul was not reconciled to Mark, and

had a better opinion of him than he had had formerly. 3. Paul orders Timothy to come to him, bids him as he came through Troas to bring with him thence those things which he had left behind him there (v. 13), the cloak he had left there, which, it may be, Paul had the more occasion for in a cold prison. Paul was guided by divine inspiration, and yet he would have his books with him. 4. He mentions *Alexander*, and the mischief that he had done him, vv. 14, 15. This is he who is spoken of Acts xix. 33. He cautions Timothy to take heed of him: "*Of whom be thou aware also*, that he do not, under pretence of friendship, betray thee to mischief." It is dangerous having any thing to do with those who would be enemies to such a man as Paul.

CONCLUSION (vv. 16–22)

Here, I. He gives Timothy an account of his own present circumstances.

1. He had lately been called to appear before the emperor, upon his appeal to Cæsar; and then *no man stood with him* (v. 16), to plead his cause, to bear testimony for him, or so much as to keep him in countenance, but *all men forsook him*.

2. *Notwithstanding this God stood by him* (v. 17), gave him extraordinary wisdom and courage, to enable him to speak so much the better himself. *And that all the Gentiles might hear*; the emperor himself and the great men who would never have heard Paul preach if he had not been brought before them. *And I was delivered out of the mouth of the lion*, that is, of Nero (as some

think) or some other judge. *And the Lord shall deliver me from every evil work*. See how Paul improved his experiences: "*He that hath delivered doth deliver, and we trust he will yet deliver*, will deliver me *from every evil work*, from any ill done to me by others. *And shall preserve me to his heavenly kingdom*." And for this he gives glory to God, rejoicing in hope of the glory of God.

II. He sends salutations to *Aquila, and Priscilla, and the household of Onesiphorus, v*. 19. He mentions his leaving *Trophimus sick at Miletus* (*v*. 20), by which it appears that though the apostles healed all manner of diseases miraculously, for the confirmation of their doctrine, yet they did not exert that power upon their own friends, lest it should have looked like a collusion.

III. He hastens Timothy to *come to him before winter* (*v*. 21), because he longed to see him, and because in the winter the journey or voyage would be more dangerous.

IV. He sends commendations to him from *Eubulus, Pudens, Linus, Claudia,* and all the *brethren*.

V. He concludes with a prayer, that the *Lord Jesus would be with his spirit*.

THE EPISTLE OF ST. PAUL TO

TITUS

CHAPTER ONE

GREETINGS (vv. 1–5)

Here is the preface to the epistle, showing,

I. The writer. *Paul*, a Gentile name taken by the apostle of the Gentiles, Acts xiii. 9, 46, 47.

II. The person written to, who is described, 1. By his name, *Titus*, a Gentle Greek, yet called both to the faith and ministry. Observe, the grace of God is free and powerful. What worthiness or preparation was there in one of heathen stock and education? 2. By his spiritual relation to the apostle: *My own* (or *my genuine*) *son*, not by natural generation, but by supernatural regeneration. *I have begotten you through the gospel*, said he to the Corinthians, 1 Cor. iv. 15. "*My own son after the common faith*, that faith which is common to all the regenerate, and which thou hast in truth, and expressest to the life." This might be said to distinguish Titus from hypocrites and false teachers, and to recommend him to the regard of the Cretans, as being among them a lively image of the apostle himself, in faith, and life, and heavenly doctrine.

III. The salutation and prayer, wishing all blessings to him: *Grace, mercy, and peace, from God the Father, and the Lord Jesus Christ our Saviour*.

Thus far is the preface to the epistle; then follows the entrance into the matter, by signifying the end of Titus's being left in Crete:

I. More generally: *For this cause left I thee in Crete, that thou shouldst set in order the things that are wanting*. Titus was to go on in settling what the apostle himself had not time for, in his short stay there.

II. In special: *To ordain elders in every city*, that is, ministers, who were mostly out of the elder and most understanding and experienced Christians; or, if younger in years, yet such as were grave and solid in their deportment and manners. These were to be set where there was any fit number of Christians, as in larger towns and cities was usually the case; though villages, too, might have them where there were Christians enough for it. These presbyters or elders were to have the ordinary and stated care and charge of the churches; to feed and govern them, and perform all pastoral work and duty in and towards them.

III. The rule of his proceeding: *As I had appointed thee*, probably when he was going from him, and in the presence and hearing of others, to which he may now refer, not so much for Titus's own sake as for the people's, that they might the more readily yield obedience to Titus.

ORDINATION (*vv.* 6–16)

The apostle here gives Titus directions about ordination, showing whom he should ordain, and whom not.

I. Of those whom he should ordain. He points out their qualifications and virtues; such as respect their life and manners, and such as relate to their doctrine: the former in the sixth, seventh, and eighth verses, and the latter in the ninth.

1. Their qualifications respecting their life and manners are,

(1) More general: *If any be blameless.* The meaning is, He must be one who lies not under an ill character; but rather must have a good report.

(2) More particularly.

[1] There is his relative character. In his own person, he must be of conjugal chastity: *The husband of one wife.* And, as to his children, *having faithful children*, obedient and good, brought up in the true Christian faith, and living according to it, at least as far as the endeavours of the parents can avail. *Not accused of riot, nor unruly*, not justly so accused, as having given ground and occasion for it, for otherwise the most innocent may be falsely so charged; they must look to it therefore that there be no colour for such censure. The ground of this qualification is shown from the nature of his office (*v.* 7): *For a bishop must be blameless, as the steward of God.* Those before termed presbyters, or elders, are in this verse styled bishops; and such they were, having no ordinary fixed and standing officers above them.

[2] The more absolute ones are expressed, *First*, Negatively, showing what an elder or bishop must not be: *Not self-willed. Not soon angry, not one of a hasty angry temper*, soon and easily provoked and inflamed. *Not given to wine*; there is no greater reproach on a minister than to be a wine-bibber, one who loves it, and gives himself undue liberty this way who *continues at the wine or strong drink till it inflames him.* Seasonable and moderate use of this, as of the other good creatures of God, is not unlawful. But excess therein is shameful in all, especially in a minister. *No striker*, in any quarrelsome or contentious manner, not injuriously nor out of revenge, with cruelty or unnecessary roughness. *Not given to filthy lucre*; not greedy of it (as 1 Tim. iii. 3). But, *Secondly*, Positively: he must be (*v.* 8) *a lover of hospitality*, as an evidence that he is not given to filthy lucre. *A lover of good men*, or of *good things*; ministers should be exemplary in both; this will evince their open piety, and likeness to God and their Master Jesus Christ. *Holy* in what concerns religion; one who reverences and worships God, and is of a spiritual and heavenly conversation. *Temperate*; it comes from a word that signifies *strength*, and denotes one who has power over his appetite and affections, or, in things lawful, can, for good ends, restrain and hold them in.

2. As to doctrine,

(1) Here is his duty: *Holding fast the faithful word, as he has been taught*, keeping close to the doctrine of Christ, *the word of his grace.*

(2) Here is the end: *That he may be able, by sound doctrine, both to exhort, and to convince the gainsayers*, to persuade and draw others to the true faith, and to convince the contrary-minded.

II. The apostle's directory shows whom he should reject or avoid.

1. From bad teachers. (1) Those false teachers are described. They were *unruly*, headstrong and ambitious of power. (2) Here is the apostle's direction how to deal with them (*v.* 11): *Their mouths must be stopped*; not by outward force (Titus had no such power, nor was this the gospel method), but by confutation and conviction, showing them their error, *not giving place to them even for an hour*.

III. In reference to their people or hearers, who are described from ancient testimony given of them.

1. Here is the witness (*v.* 12): *One of themselves, even a prophet of their own*, that is, one of the Cretans, not of the Jews, Epimenides a Greek poet, likely to know and unlikely to slander them.

2. Here is the matter of his testimony: *The Cretans are always liars, evil beasts, slow bellies.* Even to a proverb, they were infamous for falsehood and lying.

3. Here is the verification of this by the apostle himself: *v.* 13. This witness is true.

4. He instructs Titus how to deal with them: *Wherefore rebuke them sharply.* When Paul wrote to Timothy he bade him instruct with meekness; but now, when he writes to Titus, he bids him rebuke them sharply. The Cretans' sins and corruptions were many, great, and habitual; therefore they must be

rebuked sharply. But that such direction might not be misconstrued,

5. Here is the end of it noted: *That they may be sound in the faith* (*v.* 14), *not giving heed to Jewish fables, and commandments of men, that turn from the truth.*

6. He gives the reasons of this, from the liberty we have by the gospel from legal observances, and the evil and mischief of a Jewish spirit under the Christian dispensation in the last two verses. To good Christians that are sound in the faith and thereby purified *all things are pure.*

CHAPTER TWO

GENERAL DUTIES (*vv.* 1–10)

Now here he exhorts him,

I. Generally, to a faithful discharge of his own office: and then,

II. Specially and particularly, he instructs him to apply this sound doctrine to several sorts of persons, from *vv.* 2–10.

1. To the aged men. By aged men some understand elders by office, including deacons, &c. But all old disciples of Christ must conduct themselves in every thing agreeably to the Christian doctrine.

2. To the aged women. These also must be instructed and warned. They must *be in behaviour as becometh holiness*: both men and women must accommodate their behaviour to their profession.

3. There are lessons for young women also, whom the aged women must teach, instructing and advising them in the duties of religion according to their years. These young women the more aged must

teach, (1) To bear a good personal character: *To be sober and discreet.* (2) *To love their husbands, and to be obedient to them*: and where there is true love this will be no difficult command. (3) *And to love their children*, not with a natural affection only, but a spiritual, a love springing from a holy sanctified heart and regulated by the word. The reason is added: *That the word of God may not be blasphemed.* Failures in such relative duties would be greatly to the reproach of Christianity.

4. Here is the duty of young men. They are apt to be eager and hot, thoughtless and precipitant; therefore they must be earnestly called upon and exhorted to be considerate; not rash; advisable and submissive, not wilful and headstrong; humble and mild, not haughty and proud; for there are more young people ruined by pride than by any other sin.

5. With these instructions to Titus, the apostle inserts some directions to himself. He could not expect so successfully to teach others, if he did not conduct himself well both in his conversation and preaching. (1) Here is direction for his manner of life: *In all things showing thyself a pattern of good works, v.* 7. Without this, he would pull down with one hand what he built with the other. And here is direction, (2) For his teaching and doctrine, as well as for his life: *In doctrine showing uncorruptness, gravity, sincerity, sound speech, that cannot be condemned, vv.* 7, 8. They must make it appear that the design of their preaching is purely to advance the honour of God, the interest of Christ and his kingdom, and the welfare and happiness of souls.

6. The directions respecting servants. Servants must know and do their duty to their earthly masters, but with an eye to their heavenly one: and Titus must not only instruct and warn earthly masters of their duties, but servants also of theirs, both in his public preaching and private admonitions.

THE DESIGN OF THE GOSPEL (*vv.* 11–15)

Here we have the grounds or considerations upon which all the foregoing directions are urged, taken from the nature and design of the gospel, and the end of Christ's death.

I. This is the very aim and business of Christianity, to instruct, and help, and form persons, under all distinctions and relations, to a right frame and conduct. For this,

1. They are put under the dispensation of *the grace of God*, so the gospel is called, Eph. iii. 2. Now grace is obliging and constraining to goodness.

2. This gospel grace *brings salvation* (reveals and offers it to sinners and ensures it to believers)— salvation from sin and wrath, from death and hell. Hence it is called *the word of life.*

3. *It hath appeared*, or shone out more clearly and illustriously than ever before. For,

4. It hath appeared *to all men*; not to the Jews only, but gospel grace is open to all, and all are invited to come and partake of the benefit of it, Gentiles as well as Jews.

5. This gospel revelation is to *teach*. For it teaches us,

(1) To abandon sin: *Denying ungodliness and worldly lusts*; to renounce and have no more to do with these. And then,

(2) To make conscience of that which is good: *To live soberly, righteously, and godly*, &c. Religion is not made up of negatives only; there must be doing good as well as eschewing evil; in these conjunctly is sincerity proved and the gospel adorned.

(3) To look for the glories of another world, to which a sober, righteous, and godly life in this is preparative: *Looking for that blessed hope, and the glorious appearing of the great God and our Saviour Jesus Christ*. And herewith is connected another ground, namely,

II. From the end of Christ's death: *Who gave himself for us, that he might redeem us from all iniquity, and purify unto himself a peculiar people, zealous of good works, v.* 14. To bring us to holiness and happiness was the end of Christ's death, as well as the scope of his doctrine.

CHAPTER THREE

GOOD WORKS (*vv.* 1–8)

Here is the fourth thing in the matter of the epistle. The apostle had directed Titus in reference to the particular and special duties of several sorts of persons; now he bids him exhort to what concerned them more in common, namely, to quietness and submission to rulers, and readiness to do good, and to equitable and gentle behaviour towards all men—things comely

and ornamental of religion; he must therefore put them in mind of such things. Here are the duties themselves, and the reasons of them.

I. The duties themselves, which they were to be reminded of. 1. *Put them in mind to be subject to principalities and powers, to obey magistrates.* Magistracy is God's ordinance for the good of all, and therefore must be regarded and submitted to by all; not for wrath and by force only, but willingly and for conscience' sake. And, 2. *To be ready to every good work.* The precept regards doing good in all kinds, and on every occasion that may offer, whether respecting God, ourselves, or our neighbour—What may bring credit to religion in the world. And, 3. *To speak evil of no man: to revile*, or *curse*, or *blaspheme none*: or (as our translation more generally) *to speak evil of none*, unjustly and falsely. If no good can be spoken, rather than speak evil unnecessarily, say nothing. And, 4. *To be no brawlers; no fighters*, either with hand or tongue, no quarrelsome contentious persons, apt to give or return ill and provoking language. Wherefor it follows, 5. *But gentle; equitable and just*, or candid and fair in constructions of things, not taking words or actions in the worst sense; and for peace sometimes yielding somewhat of strict right. And, 6. *Showing all meekness to all men.* We must be of a mild disposition, and not only have meekness in our hearts, but show it in our speech and conduct. Thus of the duties themselves, which Titus was to put people in mind of: for which,

389

II. He adds the reasons, which are derived

1. From their own past condition. Consideration of men's natural condition is a great means and ground of equity and gentleness, and all meekness, towards those who are yet in such a state. This has a tendency to abate pride and work pity and hope in reference to those who are yet unconverted. And he reasons,

2. From their present state. "We are delivered out of that our miserable condition by no merit nor strength of our own; but only by the mercy and free grace of God, and merit of Christ, and operation of his Spirit. Therefore we have no ground, in respect of ourselves, to contemn those who are yet unconverted, but rather to pity them, and cherish hope concerning them, that they, though in themselves as unworthy and unmeet as we were, yet may obtain mercy, as we have: and so upon this occasion the apostle again opens the causes of our salvation, *vv.* 4–7.

(1) We have here the prime author of our salvation—God the Father, therefore termed here *God our Saviour.*

(2) The spring and rise of it—the divine *philanthropy*, or *kindness and love of God to man.* By grace we are saved from first to last.

(3) Here is the means, or instrumental cause—the shining out of this love and grace of God in the gospel, *after it appeared*, that is, in the word.

(4) False grounds and motives are here removed: *Not by works of righteousness which we have done, but according to his mercy, he saved*

us; not for foreseen works of ours, but his own free grace and mercy alone.

(5) Here is the formal cause of salvation, or that wherein it lies, the beginnings of it at least—in regeneration or spiritual renewing, as it is here called.

(6) Here is the outward sign and seal thereof in baptism, called therefore *the washing of regeneration.* The work itself is inward and spiritual; but it is outwardly signified and sealed in this ordinance.

(7) Here is the principal efficient, namely, the Spirit of God; it is the *renewing of the Holy Ghost.*

(8) Here is the manner of God's communicating this Spirit in the gifts and graces of it; not with a scanty and niggardly hand, but most freely and plentifully: *Which he shed on us abundantly.*

(9) Here is the procuring cause of all, namely, Christ: *Through Jesus Christ our Saviour.* He it is who purchased the Spirit and his saving gifts and graces. All come through him, and through him as a Saviour, whose undertaking and work it is to bring to grace and glory.

(10) Here are the ends why we are brought into this new spiritual condition, namely, justification, and heirship, and hope of eternal life: *That, being justified by his grace, we should be made heirs according to the hope of eternal life.*

III. The apostle, having opened the duties of Christians in common, with the reasons respecting themselves, adds another from their goodness and usefulness to men. These things are good in themselves, and the teaching of them useful to mankind, making persons a common good in their places.

CONCLUSION (vv. 9–15)

Here is the fifth and last thing in the matter of the epistle: what Titus should avoid in teaching; how he should deal with a heretic; with some other directions. Observe,

1. That the apostle's meaning might be more clear and full, and especially fitted to the time and state of things in Crete, and the many judaizers among them, he tells Titus what, in teaching, he should shun, v. 9. Idle and foolish enquiries, tending neither to God's glory nor the edification of men, must be shunned.—*And genealogies* (of the gods, say some, that the heathen poets made such noise about; or rather those that the Jews were so curious in).—*And contentions, and strivings about the law*. There were those who were for the Mosaic rites and ceremonies, and would have them continued in the church, though by the gospel

and the coming of Christ they were superseded and done away. Titus must give no countenance to these, but avoid and oppose them.

II. But because, after all, there will be *heresies* and *heretics* in the church, the apostle next directs Titus what to do in such a case, and how to deal with such, v. 10. "Admonish him once and again, that, if possible, he may be brought back, and thou mayest gain thy brother; but, if this will not reduce him, that others be not hurt, cast him out of the communion, and warn all Christians to avoid him.—*Knowing that he that is such is subverted* (turned off from the foundation) *and sinneth* grievously, being *self-condemned*.

III. The apostle subjoins some further directions, vv. 12, 13.

IV. The apostle concludes with salutations and benedictions, v. 5. Though perhaps not personally known (some of them at least), yet all by Paul testify their love and good wishes to Titus, owning him thereby in his work, and stimulating him to go on therein.

PHILEMON

CHAPTER ONE
GREETINGS (vv. 1–7)

I. In the first two verses of the preface we have the persons from and to whom it is written.

1. The persons writing: Paul, the principal, who calls himself *a prisoner of Jesus Christ*, that is, for Jesus Christ, and Timothy. What could be denied to two such petitioners?

2. The persons written to are *Philemon and Apphia*, and with them Archippus, and the church in Philemon's house. Philemon, the master of Onesimus, a slave, was the principal, to whom the letter is inscribed, the head of the family, in whom were the authority and power of taking in or shutting out, and whose property Onesimus was: with him therefore chiefly lay the business. Next to this inscription is,

II. The apostle's salutation of those named by him (*v.* 3): *Grace to you and peace from God our Father and the Lord Jesus Christ*.

III. He expresses the singular affection he had for him, by thanksgiving and prayer to God in his behalf, and the great joy for the many good things he knew and heard to be in him, *vv.* 4–7. The apostle's thanksgiving and prayer for Philemon are here set forth by the object, circumstance, and matter of them, with the way whereby much of the knowledge of Philemon's goodness came to him.

1. Here is the object of Paul's praises and prayers for Philemon: *I thank my God, making mention of thee in my prayers, v.* 4.

2. Here is the circumstance: *Always making mention of thee. Always*—usually, not once or twice only, but frequently.

3. Here is the matter both of his praises and prayers, in reference to Philemon.

(1) Of his praises. [1] He thanks God for the love which he heard Philemon had towards the Lord Jesus. [2] For his faith in Christ also. Love to Christ, and faith in him, are prime Christian graces, for which there is great ground of praise to God, where he has blessed any with them. [3] He praises God likewise for Philemon's love to all the saints. These two must go together; for he who *loveth him that begat must and* will *love those also that are begotten of him*. Mere external differences are nothing here. Paul calls a poor converted slave *his bowels*. We must love, as God does, all saints.

(2) The apostle joins prayer with his praises, that the fruits of Philemon's faith and love might be more and more conspicuous, so that the communication of them might constrain others to the

acknowledgment of the all good things that were in him and in his house towards Christ Jesus.

4. He adds a reason, both of his prayer and his praises (*v.* 7): *For "we have great joy and consolation in thy love, because the bowels of the saints are refreshed by thee, brother."*

PAUL'S PLEA (*vv.* 8–25)

We have here,

I. The main business of the epistle, which was to plead with Philemon on behalf of Onesimus, that he would receive him and be reconciled to him. Many arguments Paul urges for this purpose, *vv.* 8–21. The

1st Argument is taken from what was before noted: "Seeing so much good is reported of thee and found in thee, especially thy love to all saints, now let me see it on a fresh and further occasion; *refresh the bowels of Onesimus and mine also*, in forgiving and receiving him, who is now a convert, and so a saint indeed, and meet for thy favour and love." The

2nd Argument is from the authority of him that was now making this request to him: *I might be very bold in Christ to enjoin thee that which is convenient, v.* 8. The apostles had under Christ great power in the church over the ordinary ministers, as well as the members of it, for edification; they might require of them what was fit, and were therein to be obeyed, which Philemon should consider. This was a matter within the compass of the apostle's power to require, though he would not in this

instance act up to it. Wherefore this may be a

3rd Argument, Waiving the authority which yet he had to require, he chooses to entreat it of him (*v.* 9): *Yet for love's sake I rather beseech thee.* And especially, which may be a

4th Argument, When any circumstance of the person pleading gives additional force to his petition, as here: *Being such a one as Paul the aged, and now also a prisoner of Jesus Christ.* The request of an aged apostle, and now suffering for Christ and his gospel, should be tenderly considered. He makes also a

5th Argument. From the spiritual relation now between Onesimus and himself: *I beseech thee for my son Onesimus, whom I have begotten in my bonds, v.* 10. Paul makes an argument to Philemon from this dear relation that now was between Onesimus and him, his son begotten in his bonds. And a

6th Argument is from Philemon's own interest: *Who in time past was to thee unprofitable, but now profitable to thee and to me, v.* 11. There seems an allusion to the name Onesimus, which signifies *profitable*. Now he will answer to his name. This then is the argument here urged: "It will now be for thy advantage to receive him: thus changed, as he is, thou mayest expect him to be a dutiful and faithful servant, though in time past he was not so." Whereupon,

7th Argument, He urges Philemon from the strong affection that he had to Onesimus. He had mentioned the spiritual relation before, *My son begotten in my bonds*; and now he signifies how dear he was to him: *Thou therefore receive him, that is my own bowels*, v. 12. And again, an

8*th Argument* is from the apostle's denying himself in sending back Onesimus: though he might have presumed upon Philemon's leave to detain him longer, yet he would not, vv. 13, 14. And he further urges,

9*th Argument*, That such a change was now wrought in Onesimus that Philemon needed not fear his ever running from him, or injuring him any more. And, besides interest, a

10*th Argument* is taken from the capacity under which Onesimus now would return, and must be received by Philemon (v. 16): "*Not now as a servant* (that is, not merely or so much), *but above a servant* (in a spiritual respect), *a brother beloved*, one to be owned as a brother in Christ, and to be beloved as such, upon account of this holy change that is wrought in him, and one therefore who will be useful unto thee upon better principles and in a better manner than before, who will love and promote the best things in thy family, be a blessing in it, and help to keep up the church that is in thy house." This argument is strengthened by another, the

11*th Argument*, From the communion of saints: *If thou count me therefore a partner, receive him as myself*, v. 17. There is a fellowship among saints; they have interest one in another, and must love and act accordingly. The answer to this makes a

12*th Argument*, A promise of satisfaction to Philemon: *If he hath*

wronged thee, or oweth thee aught, &c., vv. 18, 19. Here are three things:

(1) A confession of Onesimus's debt to Philemon: *If he hath wronged thee, or oweth thee aught.* It is not an *if* of doubting, but of concession; *seeing he hath wronged thee*, and thereby has become indebted to thee; such as *if* as Col. iii. 1 and 2 Pet. ii. 4, &c. And,

(2) Paul here engages for satisfaction: *Put that on my account; I Paul have written it with my own hand, I will repay it*. It was much that Paul, who lived on contributions himself, would undertake to make good all loss by an evil servant to his master; but hereby he expresses his real and great affection for Onesimus, and his full belief of the sincerity of his conversion; and he might have hope that, notwithstanding this generous offer, Philemon would not insist on it, but freely remit all, considering,

(3) The reason of things between him and Philemon: "*Albeit, I do not say to thee how thou owest unto me even thy own self besides*; thou wilt remember, without my reminding thee, that thou art on other accounts more in debt to me than this comes to." Modesty in self-praises is true praise. Further, a

13*th Argument* is from the joy and comfort the apostle hereby would have on Philemon's own account, as well as on Onesimus's in such a seasonable and acceptable fruit of Philemon's faith and obedience: *Yea, brother, let me have joy of thee in the Lord: refresh my bowels in the Lord*, v. 20. And, once more, his last, which is the

14*th Argument*, Lies in the good

hope and opinion which he expresses of Philemon: *Having confidence in thy obedience, I wrote unto thee, knowing that thou wilt also do more than I say, v.* 21. Good thoughts and expectations of us more strongly move and engage us to do the things expected from us.

Thus far is the substance and body of the epistle. We have,

II. The conclusion, where,

1. He signifies his good hope of deliverance, through their prayers, and that shortly he might see them, desiring Philemon to make provision for him.

2. He sends salutations from one who was his fellow-prisoner, and four more who were his fellow-labourers, *vv.* 23, 24.

3. Here is the apostle's closing prayer and benediction, *v.* 25.

THE EPISTLE TO THE

HEBREWS

CHAPTER ONE

SPOKEN THROUGH A SON
(vv. 1–3)

Here the apostle begins with a general declaration of the excellency of the gospel dispensation above that of the law. Observe,

I. The way wherein God communicated himself and his will to men under the Old Testament. We have here an account, 1. Of the persons by whom God delivered his mind under the Old Testament; they were *the prophets*. 2. The persons to whom God spoke by the prophets: *To the fathers*, to all the Old-Testament saints who were under that dispensation. 3. The order in which God spoke to men in those times that went before the gospel, those past times: he spoke to his ancient people *at sundry times and in divers manners*.

II. God's method of communicating his mind and will under the New-Testament dispensation. There was first the natural revelation; then the patriarchal, by dreams, visions, and voices; then the Mosaic, in the law given forth and written down; then the prophetic, in explaining the law, and giving clearer discoveries of Christ: but now we must expect no new revelation, but only more of the Spirit of Christ to help us better to understand what is already re-vealed. Now the excellency of the gospel revelation above the former consists in two things:

1. It is the final, the finishing revelation, given forth in the last days of divine revelation, to which nothing is to be added, but the canon of scripture is to be settled and sealed.

2. It is a revelation which God has made by his Son, the most excellent messenger that was ever sent into the world. And here we have an excellent account of the glory of our Lord Jesus Christ.

(1) The glory of his office, and that in three respects: [1] God hath appointed him to be heir of all things. [2] By him God made the worlds, both visible and invisible, the heavens and the earth; not as an instrumental cause, but as his essential word and wisdom. [3] He upholds all things by the word of his power: he keeps the world from dissolving. *By him all things consist.*

(2) Hence the apostle passes to the glory of the person of Christ, who was able to execute such an office: *He was the brightness of his Father's glory, and the express image of his person*, v. 3. [1] He is, in person, the Son of God, the only-begotten Son of God, and as such he must have the same nature. [2] The person of the Son is the glory of the Father, shining forth

396

with a truly divine splendour. [3] The person of the Son is the true image and character of the person of the Father; being of the same nature, he must bear the same image and likeness.

(3) From the glory of the person of Christ he proceeds to mention the glory of his grace; his condescension itself was truly glorious. The sufferings of Christ had this great honour in them, to be a full satisfaction for the sins of his people: *By himself he purged away our sins.*

(4) From the glory of his sufferings we are at length led to consider the glory of his exaltation: *When by himself he had purged away our sins, he sat down at the right hand of the Majesty on high,* at his Father's right hand.

Now it was by no less a person than this that God in these last days spoke to men; and, since the dignity of the messenger gives authority and excellency to the message, the dispensations of the gospel must therefore exceed, very far exceed, the dispensation of the law.

BETTER THAN THE ANGELS
(vv. 4–14)

Here observe,

I. The superior nature of Christ is proved from his superior name. The scripture does not give high and glorious titles without a real foundation and reason in nature.

II. Here are several passages of scripture cited, in which those things are said of Christ that were never said of the angels.

1. It was said of Christ, *Thou art my Son, this day have I begotten thee* (Ps. ii. 7), which may refer to his eternal generation, or to his resurrection, or to his solemn inauguration into his glorious kingdom at his ascension and session at the right hand of the Father. Now this was never said concerning the angels, and therefore by inheritance he has a more excellent nature and name than they.

2. It is said concerning Christ, but never concerning the angels, *I will be to him a Father, and he shall be to me a Son*; taken from 2 Sam. vii. 14.

3. It is said of Christ, *When God bringeth his First-begotten into the world, let all the angels of God worship him.* God will not suffer an angel to continue in heaven who will not be in subjection to Christ, and pay adoration to him.

4. God has said concerning Christ, *Thy throne, O God, is for ever and ever, &c., vv.* 8–12. But of the angels he has only said that *he hath made them spirits, and his ministers a flame of fire, v.* 7. Now, upon comparing what he here says of the angels with what he says to Christ, the vast inferiority of the angels to Christ will plainly appear.

(1) What does God say here of the angels? *He maketh his angels spirits, and his ministers a flame of fire.* This we have in Ps. civ. 4. But observe,

(2) How much greater things are said of Christ by the Father. Here two passages of scripture are quoted.

[1] One of these is out of Ps. xlv. 6, 7, where God declares of Christ, *First,* His true and real divinity, and that with much pleasure and

affection, not grudging him that glory: *Thy throne, O God. Secondly,* God declares his dignity and dominion, as having a throne, a kingdom, and a sceptre of that kingdom. *Thirdly,* God declares the eternal duration of the dominion and dignity of Christ, founded upon the divinity of his person: *Thy throne, O God, is for ever and ever. Fourthly,* God declares of Christ the perfect equity of his administration, and of the execution of his power, through all the parts of his government. *Fifthly,* God declares of Christ how he was qualified for the office of Mediator, and how he was installed and confirmed in it (*v.* 9): *Therefore God, even thy God, hath anointed thee with the oil of gladness above thy fellows.*

[2] The other passage of scripture in which is the superior excellence of Christ to the angels is taken out of Ps. cii. 25–27, and is recited in *vv.* 10–12, where the omnipotence of the Lord Jesus Christ, is declared as it appears both in creating the world and in changing it.

First, In creating the world (*v.* 10): *And thou, Lord, in the beginning hast laid the foundation of the earth, and the heavens are the work of thy hands.* The Lord Christ had the original right to govern the world, because he made the world in the beginning.

Secondly, In changing the world that he has made; and here the mutability of this world is brought in to illustrate the immutability of Christ. Christ is immutable and immortal: his years shall not fail. This may comfort us under all decays of nature that we may observe in ourselves or in our friends, though our flesh and heart fail and our days are hastening to an end.

III. The superiority of Christ to the angels appears in this, that God never said to the angels what he has said to Christ, *vv,* 13, 14.

-1. What has God said to Christ? He has said, "*Sit thou at my right hand, till I make thy enemies thy footstool,* Ps. cx. 1. Receive thou glory, dominion, and rest; and remain in the administration of thy mediatorial kingdom until all thy enemies shall either be made thy friends by conversion or thy footstool."

2. What has God said to the angels? He never said to them, as he said to Christ, *Sit you at my right hand*; but he has said of them here that *they are ministering spirits, sent forth to minister for those who shall be the heirs of salvation.* Angels are ministering spirits under the blessed Trinity, to execute the divine will and pleasure; they are the ministers of divine Providence.

CHAPTER TWO

DANGER OF NEGLECT
(*vv.* 1–4)

He now comes to apply this doctrine both by way of exhortation and argument.

I. By way of exhortation: *Therefor we ought to give the more diligent heed to the things which we have heard, v.* 1. This is the first way by which we are to show our esteem of Christ and of the gospel.

II. By way of argument, he adds strong motives to enforce the exhortation.

1. From the great loss we shall sustain if we do not take this earnest heed to the things which we have heard: *We shall let them slip.*

2. Another argument is taken from the dreadful punishment we shall incur if we do not do this duty, a more dreadful punishment than those fell under who neglected and disobeyed the law, *vv.* 2, 3. Here observe, (1) How the law is described: it was the *word spoken by angels, and declared to be stedfast.* It was the word spoken by angels, because given by the ministration of angels, they sounding the trumpet, and perhaps forming the words according to God's direction. (2) How the gospel is described. It is salvation, a great salvation; so great salvation that no other salvation can compare with it. (3) How sinning against the gospel is described: it is declared to be a *neglect of this great salvation*; it is a contempt put upon the saving grace of God in Christ, making light of it, not caring for it. Let us all take heed that we be not found among those wretched sinners who neglect the grace of the gospel. (4) How the misery of such sinners is described: it is declared to be unavoidable (*v.* 3): *How shall we escape?*

3. Another argument to enforce the exhortation is taken from the dignity and excellency of the person by whom the gospel began to be spoken (*v.* 3): *It began at first to be spoken by the Lord.* This great Lord of all was the first who began to speak it plainly and clearly, without types and shadows as it was before he came.

4. Another argument is taken from the character of those who were witnesses to Christ and the gospel (*vv.* 3, 4): *It was confirmed to us by those that heard him, God also bearing them witness.* It was the will of God that we should have sure footing for our faith, and a strong foundation for our hope in receiving the gospel. As at the giving forth of the law there were signs and wonders, by which God testified the authority and excellency of it, so he witnessed to the gospel by more and greater miracles, as to a more excellent and abiding dispensation.

THE SON OF MAN (*vv.* 5–9)

The apostle, having made this serious application of the doctrine of the personal excellency of Christ above the angels, now returns to that pleasant subject again, and pursues it further (*v.* 5): *For to the angels hath he not put in subjection the world to come, whereof we speak.*

I. Here the apostle lays down a negative proposition, including a positive one—That the state of the gospel-church, which is here called *the world to come*, is *not subjected to the angels*, but under the special care and direction of the Redeemer himself.

II. We have a scripture-account of that blessed Jesus to whom the gospel world is put into subjection. It is taken from Ps. viii. 4–6, *But one in a certain place testified, saying, What is man, that thou art mindful of him? or the Son of man, that thou visitest him?* &c. These words are to be considered both as applicable to mankind in general, and as applied here to the Lord Jesus Christ.

1. As applicable to mankind in general, (1) In remembering them, or being mindful of them, when yet they had no being but in the counsels of divine love. (2) In visiting them. God's purpose of favours for men is productive of gracious visits to them; he comes to see us, how it is with us, what we ail, what we want, what dangers we are exposed to, what difficulties we have to encounter; and by his visitation our spirit is preserved. (3) In making man the head of all the creatures in this lower world. (4) In crowning him with glory and honour, the honour of having noble powers and faculties of soul, whereby he is allied to both worlds, capable of serving the interests of both worlds, and of enjoying the happiness of both. (5) In giving him right to and dominion over the inferior creatures.

2. As applied to the Lord Jesus Christ, and the whole that is here said can be applied only to him, *vv.* 8, 9. God crowned the human nature of Christ with glory and honour, in his being perfectly holy, and having the Spirit without measure, and by union with the divine nature in the second person of the Trinity, the fulness of the Godhead dwelling in him bodily.

CAPTAIN OF SALVATION
(*vv.* 10–13)

Having mentioned the death of Christ, the apostle here proceeds to prevent and remove the scandal of the cross; and this he does by show-

ing both how it became God that Christ should suffer and how much man should be benefited by those sufferings.

I. How it became God that Christ should suffer, *v.* 10. Here,

1. God is described as the final end and first cause of all things, and as such it became him to secure his own glory in all that he did.

2. He is declared to have acted up to this glorious character in the work of redemption, as to the choice both of the end and of the means.

(1) In the choice of the end; and that was to bring many sons to glory, to present glory in enjoying the glorious privileges of the gospel, and to future glory in heaven, which will be glory indeed, an exceeding eternal weight of glory.

(2) In the choice of the means. [1] In finding out such a person as should be the captain of our salvation; those that are saved must come to that salvation under the guidance of a captain and leader sufficient for that purpose. [2] In making this captain of our salvation perfect through sufferings. That is, he perfected the work of our redemption by shedding his blood, and was thereby perfectly qualified to be a Mediator between God and man. He found his way to the crown by the cross, and so must his people too.

II. He shows how much they would be benefited by the cross and sufferings of Christ. Hereby they are brought into a near union with Christ, and into a very endearing relation.

1. Into a near union (*v.* 11): *Both he that sanctifieth and those that are*

sanctified are all of one. How? Why, (1) They are all of one heavenly Father, and that is God. (2) They are of one earthly father, Adam. Christ and believers have the same human nature. (3) Of one spirit, one holy and heavenly disposition; the same mind is in them that was in Christ, though not in the same measure; the same Spirit informs and actuates the head and all the members.

2. Into an endearing relation. This results from the union.

(1) He declares what this relation is: he and believers being all of one, he therefore is not ashamed to call them *brethren*.

(2) He illustrates this from three texts of scripture.

[1] The first is out of Ps. xxii. 22. Now here it is foretold, *First*, That Christ should have a church or *congregation* in the world, a company of volunteers, freely willing to follow him. *Secondly*, That these should not only be brethren to one another, but to Christ himself. *Thirdly*, That he would declare his Father's name to them, that is, his nature and attributes, his mind and will. *Fourthly*, That Christ would sing praise to his Father in the church.

[2] The second scripture is quoted from Ps. xviii. 2, *And again, I will put my trust in him*. He suffered and trusted as our head and president. His brethren must suffer and trust too.

[3] The third scripture is taken from Isa. viii. 18, *Behold, I and the children which God hath given me*. this proves Christ really and truly man, for parents and children are of the same nature.

A FAITHFUL HIGH PRIEST
(*vv*. 14–18)

Here the apostle proceeds to assert the incarnation of Christ, as taking upon him not the nature of angels, but the seed of Abraham; and he shows the reason and design of his so doing.

I. The incarnation of Christ is asserted (*v*. 16). Now Christ resolving to recover the seed of Abraham and raise them up from their fallen state, he took upon him the human nature from one descended from the loins of Abraham, that the same nature that had sinned might suffer, to restore human nature to a state of hope and trial.

II. The reasons and designs of the incarnation of Christ are declared.

1. *Because the children were partakers of flesh and blood, he must take part of the same, and be made like his brethren, vv*. 14, 15. For no higher nor lower nature than man's that had sinned could so suffer for the sin of man as to satisfy the justice of God.

2. He became man that he might die; as God he could not die, and therefore he assumed another nature and state.

3. That *through death he might destroy him that had the power of death, that is, the devil, v*. 14. Now Christ has so far destroyed him who had the power of death that he can keep none under the power of spiritual death; nor can he draw any into sin, nor execute the sentence upon any but those who choose and continue to be his willing slaves, and persist in their enmity to God.

4. That he might deliver his own people from the slavish fear of death to which they are often subject. Christ became man, and died, to deliver them from those perplexities of soul, by letting them know that death is not only a conquered enemy, but a reconciled friend, not sent to hurt the soul, or separate it from the love of God, but to put an end to all their grievances and complaints, and to give them a passage to eternal life and blessedness; so that to them death is not now in the hand of Satan, but in the hand of Christ.

5. Christ must be made like unto his brethren, that he might be a merciful and faithful high priest in things pertaining to the justice and honour of God and to the support and comfort of his people. He must be faithful to God and merciful to men. Christ is ready and willing to succour those who under their temptations apply to him; and he became man, and was tempted, that he might be every way qualified to succour his people.

CHAPTER THREE

A SON IN HIS HOUSE

(*vv.* 1–6)

In these verses we have the application of the doctrine laid down in the close of the last chapter concerning the priesthood of our Lord Jesus Christ. And observe,

I. In how fervent and affectionate a manner the apostle exhorts Christians to have this high priest much in their thoughts. That this exhortation might be made the more effectual, observe,

1. The honourable compellation used towards those to whom he wrote: *Holy brethren, partakers of the heavenly calling.*

2. The titles he gives to Christ, whom he would have them consider; (1) As the apostle of our profession, a messenger and a principal messenger sent of God to men, upon the most important errand. (2) Not only the apostle, but the high priest too, of our profession, upon whose satisfaction and intercession we profess to depend for pardon of sin, and acceptance with God. (3) As Christ, the Messiah, anointed and every way qualified for the office both of apostle and high priest.

II. We have the duty we owe to him who bears all these high and honourable titles, and that is to consider him as thus characterized. Consider what he is in himself, what he is to us, and what he will be to us hereafter and for ever.

III. We have several arguments drawn up to enforce this duty of considering Christ the apostle and high priest of our profession.

1. The first is taken from his fidelity, *v.* 2. He was faithful to him that appointed him, as Moses was in all his house.

2. Another argument is taken from the superior glory and excellence of Christ above Moses (*vv.* 3–6); therefore they were more obliged to consider Christ. (1) Christ was a maker of the house, Moses but a member in it. (2) Christ was the master of this house, as well as the maker, *vv.* 5, 6. This house is styled his house, as the Son of God.

We have here a direction what those must do who would partake of the dignity and privileges of the household of Christ. *First,* They must take the truths of the gospel into their heads and hearts. *Secondly,* They must build their hopes of happiness upon those truths. *Thirdly,* They must make an open profession of those truths. *Fourthly,* They must so live up to them as to keep their evidences clear, that they may rejoice in hope, and then they must in all persevere to the end.

HARDENED HEARTS
(*vv.* 7–19)

Here the apostle proceeds in pressing upon them serious counsels and cautions to the close of the chapter; and he recites a passage out of Ps. xcv. 7, &c. where observe,

I. What he counsels them to do — to give a speedy and present attention to the call of Christ.

II. What he cautions them against — hardening their hearts, turning the deaf ear to the calls and counsels of Christ.

III. Whose example he warns them by — that of the Israelites their fathers in the wilderness.

IV. What use the apostle makes of their awful example, *vv.* 12, 13, &c. He gives the Hebrews a proper caution, and enforces it with an affectionate compellation.

1. He gives the Hebrews a proper caution; the word is, *Take heed, look to it.*

2. He enforces the admonition with an affectionate compellation: *Take heed, brethren, lest there be in any of you an evil heart of unbelief in departing from the living God.*

Here observe, (1) A heart of unbelief is an evil heart. Unbelief is a great sin, it vitiates the heart of man. (2) An evil heart of unbelief is at the bottom of all our sinful departures from God.

3. He subjoins good counsel to the caution, and advises them to that which would be a remedy against this evil heart of unbelief — that they should *exhort one another daily, while it is called to-day, v.* 13.

4. He comforts those who not only set out well, but hold on well, and hold out to the end (*v.* 14).

5. The apostle resumes what he had quoted before from Ps. xcv. 7, &c., and he applies it closely to those of that generation, *vv.* 15, 16, &c. While it is said, *To-day if you will hear,* &c.; as if he should say, "What was recited before from that scripture belonged not only to former ages, but to you now, and to all who shall come after you; that you take heed you fall not into the same sins, lest you fall under the same condemnation."

6. The apostle puts some queries upon what had been before mentioned, and gives proper answers to them (*vv.* 17–19). Whence observe, (1) God is grieved only with those of his people who sin against him, and continue in sin. (2) God is grieved and provoked most by sins publicly committed by the generality of a nation. (3) Though God grieves long, and bears long, when pressed with the weight of general and prevailing wickedness, yet he will at length ease himself of public offenders by public judgments. (4) Unbelief (with rebellion which is the consequent of it) is the great damning sin of the world.

CHAPTER FOUR

THE PERFECT REST (vv. 1–10)

Here, I. The apostle declares that our privileges by Christ under the gospel are not only as great, but greater than those enjoyed under the Mosaic law. He specifies this, that we have a promise left us of entering into his rest; that is, of entering into a covenant-relation to Christ, and a state of communion with God through Christ, and of growing up therein, till we are made perfect in glory.

II. He demonstrates the truth of his assertion, that we have as great advantages as they. For says he (v. 2), *To us was the gospel preached as well as unto them.*

III. He again assigns the reason why so few of the ancient Jews profited by that dispensation of the gospel which they enjoyed, and that was their want of faith: *The word preached did not profit them because it was not mixed with faith in those that heard him, v. 2.*

IV. On these considerations the apostle grounds his repeated and earnest caution and counsel that those who enjoy the gospel should maintain a holy fear and jealousy over themselves, lest latent unbelief should rob them of the benefit of the word, and of that spiritual rest which is discovered and tendered in the gospel.

V. The apostle confirms the happiness of all those who truly believe the gospel; and this he does,

1. By asserting so positively the truth of it, from the experience of himself and others: *"We, who have believed, do enter into rest, v. 3."*

2. He illustrates and confirms it

that those who believe are thus happy, and do enter into rest. (1) From God's finishing his work of creation, and so entering into his rest (vv. 3, 4), appointing our first parents to rest the seventh day, to rest in God. (2) From God's continuing the observance of the sabbath, after the fall, and the revelation of a Redeemer. (3) From God's proposing Canaan as a typical rest for the Jews who believed: and as those who did believe, Caleb and Joshua, did actually enter into Canaan; so those who now believe shall enter into rest. (4) From the certainty of another rest besides that seventh day of rest instituted and observed both before and after the fall. For the Psalmist has spoken of another day and another rest, whence it is evident that there is a more spiritual and excellent sabbath remaining for the people of God than that into which Joshua led the Jews (vv. 6–9). Every true believer hath ceased from his own works of sin, from relying on his own works of righteousness, and from the burdensome works of the law, as God and Christ have ceased from their works of creation and redemption.

VI. The apostle confirms the misery of those who do not believe; they shall never enter into this spiritual rest, either of grace here or glory hereafter.

A COMPASSIONATE PRIEST (vv. 11–16)

In this latter part of the chapter the apostle concludes, first, with a serious repeated exhortation, and then with proper and powerful motives.

I. Here we have a serious exhortation: *Let us labour therefore to enter into that rest, v.* 11.

II. Here we have proper and powerful motives to make the advice effectual, which are drawn,

1. From the dreadful example of those who have already perished by unbelief: *Lest any man fall after the same example of unbelief.*

2. From the great help and advantage we may have from the word of God to strengthen our faith, and excite our diligence, that we may obtain this rest: *The word of God is quick and powerful, v.* 12. Now of this word it is said, (1) That it is *quick*; it is very lively and active, in all its efforts, in seizing the conscience of the sinner, in cutting him to the heart, and in comforting him and binding up the wounds of the soul. (2) It is *powerful.* When God sets it home by his Spirit, it convinces powerfully, converts powerfully, and comforts powerfully. (3) It is *sharper than any two-edged sword*; it cuts both ways; it is *the sword of the Spirit,* Eph. vi. 17. It is the two-edged sword that cometh out of the mouth of Christ, Rev. i. 16. It is sharper than any two-edged sword, for it will enter where no other sword can, and make a more critical dissection. (4) It is *a discerner of the thoughts and intents of the heart,* even the most secret and remote thoughts and designs. It will uncover to men the variety of their thoughts and purposes. The word will turn the inside of a sinner out, and let him see all that is in his heart.

3. From the perfections of the Lord Jesus Christ, both of his person and office.

(1) His person, particularly his omniscience: *Neither is there any creature that is not manifest in his sight, v.* 13. We shall have to do with him as one who will determine our everlasting state. This omniscience of Christ, and the account we owe of ourselves to him, should engage us to persevere in faith and obedience till he has perfected all our affairs.

(2) We have an account of the excellency and perfection of Christ, as to his office, and this particular office of our high priest.

[1] What kind of high priest Christ is (*v.* 14): *Seeing we have such a high priest*; that is, *First,* A great high priest, much greater than Aaron, or any of the priests of his order. The greatness of our high priest is set forth, 1. By his having passed into the heavens. The high priest under the law, once a year, went out of the people's sight within the veil, into the holiest of all, where were the sacred signals of the presence of God; but Christ once for all has passed into the heavens, to take the government of all upon him. 2. The greatness of Christ is set forth by his name, *Jesus*—a physician and a Saviour, and one of a divine nature, the Son of God by eternal generation; and therefore having divine perfection, able to save to the uttermost all who come to God by him. *Secondly,* He is not only a great, but a gracious high priest, merciful, compassionate, and sympathizing with his people: *We have not a high priest who cannot be touched with the feeling of our infirmities, v.* 15. *Thirdly,* He is a sinless high priest: *He was in all things tempted as we*

are, yet without sin. He was tempted by Satan, but he came off without sin. He was holy, harmless, and undefiled; and such a high priest became us. Having thus told us what a one our high priest is, the apostle proceeds to show us,

[2] How we should demean ourselves towards him. *First,* Let us hold fast our profession of faith in him, *v.* 14. Let us never deny him, never be ashamed of him before men. *Secondly,* We should encourage ourselves, by the excellency of our high priest, to come boldly to the throne of grace, *v.* 16. The office of Christ, as being our high priest, and such a high priest, should be the ground of our confidence in all our approaches to the throne of grace. Had we not a Mediator, we could have no boldness in coming to God; for we are guilty and polluted creatures. We must either go in the hand of a Mediator or our hearts and hopes will fail us. We have boldness to enter into the holiest by the blood of Jesus.

CHAPTER FIVE

THE OBEDIENT SON (*vv.* 1–9)

We have here an account of the nature of the priestly office in general, though with an accommodation to the Lord Jesus Christ. We are told,

I. Of what kind of beings the high priest must be. He must be taken from among men; he must be a man, one of ourselves, bone of our bone, flesh of our flesh, and spirit of our spirits, a partaker of our nature, and a standard-bearer

among ten thousand. This implies, 1. That man had sinned. 2. That God would not admit sinful man to come to him immediately and alone, without a high priest, who must be taken from among men. 3. That God was pleased to take one from among men, by whom they might approach God in hope, and he might receive them with honour. 4. That every one shall now be welcome to God that comes to him by this his priest.

II. For whom every high priest is ordained: *For men in things pertaining to God,* for the glory of God and the good of men, that he might come between God and man.

III. For what purpose every high priest was ordained: *That he might offer both gifts and sacrifices for sin.*

1. This intimates, (1) That all we bring to God must be free and not forced; it must be a gift; it must be given and not taken away again. (2) That all we bring to God must go through the high priest's hands, as the great agent between God and man.

2. That he might offer sacrifices for sin; that is, the offerings that were appointed to make atonement, that sin might be pardoned and sinners accepted. Thus Christ is constituted a high priest for both these ends.

IV. How this high priest must be qualified, *v.* 2.

1. He must be one that can have compassion on two sorts of persons: (1) *On the ignorant,* or those that are guilty of sins of ignorance. (2) *On those that are out of the way,* out of the way of truth, duty, and happiness; and he must be one who

406

has tenderness enough to lead them back from the by-paths of error, sin, and misery.

2. He must also be compassed with infirmity; and so be able from himself feelingly to consider our frame, and to sympathize with us. Thus Christ was qualified.

V. How the high priest was to be called of God. He must have both an internal and external call to his office: *For no man taketh this honour to himself (v. 4)*, that is, no man ought to do it, no man can do it legally; if any does it, he must be reckoned a usurper, and treated accordingly.

VI. How this is brought home and applied to Christ: *So Christ glorified not himself, v. 5.*

VII. The apostle prefers Christ before Aaron, both in the manner of his call and in the holiness of his person. 1. In the manner of his call, in which God said unto him, *Thou art my Son, this day have I begotten thee* (quoted from Ps. ii. 7), referring to his eternal generation as God. Now God never said thus to Aaron. Another expression that God used in the call of Christ we have in Ps. cx. 4, *Thou art a priest for ever, after the order of Melchisedec, v.* 6. God the Father appointed him a priest of a higher order than that of Aaron. The priesthood of Aaron was to be but temporary; the priesthood of Christ was to be perpetual: the priesthood of Aaron was to be successive, descending from the fathers to the children; the priesthood of Christ, after the order of Melchisedec, was to be personal, and the high priest immortal as to his office, without descent, having neither beginning

of days nor end of life, as it is more largely described in the seventh chapter, and will be opened there. 2. Christ is here preferred to Aaron in the holiness of his person. Other priests were to offer up sacrifices, as for the *sins of others, so for themselves, v.* 3. But Christ needed not to offer for sins for himself, *for he had done no violence,* neither was there *any deceit in his mouth,* Isa. liii. 9. And such a high priest became us.

VIII. We have an account of Christ's discharge of this his office, and of the consequences of that discharge, *vv.* 7–9.

1. The discharge of his office of the priesthood (*v.* 7): *Who in the days of his flesh, when he had offered up prayers and supplications*, &c.

2. The consequences of this discharge of his office, *vv.* 8, 9, &c.

(1) By these his sufferings *he learned obedience, though he was a Son, v.* 8. Here observe, [1] The privilege of Christ: *He was a Son;* the only-begotten of the Father. [2] Christ made improvement by his sufferings. By his passive obedience, he learned active obedience; that is, he practised that great lesson, and made it appear that he was well and perfectly learned in it. We need affliction, to teach us submission.

(2) By these his sufferings he was made perfect, and became the author of eternal salvation to all who obey him, *v.* 9. To those who obey him, devoting themselves to him, denying themselves, and taking up their cross, and following him, he will be the author, the grand cause of their salvation, and they shall own him as such for ever.

TRUE TEACHING (*vv.* 10–14)

Here the apostle returns to what he had in *v.* 6 cited out of Ps. cx., concerning the peculiar order of the priesthood of Christ, that is, the order of Melchisedec. And here,

I. He declares he had many things which he could say to them concerning this mysterious person called Melchisedec, whose priesthood was eternal, and therefore the salvation procured thereby should be eternal also. We have a more particular account of this Melchisedec in *ch.* vii.

II. He assigns the reason why he did not say all those things concerning Christ, our Melchisedec, that he had to say, and what it was that made it so difficult for him to utter them, namely, the dullness of the Hebrews to whom he wrote: *You are dull of hearing.* Dull hearers make the preaching of the gospel a difficult thing.

III. He insists upon the faultiness of this infirmity of theirs. It was not a mere natural infirmity, but it was a sinful infirmity, and more in them than others, by reason of the singular advantages they had enjoyed for improving in the knowledge of Christ.

IV. The apostle shows how the various doctrines of the gospel must be dispensed to different persons. There are in the church babes and persons of full age (*vv.* 12–14), and there are in the gospel milk and strong meat. The deeper mysteries of religion belong to those that are of a higher class in the school of Christ, who have learned the first principles and well improved them.

CHAPTER SIX

FIRST PRINCIPLES (*vv.* 1–8)

We have here the apostle's advice to the Hebrews—that they would grow up from a state of childhood to the fulness of the stature of the new man in Christ.

I. The apostle mentions several foundation-principles, which must be well laid at first, and then built upon; neither his time nor theirs must be spent in laying these foundations over and over again. These foundations are six:

1. Repentance from dead works, that is, conversion and regeneration, repentance from a spiritually dead state and course.

2. Faith towards God, a firm belief of the existence of God, of his nature, attributes, and perfections, the trinity of persons in the unity of essence, the whole mind and will of God as revealed in his word, particularly what relates to the Lord Jesus Christ.

3. The doctrine of baptisms, that is, of being baptized by a minister of Christ with water, in the name of the Father, and of the Son, and of the Holy Ghost, as the initiating sign or seal of the covenant of grace. And the doctrine of an inward baptism, that of the Spirit sprinkling the blood of Christ upon the soul, for justification, and the graces of the Spirit for sanctification.

4. Laying on of hands, on persons passing solemnly from their initiated state by baptism to the confirmed state, by returning the answer of a good conscience towards God, and sitting down at the Lord's table. Or by this may be

meant ordination of persons to the ministerial office.

5. The resurrection of the dead, that is, of dead bodies; and their re-union with their souls.

6. Eternal judgment, determining the soul of every one, when it leaves the body at death, and both soul and body at the last day, to their eternal state.

II. The apostle declares his readiness and resolution to assist the Hebrews in building themselves up on these foundations till they arrive at perfection: *And this we will do, if God permit, v. 3.*

III. He shows that this spiritual growth is the surest way to prevent that dreadful sin of apostasy from the faith. And here,

1. He shows how far persons may go in religion, and, after all, fall away, and perish for ever, *vv.* 4, 5. (1) They may be *enlightened.* Some of the ancients understand this of their being baptized; but it is rather to be understood of notional knowledge and common illumination, of which persons may have a great deal, and yet come short of heaven. (2) They may *taste of the heavenly gift*, feel something of the efficacy of the Holy Spirit in his operations upon their souls. (3) They may be *made partakers of the Holy Ghost*, that is, of his extraordinary and miraculous gifts. (4) They may *taste of the good word of God*; they may have some relish of gospel doctrines. (5) They may have *tasted of the powers of the world to come*; they may have been under strong impressions concerning heaven and hell. Now hence observe, [1] These great things are spoken here of those who may fall way; yet it is

not here said of them that they were truly converted, or that they were justified; there is more in true saving grace than in all that is here said of apostates. [2] This therefore is no proof of the final apostasy of true saints. These indeed may fall frequently and foully, but yet they will not totally nor finally from God.

2. The apostle describes the dreadful case of such as fall away after having gone so far in the profession of religion. (1) The greatness of the sin of apostasy. It is *crucifying the Son of God afresh, and putting him to open shame*. They do what in them lies to represent Christ and Christianity as a shameful thing, and would have him to be a public shame and reproach. This is the nature of apostasy. (2) The great misery of apostates. [1] It is impossible to renew them again unto repentance. God can renew them to repentance, but he seldom does it; and with men themselves it is impossible. [2] Their misery is exemplified by a proper similitude, taken from the ground that after much cultivation brings forth nothing but briers and thorns.

I. He freely and openly declares the good hope he had concerning them, that they would endure to the end: *But beloved, we are persuaded better things of you, v. 9.*

II. He proposes arguments and encouragements to them to go on in the way of their duty. 1. That God had wrought a principle of holy love and charity in them, which had discovered itself in suitable works that would not be forgotten of God: *God is not unrighteous to forget your labour of love, v.* 10. 2. Those who expect a gracious reward for the labour of love must continue in it as long as they have ability and opportunity. 3. Those who persevere in a diligent discharge of their duty shall attain to the full assurance of hope in the end.

III. He proceeds to set before them caution and counsel how to attain this full assurance of hope to the end. 1. That they should not be slothful. 2. That they would follow the good examples of those who had gone before, *v.* 12.

IV. The apostle closes the chapter with a clear and full account of the assured truth of the promises of God, *v.* 13, *to the end.* They are all confirmed by the oath of God, and they are all founded in the eternal counsel of God, and therefore may be depended upon.

1. They are all confirmed by the oath of God. Now, if God would condescend to take an oath to his people, he will surely remember the nature and design of it.

2. The promises of God are all founded in his eternal counsel; and this counsel of his is an immutable counsel.

3. The promises of God, which are founded upon these immutable counsels of God, and confirmed by the oath of God, may safely be depended upon; for here we have two immutable things, the counsel and the oath of God, in which it is impossible for God to lie, contrary to his nature as well as to his will. Gospel hope is our anchor (*v.* 19). It is sure and stedfast, or else it could not keep us so. *First,* It is sure in its own nature; for it is the special work of God in the soul. *Secondly,* It is stedfast as to its object; it is an anchor that has taken good hold, it enters that which is within the veil; it is an anchor that is cast upon the rock, the Rock of ages.

CHAPTER SEVEN

MELCHISEDEC, THE PRIEST
(*vv.* 1–10)

The foregoing chapter ended with a repetition of what had been cited once and again before out of Ps. cx. 4, *Jesus, a high priest for ever, after the order of Melchisedec.*

I. The great question that first offers itself is, Who was this Melchisedec? All the account we have of him in the Old Testament is in Gen. xiv. 18, &c., and in Ps. cx. 4. Indeed we are much in the dark about him; God has thought fit to leave us so, that this Melchisedec might be a more lively type of him whose generation none can declare.

1. Many Christian writers have thought him to be Jesus Christ himself, appearing by a special dispensation and privilege to Abraham in the flesh, and who was known to Abraham by the name *Melchisedec*, which agrees very well to Christ, and to what is said, John viii. 56, *Abraham saw* his *day and rejoiced.* Much may be said for this opinion, and what is said in *v.* 3 does not seem to agree with any mere man; but then it seems strange to make Christ a type of himself. The most general opinion is that he was a Canaanite king, who reigned in Salem, and kept up religion and the worship of the true God; that he was raised to be a type of Christ, and was honoured by Abraham as such.

2. But we shall leave these conjectures, and labour to understand, as far as we can, what is here said of him by the apostle, and how Christ is represented thereby, *vv.* 1–3. (1) Melchisedec was a king, and so is the Lord Jesus—a king of God's anointing. (2) That he was *king of righteousness*: his name signifies *the righteous king.* Jesus Christ is a rightful and a righteous king—rightful in his title, righteous in his government. (3) He was king of Salem, that is, king of peace; first king of righteousness, and after that king of peace. So is our Lord Jesus. (4) He was *priest of the most high God*, qualified and anointed in an extraordinary manner to be his priest among the Gentiles. So is the Lord Jesus. (5) He was *without father, without mother, without descent, having neither beginning of days nor end of life, v.* 3. This must not be understood according to the letter. His priesthood is without descent, did not descend to him from another, nor from him to another, but is personal and perpetual. (6) That he *met Abraham returning from the slaughter of the kings, and blessed him.* The incident is recorded Gen. xiv. 18, &c. He brought forth bread and wine to refresh Abraham and his servants when they were weary; he gave as a king, and blessed as a priest. Thus our Lord Jesus meets his people in their spiritual conflicts, refreshes them, renews their strength, and blesses them. (7) That *Abraham gave him a tenth part of all* (*v.* 2), that is, as the apostle explains it, of all *the spoils.* And thus are we obliged to make all possible returns of love and gratitude to the Lord Jesus for all the rich and royal favours we receive from him. (8) That this Melchisedec was *made like unto the Son of God, and abideth a priest continually.* He bore the image of God in his piety and authority, and stands upon record as an immortal high priest; the ancient type of him who is the eternal and only-begotten of the Father, who abideth a priest for ever.

II. Let us now consider (as the apostle advises) how great this Melchisedec was, and how far his priesthood was above that of the order of Aaron (*vv.* 4, 5, &c.): *Now consider how great this man was,* &c. The greatness of this man and his priesthood appears, 1. From Abraham's paying the tenth of the spoils unto him. 2. From Melchisedec's blessing of Abraham, *who had the promises; and, without contradiction, the less is blessed of the greater, vv.* 6, 7. (2) Melchisedec's greater honour—in that it was his place and privilege to bless Abraham; and it is an incontested maxim *that the less is blessed of the greater, v.* 7. He who gives the blessing is greater than he who receives it.

A GREATER PRIEST
(*vv.* 11–28)

Here,

I. It is asserted that perfection could not come by the Levitical priesthood and the law.

II. That therefore another priest must be raised up, after the order of Melchisedec, by whom, and his law of faith, perfection might come to all who obey him.

III. It is asserted that the priesthood being changed there must of necessity be a change of the law; there being so near a relation between the priesthood and the law, the dispensation could not be the same under another priesthood; a new priesthood must be under a new regulation, managed in another way, and by rules proper to its nature and order.

IV. It is not only asserted, but proved, that the priesthood and law are changed, *vv.* 13, 14. The priesthood and law by which perfection could not come are abolished, and a priest has arisen, and a dispensation is now set up, by which true believers may be made perfect (*vv.* 15–21). Observe the description we have of the personal holiness of Christ expressed in various terms, all of which some learned divines consider as relating to his perfect purity. [1] He is holy, perfectly free from all the habits or principles of sin, not having the least disposition to it in his nature; no sin dwells in him, though it does in the best of Christians, not the least sinful inclination. [2] He is harmless, perfectly free from all actual transgression, has done no violence, nor is there any deceit in his mouth, never did the least wrong to God or man. [3] He is undefiled, he was never accessory to other men's sins. [4] He is separate from sinners, not only in his present state, but in his personal purity. Christ was, by his ineffable conception in the virgin, separate from sinners; though he took a true human nature, yet the miraculous way in which it was conceived set him upon a separate footing from

all the rest of mankind. [5] He is made higher than the heavens. Most expositors understand this concerning his state of exaltation in heaven, at the right hand of God, to perfect the design of his priesthood. But Dr. Goodwin thinks this may be very justly referred to the personal holiness of Christ, which is greater and more perfect than the holiness of the hosts of heaven.

CHAPTER EIGHT
CHRIST'S PRIESTHOOD
(*vv.* 1–5)

Here is, I. A summary recital of what had been said before concerning the excellency of Christ's priesthood, showing what we have in Christ, where he now resides, and what sanctuary he is the minister of, *vv.* 1, 2.

II. The apostle sets before the Hebrews the necessary parts of Christ's priesthood, or what it was that belonged to that office, in conformity to what every high priest is ordained to, *vv.* 3, 4. 1. *Every high priest is ordained to offer gifts and sacrifices.* It necessarily belongs to the priesthood of Christ that he should have somewhat to offer; and he, as the antitype, had himself to offer, his human nature upon the altar of his divine nature, as the great atoning sacrifice that finished transgression, and made an end of sin once for all. 2. Christ must now execute his priesthood in heaven, in the holy of holies, the true tabernacle which the Lord hath fixed. For, (1) *If Christ were on earth, he would not be a priest* (*v.* 4), that is, not according to the Levitical law, as not being of the line of that priesthood; and so long as that priesthood continued there must be a strict regard paid to the divine institution in every thing. (2) All the services of the priest, under the law, as well as every thing in that tabernacle which was framed according to the pattern in the mount, were only exemplars and shadows of heavenly things, *v.* 5.

THE NEW COVENANT
(*vv.* 6–13)

Now observe,

I. What is here said of the old covenant, or rather of the old dispensation of the covenant of grace: of this it is said, 1. That it was made with the fathers of the Jewish nation at mount Sinai (*v.* 9), and Moses was the Mediator of that covenant. 2. That this covenant was not found faultless (*vv.* 7, 8); it was a dispensation of darkness and dread, tending to bondage, and only a schoolmaster to bring us to Christ; it was perfect in its kind, and fitted to answer its end, but very imperfect in comparison of the gospel. 3. That it was not sure or stedfast; *for the Jews continued not in that covenant, and the Lord regarded them not, v.* 13. God will regard those who remain in his covenant, but will reject those who cast away his yoke from them. 4. That it is decayed, grown old, and vanisheth away, *v.* 13.

II. What is here said of the New-Testament dispensation, to prove the superior excellency of Christ's ministry. It is said,

1. That it is a better covenant (*v.* 6), without fault, well ordered in all things. It requires nothing but what it promises grace to perform.

2. That it is established upon better promises, more clear and express, more spiritual, more absolute.

3. It is a new covenant, even that new covenant that God long ago declared he would make with the house of Israel, that is, all the Israel of God; this was promised in Jer. xxxi. 31, 32, and accomplished in Christ.

4. Here,

(1) God articles with his people *that he will put his laws into their minds and write them in their hearts, v.* 10. He once wrote his laws to them, now he will write his laws in them.

(2) He articles with them to take them into a near and very honourable relation to himself.

(3) He articles with them that they shall grow more acquainted with their God (*v.* 11): *They shall all know me from the least to the greatest,* insomuch that there shall not be so much need of one neighbour teaching another the knowledge of God.

(4) God articles with them about the pardon of their sins, as what always accompanies the true knowledge of God (*v.* 12): *For I will be merciful to their unrighteousness,* &c.

CHAPTER NINE
THE TABERNACLE (*vv.* 1–7)

Here, I. The apostle gives an account of the tabernacle, that place of worship which God appointed to be pitched on earth.

II. From the description of the

place of worship in the Old-Testament dispensation, the apostle proceeds to speak of the duties and services performed in those places, v. 6. When the several parts and furniture of the tabernacle were thus settled, then what was to be done there?

1. The ordinary priests went always into the first tabernacle, to accomplish the service of God.

2. Into the second, the interior part, went the high priest alone, v. 7. This part was an emblem of heaven, and Christ's ascension thither.

A GREATER TABERNACLE
(vv. 8–14)

Now here are several things mentioned as the things that the Holy Ghost signified and certified to his people in the tabernacle.

I. That the way into the holiest of all was not yet made manifest, while the first tabernacle was standing, v. 8.

II. That the first tabernacle was only a figure for the time then present, v. 9.

III. That none of the gifts and sacrifices there offered could make the offerers perfect as pertaining to conscience (v. 9). He could not be saved by them from sin or hell, as all those are who believe in Christ.

IV. The Holy Ghost hereby signifies that the Old-Testament institutions were but external carnal ordinances imposed upon them until the time of reformation, v. 10.

V. The Holy Ghost signifies to us hereby that we never make the right use of types but when we apply them to the antitype. For,

1. *Christ is a high priest of good things to come*, by which may be understood, (1) All the good things that were to come during the Old Testament, and now have come under the New. (2) All the good things yet to come and to be enjoyed in a gospel state, when the promises and prophecies made to the gospel church in the latter days shall be accomplished. (3) Of all the good things to come in the heavenly state, which will perfect both the Testaments.

2. Christ is a high priest *by a greater and more perfect tabernacle* (v. 11), *a tabernacle not made with hands, that is to say, not of this building*, but his own body, or rather human nature, conceived by the Holy Ghost overshadowing the blessed virgin. This was a new fabric, a new order of building, infinitely superior to all earthly structures, not excepting the tabernacle of the temple itself.

3. Christ, our high priest, has entered into heaven, not as their high priest entered into the holiest, with the blood of bulls and of goats, but by his own blood, typified by theirs, and infinitely more precious. And this,

4. Not for one year only, which showed the imperfection of that priesthood, that it did but typically obtain a year's reprieve or pardon. But our high priest entered into heaven *once for all*, and has obtained not a yearly respite, but eternal redemption.

5. The Holy Ghost further signified and showed what was the efficacy of the blood of the Old-Testament sacrifices, and thence is inferred the much greater efficacy

of the blood of Christ. (1) The efficacy of the blood of the legal sacrifices extended to the purifying of the flesh (*v.* 13): it freed the outward man from ceremonial uncleanness and from temporal punishment. (2) He infers very justly hence the far greater efficacy of the blood of Christ (*v.* 14): *How much more shall the blood of Christ*, &c. For, *First*, It is sufficient to purge the conscience from dead works, it reaches to the very soul and conscience, the defiled soul, defiled with sin, which is a dead work, proceeds from spiritual death, and tends to death eternal. *Secondly*, It is sufficient to enable us to serve the living God, not only by purging away that guilt which separates between God and sinners, but by sanctifying and renewing the soul through the gracious influences of the Holy Spirit, purchased by Christ for this purpose, that we might be enabled to serve the living God in a lively manner.

PURGED WITH BLOOD
(*vv.* 15–22)

In these verses the apostle considers the gospel under the notion of a will or testament, the new or last will and testament of Christ, and shows the necessity and efficacy of the blood of Christ to make this testament valid and effectual.

I. The gospel is here considered as a testament, the new and last will and testament of our Lord and Saviour Jesus Christ. It is observable that the solemn transactions that pass between God and man are sometimes called a covenant, here a testament. A testament is a voluntary act and deed of a single person, duly executed and witnessed, bestowing legacies on such legatees as are described and characterized by the testator, and which can only take effect upon his death.

II. To make this New Testament effectual, it was necessary that Christ should die; the legacies accrue by means of death. The method taken by Moses, according to the direction he had received from God, is here particularly related. (1) Moses spoke every precept to all the people, according to the law, *v.* 19. He published to them the tenour of the covenant, the duties required, the rewards promised to those who did their duty, and the punishment threatened against the transgressors, and he called for their consent to the terms of the covenant; and this in an express manner. (2) Then he took the blood of calves and of goats, with water, and scarlet wool, and hyssop, and applied this blood by sprinkling it. Now with these Moses sprinkled, [1] The book of the law and covenant, to show that the covenant of grace is confirmed by the blood of Christ and made effectual to our good. [2] The people, intimating that the shedding of the blood of Christ will be no advantage to us if it be not applied to us. [3] He sprinkled the tabernacle and all the utensils of it, intimating that all the sacrifices offered up and services performed there were accepted only through the blood of Christ, which procures the remission of that iniquity that cleaves to our holy things, which could not have been remitted but by that atoning blood.

ONE SACRIFICE FOR EVER
(vv. 23–28)

In this last part of the chapter, the apostle goes on to tell us what the Holy Ghost has signified to us by the legal purifications of the patterns of the things in heaven, inferring thence the necessity of better sacrifices to consecrate the heavenly things themselves.

I. The necessity of purifying the patterns of the things in heaven, v. 23.

II. The necessity that the heavenly things themselves should be purified with better sacrifices than of bulls and goats. Now it is very evident that the sacrifice of Christ is infinitely better than those of the law, 1. From the places in which the sacrifices under the law, and that under the gospel, were offered. Christ's sacrifice, though offered upon earth, was by himself carried up into heaven, and is there presented in a way of daily intercession; for he appears in the presence of God for us. 2. From the sacrifices themselves, v. 26. Those under the law were the lives and blood of other creatures of a different nature from the offerers; but the sacrifice of Christ was the oblation of himself; he offered his own blood, truly called, by virtue of the hypostatical union, *the blood of God*; and therefore of infinite value. 3. From the frequent repetition of the legal sacrifices. This showed the imperfection of that law. It is the honour and perfection of Christ's sacrifice that, being once offered, it was sufficient to all the ends of it. 4. From the inefficacy of the legal sacrifices, and the efficacy of Christ's sacrifice.

III. The apostle illustrates the argument from the appointment of God concerning men (vv. 27, 28), and observes something like it in the appointment of God concerning Christ.

1. The appointment of God concerning men contains in it two things: (1) That they must once die, or, at least, undergo a change equivalent to death. (2) It is appointed to men that after death they shall come to judgment, to a particular judgment immediately after death.

2. The appointment of God concerning Christ, bearing some resemblance to the other. (1) He must be once offered, to bear the sins of many, of all the Father had given to him, of all who should believe in his name. (2) It is appointed that Christ shall appear the second time without sin, to the salvation of those who look for him.

CHAPTER TEN
INEFFECTIVE SACRIFICES
(vv. 1–6)

Here the apostle, by the direction of the Spirit of God, sets himself to lay low the Levitical dispensation. As,

I. That the law had a shadow, and but a shadow, of good things to come; and who would dote upon a shadow, though of good things, especially when the substance has come?

II. That the law was not the very image of the good things to come. The law did not go so far, but was only a shadow. The law was a very rough draught of the great design of divine grace, and therefore not to be so much doted on.

III. The legal sacrifices, being offered year by year, could never make the comers thereunto perfect; for then there would have been an end of offering them, *vv.* 1, 2.

IV. As the legal sacrifices did not of themselves take away sin, so it was impossible they should, *v.* 4. There was an essential defect in them. 1. They were not of the same nature with us who sinned. 2. They were not of sufficient value to make satisfaction for the affronts offered to the justice and government of God. 3. The beasts offered up under the law could not consent to put themselves in the sinner's room and place. The atoning sacrifice must be one capable of consenting, and must voluntarily substitute himself in the sinner's stead: Christ did so.

V. There was a time fixed and foretold by the great God, and that time had now come, when these legal sacrifices would be no longer accepted by him nor useful to men.

THE OFFERING OF CHRIST
(*vv.* 7–18)

Here the apostle raises up and exalts the Lord Jesus Christ, as high as he had laid the Levitical priesthood low. He recommends Christ to them as the true high priest, the true atoning sacrifice, the antitype of the rest: and this he illustrates,

I. From the purpose and promise of God concerning Christ, which are frequently recorded in the volume of the book of God, *v.* 7.

II. From what God had done in preparing a body for Christ (that is, a human nature), that he might

be qualified to be our Redeemer and Advocate.

III. From the readiness and willingness that Christ discovered to engage in this work, when no other sacrifice would be accepted, *vv.* 7–9.

IV. From the errand and design upon which Christ came; and this was to do the will of God, not only as a prophet to reveal the will of God, not only as a king to give forth divine laws, but as a priest to satisfy the demands of justice, and to fulfil all righteousness.

V. From the perfect efficacy of the priesthood of Christ (*v.* 14): *By one offering he hath for ever perfected those that are sanctified*; he has delivered and will perfectly deliver those that are brought over to him, from all the guilt, power, and punishment of sin, and will put them into the sure possession of perfect holiness and felicity.

VI. From the place to which our Lord Jesus is now exalted, the honour he has there, and the further honour he shall have: *This man, after he had offered one sacrifice for sins, for ever sat down at the right hand of God, henceforth expecting till his enemies be made his footstool, vv.* 12, 13. The Father acquiesces and is satisfied in him; he is satisfied in his Father's will and presence; this is his rest for ever; here he will dwell, for he has both desired and deserved it.

VII. The apostle recommends Christ from the witness the Holy Ghost has given in the scriptures concerning him; this relates chiefly to what should be the happy fruit and consequence of his humiliation and sufferings, which in general is that new and gracious covenant that is founded upon his satisfaction, and sealed by his blood (*v.* 15).

THE CONSECRATED WAY
(*vv.* 19–39)

I. Here the apostle sets forth the dignities of the gospel state. The privileges are, 1. Boldness to enter into the holiest. 2. A high priest over the house of God, even this blessed Jesus, who presides over the church militant, and every member thereof on earth, and over the church triumphant in heaven.

II. The apostle tells us the way and means by which Christians enjoy such privileges, and, in general, declares it to be *by the blood of Jesus*, by the merit of that blood which he offered up to God as an atoning sacrifice. Now the apostle, having given this general account of the way by which we have access to God, enters further into the particulars of it, *v.* 20. As, 1. It is the only way; there is no way left but this. 2. It is a new way, both in opposition to the covenant of works and to the antiquated dispensation of the Old Testament; *the last way* that will ever be opened to men. 3. It is a living way. It would be death to attempt to come to God in the way of the covenant of works; but this way we may come to God, and live. 4. It is a way that Christ has consecrated for us through the veil, that is, his flesh. Our way to heaven is by a crucified Saviour; his death is to us the way of life. To those who believe this he will be precious.

III. He proceeds to show the Hebrews the duties binding upon them on account of these privi-

leges, which were conferred in such an extraordinary way, *vv.* 22, 23, &c.

1. They must draw near to God, and that in a right manner. (1) With a true heart, without any allowed guile or hypocrisy. (2) In full assurance of faith, with a faith grown up to a full persuasion that when we come to God by Christ we shall have audience and acceptance. And, (3) Having our hearts sprinkled from an evil conscience, by a believing application of the blood of Christ to our souls. (4) Our bodies washed with pure water, that is, with the water of baptism, or with the sanctifying virtue of the Holy Spirit.

2. The apostle exhorts believers to hold fast the profession of their faith, *v.* 23. The motive or reason enforcing this duty: *He is faithful that hath promised.* God has made great and precious promises to believers, and he is a faithful God, true to his word; there is no falseness nor fickleness with him, and there should be none with us.

IV. We have the means prescribed for preventing our apostasy, and promoting our fidelity and perseverance, *vv.* 24, 25. &c. He mentions several; as, 1. That we should *consider one another, to provoke to love and to good works.* Christians ought to have a tender consideration and concern for one another. 2. *Not to forsake the assembling of ourselves together*, *v.* 25. It is the will of Christ that his disciples should assemble together, sometimes more privately for conference and prayer, and in public for hearing and joining in all the ordinances of gospel worship. There were in the apostles' times, and should be in every age, Christian assemblies for the worship of God, and for mutual edification. 3. To exhort one another, to exhort ourselves and each other, to warn ourselves and one another of the sin and danger of backsliding, to put ourselves and our fellow-christians in mind of our duty, of our failures and corruptions, to watch over one another, and be jealous of ourselves and one another with a godly jealousy. 4. That we should observe the approaching of times of trial, and be thereby quickened to greater diligence: *So much the more, as you see the day approaching*.

V. Having mentioned these means of establishment, the apostle proceeds, in the close of the chapter, to enforce his exhortations to perseverance, and against apostasy, by many very weighty considerations, *vv*. 26, 27, &c.

1. From the description he gives of the sin of apostasy. It is *sinning wilfully after we have received the knowledge of the truth*, sinning wilfully against that truth of which we have had convincing evidence. It is total apostasy.

2. From the dreadful doom of such apostates. (1) There remains no more sacrifice for such sins, no other Christ to come to save such sinners; they sin against the last resort and remedy. (2) There remains for them only a certain fearful looking for of judgment, *v.* 27.

3. From the methods of divine justice with those who despised Moses's law, that is, sinned presumptuously, despising his authority, his threatenings and his power.

Here he refers to their own consciences, to judge how much sorer punishment the despisers of Christ (after they have professed to know him) are likely to undergo; and they may judge of the greatness of the punishment by the greatness of the sin. How dreadful is the case when not only the justice of God, but his abused grace and mercy call for vengeance!

4. From the description we have in the scripture of the nature of God's vindictive justice, *v.* 30. Vindictive justice is a glorious, though terrible attribute of God; it belongs to him, and he will use and execute it upon the heads of such sinners as despise his grace; he will avenge himself, and his Son, and Spirit, and covenant, upon apostates. And how dreadful then will their case be!

5. He presses them to perseverance by putting them in mind of their former sufferings for Christ: *But call to mind the former days, in which, after you were illuminated, you endured a great fight of afflictions, v.* 32. In the early days of the gospel there was a very hot persecution raised up against the professors of the Christian religion, and the believing Hebrews had their share of it.

What was it that enabled them to bear up under their sufferings? They knew in themselves that they had in heaven a better and a more enduring substance.

6. He presses them to persevere, from that recompence of reward that waited for all faithful Christians (*v.* 35): *Cast not away therefore your confidence, which hath great recompence of reward*. Observe, The

greatest part of the saints' happiness is in promise. They must first do the will of God before they receive the promise; and, after they have done the will of God, they have need of patience to wait for the time when the promise shall be fulfilled; they have need of patience to live till God calls them away. The Christian's present conflict may be sharp, but it will be soon over.

7. He presses them to perseverance, by telling them that this is their distinguishing character and will be their happiness; whereas apostasy is the reproach, and will be the ruin, of all who are guilty of it (*vv*. 38, 39): *Now the just shall live by faith*, &c. The apostle concludes with declaring his good hope concerning himself and these Hebrews, that they should not forfeit the character and happiness of the just, and fall under the brand and misery of the wicked (*v*. 39): *But we are not*, &c.

CHAPTER ELEVEN
NATURE OF FAITH (*vv*. 1–3)

Here we have, I. A definition or description of the grace of faith in two parts. 1. It *is the substance of things hoped for*. Faith and hope go together; and the same things that are the object of our hope are the object of our faith. It is a firm persuasion and expectation that God will perform all that he has promised to us in Christ. 2. It is *the evidence of things not seen*. Faith demonstrates to the eye of the mind the reality of those things that cannot be discerned by the eye of the body.

II. An account of the honour it reflects upon all those who have lived in the exercise of it (*v*. 2): *By it the elders obtained a good report* — the ancient believers, who lived in the first ages of the world.

III. We have here one of the first acts and articles of faith, which has a great influence on all the rest, and which is common to all believers in every age and part of the world, namely, the creation of the *worlds by the word of God*, not out of pre-existent matter, but out of nothing, *v*. 3. By faith we understand much more of the formation of the world than ever could be understood by the naked eye of natural reason. Now what does faith give us to understand concerning *the worlds*, that is, the upper, middle, and lower regions of the universe? 1. *That these worlds were* not eternal, nor did they produce themselves, but they were made by another. 2. That the maker of the worlds is God; he is the maker of all things; and whoever is so must be God. 3. That he made the world with great exactness. 4. That God made the world by his word, that is, by his essential wisdom and eternal Son, and by his active will, saying, *Let it be done, and it was done*, Ps. xxxiii. 9. 5. That the world was thus framed out of nothing, out of no pre-existent matter. These things we understand by faith.

EXAMPLES OF FAITH
(*vv*. 4–31)

The apostle, having given us a more general account of the grace of faith, now proceeds to set before us some illustrious examples of it in the Old-Testament times, and these may be divided into two classes: 1. Those whose names are mentioned, and the particular exercise and actings of whose faith are specified. 2. Those whose names are barely mentioned, and an account given in general of the exploits of their faith, which it is left to the reader to accommodate, and apply to the particular persons from what he gathers up in the sacred story. We have here those whose names are not only mentioned, but the particular trials and actings of their faith are subjoined.

1. The leading instance and example of faith here recorded is that of Abel, one of the first saints, and the first martyr for religion, of all the sons of Adam, one who lived by faith, and died for it, and therefore a fit pattern for the Hebrews to imitate.

II. Of the faith of Enoch, *v.* 5. He is the second of those elders that through faith have a good report. Observe,

1. What is here reported of him. In this place (and in Gen. v. 22, &c.) we read, (1) *That he walked with God*, that is, that he was really, eminently, actively, progressively, and perseveringly religious in his conformity to God, communion with God, and complacency in God. (2) *That he was translated, that he should not see death*, nor any part of him be found upon earth; for God took him, soul and body, into heaven, as he will do those of the saints who shall be found alive at his second coming. (3) *That before his translation he had this testimony, that he pleased God.* He

had the evidence of it in his own conscience, and the Spirit of God witnessed with his spirit.

2. What is here said of his faith, *v.* 6. It is said that *without* this *faith it is impossible to please God*, without such a faith as helps us to walk with God, an active faith, and that we cannot come to God unless we *believe that he is, and that he is a rewarder of those that diligently seek him.*

III. The faith of Noah, *v.* 7. Observe,

1. The ground of Noah's faith—a warning he had received from God of things as yet not seen.

2. The actings of Noah's faith, and the influence it had both upon his mind and practice. (1) Upon his mind; it impressed his soul with a fear of God's judgment: he was *moved with fear.* (2) His faith influenced his practice. His fear, thus excited by believing God's threatening, moved him to prepare an ark, in which, no doubt, he met with the scorns and reproaches of a wicked generation.

3. The blessed fruits and rewards of Noah's faith. (1) Hereby himself and his house were saved, when a whole world of sinners were perishing about them. (2) Hereby he judged and condemned the world; his holy fear condemned their security and vain confidence; his faith condemned their unbelief; his obedience condemned their contempt and rebellion. (3) Hereby *he became an heir of the righteousness which is by faith.* [1] He was possessed of a true justifying righteousness; he was *heir to it*: and, [2] This his right of inheritance was through faith in Christ, as *a*

member of Christ, a child of God, and, if a child, then an heir.

IV. The faith of Abraham, the friend of God, and father of the faithful, in whom the Hebrews boasted, and from whom they derived their pedigree and privileges; and therefore the apostle, that he might both please and profit them, enlarges more upon the heroic achievements of Abraham's faith than of that of any other of the patriarchs; and in the midst of his account of the faith of Abraham he inserts the story of Sarah's faith, whose daughters those women are that continue to do well. Observe,

1. The ground of Abraham's faith, the call and promise of God, *v* 8.

2. The exercise of Abraham's faith: he yielded an implicit regard to the call of God. (1) *He went out, not knowing whither he went.* (2) *He sojourned in the land of promise as in a strange country.* This was an exercise of his faith.

3. The supports of Abraham's faith (*v.* 10): *He looked for a city that hath foundations, whose builder and maker is God.* It was a support to him under all the trials of his sojourning state, helped him patiently to bear all the inconveniences of it, and actively to discharge all the duties of it, persevering therein unto the end.

V. In the midst of the story of Abraham, the apostle inserts an account of the faith of Sarah. Here observe,

1. The difficulties of Sarah's faith, which were very great.

2. The actings of her faith. Her unbelief is pardoned and forgotten, but her faith prevailed and is recorded: *She judged him faithful, who had promised, v.* 11.

3. The fruits and rewards of her faith. (1) *She received strength to conceive seed.* (2) *She was delivered of a child,* a man-child, a child of the promise, the comfort of his parents' advanced years, and the hope of future ages. (3) From them, by this son, sprang a numerous progeny of illustrious persons, *as the stars of the sky* (*v.* 12)—a great, powerful, and renowned nation.

VI. The apostle proceeds to make mention of the faith of the other patriachs, Isaac and Jacob, and the rest of his happy family, *v.* 13.

VII. Now after the apostle has given this account of the faith of others, with Abraham, he returns to him again, and gives us an instance of the greatest trial and act of faith that stands upon record, either in the story of the father of the faithful or of any of his spiritual seed; and this was his offering up Isaac: *By faith Abraham, when he was tried, offered up Isaac; and he that had received the promises offered up his only-begotten son, v.* 17.

VIII. Of the faith of Isaac, *v.* 20. Something of him we had before interwoven with the story of Abraham; here we have something of a distinct nature—that by faith he blessed his two sons, Jacob and Esau, *concerning things to come.* Here observe,

1. The actings of his faith: He *blessed Jacob and Esau concerning things to come.* He blessed them; that is, he resigned them up to God in covenant.

2. The difficulties Isaac's faith struggled with. (1) He seemed to

have forgotten how God had determined the matter at the birth of these his sons, Gen. xxv. 23. (2) He acted in this matter with some reluctance. We now go on to,

IX. The faith of Jacob (*v.* 21), who, *when he was dying, blessed both the sons of Joseph, and worshipped, leaning upon the top of his staff.* There were a great many instances of the faith of Jacob; his life was a life of faith, and his faith met with great exercise.

X. The faith of Joseph, *v.* 22. And here also we consider,

1. What he did by his faith: *He made mention of the departing of the children of Israel, and gave commandment concerning his bones.* The passage is out of Gen. l. 24, 25.

2. When it was that the faith of Joseph acted after this manner; namely, as in the case of Jacob, when he was dying.

XI. The faith of the parents of Moses, which is cited from Exod. ii. 3, &c.

XII. The faith of Moses himself (*vv.* 24, 25, &c.), here observe,

1. An instance of his faith in conquering the world.

(1) He *refused to be called the son of Pharaoh's daughter*, whose foundling he was, and her fondling too; she had adopted him for her son, and he refused it.

(2) He chose *rather to suffer affliction with the people of God than to enjoy the pleasures of sin for a season, v.* 25. He was willing to take his lot with the people of God here, though it was a suffering lot, that he might have his portion with them hereafter, rather than to enjoy all the sensual sinful pleasures of Pharaoh's court, which would be

but for a season, and would then be punished with everlasting misery.

(3) He accounted *the reproaches of Christ greater riches than the treasures of Egypt, v.* 26. See how Moses weighed matters: in one scale he put the worst of religion—*the reproaches of Christ*, in the other scale the best of the world—*the treasures of Egypt*; and in his judgment, directed by faith, the worst of religion weighed down the best of the world.

2. The circumstance of time is taken notice of, when Moses by his faith gained this victory over the world, in all its honours, pleasures, and treasures: *When he had come to years* (*v.* 24). It was not the act of a child, that prefers counters to gold, but it proceeded from mature deliberation.

3. What it was that supported and strengthened the faith of Moses to such a degree as to enable him to gain such a victory over the world: *He had respect unto the recompence of reward*, that is, say some, the deliverance out of Egypt; but doubtless it means much more— the glorious reward of faith and fidelity in the other world.

4. We have another instance of the faith of Moses, namely, in forsaking Egypt: *By faith he forsook Egypt, not fearing the wrath of the king, v.* 27.

5. We have yet another instance of the faith of Moses, in keeping *the passover and sprinkling of blood, v.* 28. The account of this we have in Exod. xii. 13–23. Though all Israel kept this passover, yet it was by Moses that God delivered the institution of it; and, though it was a great mystery, Moses by faith

Examples of Faith

both delivered it to the people and kept it that night in the house where he lodged.

XIII. The next instance of faith is that of the Israelites passing through the Red Sea under the conduct of Moses their leader, *v.* 29. The story we have in Exodus, *ch.* xiv. Observe,

1. The preservation and safe passage of the Israelites through the Red Sea, when there was no other way to escape from Pharaoh and his host, who were closely pursuing them.

2. The destruction of the Egyptians. They, presumptuously attempting to follow Israel through the Red Sea, being thus blinded and hardened to their ruin, were all drowned. Their rashness was great, and their ruin was grievous.

XIV. The next instance of faith is that of the Israelites, under Joshua their leader, before the walls of Jericho. The story we have Josh. vi. 5, &c. God can and will in his own time and way cause all the powerful opposition that is made to his interest and glory to fall down, and the grace of faith is mighty through God for the pulling down of strong-holds; he will make Babylon fall before the faith of his people, and, when he has some great thing to do for them, he raises up great and strong faith in them.

XV. The next instance is the faith of Rahab, *v.* 31. Among the noble army of believing worthies, bravely marshalled by the apostle, Rahab comes in the rear, to show *that God is no respecter of persons.* Here consider,

1. Who this Rahab was. (1) She was a Canaanite, a *stranger to the commonwealth of Israel*, and had but little help for faith, and yet she was a believer; the power of divine grace greatly appears when it works without the usual means of grace. (2) She was a harlot, and lived in a way of sin; and yet she believed that the greatness of sin, if truly repented of, shall be no bar to the pardoning mercy of God.

2. What she did by her faith: *She received the spies in peace*, the men that Joshua had sent to spy out Jericho, Josh. ii. 6, 7.

3. What she gained by her faith. She escaped perishing with those that believed not. Singular faith, when the generality are not only unbelievers, but against believers, will be rewarded with singular favours in times of common calamity.

THE HEROES OF FAITH
(*vv.* 32–40)

The apostle now concludes his narrative with a more summary account of another set of believers, where the particular acts are not ascribed to particular persons by name, but left to be applied by those who are well acquainted with the sacred story; and, like a divine orator, he prefaces this part of the narrative with an elegant expostulation: *What shall I say more? Time would fail me.*

I. In this summary account the apostle mentions,

1. Gideon, whose story we have in Judges vi. 11, &c.

2. Barak, another instrument raised up to deliver Israel out of the hand of Jabin, king of Canaan, Judg. iv.

3. Samson, another instrument that God raised up to deliver Israel from the Philistines: his story we have in Judges xiii., xiv., xv., and xvi., and from it we learn that the grace of faith is the strength of the soul for great service.

4. Jephthah, whose story we have, Judg. xi., before that of Samson. He was raised up to deliver Israel from the Ammonites.

5. David, that great man after God's own heart. Few ever met with greater trials, and few ever discovered a more lively faith.

6. Samuel, raised up to be a most eminent prophet of the Lord to Israel, as well as a ruler over them. God revealed himself to Samuel when he was but a child, and continued to do so till his death.

7. To Samuel he adds, *and of the prophets*, who were extraordinary ministers of the Old-Testament church. Now a true and strong faith was very requisite for the right discharge of such an office as this.

II. Having done naming particular persons, he proceeds to tell us what things were done by their faith.

1. *By faith they subdued kingdoms*, v. 33. The interests and powers of kings and kingdoms are often set up in oppositin to God and his people.

2. They *wrought righteousness*, both in their public and personal capacities.

3. They *obtained promises*, both general and special. It is faith that gives us an interest in the promises; it is by faith that we have the comfor of the promises; and it is by faith that we are prepared to wait for the promises, and in due time to receive them.

4. They *stopped the mouths of lions*; so did Samson, Judg. xiv. 5, 6, and David, 1 Sam. xvii. 34, 35, and Dan. vi. 22.

5. They *quenched the violence of the fire*, v. 34. So Moses, by the prayer of faith, quenched the fire of God's wrath that was kindled against the people of Israel, Num. xi. 1, 2. So did the three children, or rather mighty champions, Dan. III. 17–27.

6. They *escaped the edge of the sword*. The swords of men are held in the hand of God, and he can blunt the edge of the sword, and turn it away from his people against their enemies when he pleases.

7. *Out of weakness they were made strong*. From national weakness, into which the Jews often fell by their unbelief. From bodily weakness; thus Hezekiah (Isa. xxxviii. 15, 16). And it is the same grace of faith that from spiritual weakness helps men to recover and renew their strength.

8. They *grew valiant in fight*. True faith gives truest courage and patience, as it discerns the strength of God, and thereby the weakness of all his enemies. And they were not only valiant, but successful.

9. *Women received their dead raised to life again*, v. 35. So did the widow of Zarepath (1 Kings xvii. 23), and the Shunamite, 2 Kings iv. 36.

III. The apostle tells us what these believers endured by faith. 1. They *were tortured, not accepting deliverance*, v. 35. 2. They endured *trials of cruel mockings and scourgings, and bonds and imprisonment*, v. 36. 3. They were put to death in the most cruel manner. 4. Those who escaped death were used so ill that death might seem more eligible than such a life. Such sufferings as these they endured then for their faith; and such they endured through the power of the grace of faith.

IV. What they obtained by their faith. 1. A most honourable character and commendation from God, the true Judge and fountain of honour—that *the world was not worthy* of such men; the world did not deserve such blessings; they did not know how to value them, nor how to use them. 2. They *obtained a good report* (*v*. 39) of all good men, and of the truth itself, and have the honour to be enrolled in this sacred calendar of the Old-Testament worthies, God's witnesses. 3. They obtained an interest in the promises, though not the full possession of them. They had a title to the promises, though they received not the great things promised. He tells the Hebrews that God had *provided some better things for* them (*v*. 40), and therefore they might be assured that he expected at least as good things from them; and that since the gospel is the end and perfection of the Old Testament, which had no excellency but in its reference to Christ and the gospel, it was expected that their faith should be as much more perfect than the faith of the Old-Testament saints.

CHAPTER TWELVE

LOOKING TO JESUS (*vv*. 1–3)

Here observe what is the great duty which the apostle urges upon the Hebrews, and which he so much desires they would comply with,

and that is, to *lay aside every weight, and the sin that did so easily beset them, and run with patience the race set before them*. The duty consists of two parts, the one preparatory, the other perfective.

I. Preparatory: *Lay aside every weight, and the sin*, &c. 1. *Every weight*, that is, all inordinate affection and concern for the body, and the present life and world. 2. *The sin that doth so easily beset us*; the sin that has the greatest advantage against us, by the circumstances we are in, our constitution, our company.

II. Perfective: *Run with patience the race that is set before us*. The apostle speaks in the gymnastic style, taken from the Olympic and other exercises.

1. Christians have a race to run, a race of service and a race of sufferings, a course of active and passive obedience.

2. This race is set before them; it is marked out unto them, both by the word of God and the examples of the faithful servants of God, that cloud of witnesses with which they are compassed about.

3. This race must be run with patience and perseverance.

4. Christians have a greater example to animate and encourage them in their Christian course than any or all who have been mentioned before, and that is the Lord Jesus Christ: *Looking unto Jesus, the author and finisher of our faith, v.* 2. Here observe,

(1) What our Lord Jesus is to his people: he is *the author and finisher of* their *faith*—the beginning, perfecter, and rewarder of it.

(2) What trials Christ met with in

his race and course. [1] He *endured the contradiction of sinners against himself* (v. 3); he bore the opposition that they made to him, both in their words and behaviour. [2] He *endured the cross*—all those sufferings that he met with in the world. [3] He *despised the shame*. All the reproaches that were cast upon him, both in his life and at his death, he despised.

(3) What it was that supported the human soul of Christ under these unparalleled sufferings; and that was *the joy that was set before him*. He had something in view under all his sufferings, which was pleasant to him. This was the joy that was set before him.

(4) The reward of his suffering: he *has sat down at the right hand of the throne of God*.

(5) What is our duty with respect to this Jesus. We must, [1] Look unto him; that is, we must set him continually before us as our example, and our great encouragement; we must look to him for direction, for assistance, and for acceptance, in all our sufferings. [2] We must consider him, meditate much upon him, and reason with ourselves from his case to our own.

(6) The advantage we shall reap by thus doing: it will be a means to prevent our weariness and fainting (v. 3).

CHASTENING (vv. 4–17)

Here the apostle presses the exhortation to patience and perseverance by an argument taken from the gentle measure and gracious nature of those sufferings which the believing Hebrews endured in their Christian course.

I. From the gentle and moderate degree and measure of their sufferings: *You have not yet resisted unto blood, striving against sin*, v. 4. Observe,

1. He owns that they had suffered much, they had been striving to an agony against sin.

2. He puts them in mind that they might have suffered more, that they had not suffered as much as others; for they had *not yet resisted unto blood*, they had not been called to martyrdom as yet, though they knew not how soon they might be.

II. He argues from the peculiar and gracious nature of those sufferings that befall the people of God. Observe,

1. Those afflictions which may be truly persecution as far as men are concerned in them are fatherly rebukes and chastisements as far as God is concerned in them.

2. God has directed his people how they ought to behave themselves under all their afflictions; they must avoid the extremes that many run into. (1) They must not despise the chastening of the Lord. Those who make light of affliction make light of God and make light of sin. (2) They must not faint when they are rebuked; they must not despond and sink under their trial, nor fret and repine, but bear up with faith and patience. (3) If they run into either of these extremes, it is a sign they have forgotten their heavenly Father's advice and exhortation, which he has given them in true and tender affection.

3. Afflictions, rightly endured, though they may be the fruits of God's displeasure, are yet proofs of his paternal love to his people

and care for them (*vv.* 6, 7): *Whom the Lord loveth he chasteneth, and scourgeth every sin whom he receiveth.*

4. Those that are impatient under the discipline of their heavenly Father behave worse towards him than they would do towards earthly parents, *vv.* 9, 10.

5. The children of God, under their afflictions, ought not to judge of his dealings with them by present sense, but by reason, and faith, and experience: *No chastening for the present seemeth to be joyous, but grievous; nevertheless afterwards it yieldeth the peaceable fruits of righteousness, v.* 11.

6. Where afflictions and sufferings for the sake of Christ are not considered by men as the chastisement of their heavenly Father, and improved as such, they will be a dangerous snare and temptation to apostasy, which every Christian should most carefully watch against (*vv.* 15, 16): *Looking diligently lest any man fail of the grace of God,* &c.

[2] The apostle backs the caution with an awful example, and that is, that of Esau, who though born within the pale of the church, and having the birthright as the eldest son, and so entitled to the privilege of being prophet, priest, and king, in his family, was so profane as to despise these sacred privileges, and to sell his birthright for a morsel of meat. Where observe, *First,* Esau's sin. He profanely despised and sold the birthright, and all the advantages attending it. So do apostates, who to avoid persecution, and enjoy sensual ease and pleasure, though they bore the character of the children of God, and had a visible right to the blessing and inheritance, give up all pretensions thereto. *Secondly,* Esau's punishment, which was suitable to his sin. His conscience was convinced of his sin and folly, when it was too late: *He would afterwards have inherited the blessing,* &c. His punishment lay in two things: 1. He was condemned by his own conscience; he now saw that the blessing he had made so light of was worth the having, worth the seeking, though with much carefulness and many tears. 2. He was rejected of God: *He found no place of repentance* in God nor in his father; the blessing was given to another, even to him to whom he sold it for a mess of pottage. Esau, in his great wickedness, had made the bargain, and God, in his righteous judgment, ratified and confirmed it, and would not suffer Isaac to reverse it.

We may hence learn, [1] That apostasy from Christ is the fruit of preferring the gratification of the flesh to the blessing of God and the heavenly inheritance [2] Sinners will not always have such mean thoughts of the divine blessing and inheritance as now they have. [3] When the day of grace is over (as sometimes it may be in this life), they will find no place for repentance: they cannot repent aright of their sin; and God will not repent of the sentence he has passed upon them for their sin.

THE EARTH SHAKEN
(*vv.* 18–29)

Here the apostle goes on to engage the professing Hebrews to perseverance in their Christian course and conflict, and not to relapse again into Judaism.

I. He shows how much the gospel church differs from the Jewish church, and how much it excels. And here we have a very particular description of the state of the church under the Mosaic dispensation, *vv.* 18–21. 1. It was a gross sensible state. Mount Sinai, constituted, was a *mount that might be touched* (*v.* 18), a gross palpable place; so was the dispensation. 2. It was a dark dispensation. Upon that mount there were blackness and darkness, and that church-state was covered with dark shadows and types. 3. It was a dreadful and terrible dispensation; the Jews could not bear the terror of it. 4. It was a limited dispensation; all might not approach to that mount, but only Moses and Aaron. 5. It was a very dangerous dispensation. The mount burned with fire, and whatever man or beast touched the mount must *be stoned, or thrust through with a dart*, *v.* 20.

II. He shows how much the gospel church represents the church triumphant in heaven, what communication there is between the one and the other. The gospel church is called *mount Zion, the heavenly Jerusalem, which is free*, in opposition to mount Sinai, which tendeth to bondage, Gal. iv. 24. Now, in coming to mount Zion, believers come into heavenly places, and into a heavenly society.

1. Into heavenly places. (1) *Unto the city of the living God.* God has taken up his gracious residence in the gospel church, which on that account is an emblem of heaven.

(2) To *the heavenly Jerusalem* as born and bred there, as free denizens there. Here believers have clearer views of heaven, plainer evidences for heaven, and a greater meetness and more heavenly temper of soul.

2. To a heavenly society. (1) *To an innumerable company of angels*, who are of the same family with the saints, under the same head, and in a great measure employed in the same work. (2) *To the general assembly and church of the first-born, that are written in heaven*, that is, to the universal church, however dispersed. (3) *To God the Judge of all*, that great God who will judge both Jew and Gentile according to the law they are under. (4) *To the spirits of just men made perfect.* Believers have union with departed saints in one and the same head and Spirit, and a title to the same inheritance, of which those on earth are heirs, those in heaven possessors. (5) *To Jesus the Mediator of the new covenant, and to the blood of sprinkling, that speaketh better things than that of Abel.* This is none of the least of the many encouragements there are to perseverance in the gospel state, since it is a state of communion with Christ the Mediator of the new covenant, and of communication of his blood, that speaketh better things than the blood of Abel. This is speaking blood, and it speaks better things than that of Abel. *First*, It speaks to God in behalf of sinners; it pleads not for vengeance, as the blood of Abel did on him who shed it, but for mercy. *Secondly*, To sinners, in the name of God. It speaks pardon to their

sins, peace to their souls; and bespeaks their strictest obedience and highest love and thankfulness.

III. The apostle, having thus enlarged upon the argument to perseverance taken from the heavenly nature of the gospel church state, closes the chapter by improving the argument in a manner suitable to the weight of it (*vv* 25, &c.): *See then that you refuse not him that speaketh*—that speaketh by his blood; and not only speaketh after another manner than the blood of Abel spoke from the ground, but than God spoke by the angels, and by Moses spoke on mount Sinai; then he spoke on earth, now he speaks from heaven.

And hence the apostle justly concludes, [1] How necessary it is for us to obtain *grace from God, to serve him acceptably*: if we be not accepted of God under this dispensation, we shall never be accepted at all; and we lose all our labour in religion if we be not accepted of God. [2] We cannot worship God acceptably, unless we worship him with *godly reverence and fear*. As faith, so holy fear, is necessary to acceptable worship. [3] It is only the grace of God that enables us to worship God in a right manner: nature cannot come up to it. [4] God is the same just and righteous God under the gospel that he appeared to be under the law.

CHAPTER THIRTEEN
VARIOUS DUTIES (*vv.* 1–17)

Now the apostle calls the believing Hebrews to the performance of many excellent duties, in which it becomes Christians to excel.

I. To brotherly love (*v.* 1), by which he does not only mean a general affection to all men, as our brethren by nature, nor that more limited affection which is due to those who are of the same immediate parents, but that special and spiritual affection which ought to exist among the children of God. Christians should always love and live as brethren, and the more they grow in devout affection to God their heavenly Father the more they will grow in love to one another for his sake.

II. To hospitality: *Be not forgetful to entertain strangers for his sake, v.* 2. We must add to brotherly kindness charity. Here observe, 1. The duty required—*to entertain strangers*, both those that are strangers to the commonwealth of Israel, and strangers to our persons. Though we know not who they are, nor whence they come, yet, seeing they are without any certain dwelling place, we should allow them room in our hearts and in our houses, as we have opportunity and ability. 2. The motive: *Thereby some have entertained angels unawares*; so Abraham did (Gen. xviii.), and Lot (Gen. xix.), and one of those that Abraham entertained was the Son of God; and, though we cannot suppose this will ever be our case, yet what we do to strangers, in obedience to him, he will reckon and reward as done to himself. Matt. xxv. 35, *I was a stranger, and you took me in.*

III. To Christian sympathy: *Remember those that are in bonds, v.* 3. Here observe,

1. The duty—to *remember those that are in bonds* and in *adversity*.

2. The reason of the duty: *As being yourselves in the body*; not only in the body natural, and so liable to the like sufferings, and you should sympathise with them now that others may sympathise with you when your time of trial comes; but in the same mystical body, under the same head, *and if one member suffer all the rest suffer with it*, 1. Cor. xii. 26.

IV. To purity and chastity, *v.* 4. Here you have, 1. A recommendation of God's ordinance of marriage, that it *is honourable in all*, and ought to be so esteemed by all, and not denied to those to whom God has not denied it. 2. A dreadful but just censure of impurity and lewdness: *Whoremongers and adulterers God will judge.*

V. To Christian contentment, *vv.* 5, 6. Here observe, 1. The sin that is contrary to this grace and duty—*covetousness*, an over eager desire of the wealth of this world, envying those who have more than we. 2. The duty and grace that is contrary to covetousness—being satisfied and pleased *with such things as we have.* 3. What reason Christians have to be contented with their lot. (1) *God hath said, I will never leave thee, nor forsake thee, vv.* 5, 6. (2) From this comprehensive promise they may assure themselves of help from God: *So that we may boldly say, The Lord is my helper; I will not fear what man shall do unto me, v.* 6. Men can do nothing against God, and God can make all that men do against his people to turn to their good.

VI. To the duty Christians owe to their ministers, and that both to those that are dead and to those that are yet alive.

1. To those that are dead: *Remember those that have had the rule over you, v.* 7. Here observe,

(1) The description given of them. They were such as had the rule over them, and had spoken to them the word of God; their guides and governors, who had spoken to them the word of God.

(2) The duties owing to them, even when they were dead.

[1] "*Remember them*—their preaching, their praying, their private counsel, their example."

[2] "*Follow* their *faith*; be stedfast in the profession of the faith they preached to you, and labour after the grace of faith by which they lived and died so well." Now this duty of following the same true faith in which they had been instructed the apostle enlarges much upon, and presses them earnestly to it, not only from the remembrance of their faithful deceased guides, but from several other motives.

First, From the immutability and eternity of the Lord Jesus Christ.

Secondly, From the nature and tendency of those erroneous doctrines that they were in danger of falling in with.

Observe,

(*a*) The Christian church has its altar. It was objected against the primitive Christians that their assemblies were destitute of an altar; but this was not true. *We have an altar*, not a material altar, but a personal one, and that is Christ; he is both our altar, and our sacrifice; he sanctifies the gift.

(*b*) This altar furnishes out a feast for true believers, a feast upon the sacrifice, spiritual strength and growth, and holy delight and pleasure.

(*c*) Those who adhere to the tabernacle or the Levitical dispensation, or return to it again, exclude themselves from the privileges of this altar, from the benefits purchased by Christ.

VII. To improve this argument (*vv*. 13-15) in suitable advices. *First, Let us go forth therefore unto him without the camp*; go forth from the ceremonial law, from sin, from the world, from ourselves, our very bodies, when he calls us. *Secondly*, Let us be willing to *bear his reproach*, be willing to be accounted the offscouring of all things, not worthy to live, not worthy to die a common death. *Thirdly*, Let us make a right use of this altar; not only partake of the privileges of it, but discharge the duties of the altar, as those whom Christ has made priests to attend on this altar.

2. Having thus told us the duty Christians owe to their deceased ministers, which principally consists in following their faith and not departing from it, the apostle tells us what is the duty that people owe to their living ministers (*v*. 17) and the reasons of that duty: (1) The duty—to obey them, and submit themselves to them. (2) The motives to this duty. [1] They have the rule over the people; their office, though not magisterial, yet is truly authoritative. [2] They watch for the souls of the people,

not to ensnare them, but to save them. [3] They must give an account how they have discharged their duty, and what has become of the souls committed to their trust, whether any have been lost through their neglect, and whether any of them have been brought in and built up under their ministry. [4] They would be glad to give a good account of themselves and their hearers. [5] If they give up their account with grief, it will be the people's loss as well as theirs.

CONCLUSION (*vv*. 18-25)

Here, I. The apostle recommends himself, and his fellow-sufferers, to the prayers of the Hebrew believers (*v*. 18): "*Pray for us*; for me and Timothy" (mentioned *v*. 23), "and for all those of us who labour in the ministry of the gospel."

II. He offers up his prayers to God for them, being willing to do for them as he desired they should do for him: *Now the God of peace*, &c., *v*. 20.

III. He gives the Hebrews an account of Timothy's liberty and his hopes of seeing them with him in a little time, *v*. 23. It seems, Timothy had been a prisoner, doubtless for the gospel, but now he was set at liberty.

IV. Having given a brief account of this his letter, and begged their attention to it (*v*. 22), he closes with salutations, and a solemn, though short benediction.

432

THE GENERAL EPISTLE OF

JAMES

CHAPTER ONE
FAITH AND PATIENCE
(vv. 1–12)

Here is an apostle writing to the scattered; an epistle from God to them, when driven away from his temple, and seemingly neglected by him. It was the desire of this apostle's heart that those who were scattered might be comforted— that they might do well and fare well, and be enabled to rejoice even in their distresses.

We now come to consider the matter of this epistle. In this paragraph we have the following things to be observed:

I. The suffering state of Christians in this world is represented. 1. It is implied that troubles and afflictions may be the lot of the best Christians, even of those who have the most reason to think and hope well of themselves. 2. These outward afflictions and troubles are temptations to them. The devil endeavours by sufferings and crosses to draw men to sin and to deter them from duty, or unfit them for it. 3. These temptations may be numerous and various: *Divers temptations*, as the apostle speaks. 4. The trials of a good man are such as he does not create to himself, nor sinfully pull upon himself; but they are such as he is said to fall into.

II. The graces and duties of a state of trial and affliction are here pointed out to us.

1. One Christian grace to be exercised is joy: *Count it all joy, v.* 2. We must not sink into a sad and disconsolate frame of mind, which would make us faint under our trials.

2. Faith is a grace that one expression supposes and another expressly requires: *Knowing this, that the trial of your faith, v.* 3; and then in *v.* 6, *Let him ask in faith.* There must be a sound believing of the great truths of Christianity, and a resolute cleaving to them, in times of trial.

3. There must be patience: *The trial of faith worketh patience.* The trying of one grace produces another; and the more the suffering graces of a Christian are exercised the stronger they grow. *Tribulation worketh patience*, Rom. v. 3.

4. Prayer is a duty recommended also to suffering Christians; and here the apostle shows, (1) What we ought more especially to pray for— wisdom: *If any lack wisdom, let him ask of God.* We should not pray so much for the removal of an affliction as for wisdom to make a right use of it. (2) In what way this is to be obtained—upon our petitioning or asking for it. Let us confess our want of wisdom to God and daily ask it of him. (3) We have the greatest encouragement to do

this: *he giveth to all men liberally, and upbraideth not.* Yea, it is expressly promised that *it shall be given, v.* 5. But, (4) There is one thing necessary to be observed in our asking, namely, that we do it with a believing, steady mind: *Let him ask in faith, nothing wavering, v.* 6.

5. That oneness, and sincerity of intention, and a steadiness of mind, constitute another duty required under affliction: *He that wavereth is like a wave of the sea, driven with the wind, and tossed.* Now, for the cure of a wavering spirit and a weak faith, the apostle shows the ill effects of these, (1) In that the success of prayer is spoiled hereby: *Let not that man think that he shall receive any thing of the Lord, v.* 7. (2) A wavering faith and spirit has a bad influence upon our conversations. *A double-minded man is unstable in all his ways, v.* 8.

III. The holy humble temper of a Christian, both in advancement and debasement, is described: and both poor and rich are directed on what grounds to build their joy and comfort, *vv.* 9–11. Here we may observe, 1. Those of low degree are to be looked upon as brethren: *Let the brother of low degree,* &c. Poverty does not destroy the relation among Christians. 2. Good Christians may be rich in the world, *v.* 10. 3. Both these are allowed to rejoice. No condition of life puts us out of a capacity of rejoicing in God. 4. Observe what reason rich people have, notwithstanding their riches, to be humble and low in their own eyes, because both they and their riches are passing away: *As the flower of the grass he shall*

pass away. He, and his wealth with him, *v.* 11.

IV. A blessing is pronounced on those who endure their exercises and trials, as here directed: *Blessed is the man that endureth temptation, v.* 12. The crown of life is promised not only to great and eminent saints, but to all those who have the love of God reigning in their hearts.

TEMPTATION (*vv.* 13–18)

I. We are here taught that God is not the author of any man's sin. Whoever they are who raise persecutions against men, and whatever injustice and sin they may be guilty of in proceeding against them, God is not to be charged with it. As God cannot be tempted with evil himself, so neither can he be a tempter of others.

II. We are taught where the true cause of evil lies, and where the blame ought to be laid (*v.* 14): *Every man is tempted* (in an ill sense) *when he is drawn away of his own lust, and enticed.* In other scriptures the devil is called *the tempter,* and other things may sometimes concur to tempt us; but neither the devil nor any other person or thing is to be blamed so as to excuse ourselves; for the true original of evil and temptation is in our own hearts.

III. We are taught yet further that, while we are the authors and procurers of all sin and misery to ourselves, *God is the Father and fountain of all good, vv.* 16, 17. We must own God as the author of all the powers and perfections that are in the creature, and the giver of all the benefits which we have in and by those powers and perfections: but none of their darknesses, their imperfections, or their ill actions are to be charged on the Father of lights; from him proceeds every good and perfect gift, both pertaining to this life and that which is to come. As every good gift is from God, so particularly the renovation of our natures, our regeneration, and all the holy happy consequences of it, must be ascribed to him (*v.* 18): *Of his own will begat he us with the word of truth.* The end and design of God's giving renewing grace is here laid down: *That we should be a kind of first-fruits of his creatures* — that we should be God's portion and treasure, and a more peculiar property to him, as the first-fruits were; and that we should become holy to the Lord, as the first-fruits were consecrated to him.·

DOERS OF THE WORD
(*vv.* 19–27)

In this part of the chapter we are required,

I. To restrain the workings of passion. *Wherefore, my beloved brethren, let every man be swift to hear, slow to speak, slow to wrath, v.* 19. Instead of censuring God under our trials, let us open our ears and hearts to hear what he will say to us. People are often stiff in their own opinions because they are not willing to hear what others have to offer against them: whereas we should be swift to hear reason and truth on all sides, and be slow to speak any thing that should prevent this: and, when we do speak, there should be nothing of wrath; for a soft answer turneth away wrath.

II. A very good reason is given for suppressing anger: *For the wrath of man worketh not the righteousness of God, v.* 20. *Wrath* is a human thing, and the wrath of man stands opposed to the righteousness of God.

III. We are called upon to suppress other corrupt affections, as well as rash anger: *Lay aside all filthiness and superfluity of naughtiness, v.* 21. The word here translated *filthiness* signifies those lusts which have the greatest turpitude and sensuality in them; and the words rendered *superfluity of naughtiness* may be understood of the overflowings of malice or any other spiritual wickednesses. Observe, from the foregoing parts of this chapter, the laying aside of all filthiness is what a time of temptation and affliction calls for, and is necessary to the avoiding of error, and the right receiving and improving of the word of truth: for,

IV. We are here fully, though briefly, instructed concerning hearing the word of God.

1. We are required to prepare ourselves for it (*v.* 21), to get rid of every corrupt affection and of every prejudice and prepossession, and to lay aside those sins which pervert the judgment and blind the mind.

2. We are directed how to hear it: *Receive with meekness the engrafted word, which is able to save your souls.* (1) In hearing the word of God, we are to receive it — assent to the truths of it — consent to the laws of it. (2) We must therefore yield ourselves to the word of God, with most submissive, humble, and tractable tempers: this is to *receive it with meekness.* (3) In all our

hearing we should aim at the salvation of our souls.

3. We are taught what is to be done after hearing (*v.* 22): *But be you doers of the word, and not hearers only, deceiving your own selves.* Observe here, (1) Hearing is in order to do; the most attentive and the most frequent hearing of the word of God will not avail us, unless we be also doers of it. Observe, (2) Bare hearers are self-deceivers; the original word signifies men's arguing sophistically to themselves; their reasoning is manifestly deceitful and false when they would make one part of their work discharge them from the obligation they lie under to another.

4. The apostle shows what is the proper use of the word of God, who they are that do not use it as they ought, and who they are that do make a right use of it, *vv.* 23–25. Let us consider each of these distinctly. (1) The use we are to make of God's word may be learnt from its being compared to a glass, in which a man may *behold his natural face*. As a looking-glass shows us the spots and defilements upon our faces, that they may be remedied and washed off, so the word of God shows us our sins, that we may repent of them and get them pardoned; it shows us what is amiss, that it may be amended. (2) We have here an account of those who do not use this glass of the word as they ought: *He that beholds himself, and goes his way, and straightway forgets what manner of man he was, v.* 24. This is the true description of one who hears the word of God and does it not. (3) Those also are described, and

pronounced blessed, who hear aright, and who use the glass of God's word as they should do (*v.* 25): *Whoso looketh into the perfect law of liberty, and continueth therein,* &c. Observe here, [1] The gospel is a law of liberty, or, as Mr. Baxter expresses it, *of liberation,* giving us deliverance from the Jewish law, and from sin and guilt, and wrath and death. [2] It is a perfect law; nothing can be added to it. [3] In hearing the word, we look into this perfect law; we consult it for counsel and direction; we look into it, that we may thence take our measures. [4] Then only do we look into the law of liberty as we should when we *continue therein.* [5] Those who thus do, and *continue in the law and word of God,* are, and *shall be, blessed in their deed; blessed in all their ways,* according to the first psalm, to which, some think, James here alludes.

V. The apostle next informs us how we may distinguish between a vain religion and that which is pure and approved of God. Here it is plainly and peremptorily declared,

1. What is a vain religion: *If any man among you seemeth to be religious, and bridleth not his tongue, but deceives his own heart, this man's religion is vain.* The man who has a detracting tongue cannot have a truly humble gracious heart. He who delights to injure his neighbour in vain pretends to love God; therefore a reviling tongue will prove a man a hypocrite.

2. It is here plainly and peremptorily declared wherein true religion consists: *Pure religion and undefiled before God and the Father is this, v.* 27. *Visiting the fatherless and*

widows in their affliction. Visiting is here put for all manner of relief which we are capable of giving to others; and fatherless and widows are here particularly mentioned, because they are generally most apt to be neglected or oppressed: but by them we are to understand all who are proper objects of charity, all who are in affliction. It is very remarkable that if the sum of religion be drawn up in two articles this is one—to be charitable and relieve the afflicted. Observe, (4) An unspotted life must accompany an unfeigned love and charity: *To keep himself unspotted from the world.* The world is apt to spot and blemish the soul, and it is hard to live in it, and have to do with it, and not be defiled; but this must be our constant endeavour. Herein consists pure and undefiled religion. The very things of the world too much taint our spirits, if we are much conversant with them; but the sins and lusts of the world deface and defile them very woefully indeed. James comprises *all that is in the world*, which we are not to love, under three heads: *the lust of the flesh, the lust of the eyes, and the pride of life*; and to keep ourselves unspotted from all these is to keep ourselves unspotted from the world. May God by his grace keep both our hearts and lives clean from the love of the world, and from the temptations of wicked worldly men.

CHAPTER TWO

SNOBBERY REBUKED (*vv.* 1–7)

The apostle is here reproving a very corrupt practice. He shows how much mischief there is in the sin of *respect of persons.* Here we have,

I. A caution against this sin laid down in general: *My brethren, have not the faith of our Lord Jesus Christ, the Lord of glory, with respect of persons, v.* 1. You should not make men's outward and worldly advantages the measure of your respect. In professing the faith of our Lord Jesus Christ, we should not show respect to men, so as to cloud or lessen the glory of our glorious Lord.

II. We have this sin described and cautioned against, by an instance or example of it (*vv.* 2, 3): *For if there come into your assembly a man with a gold ring,* &c. In matters of religion, rich and poor stand upon a level; no man's riches set him in the least nearer to God, nor does any man's poverty set him at a distance from God. *With the Most High there is no respect of persons*, and therefore in matters of conscience there should be none with us. All undue honouring of worldly greatness and riches should especially be watched against in Christian societies.

III. We have the greatness of this sin set forth, *vv.* 4, 5. It is great partiality, it is injustice, and it is to set ourselves against God, who has chosen the poor, and will honour and advance them (if good), let who will despise them. Again, take notice that many poor of the world are rich in faith; thus the poorest may become rich; and this is what they ought to be especially ambitious of. It is expected from those who have wealth and estates that they be rich in good works, because the more they have the more they have to do good with; but it is expected from the poor in the world that they be rich in faith, for the less they have here the more they may, and should, live in the believing expectation of better things in a better world. After such considerations as these, the charge is cutting indeed: *But you have despised the poor*, v. 6. "*Do not rich men oppress you, and draw you before the judgment-seat? Do not they blaspheme that worthy name by which you are called?* v. 7. Consider how commonly riches are the incentives of vice and mischief, of blasphemy and persecution: consider how many calamities you yourselves sustain, and how great reproaches are thrown upon your religion and your God by men of wealth, and power, and worldly greatness; and this will make your sin appear exceedingly sinful and foolish.

THE ROYAL LAW (*vv.* 8–13)

Here,

I. We have the law that is to guide us in all our regards to men set down in general. *If you fulfil the royal law, according to the scripture, Thou shalt love thy neighbour as thyself, you do well*, v. 8. Observe hence, 1. The rule for Christians to walk by is settled in the scriptures: *If according to the scriptures*, &c. 2. The scripture gives us this as a law, to love our neighbour as ourselves. 3. This law is a royal law, it comes from the King of kings. 4. A pretence of observing this royal law, when it is interpreted with partiality, will not excuse men in any unjust proceedings.

II. This general law is to be considered together with a particular law: "*If you have respect to persons, you commit sin, and are convinced of the law as transgressors,*" v. 9. The very royal law itself, rightly explained, would serve to convict them, because it teaches them to put themselves as much in the places of the poor as in those of the rich, and so to act equitably towards one as well as the other. Hence he proceeds,

III. To show the extent of the law, and how far obedience must be paid to it. They must fulfil the royal law, have a regard to one part as well as another, otherwise it would not stand them in stead, when they pretended to urge it as a reason for any particular actions: *For whosoever shall keep the whole law, and yet offend in one point, is guilty of all,* v. 10.

IV. James directs Christians to govern and conduct themselves more especially by the law of Christ. *So speak and so do as those that shall be judged by the law of liberty, v.* 12. This will teach us, not only to be just and impartial, but very compassionate and merciful to the poor; and it will set us perfectly free from all sordid and undue regards to the rich. The consideration of our being judged by the gospel should engage us more especially to be merciful in our regards to the poor (v. 13): *For he shall have judgment without mercy that hath shown no mercy; and mercy rejoiceth against judgment.*

FAITH AND WORKS(*vv.* 14–26)

It is here proved at large that a man is justified, not by faith only, but by works. Now,

438

I. Upon this arises a very great question, namely, how to reconcile Paul and James. Paul, in his epistles to the Romans and Galatians, seems to assert the directly contrary thing to what James here lays down, saying it often, and with a great deal of emphasis, *that we are justified by faith only, and not by the works of the law*. Many ways might be mentioned which have been invented among learned men to make the apostles agree; but it may be sufficient only to observe these few things following: 1. When Paul says that *a man is justified by faith, without the deeds of the law* (Rom. iii. 28), he plainly speaks of another sort of work than James does, but not of another sort of faith. Paul speaks of works wrought in obedience to the law of Moses, and before men's embracing the faith of the gospel. But James speaks of works done in obedience to the gospel, and as the proper and necessary effects and fruits of sound believing in Christ Jesus. 2. Paul not only speaks of different works from those insisted on by James, but he speaks of a quite different use that was made of good works from what is here urged and intended. Paul had to do with those who depended on the merit of their works in the sight of God, and thus he might well make them of no manner of account. James had to do with those who cried up faith, but would not allow works to be used even as evidences; they depended upon a bare profession, as sufficient to justify them. 3. The justification of which Paul speaks is different from that spoken of by James; the one speaks of our persons being justified before God, the other speaks of our faith being justified before men.

II. Having thus cleared this part of scripture from every thing of a contradiction to other parts of it, let us see what is more particularly to be learnt from this excellent passage of James; we are taught,

1. That faith without works will not profit, and cannot save us. *What doth it profit, my brethren, if a man say he hath faith, and have not works? Can faith save him?* For a man to have faith, and to say he has faith, are two different things; the apostle does not say, *If a man have faith without works*, for that is not a supposable case; the drift of this place of scripture is plainly to show that an opinion, or speculation, or assent, without works, is not faith; but the case is put thus, *If a man say he hath faith*, &c.

2. "*If a brother or a sister be naked, and destitute of daily food, and one of you say unto them, Depart in peace, be you warmed and filled, notwithstanding you give them not those things which are needful to the body, what doth it profit?* vv.* 15–17. What will such a charity as this, that consists in bare words, avail either you or the poor? Will you come before God with such empty shows of charity as these? "*Even so faith, if it hath not works, is dead, being alone*," *v.* 17. We are too apt to rest in a bare profession of faith, and to think that this will save us; it is a cheap and easy religion to say, "We believe the articles of the Christian faith;" but it is a great delusion to imagine that this is enough to bring us to heaven.

3. We are taught to compare a

faith boasting of itself without works and a faith evidenced by works, by looking on both together, to try how this comparison will work upon our minds. And this is the evidence according to which Christ will proceed at the day of judgment. *The dead were judged according to their works*, Rev. xx. 12. How will those be exposed then who boast of that which they cannot evidence, or who go about to evidence their faith by any thing but works of piety and mercy!

4. We are taught to look upon a faith of bare speculation and knowledge as the faith of devils: *Thou believest that there is one God; thou doest well; the devils also believe, and tremble, v.* 19. They tremble, not out of reverence, but hatred and opposition to that one God on whom they believe. To rehearse that article of our creed, therefore, *I believe in God the Father Almighty*, will not distinguish us from devils at last, unless we now give up ourselves to God as the gospel directs, and love him, and delight ourselves in him, and serve him, which the devils do not, cannot do.

5. We are taught that he who boasts of faith without works is to be looked upon at present as a foolish condemned person. *But wilt thou know, O vain man, that faith without works is dead? v.* 20. Faith without works is said to be *dead*, not only as void of all those operations which are the proofs of spiritual life, but as unavailable to eternal life: such believers as rest in a bare profession of faith *are dead while they live.*

6. We are taught that a justifying faith cannot be without works, from two examples, Abraham and Rahab.

(1) The first instance is that of Abraham, the father of the faithful, and the prime example of justification, to whom the Jews had a special regard (*v.* 21). Paul, on the other hand, says (in *ch.* iv. of the epistle to the Romans) that Abraham *believed, and it was counted to him for righteousness.* But these are well reconciled, by observing what is said in Heb. xi., which shows that the faith both of Abraham and Rahab was such as to produce those good works of which James speaks, and which are not to be separated from faith as justifying and saving. By what Abraham did, it appeared that he truly believed.

(2) The second example of faith's justifying itself and us with and by works is Rahab: *Likewise also was not Rahab the harlot justified by works, when she had received the messengers, and had sent them out another way? v.* 25. The former instance was of one renowned for his faith all his life long. This is of one noted for sin, whose faith was meaner and of a much lower degree; so that the strongest faith will not do, nor the meanest be allowed to go without works. This Rahab believed the report she had heard of God's powerful presence with Israel; but that which proved her faith sincere was, that, to the hazard of her life, she *received the messengers, and sent them out another way.*

7. And now, upon the whole matter, the apostle draws this conclusion, *As the body without the spirit is dead, so faith without works*

is dead also, v. 26. These words are read differently; some reading them, *As the body without the breath is dead, so is faith without works*: and then they show that works are the companions of faith, as breathing is of life. Others read them, *As the body without the soul is dead, so faith without works is dead also*: and then they show that as the body has no action, nor beauty, but becomes a loathsome carcase, when the soul is gone, so a bare profession without works is useless, yea, loathsome and offensive. Let us then take heed of running into extremes in this case.

CHAPTER THREE
THE TONGUE (*vv.* 1–12)

Those who set up faith in the manner the former chapter condemns are most apt to run into those sins of the tongue which this chapter condemns. And indeed the best need to be cautioned against a dictating, censorious, mischievous use of their tongues. We are therefore taught,

I. Not to use our tongues so as to lord it over others: *My brethren, be not many masters*, &c., *v.* 1. These words do not forbid doing what we can to direct and instruct others in the way of their duty or to reprove them in a Christian way for what is amiss; but we must not affect to speak and act as those who are continually assuming the chair, we must not prescribe to one another, so as to make our own sentiments a standard by which to try all others, because God gives various gifts to men, and expects from each according to that measure of light which he gives.

II. We are taught to govern our tongue so as to prove ourselves perfect and upright men, as such as have an entire government over ourselves: *If any man offend not in word, the same is a perfect man, and able also to bridle the whole body*. It is here implied that he whose conscience is affected by tongue-sins, and who takes care to avoid them, is an upright man, and has an undoubted sign of true grace. But, on the other hand, *if a man seemeth to be religious* (as was declared in the first chapter) *and bridleth not his tongue*, whatever profession he makes, *that man's religion is vain*. Further, he that offends not in word will not only prove himself a sincere Christian, but a very much advanced and improved Christian. For the wisdom and grace which enable him to rule his tongue will enable him also to rule all his actions. This we have illustrated by two comparisons: 1. The governing and guiding of all the motions of a horse, by the bit which is put into his mouth. 2. The governing of a ship by the right management of the helm.

III. We are taught to dread an unruly tongue as one of the greatest and most pernicious evils. It is compared to a little fire placed among a great deal of combustible matter, which soon raises a flame and consumes all before it: *Behold, how great a matter a little fire kindleth! And the tongue is a fire, a world of iniquity*, &c., *vv.* 5, 6.

IV. We are next taught how very difficult a thing it is to govern the tongue: *For every kind of beasts, and of birds, and of serpents, and of things in the sea, is tamed, and hath been tamed, of mankind. But the tongue can no man tame, vv.* 7, 8. The apostle does not intend to represent it as a thing impossible, but as a thing extremely difficult, which therefore will require great watchfulness, and pains, and prayer, to keep it in due order.

V. We are taught to think of the use we make of our tongues in religion and in the service of God, and by such a consideration to keep it from cursing, censuring, and every thing that is evil on other occasions. How absurd is it that those who use their tongues in prayer and praise should ever use them in cursing, slandering, and the like!

WISDOM FROM ABOVE
(*vv.* 13–18)

I. We have here some account of true wisdom, with the distinguishing marks and fruits of it: *Who is a wise man, and endued with knowledge among you? Let him show out of a good conversation his works with meekness of wisdom, v.* 13. Now where this is the happy case of any there will be these following things: 1. A good way of life. If we are wiser than others, this should be evidenced by the goodness of our behaviour, not by the roughness or vanity of it. 2. True wisdom may be known by its works. The conversation here does not refer only to words, but to the whole of men's practice. 3. True wisdom may be known by the meekness of the spirit and temper: *Let him show with meekness,* &c. It is a great instance of wisdom prudently to bridle our

own anger, and patiently to bear the anger of others.

II. We have the glorying of those taken away who are of a contrary character to that now mentioned, and their wisdom exposed in all its boasts and productions: "*If you have bitter envying and strife in your hearts, glory not,* &c., *vv.* 14–16. Pretend what you will, and think yourselves ever so wise, yet you have abundance of reason to cease your glorying, if you run down love and peace, and give way to bitter envying and strife. For observe, whence such wisdom cometh: *It descendeth not from above,* but ariseth from beneath; and, to speak plainly, it is *earthly, sensual, devilish, v.* 15.

III. We have the lovely picture of that wisdom which is from above more fully drawn, and set in opposition to this which is from beneath: *But the wisdom that is from above is first pure, then peaceable,* &c., *vv.* 17, 18. It consists of these several things: 1. It is pure, without mixture of maxims or aims that would debase it. 2. The wisdom that is from above is peaceable. Peace follows purity, and depends upon it. 3. It is gentle, not standing upon extreme right in matters of property; not being rude and overbearing in conversation, nor harsh and cruel in temper. 4. Heavenly wisdom is *easy to be entreated,* it is very *persuadable,* either to what is good or from what is evil. 5. Heavenly wisdom is full of mercy and good fruits, inwardly disposed to every thing that is kind and good. 6. Heavenly wisdom is without partiality. The wisest men are least apt to be censurers. 7. That wisdom which is from above is without hypocrisy. It has no disguises nor deceits.

CHAPTER FOUR
CAUSES OF WAR (*vv.* 1–10)

I. The apostle here reproves the Jewish Christians for their wars, and for their lusts as the cause of them: *Whence come wars and fightings among you? Come they not hence, even of your lusts that war in your members, v.* 1. Hereupon, our apostle informs them that the origin of their wars and fightings was not (as they pretended) a true zeal for their country, and for the honour of God, but that their prevailing lusts were the cause of all. Impetuous passions and desires first war in their members, and then raise feuds in their nation. Apply this to private cases, and may we not then say of fightings and strifes among relations and neighbours that they come from those lusts which war in the members? Sinful desires and affections generally exclude prayer, and the working of our desires towards God: "*You fight and war, yet you have not, because you ask not.*" You fight, and do not succeed, because you do not pray: you do not consult God in your undertakings, whether he will allow of them or not. Let us learn hence, in the management of all our worldly affairs and in our prayers to God for success in them, to see that our ends be right.

II. We have fair warning to avoid all criminal friendships with this world: *You adulterers and adulteresses, know you not that the friend-*ship *of the world is enmity with God? v.* 4. Worldly people are here called adulterers and adulteresses, because of their perfidiousness to God, while they give their best affections to the world. *You cannot serve God and mammon*, Matt. vi. 24. Hence arise wars and fightings, even from this adulterous idolatrous love of the world, and serving of it; for what peace can there be among men, so long as there is enmity towards God? or who can fight against God, and prosper?

III. We are taught to observe the difference God makes between pride and humility. *God resisteth the proud, but giveth grace unto the humble, v.* 6. Grace, as opposed to disgrace, is honour; this God gives to the humble; and, where God gives grace to be humble, there he will give all other graces, and, as in the beginning of this sixth verse, he will *give more grace*.

IV. We are taught to submit ourselves entirely to God: *Submit yourselves therefore to God. Resist the devil, and he will flee from you, v.* 7. Christians should forsake the friendship of the world, and watch against that envy and pride which they see prevailing in natural men, and should by grace learn to glory in their submissions to God. If we basely yield to temptations, the devil will continually follow us; but if we *put on the whole armour of God*, and stand it out against him, he will be gone from us. Resolution shuts and bolts the door against temptation.

V. We are directed how to act towards God, in our becoming submissive to him, *vv.* 8–10. 1. *Draw nigh to God.* The heart that has rebelled must be brought to the foot of God; the spirit that was distant and estranged from a life of communion and converse with God must become acquainted with him. 2. *Cleanse your hands.* He who comes unto God must have clean hands. Paul therefore directs to *lift up holy hands without wrath and doubting* (1 Tim. ii. 8), hands free from blood, and bribes, and every thing that is unjust or cruel, and free from every defilement of sin: he is not subject to God who is a servant of sin. 3. The hearts of the double-minded must be purified. Those who halt between God and the world are here meant by *the double-minded.* To *purify the heart* is to be sincere, and to act upon this single aim and principle, rather to please God than to seek after any thing in this world. 4. *Be afflicted, and mourn, and weep.* This may be taken either as a prediction of sorrow or a prescription of seriousness. 5. "*Humble yourselves in the sight of the Lord.* Let the inward acts of the soul be suitable to all those outward expressions of grief, affliction, and sorrow, before mentioned."

VI. We have great encouragement to act thus towards God: *He will draw nigh to those that draw nigh to him* (v. 8), *and he will lift up* those who humble themselves in his sight, *v.* 10.

WARNING AGAINST OVER-CONFIDENCE
(vv. 11–17)

In this part of the chapter,

I. We are cautioned against the sin of evil-speaking: *Speak not evil one of another, brethren, v.* 11. He

who is guilty of the sin here cautioned against is not a doer of the law, but a judge; he assumes an office and a place that do not belong to him, and he will be sure to suffer for his presumption in the end. God, the Lawgiver, has reserved the power of passing the final sentence on men wholly to himself.

II. We are cautioned against a presumptuous confidence of the continuance of our lives, and against forming projects thereupon with assurance of success, *vv.* 13, 14. We can fix the hour and minute of the sun's rising and setting tomorrow, but we cannot fix the certain time of a vapour's being scattered; such is our life: *it appears but for a little time, and then vanisheth away.*

III. We are taught to keep up a constant sense of our dependence on the will of God for life, and all the actions and enjoyments of it: *You ought to say, If the Lord will, we shall live, and do this, or that, v.* 15. The apostle, having reproved them for what was amiss, now directs them how to be and do better. All our actions and designs are under the control of Heaven. Therefore both our counsels for action and our conduct in action should be entirely referred to God; all we design and all we do should be with a submissive dependence on God.

IV. We are directed to avoid vain boasting, and to look upon it not only as a weak, but a very evil thing. *You rejoice in your boastings; all such rejoicing is evil, v.* 16. They promised themselves life and prosperity, and great things in the world, without any just regard to God; and then they boasted of these things. If we rejoice in our own vain confidences and presumptuous boasts, this is evil: it is an evil carefully to be avoided by all wise and good men.

V. We are taught, in the whole of our conduct, to act up to our own convictions, and, whether we have to do with God or men, to see that we never go contrary to our own knowledge (*v.* 17).

CHAPTER FIVE

WARNING TO THE RICH
(*vv.* 1–11)

The apostle is here addressing first sinners and then saints.

I. Let us consider the address to sinners; and here we find James seconding what his great Master had said: *Woe unto you that are rich; for you have received your consolation*, Luke vi. 24.

1. He foretells the judgments of God that should come upon them, *vv.* 1–3). Their misery shall arise from the very things in which they placed their happiness. "Corruption, decay, rust, and ruin, will come upon all your goodly things: *Your riches are corrupted and your garments are motheaten, v.* 2. They think to heap up treasure for their latter days, to live plentifully upon when they come to be old; but, alas! they are only heaping up treasures to become a prey to others (as the Jews had all taken from them by the Romans), and treasurers that will prove at last to be only treasures of wrath, *in the day of the revelation of the righteous judgment of God.*

2. The apostle shows what those sins are which should bring such miseries. (1) Covetousness is laid to the charge of this people; they laid by their garments till they bred moths and were eaten; they hoarded up their gold and silver till they were rusty and cankered. God gives us our worldly possessions that we may honour him and do good with them; but if, instead of this, we sinfully hoard them up, through an undue affection towards them, or a distrust of the providence of God for the future, this is a very heinous crime. (2) Another sin charged upon those against whom James writes is oppression: *Behold, the hire of the labourers, who have reaped down your fields, which is of you kept back by fraud, crieth,* &c., *v.* 4. Those who have wealth in their hands get power into their hands, and then they are tempted to abuse that power to oppress such as are under them. This is a crying sin, an iniquity that cries so as to reach the ears of God; and, in this case, God is to be considered as *the Lord of sabaoth,* or *the Lord of hosts,* a phrase often used in the Old-Testament, when the people of God were defenceless and wanted protection, and when their enemies were numerous and powerful. (3) Another sin here mentioned is sensuality and voluptuousness. *You have lived in pleasure on the earth, and been wanton, v.* 5. God does not forbid us to use pleasure; but to live in them as if we lived for nothing else is a very provoking sin. (4) Another sin here charged on the rich is persecution: *You have condemned and killed the just, and he*

doth not resist you, v. 6. This fills up the measure of their iniquity. They oppressed and acted very unjustly, to get estates; when they had them, they gave way to luxury and sensuality, till they had lost all sense and feeling of the wants or afflictions of others; and then they persecute and kill without remorse.

II. We have next subjoined an address to saints.

1. Attend to your duty: *Be patient (v. 7), establish your hearts (v. 8), grudge not one against another, brethren, v. 9.* Consider well the meaning of these three expressions: (1) *"Be patient*—bear your afflictions without murmuring, your injuries without revenge; and, though God should not in any signal manner appear for you immediately, wait for him. (2) *"Establish your hearts*—let your faith be firm, without wavering, your practice of what is good constant and continued, without tiring, and your resolutions for God and heaven fixed, in spite of all sufferings or temptations." (3) *Grudge not one against another.* Those who are in the midst of common enemies, and in any suffering circumstances, should be more especially careful not to grieve nor to groan against one another, otherwise judgments will come upon them as well as others; and the more such grudgings prevail the nearer do they show judgment to be.

2. Consider what encouragement here is for Christians to be patient, to establish their hearts, and not to grudge one against another. And, (1) "Look to the example of the husbandman: *He waits for the precious fruit of the earth, and hath long patience for it, until he receive the early and latter rain.*" (2) "Think how short your waiting time may possibly be: *The coming of the Lord draweth nigh, v. 8; behold, the Judge standeth before the door, v. 9.* (3) The danger of our being condemned when the Judge appears should excite us to mind our duty as before laid down; *Grudge not, lest you be condemned.* (4) We are encouraged to be patient by the example of the prophets (*v. 10*). Those who were the greatest examples of suffering affliction were also the best and greatest examples of patience. (5) Job also is proposed as an example for the encouragement of the afflicted. In the case of Job you have an instance of a variety of miseries, and of such as were very grievous; but under all he could bless God, and, as to the general bent of his spirit, he was patient and humble: and what came to him in the end? Why, truly, God accomplished and brought about those things for him which plainly prove that *the Lord is very pitiful, and of tender mercy.*

PRAYER THAT WORKS
(*vv. 12–20*)

I. The sin of swearing is cautioned against: *But above all things, my brethren, swear not, &c., v. 12.* All customary needless swearing is undoubtedly forbidden, and all along in scripture condemned, as a very grievous sin.

2. *But let your yea be yea, and your nay nay; lest you fall into condemnation;* that is, let it be known that you keep to truth, and

are firm to your word, and by this means you will find there is no need to swear to what you say.

II. As Christians we are taught to suit ourselves to the dispensations of Providence (*v.* 13): *Is any among you afflicted? Let him pray. Is any merry? Let him sing psalms.* Our condition in this world is various; and our wisdom is to submit to its being so, and to behave as becomes us both in prosperity and under affliction.

III. We have particular directions given as to sick persons, and *healing pardoning mercy promised* upon the observance of those directions. *If any be sick,* they are required, 1. To *send for the elders, the presbyters,* pastors or ministers *of the church, vv.* 14, 15. It lies upon sick people as a duty to send for ministers, and to desire their assistance and their prayers. 2. It is the duty of ministers to pray over the sick, when thus desired and called for. 3. In the times of miraculous healing, the *sick were to be anointed with oil in the name of the Lord,* and some have thought that it should not be wholly laid aside in any age, but that where there are extraordinary measures of faith in the person anointing, and in those who are anointed, an extraordinary blessing may attend the observance of this direction for the sick. However that be, there is one thing carefully to be observed here, that the saving of the sick is not ascribed to the *anointing with oil,* but to prayer: *The prayer of faith shall save the sick,* &c., *v.* 15. So that, 4. Prayer over the sick must proceed from, and be accompanied with, a lively faith. 5. We

should observe the success of prayer. The Lord shall raise up; that is, if he be a person capable and fit for deliverance, and if God have any thing further for such a person to do in the world. *And, if he have committed sins, they shall be forgiven him*; that is, where sickness is sent as a punishment for some particular sin, that sin shall be pardoned, and in token thereof the sickness shall be removed.

IV. Christians are directed to *confess their faults one to another, and so to join in their prayers with and for one another, v.* 16. Some expositors connect this with *v.* 14. As if when sick people send for ministers to pray over them they should then confess their faults to them. Indeed, where any are conscious that their sickness is a vindictive punishment of some particular sin, and they cannot look for the removal of their sickness without particular applications to God for the pardon of such a sin, there it may be proper to acknowledge and tell his case, that those who pray over him may know how to plead rightly for him. But the confession here required is that of Christians to one another, and not to a priest. Where persons have injured one another, acts of injustice must be confessed to those against whom they have been committed.

V. The great advantage and efficacy of prayer are declared and proved: *The effectual fervent prayer of a righteous man availeth much,* whether he pray for himself or for others: witness the example of Eljiah, *vv.* 17, 18. He who prays must be a righteous man; not righteous in an absolute sense (for this Elias was not, who is here made a pattern to us), but righteous in a gospel sense; not loving nor approving of any known iniquity. *If I regard iniquity in my heart, the Lord will not hear my prayer*, Ps. lxvi. 18. Further, the prayer itself must be a fervent, in-wrought, well-wrought prayer. It must be a pouring out of the heart to God; and it must proceed from a faith unfeigned. Such prayer avails much. The power of prayer is here proved from the success of Elijah. This may be encouraging to us even in common cases, if we consider that Elijah was *a man of like passions with us*.

VI. This epistle concludes with an exhortation to do all we can in our places to promote the conversion and salvation of others, *vv.* 19, 20. It is no mark of a wise or a holy man to boast of his being free from error, or to refuse to acknowledge when he is in an error. But if any do err, be they ever so great, you must not be afraid to show them their error; and, be they ever so weak and little, you must not disdain to make them wiser and better. If they err from the truth, that is, from the gospel (the great rule and standard of truth), whether it be in opinion or practice, you must endeavour to bring them again to the rule. He who thus converteth a sinner from the error of his ways *shall save a soul from death.* There is a soul in the case; and what is done towards the salvation of the soul shall certainly turn to good account. And then, by such conversion of heart and life, a *multitude of sins shall be hid. Those that turn many to righteousness*, and those who help to do so, *shall shine as the stars for ever and ever.*

THE FIRST EPISTLE GENERAL OF

PETER

CHAPTER ONE

GREETINGS AND BLESSINGS (vv. 1–5)

In this inscription we have three parts:

I. The author of it, described, 1. By his name—*Peter*. His first name was *Simon*, and Jesus Christ gave him the surname of *Peter*, which signifies *a rock*, as a commendation of his faith, and to denote that he should be an eminent pillar in the church of God, Gal. ii. 9. 2. By his office—*an apostle of Jesus Christ*.

II. The persons to whom this epistle was addressed, and they are described,

1. By their external condition— *Strangers dispersed throughout Pontus, Galatia*, &c. They were chiefly Jews.

2. They are described by their spiritual condition: *Elect according to the foreknowledge of God the Father*, &c. These poor strangers, who were oppressed and despised in the world, were nevertheless in high esteem with the great God, and in the most honourable state that any person can be in during this life; for they were,

III. The salutation follows: *Grace unto you, and peace be multiplied.* The blessings desired for them are *grace and peace*. The increase of grace and peace is from

God. Where he gives true grace he will give more grace.

Next we have,

IV. A congratulation of the dignity and happiness of the state of these believers, brought in under the form of a thanksgiving to God. Other epistles begin in like manner, 2. Cor. i. 3; Eph. i. 3. Here we have,

1. The duty performed, which is blessing God. A man blesses God by a just acknowledgment of his excellency and blessedness.

2. The object of this blessing described by his relation to Jesus Christ: *The God and Father of our Lord Jesus Christ*. Here are three names of one person, denoting his threefold office. (1) He is *Lord*, a universal king or sovereign. (2) *Jesus*, a priest or Saviour. (3) *Christ*, a prophet, anointed with the Spirit and furnished with all gifts necessary for the instruction, guidance, and salvation of his church.

3. The reasons that oblige us to this duty of blessing God, which are comprised in *his abundant mercy*.

V. Having congratulated these people on their new birth, and the hope of everlasting life, the apostle goes on to describe that life under the notion of *an inheritance*, a most proper way of speaking to these people; for they were poor and persecuted, perhaps turned out of their inheritances to which they were born; to allay this grievance, he tells them they were new-born to a new inheritance, infinitely better than what they had lost. Here note,

1. Heaven is the undoubted inheritance of all the children of God. This inheritance is not our purchase, but our Father's gift; not wages we merit, but the effect of grace.

2. The incomparable excellencies of this inheritance, which are four: (1) It is incorruptible, in which respect it is like its Maker, who is called the *incorruptible God*, Rom. i. 23. (2) This inheritance is unde-filed, like the great high priest that is now in possession of it, who is *holy, harmless, and undefiled*, Heb. vii. 26. (3) It fadeth not away, but always retains its vigour and beauty. (4) "*Reserved in heaven for you.*" This inheritance is preserved for them, and none but them; all the rest will be shut out for ever.

VI. This inheritance being de-scribed as future, and distant both in time and place, the apostle supposes some doubt or uneasiness yet to remain upon the minds of these people, whether they might not possibly fall short by the way. To this he answers that they should be safely guarded and conducted thither; they should be kept and preserved from all such destructive temptations and injuries as would prevent their safe arrival at eternal life. The blessing here promised is preservation: You *are kept*; the author of it is *God*; the means in us made use of for that end are our own *faith* and care; the end to which we are preserved is *salvation*; and the time when we shall see the

safe end and issue of all is *the last time.*

FAITH ON TRIAL (*vv.* 6–9)

The first word, *wherein*, refers to the apostle's foregoing discourse about the excellency of their present state, and their grand expectations for the future.

I. The apostle grants they were in great affliction, and propounds several things in mitigation of their sorrows. 1. Every sound Christian has always something wherein he may greatly rejoice. 2. The chief joy of a good Christian arises from things spiritual and heavenly, from his relation to God and to heaven. 3. The best Christians, those who have reason greatly to rejoice, may yet be in great heaviness through manifold temptations. 4. The afflic-tions and sorrows of good people are but for a little while, they are but for a season; though they may be smart, they are but short. 5. Great heaviness is often necessary to a Christian's good: *If need be, you are in heaviness.* God does not afflict his people willingly, but acts with judgment, in proportion to our needs.

II. He expresses the end of their afflictions and the ground of their joy under them, *v.* 7. The end of good people's afflictions is *the trial of their faith*. As to the nature of this trial, it is *much more precious than of gold that perisheth, though it be tried with fire*. The effect of the trial is this, it will *be found unto praise, honour, and glory at the appearing of Jesus Christ*.

III. He particularly commends the faith of these primitive Chris-tians upon two accounts:

1. The excellency of its object, the unseen Jesus.

2. On account of two notable productions or effects of their faith, *love* and *joy*, and this joy so great as to be above description: *You rejoice with joy unspeakable, and full of glory.* Learn,

(1) The faith of a Christian is properly conversant about things revealed, but not seen.

(2) True faith is never alone, but produces a strong love to Jesus Christ.

(3) Where there are true faith and love to Christ there is, or may be, *joy unspeakable and full of glory.* This joy is inexpressible, it cannot be described by words; the best discovery is by an experimental taste of it; it is *full of glory*, full of heaven. Well might these primitive Christians rejoice with joy unspeakable, since they were every day *receiving the end of their faith, the salvation of their souls v.* 4.

THE AUTHORITY OF THE PROPHETS (*vv.* 10–12)

Because they were Jews, and had a profound veneration for the Old Testament, he produces the authority of the prophets to convince them that the doctrine of salvation by faith in Jesus Christ was no new doctrine, but the same which the old prophets did enquire and search diligently into. Note,

I. Who made this diligent search —*the prophets*, who were persons inspired by God either to do or to say things extraordinary, above the reach of their own studies and abilities, as foretelling things to come, and revealing the will of God, by the direction of the Holy Spirit.

II. The object of their search, which was *salvation*, and *the grace of God which should come unto you.*

III. The manner of their enquiry: they *enquired and searched diligently.*

IV. The particular matters which the ancient prophets chiefly searched into, which are expressed in *v.* 11. Jesus Christ was the main subject of their studies; and, in relation to him, they were most inquisitive into,

1. His humiliation and death, and the glorious consequences of it.

2. The time, and the manner of the times, wherein the Messiah was to appear. The works here ascribed to the Holy Ghost prove him to be God. He *did signify*, discover, and manifest to the prophets, many hundred years *beforehand, the sufferings of Christ*, with a multitude of particular circumstances attending them; and he did also *testify*, or give proof and evidence beforehand, of the certainty of that event, by inspiring the prophets to reveal it, to work miracles in confirmation of it, and by enabling the faithful to believe it.

V. The success with which their enquiries were crowned. They were informed that these things should not come to pass in their time, but yet all was firm and certain, and should come to pass in the times of the apostles. The mysteries of the gospel, and the methods of man's salvation, are so glorious that the blessed angels earnestly desire to look into them; they are curious, accurate, and industrious in prying into them; they consider the whole scheme of man's redemption with deep attention and admiration, particularly the points the apostle had been discoursing of: *Which things the angels desire to* stoop down and *look into*, as *the cherubim* did continually *towards the mercy-seat*.

TRUE HOLINESS (*vv.* 13–23)

Here the apostle begins his exhortations to those whose glorious state he had before described.

I. He exhorts them to sobriety and holiness.

1. *Wherefore gird up the loins of your mind*, &c., *v.* 13. As if he had said, You have a journey to go, a race to run, a warfare to accomplish, and a great work to do; as the traveller, the racer, the warrior, and the labourer, gather in, and gird up, their long and loose garments, that they may be more ready, prompt, and expeditious in their business, so do you by your minds, your inner man, and affections seated there." *Be sober*, be vigilant against all your spiritual dangers and enemies. Be sober-minded also in opinion, as well as in practice, and humble in your judgment of yourselves." *And hope to the end, for the grace that is to be brought to you at the revelation of Jesus Christ*. Hope perfectly, trust without doubting to that grace which is now offered to you by the gospel.

2. *As obedient children*, &c., *v.* 14. These words may be taken as a rule of holy living, which is both positive—"You ought to live *as obedient children*, as those whom God hath adopted into his family, and regenerated by his grace;" and negative—"You must *not fashion yourselves according to the former lusts, in your ignorance*." Or the

words may be taken as an argument to press them to holiness from the consideration of what they now are, children of obedience, and what they were when they lived in lust and ignorance.

3. *But as he who hath called you*, &c., *vv.* 15, 16. Here is a noble rule enforced by strong arguments: *Be you holy in all manner of conversation*. Who is sufficient for this? And yet it is required in strong terms, and enforced by three reasons, taken from the grace of God in calling us, —from his command, *it is written*, —and from his example. *Be you holy, for I am holy*.

4. *If you call on the Father*, &c., *v.* 17. The apostle does not there express any doubt at all whether these Christians would call upon their heavenly Father, but supposes they would certainly do it, and from this argues with them to *pass the time of their sojourning here in fear*: "If you own the great God as a Father and a Judge, you ought to live the time of your sojourning here in his fear." The judgment of God will be without respect of persons: *According to every man's work*. We are obliged to faith, holiness, and obedience, and our works will be an evidence whether we have complied with our obligations or not.

5. The apostle having exhorted them to *pass the time of their sojourning in the fear of God* from this consideration, that they *called on the Father*, he adds (*v.* 18) a second argument: *Because* or *forasmuch as you were not redeemed with corruptible things*, &c. Herein he puts them in mind, (1) That they were redeemed, or brought back

again, by a ransom paid to the Father. (2) What the price paid for their redemption was: *Not with corruptible things, as silver and gold, but with the precious blood of Christ.* (3) From what they were redeemed: *From a vain conversation received by tradition.* (4) They knew this: *Forasmuch as you know*, and cannot pretend ignorance of this great affair.

6. Having mentioned the price of redemption, the apostle goes on to speak of some things relating both to the Redeemer and the redeemed, *vv.* 20, 21.

(1) The Redeemer is further described, not only as a Lamb without spot, but as one, [1] That was *fore-ordained before the foundation of the world*, fore-ordained or foreknown. When prescience is ascribed to God, it implies more than bare prospect or speculation. It imports an act of the will, a resolution that the thing shall be, Acts ii. 23. [2] That was *manifested in these last days for them.* He was manifested or demonstrated to be that Redeemer whom God had fore-ordained. [3] That was raised from the dead by the Father, who gave him glory.

(2) The redeemed are also described here by their faith and hope, the cause of which is Jesus Christ: "*You do by him believe in God*—by him as the author, encourager, support, and finisher of your faith; your faith and hope now may be in God, as reconciled to you by Christ the Mediator."

(3) From all this we learn, [1] The decree of God to send Christ to be a Mediator was from everlasting, and was a just and merciful decree,

which yet does not at all excuse man's sin in crucifying him, Acts ii. 23. God had purposes of special favour towards his people long before he made any manifestations of such grace to them [2] Great is the happiness of the last times in comparison with what the former ages of the world enjoyed. [3] The redemption of Christ belongs to none but true believers.

II. He exhorts them to brotherly love.

1. He supposes that the gospel had already had such an effect upon them as to purify their souls while they obeyed it through the Spirit, and that it had produced at least an *unfeigned love of the brethren*; and thence he argues with them to proceed to a higher degree of affection, to love one another with a pure heart fervently, *v.* 22.

2. He further presses upon Christians the duty of loving one another with a pure heart fervently from the consideration of their spiritual relation; they are all *born again, not of corruptible seed, but incorruptible*, &c. Hence we may learn, (1) That all Christians are born again. (2) The word of God is the great means of regeneration, Jam. i. 18. The grace of regeneration is conveyed by the gospel. (3) This new and second birth is much more desirable and excellent than the first. (4) Those that are regenerate should love one another with a pure heart fervently.

A WORD FOR EVER
(*vv.* 24, 25)

The apostle having given an account of the excellency of the renewed spiritual man as born again, not of corruptible but incorruptible seed, he now sets before us the vanity of the natural man, taking him with all his ornaments and advantages about him: *For all flesh is as grass, and all the glory of man as the flower of grass*; and nothing can make him a solid substantial being but the being born again of the incorruptible seed, the word of God, which will transform him into a most excellent creature, whose glory will not fade like a flower, but shine like an angel; and this word is daily set before you in the preaching of the gospel.

CHAPTER TWO
THE MILK OF THE WORD
(*vv.* 1–3)

The holy apostle pursues his discourse, and very properly comes in with this necessary advice, *Wherefore laying aside all malice*, &c.

I. His advice is to lay aside or put off what is evil, as one would do an old rotten garment: "Cast it away with indignation never put it on more."

II. The apostle goes on to direct to wholesome and regular food, that they may grow thereby. The duty exhorted to is a strong and constant desire for the *word of God*, which word is here called *reasonable milk*, only, this phrase not being proper English, our translators rendered it *the milk of the word*, by which we are to understand food proper for the soul, or a reasonable creature, whereby the mind, not the body, is nourished and strengthened. This milk of the word must be *sincere*, not adulter-

ated by the mixtures of men, who often corrupt the word of God, 2 Cor. ii. 17. The manner in which they are to desire this sincere milk of the word is stated thus: *As newborn babes*. He puts them in mind of their regeneration. A new life requires suitable food. They, being newly born, must desire the milk of the word.

III. He adds an argument from their own experience: *If so be*, or *since that*, or *forasmuch as, you have tasted that the Lord is gracious, v.* 3. The apostle does not express a doubt, but affirms that these good Christians had tasted the goodness of God, and hence argues with them. "You ought to lay aside these vile sins (*v.* 1); you ought to desire the word of God; you ought to grow thereby, since you cannot deny but that you have tasted that the Lord is gracious."

THE PEOPLE OF GOD
(*vv.* 4–12)

I. The apostle here gives us a description of Jesus Christ as a living stone.

1. In this metaphorical description of Jesus Christ, he is called a stone, to denote his invincible strength and everlasting duration, and to teach his servants that he is their protection and security, the foundation on which they are built, and a rock of offence to all their enemies. He is the living stone, having eternal life in himself, and being the prince of life to all his people.

2. Having described Christ as the foundation, the apostle goes on to speak of the superstructure, the materials built upon him: *You also,*

as living stones, *are built up*, v. 6. Christ, the foundation, is a living stone. Christians are lively stones, and these make a spiritual house, and they are a holy priesthood; and, though they have no bloody sacrifices of beasts to offer, yet they have much better and more acceptable, and they have an altar too on which to present their offerings; for they offer spiritual sacrifices, acceptable to God by Jesus Christ.

II. He confirms what he had asserted of Christ being a *living stone*, &c., from Isa. xxviii. 16. The constituting of Christ Jesus head of the church is an eminent work of God: *I lay in Zion*. Jesus Christ is the chief corner-stone that God hath laid in his spiritual building. The corner-stone stays inseparably with the building, supports it, unites it, and adorns it. So does Christ by his holy church, his spiritual house.

III. He deduces an important inference, *v.* 7. Jesus Christ is said to be the chief corner-stone. Hence the apostle infers with respect to good men, "To you therefore who believe he is precious, or he is an honour. Christ is the crown and honour of a Christian; you who believe will be so far from being ashamed of him that you will boast of him and glory in him for ever." As to wicked men, the disobedient will go on to disallow and reject Jesus Christ; but God is resolved that he shall be, in despite of all opposition, the head of the corner.

IV. The apostle adds a further description, still preserving the metaphor of a stone, *v.* 8. The words are taken from Isa. viii. 13, 14. Observe,

1. The builders, the chief-priests, refused him, and the people followed their leaders; and so Christ became to them *a stone of stumbling, and a rock of offence*, at which they stumbled and hurt themselves; and in return he fell upon them as a mighty stone or rock, and punished them with destruction. Matt. xxi. 44, *Whosoever shall fall on this stone shall be broken; but on whomsoever it shall fall it will grind him to powder.*

2. Those who received him were highly privileged, *v.* 9. The Jews were exceedingly tender of their ancient privileges, of being the only people of God, taken into a special covenant with him, and separated from the rest of the world. "Now," say they, "if we submit to the gospel-constitution, we shall lose all this, and stand upon the same level with the Gentiles."

(1) To this objection the apostle answers, that if they did not submit they were ruined (*vv.* 7, 8), but that if they did submit they should lose no real advantage, but continue still what they desired to be, *a chosen generation, a royal priesthood*, &c. Learn, [1] All true Christians *are a chosen generation*; they all make one family, a sort and species of people distinct from the common world, of another spirit, principle, and practice, which they could never be if they were not chosen in Christ to be such, and sanctified by his spirit. [2] All the true servants of Christ are a royal priesthood, separated from sin and sinners, consecrated to God, and offering to God spiritual services and oblations, acceptable to God through Jesus Christ. [3] All

Christians, wheresoever they be, compose one holy nation, collected under one head, agreeing in the same manners and customs, and governed by the same laws; and they are a holy nation, because consecrated and devoted to God, renewed and sanctified by his Holy Spirit. [4] It is the honour of the servants of Christ that they are God's peculiar people. They are the people of his acquisition, choice, care, and delight.

(2) To make this people content, and thankful for the great mercies and dignities brought unto them by the gospel, the apostle advises them to compare their former and their present state. Time was when they were not a people, nor had they obtained mercy, but they were solemnly disclaimed and divorced (Jer. iii. 8; Hos. i. 6, 9); but now they are taken in again to be the people of God, and have obtained mercy.

V. He warns them to beware of fleshly lusts, *v.* 11. The duty is to abstain from, and to suppress, the first inclination or rise of fleshly lusts. These Christians ought to avoid, considering, 1. The respect they have with God and good men: They are *dearly beloved*. 2. Their condition in the world: *They are strangers and pilgrims*. 3. The mischief and danger these sins do: "*They war against the soul*; and therefore your souls ought to war against them."

VI. He exhorts them further to adorn their profession by an honest manner of life. Their behaviour in every turn, every instance, and every action of their lives, ought to be honest; that is,

good, lovely, decent, amiable, and without blame.

SUBMISSION (*vv.* 13–25)

I. The case of subjects. Christians were not only reputed innovators in religion, but disturbers of the state; it was highly necessary, therefore, that the apostle should settle the rules and measures of obedience to the civil magistrate, which he does here, where,

1. The duty required is submission, which comprises loyalty and reverence to their persons, obedience to their just laws and commands, and subjection to legal penalties.

2. The persons or objects to whom this submission is due are described, (1) More generally: *Every ordinance of man.* (2) Particularly: *To the king, as supreme.*

3. The reasons to enforce this duty are,

(1) *For the Lord's sake*, who has ordained magistracy for the good of mankind, who has required obedience and submission (Rom. xiii.), and whose honour is concerned in the dutiful behaviour of subjects to their sovereigns.

(2) From the end and use of the magistrate's office, which are, to punish evil-doers, and to praise and encourage all those that do well.

(3) Another reason why Christians should submit to the civil magistrate is because it *is the will of God*, and consequently their duty; and because it is the way to put to silence the malicious slanders of ignorant and foolish men, *v.* 15.

(4) He reminds them of the spiritual nature of Christian liberty. They were free spiritually from the

bondage of sin and Satan, and the ceremonial law; but they must not make their Christian liberty a cloak or covering for any wickedness, or for the neglect of any duty towards God or towards their superiors, but must still remember they were *the servants of God.*

4. The apostle concludes his discourse concerning the duty of subjects with four admirable precepts: (1) *Honour all men.* A due respect is to be given to all men. (2) *Love the brotherhood.* All Christians are a fraternity, united to Christ the head. (3) *Fear God* with the highest reverence, duty, and submission. (4) *Honour the king* with that highest honour that is peculiarly due to him above other men.

II. The case of servants wanted and apostolical determination as well as that of subjects, for they imagined that their Christian liberty set them free from their unbelieving and cruel masters; to this the apostle answers, *Servants, be subject, v.* 18. Observe,

I. He orders them to *be subject,* to do their business faithfully and honestly, to conduct themselves with reverence and affection, and to submit patiently to hardships and inconveniences.

2. Having charged them to be subject, he condescends to reason with them about it.

(1) If they were patient under their hardships, while they suffered unjustly, and continued doing their duty to their unbelieving and untoward masters, this would be acceptable to God, and he would reward all that they suffered for conscience towards him; but to be

patient when they were justly chastised would deserve no commendation at all; it is only *doing well, and suffering patiently for that, which is acceptable with God, vv.* 19, 20.

(2) More reasons are given to encourage Christian servants to patience under unjust sufferings, *v.* 21. [1] From their Christian calling and profession: *Hereunto were you called.* [2] From the example of Christ, who *suffered for us,* and so became our *example, that we should follow his steps,* whence learn,

3. The example of Christ's subjection and patience is here explained and amplified: *Christ suffered,* (1) Wrongfully, and without cause; for he *did no sin, v.* 22. (2) Patiently: *When he was reviled, he reviled not again* (*v.* 23). *But committed* both *himself* and his cause *to God that judgeth righteously,* who would in time clear his innocency, and avenge him on his enemies.

4. Lest any should think, from what is said, *vv.* 21–23, that Christ's death was designed merely for an example of patience under sufferings, the apostle here adds a more glorious design and effect of it: *Who his own self,* &c., where note, (1) The person suffering—Jesus Christ: *His own self—in his own body.* (2) The sufferings he underwent were *stripes,* wounds, and death, *the death of the cross*—servile and ignominious punishments! (3) The reason of his sufferings: He *bore our sins,* which teaches, [1] That Christ, in his sufferings, stood charged with our sins, as one who had undertaken to put them away by *the sacrifice of*

himself, Isa. liii. 6. [2] That he bore the punishment of them, and thereby satisfied divine justice. [3] That hereby he takes away our sins, and removes them away from us. (4) Christ was bruised and crucified as an expiatory sacrifice, and *by his stripes we are healed*.

5. The apostle concludes his advice to Christian servants, by putting them in mind of the difference between their former and present condition, *v*. 25. They *were as sheep going astray, but are now returned*. The word is passive, and shows that the return of a sinner is the effect of divine grace.

CHAPTER THREE
HUSBANDS AND WIVES
(*vv*. 1–7)

The apostle having treated of the duties of subjects to their sovereigns, and of servants to their masters, proceeds to explain the duty of husbands and wives.

I. Lest the Christian matrons should imagine that their conversion to Christ, and their interest in all Christian privileges, exempted them from subjection to their pagan or Jewish husbands, the apostle here tells them,

1. In what the duty of wives consists.

(1) In *subjection*, or an affectionate submission to the will, and obedience to the just authority, of *their own husbands*.

(2) In *fear*, or reverence to their husbands, Eph. v. 33.

(3) In a *chaste conversation*, which their unbelieving husbands would accurately observe and attend to.

(4) In preferring the ornaments of the mind to those of the body.

2. The duties of Christian wives being in their nature difficult, the apostle enforces them by the example, (1) Of the holy women of old, who trusted in God, *v*. 5. (2) Of Sara, who obeyed her husband, and followed him when he went from Ur of the Chaldeans, *not knowing whither he went*, and *called him lord*.

II. The husband's duty to the wife comes next to be considered.

1. The particulars are, (1) *Cohabitation*, which forbids unnecessary separation, and implies a mutual communication of goods and persons one to another, with delight and concord. (2) *Dwelling with the wife according to knowledge*; not according to lust, as brutes; nor according to passion, as devils; but according to knowledge, as wise and sober men, who know the word of God and their own duty. (3) *Giving honour to the wife*—giving due respect to her.

2. The reasons are, Because she is *the weaker vessel* by nature and constitution, and so ought to be defended. They are *heirs together of the grace of life*, of all the blessings of this life and another, and therefore should live peaceably and quietly one with another, and, if they do not, their prayers one with another and one for another will be hindered, so that often "you will not pray at all, or, if you do, you will pray with a discomposed ruffled mind, and so without success."

FRIENDS AND ENEMIES
(*vv*. 8–15)

The apostle here passes from special to more general exhortations.

I. He teaches us how Christians and friends should treat one another. He advises Christians to *be all of one mind*, to be unanimous in the belief of the same faith, and the practice of the same duties of religion; and, whereas the Christians at that time were many of them in a suffering condition, he charges them to *have compassion one of another*, to *love as brethren*, to *pity* those who were in distress, and to *be courteous* to all.

II. He instructs us how to behave towards enemies. The apostle knew that Christians would *be hated* and evil-entreated *of all men for Christ's sake*; therefore,

1. He warns them not to return *evil for evil, nor railing for railing*; but, on the contrary, "when they rail at you, do you bless them; when they give you evil words, do you give them good ones; for Christ has both by his word and example called you to bless those that curse you, and has settled a blessing on you as your everlasting inheritance, though you were unworthy."

2. He gives an excellent prescription for a comfortable happy life in this quarrelsome ill-natured world (*v.* 10): it is quoted from Ps. xxxiv. 12–14. Avoid doing any real damage or hurt to your neighbour, but be ever ready to do good, and to overcome evil with good; seek peace with all men, and pursue it, though it retire from you.

3. He shows that Christians need not fear that such patient inoffensive behaviour as is prescribed will invite and encourage the cruelty of their enemies, for God will thereby be engaged on their side: *For the eyes of the Lord are over the righteous* (*v.* 12).

4. This patient humble behaviour of Christians is further recommended and urged from two considerations: (1) This will be the best and surest way to prevent suffering; for *who is he that will harm you? v.* 13. (2) This is the way to improve sufferings. "*If you be followers of that which is good*, and yet *suffer*, this is suffering for righteousness' sake (*v.* 14), and will be your glory and your happiness, as it entitles you to the blessing promised by Christ (Matt. v. 10). When this principle is laid deeply into your hearts, the next thing, as to men, is to be always ready, that is, able and willing, *to give an answer*, or make an apology or defence, of the faith you profess, and that *to every man that asketh a reason of your hope*, what sort of hope you have, for which you suffer such hardships in the world. These confessions of our faith ought to be made *with meekness and fear*; apologies for our religion ought to be made with modesty and meekness, in the fear of God, with jealousy over ourselves, and reverence to our superiors.

OUR SUFFERINGS AND CHRIST'S (*vv.* 16–20)

The confession of a Christian's faith cannot credibly be supported but by the two means here specified —*a good conscience* and a *good conversation*. Conscience is good when it does its office well, when it is kept pure and uncorrupt, and clear from guilt; then it will justify you, though men accuse you. *A good conversation in Christ* is a holy life, according to the doctrine and example of Christ.

Then, I. The example of Christ is proposed as an argument for patience under sufferings. In the case of our Lord's suffering, it was the just that suffered for the unjust; he substituted himself in our room and stead, and bore our iniquities. He that knew no sin suffered instead of those that knew no righteousness. The merit and perfection of Christ's sacrifice were such that for him to suffer once was enough. The legal sacrifices were repeated from day to day, and from year to year; but the sacrifice of Christ, once offered, purgeth away sin, Heb. vii. 27; ix. 26, 28; x. 10, 12, 14. If he once suffered, and then entered into glory, shall not we be patient under trouble, since it will be but a little time and we shall follow him to glory?

II. The apostle passes from the example of Christ to that of the old world, and sets before the Jews, to whom he wrote, the different event of those who believed and obeyed Christ preaching by Noah, from those that continued disobedient and unbelieving, intimating to the Jews that they were under a like sentence.

1. For the explication of this we may notice, (1) The preacher— Christ Jesus, who has interested himself in the affairs of the church and of the world ever since he was first promised to Adam, Gen. iii. 15. (2) The hearers. Because they were dead and disembodied when the apostle speaks of them, therefore he properly calls them spirits now *in prison*; not that they were *in prison when Christ preached to*

them. (3) The sin of these people: They were *disobedient*, that is, *rebellious*, *unpersuadable*, and *unbelieving*, as the word signifies; this their sin is aggravated from the patience and *long-suffering of God* (which *once waited* upon them for 120 years together, *while Noah was preparing the ark*, and by that, as well as by his preaching, giving them fair warning of what was coming upon them. (4) The event of all: Their bodies were drowned, and their spirits cast into hell, which is called a prison (Matt. v. 25; 2 Pet. ii. 4, 5); but Noah and his family, who believed and were obedient, *were saved in the ark*.

2. From the whole we learn that, (1) God takes exact notice of all the means and advantages that people in all ages have had for the salvation of their souls; it is put to the account of the old world that Christ offered them his help, sent his Spirit, gave them fair warning by Noah, and waited a long time for their amendment. (2) Though the patience of God wait long upon sinners, yet it will expire at last; it is beneath the majesty of the great God always to wait upon man in vain. (3) The spirits of disobedient sinners, as soon as they are out of their bodies, are committed to the prison of hell, whence there is no redemption. (4) The way of the most is neither the best, the wisest, nor the safest way to follow.

BAPTISM'S MEANING
(*vv.* 21, 22)

Noah's salvation in the ark upon the water prefigured the salvation of all good Christians in the church by baptism.

· I. Peter declares what he means by saving baptism; not the outward ceremony of washing with water, which, in itself, does no more than put away the filth of the flesh, but it is that baptism wherein there is a faithful answer or restipulation of a resolved good conscience, engaging to believe in, and be entirely devoted to, God, the Father, Son, and Holy Ghost, renouncing at the same time the flesh, the world, and the devil.

II. The apostle shows that the efficacy of baptism to salvation depends not upon the work done, but upon the resurrection of Christ, which supposes his death, and is the foundation of our faith and hope, to which we are rendered conformable by dying to sin, and rising again to holiness and newness of life.

III. The apostle, having mentioned the death and resurrection of Christ, proceeds to speak of his ascension, and sitting at the right hand of the Father, as a subject fit to be considered by these believers for their comfort in their suffering condition, *v.* 22.

CHAPTER FOUR
CEASING FROM SIN (*vv.* 1–3)

The apostle here draws a new inference from the consideration of Christ's sufferings. As he had before made use of it to persuade to patience in suffering, so here to mortification of sin. Observe,

I. How the exhortation is expressed. The supposition is *that Christ had suffered* for us in the flesh, or in his human nature. The consequent or inference is, "*Arm* and fortify *yourselves likewise with*

the same mind, courage, and resolution." The word flesh in the former part of the verse signifies Christ's human nature, but in the latter part it signifies man's corrupt nature. So the sense is, "As Christ suffered in his human nature, do you, according to your baptismal vow and profession, make your corrupt nature suffer, by putting to death the body of sin by self-denial and mortification; for, if you do thus suffer, you will be conformable to Christ in his death and resurrection, and will *cease from sin.*"

II. How it is further explained, *v.* 2. The apostle explains what he means by being dead to sin, and ceasing from sin, both negatively and positively. Negatively, a Christian ought *no longer to live the rest of his time in the flesh,* to the sinful lusts and corrupt desires of carnal wicked men; but, positively, he ought to conform himself to the revealed will of the holy God.

III. How it is enforced (*v.* 3): *For the time past of our life may suffice us to have wrought the will of the Gentiles,* &c. Here the apostle argues from equity. "It is but just, equal, and reasonable, that as you have hitherto all the former part of your life served sin and Satan, so you should now serve the living God."

A VISIBLE CHANGE (*vv.* 4–6)

I. Here you have the visible change wrought in those who in the foregoing verse were represented as having been in the former part of their life very wicked. They no longer run on in the same courses, or with the same companions, as they used to do. Hereupon observe the conduct of their wicked acquaintance towards them. 1. *They think it strange*, they are surprised and wonder at it, as at something new and unusual, that their old friends should be so much altered. 2. *They speak evil of them*. Their surprise carries them to blasphemy. They speak evil of their persons, of their way, their religion, and their God.

II. For the comfort of the servants of God, it is here added,

1. That all wicked people, especially those who speak evil of such as are not as bad as themselves, shall *give an account*.

2. That *for this cause was the gospel preached also to those that are dead, that they might be judged according to men in the flesh, but live according to God in the Spirit, v.* 6. Some understand this difficult place thus: *For this cause was the gospel preached* to all the faithful of old, who are now dead in Christ, that thereby they might be taught and encouraged to bear the unrighteous judgments and persecutions which the rage of men put upon them *in the flesh, but might live in the Spirit unto God.* Others take the expression, *that they might be judged according to men in the flesh*, in a spiritual sense, thus: The gospel was preached to them, to judge them, condemn them, and reprove them, for the corruption of their natures, and the viciousness of their lives, while they lived after the manner of the heathen or the mere natural man; and that, having thus mortified their sins, they might live according to God, a new and spiritual life.

GOOD STEWARDS (*vv.* 7–11)

We have here an awful position or doctrine, and an inference drawn from it. The position is that the *end of all things is at hand*. The inference from this comprises a series of exhortations.

1. To sobriety and watchfulness: *Be you therefore sober, v.* 7.

2. To charity: *And above all things have fervent charity among yourselves, v.* 8. Here is a noble rule in Christianity. Christians ought to love one another, which implies an affection to their persons, a desire of their welfare, and a hearty endeavour to promote it.

3. To hospitality, *v.* 9. The hospitality here required is a free and kind entertainment of strangers and travellers.

4. To the improvement of talents, *v.* 11.

(1) The rule is that whatever gift, ordinary or extraordinary, whatever power, ability, or capacity of doing good is given to us, we should minister, or do service, with the same *one to another*, accounting ourselves not masters, but only *stewards of the manifold grace*, or the various gifts, of God.

(2) The apostle exemplifies his direction about gifts in two particulars—speaking and ministering, concerning which he gives these rules: [1] *If any man*, whether a minister in public or a Christian in private conference, *speak* or teach, he must do it *as the oracles of God*, which direct us as to the matter of our speech. [2] *If any man minister*, either as a deacon, distributing the alms of the church and taking care of the poor, or as a private person,

by charitable gifts and contributions, *let him do it as of the ability which God giveth.* He who has received plenty and ability from God ought to minister plentifully, and according to his ability.

SUFFERING AS A CHRISTIAN (*vv.* 12–19)

The frequent repetition of counsel and comfort to Christians, considered as sufferers, in every chapter of this epistle, shows that the greatest danger these new converts were in arose from the persecutions to which their embracing Christianity exposed them. An unmortified spirit is very unfit to bear trials. Observe,

I. The apostle's kind manner of address to these poor despised Christians: they were his *beloved,* *v.* 9.

II. His advice to them, relating to their sufferings, which is,

1. That they should not think them strange, nor be surprised at them, as if some unexpected event befell them; for,

(1) Though they be sharp and fiery, yet they are designed only to try, not to ruin them, to try their sincerity, strength, patience, and trust in God.

(2) From the fiery trial the apostle descends to a lower degree of persecution—that of the tongue by slander and reproach, *v.* 14. He supposes that this sort of suffering would fall to their lot: they would be reviled, evil-spoken of, and slandered for the name or sake of Christ. In such case he asserts, *Happy are you.* By your patience and fortitude in suffering, by your dependence upon the promises of God, and adhering to the word which the Holy Spirit hath revealed, *he is on your part glorified;* but by the contempt and reproaches cast upon you *the Spirit itself* is evil-spoken of and blasphemed."

2. That they should take care they did not suffer justly, as evil-doers, *v.* 15. One would think such a caution as this needless to such an excellent set of Christians as these were. But their enemies charged them with these and other foul crimes: therefore the apostle, when he was settling the rules of the Christian religion, thought these cautions necessary, forbidding every one of them to hurt the life or the estate and property of any one, or to do any sort of evil, or, without call and necessity, to play the *bishop in another man's charge,* or busy himself *in other men's matters.* To this caution he adds a direction, *that if any man suffer* for the cause of Christianity, and with a patient Christian spirit, he ought not to account it a shame, but an honour to him; and ought to glorify God who hath thus dignified him, *v.* 16.

3. That their trials were now at hand, and they should stand prepared accordingly, *vv.* 17, 18.

(1) He tells them that the time had come when *judgment must begin at the house of God.* The usual method of Providence has been this: When God brings great calamities and sore judgments upon whole nations, he generally begins with his own people, Isa. x. 12; Jer. xxv. 29; Ezek. ix. 6. "Such a time of universal calamity is now at hand, which was foretold by our Saviour, Matt. xxiv, 9, 10. This renders all the foregoing exhorta-

tions to patience necessary for you."

(2) He intimates the irremediable doom of the wicked: *If the righteous scarcely be saved, where shall the ungodly and sinner appear*, *v.* 18. This whole verse is taken from Prov. xi. 31.

4. That when called to suffer, *according to the will of God*, they should look chiefly to the safety of their souls, which are put into hazard by affliction, and cannot be kept secure otherwise than by *committing them to God*, who will undertake the charge, if we commit them to him in well-doing; for he is their Creator, and has out of mere grace made many kind promises to them of eternal salvation, in which he will show himself faithful and true, *v.* 19.

CHAPTER FIVE

ADVICE TO ELDERS (*vv.* 1–4)

Here we may observe,

I. The persons to whom this exhortation is given—to the presbyters, pastors, and spiritual guides of the church, elders by office, rather than by age, ministers of those churches to whom he wrote this epistle.

II. The person who gives this exhortation—the apostle Peter: *I exhort*; and, to give force to this exhortation, he tells them he was their brother-presbyter or fellow-elder, and so puts nothing upon them but what he was ready to perform himself. He was also *a witness of the sufferings of Christ*, being with him in the garden, attending him to the palace of the high-priest, and very likely being a spectator of his suffering upon the

cross, at a distance among the crowd, Acts iii. 15. He adds that he was also *a partaker of the glory* that was in some degree revealed at the transfiguration (Matt. xvii. 1–3), and shall be completely enjoyed at the second coming of Jesus Christ.

III. The pastor's duty described, and the manner in which that duty ought to be performed. The pastoral duty is three-fold: 1. *To feed the flock*, by preaching to them the sincere word of God, and ruling them according to such directions and discipline as the word of God prescribes. 2. The pastors of the church must *take the oversight thereof*. 3. They must be *examples to the flock*, and practise the holiness, self-denial, mortification, and all other Christian duties, which they preach and recommend to their people.

IV. In opposition to that filthy lucre which many propose to themselves as their principal motive in undertaking and discharging the pastoral office, the apostle sets before them the crown of glory designed by the great shepherd, Jesus Christ, for all his faithful ministers.

HUMILITY (*vv.* 5–7)

Having settled and explained the duty of the pastors or spiritual guides of the church, the apostle comes now to instruct the flock,

I. How to behave themselves to their ministers and to one another. He exhorts those that are younger and inferior to *submit themselves to the elder*, to give due respect and reverence to their persons, and to yield to their admonitions, reproof, and authority, enjoining and commanding what the word of God requires, Heb. xiii. 17. As to one another, the rule is that they should all *be subject one to another*, so far as to receive the reproofs and counsels one of another, and be ready to *bear one another's burdens*, and perform all the offices of friendship and charity one to another. He advises them to *be clothed with humility*. Observe, Humility is the great preserver of peace and order in all Christian churches and societies, consequently pride is the great disturber of them, and the cause of most dissensions and breaches in the church.

II. The apostle, knowing that these Christians were already under very hard circumstances, rightly supposes that what he had foretold of greater hardships yet coming might excite in them abundance of care and fear about the event of these difficulties. His advice is to *cast all their care*, or *all care of themselves, upon God*. Learn, 1. The best of Christians are apt to labour under the burden of anxious and excessive care; the apostle calls it, *all your care*, intimating that the cares of Christians are various and of more sorts than one: personal cares, family cares, cares for the present, cares for the future, cares for themselves, for others, and for the church. The best remedy against immoderate care is to *cast our care upon God*, and resign every event to his wise and gracious determination.

RESISTING THE DEVIL
(vv. 8, 9)

Here the apostle does three things:
I. He shows them their danger

from an enemy more cruel and restless than even the worst of men, whom he describes.

1. By his characters and names.
2. By his business: *He walks about, seeking whom he may devour*; his whole design is to devour and destroy souls.

II. Hence he infers that it is their duty, 1. To *be sober*, and to govern both the outward and the inward man by the rules of temperance, modesty, and mortification. 2. To *be vigilant*; not secure or careless, but rather suspicious of constant danger from this spiritual enemy, and, under that apprehension, to be watchful and diligent to prevent his designs and save our souls. 3. To resist him *stedfast in the faith*.

III. He tells them that their care was not singular, for they knew that the like afflictions befell their brethren in all parts of the world, and that all the people of God were their fellow-soldiers in this warfare.

PRAYER (vv. 10–14)

We now come to the conclusion of this epistle, which,

I. The apostle begins with a most weighty prayer, which he addresses to God as *the God of all grace*, the author and finisher of every heavenly gift and quality, acknowledging, on their behalf, that God had already called them to be partakers of that eternal glory, which, being his own, he had promised and settled upon them, through the merit and intercession of Jesus Christ.

II. He recapitulates the design of his writing this epistle to them (v. 12), which was, 1. To testify, and in the strongest terms to assure them, that the doctrine of salvation, which he had explained and they had embraced, was the true account of the grace of God, foretold by the prophets and published by Jesus Christ. 2. To exhort them earnestly that, as they had embraced the gospel, they would continue stedfast in it, notwithstanding the arts of seducers, or the persecutions of enemies.

III. He recommends *Silvanus*, the person by whom he sent them this brief epistle, as a brother whom he esteemed faithful and friendly to them, and hoped they would account him so, though he was a minister of the uncircumcision.

IV. He closes with salutations and a solemn benediction. He exhorts them to fervent love and charity one towards another, and to express this by giving *the kiss of peace* (*v.* 14), according to the common custom of those times and countries, and so concludes with a benediction, which he confines to those *that are in Christ Jesus*, united to him by faith and sound members of his mystical body.

THE SECOND EPISTLE GENERAL OF

PETER

CHAPTER ONE
GREETINGS (*vv.* 1–4)

The apostle Peter, being moved by the Holy Ghost to write once more to those who from among the Jews were turned to faith in Christ, begins this second epistle with an introduction, wherein the same persons are described and the same blessings are desired that are in the preface to his former letter. Observe, (1) The fountain of all spiritual blessings is the divine power of Jesus Christ, who could not discharge all the office of Mediator, unless he was God as well as man. (2) All things that have any relation to, and influence upon, the true spiritual life, the life and power of godliness, are from Jesus Christ; *in him all fulness dwells*, and it is from him that we receive, *and grace for grace* (John i. 16). (3) Knowledge of God, and faith in him, are the channel whereby all spiritual supports and comforts are conveyed to us; but then we must own and acknowledge God as the author of our effectual calling, for so he is here described: *Him that hath called us to glory and virtue.* (4) In the fourth verse the apostle goes on to encourage their faith and hope in looking for an increase of grace and peace, because the same glory and virtue are employed and evidenced in giving the promises of the gospel that are exercised in our effectual calling.

ADDITIONS TO FAITH
(*vv.* 5–11)

In these words the apostle comes to the chief thing intended in this epistle—to excite and engage them to advance in grace and holiness.

I. Here we cannot but observe how the believer's way is marked out step by step. 1. He must get *virtue*, by which some understand *justice*; and then the *knowledge, temperance, and patience* that follow, being joined with it, the apostle may be supposed to put them upon pressing after the four cardinal virtues, or the four elements that go to the making up of every virtue or virtuous action. 2. The believer must add *knowledge* to his virtue, prudence to his courage. Every believer must labour after the knowledge and wisdom that are profitable to direct, both as to the proper method and order wherein all Christian duties are to be performed and as to the way and manner of performing them. 3. We must add *temperance* to our knowledge. We must be sober and moderate in our love to, and use of, the good things of this life. 4. Add to temperance *patience*, which must *have its perfect work*, or we cannot *be perfect and entire, wanting nothing*

(Jam. i. 4). 5. To patience we must add *godliness*, and this is the very thing which is produced by patience, for that works experience, Rom. v. 4. Hereby they are brought to the child-like fear and reverential love wherein true godliness consists: to this, 6. We must add *brotherly-kindness*, a tender affection to all our fellow-christians. 7. *Charity*, or a love of good-will to all mankind, must be added to the love of delight which we have for those who are the children of God.

II. All the forementioned graces must be had, or we shall not be *thoroughly furnished for all good works*—for the duties of the first and second table, for active and passive obedience, and for those services wherein we are to imitate God as well as for those wherein we only obey him—and therefore to engage us to an industrious and unwearied pursuit of them, the apostle sets forth the advantages that redound to all who success-fully labour so as to get these things to *be and abound in them*, *vv.* 8–11.

THE PRESENT TRUTH
(*vv.* 12–15)

I. The importance and advantage of progress and perseverance in grace and holiness made the apostle to be very diligent in doing the work of a minister of Christ, that he might thereby excite and assist them to be diligent in the duty of Christians.

II. The apostle, being set upon the work, tells us (*v.* 14) what makes him earnest in this matter, even the knowledge he had, not only that he must certainly, but also that he must shortly, *put off this taber-nacle*.

THE HOLY MOUNT
(*vv.* 16–18)

Here we have the reason of giving the foregoing exhortation, and that with so much diligence and serious-ness. These things are not idle tales, or a vain thing, but of un-doubted truth and vast concern. The gospel is not a *cunningly devised fable*. 1. The preaching of the gospel is a making known the power of Christ, that he is able to save to the uttermost all who come to God by him. He is the mighty God, and therefore can save from both the guilt and the filth of sin. 2. The coming of Christ also is made known by the preaching of the gospel. 3. And though this gospel of Christ has been blas-phemously called a *fable*, yet our apostle proves that it is of the greatest certainty and reality, in-asmuch as during our blessed Saviour's abode here on earth, when he took on him the form of a servant and was found in fashion as a man, he sometimes manifested himself to be God, and particu-larly to our apostle and the two sons of Zebedee, who *were eye-witnesses of his divine majesty, when he was transfigured before them*. This Peter, James, and John, were eye-witnesses of, and therefore might and ought to attest; and surely their testimony is true, when they witness what they have seen with their eyes, yea, and heard with their ears: for, besides the visible glory that Christ was invested with here on earth, there was an audible voice from heaven.

A SURE WORD (*vv*. 19–21)

Here note,

I. The description that is given of the scriptures of the Old Testament: they are called *a more sure word of prophecy. Moses and the prophets* more powerfully persuade than even miracles themselves, Luke xvi. 31. How firm and sure should our faith be, who have such a firm and sure word to rest upon! All the prophecies of the Old Testament are more sure and certain to us who have the history of the most exact and minute accomplishment of them.

II. The encouragement the apostle gives us to search the scriptures. He tells us, *We do well if we take heed to them*; that is, apply our minds to understand the sense, and our hearts to believe the truth, of this sure word, yea, bend ourselves to it, that we may be moulded and fashioned by it. When the light of the scripture is darted into the blind mind and dark understanding by the Holy Spirit of God, then the *spiritual day dawns and the day-star arises in that soul.*

III. The apostle lays down one thing as previously necessary to our giving heed to, and getting good by, the scriptures, and that is the knowing that all prophecy is of divine origin. Now this important truth he not only asserts, but proves. 1. Observe, No scripture prophecy is of private interpretation (or a man's own proper opinion, an explication of his own mind), but the revelation of the mind of God. This was the difference between the prophets of the Lord and the false prophets who have been in the world. 2. This

important truth of the divine origin of the scriptures (that what is contained in them is the mind of God and not of man) is to be known and owned by all who will give heed to the sure word of prophecy. 3. The divinity of the scriptures must be known and acknowledged in the first place, before men can profitably use them, before they can give good heed to them.

IV. Seeing it is so absolutely necessary that persons be fully persuaded of the scripture's divine origin, the apostle (*v*. 21) tells us how the Old Testament came to be compiled, and that, 1. Negatively: *It came not by the will of man.* Neither the things themselves that are recorded, and make up the several parts of the Old Testament, are the opinions of men, nor was the will of any of the prophets or penmen of the scriptures the rule or reason why any of those things were written which make up the canon of the scripture. 2. Affirmatively: *Holy men of God spoke as they were moved by the Holy Ghost.* So that the very words of scripture are to be accounted the words of the Holy Ghost, and all the plainness and simplicity, all the power and virtue, all the elegance and propriety, of the very words and expressions are to be regarded by us as proceeding from God.

CHAPTER TWO

FALSE TEACHERS (*vv*. 1–3)

I. In all ages of the church, and under all dispensations, when God sends true prophets, the devil sends some to seduce and deceive, false prophets in the Old Testament, and false Christs, false apostles, and seducing teachers, in the New.

II. He proceeds, in the second verse, to tell us the consequence with respect to others; and here we may learn, 1. Corrupt leaders seldom lack many to follow them; though the way of error is a pernicious way, yet many are ready to walk therein. 2. The spreading of error will bring up an evil report on the way of truth; that is, the way of salvation by Jesus Christ, who is *the way, the truth, and the life*.

III. Observe, in the next place, the method seducers take to draw disciples after them: they use *feigned words*; they flatter, and by good words and fair speeches deceive the hearts of the simple.

THE JUDGMENT OF GOD
(*vv.* 3–6)

I. See how God dealt with the angels who sinned. Observe, 1. No excellency will exempt a sinner from punishment. 2. By how much the more excellent the offender, by so much the more severe the punishment. 3. Sin debases and degrades the persons who commit it. 4. Those who rebel against the God of heaven shall all be sent down to hell. 5. Sin is the work of darkness, and darkness is the wages of sin. 6. As sin binds men over to punishment, so misery and torment hold men under punishment. 7. The last degree of torment is not till the day of judgment.

II. See how God dealt with the old world, even in much the same way that he dealt with the angels.

He spared not the old world. Observe what was the procuring cause of this: *it was a world of ungodly men*. Ungodliness puts men out of the divine protection, and exposes them to utter destruction.

III. See how God dealt with Sodom and Gomorrah; though they were situated in a country like the garden of the Lord, yet, if in such a fruitful soil they abound in sin, God can soon turn a fruitful land into barrenness and a well-watered country into dust and ashes. Let us take warning by all the instances of God's taking vengeance, which are recorded for our admonition, and to prevent our promising ourselves impunity, though we go on in a course of sin.

DELIVERANCE (*vv.* 7–9)

Here observe, 1. The character given of Lot; he is called *a just man*. And here is a just man in the midst of a most corrupt and profligate generation universally gone off from all good. 2. The impression the sins of others made upon this righteous man. Though the sinner takes pleasure in his wickedness, it is a grief and vexation to the soul of the righteous. 3. Here is particular mention of the duration and continuance of this good man's grief and vexation: it was *from day to day*. It is here presupposed that the righteous must have their temptations and trials. The devil and his instruments will thrust sore at them, that they may fall; and, if we will get to heaven, it must be through many tribulations. It is therefore our duty to reckon upon and prepare for them.

DANGERS OF APOSTASY AND ERROR (*vv.* 10–22)

But why will God thus deal with these false teachers? This he shows in what follows.

I. *These walk after the flesh*; they follow the devices and desires of their own hearts, they give up themselves to the conduct of their own fleshly mind, refusing to make their reason stoop to divine revelation, and to *bring every thought to the obedience of Christ*; they, in their lives, act directly contrary to God's righteous precepts, and comply with the demands of corrupt nature.

II. This he aggravates, by setting forth the very different conduct of more excellent creatures, even the *angels*. Let us, who pray that God's *will may be done on earth as it is in heaven*, imitate the angels in this particular; if we complain of wicked men, let it be to God, and that not with rage and reviling, but with compassion and composedness of mind, that may evidence that we belong to him who is meek and merciful.

III. The apostle, having shown (*v.* 11) how unlike seducing teachers are to the most excellent creatures, proceeds (*v.* 12) to show how they are to the most inferior: they are *like the horse and mule, which have no understanding*; they are *as natural brute beasts, made to be taken and destroyed.*

IV. The apostle (*vv.* 15, 16) proves that they are *cursed children*, even such covetous persons as *the Lord abhors*, by showing, 1. They *have forsaken the right way*; and it cannot be but such self-seekers must be out of the right way, which is a self-denying way. 2. They have gone into a wrong way: they have erred and strayed from the way of life, and gone over into the path which leads to death, and takes hold of hell; and this he makes out by showing it to be *the way of Balaam, the son of Bosor*. Balaam was indeed restrained from actually *cursing the people*, but he had so strong a desire after the honours and riches that were promised him that he went as far as he could, and did his utmost to get from under the restraint that was upon him.

V. The apostle proceeds (*v.* 17) to a further description of seducing teachers, whom he sets forth,

1. As *wells*, or fountains, *without water*. In vain then are all our expectations of being fed and filled with knowledge and understanding by those who are themselves ignorant and empty.

2. As *clouds carried with a tempest*. When we see a cloud we expect a refreshing shower from it; but these are clouds which yield no rain, for they are driven with the wind, but not of the Spirit, but the stormy wind or tempest of their own ambition and covetousness. To prevent these men's gaining proselytes, he tells us that, in the midst of all their talk of liberty, they themselves are the vilest slaves, for they are the servants of corruption; their own lusts have got a complete victory over them, and they are actually in bondage to them, making *provision for the flesh*, to satisfy its cravings, comply with its directions, and obey its commands. Their minds and hearts

are so far corrupted and depraved that they have neither power nor will to refuse the task that is imposed on them. They are conquered and captivated by their spiritual enemies, and yield their members servants of unrighteousness: and what a shame it is to be overcome and commanded by those who are themselves *the servants of corruption, and slaves to their own lusts!*

VI. The apostle, in the last two verses of the chapter, sets himself to prove that a state of apostasy is worse than a state of ignorance; for it is a *condemning of the way of righteousness*, after they have had some knowledge of it, and expressed some liking to it; it carries in it a declaring that they have found some iniquity in the way of righteousness and some falsehood in the word of truth.

CHAPTER THREE
THE LAST DAYS (vv. 1–7)

That the apostle might the better reach his end in writing this epistle, which is to make them steady and constant in a fiducial and practical remembrance of the doctrine of the gospel, he, 1. Expresses his special affection and tenderness for them, by calling them *beloved*. 2. He evinces a sincere love to them, and hearty concern for them, by writing the same thing to them, though in other words. 3. The better to recommend the matter, he tells them that what he would have them to remember are, (1) *The words spoken by the holy prophets*, who were divinely inspired, both en-

lightened and sanctified by the Holy Ghost. (2) *The commandments of the apostles of the Lord and Saviour*; and therefore the disciples and servants of Christ ought to regard what those who are sent by him have declared unto them to be the will of their Lord.

To quicken and excite us to a serious minding and firm adhering to what God has revealed to us by the prophets and apostles, we are told that there will be *scoffers*, men who will *make a mock of sin*, and of salvation from it. Now to prevent the true Christian's being overcome, when attacked by these scoffers, we are told,

I. What sort of persons they are: they *walk after their own lusts*, they follow the devices and desires of their own hearts, and carnal corrupt affections, not the dictates and directions of right reason and an enlightened well-informed judgment.

II. We also are forewarned how far they will proceed: they will attempt to shake and unsettle us, even as to our belief of Christ's second coming; they will scoffingly say, *Where is the promise of his coming?* v. 4.

III. We are also forewarned of the method of their reasoning, for while they laugh they will pretend to argue too. To this purpose they add that *since the fathers fell asleep all things continue as they were from the beginning of the creation*, v. 4. This is a subtle, though not a solid way of reasoning; it is apt to make impressions upon weak minds, and especially upon wicked hearts. *Because sentence against them is not speedily executed*, therefore they flatter themselves that it never will.

IV. Here is the falsehood of their argument detected. Whereas they confidently had said there had not been any change *from the beginning of the creation*, the apostle puts us in remembrance of a change already past, which, in a manner, equals that which we are called to expect and look for, which was the drowning of the world in the days of Noah. He mentions the one as what God has done, to convince and persuade us the rather to believe that the other both may be and will be.

1. We begin with the apostle's account of the destruction which has once already come upon the world (*vv.* 5, 6).

2. What the apostle says of the destructive change which is yet to come upon it: *The heavens and the earth, which now are, by the same word are kept in store, reserved unto fire against the day of judgment and perdition of ungodly men, v.* 7. Here we have an awful account of the final dissolution of the world, and which we are yet more nearly concerned in. Let therefore the scoffers, who laugh at the coming of our Lord to judgment, at least consider that it *may be*. There is nothing said of it in the word of God but what is within reach of the power of God. Now that which he has said, and which he will certainly make good, is that *the heavens and the earth which now are kept in store*, not to be, what earthly minds would wish to have them, treasures for us, but to be what God will have them, in his treasury, securely lodged and kept safely for his purposes. It follows, they are *reserved unto fire*.

A DAY—OR A THOUSAND YEARS (*v.* 8)

Here we may observe,

I. The truth which the apostle asserts—*that with the Lord one day is as a thousand years, and a thousand years are as one day*. Though, in the account of men, there is a great deal of difference between a day and a year, and a vast deal more between one day and a thousand years, yet in the account of God, who inhabits eternity, in which there is no succession, there is no difference; for all things past, present, and future, are ever before him, and the delay of a thousand years cannot be so much to him as the deferring of any thing for a day or an hour is to us.

II. The importance of this truth. If men have no knowledge or belief of the eternal God, they will be very apt to think him such a one as themselves. Yet how hard is it to conceive of eternity! It is therefore not very easy to attain such a knowledge of God as is absolutely necessary.

THE DAY OF THE LORD (*vv.* 9–10)

We are here told that *the Lord is not slack*—he does not delay beyond the appointed time. But the apostle assures us,

I. That what men count slackness is truly *long-suffering*, and that *to us-ward*; it is giving more time to his own people, *whom he has chosen before the foundation of the world*, many of whom are not as yet converted; and those who are in a state of grace and favour with God are to advance in knowledge and holiness.

II. *The day of the Lord will come as a thief in the night*, v. 10. Here we may observe, 1. The certainty of the day of the Lord. 2. The suddenness of this day: It *will come as a thief in the night*, at a time when men are sleeping and secure, and have no manner of apprehension or expectation of the day of the Lord, any more than men have of a thief when they are in a deep sleep, in the dark and silent night.

NEW HEAVEN, NEW EARTH
(*vv.* 11–18)

The apostle, having instructed them in the doctrine of Christ's second coming,

I. Takes occasion thence to exhort them to purity and godliness in their whole conversation: all the truths which are revealed in scripture should be improved for our advancement in practical godliness: this is the effect that knowledge must produce, or we are never the better for it. Here we must take notice, 1. What true Christians look for: *new heavens and a new earth*, in which a great deal more of the wisdom, power and goodness of our great God and Saviour Jesus Christ will be clearly discerned than we are able to discover in what we now see. 2. What is the ground and foundation of this expectation and hope—*the promise of God*. To look for any thing which God has not promised is presumption; but if our expectations are according to the promise, both as to the things we look for

and the time and way of their being brought about, we cannot meet with a disappointment.

II. As in *v.* 11 he exhorts to holiness from the consideration that *the heavens and the earth shall be dissolved*, so in *v.* 14 he resumes his exhortation from the consideration that they shall be again renewed. Get ready to *appear before the judgment-seat of Christ*: and see to it,

1. "That you be *found of him in peace*, in a state of peace and reconciliation with God through Christ, in whom alone God is *reconciling the world to himself.*"

2. That you be *found of Christ without spot, and blameless. Follow after holiness* as well as peace.

III. He mentions Paul as one who had an uncommon measure of wisdom given unto him. But the apostle Peter proceeds to tell us that in those things which are to be met with in Paul's epistles there are some things hard to be understood. Among the variety of subjects treated of in scripture, some are not easy to be understood because of their own obscurity, such are prophecies; others cannot be so easily understood because of their excellency and sublimity, as the mysterious doctrines; and others are with difficulty taken in because of the weakness of men's minds, such are the things of the Spirit of God, mentioned 1 Cor. ii. 14. And here the unlearned and unstable make wretched work; for they wrest and torture the scriptures, to make them speak what the Holy Ghost did not intend.

IV. The apostle gives them a word of caution, *vv.* 17, 18, where,

1. He intimates that the knowledge we have of these things should make us very wary and watchful.

2. That we may the better avoid being led away, the apostle directs us what to do, *v.* 18. And, (1) We must *grow in grace.* (2) We must grow *in the knowledge of our Lord Jesus Christ. To him be glory both now and for ever. Amen.*

JOHN

CHAPTER ONE

THE APOSTOLIC TESTIMONY
(vv. 1–4)

The apostle begins,

I. With an account or character of the Mediator's person, 1. *As the Word of life*, v. 1. In the gospel these two are disjoined, and he is called first *the Word*, John i. 1, and afterwards *Life. In him was life, and that life was* (efficiently and objectively) *the light of men*, John i. 4. Here both are conjoined: *The Word of life*, the vital Word. 2. *As eternal life*. His duration shows his excellency. He was from eternity; and so is, in scripture-account, necessary, essential, uncreated life. 3. *As life manifested* (v. 2), manifested in the flesh, manifested to us. The eternal life would assume mortality, would put on flesh and blood (in the entire human nature), and so dwell among us and converse with us, John i. 14.

II. With the evidences and assurances that the apostle and his brethren had of the Mediator's presence in this world. *The life, the word of life, the eternal life*, as such, could not be seen and felt; but the life manifested might be, and was so. The divine life, or Word incarnate, presented and evinced itself to the very senses of the apostles. As, 1. To their ears: *That which we have heard, vv.* 1, 3. 2. To their eyes: *That which we have seen*

with our eyes, vv. 1–3. 3. To their internal sense, to the eyes of their mind; for so (possibly) may the next clause be interpreted: *Which we have looked upon*. 4. To their hands and sense of feeling: *And our hands have handled* (touched and felt) *of the Word of life*. This surely refers to the full conviction our Lord afforded his apostles of the truth, reality, solidity, and organization of his body, after his resurrection from the dead.

III. With a solemn assertion and attestation of these grounds and evidences of the Christian truth and doctrine. The apostles publish these assurances for our satisfaction: *We bear witness, and show unto you, v.* 2. *That which we have seen and heard declare we unto you, v.* 3.

IV. With the reason of the apostle's exhibiting and asserting this summary of sacred faith. This reason is twofold:

1. That the believers of it may be advanced to the same happiness with them (with the apostles themselves): *That which we have seen and heard declare we unto you, that you may have fellowship with us, v.* 3. We see there is a fellowship or communion that runs through the whole church of God. There may be some personal distinctions and peculiarities, but there is a communion (or common participation of privilege and dignity) belonging

to all saints, from the highest apostle to the lowest believer. *And truly our fellowship* (or communion) *is with the Father and his Son Jesus Christ.*

2. That believers may be enlarged and advanced in holy joy: *And these things write we unto you that your joy may be full, v.* 4. The gospel dispensation is not properly a dispensation of fear, sorrow, and dread, but of peace and joy.

TRUE FELLOWSHIP (*vv.* 5–7)

I. Here is the message or report that the apostle avers to come from the Lord Jesus: *This then is the message which we have heard of him* (*v.* 5), of his Son Jesus Christ. What was communicated to them they were solicitous to impart: *This then is the message which we have heard of him, and declare unto you.—That God is light, and in him is no darkness at all, v.* 5. This report asserts the excellency of the divine nature. He is all that beauty and perfection that can be represented to us by light. There is no defect or imperfection, no mixture of any thing alien or contrary to absolute excellency, no mutability or capacity of any decay in him: *In him is no darkness at all, v.* 5.

II. There is a just conclusion to be drawn from this message and report. This conclusion issues into two branches: 1. For the conviction of such as have no true fellowship with God: *If we say we have fellowship with him, and walk in darkness, we lie, and do not the truth.* It is known that to walk, in scripture account, is to order and frame the course and actions of the moral life, that is, of the life so far as it is

capable of subjection to the divine law. *To walk in darkness* is to live and act according to such ignorance, error, and erroneous practice, as are contrary to the fundamental dictates of our holy religion. Now there may be those who may pretend to great attainments and enjoyments in religion; they may profess to have communion with God; and yet their lives may be irreligious, immoral, and impure. To such the apostle would not fear to give the lie: *They lie, and do not the truth.* 2. For the conviction and consequent satisfaction of those that are near to God: *But, if we walk in the light, we have fellowship one with another, and the blood of Jesus Christ his Son cleanseth us from all sin.* Those that so walk show that they know God, that they have received of the Spirit of God, and that the divine impress or image is stamped upon their souls. *Then we have fellowship one with another,* they with us and we with them, and both with God, in his blessed communications to us. And this is one—that his Son's blood or death is applied or imputed to us: *The blood of Jesus Christ his Son cleanseth us from all sin.* His blood applied to us discharges us from the guilt of all sin, both original and actual, inherent and committed: and so far we stand righteous in his sight.

CONFESSION (*vv.* 8–10)

Here, I. The apostle, having supposed that even those of this heavenly communion have yet their sin, proceeds here to justify that supposition, and this he does by showing the dreadful consequences of denying it, and that in two particulars: 1. *If we say, We have no sin, we deceive ourselves, and the truth is not in us, v.* 8. We must beware of deceiving ourselves in denying or excusing our sins. 2. *If we say, We have not sinned, we make him a liar, and his word is not in us, v.* 10. The denial of our sin not only deceives ourselves, but reflects dishonour upon God. It challenges his veracity. He has abundantly testified of, and testified against, the sin of the world.

II. The apostle then instructs the believer in the way to the continued pardon of his sin. Here we have, 1. His duty in order thereto: *If we confess our sins, v.* 9. Penitent confession and acknowledgment of sin are the believer's business, and the means of his deliverance from his guilt. And, 2. His encouragement thereto, and assurance of the happy issue. This is the veracity, righteousness, and clemency of God, to whom he makes such confession: *He is faithful and just to forgive us our sins, and to cleanse us from all unrighteousness, v.* 9. God is faithful to his covenant and word, wherein he has promised forgiveness to penitent believing confessors.

CHAPTER TWO

OUR ADVOCATE (*vv.* 1, 2)

These verses relate to the concluding subject of the foregoing chapter, in which the apostle proceeds upon the supposition of the real Christian's sin. And here he gives them both dissuasion and support.

I. Dissuasion. He would leave no room for sin: "*My little children,* these things write I unto you, that you sin not, v.* 1. The design or purport of this letter, the design of what I have just said concerning communion with God and the overthrow of it by an irreligious course, is to dissuade and drive you from sin." *But, if a man sin,* he may know his help and cure. And so we see,

II. The believer's support and relief in case of sin: *And* (or *but*) *if any man sin* (any of us, or of our foresaid communion), *we have we an Advocate with the Father,* &c., *v.* 1. Believers themselves, those that are advanced to a happy gospel-state, have yet their sins. And this must be the support, satisfaction, and refuge of believers (or real Christians) in or upon their sins: *We have an Advocate.* The original name is sometimes given to the Holy Ghost, and then it is rendered, *the Comforter.* He acts within us; he puts pleas and arguments into our hearts and mouths; and so is our advocate, by teaching us to intercede for ourselves. But here is an advocate outside us, in heaven and with the Father. The proper office and business of an advocate is with the judge; with him he pleads the client's cause. The Judge with whom our advocate pleads is the Father, his Father and ours. *And he is the propitiation for our sins, v.* 2. He is the expiatory victim, the propitiatory sacrifice that has been offered to the Judge for all our offences against his majesty, and law, and government. The Mediator of intercession, the Advocate for us, is the Mediator of redemption, the propitiation for our sins. It is his propitiation that he pleads. *He is the propitiation for our sins; and not for ours only* (not only for the sins of us Jews, us that are Abraham's seed according to the flesh), *but also for those of the whole world* (v. 2); not only for the past, or us present believers, but for the sins of all who shall hereafter believe on him or come to God through him.

ABIDING IN HIM (*vv.* 3–6)

These verses may seem to relate to the seventh verse of the former chapter. Here now succeeds the trial or test of our light and of our love.

I. The trial of our light: *And hereby we do know that we know him, if we keep his commandments, v.* 3. A careful conscientious obedience to his commands shows that the apprehension and knowledge of these things are graciously impressed upon the soul; and therefore it must follow in the reverse that *he that saith, I know him, and keepeth not his commandments, is a liar, and the truth is not in him, v.* 4.

II. The trial of our love: *But whoso keepeth his word in him verily is the love of God perfected*; *hereby know we that we are in him, v.* 5. To keep the word of God, or of Christ, is sacredly to attend thereto in all the conduct and motion of life; in him that does so is the love of God perfected.

BROTHERLY LOVE (*vv.* 7–11)

The precept of fraternal love is recommended,

I. As an old one: *I write no new commandment unto you, but an old commandment, which you had from the beginning, v.* 7. In the state of

sin and promised recovery, they must love one another as related to God their Maker, as related to each other by blood, and as partners in the same hope.

II. As a new one: "*Again, a new commandment I write unto you.*" We should see that that grace or virtue which was true in Christ be true also in us; we should be conformable to our head. 1. He who wants such love in vain pretends his light: *He that saith he is in the light, and hateth his brother, is in darkness even until now, v.* 9. 2. He who is governed by such love approves his light to be good and genuine: *He that loveth his brother* (as his brother in Christ) *abideth in the light, v.* 10. He sees the foundation and reason of Christian love; he discerns the weight and value of the Christian redemption; he sees how meet it is that we should love those whom Christ hath loved; and then the consequence will be that *there is no occasion of stumbling in him* (v. 10); he will be no scandal, *no stumbling-block, to his brother.* 3. Hatred is a sign of spiritual darkness: *But he that hateth his brother is in darkness, v.* 11. Spiritual light is instilled by the Spirit of grace, and one of *the first-fruits of that Spirit is love*; he then who is possessed with malignity towards a Christian brother must needs be destitute of spiritual light; consequently *he walks in darkness* (v. 11).

LOVE OF THE WORLD
(*vv.* 12–17)

I. We have the address itself made to the various forms and ranks in the church of Christ. In this distribution the apostle addresses,

1. The lowest in the Christian school: *I write unto you, little children*, v. 12. He addresses *the children* in Christianity upon two accounts: (1) *Because their sins were forgiven them for his name's sake*, v. 12. The youngest sincere disciple is pardoned. (2) Because of their knowledge of God: *I write unto you, little children, because you have known the Father*, v. 13. Children are wont to know none so soon as their father. Next he addresses,

2. Those of the highest station and stature, to the seniors in Christianity, to whom he gives an honourable appellation: *I write unto you, fathers (vv.* 13, 14), *unto you old disciples*, Acts xxi. 16. Those that are of longest standing in Christ's school have need of further advice and instruction; none are too old to learn. He writes to them upon the account of their knowledge: *I write unto you, fathers, because you have known him that is from the beginning, vv.* 13, 14. Then,

3. To the middle age of Christians, to those who are in their bloom and flower: *I write unto you, young men, vv.* 13, 14. There are the adult in Christ Jesus, those that have arrived at the strength of spirit and sound sense and can discern between good and evil. The apostle applies to them upon these accounts: (1) Upon the account of their martial exploits. Dexterous soldiers they are in the camp of Christ: *Because you have overcome the wicked one*, v. 13. (2) Upon the account of their strength, discovered in this their achievement: *Because you are strong, and you have overcome the wicked one*, v. 14. (3) Because of their acquain-

tance with the word of God: *And the word of God abideth in you*, v. 14.

II. We have a caution fundamental to vital practical religion: "*Love not the world, neither the things that are in the world*, v. 15. Be crucified to the world, be mortified to the things, to the affairs and enticements, of it." The several degrees of Christians should unite in this, in being dead to the world. These reasons are taken,

1. From the inconsistency of this love with the love of God: *If any man love the world, the love of the Father is not in him*, v. 15.

2. From the prohibition of worldly love or lust; it is not ordained of God: *It is not of the Father, but is of the world*, v. 16.

3. From the vain and vanishing state of earthly things and the enjoyment of them. *And the world passeth away, and the lust thereof*, v. 17.

4. From the immortality of the divine lover, the lover of God: *But he that doeth the will of God*, which must be the character of the lover of God, in opposition to this lover of the world, *abideth for ever*, v. 17.

ANTICHRISTS (*vv.* 18, 19)

Here is, I. A moral prognostication of the time; the end is coming: *Little children, it is the last time*, v. 18. It is meet that the disciples should be warned of the haste and end of time, and apprised as much as may be of the prophetic periods of time.

II. The sign of this last time: *Even now there are many antichrists* (v. 18), many that oppose the person, doctrine, and kingdom of Christ. Let the prediction that we see there has been of seducers arising in the Christian world fortify us against their seduction.

III. Some account of these seducers or antichrists. 1. More positively. They were once entertainers or professors of apostolical doctrine: *"They went out from us (v. 19), from our company and communion."* 2. More privatively. "They were not inwardly such as we are: *But they were not of us*; they had not *from the heart obeyed the form of sound doctrine delivered to them*; they were not of our union with Christ the head." *But* this was done (or *they went out*) *that they might be made manifest that they were not all of us, v.* 19. The church knows not well who are its vital members and who are not; and therefore the church, considered as internally sanctified, may well be styled *invisible*.

THE ANOINTING (vv. 20–17)

Here, I. The apostle encourages the disciples (to whom he writes) in these dangerous times, in this hour of seducers; he encourages them in the assurance of their stability in this day of apostasy: *But you have an unction from the Holy One, and you know all* things. We see, 1. The blessing wherewith they were enriched—an unguent from heaven: *You have an unction.* 2. From whom this blessing comes—*from the Holy One*, either from the Holy Ghost or from the Lord Christ. 3. The effect of this unction—it is a spiritual eyesalve; it enlightens and strengthens the eyes of the understanding.

II. The apostle indicates to them the mind and meaning with which he wrote to them. 1. By way of

negation; not as suspecting their knowledge, or supposing their ignorance in the grand truths of the gospel. 2. By way of assertion and acknowledgment, as relying upon their judgment in these things: *But because you know it* (you know *the truth in Jesus), and that no lie is of the truth.*

III. The apostle further arraigns these seducers who had newly arisen. 1. They are *liars*, egregious opposers of sacred truth: *Who is a liar*, or the liar, the notorious liar of the time and age in which we live, *but he that denieth that Jesus is the Christ?* 2. They are direct enemies to God as well as to the Lord Christ; *He is antichrist who denieth the Father and the Son, v.* 22. He that opposes Christ denies the witness and testimony of the Father, and the seal that he hath given to his Son; *for him hath God the Father sealed*, John vi. 27.

IV. Hereupon the apostle advises and persuades the disciples to continue in the old doctrine at first communicated to them: *Let that therefore abide in you which you have heard from the beginning, v.* 24. Truth is older than error. True Christians have an inward confirmation of the divine truth they have imbibed: the Holy Spirit has imprinted it on their minds and hearts. The unction, the pouring out of the gifts of grace upon sincere disciples, is a seal to the truth and doctrine of Christ, since none giveth that seal but God. It is better than human instruction: *"And you need not that any man teach you, v.* 27." The divine unction does not supersede ministerial teaching, but surmount it.

It teaches you to abide in Christ; and, as it teaches you, it secures you; it lays a restraint upon your minds and hearts, that you may not revolt from him.

ABIDE IN HIM (vv. 28, 29)

From the blessing of the sacred unction the apostle proceeds in his advice and exhortation to constancy in and with Christ: *And now, little children, abide in him, v.* 28. This duty of perseverance and constancy in trying times is strongly urged by the two following considerations: 1. From the consideration of his return at the great day of account: *That when he shall appear we may have confidence, and not be ashamed before him at his coming, v.* 28. At his public appearance he will shame all those who have abandoned him, by professing before men and angels that he is ashamed of them, Mark viii. 38. To the same advice and exhortation he proceeds, 2. From the consideration of the dignity of those who still adhere to Christ and his religion: *If you know that he is righteous, you know that every one that doeth righteousness is born of him, v.* 29. He that doeth righteousness may here be justly enough assumed as another name for him that abideth in Christ. For he that abideth in Christ abideth in the law and love of Christ, and consequently in his allegiance and obedience to him.

CHAPTER THREE

THE PURE HOPE (vv. 1–3)

The apostle, having shown the dignity of Christ's faithful followers, that they are born of him and thereby nearly allied to God, now here,

I. Breaks forth into the admiration of that grace that is the spring of such a wonderful vouchsafement. Thence the apostle,

II. Infers the honour of believers above the recognition of the world. Unbelievers know little of them. *Therefore* (or wherefore, upon this score) *the world knoweth us not, v.* 1. Little does the world perceive the advancement and happiness of the genuine followers of Christ. Then the apostle,

III. Exalts these persevering disciples in the prospect of the certain revelation of their state and dignity. *But we know that when he shall appear we shall be like him.* When the head of the church, the only-begotten of the Father, shall appear, his members, the adopted of God, shall appear and be manifested together with him. *We shall be like him, for we shall see him as he is.* Their likeness will be the cause of that sight which they shall have of him. Their likeness shall enable them to see him as the blessed do in heaven. Then the apostle,

IV. Urges the engagement of these sons of God to the prosecution of holiness: *And every man that hath this hope in him purifies himself even as he is pure, v.* 3. The sons of God know that their Lord is holy and pure; he is of purer heart and eyes than to admit any pollution or impurity to dwell with him. Those then who hope to live with him must study the utmost purity from the world, and flesh, and sin; they must grow in grace and holiness.

MARKS OF GOD'S PEOPLE
(*vv.* 4–10)

The apostle now proceeds to fill his own mouth and the believer's mind with multiplied arguments against sin. And so he reasons and argues,

I. From the nature of sin and the intrinsic evil of it. It is contrary to the divine law: *Whosoever committeth sin transgresseth also* (or *even*) *the law; for sin is the transgression of the law*, or is lawlessness, *v.* 4. The current commission of sin now is the rejection of the divine law, and this is the rejection of the divine authority, and consequently of God himself.

II. From the design and errand of the Lord Jesus in and to this world, which was to remove sin: *And you know that he was manifested to take away our sins, and in him is no sin*, *v.* 5. Those that expect communion with Christ above should study communion with him here in the utmost purity.

III. From the opposition between sin and a real union with or adhesion to the Lord Christ: *Whosoever abideth in him sinneth not*, *v.* 6. To sin here is the same as to commit sin (*vv.* 8, 9), and to commit sin is to practise sin. He that abideth in Christ continues not in the practice of sin.

IV. From the connection between the practice of righteousness and a state of righteousness, intimating that the practice of sin and a justified state are inconsistent.

V. From the relation between the sinner and the devil. 1. As elsewhere sinners and saints are distinguished, *so to commit sin* is here

so to practise it as sinners do, that are distinguished from saints, to live under the power and dominion of it; and he who does so *is of the devil*. And thereupon we must see how he argues, 2. From the design and office of the Lord Christ against the devil: *For this purpose the Son of God was manifested, that he might destroy the works of the devil*, *v.* 8. Let not us serve or indulge what the Son of God came to destroy.

VI. From the connection between regeneration and the relinquishment of sin: *Whosoever is born of God doth not commit sin. Such a one committeth not sin*, does not work iniquity nor practise disobedience, which is contrary to his new nature and the regenerate complexion of his spirit; for, as the apostle adds, *his seed remaineth in him*, either the word of God in its light and power *remaineth in him* (as 1 Pet. i. 23), or, *that which is born of the Spirit is spirit*; the spiritual seminal principle of holiness remaineth in him. *He therefore cannot sin*, in the sense in which the apostle says, *he cannot commit sin*. He cannot continue in the course and practice of sin. He cannot so sin as to denominate him a sinner in opposition to a saint or servant of God. Again, he cannot sin comparatively, as he did before he was born of God, and as others do that are not so. And the reason is *because he is born of God*, which will amount to all this inhibition and impediment.

VII. From the discrimination between the children of God and the children of the devil. They have their distinct characters. *In this the*

children of God are manifest and the
children of the devil, v. 10.

LOVING ONE ANOTHER
(vv. 11–13)

The apostle, having intimated that
one mark of the devil's children is
hatred of the brethren, takes
occasion thence,

I. To recommend fraternal Christian love, and that from the excellence, or antiquity, or primariness
of the injunction relating thereto.

II. To dissuade from what is
contrary thereto, all ill-will towards
the brethren, and that by the
example of Cain. His envy and
malignity should deter us from
harbouring the like passion. And
then,

III. To infer that it is no wonder
that good men are so served now:
*Marvel not, my brethren, if the
world hate you*, v. 13. The serpentine
nature still continues in the world.

THE MARK OF LOVE
(vv. 14–19)

The beloved apostle can scarcely
touch upon the mention of sacred
love, but he must enlarge upon the
enforcement of it, as here he does
by divers arguments and incentives
thereto; as,

I. That it is a mark of our
evangelical justification, of our
transition into a state of life: *We
know that we have passed from
death to life, because we love the
brethren*, v. 14. But this love,

1. Supposes a general love to
mankind: the law of Christian love,
in the Christian community, is
founded on the catholic law, in the
society of mankind, *Thou shalt love
thy neighbour as thyself*.

2. It includes a peculiar love to
the Christian society, to the catholic
church, and that for the sake of her
head, as being his body, as being
redeemed, justified, and sanctified
in and by him.

II. The hatred of our brethren is,
on the contrary, a sign of our
deadly state, of our continuance
under the legal sentence of death:
He that loveth not his brother (his
brother in Christ) *abideth in death*,
v. 14. He yet stands under the
curse and condemnation of the law.

III. The example of God and
Christ should inflame our hearts
with this holy love: *Hereby perceive
we the love of God, because he laid
down his life for us; and we ought to
lay down our lives for the brethren*,
v. 16. Surely we should love those
whom God hath loved, and so
loved; and we shall certainly do so
if we have any love for God.

IV. The apostle, having proposed
this flaming constraining example
of love, and motive to it, proceeds to
show us what should be the temper and effect of this our Christian
love. And, 1. It must be, in the
highest degree, so fervent as to
make us willing to suffer even to
death for the good of the church,
for the safety and salvation of the
dear brethren: *And we ought to lay
down our lives for the brethren*
(v. 16). 2. It must be, in the next
degree, compassionate, liberal, and
communicative to the necessities of
the brethren: For *whoso hath this
world's good, and seeth his brother
have need, and shutteth up his bowels
of compassion from him, how dwelleth the love of God in him?* v. 17.

V. This love will evince our sincerity in religion, and give us hope towards God: *And hereby we know that we are of the truth, and shall assure our hearts before him*, v. 19.

CONSCIENCE AND CONFIDENCE (vv. 20–22)

The apostle, having intimated that there may be, even among us, such a privilege as an assurance or sound persuasion of heart towards God, proceeds here,

I. To establish the court of conscience, and to assert the authority of it: *For, if our heart condemn us, God is greater than our heart, and knoweth all things*, v. 20. Our heart here is our self-reflecting judicial power. This power can act as witness, judge, and executioner of judgment; it either accuses or excuses, condemns or justifies; it is set and placed in this office by God himself. 1. If conscience condemn us, God does so too: *For, if our heart condemn us, God is greater than our heart, and knoweth all things*, v. 20. Or, 2. If conscience acquit us, God does so too: *Beloved, if our heart condemn us not, then have we confidence towards God* (v. 21), then have we assurance that he accepts us now, and will acquit us in the great day of account.

II. To indicate the privilege of those who have a good conscience towards God. They have interest in heaven and in the court above; their suits are heard there: *And whatsoever we ask we receive of him*, v. 22.

HIS COMMANDMENT (vv. 23, 24)

The apostle, having mentioned keeping the commandments, and pleasing God, as the qualification

of effectual petitioners in and with Heaven, here suitably proceeds.

I. To represent to us what those commandments primarily and summarily are; they are comprehended in this double one: *And this is his commandment, That we should believe on the name of his Son Jesus Christ, and love one another, as he gave us commandment*, v. 23.

II. To represent to us the blessedness of obedience to these commands. The obedient enjoy communion with God: *And he that keepeth his commandments*, and particularly those of faith and love, *dwelleth in him, and he in him*, v. 24.

CHAPTER FOUR

TEST THE SPIRITS (vv. 1–3)

The apostle, having said that God's dwelling in and with us may be known by *the Spirit that he hath given us*, intimates that that Spirit may be discerned and distinguished from other spirits that appear in the world; and so here,

I. He calls the disciples, to whom he writes, to caution and scrutiny about the spirits and spiritual professors that had now risen. A reason is given for this trial: *Because many false prophets have gone out into the world*, v. 1. It should not seem strange to us that false teachers set themselves up in the church: it was so in the apostles' times; fatal is the spirit of delusion, sad that men should vaunt themselves for prophets and inspired preachers that are by no means so!

II. He gives a test whereby the disciples may try these pretending spirits. These spirits set up for prophets, doctors, or dictators in religion, and so they were to be tried by their doctrine; and the test whereby in that day, or in that part of the world where the apostle now resided (for in various seasons, and in various churches, tests were different), must be this: *Hereby know you the Spirit of God, Every spirit that confesseth that Jesus Christ has come in the flesh* (or *that confesseth Jesus Christ that came in the flesh) is of God, v.* 2. Jesus Christ is to be confessed as the Son of God, the eternal life and Word, that was with the Father from the beginning; as the Son of God that came into, and came in, our human mortal nature, and therein suffered and died at Jerusalem. He who confesses and preaches this, by a mind supernaturally instructed and enlightened therein, does it by the Spirit of God, or God is the author of that illumination. On the contrary, *"Every spirit that confesseth not that Jesus Christ has come in the flesh* (or *Jesus Christ that came in the flesh) is not of God, v.* 3.

TRUTH AND ERROR
(*vv.* 4–6)

In these verses the apostle encourages the disciples against the fear and danger of this seducing antichristian spirit, and that by such methods as these: 1. He assures them of a more divine principle in them: *"You are of God, little children, v.* 4. *You are God's little children. We are of God, v.* 6. 2. He gives them hope of victory: *"And have overcome them, v.* 4. You have hitherto overcome these deceivers and their temptations, and there is good ground of hope that you will do so still, and that upon these two

accounts:"—(1) "There is a strong preserver within you: *Because greater is he that is in you than he that is in the world," v.* 4. (2) You are not of the same temper with these deceivers. The Spirit of God hath framed your mind for God and heaven; *but they are of the world.* Then, 3. He represents to them that though their company might be the smaller, yet it was the better; they had more divine and holy knowledge: *"He that knoweth God heareth us."* As, on the contrary, *"He that is not of God heareth not us.* He who knows not God regards not us. He that is not *born of God* (walking according to his natural disposition) walks not with us."

GOD IS LOVE (*vv.* 7–13)

As *the Spirit of truth* is known by doctrine (thus spirits are to be tried), it is known by love likewise; and so here follows a strong fervent exhortation to holy Christian love: *Beloved, let us love one another, v.* 7. This exhortation is pressed and urged with variety of argument: as,

I. From the high and heavenly descent of love: *For love is of God.* He is the fountain, author, parent, and commander of love; it is the sum of his law and gospel: *And every one that loveth* (whose spirit is framed to judicious holy love) *is born of God, v.* 7. The Spirit of God is the Spirit of love. Love comes down from heaven.

II. Love argues a true and just apprehension of the divine nature: *He that loveth knoweth God, v.* 7. He *that loveth not knoweth not God, v.* 8. What attribute of the divine Majesty so clearly shines in all the world as his communicative goodness, which is love. His love must needs shine among his primary brightest perfections; *for God is love* (*v.* 8), his nature and essence are love, his will and works are primarily love. Then,

III. Divine love to the brethren should constrain ours: *Beloved* (I would adjure you by your interest in my love to remember), *if God so loved us, we ought also to love one another*, *v.* 11. This should be an invincible argument.

IV. The Christian love is an assurance of the divine inhabitation: *If we love one another, God dwelleth in us*, *v.* 12.

V. Herein the divine love attains a considerable end and accomplishment in us: "*And his love is perfected in us*," *v.* 12. It has obtained its completion in and upon us. God's love is not perfected in him, but in and with us.

DIVINE LOVE (*vv.* 14–16)

Since faith in Christ works love to God, and love to God must kindle love to the brethren, the apostle here confirms the prime article of the Christian faith as the foundation of such love. Here,

I. He proclaims the fundamental article of the Christian religion, which is so representative of the love of God: *And we have seen, and do testify, that the Father sent the Son to be the Saviour of the world*, *v.* 14. Thereupon,

II. The apostle states the excellency, or the excellent privilege attending the due acknowledgment of this truth: *Whosoever shall confess that Jesus is the Son of God, God dwelleth in him, and he in God,*

v. 15. This confession seems to include faith in the heart as the foundation of it, acknowledgment with the mouth to the glory of God and Christ, and profession in the life and conduct, in opposition to the flatteries or frowns of the world. Then,

III. The apostle applies this to the excitation of holy love. God's love is thus seen and exerted in Christ Jesus; *and* thus *have we known and believed the love that God hath to us*, *v.* 16. Hence we may learn,

1. That *God is love* (*v.* 16); he is essential boundless love.

2. That hereupon *he that dwelleth in love dwelleth in God, and God in him*, *v.* 16. There is great communion between the God of love and the loving soul.

PERFECT LOVE (*vv.* 17–21)

The apostle, having thus excited and enforced sacred love from the great pattern and motive of it, proceeds to recommend it further by other considerations; and he recommends it in both the branches of it, both as love to God, and love to our brother or Christian neighbour.

I. As love to God. Love to God seems here to be recommended on these accounts: 1. It will give us peace and satisfaction of spirit in the day when it will be most needed, or when it will be the greatest pleasure and blessing imaginable: *Herein is our love made perfect, that we may have boldness in the day of judgment*, *v.* 17. Possibly here by the love of God may be meant our *love to God*, which is *shed abroad upon our hearts by the Holy Ghost*;

this is the foundation of our hope, or of our assurance that our hope will hold good at last. He will give the crown of righteousness to all that love his appearing. And we have this boldness towards Christ because of our conformity to him: *Because as he is so are we in this world*, v. 17. 2. It prevents or removes the uncomfortable result and fruit of servile fear: *There is no fear in love* (v. 18); so far as love prevails, fear ceases. There is a being afraid of God, which arises from a sense of guilt, and a view of his vindictive perfections; in the view of them, God is represented as a consuming fire; and so fear here may be rendered *dread: There is no dread in love*. Love considers its objects as good and excellent, and therefore amiable, and worthy to be beloved. Those who perfectly love God are, from his nature, and counsel, and covenant, perfectly assured of his love, and consequently are perfectly free from any dismal dreadful suspicions of his punitive power and justice, as armed against them; they well know that God loves them, and they thereupon triumph in his love. 3. From the source and rise of it, which is the antecedent love of God: *We love him, because he first loved us*, v. 19. His love is the incentive, the motive, and moral cause of ours.

II. As love to our brother and neighbour in Christ; such love is argued and urged on these accounts: 1. As suitable and consonant to our Christian profession. How shall the hater of a visible image of God pretend to love the unseen original, the invisible God himself? 2. As suitable to the express law of God, and the just reason of it: *And this commandment have we from him, that he who loveth God love his brother also*, v. 21.

CHAPTER FIVE

THE VICTORY OF FAITH
(vv. 1–5)

I. The apostle having, in the conclusion of the last chapter, as was there observed, urged Christian love upon those two accounts, as suitable to Christian profession and as suitable to the divine command, here adds a third: Such love is suitable, and indeed demanded, by their eminent relation; our Christian brethren or fellow-believers are nearly related to God; they are his children: *Whosoever believeth that Jesus is the Christ is born of God*, v. 1.

II. The apostle shows, 1. How we may discern the truth, or the true evangelical nature of our love to the regenerate. The ground of it must be our love to God, whose they are: *By this we know that we love the children of God, when we love God*, v. 2. 2. How we may learn the truth of our love to God—it appears in our holy obedience: *When we love God, and keep his commandments*, v. 2. 3. What is and ought to be the result and effect of regeneration—an intellectual spiritual conquest of this world: *For whatsoever is born of God*, or, as in some copies, whosoever *is born of God, overcometh the world*, v. 4. He that is born of God is born *for* God, and consequently for another world. Faith is the cause of victory, the means, the instrument, the spiritual armour and artillery by which we overcome.

III. The apostle concludes that it is the real Christian that is the true conqueror of the world: *Who is he then that overcometh the world, but he that believeth that Jesus is the Son of God? v.* 5. It is the world that lies in our way to heaven, and is the great impediment to our entrance there. But he who believes that Jesus is the Son of God believes therein that Jesus came from God to be the Saviour of the world, and powerfully to conduct us from the world to heaven, and to God, who is fully to be enjoyed there. And he who so believes must needs by this faith overcome the world.

THE THREE WITNESSES
(vv. 6–9)

The Lord Jesus brings his credentials along with him, and he brings them in the way by which he came and in the witness that attends him.

I. In the way and manner by which he came; not barely by which he came into the world, but by and with which he came, and appeared, and acted, as a Saviour in the world: *This is that came by water and blood. Jesus Christ came with water and blood,* as the notes and signatures of the true effectual Saviour of the world; and he came by water and blood as the means by which he would heal and save us. (1) Inwardly, from the power and pollution of sin in our nature. For our cleansing from this we need spiritual water; such as can reach the soul and the powers of it. Accordingly, there is in and by Christ Jesus *the washing of regeneration and the renewing of the Holy Ghost.* (2) We are defiled outwardly, by the guilt and condemning power of sin upon our persons. From this we must be purged by atoning blood. It is the law or determination in the court of heaven *that without shedding of blood there shall be no remission,* Heb. ix. 22. The Saviour from sin therefore must come with blood. He who comes by water and blood is an accurate perfect Saviour. And this is he who comes by water and blood, even Jesus Christ! But we see his credentials also.

II. In the witness that attends him, and that is, the divine Spirit, that Spirit to whom the perfecting of the works of God is usually attributed: *And it is the Spirit that beareth witness, v.* 6. *Because* (or for) *there are three that bear record in heaven, the Father, the Word, and the Holy Ghost, and these three are one.*

To these there is opposed, though with them joined, a trinity of witnesses on earth, such as continue here below: *And there are three that bear witness on earth, the spirit, the water, and the blood; and these three agree in one, v.* 8. [1] Of these witnesses the first is the *spirit.* This must be distinguished from the person of the Holy Ghost, who is in heaven. We must say then, with the Saviour (according to what is reported by this apostle), *that which is born of the Spirit is spirit,* John iii. 6. The regeneration or renovation of souls is a testimony to the Saviour. It is his actual though initial salvation. It is a testimony on earth, because it continues with the church here, and is not performed in that conspicuous astonishing manner in which signs from heaven are accomplished. To this Spirit belong not only the regeneration and conversion of the church, but its progressive sanctification, victory over the world, her peace, and love, and joy, and all that grace by which she is made meet for the inheritance of the saints in light. [2] The second is the *water*. This was before considered as a means of salvation, now as a testimony to the Saviour himself, and intimates his purity and purifying power. [3] The third witness is the blood; this he shed, and this was our ransom. This testifies for Jesus Christ, *First*, In that it sealed up and finished the sacrifices of the Old Testament, *Christ, our Passover, was sacrificed for us. Secondly,* In that it confirmed his own predictions, and the truth of all his ministry and doctrine, John xviii. 37. *Thirdly,* In that it showed unparalleled love to God, in that he would die a sacrifice to his honour and glory, in making atonement for the sins of the world, John xiv. 30, 31. *Fourthly,* In that it demonstrated unspeakable love to us; and none will deceive those whom they entirely love, John xiv. 13–15. *Fifthly,* In that it demonstrated the disinterestedness of the Lord Jesus as to any secular interest and advantage. No impostor and deceiver ever proposes to himself contempt and a violent cruel death, John xviii. 36. *Sixthly,* In that it lays obligation on his disciples to suffer and die for him. *Seventhly,* The benefits accruing and procured by his blood (well understood) must immediately demonstrate that he is indeed the Saviour of the world. And then, *Eighthly,* These are signified and sealed in the institution of his own supper: *This is my blood of the New Testament* (which ratifies the New Testament), *which is shed for many, for the remission of sins,* Matt. xxiv. 28. Such are the witnesses on earth.

III. The apostle justly concludes, *If we receive the witness of men, the witness of God is greater; for this is the witness of God, that he hath testified of his Son, v.* 9. God, *that cannot lie,* hath given sufficient assurance to the world that Jesus Christ is his Son, the Son of his love, and Son by office, to reconcile and recover the world unto himself; he testified therefore the truth and divine origin of the Christian religion, and that it is the sure appointed way and means of bringing us to God.

CHRISTIAN ASSURANCE
(*vv.* 10–13)

In these words we may observe,

I. The privilege and stability of the real Christian: *He that believeth on the Son of God,* hath been prefailed with unfeignedly to cleave to him for salvation, *hath the witness in himself, v.* 10.

II. The aggravation of the unbeliever's sin, the sin of unbelief: *He that believeth not God hath made him a liar.* He does, in effect, give God the lie, *because he believeth not the record that God gave of his Son, v.* 10.

III. The matter, the substance, or contents of all this divine testimony concerning Jesus Christ: *And this is the record, that God hath given to us eternal life, and this life is in his Son*, *v.* 11. This is the sum of the gospel. This is the sum and epitome of the whole record given us by all the aforesaid six witnesses.

IV. The end and reason of the apostle's preaching this to believers. 1. For their satisfaction and comfort: *These things have I written unto you that believe on the name of the Son of God, that you may know that you have eternal life*, *v.* 13. These believers may come to know that they have eternal life, and should be quickened, encouraged, and comforted, in the prospect of it. 2. For their confirmation and progress in their holy faith: *And that you may believe on the name of the Son of God* (*v.* 13), may go on believing. Believers must persevere, or they do nothing.

MORTAL SIN (*vv.* 14–17)

Here we have,

I. A privilege belonging to faith in Christ, namely, audience in prayer: *This is the confidence that we have in him, that, if we ask any thing according to his will, he heareth us*, *v.* 14. The Lord Christ emboldens us to come to God in all circumstances, with all our supplications and requests. It is not fit that we should ask what is contrary either to his majesty and glory or to our own good, who are his and dependent on him. And then we may have confidence that the prayer of faith shall be heard in heaven.

II. The advantage accruing to us by such privilege: *If we know that he heareth us, whatsoever we ask, we know that we have the petitions that we desired of him*, *v.* 15. Great are the deliverances, mercies, and

blessings, which the holy petitioner needs.

III. Direction in prayer in reference to the sins of others: *If any man see his brother sin a sin which is not unto death, he shall ask, and he shall give him life for those that sin not unto death. There is a sin unto death: I do not say that he shall pray for it*, *v.* 16. Here we may observe, 1. We ought to pray for others as well as for ourselves. 2. There is a great distinction in the heinousness and guilt of sin: *There is a sin unto death* (*v.* 16), *and there is a sin not unto death*, *v.* 17. (1) *There is a sin unto death.* All sin, as to the merit and legal sentence of it, is unto death. But there is a sin unto death in opposition to such sin as is here said *not to be unto death*. There is therefore, (2) *A sin not unto death.* This surely must include all such sin as by divine or human constitution may consist with life; in the human constitution with temporal or corporal life, in the divine constitution with corporal or with spiritual life. There are sins which, by divine constitution, are inconsistent with spiritual and evangelical life, with spiritual life in the soul and with an evangelical right to life above. Such are total impenitence and unbelief for the present. Final impenitence and unbelief are infallibly to death eternal, as also a blaspheming of the Spirit of God in the testimony that he has given to Christ and his gospel, and a total apostasy from the light and convictive evidence of the truth of the Christian religion. These are sins involving the guilt of everlasting death. Then comes,

IV. The application of the direction for prayer according to the different sorts of sin thus distinguished. The prayer is supposed to be for life: *He shall ask, and he* (God) *shall give them life*. Life is to be asked of God. In the case of a brother's sin, which is not (in the manner already mentioned) unto death, we may in faith and hope pray for him; and particularly for the life and soul and body. But, in case of the sin unto death in the forementioned ways, we have no allowance to pray.

CONCLUSION (*vv.* 18–21)

Here we have,

I. A recapitulation of the privileges and advantages of sound Christian believers. 1. They are secured against sin, against the fulness of its dominion or the fulness of its guilt: *We know that whosoever is born of God* (and the believer in Christ is born of God, *v.* 1) *sinneth not* (*v.* 18). 2. They are fortified against the devil's destructive attempts: *He that is begotten of God keepeth himself,* that is, is enabled to guard himself, *and the wicked one toucheth him not* (*v.* 18), that is, that the wicked one may not touch him, namely, to death. 3. They are on God's side and interest, in opposition to the state of the world: *And we know that we are of God, and the whole world lieth in wickedness, v.* 19. Mankind are divided into two great parties or dominions, that which belongs to God and that which belongs to wickedness or to the wicked one. The Christian believers belong to God. 4. They are enlightened in the knowledge of the true eternal God: "*And we know that the Son of God has come, and has given us an understanding, that we may know him that is true, v.* 20. 5. They have a happy union with God and his Son: "*And we are in him that is true, even* (or and) *in his Son Jesus Christ," v.* 20. The Son leads us to the Father, and we are in both, in the love and favour of both, in covenant and federal alliance with both, in spiritual conjunction with both by the inhabitation and operation of their Spirit: and, that you may know how great a dignity and felicity this is, you must remember that this true one is *the true God and eternal life.* Then we have,

II. The apostle's concluding monition: "*Little children*" (dear children, as it has been interpreted), "*keep yourselves from idols, v.* 21. Since you know the true God, and are in him, let your light and love guard you against all that is advanced in opposition to him, or competition with him. Flee from the false gods of the heathen world. They are not comparable to the God whose you are and whom you serve."

JOHN

SALUTATION (vv. 1–4)

Ancient epistles began, as here, with salutation and good wishes: religion consecrates, as far as may be, old forms, and turns compliments into real expressions of life and love. Here we have, as usually.

I. The saluter, not expressed by name, but by a chosen character: *The elder*.

II. The saluted—a noble Christian matron, and her children: *To the elect lady and her children*. This *lady and her children* are further notified by the respect paid them, and that, 1. By the apostle himself: *Whom I love in the truth*, or in truth, whom I sincerely and heartily love. 2. By all her Christian acquaintance, all the religious who knew her: *And not I only, but also all those that have known the truth*.

III. The salutation, which is indeed an apostolical benediction: *Grace be with you, mercy, and peace, from God the Father and from the Lord Jesus Christ, the Son of the Father, in truth and love, v. 3*. Sacred love pours out blessings upon this honourable Christian family; to those who have shall more be given.

IV. The congratulation upon the prospect of the exemplary behaviour of other children of this excellent lady. Happy parent, who was blessed with such a numerous religious offspring! *I rejoiced greatly that I found of thy children walking in the truth, as we have received commandment from the Father, v. 4*. We see here also the rule of true walking: *the commandment of the Father*. Then is our walk true, our converse right, when it is managed by the word of God.

TRUE LOVE (vv. 5, 6)

We come now more into the design and substance of the epistle; and here we have,

I. The apostle's request: *Now, I beseech thee, lady*.

1. This love is recommended, (1) From the obligation thereto—*the commandment*. Divine command should sway our mind and heart. (2) From the antiquity of the obligation: *Not as though I wrote a new commandment unto thee, but that which we had from the beginning, v. 5*.

2. Then this love is illustrated from the fruitful nature of it: *And this is love, that we walk after his commandments, v. 5*. This is the test of our love to God, our obedience to him.

DECEIVERS (vv. 7–9)

In this principal part of the epistle we find,

I. The ill news communicated to the lady—seducers are abroad: *For many deceivers have entered into the world.* Now here is, 1. The description of the deceiver and his deceit — he *confesses not that Jesus Christ has come in the flesh* (*v.* 7); he brings some error or other concerning the person of the Lord Jesus. 2. The aggravation of the case — such a one is *a deceiver and an antichrist* (*v.* 7); he deludes souls and undermines the glory and kingdom of the Lord Christ.

II. The counsel given to this elect household hereupon. Now care and caution are needful: *Look to yourselves, v.* 8. Two things they must beware of: 1. *That they lose not what they have wrought* (*v.* 8), what they have done or what they have gained. 2. That they lose not their reward, none of it, no portion of that honour, or praise, or glory that they once stood fair for.

III. The reason of the apostle's counsel, and of their care and caution about themselves, which is twofold: 1. The danger and evil of departure from gospel light and revelation; it is in effect and reality a departure from God himself: *Whosoever transgresseth* (transgresseth at this dismal rate), *and abideth not in the doctrine of Christ, hath not God.* 2. The advantage and happiness of firm adherence to Christian truth; it unites us to Christ (the object or subject-matter of that truth), and thereby to the Father also; for they are one.

A WARNING (*vv.* 10–13)

Here, I. Upon due warning given concerning seducers, the apostle gives direction concerning the treatment of such. They are not to be entertained as the ministers of Christ. The Lord Christ will distinguish them from such, and so would he have his disciples. The direction is negative. 1. Support them not. These deceivers might possibly expect the same reception with others, or with the best who came there (as the blind are often bold enough), but the apostle allows it not: "Do not welcome them into your family." 2. Bless not their enterprises: *Neither bid him God speed.* Attend not their service with your prayers and good wishes. Then,

II. Here is the reason of such direction, forbidding the support and patronage of the deceiver: *For he that biddeth him God speed is partaker of his evil deeds.* Favour and affection partake of the sin.

The apostle concludes this letter with an adjournment of many things to personal conference: *Having many things to write unto you I would not write with paper and ink; but I trust to come unto you, and speak face to face, that our joy may be full.* Here it is supposed that some things are better spoken than written.

THE THIRD EPISTLE OF

JOHN

SALUTATION (*vv.* 1, 2)

Here we see, I. The sacred penman
who writes and sends the letter; not
here indeed notified by his name,
but a more general character: *The
elder.*

II. The person saluted and
honoured by the letter. The former
is directed to an elect lady, this to a
choice gentleman; such are worthy
of esteem and value. He is notified,
1. By his name, — *Gaius.* Then, 2. By
the kind expressions of the apostle
to him: *The well-beloved,* and *whom
I love in the truth.*

III. The salutation or greeting,
containing a prayer, introduced by
an affectionate compellation — *Beloved,* thou beloved one in Christ.
Grace and health are two rich companions; grace will improve health,
health will employ grace.

THE FAITHFUL MAN
(*vv.* 3–8)

In these verses we have,

I. The good report that the
apostle had received concerning
this friend of his: *The brethren came
and testified of the truth that is in
thee* (*v.* 3), *who have borne witness
of thy charity before the church,
v.* 6.

II. The report the apostle himself
gives of him, introduced by an
endearing appellation again: *Be-

loved, thou doest faithfully whatsoever thou doest to the brethren, and
to strangers, v.* 5. 1. He was hos-
pitable, good to the brethren, even
to strangers; it was enough to
recommend them to Gaius's house
that they belonged to Christ. 2. He
seems to have been of a catholic
spirit; he could overlook the petty
differences among serious Christians, and be communicative to all
who bore the image and did the
work of Christ. And, 3. He was
conscientious in what he did.

III. The apostle's joy therein, in
the good report itself, and the good
ground of it: *I rejoiced greatly when
the brethren came and testified, &c.,
v.* 3. *I have no greater joy than to
hear that my children walk in the
truth,* in the prescripts of the
Christian religion. The best evidence of our having the truth is our
walking in the truth.

IV. The direction the apostle
gives his friend concerning further
treatment of the brethren that were
with him: *Whom if thou bring forward on their journey, after a godly
sort, thou shalt do well.* It seems to
have been customary in those days
of love to attend travelling ministers and Christians, at least some
part of their road, 1 Cor. xvi. 6.

V. The reasons of this directed
conduct; these are two: 1. *Because
that for his name's sake these
brethren went forth, taking nothing*

495

of the Gentiles. It appears thus that these were ministerial brethren. 2. *We ought therefore to receive such, that we may be fellow-helpers to the truth*, to true religion. The institution of Christ is the true religion; it has been attested by God. Those that are true in it and true to it will earnestly desire, and pray for, and contribute to, its propagation in the world.

A MALICIOUS ENEMY
(*vv.* 9–11)

I. Here is a very different example and character, an officer, a minister in the church, less generous, catholic, and communicative than the private Christians. In reference to this minister, we see,

1. His name—a Gentile name: *Diotrephes*, attended with an unchristian spirit.

2. His temper and spirit—full of pride and ambition: *He loves to have the pre-eminence.*

3. His contempt of the apostle's authority, and letter, and friends. (1) Of his authority: *The deeds which he doeth* contrary to our appointment, *prating against us with malicious words.* Malice and ill-will in the heart will be apt to vent themselves by the lips. The heart and mouth are both to be watched. (2) Of his letter: "*I wrote to the church* (*v.* 9), namely, in recommendation of such and such brethren. *But Diotrephes receiveth us not*, admits not our letter and testimony therein." This seems to be the church of which Gaius was a member. (3) Of his friends, the brethren he recommended: *Neither doth he himself*

receive the brethren, and forbiddeth those that would, and casteth them out of the church, v. 10. Many are cast out of the church who should be received there with satisfaction and welcome. But woe to those who cast out the brethren whom the Lord Christ will take into his own communion and kingdom!

4. The apostle's menace of this proud domineerer: *Wherefore, if I come, I will remember his deeds which he doeth* (*v.* 10), will remember to censure them.

II. Here is counsel upon that different character, dissuasion from copying such a pattern, and indeed any evil at all: *Beloved, follow not that which is evil, but that which is good, v.* 11.

CONCLUSION (*vv.* 12–14)

Here we have, I. The character of another person, one *Demetrius*, not much known otherwise. But here his name will live. It is well for those who are commended when those who commend them can appeal to the consciences of those who knew them most.

II. The conclusion of the epistle, in which we may observe, 1. The referring of some things to personal interview: *I have many things to write, but I will not with ink and pen, but I trust I shall shortly see thee, vv.* 13, 14. 2. The benediction: *Peace be to you*; all felicity attend you. 3. The public salutation sent to Gaius: *Our friends salute thee.* 4. The apostle's particular salutation of the Christians in Gaius's church or vicinity: *Greet the friends by name.*

THE GENERAL EPISTLE OF

JUDE

GREETINGS (vv 1, 2)

Here we have the preface or introduction, in which,

I. We have an account of the penman of this epistle, *Jude*, or *Judas*, or Judah. He was an apostle, a faithful servant of Jesus Christ.

II. We are here informed to whom this epistle is directed; namely, to all those *who are sanctified by God the Father, and preserved in Jesus Christ, and called.*

III. We have the apostolical benediction: *Mercy to you,* &c. From the mercy, peace, and love of God all our comfort flows, all our real enjoyment in this life, all our hope of a better.

BEWARE OF INFILTRATORS (vv. 3–7)

We have here, I. The design of the apostle in writing this epistle to the lately converted Jews and Gentiles; namely, to establish them in the Christian faith. Here observe, 1. The gospel salvation is a common salvation, that is, in a most sincere offer and tender of it to all mankind to whom the notice of it reaches: for so the commission runs (Mark xvi. 15, 16). 2. This common salvation is the subject-matter of the faith of all the saints. It is the faith once, *or at once, once for all, delivered to the saints,* to which nothing can be added, from which nothing

may be detracted, in which nothing more or less should be altered. 3. The apostles and evangelists all wrote to us of this common salvation. 4. Those who preach or write of the common salvation should give all diligence to do it well: they should not allow themselves to offer to God or his people that which costs them nothing, or next to nothing, little or no pains or thought, 2 Sam. xxiv. 24. This were to treat God irreverently, and man unjustly. 5. Those who have received the doctrine of this common salvation must contend earnestly for it. *Earnestly,* not *furiously.* Those who strive for the Christian faith, or in the Christian course, must strive lawfully, or they lose their labour, and run great hazard of losing their crown, 2 Tim. ii. 5.

II. The occasion the apostle had to write to this purport. As evil manners give rise to good laws, so dangerous errors often give just occasion to the proper defence of important truths. Here observe, 1. Ungodly men are the great enemies of the faith of Christ and the peace of the church. 2. Those are *the worst of ungodly men who turn the grace of God into lasciviousness,* who take encouragement to sin more boldly because the grace of God has abounded, and still abounds, so wonderfully, who are hardened in their impieties by the extent and fulness of gospel grace, the design of which is to reduce men from sin, and bring them unto God. 3. Those who turn the grace of God into lasciviousness do in effect *deny the Lord God, and our Lord Jesus Christ*; that is, they deny both natural and revealed religion. 4. Those who turn the grace of God into lasciviousness are ordained unto condemnation. They sin against the last, the greatest, and most perfect remedy; and so are without excuse. 5. We ought to contend earnestly for the faith, in opposition to those who would corrupt or deprave it, such as have *crept in unawares*. Whoever may attempt to corrupt the faith, we ought to contend earnestly against them.

III. The fair warning which the apostle, in Christ's name, gives to those who, having professed his holy religion, do afterwards desert and prove false to it, *vv. 5–7*. We have here a recital of the former judgments of God upon sinners, with design to awaken and terrify those to whom warning is given in this epistle.

Now what are these things which we Christians need to be put in remembrance of?

1. The destruction of the unbelieving Israelites in the wilderness, *v. 5*.

2. We are here put in remembrance of the fall of the angels, *v. 6*. There were a great number of the angels who *left their own habitation*; that is, who were not pleased with the posts and stations the supreme Monarch of the universe had assigned and allotted to them. Thus they quitted their post, and rebelled

against God, their Creator and sovereign Lord. But God did not spare them (high and great as they were). There is, undoubtedly there is, a judgment to come; the fallen angels are *reserved to the judgment of the great day*; and shall fallen men escape it? Surely not.

3. The apostle here calls to our remembrance the destruction of Sodom and Gomorrah, *v. 7. Even as*, &c. Their ruin is a particular warning to all people to take heed of, and fly *from, fleshly lusts that war against the soul*, 1 Pet. ii. 11.

WARNINGS FROM THE PAST
(*vv. 8–15*)

The apostle here exhibits a charge against deceivers who were now seducing the disciples of Christ from the profession and practice of his holy religion. Here,

I. The character of these deceivers is described.

1. They *defile the flesh*. The flesh or body is the immediate seat, and often the irritating occasion, of many horrid pollutions.

2. They *despise dominion, and speak evil of dignities*, are of a disturbed mind and a seditious spirit, forgetting that *the powers that be are ordained of God*, Rom. xiii. 1.

On this occasion the apostle brings in *Michael the archangel*, &c., *v. 9*. Interpreters are at a loss what is here meant by *the body of Moses*. Some think that the devil contended that Moses might have a public and honourable funeral, that the place where he was interred might be generally known, hoping thereby to draw the Jews, so naturally prone thereto, to a new and fresh instance of idolatry. Dr.

Scott thinks that by the body of Moses we are to understand the Jewish church, whose destruction the devil strove and contended for, as the Christian church is called the body of Christ in the New-Testament style. Others bring other interpretations, which I will not here trouble the reader with. Though this contest was mightily eager and earnest, and Michael was victorious in the issue, yet he would not *bring a railing accusation against the devil himself*; he knew a good cause needed no such weapons to be employed in its defence. Truth needs no supports from falsehood or scurrility. So the lesson hence is that we ought to stand up in defence of those whom God owns, how severe soever Satan and his instruments may be in their censures of them and their conduct.

3. *They speak evil of the things which they know not*, &c., *v.* 10. Observe, Those who speak evil of religion and godliness *speak evil of the things which they know not*; for, if they had known them, they would have spoken well of them.

4. In *v.* 11 the apostle represents them as followers *of Cain*, and in *vv.* 12, 13, as atheistical and profane people, who thought little, and perhaps believed not much, of God or a future world—as greedy and covetous, who, so they could but gain present worldly advantages, cared not what came next—rebels against God and man, who, like Core, ran into attempts in which they must assuredly perish, as he did. Of such the apostle further says, (1) *These are spots in your feasts of charity*—the *love-feasts*, so much spoken of by the ancients.

They happened, by whatever means or mischance, to be admitted among them, but were spots in them, defiled and defiling. (2) *When they feast with you, they feed themselves without fear*. Arrant gluttons, no doubt, they were; such as minded only the gratifying of their appetites with the daintiness and abundance of their fare; they had no regard to Solomon's caution, Prov. xxiii. 2. (3) *Clouds they are without water*, which promise rain in time of drought, but perform nothing of what they promise. (4) *Trees whose fruit withereth*, &c. Trees they are, for they are planted in the Lord's vineyard, yet fruitless ones. (5) *Raging waves of the sea*, boisterous, noisy, and clamorous; full of talk and turbulency, but with little (if any) sense or meaning. (6) *Wandering stars*, planets that are erratic in their motions, keep not that steady regular course which the fixed ones do, but shift their stations, that one has sometimes much ado to know where to find them.

II. The doom of this wicked people is declared: *To whom is reserved the blackness of darkness for ever.*

Of the prophecy of Enoch (*vv.* 14, 15) we have no mention made in any other part or place of scripture; yet now it is scripture that there was such prophecy. Observe, 1. Christ's coming to judgment was prophesied of as early as the middle of the patriarchal age, and was therefore even then a received and acknowledged truth.—*The Lord cometh with* his holy myriads, including both angels and the spirits of just men made perfect.

2. It was spoken of then, so long ago, as a thing just at hand.

ENCOURAGEMENT
(vv. 16–25)

Here, I. The apostle enlarges further on the character of these evil men and seducers: they *are murmurers, complainers*, &c., *v.* 16. Observe, A murmuring complaining temper, indulged and expressed, lays men under a very bad character; such are very weak at least, and for the most part very wicked.

II. He proceeds to caution and exhort those to whom he is writing, *vv.* 17–23. Here,

1. He calls them to remember how they had been forewarned: *But, beloved, remember*, &c., *v.* 17.

2. He guards them against seducers by a further description of their odious character: *These are those who separate*, &c., *v.* 19. Observe, (1) Sensualists are the worst separatists. They separate themselves from God, and Christ, and his church, to the devil, the world, and the flesh, by their ungodly courses and vicious practices. (2) Sensual men have not the Spirit, that is, of God and Christ, the Spirit of holiness, which whoever *has not, is none of Christ's*, does not belong to him, Rom. viii. 9. (3) The worse others are the better should we endeavour and approve ourselves to be.

3. He exhorts them to persevering constancy in truth and holiness.

(1) *Building up yourselves in your most holy faith, v.* 20. Observe, The way to hold fast our profession is to hold on in it. Having laid our foundation well in a sound faith,

and a sincere upright heart, we must build upon it, make further progress continually.

(2) *Praying in the Holy Ghost.* Observe, [1] Prayer is the nurse of faith; the way to *build up ourselves in our most holy faith* is to *continue instant in prayer*, Rom. xii. 12. [2] Our prayers are then most likely to prevail when we *pray in the Holy Ghost*, that is, under his guidance and influence.

(3) *Keep yourselves in the love of God, v.* 21. [1] "Keep up the grace of love to God in its lively vigorous actings and exercises in your souls." [2] "Take heed of throwing yourselves out of the love of God to you, or its delightful, cheering, strengthening manifestations; keep yourselves in the way of God, if you would continue in his love."

(4) *Looking for the mercy*, &c. [1] Eternal life is to be looked for only through *mercy*; mercy is our only plea, not merit. [2] It is said, not only through the mercy of God as our Creator, but through the mercy *of our Lord Jesus Christ* as Redeemer; all who come to heaven must come thither through our Lord Jesus Christ. [3] A believing expectation of eternal life will arm us against the snares of sin (2 Pet. iii. 14); a lively faith of the blessed hope will help us to mortify our cursed lusts.

4. He directs them how to behave towards erring brethren: *And of some have compassion*, &c., *vv.* 22, 23. Observe, (1) We ought to do all we can to rescue others out of the snare of the devil, that they may be saved from (or recovered, when entangled therein, out of) dangerous errors, or pernicious

practices. (2) This must be done with *compassion, making a difference.* How is that? We must distinguish between the weak and the wilful. *Others save with fear,* urging upon them *the terrors of the Lord. Hating even the garment spotted with the flesh,* that is, keeping yourselves at the utmost distance from what is or appears evil, and designing and endeavouring that others may do so too.

III. The apostle concludes this epistle with a solemn ascription of glory to the great God, *vv.* 24, 25. Note, 1. Whatever is the subject or argument we have been treating of, ascribing glory to God is fittest for us to conclude with. 2. God is able, and he is as willing as able, *to keep us from falling, and to present us faultless before the presence of his glory*; not as those who never have been faulty, but as those whose faults shall not be imputed, to their ruin, which, but for God's mercy and a Saviour's merits they might most justly have been.

THE

REVELATION OF ST. JOHN

THE DIVINE

CHAPTER ONE
THE FAITHFUL WITNESS
(vv. 1–8)

Our Lord Jesus is the great trustee of divine revelation; it is to him that we owe the knowledge we have of what we are to expect from God and what he expects from us. This revelation Christ *sent and signified by his angel*. Observe here the admirable order of divine revelation. God gave it to Christ, and Christ employed an angel to communicate it to the churches. The angels *signified it to the apostle John*. John was the apostle chosen for this service. Some think he was the only one surviving, the rest having sealed their testimony with their blood. This was to be the last book of divine revelation; and therefore notified to the church by the last of the apostles. John was the beloved disciple.

The evangelists give us an account of the things that are past; prophecy gives us an account of things to come. These future events are shown, not in the clearest light in which God could have set them, but in such a light as he saw most proper, and which would best answer his wise and holy purposes. We have in this revelation a general idea of the methods of divine providence and government in and about the church, and many good lessons may be learned hereby. These events (it is said) were such as should come to pass not only *surely*, but *shortly*; that is, they would begin to come to pass very shortly, and the whole would be accomplished in a short time. For now the last ages of the world had come.

We have here an apostolic benediction on those who should give a due regard to this divine revelation; and this benediction is given more generally and more especially.

I. More generally, to all who either read or hear the words of the prophecy.

II. The apostolic benediction is pronounced more especially and particularly to the seven Asian churches, *v.* 4. These seven churches are named in *v.* 11, and distinct messages sent to each of them respectively in the chapters following. Observe the particular account we have here of Christ, *v.* 5. [1] He *is the faithful witness*; he was from eternity a witness to all the counsels of God (John i. 18), and he was in time a faithful witness to the revealed will of God, who has now spoken to us by his Son. [2] He is the first-begotten or first-born from the dead, or the first parent

502

and head of the resurrection. [3] He is the prince of the kings of the earth. This is good news to the church, and it is good evidence of the Godhead of Christ, who is King of kings and Lord of lords. [4] He is the great friend of his church and people. He has loved them, and, in pursuance of that everlasting love, he has, *First, Washed them from their sins in his own blood.* Sins leave a stain upon the soul, a stain of guilt and of pollution. Nothing can fetch out this stain but the blood of Christ. *Secondly,* He has *made them kings and priests to God and his Father.* Having justified and sanctified them, he makes them kings to his Father; that is, in his Father's account, with his approbation, and for his glory. He hath made them priests, given them access to God, enabled them to enter into the holiest and to offer spiritual and acceptable sacrifices, and has given them an unction suitable to this character; and for these high honours and favours they are bound to ascribe to him dominion and glory for ever. [5] He will be the Judge of the world: *Behold, he cometh, and every eye shall see him, v.* 7. This book, the Revelation, begins and ends with a prediction of the second coming of the Lord Jesus Christ. He will come publicly: *Every eye shall see him,* the eye of his people, the eye of his enemies, every eye, yours and mine. [6] This account of Christ is ratified and confirmed by himself, *v.* 8. Here our Lord Jesus justly challenges the same honour and power that is ascribed to the Father, *v.* 4. He is the beginning and the end; all

things are from him and for him; he is the Almighty; he is the same eternal and unchangeable one. And surely whoever presumes to blot out one character of this name of Christ deserves to have his name blotted out of the book of life. Those that honour him he will honour; but those who despise him shall be lightly esteemed.

VISION OF CHRIST (*vv.* 9–20)

We have now come to that glorious vision which the apostle had of the Lord Jesus Christ, when he came to deliver this revelation to him, where observe,

I. The account given of the person who was favoured with this vision. He describes himself, 1. By his present state and condition. He was *the brother and companion of these churches in tribulation, and in the kingdom and patience of Christ.* He was, at their time, as the rest of true Christians were, a persecuted man, banished, and perhaps imprisoned, for his adherence to Christ. 2. By the place where he was when he was favoured with this vision: he was in *the isle Patmos.* 3. The day and time in which he had this vision: it was *the Lord's day,* the day which Christ had separated and set apart for himself, as the eucharist is called *the Lord's supper.* Surely this can be no other than the Christian sabbath, the first day of the week, to be observed in remembrance of the resurrection of Christ. 4. The frame that his soul was in at this time: *He was in the Spirit.* He was not only in a rapture when he received the vision, but before he received it; he was in a serious, heavenly, spiritual frame, under the blessed gracious influences of the Spirit of God. God usually prepares the souls of his people for uncommon manifestations of himself, by the quickening sanctifying influences of his good Spirit.

II. The apostle gives an account of what he heard when thus in the Spirit. An alarm was given as with the sound of a trumpet, and then *he heard a voice*, the voice of Christ applying to himself the character before given, *the first and the last*, and commanding the apostle to commit to writing the things that were now to be revealed to him, and to send it immediately *to the seven Asian churches*, whose names are mentioned.

III. We have also an account of what he saw. *He turned to see the voice*, whose it was and whence it came; and then a wonderful scene of vision opened itself to him.

1. He saw a representation of the church under the emblem of *seven golden candlesticks*, as it is explained in the last verse of the chapter. The churches are compared to candlesticks, because they hold forth the light of the gospel to advantage.

2. He saw a representation of the Lord Jesus Christ in the midst of the golden candlesticks; for he has promised to be with his churches always to the end of the world, filling them with light, and life, and love, for he is the very animating informing soul of the church. And here we observe,

(1) The glorious form in which Christ appeared in several particulars. [1] He was *clothed with a garment down to the foot*, a princely and priestly robe, denoting righteousness and honour. [2] *He was girt about with a golden girdle*, the breast-plate of the high priest, on which the names of his people are engraven; he was ready girt to do all the work of a Redeemer. [3] *His head and hairs were white like wool or snow.* He was the Ancient of days; his hoary head was no sign of decay, but was indeed a crown of glory. [4] *His eyes were as a flame of fire*, piercing and penetrating into the very hearts and reins of men, scattering terrors among his adversaries. [5] *His feet were like unto fine burning brass*, strong and stedfast, supporting his own interest, subduing his enemies, and treading them to powder. [6] *His voice was as the sound of many waters*, of many rivers falling in together. He can and will make himself heard to those who are afar off as well as to those who are near. [7] *He had in his right hand seven stars*, that is, the ministers of the seven churches, who are under his direction, have all their light and influence from him, and are secured and preserved by him. [8] *Out of his mouth went a two-edged sword*, his word, which both wounds and heals, strikes at sins on the right hand and on the left, [9] *His countenance was as the sun shining*, its strength too bright and dazzling for mortal eyes to behold.

(2) The impression this appearance of Christ made upon the apostle John (*v.* 17): *He fell at the feet of Christ as dead*; he was overpowered with the greatness of the lustre and glory in which Christ appeared.

He laid his hand upon him, v. 17. He raised him up; he did not plead against him with his great power, but he put strength into him, he spoke kind words to him. And here he acquaints him, *First,* With his divine nature: *The first and the last. Secondly,* With his former sufferings: *I was dead;* the very same that his disciples saw upon the cross dying for the sins of men. *Thirdly,* With his resurrection and life: *"I live, and am alive for evermore,* have conquered death and opened the grave, and am partaker of an endless life." *Fourthly,* With his office and authority: *I have the keys of hell and of death,* a sovereign dominion in and over the invisible world. *Fifthly,* With his will and pleasure: *Write the things which thou hast seen, and the things which are, and which shall be hereafter. Sixthly,* With the meaning of the seven stars, that *they are the ministers of the churches;* and of the seven candlesticks, that *they are the seven churches,* to whom Christ would now send by him particular and proper messages.

CHAPTER TWO
MESSAGE FOR EPHESUS
(vv. 1–7)

We have here,

I. The inscription, where observe, 1. To whom the first of these epistles is directed: *To the church of Ephesus,* a famous church planted by the apostle Paul (Acts xix.), and afterwards watered and governed by John, who had his residence very much there.

II. The contents of the epistle, in which, as in most of those that follow, we have,

1. The commendation Christ gave this church, ministers and members, which he always brings in by declaring that he knows their works, and therefore both his commendation and reprehension are to be strictly regarded; for he does not in either speak at a venture: he knows what he says. Now the church of Ephesus is commended, (1) For their diligence in duty: *I know thy works, and thy labour, v.* 2. (2) For their patience in suffering: *Thy labour and thy patience, v.* 2. It is not enough that we be diligent, but we must be patient, and endure hardness as good soldiers of Christ. (3) For their zeal against what was evil: *Thou canst not bear those that are evil, v.* 2.

2. The rebuke given to this church: *Nevertheless, I have somewhat against thee, v.* 4. The sin that Christ charged this church with was their decay and declension in holy love and zeal: *Thou hast left thy first love;* not left and forsaken the object of it, but lost the fervent degree of it that at first appeared.

3. The advice and counsel given them from Christ: *Remember therefore whence thou hast fallen, and repent,* &c. (1) Those that have lost their first love *must remember whence they have fallen;* they must compare their present with their former state, and consider how much better it was with them then than now. (2) They must repent. They must be inwardly grieved and ashamed for their sinful declension and judge and condemn themselves for it. (3) They must return and do their first works. They must

endeavour to revive and recover their first zeal, tenderness, and seriousness, and must pray as earnestly, and watch as diligently, as they did when they first set out in the ways of God.

4. This good advice is enforced and urged, (1) By a severe threatening, if it should be neglected: *I will come unto thee quickly, and remove thy candlestick out of its place.* (2) By an encouraging mention that is made of what was yet good among them: *This thou hast, that thou hatest the deeds of the Nicolaitans, which I also hate,* v. 6. The Nicolaitans were a loose sect who sheltered themselves under the name of Christianity. They held hateful doctrines, and they were guilty of hateful deeds, hateful to Christ and to all true Christians; and it is mentioned to the praise of the church of Ephesus that they had a just zeal and abhorrence of those wicked doctrines and practices.

III. We have the conclusion of this epistle, in which, as in those that follow, we have,

1. A call to attention: *He that hath an ear, let him hear what the Spirit saith unto the churches.*

2. A promise of great mercy to those who overcome.

SMYRNA (*vv.* 8–11)

We now proceed to the second epistle sent to another of the Asian churches, where, as before, observe,

I. The superscription, telling us to whom it was more expressly and immediately directed: *To the angel of the church in Smyrna,* a place well known at this day by our merchants, a city of great trade and wealth,

perhaps the only city of all the seven that is still known by the same name.

II. The subject-matter of this epistle to Smyrna, where, after the common declaration of Christ's omniscience, and the perfect cognizance he has of all the works of men and especially of his churches, he takes notice,

1. Of the improvement they had made in their spiritual state. This comes in in a short parenthesis; yet it is very emphatic: *But thou art rich* (v. 9), poor in temporals, but rich in spirituals—poor in spirit, and yet rich in grace.

2. Of their sufferings: *I know thy tribulation and thy poverty*—the persecution they underwent, even to the spoiling of their goods.

3. He knows the wickedness and the falsehood of their enemies: *I know the blasphemy of those that say they are Jews, but are not*; that is, of those who pretend to be the only peculiar covenant-people of God, as the Jews boasted themselves to be, even after God had rejected them; or of those who would be setting up the Jewish rites and ceremonies, which were now not only antiquated, but abrogated; these may say that they only are the church of God in the world, when indeed *they are the synagogue of Satan.*

4. He foreknows the future trials of his people, and forewarns them of them, and fore-arms them against them. (1) He forewarns them of future trials: *The devil shall cast some of you into prison, and you shall have tribulation,* v. 10. (2) Christ fore-arms them against these approaching troubles, [1] By his

counsel: *Fear none of these things.*
[2] By showing them how their
sufferings would be alleviated and
limited. *First,* They should not be
universal. It would be some of
them, not all, who should be cast
into prison, those who were best
able to bear it and might expect to
be visited and comforted by the
rest. *Secondly,* They were not to be
perpetual, but for a set time, and a
short time: *Ten days.* It should not
be everlasting tribulation. *Thirdly,*
It should be to try them, not to
destroy them, that their faith, and
patience, and courage, might be
proved and improved, and be found
to honour and glory. [3] By proposing and promising a glorious
reward to their fidelity: *Be thou
faithful to death, and I will give thee
a crown of life.* The life so worn out
in his service, or laid down in his
cause, shall be rewarded with
another and a much better life that
shall be eternal.

III. The conclusion of this message, and that, as before, 1. With a
call to universal attention, that all
men, all the world, should hear
what passes between Christ and his
churches. 2. With a gracious
promise to the conquering Christian: *He that overcometh shall not
be hurt of the second death,* v. 11.
The second death shall have no
power over those who are *partakers
of the first resurrection*: the first
death shall not hurt them, and the
second death shall have no power
over them.

PERGAMOS (vv. 12–17)

Here also we are to consider,

I. To whom it was sent: *To the
angel of the church of Pergamos.*

Whether this was a city raised up
out of the ruins of old Troy, or
some other city of the same name,
is neither certain nor material. It
was a place where Christ had called
and constituted a gospel church, by
the preaching of the gospel and the
grace of his Spirit making the word
effectual. The church of Pergamos
was infested with men of corrupt
minds, who did what they could to
corrupt both the faith and manners
of the church; and Christ, being
resolved to fight against them by
the sword of his word, takes the
title of him that *hath the sharp
sword with two edges.*

II. From the inscription we
proceed to the contents of the
epistle, in which the method is
much the same as is observed in the
rest. Here,

1. Christ takes notice of the trials
and difficulties this church encountered with: *I know thy works,
and where thou dwellest,* &c. v. 13.
Some think that the Roman
governor in this city was a most
violent enemy to the Christians;
and the seat of persecution is
Satan's seat.

2. He commends their stedfastness: *Thou holdest fast my name,
and hast not denied my faith.* These
two expressions are much the same
in sense; the former may, however,
signify the effect and the latter the
cause or means.

3. He reproves them for their
sinful failures (v. 14): *But I have a
few things against thee, because thou
hast there those that hold the doctrine of Balaam,* &c., and *those that
hold the doctrine of the Nicolaitans,
which thing I hate.* There were some
who taught that it was lawful to eat

things sacrificed to idols, and that simple fornication was no sin; they, by an impure worship, drew men into impure practices, as Balaam did the Israelites.

4. He calls them to repentance: *Repent, or else I will come unto thee quickly,* &c., v. 16. The word of God will take hold of sinners, sooner or later, either for their conviction or their confusion.

III. We have the conclusion of this epistle, where, after the usual demand of universal attention, there is the promise of great favour to those that overcome. They shall *eat of the hidden manna, and have the new name, and the white stone, which no man knoweth, saving he that receiveth it,* v. 17. The stone alludes to the ancient custom of giving a white stone to those acquitted on trial and a black stone to those condemned.

THYATIRA (*vv.* 18–29)

I. To whom it is directed: *To the angel of the church of Thyatira,* a city of the proconsular Asia, bordering upon Mysia on the north and Lydia on the south, a town of trade. *The Son of God* is here described as having *eyes like a flame of fire, and feet like as fine brass.* His general title is here, *the Son of God,* that is, the eternal and only-begotten Son of God. The description we have here of him is in two characters: (1) That his eyes are like a flame of fire, signifying his piercing, penetrating, perfect knowledge. (2) That his feet are like fine brass, that the outgoings of his providence are steady, awful, and all pure and holy.

II. The contents or subject-matter

of this epistle, which, as the rest, includes,

1. The honourable character and commendation Christ gives of this church. Now in this church Christ makes honourable mention, (1) Of their *charity,* either more general, a disposition to do good to all men, or more special, to the household of faith: there is no religion where there is no charity. (2) Their *service,* their ministration; this respects chiefly the officers of the church, who had laboured in the word and doctrine. (3) Their *faith,* which was the grace that actuated all the rest, both their charity and their service. (4) Their *patience.* (5) Their growing fruitfulness: their last works were better than the first.

2. A faithful reproof for what was amiss. This is not so directly charged upon the church itself as upon some wicked seducers who were among them; the church's fault was that she connived too much at them.

(1) These wicked seducers are compared to Jezebel, and called by her name. The sin of these seducers was that they attempted to draw the servants of God into fornication, and to offer sacrifices to idols.

(2) Now why should the wickedness of this Jezebel be charged upon the church of Thyatira? Because that church suffered her to seduce the people of that city. But how could the church help it? They had not, as a church, civil power to banish or imprison her; but they had ministerial power to censure and to excommunicate her: and it is probable that neglecting to use the power they had made them sharers in her sin.

3. The punishment of this seducer, this Jezebel, *vv.* 22, 23, in which is couched a prediction of the fall of Babylon. (1) *I will cast her into a bed*, into a bed of pain. (2) *I will kill her children with death*; that is, the second death, which does the work effectually, and leaves no hope of future life.

4. The design of Christ in the destruction of these wicked seducers, and this was the instruction of others, especially of his churches.

5. The encouragement given to those who keep themselves pure and undefiled: *But to you I say, and unto the rest*, &c., *v.* 24. Christ is coming to put an end to all the temptations of his people; and, if they hold fast faith and a good conscience till he come, all the difficulty and danger will be over.

III. We now come to the conclusion of this message, *vv.* 26–29. Here we have, 1. The promise of an ample reward to the persevering victorious believer, in two parts: (1) Very great power and dominion over the rest of the world: *Power over the nations*, which may refer either to the time when the empire should turn Christian, or to the other world, when believers shall sit down with Christ on his throne of judgment. (2) Knowledge and wisdom, suitable to such power and dominion: *I will give him the morning-star*. Christ is the morning-star. He brings day with him into the soul, the light of grace and of glory; and he will give his people that perfection of light and wisdom. 2. This epistle ends with the usual demand of attention: *He that hath an ear let him hear what the Spirit saith unto the churches.*

CHAPTER THREE

THE CHURCH OF SARDIS
(*vv.* 1–6)

Here is, I. To whom this letter is directed: *To the angel of the church of Sardis*, an ancient city of Lydia, on the banks of the mountain Tmolus, said to have been the chief city of Asia the Less, and the first city in that part of the world that was converted by the preaching of John; and, some say, the first that revolted from Christianity, and one of the first that was laid in its ruins, in which it still lies, without any church or ministry. The Lord Jesus here assumes the character of him *that hath the seven spirits of God, and the seven stars*, taken out of *ch.* i. 4, where *the seven spirits are said to be before the throne.*

II. The body of this epistle. There is this observable in it, that whereas in the other epistles Christ begins with commending what is good in the churches, and then proceeds to tell them what is amiss, in this (and in the epistle to Laodicea) he begins,

1. With a reproof, and a very severe one: *I know thy works, that thou hast a name that thou livest, and art dead.* Hypocrisy, and a lamentable decay in religion, are the sins charged upon this church, by one who knew her well, and all her works.

2. Our Lord proceeds to give this degenerate church the best advice: *Be watchful, and strengthen the things*, &c., *v.* 2. (1) He advises them to be upon their watch. The cause of their sinful deadness and declension was that they had let down their watch. (2) To strengthen

the things that remain, and that are ready to die. Some understand this of persons; there were some few who had retained their integrity, but they were in danger of declining with the rest. Or it may be understood of practices, as it follows: *I have not found thy works perfect before God*, not filled up; there is something wanting in them. (3) To recollect themselves, and *remember how they have received and heard* (*v.* 3); not only to remember what they had received and heard, but how they had received and heard, what impressions the mercies of God had made upon their souls at first. (4) To hold fast what they had received, that they might not lose all, *and repent* sincerely that they had lost so much of the life of religion, and had run the risk of losing all.

3. Christ enforces his counsel with a dreadful threatening in case it should be despised: *I will come unto thee as a thief, and thou shalt not know the hour, v.* 3.

4. Our blessed Lord does not leave this sinful people without some comfort and encouragement: *In the midst of judgment he remembers mercy* (*v.* 4), and here, (1) He makes honourable mention of the faithful remnant in Sardis, though but small. (2) He makes a very gracious promise to them: *They shall walk with me in white, for they are worthy*—in the *stola*, the white robes of justification, and adoption, and comfort, or in the white robes of honour and glory in the other world.

III. We now come to the conclusion of this epistle, in which, as before, we have,

1. A great reward promised to the conquering Christian (*v.* 5), and it is very much the same with what has been already mentioned: *He that overcometh shall be clothed in white raiment*. Now to this is added another promise very suitable to the case: *I will not blot his name out of the book of life, but will confess his name before my Father, and before his angels.*

2. The demand of universal attention finishes the message.

PHILADELPHIA (*vv.* 7–13)

Observe,

I. For whom the letter was more immediately designed: *The angel of the church of Philadelphia*; this also was a city in Asia Minor, seated upon the borders of Mysia and Lydia, and had its name from that brotherly love for which it was eminent.

2. By whom this letter was signed; even by the same Jesus who is alone the universal head of all the churches; and here observe by what title he chooses to represent himself to this church: *He that is holy, he that is true, he that hath the key of David*, &c. Observe, (1) The acts of his government. [1] He opens. He opens a door of opportunity to his churches; he opens a door of utterance to his ministers; he opens a door of entrance, opens the heart; he opens a door of admission into the visible church, laying down the terms of communion; and he opens the door of admission into the church triumphant, according to the terms of salvation fixed by him. [2] He shuts the door. When he pleases, he shuts the door of opportunity and the

door of utterance, and leaves obstinate sinners shut up in the hardness of their hearts; he shuts the door of church-fellowship against unbelievers and profane persons; and he shuts the door of heaven against the foolish virgins who have slept away their day of grace, and against the workers of iniquity, how vain and confident soever they may be. (2) The way and manner in which he performs these acts, and that is absolute sovereignty, independent upon the will of men, and irresistible by the power of men.

II. The subject-matter of this epistle, where,

1. Christ puts them in mind of what he had done for them: *I have set before thee an open door, and no man can shut it, v.* 8. I have set it open, though there be many adversaries.

2. This church is commended: *Thou hast a little strength, and hast kept my word, and hast not denied my name, v.* 8. In this there seems to be couched a gentle reproof. True grace, though weak, has the divine approbation; but, though Christ accepts a little strength, yet believers should not rest satisfied in a little, but should strive to grow in grace, to be *strong in faith, giving glory to God.*

3. Here is a promise of the great favour God would bestow on this church, *vv.* 9, 10. This favour consists in two things:

(1) Christ would make this church's enemies subject to her. [1] Those enemies are described to be such as *said they were Jews,* but lied in saying so—pretended to be the only and peculiar people of

God, but were really *the synagogue of Satan.* [2] Their subjection to the church is described: *They shall worship at thy feet;* not pay a religious and divine honour to the church itself, nor to the ministry of it, but shall be convinced that they have been in the wrong, that this church is in the right and is beloved of Christ.

(2) Another instance of favour that Christ promises to this church is persevering grace in the most trying times (*v.* 10), and this as the reward of their past fidelity. *To him that hath shall be given.*

4. Christ calls the church to that duty which he before promised he would enable her to do, and that is, to persevere, *to hold fast that which she had.*

III. The conclusion of this epistle, *vv.* 12, 13. Here,

1. After his usual manner, our Saviour promises a glorious reward to the victorious believer, in two things: (1) He shall be a monumental *pillar in the temple of God;* not a pillar to support the temple (heaven needs no such props), but a monument of the free and powerful grace of God. (2) On this monumental pillar there shall be an honourable inscription, as in those cases is usual.

2. The epistle is closed up with the demand of attention: *He that hath an ear, let him hear what the Spirit saith unto the churches,* how Christ loves and values his faithful people, how he commends, and how he will crown their fidelity.

LAODICEA (*vv.* 14–22)

We now come to the last and worst of all the seven Asian churches, the reverse of the church of Philadelphia; for, as there was nothing reproved in that, here is nothing commended in this, and yet this was one of *the seven golden candlesticks*, for a corrupt church may still be a church. Here we have, as before,

I. To whom: *To the angel of the church of Laodicea*. This was a once famous city near the river Lycus, had a wall of vast compass, and three marble theatres, and, like Rome, was built on seven hills. 2. From whom this message was sent. Here our Lord Jesus styles himself *the Amen, the faithful and true witness, the beginning of the creation of God. The beginning of the creation of God*, either of the first creation, and so he is the beginning, that is, the first cause, the Creator, and the Governor of it; or of the second creation, the church; and so he is the head of that body, the first-born from the dead, as it is in *ch.* i. 5, whence these titles are taken.

II. The subject-matter, in which observe,

1. The heavy charge drawn up against this church, ministers and people, by one who knew them better than they knew themselves: *Thou art neither cold nor hot*, but worse than either; *I would thou wert cold or hot, v.* 15. Lukewarmness or indifference in religion is the worst temper in the world. If religion is a real thing, it is the most excellent thing, and therefore we should be in good earnest in it.

2. A severe punishment threatened: *I will spue thee out of my mouth.* He is sick of them, and cannot long bear them.

3. We have one cause of this

indifference and inconsistency in religion assigned, and that is self-conceitedness or self-delusion. They thought they were very well already, and therefore they were very indifferent whether they grew better or no: *Because thou sayest, I am rich, and increased with goods*, &c., *v.* 17.

4. We have good counsel given by Christ to this sinful people, and that is that they drop their vain and false opinion they had of themselves, and endeavour to be that really which they would seem to be: *I counsel thee to buy of me*, &c., *v.* 18. How can those that are poor buy gold? Just as they may buy of Christ wine and milk, that is, *without money and without price*, Isa. lv. 1. These people were naked; Christ tells them where they might have clothing, and such as would cover the shame of their nakedness. They were blind; and he *counsels them to buy of him eye-salve, that they might see*, to give up their own wisdom and reason, which are but blindness in the things of God, and resign themselves to his word and Spirit, and their eyes shall be opened to see their way and their end, their duty and their true interest.

5. Here is added great and gracious encouragement to this sinful people to take the admonition and advice well that Christ had given them, *vv.* 19, 20. He tells them, (1) It was given them in true and tender affection: "*Whom I love, I rebuke and chasten.*" (2) If they would comply with his admonitions, he was ready to make them good to their souls: *Behold, I stand at the door and knock*, &c., *v.* 20. Here observe, [1] Christ is gra-

ciously pleased by his word and Spirit to come to the door in the heart of sinners; he draws near to them in a way of mercy, ready to make them a kind visit. [2] He finds this door shut against him; the heart of man is by nature shut up against Christ by ignorance, unbelief, sinful prejudices. [3] When he finds the heart shut, he does not immediately withdraw, but he waits to be gracious. [4] He uses all proper means to awaken sinners, and to cause them to open to him: he calls by his word, he knocks by the impulses of his Spirit upon their conscience. [5] Those who open to him shall enjoy his presence, to their great comfort and advantage.

III. We now come to the conclusion of this epistle; and here we have as before,

1. The promise made to the overcoming believer. *They shall sit down with me on my throne, as I also overcame, and have sat down with my Father on his throne, v.* 21.

2. All is closed up with the general demand of attention (*v.* 22). Thus end the messages of Christ to the Asian churches, the epistolary part of this book. We now come to the prophetical part.

CHAPTER FOUR

VISION OF HEAVEN (*vv.* 1–8)

We have here an account of a second vision with which the apostle John was favoured. Observe,

I. The preparation made for the apostle's having this vision.

1. *A door was opened in heaven.* Hence we learn, (1) Whatever is transacted on earth is first designed and settled in heaven. (2) We can know nothing of future events but what God is pleased to discover to us. But, (3) So far as God reveals his designs to us we may and ought to receive them, and not pretend to be wise above what is revealed.

2. To prepare John for the vision, a trumpet was sounded, and he was called up into heaven, to have a sight there of the things which were to be hereafter. He was called into the third heavens.

3. To prepare for this vision, *the apostle was in the Spirit.* He was in a rapture, as before (*ch.* i. 10), whether in the body or out of the body we cannot tell. Now observe,

II. The vision itself. It begins with the strange sights that the apostle saw, and they were such as these: 1. He saw *a throne set in heaven,* the seat of honour, and authority, and judgment. 2. He saw a glorious one upon the throne. This throne was not empty; there was one in it who filled it, and that was God, who is here described by those things that are most pleasant and precious in our world: *His countenance was like a jasper and a sardine-stone;* he is not described by any human features, so as to be represented by an image, but only by his transcendant brightness. 3. He saw *a rainbow about the throne, like unto an emerald, v.* 3. The rainbow was the seal and token of the covenant of providence that God made with Noah and his posterity with him, and is a fit emblem of that covenant of promise that God had made with Christ as the head of the church. 4. He saw *four-and-twenty seats* round about the throne, not empty, but filled with *four-and-twenty elders*, presbyters, representing, very probably, the whole church of God, both in the Old-Testament and in the New-Testament state. *They are clothed in white raiment*, the righteousness of the saints, both imputed and inherent; *they had on their heads crowns of gold*, signifying the honour and authority given them of God, and the glory they have with him. 5. He perceived lightnings and voices proceeding out of the throne; that is, the awful declarations that God makes to his church of his sovereign will and pleasure. 6. He saw *seven lamps of fire burning before the throne*, which are explained to be *the seven Spirits of God* (*v.* 5), the various gifts, graces, and operations of the Spirit of God in the churches of Christ. 7. He saw *before the throne a sea of glass, like unto crystal*. In the gospel church the sea or laver for purification is the blood of the Lord Jesus Christ, who cleanses from all sin, even from sanctuary-sins. In this all those must be washed that are admitted into the gracious presence of God on earth or his glorious presence in heaven. 8. He saw *four animals*, living creatures, between the throne and the circle of the elders (as seems most probable), standing between God and the people; these seem to signify the ministers of the gospel.

WORSHIP IN HEAVEN
(*vv.* 8–11)

We have considered the sights that the apostle saw in heaven: now let us observe the songs that he heard.

I. He heard the song of the four living creatures, of the ministers of the church, which refers to the prophet Isaiah's vision, *ch.* vi. And here, 1. They adore one God, and one only, *the Lord God Almighty*, unchangeable and everlasting. 2. They adore three holies in this one God, the Holy Father, the Holy Son, and the Holy Spirit; and these are one infinitely holy and eternal Being, who sits upon the throne, *and lives for ever and ever*. In this glory the prophet saw Christ, and spoke of him.

II. He heard the adorations of the *four-and-twenty elders*, that is, of the Christian people represented by them; the ministers led, and the people followed, in the praises of God, *vv.* 10, 11.

CHAPTER FIVE
THE SEALED BOOK (*vv.* 1–5)

Hitherto the apostle had seen only the great God, the governor of all things, now,

I. He is favoured with a sight of the model and methods of his government, as they are all written down in a book which he holds in his hand; and this we are now to consider as shut up and sealed in the hand of God. *Known unto God*, and to him alone, *are all his works, from the beginning of the world*; but it is his glory to conceal the matter as he pleases.

II. He heard a proclamation made concerning this sealed book. The cry or challenge proclaimed was, "*Who is worthy to open the book, and to loose the seals thereof?*" *v.* 2. None in heaven or earth could accept the challenge and undertake the task: none *in heaven*, none of the glorious holy angels, though before the throne of God, and the ministers of his providence; they with all their wisdom cannot dive into the decrees of God: none *on earth*, no man, the wisest or the best of men, none of the magicians and soothsayers, none of the prophets of God, any further than he reveals his mind to them: *none under the earth*, none of the fallen angels, none of the spirits of men departed, though they should return to our world, can open this book. Satan himself, with all his subtlety, cannot do it; the creatures cannot open it, nor look on it; they cannot read it. God only can do it.

III. He felt a great concern in himself about this matter: the apostle *wept much*; it was a great disappointment to him.

IV. The apostle was comforted and encouraged to hope this sealed book would yet be opened. Here observe, Who it was that would do the thing—the Lord Jesus Christ, called *the lion of the tribe of Judah*, according to his human nature, alluding to Jacob's prophecy (Gen. xlix. 10), and *the root of David* according to his divine nature, though a branch of David according to the flesh. He who is a middle person, God and man, and bears the office of Mediator between God and man, is fit and worthy to open and execute all the counsels of God towards men.

THE LAMB WITH THE MARKS OF DEATH (*vv.* 6–14)

Here, I. The apostle beholds this book taken into the hands of the Lord Jesus Christ, in order that it might be unsealed and opened by him. Here Christ is described, 1. By

his place and station: *In the midst of the throne, and of the four beasts, and of the elders.* 2. The form in which he appeared. Before he is called *a lion*; here he appears *as a lamb slain*. He appears with the marks of his sufferings upon him, to show that he intercedes in heaven in the virtue of his satisfaction. He appears as a *lamb, having seven horns and seven eyes*, perfect power to execute all the will of God and perfect wisdom to understand it all and to do it in the most effectual manner; *for he hath the seven Spirits of God.* 3. He is described by his act and deed: *He came, and took the book out of the right hand of him that sat on the throne* (v. 7), not by violence, nor by fraud, but he prevailed to do it (as *v.* 5), he prevailed by his merit and worthiness, he did it by authority and by the Father's appointment.

II. The apostle observes the universal joy and thanksgiving that filled heaven and earth upon this transaction.

1. The church begins the doxology, as being more immediately concerned in it (*v.* 8), the four living creatures, and *the four-and-twenty elders*, the Christian people, under their minister, lead up the chorus.

2. The doxology, thus begun by the church, is carried on by the angels; they take the second part, in conjunction with the church, *v.* 11.

3. This doxology, thus begun by the church, and carried on by the angels, is resounded and echoed by the whole creation, *v.* 13. Heaven and earth ring with the high praises of the Redeemer. Thus we have seen this sealed book passing with

great solemnity from the hand of the Creator into the hand of the Redeemer.

CHAPTER SIX

THE WHITE HORSE (*vv.* 1, 2)

Here, 1. Christ, the Lamb, opens the first seal; he now enters upon the great work of opening and accomplishing the purposes of God towards the church and the world. 2. One of the ministers of the church calls upon the apostle, with a voice like thunder, to come near, and observe what then appeared. 3. We have the vision itself, *v.* 2. (1) The Lord Jesus appears riding on *a white horse*. He rides on the white horse of a pure but despised gospel, with great swiftness through the world. (2) *He had a bow* in his hand. This bow, in the hand of Christ, abides in strength, and, like that of Jonathan, *never returns empty*. (3) *A crown was given him*, importing that all who receive the gospel must receive Christ as a king, and must be his loyal and obedient subjects. (4) *He went forth conquering, and to conquer*. As long as the church continues militant Christ will be conquering.

THE RED HORSE (*vv.* 3–8)

I. Upon opening the second seal, to which John was called to attend, *another horse* appears, of a different colour from the former, *a red horse*, *v.* 4. This signifies the desolating judgment of war; he that sat upon this red horse had *power to take peace from the earth, and that the* inhabitants of *the earth should kill one another*.

II. Upon opening the third seal, which John was directed to observe, another horse appears, different from the former, *a black horse*, signifying famine, that terrible judgment; *and he that sat on the horse had a pair of balances in his hand* (*v.* 5), signifying that men must now eat their bread by weight, as was threatened (Lev. xxvi. 26).

III. Upon opening the fourth seal, which John is commanded to observe, there appears another horse, of a pale colour. Here observe, 1. The name of the rider— *Death*, the king of terrors; the pestilence, which is death in its empire, death reigning over a place or nation, death on horseback, marching about, and making fresh conquests every hour. 2. The attendants or followers of this king of terrors—*hell*, a state of eternal misery to all those who die in their sins; and, in times of such a general destruction, multitudes go down unprepared into the valley of destruction.

IV. After the opening of these seals of approaching judgments, and the distinct account of them, we have this general observation, that God *gave power to them over the fourth part of the earth, to kill with the sword, and with hunger, and with death, and with the beasts of the earth*, *v.* 8. He gave them power, that is, those instruments of his anger, or those judgments themselves. To the three great judgments of war, famine, and pestilence, is here added *the beasts of the earth*, another of God's sore judgments, mentioned Ezek. xiv. 21, and mentioned here the last, because, when a nation is depopulated by the sword, famine, and pestilence, the small remnant that continue in a waste and howling wilderness encourage the wild beasts to make head against them, and they become an easy prey.

THE DAY OF WRATH
(vv. 9–17)

In the remaining part of this chapter we have the opening of the fifth and the sixth seals.

I. The fifth seal. Here observe,

1. The sight this apostle saw at the opening of the fifth seal; it was a very affecting sight (v. 9): *I saw under the altar the souls of those that were slain for the word of God, and for the testimony which they held.* He saw the souls of the martyrs. Here observe, (1) Where he saw them—*under the altar*; at the foot of the altar of incense, in the most holy place; he saw them in heaven, at the foot of Christ. (2) What was the cause in which they suffered— *the word of God and the testimony which they held,* for believing the word of God, and attesting or confessing the truth of it; this profession of their faith they held fast without wavering, even though they died for it.

2. The cry he heard: *How long, O Lord, holy and true, dost thou not judge and avenge our blood on those that dwell on the earth?* v. 10. Observe, Even *the spirits of just men made perfect* retain a proper resentment of the wrong they have sustained by their cruel enemies; and though they die in charity, praying, as Christ did, that God would forgive them, yet they are desirous that God will take a just revenge upon the sin of persecution, even while he pardons and saves the persecutors.

3. He observed the kind return that was made to this cry (v. 11), both what was given to them and what was said to them. (1) What was given to them—*white robes,* the robes of victory and of honour; their present happiness was an abundant recompence of their past sufferings. (2) What was said to them—that they should be satisfied, and easy in themselves, for it would not be long ere the number of their fellow-sufferers *should be fulfilled.*

II. We have here the sixth seal opened, v. 12. Some refer this to the great revolutions in the empire at Constantine's time, the downfall of paganism; others, with great probability, to the destruction of Jerusalem, as an emblem of the general judgment, and destruction of the wicked, at the end of the world. Here observe,

1. The tremendous events that were hastening; and here are several occurrences that contribute to make that day and dispensation very dreadful: (1) *There was a great earthquake.* (2) *The sun became black as sackcloth of hair,* either naturally, by a total eclipse, or politically, by the fall of the chief rulers and governors of the land. (3) *The moon* should *become as blood*; the inferior officers, or their military men, should be all wallowing in their own blood. (4) *The stars of heaven shall fall to the earth* (v. 13), and that *as a fig-tree casteth her untimely figs, when she is shaken of a mighty wind.* The stars may signify all the men of note and influence among them, though in lower spheres of activity; there

should be a general desolation. (5) *The heaven* should *depart as a scroll when it is rolled together.* This may signify that their ecclesiastical state should perish and be laid aside for ever. (6) *Every mountain and island shall be moved out of its place.* This leads to,

2. The dread and terror that would seize upon all sorts of men in that great and awful day, *v.* 15. When that day shall come, the most stout-hearted sinners will not be able to stand before him: all these terrors actually fell upon the sinners in Judea and Jerusalem in the day of their destruction, and they will all, in the utmost degree, fall upon impenitent sinners, at the general judgment of the last day.

CHAPTER SEVEN

BEFORE THE THRONE

(*vv.* 1–12)

Here we have, I. An account of the restraint laid upon the winds. By these winds we suppose are meant those errors and corruptions in religion which would occasion a great deal of trouble and mischief to the church of God.

II. An account of the sealing of the servants of God, where observe, 1. To whom this work was committed—to an angel, *another angel.* 2. How they were distinguished—the seal of God was set upon their foreheads, a seal known to him, and as plain as if it appeared in their foreheads; by this mark they were set apart for mercy and safety in the worst of times. 3. The number of those that were sealed, where observe, (1) A particular account of those that were

sealed of the twelve tribes of Israel—twelve thousand out of every tribe, the whole sum amounting to *a hundred and forty-four thousand.* Some take these to be a select number of the Jews who were reserved for mercy at the destruction of Jerusalem; others think that time was past, and therefore it is to be more generally applied to God's chosen remnant in the world. (2) A general account of those who were saved out of other nations (*v.* 9): *A great multitude, which no man could number, of all nations, and kindreds, and people, and tongues.* Though these are not said to be sealed, yet they were selected by God out of all nations, and brought into his church, and there stood before the throne.

III. We have the songs of saints and angels on this occasion, *vv.* 9–12, where observe,

1. The praises offered up by the saints (and, as it seems to me, by the Gentile believers) for the care of God in reserving so large a remnant of the Jews, and saving them from infidelity and destruction. Here observe, (1) The posture of these praising saints: they *stood before the throne, and before the Lamb,* before the Creator and the Mediator. (2) Their habit: they were *clothed with white robes, and had palms in their hands*; they were invested with the robes of justification, holiness, and victory, and had palms in their hands, as conquerors used to appear in their triumphs. (3) Their employment: they *cried with a loud voice, saying, Salvation to our God who sitteth upon the throne, and to the Lamb.*

2. Here is the song of the angels (*vv*. 11, 12). Here, [1] They acknowledge the glorious attributes of God—his wisdom, his power, and his might. [2] They declare that for these his divine perfections he ought to be blessed, and praised, and glorified, to all eternity; and they confirm it by their *Amen*.

THOSE IN WHITE (*vv*. 13–17)

Here we have a description of the honour and happiness of those who have faithfully served the Lord Jesus Christ, and suffered for him. Observe,

I. A question asked by one of the elders, not for his own information, but for John's instruction.

II. The answer returned by the apostle, in which he tacitly acknowledges his own ignorance, and sues to this elder for information: *Thou knowest*.

III. The account given to the apostle concerning that noble army of martyrs who stood *before the throne of God in white robes*, with palms of victory in their hands: and notice is taken here of, 1. The low and desolate state they had formerly been in. 2. The means by which they had been prepared for the great honour and happiness they now enjoyed: they had *washed their robes, and made them white in the blood of the Lamb, v*. 14. 3. The blessedness to which they are now advanced, being thus prepared for it. (1) They are happy in their station, for *they are before the throne of God night and day*; and he *dwells among them*; they are in that presence where there is fulness of joy. (2) They are happy in their employment, for they serve God

continually, and that without weakness, drowsiness, or weariness. Heaven is a state of service, though not of suffering; it is a state of rest, but not of sloth; it is a praising delightful rest. (3) They are happy in their freedom from all the inconveniences of this present life. This should moderate the Christian's sorrow in his present state, and support him under all the troubles of it.

CHAPTER EIGHT
THE SEVEN TRUMPETS
(*vv*. 1–6)

In these verses we have the prelude to the sounding of the trumpets in several parts.

I. The opening of the last seal. This was to introduce a new set of prophetical events.

II. A profound *silence in heaven for the space of half an hour*.

III. The trumpets were delivered to the angels who were to sound them.

IV. To prepare for this, another angel must first offer incense, *v*. 3. It is very probable that this other angel is the Lord Jesus, the high priest of the church, who is here described in his sacerdotal office, having a golden censer and much incense, a fulness of merit in his own glorious person, and this incense he was to offer up, *with the prayers of all the saints, upon the golden altar* of his divine nature. These prayers that were thus accepted in heaven produced great changes upon earth in return to them; the same angel that in his censer offered up the prayers of the saints in the same censer *took of the* _fire of the altar, and cast it into the earth_, and this presently caused strange commotions, _voices, and thunderings, and lightnings, and an earthquake_; these were the answers God gave to the prayers of the saints, and tokens of his anger against the world and that he would do great things to avenge himself and his people of their enemies; and now, all things being thus prepared, the angels discharge their duty.

WORMWOOD (_vv._ 7–13)

Observe, I. _The first angel sounded_ the first trumpet, and the events which followed were very dismal: _There followed hail and fire mingled with blood_, &c., _v._ 7. There was a terrible storm; but whether it is to be understood of a storm of heresies, a mixture of monstrous errors falling on the church (for in that age Arianism prevailed), or a storm or tempest of war falling on the civil state, expositors are not agreed.

II. _The second angel sounded_, and the alarm was followed, as in the first, with terrible events: _A great mountain burning with fire was cast into the sea; and the third part of the sea became blood_, _v._ 8. By this mountain some understand the leader or leaders of the heretics; others the city of Rome, which was five times sacked by the Goths and Vandals, within the compass of 137 years.

III. _The third angel sounded_, and the alarm had the like effects as before: _There fell a great star from heaven_, &c., _v._ 10. Some take this to be a political star, some eminent governor. Others take it to be an ecclesiastical star, some eminent person in the church, compared to a _burning lamp_, and they fix it upon Pelagius, who proved about this time a falling star, and greatly corrupted the churches of Christ.

IV. _The fourth angel sounded_, and the alarm was followed with further calamities. Observe, 1. The nature of this calamity; it was darkness; it fell therefore upon the great luminaries of the heaven, that give light to the world—_the sun, and the moon, and the stars_, either the guides and governors of the church, or of the state, who are placed in higher orbs than the people, and are to dispense light and benign influences to them. 2. The limitation: it was confined to a third part of these luminaries; there was some light both of the sun by day, and of the moon and stars by night, but it was only a third part of what they had before.

V. Before the other three trumpets are sounded here is solemn warning given to the world how terrible the calamities would be that should follow them, and how miserable those times and places would be on which they fell, _v._ 13.

CHAPTER NINE

THE FIFTH ANGEL (_vv._ 1–12)

Upon the sounding of this trumpet, the things to be observed are, 1. _A star falling from heaven to the earth_ Some think this star represents some eminent bishop in the Christian church, some angel of the church. 2. To this fallen star _was given the key of the bottomless pit_. Having now ceased to be a minister of Christ, he becomes the antichrist, the minister of the devil; and by the permission of Christ, who had taken from him the keys of the church, he becomes the devil's turnkey, to let loose the powers of hell against the churches of Christ. 3. Upon the opening of the bottomless pit *there arose a great smoke*, which darkened the sun and the air. The devils are the powers of darkness; hell is the place of darkness. 4. Out of this dark smoke there came a swarm of locusts, one of the plagues of Egypt, the devil's emissaries headed by antichrist, all the rout and rabble of antichristian orders, to promote superstition, idolatry, error, and cruelty; and these had, by the just permission of God, power to hurt those who had not the mark of God in their foreheads. 5. The hurt they were to do them was not a bodily, but a spiritual hurt. 6. They had no power so much as to hurt those who had the seal of God in their foreheads. 7. The power given to these factors for hell is limited in point of time: *five months*, a certain season, and but a short season, though how short we cannot tell. 8. Though it would be short, it would be very sharp. 9. These locusts were of a monstrous size and shape, *vv.* 7, 8, &c. The king and commander of this hellish squadron is here described, [1] As an angel; so he was by nature, an angel, once one of the angels of heaven. [2] *The angel of the bottomless pit*; an angel still, but a fallen angel, fallen into the bottomless pit, vastly large, and out of which there is no recovery. [3] In these infernal regions he is a sort of prince and governor, and has the powers of darkness under

his rule and command. [4] His true name is *Abaddon, Apollyon—a destroyer*, for that is his business, his design, and employment.

THE SIXTH ANGEL (*vv.* 13–21)

Here let us consider the preface to this vision, and then the vision itself.

I. The preface to this vision: *A voice was heard from the horns of the golden altar, vv.* 13, 14. These four messengers of divine judgment lay bound in the river Euphrates, a great way from the European nations. Here the Turkish power had its rise, which seems to be the story of this vision.

II. The vision itself: *And the four angels that had been bound in the great river Euphrates were now loosed, vv.* 15, 16. And here observe, 1. The time of their military operations and executions is limited to *an hour, and a day, and a month, and a year*. God will make the wrath of man praise him, and the remainder of wrath he will restrain. 2. The army that was to execute this great commission is mustered, and the number found to be of horsemen *two hundred thousand thousand*; but we are left to guess what the infantry must be. In general, it tells us, the armies of the Mahomedan empire should be vastly great; and so it is certain they were. 3. Their formidable equipage and appearance, *v.* 17. 4. The vast havoc and desolation that they made in the Roman empire, which had now become antichristian: a third part of them were killed; they went as far as their commission suffered them, and they could go no further. 5.

Their artillery, by which they made such slaughter, described *by fire, smoke, and brimstone*, issuing out of the mouths of their horses, and the stings that were in their tails. 6. Observe the impenitency of the antichristian generation under these dreadful judgments (*v*. 20).

III. From this sixth trumpet we learn, 1. God can make one enemy of the church to be a scourge and plague to another. 2. He who is the Lord of hosts has vast armies at his command, to serve his own purposes. 3. The most formidable powers have limits set them, which they cannot transgress.

CHAPTER TEN
SEVEN THUNDERS (*vv*. 1–7)

Here we have an account of another vision the apostle was favoured with, between the sounding of the sixth trumpet and that of the seventh. And we observe,

I. The person who was principally concerned in communicating this discovery to John—an angel from heaven, *another mighty angel*, who is so set forth as would induce one to think it could be no other than our Lord and Saviour Jesus Christ!

II. His station and posture: *He set his right foot upon the sea and his left foot upon the earth*, to show the absolute power and dominion he had over the world. *And he held in his hand a little book opened*, probably the same that was before sealed, but was now opened, and gradually fulfilled by him.

III. His awful voice: *He cried aloud, as when a lion roareth* (*v*. 3), and his awful voice was echoed by *seven thunders*, seven solemn and

terrible ways of discovering the mind of God.

IV. The prohibition given to the apostle, that he should not publish, but conceal what he had learned from the seven thunders, *v*. 4.

V. The solemn oath taken by this mighty angel. 1. The manner of his swearing: *He lifted up his hand to heaven, and swore by him that liveth for ever*, by himself, as God often has done, or by God as God, to whom he, as Lord, Redeemer, and ruler of the world, now appeals. 2. The matter of the oath: that *there shall be time no longer*; either, (1) That there shall be now no longer delay in fulfilling the predictions of this book. Or, (2) That when this mystery of God is finished time itself shall be no more.

THE LITTLE BOOK (*vv*. 8–11)

Here we have, I. A strict charge given to the apostle, which was, 1. That he should *go and take the little book* out of the hands of that mighty angel mentioned before. 2. To eat the book; this part of the charge was given by the angel himself, hinting to the apostle that before he should publish what he had discovered he must more thoroughly digest the predictions, and be in himself suitably affected with them.

II. An account of the taste and relish which this little book would have, when the apostle had taken it in; at first, while *in his mouth*, *sweet*. All persons feel a pleasure in looking into future events, and in having them foretold; and all good men love to receive a word from God, of what import soever it be. But, when this book of prophecy was more thoroughly digested by the apostle, the contents would be bitter; these were things so awful and terrible, such grievous persecutions of the people of God, and such desolation made in the earth, that the foresight and foreknowledge of them would not be pleasant, but painful to the mind of the apostle: thus was Ezekiel's prophecy to him, *ch.* iii. 3.

III. The apostle's discharge of the duty he was called to (*v.* 10): *He took the little book out of the angel's hand, and ate it up,* and he found the relish to be as was told him.

IV. The apostle is made to know that this book of prophecy, which he had now taken in, was not given him merely to gratify his own curiosity, or to affect him with pleasure or pain, but to be communicated by him to the world.

CHAPTER ELEVEN
MEASUREMENTS OF THE TEMPLE (*vv.* 1, 2)

This prophetical passage about measuring the temple is a plain reference to what we find in Ezekiel's vision, Ezek. xl. 3, &c. But how to understand either the one or the other is not so easy. It should seem the design of measuring the temple in the former case was in order to the rebuilding of it, and that with advantage; the design of this measurement seems to be either, 1. For the preservation of it in those times of public danger and calamity that are here foretold; or, 2. For its trial; that it may be seen how far it agrees with the

standard, or pattern, in the mount; or, 3. For its reformation; that what is redundant, deficient, or changed, may be regulated according to the true model. Observe,

I. How much was to be measured. 1. *The temple*; the gospel church in general, whether it be so built, so constituted, as the gospel rule directs, whether it be too narrow or too large, the door too wide or too strait. 2. *The altar.* That which was the place of the most solemn acts of worship may be put for religious worship in general. 3. The worshippers too must be measured, whether they make God's glory their end and his word their rule, in all their acts of worship; and whether they come to God with suitable affections, and whether their *conversation be as becomes the gospel.*

II. What was not to be measured (*v.* 2), and why it should be left out. 1. What was not to be measured: *The court which is without the temple measure it not.* 2. Why was not the outer court measured? This was no part of the temple, according to the model either of Solomon or Zerubbabel, and therefore God would have no regard to it. Those who worship in the outer court are either such as worship in a false manner or with hypocritical hearts; and these are rejected of God, and will be found among his enemies.

THE TWO WITNESSES
(*vv.* 3–13)

In this time of treading down, God has reserved to himself his faithful witnesses, who will not fail to attest the truth of his word and worship, and the excellency of his ways. Here observe,

I. The number of these witnesses: it is but a small number and yet it is sufficient. Christ sent out his disciples two by two, to preach the gospel. Some think these two witnesses are Enoch and Elijah, who are to return to the earth for a time: others, the church of the believing Jews and that of the Gentiles: it should rather seem that they are God's eminent faithful ministers, who shall not only continue to profess the Christian religion, but to preach it, in the worst of times.

II. The time of their prophesying, or bearing their testimony for Christ. *A thousand two hundred and threescore days*; that is (as many think), to the period of the reign of antichrist; and, if the beginning of that interval could be ascertained, this number of prophetic days, taking a day for a year, would give us a prospect when the end shall be.

III. Their habit, and posture: they prophesy in sackcloth, as those that are deeply affected with the low and distressed state of the churches and interest of Christ in the world.

IV. How they were supported and supplied during the discharge of their great and hard work: they stood before the God of the whole earth, and he gave them power to prophesy.

V. Their security and defence during the time of their prophesying: *If any attempted to hurt them, fire proceeded out of their mouths, and devoured them, v. 5.* God has ordained his arrows for the persecutors, and is often plaguing them while they are persecuting his people; they find it hard work to *kick against the pricks*.

VI. The slaying of the witnesses. To make their testimony more strong, they must seal it with their blood. Here observe, 1. The time when they should be killed. *When they have finished their testimony.* They are immortal, they are invulnerable, till their work be done. 2. The enemy that should overcome and slay them—*the beast that ascendeth out of the bottomless pit.* Antichrist, the great instrument of the devil, should make war against them, not only with the arms of subtle and sophistical learning, but chiefly with open force and violence; and God would permit his enemies to prevail against his witnesses for a time. 3. The barbarous usage of these slain witnesses; the malice of their enemies was not satiated with their blood and death, but pursued even their dead bodies.

VII. The resurrection of these witnesses, and the consequences thereof. Observe, 1. The time of their rising again; after they had lain dead *three days and a half* (v. 11), a short time in comparison of that in which they had prophesied. 2. The power by which they were raised: *The spirit of life from God entered into them, and they stood upon their feet.* God put not only life, but courage into them.

VIII. The ascension of the witnesses into heaven and the consequences thereof, *vv.* 12, 13. Observe, 1. Their ascension. By heaven we may understand either some more eminent station in the church, the kingdom of grace in this world, or a high place in the kingdom of glory above. 2. The consequences of their ascension—a mighty shock and convulsion in the antichristian empire and the fall of *a tenth part of the city*. Thus, when God's work and witnesses revive, the devil's work and witnesses fall before him.

THE LAST TRUMPET
(*vv.* 14–19)

We have here the sounding of the seventh and last trumpet, which is ushered in by the usual warning and demand of attention: *The second woe is past, and, behold, the third woe cometh quickly. Then the seventh angel sounded.* Here observe the effects and consequences of this trumpet, thus sounded.

I. Here were loud and joyful acclamations of the saints and angels in heaven. Observe, 1. The manner of their adorations: they rose from their seats, *and fell upon their faces, and worshipped God*; they did it with reverence and humility. 2. The matter of their adorations. (1) They thankfully recognise the right of our God and Saviour to rule and reign over all the world: *The kingdoms of this world have become the kingdoms of our Lord and of his Christ, v.* 15. They were always so in title, both by creation and purchase. (2) They thankfully observe his actual possession of them, and reign over them. (3) They rejoice that this his reign shall never end: *He shall reign for ever and ever*, till all enemies be put under his feet; none shall ever wrest the sceptre out of his hand.

II. Here were angry resentments in the world at these just appearances and actings of the power of

God (*v.* 18). *The nations were angry*; not only had been so, but were still so: their hearts rose up against God; they met his wrath with their own anger.

III. Another consequence was the opening of the temple of God in heaven. By this may be meant that here is now a more free communication between heaven and earth, prayer and praises more freely and frequently ascending and graces and blessings plentifully descending. But it rather seems to intend the church of God on earth, a heavenly temple. So, during the power of antichrist, the temple of God seemed to be shut up, and was so in a great degree; but now it was opened again.

CHAPTER TWELVE
THE WOMAN AND THE DRAGON (*vv.* 1–11)

Here we see that early prophecy eminently fulfilled in which God said he would *put enmity between the seed of the woman and the seed of the serpent*, Gen. iii. 15. You will observe,

I. The attempts of Satan and his agents to prevent the increase of the church, by devouring her offspring *as soon as it was born*: of this we have a very lively description in the most proper images.

1. We see how the church is represented in this vision. (1) As a *woman*, the weaker part of the world, but the spouse of Christ, and the mother of the saints. (2) As *clothed with the sun*, the imputed righteousness of the Lord Jesus Christ. (3) As having *the moon under her feet* (that is, the world);

she stands upon it, but lives above it. (4) As having on her head *a crown of twelve stars*, that is, the doctrine of the gospel preached by the twelve apostles, which is a crown of glory to all true believers. (5) As in travail, crying out, and *pained to be delivered*.

2. How the grand enemy of the church is represented. (1) As a *great red dragon*—a dragon for strength and terror—a red dragon for fierceness and cruelty. (2) As *having seven heads*, that is, placed on seven hills, as Rome was; and therefore it is probable that pagan Rome is here meant. (3) As having *ten horns*, divided into ten provinces, as the Roman empire was by Augustus Cæsar. (4) As having *seven crowns upon his head*, which is afterwards expounded to be seven kings, *ch.* xvii. 10. (5) As drawing with his tail a *third part of the stars in heaven*, and *casting them down to the earth*, turning the ministers and professors of the Christian religion out of their places and privileges and making them as weak and useless as he could. (6) As standing *before the woman, to devour her child as soon as it should be born*, very vigilant to crush the Christian religion in its birth and entirely to prevent the growth and continuance of it in the world.

II. The unsuccessfulness of these attempts against the church; for, 1. She was safely delivered of a *man-child* (*v.* 5), by which some understand Christ, others Constantine, but others, with greater propriety, a race of true believers, strong and united. 2. Care was taken of this child: it *was caught up to God, and to his throne*; that is,

taken into his special, powerful, and immediate protection. 3. Care was taken of the mother as well as of the child, *v.* 6. She *fled into the wilderness, a prepared* both for her safety and her sustenance.

III. The attempts of the dragon not only proved unsuccessful against the church, but fatal to his own interests; for, upon his endeavour to devour the man-child, he engaged all the powers of heaven against him (*v.* 7): *There was war in heaven*. Heaven will espouse the quarrel of the church. Here observe,

1. The seat of this war—*in heaven*, in the church, which is the *kingdom of heaven* on earth, under the care of heaven and in the same interest.

2. The parties—*Michael and his angels* on one side, and *the dragon and his angels* on the other: Christ, the great Angel of the covenant, and his faithful followers; and Satan and all his instruments.

3. The success of the battle: *The dragon and his angels fought and prevailed not*; there was a great struggle on both sides, but the victory fell to Christ and his church.

4. The triumphant song that was composed and used on this occasion, *vv.* 10, 11. The servants of God overcame Satan, [1] *By the blood of the Lamb*, as the meritorious cause. [2] *By the word of their testimony*, as the great instrument of war, *the sword of the Spirit, which is the word of God*,—by a resolute powerful preaching of the everlasting gospel.

THE DRAGON'S WAR
(*vv.* 12–17)

We have here an account of this war, so happily finished in heaven, or in the church, as it was again renewed and carried on in the wilderness, the place to which the church had fled, and where she had been for some time secured by the special care of her God and Saviour. Observe,

I. The warning given of the distress and calamity that should fall upon the inhabitants of the world in general, through the wrath and rage of the devil.

II. His second attempt upon the church now in the wilderness: *He persecuted the woman who brought forth the man-child, v.* 13. Her obscurity could not altogether protect her; the old subtle serpent, which at first lurked in paradise, now follows the church into the wilderness, and *casts out a flood of water after her, to carry her away.* This is thought to be meant of a flood of error and heresy. *The earth helped the woman, and opened her mouth, and swallowed up the flood, v.* 16. Some think we are to understand the swarms of Goths and Vandals that invaded the Roman empire, and found work for the Arian rulers, who otherwise would have been as furious persecutors as the pagan had been, and had exercised great cruelties already. The devil, being thus defeated in his designs upon the universal church, now turns his rage against particular persons and places; his malice against the woman pushes him on to *make war with the remnant of her seed.* Their fidelity to God and Christ, in doctrine, worship, and practice, was that which exposed them to the rage of Satan and his instruments; and such fidelity will expose men still,

less or more, to the end of the world, when *the last enemy shall be destroyed.*

CHAPTER THIRTEEN
THE FIRST BEAST (*vv.* 1–10)

We have here an account of the rise, figure, and progress of the first beast; and observe, 1. From what situation the apostle saw this monster. He seemed to himself to stand upon *the sea-shore,* though it is probable he was still in a rapture. 2. Whence this beast came—*out of the sea;* and yet, by the description of it, it would seem more likely to be a land-monster. 3. What was the form and shape of this beast. It was for the most part *like a leopard,* but its *feet were like the feet of a bear and its mouth as the mouth of a lion;* it had *seven heads, and ten horns, and upon its heads the name of blasphemy:* a most horrid and hideous monster! 4. The source and spring of his authority—*the dragon; he gave him his power, and seat, and great authority.* He was set up by the devil, and supported by him to do his work and promote his interest; and the devil lent him all the assistance he could. 5. A dangerous wound given him, and yet unexpectedly healed, *v.* 3. 6. The honour and worship paid to this infernal monster: *All the world wondered after the beast.* So great were the darkness, degeneracy, and madness of the world! 7. How he exercised his infernal power and policy: He had *a mouth, speaking great things, and blasphemies; he blasphemed God, the name of God, the tabernacle of God, and all those that dwell in heaven; and he made war with the* saints, *and overcame them*, and gained a sort of universal empire in the world. Thus the malice of the devil shows itself against heaven and the blessed inhabitants of heaven. These are above the reach of his power. All he can do is to blaspheme them; but the saints on earth are more exposed to his cruelty, and he sometimes is permitted to triumph over them and trample upon them. 8. The limitation of the devil's power and success, and that both as to time and persons. He is limited in point of time; his reign is *to continue forty-and-two months* (v. 5), suitable to the other prophetical characters of the reign of antichrist. He is also limited as to the persons and people that he shall entirely subject to his will and power; it will be only those *whose names are not written in the Lamb's book of life.*

THE SECOND BEAST
(vv. 11–18)

Here observe,

I. The form and shape of this second beast: *He had two horns like a lamb*, but a mouth that *spoke like the dragon.* All agree that this must be some great impostor, who, under a pretence of religion, shall deceive the souls of men.

II. The power which he exercises: *All the power of the former beast* (v. 12); he promotes the same interest, pursues the same design in substance, which is, to draw men off from worshipping the true God to worship those who by nature are no gods, and subject the souls and consciences of men to the will and authority of men, in opposition to the will of God.

III. The methods by which this second beast carried on his interests and designs; they are of three sorts: 1. Lying wonders, pretended miracles, by which they should be deceived. 2. Excommunications, anathemas, severe censures, by which they pretend to cut men off from Christ, and cast them into the power of the devil, but do indeed deliver them over to the secular power, that they may be put to death; and thus, notwithstanding their vile hypocrisy, they are justly charged with killing those whom they cannot corrupt. 3. By disfranchisement, allowing none to enjoy natural, civil, or municipal rights, who will not worship the beast.

IV. We have here *the number of the beast*, given in such a manner as shows the infinite wisdom of God, and will sufficiently exercise all the wisdom and accuracy of men: *The number* is *the number of a man*, computed after the usual manner among men, and it is 666. Only this we know, God has written *Mene Tekel* upon all his enemies; he has numbered their days, and they shall be finished, but his own kingdom shall endure for ever.

CHAPTER FOURTEEN
FOLLOWERS OF THE LAMB (vv. 1–5)

Here we have one of the most pleasing sights that can be viewed in this world—the Lord Jesus Christ at the head of his faithful adherents and attendants. Here observe, 1. How Christ appears: as a Lamb standing upon *mount Zion.*

Mount Zion is the gospel church. Christ is with his church and in the midst of her in all her troubles, and therefore she is not consumed. 2. How his people appear: very honourably. (1) As to the numbers, they are many, even all who were sealed. (2) Their distinguishing badge: they had *the name of God written in their foreheads*; they made a bold and open profession of their faith in God and Christ, and, this being followed by suitable actings, they are known and approved. (3) Their congratulations and songs of praise, which were peculiar to the redeemed (*v* 3). (4) Their character and description. [1] They are described by their chastity and purity: *They are virgins.* They had not defiled themselves either with corporal or spiritual adultery. [2] By their loyalty and stedfast adherence to Christ: *They follow the Lamb whithersoever he goes.* [3] By their former designation to this honour: *These were redeemed from among men, being the first-fruits to God, and to the Lamb, v.* 4. Here is plain evidence of a special redemption. [4] By their universal integrity and conscientiousness: *There was no guile found in them*, and *they were without fault before the throne of God.*

THE THREE ANGELS
(*vv.* 6–12)

In this part of the chapter we have three angels or messengers sent from heaven to give notice of the fall of Babylon, and of those things that were antecedent and consequent to that great event.

I. The first angel was sent on an errand antecedent to it, and that was *to preach the everlasting gospel, vv.* 6, 7.

II. The second angel follows the other and proclaims the actual fall of Babylon. By Babylon is generally understood Rome, which was before called *Sodom* and *Egypt*, for wickedness and cruelty, and is now first called *Babylon*, for pride and idolatry.

III. A third angel follows the other two, and gives warning to all of that divine vengeance which would overtake all those that obstinately adhered to the antichristian interest after God had thus proclaimed its downfall, *vv.* 9, 10.

THE HARVEST (*vv.* 13–20)

Here we have the vision of the harvest and vintage, introduced with a solemn preface. Observe,

I. The preface, *v.* 13. Here observe, (1) The description of those that are and shall be blessed—such as die in the Lord. (2) The demonstration of this blessedness: *They rest from their labours, and their works do follow them.* [1] They are blessed in their rest; they rest from all sin, temptation, sorrow, and persecution. [2] They are blessed in their recompence: *Their works follow them*; they do not go before them as their title, or price of purchase, but follow them as their evidence of having lived and died in the Lord. [3] They are happy in the time of their dying, when they have lived to see the cause of God reviving.

II. We have the vision itself, represented by a harvest and a vintage.

1. By a harvest (*vv.* 14, 15), an

emblem that sometimes signifies the cutting down of the wicked, when ripe for ruin, by the judgments of God, and sometimes the gathering in of the righteous, when ripe for heaven, by the mercy of God. This seems rather to represent God's judgments against the wicked.

2. By a vintage, *v.* 17. Some think that these two are only different emblems of the same judgment; others that they refer to distinct events of providence before the end of all things. Perhaps this great event has not yet had its accomplishment, but *the vision is for an appointed time*; and therefore, though it may seem to tarry, we are to wait for it. *But who shall live when the Lord does this?*

CHAPTER FIFTEEN

THE SEVEN VIALS (*vv.* 1–4)

Here we have the preparation of matters for the pouring out of the seven vials, which was committed to seven angels; and observe how these angels appeared to the apostle—*in heaven*; it was in a wonderful manner, and that upon account, 1. Of the work they had to do, which was to finish the destruction of antichrist. 2. The spectators and witnesses of this their commission: all *that had gotten the victory over the beast*, &c. (1) They extol the greatness of God's works, and the justice and truth of his ways, both in delivering his people and destroying their enemies. (2) They call upon all nations to render unto God their fear, glory, and worship, due to such a discovery of his truth and justice: *Who shall not fear thee? v.* 4.

SEVEN PLAGUES (*vv.* 5–8)

Observe, I. How these angels appeared—coming out of heaven to execute their commission: *The temple of the tabernacle of the testimony in heaven was opened, v.* 5.

II. How they were equipped and prepared for their work. Observe, 1. Their array: They were *clothed with pure and white linen*, and had *their breasts girded with golden girdles, v.* 6. This was the habit of the high priests when they went in to enquire of God, and came out with an answer from him. 2. Their artillery was *seven vials filled with the wrath of God*; they were armed with the wrath of God against his enemies. Now from whom did the angels receive these vials? From one of the four living creatures, one of the ministers of the true church, that is, in answer to the prayers of the ministers and people of God, and to avenge their cause, in which the angels are willingly employed.

III. The impressions these things made upon all who stood near the temple. God himself was now preaching to the church and to all the world, by terrible things in righteousness; but, when this work was done, then the churches would have rest, the temple would be opened, and the solemn assemblies gathered, edified, and multiplied.

CHAPTER SIXTEEN

PLAGUES ON LAND AND SEA (*vv.* 1–7)

We had in the foregoing chapter the great and solemn preparation that was made for the pouring out of the vials; now we have the performance of that work. Here observe,

I. That, though every thing was made ready before, yet nothing was to be put in execution without an immediate positive order from God; and this he gave out of the temple, answering the prayers of his people, and avenging their quarrel.

II. No sooner was the word of command given than it was immediately obeyed; no delay, no objection made. Now we proceed to,

(1) The first angel who poured out his vial, *v.* 2. Observe, [1] Where it fell—*upon the earth.* [2] What it produced—*noisome and grievous sores on all who had the mark of the beast.*

(2) *The second angel poured out his vial*; and here we see, [1] Where it fell—*upon the sea.* [2] What it produced: It turned the sea into blood, *as the blood of a dead man, and every living soul died in the sea.*

(3) The next angel poured out his vial; and we are told, [1] Where it fell—*upon the rivers, and upon the fountains of waters.* [2] What effect it had upon them: *It turned them into blood.* The instrument that God makes use of in this work is here called *the angel of the waters,* who extols the righteousness of God in this retaliation: *They have shed the blood of thy saints, and thou hast given them blood to drink, for they are worthy,* to which another angel answered by full consent, *v.* 7.

HEAT AND DARKNESS
(*vv.* 8–11)

In these verses we see the work going on in the appointed order.

The fourth angel poured out his vial, and that fell upon the sun. That sun which before cherished them with warm and benign influences shall now grow hot against these idolaters, and shall scorch them. The fifth angel poured out his vial, *v.* 10. And observe, 1. Where this fell—*upon the seat of the beast,* upon Rome itself, the mystical Babylon, the head of the antichristian empire. 2. What effect it had there: The whole kingdom of the beast *was full of darkness* and distress.

THE FINAL PLAGUES
(*vv.* 12–16)

The sixth angel poured out his vial; and observe,

I. Where it fell—*upon the great river Euphrates.* Some take it literally, for the place where the Turkish power and empire began. Others take it for the river Tiber; for, as Rome is mystical Babylon, Tiber is mystical Euphrates. And when Rome shall be destroyed her river and merchandise must suffer with her.

II. What did this vial produce? 1. The drying up of the river, which furnished the city with wealth, provisions, and all sorts of accommodations. 2. A way is hereby prepared *for the kings of the east.* There will be a more open communication between the western and eastern nations, which may facilitate the conversion of the Jews, and of *the fulness of the Gentiles.* 3. The last effort of the great dragon; he is resolved to have another push for it, that, if possible, he may retrieve the ruinous posture of his affairs in the world. He is now rallying his forces, recollecting all his spirits, to make one desperate sally before all be lost. This is occasioned by the pouring out of the sixth vial. Here observe, (1) The instruments he makes use of to engage the powers of the earth in his cause and quarrel: *Three unclean spirits like frogs* come forth, one *out of the mouth of the dragon*, another *out of the mouth of the beast, and* a third *out of the mouth of the false prophet*. (2) The means these instruments would use to engage the power of earth in this war. They would work pretended miracles, the old stratagem of him *whose coming is after the working of Satan, with all power, and signs, and lying wonders, and with all deceivableness of unrighteousness*, 2 Thess. ii. 9, 10. (3) The field of battle—a place called *Armageddon*; that is, say some, the mount of Megiddo. This battle required time to prepare for it, and therefore the further account of it is suspended till we come to the nineteenth chapter, *vv.* 19, 20. (4) The warning which God gives of this great and decisive trial, to engage his people to prepare for it, *v.* 15.

'IT IS DONE' (*vv.* 17–21)

Here we have an account of the seventh and last angel pouring forth his vial, contributing his part towards the accomplishment of the downfall of Babylon, which was the finishing stroke. And here, as before, observe,

I. Where this plague fell—*on the air*, upon the prince of the power of the air, that is, the devil.

II. What it produced. 1. A thankful voice from heaven, pronouncing that now the work was done. 2. A

mighty commotion on the earth—an earthquake, so great as never was before, shaking the very centre, and this ushered in by the usual concomitants of thunder and lightnings. 3. The fall of Babylon, which was divided into three parts, *called the cities of the nations* (*v.* 19).

III. How the antichristian party were affected with it. Though it fell upon them as a dreadful storm, as if the stones of the city, tossed up into the air, came down upon their heads, like hailstones of a talent weight each, yet they were so far from repenting that they blasphemed that God who thus punished them. Here was a dreadful plague of the heart, a spiritual judgment more dreadful and destructive than all the rest.

CHAPTER SEVENTEEN

FALL OF BABYLON (*vv.* 1–6)

Here we have a new vision, not as to the matter of it, for that is contemporary with what came under the three last vials; but as to the manner of description, &c. Observe, 1. The invitation given to the apostle to take a view of what was here to be represented: *Come hither, and I will show thee the judgment of the great whore*, &c., *v.* 1. Now in this observe, (1) She is named from her place of residence—*Babylon the great*. But, that we might not take it for the old Babylon literally so called, we are told there is a mystery in the name; it is some other great city resembling the old Babylon. (2) She is named from her infamous way and practice; not only a harlot, but a mother of harlots, breeding up harlots, and nursing and training them up to idolatry, and all sorts of lewdness and wickedness—the parent and nurse of all false religion and filthy conversation. 5. Her diet: she satiated herself with *the blood of the saints and martyrs of Jesus*.

VISION EXPLAINED (*vv.* 7–13)

Here we have the mystery of this vision explained. 1. This beast *was, and is not, and yet is*; that is, it *was* a seat of idolatry and persecution; *and is not*, that is, not in the ancient form, which was pagan; *and yet it is*, it is truly the seat of idolatry and tyranny, though of another sort and form. *It ascends out of the bottomless pit* (idolatry and cruelty are the issue and product of hell), and it shall return thither and go into perdition. 2. *This beast has seven heads*, which have a double signification. (1) *Seven mountains*—the seven hills on which Rome stands; and, (2) *Seven kings*—seven sorts of government. This beast makes an eighth governor, and sets up idolatry again. 3. This beast had ten horns; which are said to be *ten kings which have as yet received no kingdoms*.

DOWNFALL OF BABYLON (*vv.* 14–18)

Here we have some account of the downfall of Babylon, to be more fully described in the following chapter.

I. Here is a war begun between the beast and his followers, and the Lamb and his followers.

II. Here is a victory gained by the Lamb: *The Lamb shall overcome*.

III. Here is the ground or reason of the victory assigned; and this is

taken, 1. From the character of the Lamb: *He is King of kings and Lord of lords*. 2. From the character of his followers: *They are called, and chosen, and faithful*.

IV. The victory is justly aggrandised. 1. By the vast multitude who paid obedience and subjection to the beast and to the whore. 2. By the powerful influence which God hereby showed he had over the minds of great men.

CHAPTER EIGHTEEN

THE SIN OF BABYLON (*vv.* 1–8)

The downfall and destruction of Babylon form an event so fully determined in the counsels of God, and of such consequence to his interests and glory, that the visions and predictions concerning it are repeated. 1. Here is another angel sent from heaven, attended with great power and lustre, *v.* 1. 2. This angel publishes the fall of Babylon, as a thing already come to pass. 3. the reason of this ruin is declared (*v.* 3). The wickedness of Babylon had been very great; for she had not only forsaken the true God herself, and set up idols, but had with great art and industry drawn all sorts of men into the spiritual adultery, and by her wealth and luxury had retained them in her interest. 4. Fair warning is given to all that expect mercy from God, that they should not only *come out of her,* but be assisting in her destruction, *vv.* 4, 5.

LAMENT FOR BABYLON (*vv.* 9–24)

Here we have,

I. A doleful lamentation made by

Babylon's friends for her fall; and here observe,

1. Who are the mourners, namely, those who had been bewitched by her fornication, those who had been sharers in her sensual pleasures, and those who had been gainers by her wealth and trade.

2. What was the manner of their mourning. (1) They stood afar off, they durst not come nigh her. (2) They made a grievous outcry: *Alas! alas! that great city, Babylon, that mighty city!* (3) They wept, and *cast dust upon their heads,* v. 19. The pleasures of sin are but for a season, and they will end in dismal sorrow.

3. What was the cause of their mourning; not their sin, but their punishment.

II. An account of the joy and triumph there was both in heaven and earth at the irrecoverable fall of Babylon: while her own people were bewailing her, the servants of God were called to *rejoice over her,* v. 20. This enemy should never molest them any more, and of this they were assured by a remarkable token (v. 21): An *angel* from heaven *took up a stone like a great millstone, and cast it into the sea, saying, "Thus shall Babylon be thrown down with violence, and be found no more at all*; the place shall be no longer habitable by man, no work shall be done there, no comfort enjoyed, no light seen there, but utter darkness and desolation, as the reward of her great wickedness, first in *deceiving the nations with her sorceries,* and secondly in destroying and murdering those whom she could not deceive," v. 24. Such abominable sins deserved so great a ruin.

CHAPTER NINETEEN

PRAISE IN HEAVEN (vv. 1–10)

The fall of Babylon being fixed, finished, and declared to be irrecoverable in the foregoing chapter, this begins with a holy triumph over her, in pursuance of the order given forth: *Rejoice over her, thou heaven, and you holy apostles and prophets,* ch. xviii. 20.

The triumphant song being ended, an epithalamium, or marriage-song, begins, v. 6. Here observe,

I. The concert of heavenly music. The chorus was large and loud, *as the voice of many waters and of mighty thunderings.*

II. The occasion of this song; and that is the reign and dominion of that omnipotent God who has *redeemed his church by his own blood,* and is now in a more public manner betrothing her to himself: *The marriage of the Lamb has come,* v. 7. Some think this refers to the conversion of the Jews, which they suppose will succeed the fall of Babylon; others, to the general resurrection: the former seems more probable. Now, 1. You have here a description of the bride, how she appeared; not in the gay and gaudy dress of the mother of harlots, but *in fine linen, clean and white,* which *is the righteousness of saints*; in the robes of Christ's righteousness, both imputed for justification and imparted for sanctification. 2. The marriage-feast, which, though not particularly described (as Matt. xxii. 4), yet is declared to be such as would make all those happy who were called to it, so called as to accept the invitation, a feast made up of the promises of the gospel, *the true sayings of God, v.* 9. 3. The transport of joy which the apostle felt in himself at this vision. Here observe, (1) What honour he offered to the angel: *He fell at his feet, to worship him.* (2) How the angel refused it, and this was with some resentment: "*See thou do it not*; have a care what thou doest, thou art doing a wrong thing." (3) He gave a very good reason for his refusal: "*I am thy fellow-servant, and of thy brethren which have the testimony of Jesus*—I am a creature, thine equal in office, though not in nature."

THE WORD OF GOD
(*vv.* 11–21)

No sooner was the marriage solemnized between Christ and his church by the conversion of the Jews than the glorious head and husband of the church is called out to a new expedition, which seems to be the great battle that was to be fought at Armageddon, foretold *ch.* xvi. 16. And here observe,

I. The description of the great Commander, 1. By the seat of his empire; and that is *heaven*; his throne is there, and his power and authority are heavenly and divine. 2. His equipage: he is again described as sitting *on a white horse*, to show the equity of the cause, and certainty of success. 3. His attributes: he is *faithful and true* to his covenant and promise. 4. His armour; and that is *a vesture dipped in blood*, either his own blood, by which he purchased this mediatorial power, or the blood of his enemies, over whom he has always prevailed. 5. His name: *The Word of God*, a name that none fully

knows but himself, only this we know, that this *Word was God manifest in the flesh*; but his perfections are incomprehensible by any creature.

II. The army which he commands (*v.* 14), a very large one, made up of many armies; angels and saints followed his conduct, and resembled him in their equipage, and in their armour of purity and righteousness—chosen, and called, and faithful.

III. The weapons of his warfare —*a sharp sword* proceeding from his mouth (*v.* 15), with which *he smites the nations*, either the threatenings of the written word, which now he is going to execute, or rather his word of command calling on his followers to take a just revenge on his and their enemies, who are now put into the winepress of the wrath of God, to be trodden under foot by him.

IV. The ensigns of his authority, his coat of arms—*a name written on his vesture and thigh, King of kings, and Lord of lords*, asserting his authority and power, and the cause of the quarrel, *v.* 16.

V. An invitation given *to the fowls of heaven*, that they should come and see the battle, and share in the spoil and pillage of the field (*vv.* 17, 18).

VI. The battle joined. The enemy falls on with great fury, headed by *the beast, and the kings of the earth*; the powers of earth and hell gathered, to make their utmost effort, *v.* 19.

VII. The victory gained by the great and glorious head of the church: *The beast and the false prophet*, the leaders of the army, are taken prisoners, both he who led them by power and he who led them by policy and falsehood; these are taken and *cast into the burning lake*, made incapable of molesting the church of God any more; and their followers, whether officers or common soldiers, are given up to military execution, and made a feast for *the fowls of heaven*.

CHAPTER TWENTY

THE MILLENNIUM (*vv.* 1–10)

We have here, I. A prophecy of *the binding of Satan* for a certain term of time, in which he should have much less power and the church much more peace than before. Observe, 1. To whom this work of binding Satan is committed—to *an angel from heaven*. 2. The means he makes use of in this work: he has a *chain* and a *key, a great chain* to bind Satan, and *the key of the* prison in which he was to be confined. 3. The execution of this work, *vv.* 2, 3. (1) *He laid hold on the dragon, that old serpent, which is the devil, and Satan*. And, (2) He *cast him into the bottomless pit*, cast him down with force, and with a just vengeance, to his own place and prison, from which he had been permitted to break out, and disturb the churches, and deceive the nations; now he is brought back to that prison, and there laid in chains. (3) He is *shut up, and a seal set upon him*. (4) We have the term of this confinement of Satan—*a thousand years*, after which he was to *be loosed* again for *a little season*. The church should have a considerable time of peace and pros-

perity, but all her trials were not yet over.

II. An account of the reign of the saints for the same space of time in which Satan continued bound (*vv.* 4–6), and here observe,

1. Who those were that received such honour—those who had suffered for Christ, and all who had faithfully adhered to him.

2. The honour bestowed upon them. (1) They were raised from the dead, and restored to life. (2) *Thrones*, and power of *judgment, were given to them*; they were possessed of great honour, and interest, and authority, I suppose rather of a spiritual than of a secular nature. (3) *They reigned with Christ a thousand years*. Those who suffer with Christ shall reign with Christ.

3. The happiness of these servants of God is declared. (1) They are *blessed and holy, v.* 6. None can be blessed but those that are holy. (2) They are secured from the power of the second death. We know something of what the first death is, and it is awful; but we know not what this second death is. It must be much more dreadful; it is the death of the soul, eternal separation from God.

III. An account of the return of the church's troubles, and another mighty conflict, very sharp, but short and decisive. No sooner is Satan let loose than he falls to his old work, *deceiving the nations*, and so stirring them up to make a war with the saints and servants of God, which they would never do if he had not first deceived them. The power now permitted to him seems to be more unlimited than before.

God would, in an extraordinary and more immediate manner, fight this last and decisive battle for his people, that the victory might be complete and the glory redound to himself.

THE GREAT WHITE THRONE (*vv.* 11–15)

The utter destruction of the devil's kingdom very properly leads to an account of the day of judgment, which will determine every man's everlasting state. Here we have a description of it, where observe, 1. We behold *the throne*, and tribunal of judgment, *great* and *white*, very glorious and perfectly just and righteous. 2. The appearance of the Judge, and that is the Lord Jesus Christ, who then puts on such majesty and terror that *the earth and the heaven flee from his face, and there is no place found for them*; there is a dissolution of the whole frame of nature, 2 Pet. iii. 10. 3. The persons to be judged (*v.* 12): *The dead, small and great*; that is, young and old, low and high, poor and rich, 4. The rule of judgment settled: *The books were opened.* What books? The book of God's omniscience, who is greater than our consciences, and knows all things (there is a book of remembrance with him both for good and bad); and the book of the sinner's conscience, which, though formerly secret, will now be opened. *And another book* shall be *opened*—the book of the scriptures, the statute-book of heaven, the rule of life. 5. The cause to be tried; and that is, *the works of men*, what they have done and whether it be good or evil. 6. The issue of the trial and judg-

ment; and this will be according to the evidence of fact, and rule of judgment.

CHAPTER TWENTY-ONE

NEW JERUSALEM (*vv.* 1–8)

We have here a more general account of the happiness of the church of God in the future state, by which it seems most safe to understand the heavenly state.

I. A new world now opens to our view (*v.* 1): *I saw a new heaven and a new earth*; that is, a new universe; for we suppose the world to be made up of heaven and earth. By the new earth we may understand a new state for the bodies of men, as well as a heaven for their souls.

II. In this new world the apostle *saw the holy city, the new Jerusalem, coming down from heaven*, not locally, but as to its original: this new Jerusalem is the church of God in its new and perfect state, *prepared as a bride adorned for her husband*, beautified with all perfection of wisdom and holiness, meet for the full fruition of the Lord Jesus Christ in glory.

III. The blessed presence of God with his people is here proclaimed and admired: *I heard a great voice out of heaven, saying, Behold, the tabernacle of God is with men, &c., v.* 3.

IV. This new and blessed state will be free from all trouble and sorrow; for, 1. All the effects of former trouble shall be done away. 2. All the causes of future sorrow shall be for ever removed.

V. The truth and certainty of this blessed state are ratified by the word and promise of God, and ordered to be committed to writing, as matter of perpetual record, *vv.* 5, 6.

VI. The greatness of this future felicity is declared and illustrated, 1. By the freeness of it—it is the free gift of God: *He gives of the water of life freely*; this will not make it less but more grateful to his people. 2. The fulness of it. The people of God then lie at the fountain-head of all blessedness: they *inherit all things* (*v.* 7); enjoying God, they enjoy all things. He is all in all. 3. By the tenure and title by which they enjoy this blessedness—by right of inheritance, as *the sons of God*. 4. By the vastly different state of the wicked. Their misery helps to illustrate the glory and blessedness of the saints, and the distinguishing goodness of God towards them, *v.* 8. Thus the misery of the damned will illustrate the blessedness of those that are saved, and the blessedness of the saved will aggravate the misery of those that are damned.

THE GLORIES OF HEAVEN
(*vv.* 9–27)

We have already considered the introduction to the vision of the new Jerusalem in a more general idea of the heavenly state; we now come to the vision itself, where observe,

I. The person that opened the vision to the apostle—*one of the seven angels, that had the seven vials full of the seven last plagues, v.* 9. God has a variety of work and employment for his holy angels.

II. The place from which the apostle had this glorious view and prospect. He was taken, in ecstasy, into *a high mountain.*

III. The subject-matter of the vision—*the bride, the Lamb's wife* (*v.* 10); that is, the church of God in her glorious, perfect, triumphant state, under the resemblance of Jerusalem, having the glory of God shining in its lustre.

1. The exterior part of the city— *the wall* and *the gates*, the wall for security and the gates for entrance.

(1) The wall for security. Heaven is a safe state; those that are there are enclosed with a wall, that separates them and secures them from all evils and enemies. The foundations are described by their number and by their matter; by their number—*twelve*, alluding to the twelve apostles (*v.* 14), whose gospel doctrines are the foundations upon which the church is built, *Christ himself being the chief corner-stone*; and, as to the matter of these foundations, it was various and precious, set forth by twelve sorts of precious stones, denoting the variety and excellency of the doctrines of the gospel, or of the graces of the Holy Spirit, or the person excellencies of the Lord Jesus Christ.

(2) The gates for entrance. Heaven is not inaccessible; there is a way opened into the holiest of all; there is a free admission to all those that are sanctified; they shall not find themselves shut out. Now, as to these gates, observe, [1] Their number—*twelve gates*, answering to the twelve tribes of Israel. [2] Their guards which were placed upon them—*twelve angels*, to admit and receive the several tribes of the spiritual Israel and to keep out others. [3] The inscription on the gates—*the names of the twelve*

tribes, to show that they have a right to the tree of life, and to enter through the gates into the city. [4] The situation of the gates. As the city had four equal sides, answering to the four quarters of the world, east, west, north, and south, so on each side there were three gates, signifying that from all quarters of the earth there shall be some who shall get safely to heaven and be received there.

2. The interior part of the new Jerusalem, *vv.* 22–27. We have seen its strong wall, and stately gates, and glorious guards; now we are to be led through the gates into the city itself; and the first thing which we observe there is the street of the city, *which is of pure gold, like transparent glass, v.* 21. The saints in heaven tread upon gold. Observe,

(1) The temple of the new Jerusalem, which was no material temple, made with men's hands, as that of Solomon and Zerubbabel, but a temple altogether spiritual and divine.

(2) The light of this city. Where there is no light, there can be no lustre nor pleasure. Heaven is *the inheritance of the saints in light.* But what is that light? There is no sun nor moon shining there, *v.* 23. There is no want of the light of the sun, *for the glory of God lightens that city, and the Lamb is the light thereof.*

(3) The inhabitants of this city. They are described here several ways. [1] By their numbers— whole nations of saved souls; some out of all nations, and many out of some nations. [2] By their dignity— some of the kings and princes of the

earth: great kings. God will have some of all ranks and degrees of men to fill the heavenly mansions, high and low; and when the greatest kings come to heaven they will see all their former honour and glory swallowed up of this heavenly glory that so much excels. [3] Their continual accession and entrance into this city: *The gates shall never be shut.* There is no night, and therefore no need of shutting up the gates.

(4) The accommodations of this city: All the *glory and honour of the nations shall be brought into it.* Whatever is excellent and valuable in this world shall be there enjoyed in a more refined kind, and to a far greater degree.

(5) The unmixed purity of all who belong to the new Jerusalem, *v.* 27. [1] There the saints shall have no impure thing remaining in them. [2] There the saints shall have no impure persons admitted among them.

CHAPTER TWENTY-TWO

THE THRONE OF GOD

(*vv.* 1–5)

The heavenly state which was before described as a city, and called the new Jerusalem, is here described as a paradise. And here observe,

I. The river of paradise. The earthly paradise was well watered: no place can be pleasant or fruitful that is not so. This river is described,

1. By its fountain-head—*the throne of God and the Lamb.* 2. By its quality—*pure and clear as crystal.*

II. The tree of life, in this paradise. Such a tree there was in the earthly paradise, Gen. ii. 9. This far excels it. And now, as to this tree, observe, 1. The situation of it —*in the midst of the street, and on either side the river*; or, as it might have been better rendered, *in the midst between the terrace-walk and the river*. This tree of life is fed by the pure waters of the river that comes from the throne of God. 2. The fruitfulness of this tree. (1) It brings forth many sorts of fruit— *twelve sorts*, suited to the refined taste of all the saints. (2) It brings forth fruit at all times—*yields its fruit every month*. This tree is never empty, never barren; there is always fruit upon it. (3) The fruit is not only pleasant, but wholesome.

III. The perfect freedom of this paradise from every thing that is evil (*v.* 3): *There shall be no more curse*; no *accursed one*—no serpent there, as there was in the earthly paradise. Here is the great excellency of this paradise.

IV. The supreme felicity of this paradisaical state. 1. There the saints shall see the face of God; there they shall enjoy the beatific vision. 2. God will own them, as having his seal and name on their foreheads. 3. *They shall reign with him for ever*; their service shall be not only freedom but honour and dominion. 4. All this shall be with perfect knowledge and joy.

DIVINE CONFIRMATION
(*vv.* 6–19)

We have here a solemn ratification of the contents of this book, and particularly of this last vision (though some think it may not only refer to the whole book, but to the whole New Testament, yea, to the whole Bible, completing and confirming the canon of scripture); and here, 1. This is confirmed by the name and nature of that God who gave out these discoveries: he is *the Lord God, faithful and true*, and so are all his sayings. 2. By the messengers he chose, to reveal these things to the world; the holy angels showed them to holy men of God; and God would not employ his saints and angels in deceiving the world. 3. They will soon be confirmed by their accomplishment: they are things that must shortly be done; Christ will make haste, *he will come quickly*, and put all things out of doubt; and then those will prove the wise and happy men who have believed and kept his words. 4. By the integrity of that angel who had been the apostle's guide and interpreter in these visions. 5. By the order given to leave the book of the prophecy open, to be perused by all, that they might labour to understand it, that they might make their objections against it, and compare the prophecy with the events. God here deals freely and openly with all; he does not speak in secret, but calls every one to witness to the declarations here made, *v.* 10. 6. By the effect this book, thus kept open, will have upon men; those that are filthy and unjust will take occasion thence to be more so, but it will confirm, strengthen, and further sanctify those that are upright with God. 7. It will be Christ's rule of judgment at the great day; he will dispense rewards and punishments to men according as their works agree or disagree with the word of God.

8. It is the word of him who is the author, finisher, and rewarder of the faith and holiness of his people, *vv.* 13, 14. He is *the first and the last*, and the same from first to last, and so is his word too. 9. It is a book that condemns and excludes from heaven all wicked, unrighteous persons, and particularly *those that love and make lies* (*v.* 15), and therefore can never be itself a lie. 10. It is confirmed by *the testimony of Jesus, which is the Spirit of prophecy.* 11. It is confirmed by an open and general invitation to all to come and partake of the promises and privileges of the gospel, those streams of the water of life; these are tendered to all who feel in their souls a thirst which nothing in this world can quench. 12. It is confirmed by the joint testimony of the Spirit of God, and that gracious Spirit that is in all the true members of the church of God; *the Spirit and the bride* join in testifying the truth and excellency of the gospel. 13. It is confirmed by a most solemn sanction, condemning and cursing all who should dare to corrupt or change the word of God, either by adding to it or taking from it, *vv.* 18, 19.

FINAL PRAYER (*vv.* 20, 21)

We have now come to the conclusion of the whole, and that in three things:

I. Christ's farewell to his church. He seems now, after he has been discovering these things to his people on earth, to take leave of them, and return to heaven; but he parts with them in great kindness, and assures them it shall not be long before he comes again to them: *Behold, I come quickly.*

II. The church's hearty echo to Christ's promise, 1. Declaring her firm belief of it: *Amen, so it is,* so it shall be. 2. Expressing her earnest desire of it: *Even so, come, Lord Jesus; make haste, my beloved, and be thou like a roe, or like a young hart on the mountains of spices.* What comes from heaven in a promise should be sent back to heaven in a prayer.

III. The apostolical benediction, which closes the whole: *The grace of our Lord Jesus Christ be with you all, Amen.*

Matthew Henry's Commentary

THE FOUR GOSPELS

This is your companion volume also edited by David Winter

'A big paperback and excellent value . . . It should bring this classic commentary to a new, perhaps younger readership.'
—*Crusade* £1·00